The Political
Education of
ARNOLD
BRECHT

# The Political
# Education of
# ARNOLD
# BRECHT
## An Autobiography
## 1884-1970

PRINCETON UNIVERSITY PRESS

PRINCETON, NEW JERSEY

1970

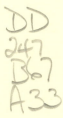
The original German edition of this autobiography
was published by Deutsche Verlags-Anstalt, Stuggart,
in 1966–1967 in two volumes: *Aus nächster Nähe,
Lebenserinnerungen eines beteiligten Beobachters* (the
years 1884–1927) and *Mit der Kraft des Geistes, Lebenserinnerungen zweite Hälfte* (the years 1927–1967).
The author has condensed and rewritten it for this
American edition.

This book has been composed in Linotype Granjon
with display in Centaur.

PRINTED IN THE UNITED STATES OF AMERICA
BY PRINCETON UNIVERSITY PRESS, PRINCETON, NEW JERSEY

*To Those Generations*
*That Have Not Yet Failed*

# INTRODUCTION

WHEN after years of concentrated effort my most voluminous book, *Political Theory: The Foundations of Twentieth-Century Political Thought,* was completed,[1] I was at long last free to turn again to other plans. Three major projects competed for priority. One—seemingly the most obvious option—was the second (special) volume of theory, parts of which were already at an advanced stage of preparation; the second, publication of my lectures on the constitutional history of mankind, an analysis of the reciprocal influences between constitutions and history; the third, some type of autobiography or memoirs, an interplay of recollections and reflections.

A writer who at the age of forty or fifty has to choose among projects of this scope can easily persuade himself that his decision concerns only the order of sequence. If he is about eighty, however, he knows that the choice of one in all probability means the death sentence for the others.

Why in these circumstances I gave priority to the autobiography calls for a word of explanation. The longer I thought over it, the more I became convinced that the other two books could be written by someone else, whereas this one only by me. I have liked to fancy, it is true, that the first volume of *Political Theory* bears my personal stamp. The second, however, was meant to be based to such an extent on the principles laid down in the former that some inspired member of our profession who agrees with them should be able to produce it in the same spirit, enriched with his own infusions. An outline of what I had planned is to be found in my article "Political Theory" in the *International Encyclopedia of the Social Sciences* (New York, 1968).

As to the constitutional history of mankind, the systematic presentation I have had in mind has not yet been forthcoming. This project, too, can well be carried through by another person, and I have no doubt that such a work will not be long in coming.

My recollections, however, can be put down by no one but me.

[1] Princeton University Press, 1959, 5th printing, 1968. German edition, 1961. Also editions in Spanish and Portuguese.

Originally I had thought only of relating a coherent story of my life, knitting together the scattered sections of the cloth from which it was cut, for my own benefit and that of friends. That would not have been very important for the world at large, was not even necessarily meant for publication, and could have been done alongside of work on weightier projects.

Yet when I had finished the first part, which dealt with my young years far removed from politics, the book turned out to become more and more a history of important political events. My life had been so closely interwoven with these events that it could not be adequately described apart from them. What I had come to see from close quarters was no longer my own personal way of life alone and its private environment, but political history from the beginning of World War I to the end of the Weimar Republic and further. Even where I had not been active myself, daily observation from central points influenced and formed me decisively.

Therewith the writing began fully to occupy my time and energies. The briefest listing of characteristic situations in which I had found myself will illustrate this, and at the same time explain the ever-growing urge I felt as a matter of professional responsibility to testify to what I had observed.

After seven years of work in the imperial Department of Justice in Berlin and half a year in the Department of Economics I received a call from the last imperial Chancellor, Prince Max von Baden, to join his staff in the Chancellery (October, 1918). I stayed there for three years under seven Chancellors (Prince Max, Ebert, Scheidemann, Bauer, Hermann Müller, Fehrenbach, Wirth) and eight revolutionary People's Commissaries in between (originally six, plus two replacements). In the Chancellery I witnessed the war's end, the debate about the Kaiser's abdication, the Revolution, the birth of the Weimar Republic, the Versailles peace negotiations, the controversy on the responsibility for Germany's collapse, the Kapp Putsch, the loss of a popular majority for democracy in the elections of 1920—deadly virus for German democracy—the unilateral disarmament, the struggle about reparations, Erzberger's assassination, Rathenau's appointment, and the beginnings of the "Policy of Fulfillment."

Only in the course of writing did I realize that apart from being the only survivor among politicians and higher staff members who at one time or other had been in the Chancellery during those three years, I was indeed the only one who had stayed there within that entire period. All others served merely during a part, generally a very small part.

Thereafter I worked for over five years in the federal Ministry of the Interior under eight ministers—two Social Democrats, three Democrats (liberals), one of the German People's Party (national-liberal), and two German Nationalists, the second of whom dismissed me because of my pro-democratic views. I witnessed Rathenau's assassination, the occupation of the Ruhr, the runaway inflation, the conflict with Bavaria, Hitler's beer-cellar putsch, the stabilization of the currency, the deceptive recovery, and, finally, the passing of three strategically important offices into the hands of men with anti-democratic and anti-republican views—the federal Presidency, the federal Ministry of the Interior, and my own office as chief of the constitutional division.

My dismissal from federal office failed to remove me from the center of political events in Germany, however. Appointed one of the leading officials of republican Prussia in Berlin and serving as Prussia's representative in the Reichsrat (Federal Council), in the official committee of twenty preparing a draft bill for Germany's reorganization (*Reichsreform*), and finally before the Supreme Constitutional Court in the conflict with the Papan government, I observed the final catastrophe of the Weimar Republic: Hitler's appointment and his gaining total power.

Temporarily arrested by Hitler's secret police and subjected to close surveillance I accepted a call to the newly founded graduate faculty of political and social science in the New School for Social Research, New York (November, 1933). A new phase of my life began, in an entirely different arena, devoted to political science rather than its practice. My share in practical politics thereafter was indeed reduced to occasional advice given in publications, memoranda, and personal discussions, as described in this book's final chapters.

Consequently, the major part of this narrative is given to the middle years of my life, those between thirty and fifty, from the beginning of World War I to Hitler's ascent to total power in Germany. The thirty-five years in the United States are dealt with more briefly, since work spent in the pursuit of theory, however important it may appear to specialists, cannot expect to encounter general interest.

The preponderance of German affairs had originally caused me to publish my memories and reflections in German. On two grounds, however, it has appeared suitable to have an English-language edition available. One is academic in character. German history from the start of World War I through the period of the Weimar democracy to the ascent of Hitler encompasses a peculiarly coherent sequence of events. Their close study leads to a number of the most puzzling problems of democracy, of political theory in general, and of history-writing—problems that are amply discussed in this book. They are sure to attract continuous attention. Just as I myself owe a good deal of my own political education to my involvement in this period's history, I felt this book might help others, not only Germans, in theirs.

The second reaches much further. This particular section of German history, from 1914 to the present, far from being simply a parochial sample of national history, has actually assumed something like the central position in the recent political history of the world at large. It is not saying too much, I think, to claim that the terminal phase of the second millennium after Christ has essentially been shaped by it and cannot correctly be apprehended without studying it.

I now must remind the reader, however, that my first purpose was writing an autobiography. Many pages are devoted to the first thirty years of my life, quite non-political in activities and atmosphere; elsewhere, too, more space is given to personal experiences and reflections than would be appropriate in a purely historical work. At first sight, this may seem to be an incompatible blend of purposes. However, reactions to the German edition have confirmed my belief that the book's intentions have not been impaired. The lyrics, drama, and epics of one particular life may be able to introduce the reader, and especially readers of the younger generations, to this portentous period of history and its perennial problems more intimately and more realistically than can purely historical studies.

An autobiography that omits the years of youth may provide good political memoirs but will be poor autobiography, and one that falsifies the record. I have tried to be as sincere as I could, not in retrospect belittling or sidetracking with the presumptive wisdom of haughty old age that which in those years had been important for my development. This is not to say that I approve of all I did or thought then. Quite the contrary, I wonder now at a good deal of it, as much as the reader may, ruefully shaking my head at times. But this is the way it was. I cannot change it; and as it was, it has formed me.

I kept no diaries. The only authentic source of these recollections is my memory, freshened up by notes, letters, memoranda, and the like still in my possession. I have not hesitated to verify data by consulting other sources of current history. In a few chapters I have used ideas and reflections from earlier publications of mine, occasionally even their wording. I am sincerely indebted for permission given me in this respect to the publishers and editors of my books *Prelude to Silence* (1944) and *Federalism and Regionalism in Germany: the Division of Prussia* (1945), both published by Oxford University Press, New York, and of my articles "Walther Rathenau and the German People," *Journal of Politics* (February, 1948) and "Die Auflösung der Weimarer Republik und die politische Wissenschaft," *Zeitschrift für Politik,* vol. 2 (1955), pp. 291 ff.

The original German edition of my autobiography was published by Deutsche Verlags-Anstalt, Stuttgart, in two volumes, the first titled *Aus nächster Nähe, Lebenserinnerungen eines beteiligten Beobachters,* covering the years from 1884 to 1927 (1966), the second, *Mit der Kraft des Geistes, Lebenserinnerungen zweite Hälfte,* 1927–1967 (1967), each about 500 pages long. The present American edition, although reduced to half the size of the German, preserves the essence of what is historically, scientifically, and humanly most important. To make this possible it omits that which was to serve purposes of documentation and verification only, especially in the two extensive appendices of the German edition, and the discussion of subjects that are of interest only to specialists. These items are easily accessible to scholars in the original edition. I have also omitted some of the purely autobiographical data, stories, anecdotes, and reflections of no significance for the understanding of the general trend of the narrative. Heavier cuts in less important chapters have made it feasible to render the most important ones in their entirety.

Chapters are numbered from the beginning to the end, whereas the German edition starts the second volume with a new numbering. Numbers in both editions are identical to Chapter 43; thereafter they diverge, partly because of the omission of some chapters. A synopsis of the relationship of the editions will be found in the Appendix.

Friendly assistants have helped me by preparing tentative transla-

tions from the German edition as a basis for me to shorten and reorganize the text and to rewrite it for non-German readers, who
would be unable to understand many historical allusions or institutional peculiarities of common knowledge to Germans, without adequate explanation; who would approach facts and implications
from their own angle of knowledge and prejudice, unless properly
warned; and who should not be bothered with details and names of
interest only to Germans. Most of the preparatory work of translation was ably done by Miss Wendy Philipson, instructor for English
at the University of München (Chapters 5 to 53, 74 to 94, 98 to the
end). Minor parts were handled equally well by Mr. Thomas
Bourke, München (Chapters 1 to 4); Mrs. Lenore Friedrich, Cambridge, Mass. (54 and 55); Mrs. Charlotte Neisser, New York (56 to
73); and Mr. Salvator Attanasio, New York (95–97). I wish to express my cordial thanks to all of them, as well as to Miss R. Miriam
Brokaw of Princeton University Press who went over the final copy,
and to Mrs. Gertrude Lederer of New York who prepared the Index.

I also wish to thank Mrs. Alice Assmus and Miss Ursula Hold-
schmidt in München, and Mrs. Johanna Brandt of New York for
their successful efforts in transcribing heavily altered manuscripts.

Finally, one word on the book's title. My original proposal was
"Participant-Observer." "Observer *of what?*" Herbert Bailey, the
publisher's editor in chief, retorted at once. What a man has observed
in eighty-five years cannot easily be summed up in a book's title. We
considered many alternatives, among them "Life Under Six Political
Regimes," "History Shaping Up For the Millennium's Final Stage,"
"Facts and Values," "From Practice To Theory," or just "Memoirs."
Any of these would have been correct, but none seemed sufficiently
specific. Mr. Bailey proposed the present title and stuck to it over my
objections that it was too personal and that its allusion to Henry
Adam's great autobiography would be considered presumptuous. He
did not share these misgivings, he said, and I can only pray that he
is right, as he usually is.

The American edition can claim independent value on the dual
ground of its more compact arrangement and its being addressed
to non-German readers.

Arnold Brecht
*New York, March 1970*

# CONTENTS

## PART XI Why into the Abyss? (1932–1933)

## PART XII From Hitler's Appointment to His Obtaining Total Power

## Part XIII  In the United States (Since 1933)

The Political
Education of
ARNOLD
BRECHT

# PART I

## The Early Years:
## Far Removed
## from Politics

# 1. As a Child at Home

FAMILIES from the upper strata of society who lived in North Germany around the turn of the century generally had little contact with politics, if we disregard occasional outbursts of patriotic feeling, hero-worship (Frederick the Great, Bismarck), and negative reactions to the opinions of *other* groups, considered "political" in contrast to one's own "objective" views.

If a boy's home was a Hanseatic town, in my case the city of Lübeck, one could be reasonably sure that the fathers of all his upper-class friends shared an outlook that could be politically classified as "National Liberal." They enthused about free trade, a flourishing industry, a strong navy, and colonies. Social Democrats were "public enemies," and heads were wagged over "ultramontane" Catholicism. This way of thinking was natural. Whoever tended farther toward the Left or the Right—*they* were the "politicians."

Once as a child in the company of my father I encountered a workers' demonstration. I asked what it was. My father explained to me that those were Social Democrats—people who aspired after higher wages and a state of the future where everyone would be equal. That struck me as being very natural. Shouldn't they be given higher wages? My father answered that was not so simple because many factories did not make sufficiently high profits to pay more; first of all, it was necessary to see to it that everyone had work and could earn a living. The answer did not quite satisfy me, and the question continued to trouble me. Whatever else demonstrations accomplish, they cause children to put questions to their parents.

I came into the world in Lübeck on the 26th of January, 1884, the same year of birth as that of Theodor Heuss, first President of the Federal Republic of Germany; the American President Harry Truman; Professor Edwin Redslob, co-founder of the Free University in Berlin; and of many others whose course of life later crossed mine. Of the house where I was born I have kept no memories, for my parents soon moved to one they had bought near the railroad station, where, opposite the Holsten Gate, my father's office was.

This house, Moislinger Allee Nr. 22, with its front- and back-garden and a square tower, which offered one of the finest views of the city's old churches and the richly wooded embankments, remained our home until my adult life.

Our father was a Protestant pastor's son—the youngest of four brothers—from a small town near Magdeburg (Ochtmersleben). As a lawyer he went into railroad administration in Berlin, married the third of four daughters of the railroad's division director from the Prussian Ministry of Commerce, Theodor Weishaupt (there was not yet a separate Ministry of Railroads). Some time afterward he went to Lübeck as president of the only large-scale private railroad yet in Germany, the Lübeck-Büchner Railroad Company. We children—the two "big ones," Edith and Gustav, and the two "little ones," Gertrud and I (there was a gap of four years between Gustav and me; our brother Rolf, the fifth child, did not enter the stage until after another twelve years)—used to issue ourselves free railroad passes by filling in the blank over our father's official seal, and so were able to make trips free of charge into pleasant surroundings, particularly the Baltic Sea, our great love. If a number of engines stood on turntables around a railroad workshop, Jürgen Fehling, lifelong friend since our schooldays and later great man of the theater, used to call it the Brecht Family Celebration Day.

Our father's brothers also had reached, each in a different profession, positions of some distinction. The oldest, an architect, was Privy Councillor to the Court of Rudolstadt; the second was a historian of high quality and Lord Mayor of Quedlinburg, where he is honored by a monument and a street-name. The third, a renowned oculist in Berlin, died at an early age; his son, later a philologist of German, Professor Walter Brecht (Vienna, Munich), was as our father's ward often in our house.

Seen as a whole, the paternal generation illustrated the frequent rise of a craftsman's family (my great grandfather was a saddler) by way of a Protestant vicarage towards the higher social strata. But we saw the older generation as personalities rather than in sociological categories. The great star in our family's sky was the grandfather, Pastor Christoph Heinrich Brecht, although we had never known him personally. He was held by us younger children in higher esteem than our mother's father, the Ministerial Director in Berlin, whose rank was a matter of complete indifference to us, and indeed, like everything "official," repulsed rather than attracted us.

In marrying my father, her elder by fifteen years, our mother at the age of twenty-one gave up not only the home and social circle of a high official in Berlin but also her studies at the Academy of Music, where she was as a gifted pianist taking lessons from Clara Schumann, the great composer's widow. The Blüthner grand piano in the drawing-room of our Lübeck house remained her spiritual habitat and her refuge from her many chores and social obligations, which she attended with a burning sense of duty, in her perfectionism sometimes stricter than our father, who had grown up with farmers' and craftsmen's sons. But she somehow managed every day to go to the piano and play, practice or give lessons to the two daughters. She never played anything but good classical pieces, especially sonatas and piano concertos by Beethoven, Mozart, Schumann, and Brahms, with great technical ability developed by diligent finger exercises, a captivatingly soft touch, and a deep understanding of the art. We two boys soon broke away from these, as we thought, boring lessons and taught ourselves to play by ear, with the occasional help of laboriously deciphered notes; so did the latecomer Rolf. Gustav also played the violin and clarinet, I the clarinet, and Rolf the cello. Sometimes we had an entire orchestra in the house. Most of the time, however, while I did my homework, I used to hear in the next room my mother's or sisters' accurate playing of good music. This became so customary to me that even now I often have sonatas or piano concertos playing from records or radio while I work. But what a world of difference between the canned music of even the greatest pianists and the warm, living flow from the piano in the next room under our mother's hands!

I was a sickly child, and as a result backward in the development of thought and speech. At the age of four I incurred a serious bout of pleurisy, as a consequence of which my heart shifted from its position and developed a valve defect which prevented me until my later school years from indulging in athletics and from performing my military service.

Gustav was physically much stronger and mentally earlier developed. A four years' age gap between brothers—especially when there is no intermediary child between them (a girl had died at birth)—is a vast chasm. To be only four when your brother is eight, only eight when he is twelve, only twelve when he is sixteen—that indeed is a sorry fate. It is only when finally the one is about twenty-three and the other twenty-seven that the age-span gradually stops having the effect of a difference between generations and eventually loses all importance.

Gustav's way of playing with me was to tyrannize me. Those games of tyranny and rebellion were to repeat themselves later between Gustav's own second and third boys, who had the same age gap. It is best described by the following scene: Wolfgang, in a fight with the younger Christoph, has thrown his brother to the floor:

"Do you admit that you're beaten?"

"No!"

Wolfgang kneels on the other's arms.

"Do you admit *now* that you're beaten?"

"No!"

"But you're lying underneath!"

"Then the winner is lying underneath!"

"But you're crying!"

"Then the winner is crying!"

Editha, six years older than I, was a sort of governess, mother's deputy, for us two little ones. Not until very much later did we build up a proper brother-sister relationship. In those early years we were for her simply incredibly stupid.

My dearest playmate, and my consolation in times of misfortune, was Gertrud, one and a half year younger than I, born in the month of roses, winsome and mild, with blue eyes and thick blond hair which, because of the curious strength of the individual strands, formed an unusual contrast to her graceful, childlike expression. By nature gay and yet pensive, she was for the parents a constant "ray of sunshine" in contrast to us "problem children," and at the same time a "little mother" because of her calm observations about the world around her. She was my confidante in all situations —understanding, discreet, always ready to help. When Gustav beat me, she wept with me. When I wanted to come home later than our parents would allow, she left the window open for me. When our parents complained about me, she defended me.

Mother's oldest sister, Anna, was married to Georg Sombart, President of the Stettin Railroad and brother of the economist, Professor Werner Sombart. Of the previous generation she represented for us the epitome of elegance and was very intent on improving our manners whenever we visited her.

The second sister, a gifted painter, was married in Berlin to the chairman of a narrow-gauge railways association, City Councillor Adalbert Erler, who was politically and socially more liberal than his sister-in-law's husband, Georg Sombart. Their son Hans Erler, later a commander and a vice-admiral in the German navy, was for his entire life a good friend of us Brecht children.

The youngest of the four sisters, Aunt Else, remained single after the death of her parents, whom she had cared for until their last breath. She was like an older sister in her mixture of good manners, intellectual freedom, and boyishness, full of tender understanding in all our joys and sorrows and always ready to accommodate and entertain us during our visits to Berlin.

Lastly, there was our mother's only brother, Uncle Ewald Weishaupt, colonel and director of the government-run rifle factory in Spandau. We had less contact with him than with our aunts, although rather more with his children, particularly his two sons; the younger of the two later became a spirited torpedo-boat commander, often in conflict with his superiors.

## 2. SCHOOLDAYS (1891–1902)

BECAUSE I had so often been ill I did not go to school until I was seven years of age; then, however, on account of my height, I was immediately put with older and quicker boys. This was at Dr. Bussenius' "preparatory school," which was the equivalent of an American grammar school, with some Latin and French added; later, boys were transferred to the Katharineum, the famous Lübeck "Gymnasium," which was almost four hundred years old.

On my first day at school, during one of the lessons, a boy from a higher class, after knocking timidly, opened the door and walked in, carrying a cane in his hand. He had to report to Mr. Sch. in this way because of insubordination during the break. The teacher ordered him to unlace and relace his boots while standing; as the boy did this, he was given several strokes of the cane on the tightest part of his trousers. Watching this took my breath away. The incident was in fact not repeated, but caning was a common means of punishment.

In the next higher class (the "Sexta") I stayed for two years at the request of my parents since I was "anyway too young." At the beginning of the second year I was being placed at the top of the class, the only time this ever happened to me at school. In the following terms I slowly dropped back to the lower third and remained there year after year, until the age of fifteen, when there was a sudden marked improvement and I rose quickly to seventh place. This seemed to me to be quite unnecessary and I cut down on work so much that I was again near the bottom, my only care being that I did not fail graduation (the "Abitur").

Corporal punishment was not used in the Katharineum, but otherwise things were all the more strange there, especially in the higher classes. We pupils had a strong code of honor among ourselves, but in our relationships with most of our old teachers—not all of them; there were remarkable exceptions of extremely popular teachers—honor had only one meaning: trying to fool them, bravely and successfully. Once I had been given two black marks on one day—a serious matter, which made my advancement seem doubtful. The mathematics teacher, Dr. Goth, who taught the last lesson that day, saw the bad marks, looked at me—I was a good mathematician—and put a good mark in the book. I was saved. A few years previously something similar, though unfortunately without the good mark, had happened in the same class to another native of Lübeck: Thomas Mann. In 1931, at the four-hundredth anniversary of the Katharineum, by which time Mann had risen to being the official speaker, the old class register was in a glass case in the exhibition room, open at the page on which the two bad marks had been entered. When we told Mann, he said: "That's going too far." There was a rumor that he had been able to make the class at that time only on the tacit understanding between school and family that he would then leave, which he did.

The century came to an end. Fifteen years old, I went on New Year's Eve into the town where the crowds were surging back and forth in Breite Strasse. I did not mingle with them, but was standing alone beneath the dark, mighty towers of St. Mary's Church when the bells rang at midnight. "No one who today sees the beginning of the new century," I thought, "will live to see its end. But these towers will still stand then as they have done for five or six centuries." A strange thrill ran through me. But before the century was half over, those eternal towers lay in ruins, the bells melted at their feet.

Three days after the new year the wedding of our eldest sister Editha took place. At the party held on the eve, one of her friends, Irmgard Behn, appeared dressed as Rautendelein—a fairy figure in a play by Hauptmann—declaiming a poem by my brother Gustav. She seemed incredibly lovely. Her cousin, the Munich sculptor Fritz Behn, Gustav, and I—we all fell in love with her at the same time. My ardent love lasted for nine months—a very long time at that age. Hopelessly for she was two years older than I, but all the more happily, I made pilgrimages almost every day over the old walls to Brehmer Strasse to see her.

In the meantime at Easter, 1900, my flamboyant final two years on school ("Prima," lower and upper section) began. School fraternities were permitted in Lübeck, a city which could allow itself such strange activities because as an independent federal state it had its own cultural sovereignty. Many of the senators had previously been members of these fraternities themselves and allowed them to continue because of pleasant memories of their own youth. Every Saturday or second Saturday we met in a reserved room of a small suburban tavern, celebrating, singing student songs, and drinking colossal amounts of beer. Every other week in winter there were dances at the homes of the most distinguished families; we visited them formally at the beginning of the winter with the tacit understanding that the parents would take turns in holding these dance evenings.

But these were matters of secondary importance compared with what really mattered to me, the theater, the old Lübeck municipal theater. I was, like Gustav four years before me, an enthusiastic theater-goer, paying sixty pfennigs for standing-room tickets, and in these two years got to know many great operas well—Wagner, Mozart, Beethoven, Verdi, Bizet—and many operettas, particularly Offenbach and Johann Strauss. A fanciful love for Alice Nova, a singer, who was ten years older than I, increased my enthusiasm. She appeared on the stage several times a week, as Adele in *Fledermaus,* as Mozart's Papagena, or Offenbach's beautiful Helen, as Thomas' Mignon, Adam's Poupée, or as an apprentice in *Meistersinger*. It was said that she came of a distinguished Bremen family and that she had thrown herself from the Rhine bridge in Cologne in order to put an end to an unhappy marriage; her husband, so the story went on, had jumped in after her and had drowned, but she was saved, had recovered, and went on to fulfill a long-felt desire: to sing and to act. In the evenings she appeared only with a lady companion who brought her to the theater and picked her up afterwards. This love story of mine also remained platonic, romantic, idealistic. Greetings in the street, when she was coming from rehearsals and I from school (I often walked up and down for a long time in order not to miss her), a few words, handshakes, a picture and a carnation—that was all.

In order to procure the money for my theater visits I coached a lower-class pupil (of whom a teacher had said to me: he is even more stupid than you) for a mark an hour and managed to learn something in the process myself, so that in the end I passed the *Abitur*, whereas he was kept down. He later became a Lübeck senator and a member of the Federal Parliament in Bonn, still a friend. A bigger problem was getting away from home in the evening. In view of my poor achievements my father announced at the beginning of my final winter at school that I must give up going to the theater until the examinations were over. This was, for the reasons I have mentioned, "impossible" for me. I invited a few of my fellow pupils to come up to my room after supper so that we might work together for the exams. We founded a "work society." Mother protested because she could not sleep. Well, I answered, then we will meet at different houses in turn. And so I went out two or three times a week—to the theater. The lie was the high price to pay for my freedom. I did not feel at the time that I was doing wrong. I very much regret that I lied to my parents. But even now I cannot quite manage penitently to regret my visits to the theater.

Of the many thousands of class hours in school I can say of only two that they had an influence on me for my whole life above and beyond the general impressions of a humanistic education. The first occurred when I was fourteen. A staff member was ill and in his place came a substitute who did not normally teach our class. He led an unprepared discussion with us, something quite outside our curriculum, about whether there were such things as superior beings and what effect they would have on us if we were to meet them. We are beings with three dimensions, he said. Let us suppose that, like shadows, we had only two—only length and width, not height as well. What could we observe if we encountered a three-dimensional being? We would perhaps bump into it. But we would not be able to envisage its third dimension; we would be able to recognize only the two dimensions familiar to us. The same would happen to us three-dimensional beings, he went on, if we were to meet a being with four dimensions. This comparison—or, more correctly, this conclusion from analogy—fascinated me. In eternally repeated sequences of thought I pictured to myself what the fourth dimension of such a being might well be and reached the conclusion that it must be *time*. We three-dimensional beings are always aware of only one moment in time. But a being with four dimensions would project into time and would be able to move about in it freely, as we do in space. I familiarized myself mentally with such a being. This was before 1900. When great scientists began to be preoccupied with Einstein's theories and with time as a fourth dimension, I was well prepared.

The other lasting impression was of a physics lesson in which Professor Goth showed us one of the first Edison phonographs: the original type of phonograph with a long horn and wax cylinder. He explained the physical process to us. No electricity could be used as an explanation or as an excuse. None was needed. The sound waves struck the membrane, a pin fastened to this engraved the vibrations on the revolving roll of wax; when the cylinder was then made to pass the pin again the membrane vibrated and produced the sounds which had been spoken. "It's all quite simple," Professor Goth concluded his demonstration, and then after a short pause added thoughtfully, passing a hand through his hair: "But that someone had the effrontery to believe that it would really work!" It was this last sentence that made the lesson so memorable for me. It became my secret cipher to the understanding of great discoveries and inventions, a source of reverence for the "effrontery" of strictly logical thought, and a continual encouragement to make myself guilty of such effrontery.

But such lessons were rare exceptions. When we left school we had had for nine years a Latin lesson every day, twice a week even two. At the end of all this hardly one of us was able to express himself fluently in Latin, or indeed, even to read a Latin text with ease. Not to succeed in teaching someone a language in nine years of daily tuition must be difficult. For this a German "Gymnasium" was necessary—and a group of pupils such as we.

History, too, remained something of a mystery to me. The collection of dates, heroes and villains, victories and defeats, conclusions of peace and breaches of faith, which were presented to us as history, had no meaning for me. There were some exceptions, as, for example, a lesson for eleven-year-old boys in which Dr. Bussenius told us, most eloquently and convincingly, of the beauty of Cleopatra; I listened to this intently. The period of history taught extended only up to the Napoleonic wars of liberation in 1813–1815; then there was a sudden leap over the internal liberation movement to the wars of 1864, 1866, 1870–1871. We did not get any further.

In our struggle against school discipline we imagined ourselves to be heroes, forerunners of a better, more creative society, far more illustrious than the petty bourgeois environment in which we lived. But I have since often regretted that I squandered the precious opportunity to learn more. I had a lot to catch up.

Nor would I wish to exaggerate the degree of our ignorance. When we left school we had learned the fundamentals of Latin, Greek, French, and English, and also of history, mathematics, and natural sciences. We had absorbed the beauty of the Greek language and the richness of its forms, the clear logic of Latin, the expressive terseness of unrhymed rhythms, not because they had been explained to us carefully, but just as independently as the beauty of the Lübeck churches in the shadow of which we had grown up; they had been natural parts of our environment, until one day or night we had the independent experience of their beauty, until we said to one another: "Look how beautiful that is."

From the first letters of words of a verse by Horace: "Si fractus illabatur orbis, impavidum ferient ruinae" ("When the earth is shattered in fragments its ruins will slay me undaunted") I formed a name which was to be my pseudonym: Sfio Ifr. No one would know what it meant.

At this time Alice Nova's farewell performance was given. She played *La Poupée* in Adam's romantic operetta. I saw the piece for the fifth time, chewing cloves during the performance, for I had read of scientific experiments, according to which an event connected with a particular smell or taste reoccurs to us with great vividness when we again come upon the same smell or taste twenty or thirty years later (not earlier). I was willing to wait that long. In fact even today cloves still immediately remind me of that farewell performance.

The beloved singer left Lübeck. At the very last moment, when the engine whistled, I climbed, armed with one of our free railroad passes valid for "any desired class," into the first class next to her second-class compartment. She leaned out the window looking at Lübeck, until it was lost to our sight and then, turning around, facetiously shook her finger at me. At the first station I asked permission to join her in her compartment. She smiled a yes. Thus for the first time I had the opportunity of talking with her at greater length. At the station in Hamburg she presented me with a large carnation from her bouquet and I took the next train back to Lübeck.

In the course of the same year she married the English baritone Whitehill, who had courted her in Lübeck, where he had begun his career. He attracted attention because—a tall, slim young man—he always went around wearing a top hat. In my third term at university I visited the couple in Bremen and spent an evening with them in the *Ratskeller*. Later I lost contact with them. Whitehill often appeared as a guest at Bayreuth.

Even after having passed the exams we continued at school from February to Easter, as was the custom. Director Schubring had us translate from Homer without preparation. I faltered over a word and asked unabashed: "Herr Direktor, what does *nebros* mean?" His answer was: "He thinks himself prepared for life and doesn't even know that *nebros* means fawn." I have never forgotten this Greek word since.

## 3. University (1902–1905)

DURING my years as a student, too, I kept aloof from politics. Sons of southern German bourgeois families often were more advanced in this respect, thanks to the more advanced democratization of political life there. Theodor Heuss, for example, who was the same age as I almost to the day, and like me in his fourth semester at the University of Berlin, was keenly politically active there, a supporter of Friedrich Naumann, while I had as little concern for politics as I had had as a schoolboy.

After groping around unsurely at the beginning in Bonn I ended up in a musical student fraternity, the Makaria. No less a person than Theodor Litt, later one of Germany's most upright philosophers, three years older and ten years more mature than I, had won me over to this by producing a pianoforte arrangement of *Tristan* and by playing the prelude to the *Meistersinger* extempore on the piano in the clubroom. I hiked, drank, laughed a lot, and, apart from music, developed a serious attitude only toward the study of law under the guidance of the great teacher Ernst Zitelmann, the only professor whose lectures I attended without fail. I was captivated by the mixture of historical and logical elements in this subject.

In the winter semester (1903–1904) in Berlin my main interest turned once more to the theater, which I had greatly missed in Bonn. From the gallery of the Royal Opera House, together with Gustav, I saw and heard Wagner's *Tristan* for the first time. Its impact has never been greater. But we liked the Metropol Theater in Behrenstrasse with its yearly "revues" almost as much. In order to save the cost of a ticket I took a part as an extra in *Lohengrin* for fifty pfennigs; Dr. Muck was the conductor, with Emmi Destinn as Elsa. At the dress rehearsal in the middle of Elsa's finest aria in the first act Dr. Muck suddenly stopped the orchestra. "One of the men of Brabant over there is wearing eye-glasses," he cried out aghast. I had put them on to see Elsa better. There were disapproving glances from all sides, including Elsa, who, however, gave a charming, understanding smile immediately afterwards. I had selected *Lohengrin* because the men of Brabant are on the stage almost without interruption with the apparent exception of the bridal scene. But even then they are present. For the bridal chamber is only a few yards deep. Behind it the stage has already been set for the trial scene with its huge lime-tree and, while Elsa and Lohengrin are left alone in the foreground by their entourage and breathe the sweet fragrances, at the back we men were sitting around the tree in the half-light behind the drop-curtain, waiting. This experience had a metaphysical significance for me. The atmosphere behind the drop-curtain has stayed with me all my life, an uncanny symbol of the fourth dimension, time. Whatever is happening around me, behind the drop-curtain I see the stage set for the trial.

In the course of my semester in Berlin and the two which followed in Göttingen there occurred a profound change in me. For the first time I began to be aware of the real nature of art, not only of music, the medium through which I had previously come close to art instinctively, but now also in painting (almost every day I spent several hours in art galleries), in drama and, above all, in *language*, in prose and in lyrical poetry, and everywhere in the relationship between form and content. Content without form now seemed to me to be water without a bucket.

Love and friendship accelerated and intensified the change. During the vacation in March between my semesters in Berlin and Göttingen, my school friend Jürgen Fehling brought me to the house of an esteemed Lübeck lawyer, descended from an old family of senators, who was at that time forty years old. I will call his wife Rezia and him, Hinrich Soederbrook, although this disguise is hardly necessary as he died fifty years ago and she, forty. Rezia wanted to invite a large company of people, for whose entertainment, on the advice of Fehling, a parody of Schiller's *Don Carlos* was to be presented. A small stage was constructed. We rehearsed and acted, Jürgen played Philipp; I, Carlos; Rezia prompted. The whole affair would not be worthy of mention, had it not been the start of a singular experience of love which strongly influenced my further development. She was at that time twenty-nine, the mother of three children between three and seven, the daughter of a Lübeck doctor and a Venezuelan lady of Spanish blood, who was a descendant of Bolivar, the liberator of South America. She had southern beauty and charm, expressive of her soul (human beauty which was not an expression of a person's soul has always repelled me), and great self-assurance in social contacts, so that for me, in otherwise humdrum hanseatic surroundings, she was a phenomenon from another world. In her bearing and gestures always a little solemn, the "beautiful stranger" in town, she loved Lübeck, yet, just as we, liked to make fun of everything philistine and petty. People from the theater and painters met at her home, also artists from Munich and Berlin, and occasionally friends from Italy or Venezuelan relatives. The sight of her, her voice and her movements, stirred me deeply. I saw her only a few times more before I went up to Göttingen for my fifth semester.

My love of Rezia seemed to me something that was its own reward. Love, *real* love, love which "conflicts with destiny," as Goethe said, was the supreme blessing, and the purer and more selfless it was, the greater the blessing. What had I to hope for from this love? What could a lanky, twenty-year-old student who, notwithstanding all his intellectual frenzy, was as yet awkward, dull, and penniless too, mean to this woman admired by so many? If indeed I might one day win her friendship, her confidence, if she might think of me with a grateful smile, then that would be enough. Everything else in life was on a totally different level.

One of the two friends who influenced my new life was Jürgen Fehling. In Göttingen I saw him every day and in the summer semester even lived with him. He had given up theology after two semesters and began to study law, mistrustfully and ready for every escape into the world of art. He had a Shakespearean richness of ideas and inspiration. It really was as though you were strolling through the fields or sitting over a pint with a nineteen-year-old Shakespeare; I cannot describe it any better.

The other was called Paul Rintelen, one of the many sons of a high-court judge. Four years older than I he had a wonderful self-assurance in making an appearance, a compelling, very melodious voice; he could read Goethe's elegies in a way no one else equaled. An ardent admirer of women, he would love both mother and daughter passionately at the same time and did not really know himself which he loved more. Abstract discussions he disliked. He could not stand Schiller, Ibsen, Wagner, or the painter Max Klinger. "Apothecaries" he called all four of them because in order to achieve their effects they would cunningly mix all sorts of ingredients. Yet to him I owed a new attitude to Goethe, one which was free from school memories, in particular to the later Goethe, to *West-östlicher Divan,* the second part of *Faust,* the *Marienbad Elegies,* and *Pandora.*

In all practical, social, and political affairs I remained as immature as I had been at school. Political activities seemed to me quite contemptible. Politics was indulged in by people different from me, people who spoiled any serious conversation because they had an answer for everything, because they *wanted* something: not conversation, not art, not love, not even truth, but something specific, always waiting for an opportunity, to go ahead with this something. As far away as possible from them! And above all from foreign policy—a book with seven seals, which only these fatuous-respectable people from the Foreign Office could decipher. To have a say in such affairs was just as ludicrous as someone wanting to step onto the stage and play in Hamlet extempore.

When I opened non-legal books, then ten to one it would be Goethe. True, I did read other things. I read everything Stendhal had written, Flaubert, Tolstoy's great novels, E. T. A. Hoffmann, Heine, Shakespeare, Hauptmann, Ibsen, Heinrich Mann, Thomas

Mann, Jens Peter Jacobsen, Hoffmannsthal, Wedekind, all the theater reviews by Alfred Kerr, and a lot of Strindberg—before he was
fashionable, not out of curiosity about his marriages but because in
him I found a first-rate attempt to explore the ways in which guilt
is logically and inexorably atoned for in human life: "How bold
then, how bad now." The cult of the aesthete and of self-flatterers
disgusted me. What I did read I usually read very slowly and carefully, as though I were writing it myself sentence by sentence. For
this reason alone I was not able to read much. In any case I read
nothing about politics, nothing about history.

We expressed our contemptuous distaste for the dominant social
ideals and the student customs about us in an entirely independent
manner of life inspired solely by our demon or genius. That is, we
engaged in what Germans call *genialisches Treiben,* generally
frowned upon and condoned exclusively in the one case of Goethe's
youth. We liked to arrange and perform parodies of great operas
and dramas, such as Carmen, Lohengrin, Meistersinger, Faust, and
we excelled in practical jokes, all far away from the serious matters
of life.

For example, there had turned up a distant acquaintance of ours,
one Herr Kraus, interested in foreign affairs, who behaved in a
high-handed fashion. From the room of a mutual friend, Eddi Berkemeyer, we wrote him the following letter, on lady's notepaper
and in a very feminine hand: "Dear Herr Kraus. From the register
of students I have learned that you are studying here at present. Do
you know that I was a friend of your dear mother's in her youth? I
am looking forward so very much to making your acquaintance
and perhaps to being of some assistance to you. I have invited a
few people to come to my house next Sunday evening at eight
o'clock. It would be a great pleasure for me if you could come.
Since there is so little time I shall not expect you to reply or to call
beforehand. Evening dress, please. Yours faithfully, Madame
Marme." We had ascertained from the directory that there was a
lady of this name living next door. On Sunday we leaned out of
the window and, lo and behold, along came Herr Kraus in a dress-
coat. "Come on up," we called. "I can't, I have an invitation," he
said proudly. Then he went in next door. After a time he came out,
looking embarrassed. But he took it good-humoredly and invited
the three of us to visit him and regaled us royally. A good diplomat!

Once, when we were playing poker at Berkemeyer's, Jürgen lost one hundred marks. It was one o'clock in the morning. Gambling debts are debts of honor. With a gloomy face he went to the desk and wrote. We had him show us the letter. It was to his eldest brother, a flourishing Lübeck attorney. "Dear Emanuel," it read, "I have done something dreadful. I have been gambling and have lost two hundred marks. Please, help me just this once. I promise that I will never gamble again. Yours, Jürgen." "But you only lost one hundred," we said. "Yes," said Jürgen, "but you only get half of what you ask for anyway." But Emanuel sent two hundred, enclosing a note in which he said that Jürgen should not make promises he would not keep; he should rather win back the money. So we suddenly had a welcome surplus which went around in the course of the following weeks.

Nonetheless, like all of us, Fehling was soon again in financial difficulties. Once he came home gloomily carrying a small blue notebook which he had just bought in order to keep a detailed account of all he spent. About six months later I found it lying on his desk. On the cover was written in Fehling's wonderful hand the word "Mammon." I opened it. The only entry read: "One notebook . . . five pfennigs."

One November day, just after the start of the winter semester, we decided at about eleven o'clock at night to run away to the station and to travel fourth class by the night train to Lübeck, in order to see the objects of our love: Jürgen, his girl friend at that time, Gertrud Sauermann, a very independent Lübeck girl, who later became a famous horsewoman; I, my distant beloved. When we arrived, we had ourselves fitted out with beards by the theater hairdresser so that our parents would know nothing of our visit. Rezia gave parties in our honor. Our disguise was not very effective. In a concert hall an old school friend tapped me on the shoulder from behind: "Hello, Brecht!" The beard at the front did not prevent people from recognizing us from behind.

Our visit had the fortunate result for me that I became an intimate younger friend of Rezia's. She and I had been sitting alone together in a corner of her blue Renaissance room with its heavy yellow curtains, talking about friendship and love, about "real" love and about Goethe's great example of taking love seriously until his old age. "I know only one kind of love," an officer had answered when she asked him what he meant by the word "love." That surprised us, for we distinguished many kinds. Our conversation and my dignified beard lured her into telling me about her life and to confess (as she put it) that the breaking off of a relationship with a Munich artist, which had threatened her marriage, had greatly depressed her. Our student prank was helping her to get over this, and for this she was grateful to us.

When we returned to Göttingen, I began to exchange letters with her. Soon we were writing daily and gradually began to address each other familiarly. The writing and receiving of these letters lifted me from the everyday world about me. Most of my letters were written at night and I would then take them to the train which came from Frankfurt and left Göttingen for Lübeck at half past one, in order to be able to post them directly into the mail coach; this involved a nightly walk over the wooded walls to the station and back. In the letters I spoke of love and art, religion and nature, human relationships (the most important thing in life), of Goethe, of plans and moods, and occasionally, but only as an exception, of my studies, my critical ideas about the nature of justice. The letters often contained poems, plans for dramas, novels, and short stories. I always wrote slowly, careful to avoid anything banal and effusive, trying to find the most appropriate expression, to put the meaningful in place of the meaningless. I struggled to attain a personal style, imitating now Goethe's prose, now Alfred Kerr's theater criticisms—a strange pair!—but gradually an individual style suited to me evolved.

When it was no longer possible to deny that I loved her, she spoke of my "first great love, which she was happy to receive." She quoted: "When you are loved you should not have time for anything else," or inscribed a picture of herself she sent me: "What annoys us in life can be enjoyed in a picture." During the Christmas vacation in Lübeck I went to her house almost every day; I also spent New Year's Eve, her birthday, there. In February she passed through Göttingen on her way to Italy; I traveled with her on the night train for an hour, as far as Kassel. On her return journey she spent two days with our small group in Göttingen. The friendship which a few months previously I had thought beyond reach had become reality.

A steady stream of literary attempts, both in verse and prose, and Rezia's moderating influence on my as yet unrestrained way of life were not all I owed to this friendship. I was lastingly influenced by the inward experiences this love gave me precisely by that which would be called its "abnormality": the lack of prospect or remedy, the impossibility of its being fulfilled in the way a man would normally desire of a love-affair, and its deep fulfillment in a different sense.

At school I had already rejected the double morality I could observe around me—uninhibited love-affairs with "lower-class" girls, and lofty, idealistic, moral pretensions in relationship with girls of one's own class of society. I was convinced that sexual union, whether with girls of a higher or lower social class, had profound and lasting psychological consequences and that at least one partner, and probably both, would suffer harm which could never again be put right unless such a love was undertaken seriously and permanently, "in heaven." Love, real love, was independent of sexual union, indeed, through sex love risked losing its transcendental character. Such opinions were regarded just as foolish then as they are today. To me, however, they were neither modern nor old-fashioned but a signpost to a better future, an eternal truth.

The Provincial Court was in Celle, and in April, 1905, Rintelen and I moved there to prepare ourselves for our first state examination. The six spring weeks on the Aller river, with daily letters, were paradise for me. I was not nervous about the exam. On the 14th of June, 1905, soon after my twenty-first birthday, I passed, with the mark "good." Another six happy weeks followed, spent partly on the Baltic, partly in Lübeck, where I was a daily visitor at Rezia's.

But what now? Should I spend my in-service training in Lübeck? My father warned me that I would then be stuck there for the rest of my life. Lübeck had, as an independent federal state, its own legal sovereignty and its own legal administration, and a Lübeck judge was a Lübeck judge; he could not be transferred to Berlin, Munich, or Weimar. My father reminded me that I was by birth a Prussian too and advised me to have my training in Prussia, in the province of Hannover, if I wished, in order to be near to Lübeck.

Thus in July, 1905, at Winsen-on-the-Luhe (situated between Hamburg and Lüneburg), I took the oath at the local court, but then immediately went on leave. I accompanied my parents to Thuringia. After that I went for two months to Leipzig in order to take my oral doctor's exam. There I lived with no social contact, except for a visit from Rezia on her return from a journey to Flor-

ence; she spent an afternoon and evening with me and left for
Lübeck at midnight.

At the invitation of my father, who wanted to lure me away from
Lübeck, I traveled to Switzerland for a week and then on to Grenoble to improve my French. But Grenoble soon bored me; I wanted
to see Paris and went there for my last six weeks. I found a cheap
room in Rue St. Jacques, on the Left Bank just in the middle of the
Latin Quarter. A new world opened up for me. Places that had previously been mere names to me—Notre Dame, Sainte Chapelle, the
Ile de St. Louis, the Louvre, the Musée Luxembourg, the Place de
la Concorde, the Champs-Elysées, the Opéra, Montmartre, the
banks and bridges of the Seine, the whole network of streets and
squares, even churchyards—were now becoming a sort of personal
possession. Every day I spent several hours in the Louvre, as I once
had done in the galleries in Berlin. At that time entry was free.
Thus I continued my private untutored study of art, attempting to
understand the history of art by merely looking, and at the same
time to gain a direct insight into the essentials of what art really is.
This was supplemented by visits to the Musée Luxembourg, where
the Impressionists were still housed at that time.

I continued to correspond with Rezia regularly. From one letter I
learned of her pride in the homage paid to her by a twenty-two-
year-old musician who had just been appointed leader of the Philharmonic at Lübeck—the beginning of a great career as a conductor. I felt that I should be near to her now, to fight for her friendship, and I counted the days and hours to my return. But at the
same time I also became aware of the strange nature of my love. I
had originally wanted nothing else but to love. The idea that my
love might be requited was so inconceivable to me that I had not
even thought about it. When in the summer our relationship became closer I reached the conclusion that I must by all means prevent her from returning my love with equal passion.

What made me think thus was not simply religious aversion to
adultery, to sin, no clearly defined moral principles. I had none. It
was my awareness of the inevitable consequences, and of my own
causative responsibility for them. I use the word "causative" ad-
visedly. For "causative" responsibility, I said to myself, was valid
even for someone who did not take "moral" responsibility very seriously. To me the most frightening aspect of her returning my love
was that my divine love would then be threatened. It would come

to an end just as surely if we had been having a secret love-affair as it would if we had thought of her separation from husband and children. The reality of life would in either case shatter all the sweetness, the poetry and sublimity of our relationship. However difficult it might be to draw a line between her affectionate friendship I wanted to have and the passionate reciprocation of love which I wanted to avoid, that distinction was to guide me. I had seen in the summer that this was not easy. Her affectionate words and gestures were now those of a mother, now of a sister or friend, now just of a woman, the distinctions blurring and merging. Physical contacts, so it seemed to me then, were ennobled and sanctified by the absolute truth of my love and by her absolute trust in me, her feeling of physical and spiritual security in my presence. But it was like walking a narrow ridge.

## 4. Unconscious Political Principles

Despite my complete lack of interest in politics at school and university, when I look back now I realize that I did hold certain beliefs which were in a way connected with politics, although I was not aware of it. Three ideals were of great importance to me, sometimes consciously, sometimes unconsciously. They were: justice, freedom, and truth. How noble it sounds to pride oneself in these principles! In the reality of life, however, my adherence was rather weak; I often sacrificed truth and justice for the sake of freedom, but seldom freedom for the sake of truth or justice.

My love of justice was genuine, though. Injustice upset and enraged me. In disputes I instinctively took the part of those who were weaker or absent. Unjust one-sided arguments did not only arouse my opposition, in a way they disgusted me. People who argued in this fashion seemed to me loathesome and stupid, more stupid than bad. In this I saw culpable stupidity. "Woe betide fools! For they could become wise. Otherwise it would be brutal to condemn them," I wrote in a sort of manifesto. In my own personal conduct I rarely hesitated to make use of those minor privileges that followed from my position as a student, or from that of my parents and friends. But as soon as I began to make a judgment on a given set of circumstances—and I was soon driven to do this, even when I myself was involved—my imagination operated in such a way that I was able to understand the point of view of other persons involved, was able to put myself in their positions, with the result that I was just to them in my opinions, and often in my actions as well.

This putting myself in other people's positions led at times to inward conflicts. Among my notes from the period there is a sheet of verse which shows how the continual weighing of conflicting arguments confused me, because it threatened the true expression of unsifted emotions. But such heretical moods did not last long. The demand for justice quickly reasserted itself.

While studying law, I began to think about the nature of justice more systematically. I did this on my own; I did not attend a single lecture on legal philosophy. There was as yet no philosophy of the scientific relativity of values. Max Weber's works on this subject did not appear until 1904, those of Radbruch and Kelsen considerably later, and in any case I did not read them until long afterward. But I struggled with the same problem: the dependence of the sense of justice either on traditions or on personal ideals and aims which conflicted with the traditions and ideals of other people. A small cardboard file on which I had written "The nature of the sense of justice" was soon filled with notes.

Fundamental axioms (axiomatically accepted principles), such as the sanctity of property and of contract, heredity and family, and the logical derivations therefrom, apparently played a decisive role in matters of justice: judgments as to whether something was just or unjust were made according to these axioms. The relationship between justice, axioms, and logic fascinated me. During my trip to Grenoble and Paris I wrote my doctoral dissertation on a legal problem in which the axioms of property, of the binding force of contracts, and of the consideration of impossibility, stood in conflict with one another. (*Sale of an article belonging to someone else,* Diss. Leipzig, 1906.)

A subsequent essay on "Contract Liability"—about a hundred printed pages long—attempted to trace the seemingly complex rules dealing with contracts in the German Civil Code of 1900 back to a few underlying principles. It was accepted without alterations for publication in *Jherings Jahrbücher* (vol. 53, 1908, pp. 213–302). My father began to treat his otherwise incomprehensibly childish and confused son with a respect that deeply moved me.

In this and in two further essays there emerged early samples of my particular interest in the influence of "impossibility," that is, of a fact in the realm of *Is,* on the realm of *Ought.* This interest had been suggested in the subtitle of my doctoral dissertation: "A contribution to the theory of impossibility." (This stimulated Rezia to write in my pianoforte arrangement of *Tristan:* "Another contribution to the theory of impossibility.") The title of one of the longest chapters of my *Political Theory,* which appeared fifty years later, is "Impossibility" (limited possibility).

A fifth piece of work—"Condition and Expectation"—threw light on another factor: *time.* A person's property rights can be disposed of not only in spacial parts, for example with landed property, but in sections of time as well, because the effect of the transfer can be postponed.

Before I discuss the transition from thoughts about justice to conscious political activity, I must come back to my youthful ideals of freedom and truth. Every boy who climbs a tree enjoys the freedom of choice of the site and the particular view he has and, not without justification, feels himself superior to people moving on a normal level. I sought such feelings everywhere. Even in later years I would climb at night into new buildings and stretch out on the builder's planks, or enter a deserted ship in the harbor, to discuss matters of importance with friends or sit alone and muse; this gave me a feeling of independence and helped me free myself of the banality of everyday thoughts.

People who appealed to authority, either their own or other people's, instead of giving reasons that convinced me or at least filled me with respect, had a bad time with me. My pet answer at twenty years of age to older persons who bragged of their age or experience was: "When you are as old as I am, then you will see that I am right." I lived and grew up in conflict with authority. Whatever I learned and devised, I learned and devised out of a sense of opposition. Once when my father had read a letter I had written in the style of a manifesto, he wrote imploring me not to read any Nietzsche for a year. I had never read Nietzsche before then. Now, of course, I read him, not much, though, only *Zarathustra;* and its beginning I read so often I never managed to finish it.

In order to enjoy my freedom more fully, I dressed differently. I wore neither the usual long tie nor the bow tie notted about a high, stiff collar, but a huge, black bow which fluttered in the wind under a collar with such a large roll a rabbit might slip into it. My hair, thick and blond, I did not wear cut short or neatly combed, as was the fashion, but falling wildly forward onto my forehead.

Since my garb made me look like a bohemian, I counteracted this by wearing a monocle instead of ordinary eyeglasses, at least for seeing into the distance (I did not need glasses for close work). I declared this to be a measure both practical and social, because it was possible to put on and take off a monocle with one hand, instead of having to execute a complicated maneuver with both, and because a monocle was cheaper than other eyeglasses. Later I gave up the fluttering tie and the roll collar, finally the monocle as well.

But now, unfortunately, I can no longer avoid the more serious aspects of my love of freedom. In order to obtain freedom I would as a boy employ any means which presented itself; to put it more bluntly: I occasionally lied, when it was necessary, and did not even have a bad conscience about it, unless it was because I had acted stupidly. I lied in the search for truth, from which I would have been cut off, if I had told the truth.

Thus the third great ideal of my youth—truth—was linked in a highly dubious manner with its opposite. I originally saw no contradiction in this. The untruthfulness against which I fought was not principally the telling of lies to other people, the "necessary lie" in the preservation of one's freedom, but lying to oneself, deep insincerity, untruthfulness which one did not admit to himself. A large number of the older generation indulged in heroic and ethical ideals, derived from the victorious wars of 1813, 1815, 1864, 1866, and 1870 and from the founding of the Empire—ideals held up to us for guidance in lofty speeches and books, dramas and poems, pictures, monuments, celebrations of the Emperor's birthday and of the battle of Sedan (1870). We were surrounded on all sides by a false bathos. By 1900 the struggle against insincerity had become characteristic of a section of the younger generation—but only of a section. In our determination to unmask insincerity we acted remorselessly.

I could not fail to see, however, that in the heroism and ethos of the old order there were things which were *not* insincere. As a student I worked out a way of thinking which I called "positive irony" (positive in the sense of "affirmative"). What is normally meant by an ironic comment is a statement which is not to be taken seriously. I, on the other hand, in using my "positive irony" would say something with a smile, *although* I meant it—for example, something heroic, virtuous, unselfish—and I meant it, although I said it. This was at the same time my reaction to the tendency of contemporary lyrics and literature toward pretentious refinements and sexual affectations, combined with a fear of ridicule. Avoid childlike simplicity, avoid naïveté! I wanted to preserve the genuine expression of genuine emotions in youth. I wrote letters, poems, and a short story in my style of positive irony.

Only gradually did I succeed in dissociating my striving for a deeper truth from a fusion with falsehood in real life, from the "necessary lie" which was supposed to preserve my freedom. The change began when I entered the university. Here there was freedom without the need to lie. The young student of law was able to study for three years, or as much longer as he liked, without taking a single exam; only in more advanced semesters did he have to hand in work for his seminars. No one checked on what he did, not even whether he really attended the lectures he had registered for (I personally did not usually attend lectures regularly).

I enjoyed this freedom as fully as my monthly allowance of 125 marks would go. In my reports home I did what was common at that time and exaggerated the portion of expenditures devoted to lecture fees. But there was no longer any cheating in my *work*. The things I wanted to know, I wanted to know; to remember, to think about, to have them ready. It was the same later with the fulfillment of my duties during my in-service training, as a young judge and as a government official. I took my duties seriously.

At the beginning of my official career my frank way of speaking and my unbureaucratic behavior were considered to be virtues and I was complimented on being a good *Hanseatic* citizen. Later, when I represented the Federal Government of Germany in negotiations at which the representatives of the States behaved in a more bureaucratic way than I did, my demeanor was appreciated as the sympathetic manner of a spokesman for the *Nation*. But afterward, when I represented Prussia, it was called typical *Prussian arrogance*. Finally when, after a long exile in America, I returned to discussions about the reorganization of Germany and debated such questions as the reciprocal withdrawal of troops from the Elbe in a quite unorthodox fashion, this attitude was termed *American freedom* or American naïveté. I myself think that I was always the same.

But in mentioning this I have gone far beyond the story of my youth. Two things still have to be added: my attitude at that time to philosophy and to religion. Everything I heard and saw of philosophy seemed to me to pass over what was essential. Love, "real" love, was essential, and so were the consequences of human actions. What could a student do, for example, when he is overpowered by the sexual urge, but does not want to find a partner in the street? Are philosophers not overpowered in that way? Anyone who says *A*, must also say *B*, and eventually *Z* too, all the way through the whole alphabet. What was the *B*, what was the *Z*, in relationship to *this A*, within *this* alphabet? Such were my questions. The philosophers did not seem to have any answers.

My Lutheran Confirmation, when I was fifteen, I had taken very seriously, deeply moved by the solemn act at the altar of St. Mary's and by my first communion. My confirmation text: "Be faithful unto death and I will give you the crown of life," has remained sacred to me all my life. But what did I really believe? Although astronomy, paleontology and biology seemed to be at one in discrediting the old, divine explanation of the world, I refused to cast off belief in God as a superstition. I mocked Haeckels' *Welträtsel* (Riddle of the Universe)—very popular during my years as a student—because in it he passed over the remaining riddles clumsily in superficial phrases. I also rejected an alternative solution which even today many of my most learned friends have chosen; they dismiss the belief in a personal God as a fairytale, but view the universe with great reverence and call this respect religion. If the universe were nothing more than a vortex of glowing masses of atoms, then I would not be able to worship it, neither the masses of atoms nor the influences they exercise upon one another, neither the gigantic spaces in which they move, nor the tremendous time that their rays need to reach us. I refused, and still refuse today, to worship sheer bigness.

If there was no benevolent God behind all this, then I did not want to degrade my reverence in the worship of glowing masses. I would rather shift it to those *human beings,* who had bestowed upon us the great creations of art and thought: Bach, Mozart, Beethoven, Schubert, Shakespeare, Goethe, the Ancient Greeks, and above all Moses and Jesus, who gave us in word and living example the Ten Commandments and the Sermon on the Mount. Nor did I want to put "Mystery" in God's place and content myself with "revering it silently," as Goethe had chosen to do. I was willing only to worship a being who could do at least that which men are capable of on a small scale: thinking, planning, acting; not the bubble of a mystery which might one day burst and leave nothing but an empty space, nor an apathetically brooding cosmos with no conscious will. I was myself a part of this and had grown beyond mere unconsciousness.

Every day and every hour we are confronted with the one alternative: that there is a thinking, planning, acting God, or that there is not. The fact that I was not able to make up my mind did not change that alternative. There cannot be a God one minute, and in the next minute none, just as fits our mood. But my realizing this did not help me to come to a decision. Science in all its exactness, science as *scientia transmissibilis,* as I have called it later, is not able to prove or disprove the existence of God. The scales that weigh the scientific arguments, in favor and against, are evenly balanced. If you, the eager reader, were in God's stead, you would probably not leave them in this state of equilibrium. When Hitler was speaking under a clear, blue sky to thousands of listeners, bragging of providence for his success, you would have sent down a thunderbolt right away from that blue sky. One beautiful summer afternoon when I was saying this to some American students, there was at that very moment a loud clap of thunder outside; a storm had gathered without our having noticed it. American students do not easily believe in miracles. They laughed and so did I.

If science were able scientifically to prove the existence of God, then our struggle with this problem would be pointless. But this does not prove either his existence or the contrary. There were times when I was convinced that there was no God. Well, then, I no longer believed in God. But even then there was something which disturbed my certainty. I prayed: "Dear God, today I have sinned against truth. I have come to the conclusion that you do not exist, but I have not been strong enough to tell the truth to myself and to others. Forgive me my untruthfulness and my weakness." Does a man who prays in this way believe in God or not? It is possible to believe and doubt at the same time, to doubt and believe on different levels. This experience later became the theme of the final chapter in my major academic work, *Political Theory.*

On no level did I ever doubt the historical truth of Jesus dying mocked and apparently powerless on the cross, Jesus, who by his very crucifixion achieved his great power on earth.

I never bothered much about whether I was immortal or not. I believed firmly in life *before* death. That was the life in which I could and must prove myself. I wanted to leave the question as to what comes afterward the secret that it is, without inquiring too closely.

In the course of my life I have put many questions to God. Almost always I have, sooner or later, had an answer. The answer did not come in actual words, but in the form of something actually happening—the consequences of good or evil.

## 5. WHEN YOU DO NOT KNOW WHAT YOU WANT— IN-SERVICE TRAINING (1906–1909)

ON my return from Paris I found Rezia unchanged in her familiarity and affection toward me. She did not care to hide the romantic fancy she had taken to the new conductor, like a schoolgirl. "And why not?" I said. "I have no claims on you. I just love you. I would rather be a conductor of Beethoven, a great actor or an extra at the Royal Opera House than a trainee in Winsen-on-the-Luhe. The great danger that you might return my love is in this way eliminated." "No," she protested, "this danger has not been eliminated."

I celebrated my twenty-second birthday in Lübeck at the end of January and then took up my post in Winsen. I stayed there until October for the prescribed nine months; then I changed over to Lüneburg for a year's training in the district court and a further four months in the public prosecutor's office. But almost every weekend I traveled to Lübeck.

The young composer—his name was Hermann Abendroth—disarmed me with his great musical ability, his lack of affectation, a certain old-fashioned element in his attitude to life, and a lack of ambition in intellectual and literary matters. Rezia lived in both our worlds, and in others too. For we were not the only frequent guests. Other musicians, singers, actors and actresses, writers, painters, who occasionally came from Munich, Berlin, or Italy and sometimes

stayed for longer periods at her home, aesthetes and intellectuals of
Lübeck society, young girls who had serious artistic ambitions, town
people of official rank too—all these came and went. Cupid's darts
sped back and forth. Whoever was tormented by unrequited love
was in his turn unhappily loved by someone else, as in the song by
Heine. No one was entirely happy in his love. Love which knew no
barriers was rather scorned. That was no real love. It was banished
from the land, so to speak, with a patronizing, "Go to bed!" Life
was a charming, yet melancholy game, both serious and facetious,
with plenty of music, many debates about art, theater, culture, and
personal philosophies, gay performances and practical jokes, but
with no clear moral concepts.

Rezia's husband, a respectable Hanseatic citizen with discreet
duelling scars which dated from his time as a member of a student
*Korps,* was to all appearances proud of the lively society of intellectuals and artists his wife drew into his home. He let her frequent
the company of us "boys" and civilize the admiration we bestowed
upon her. He used to say that, if he locked her up, he would make
a cripple of her, and he did not want that. At this time a fourth
child, a girl, was born to the couple, who looked very much like her
mother. At about the same time the only son died. Both these events
only served to increase my admiration for her. I pictured to myself
our all growing older and how we would later look back on these
years, our friendship unaltered.

The conductor was more sensible than I, in conventional terms.
He became engaged to a young actress. Our personal relations grew
very friendly and, when he later took over the Gürzenich concerts
in Cologne, we kept contact through my brother, who was the
chairman of the Cologne Musical Association.

But fundamentally I was as alone in Winsen as I had been in
Leipzig, Grenoble, and Paris. As though from a distance I looked at
myself, saw myself sitting at the bench, taking out briefs, putting
them away again, speaking to witnesses, playing cards, walking
through meadows, writing letters; it was as though I was watching
another person doing these things. Only when I was ardently pursuing some philosophical or scientific line of thought, when I was
trying to give artistic form to some idea, or when I was taking that
long walk in Lübeck from the Holsten Gate through the Burg Gate
to the Soederbrook's house—only then did this double image fade.

I now began to grow accustomed to being alone and felt myself the richer for it. I hired a piano and from now on this was always the first thing I did when I moved somewhere new. It gave me great satisfaction when I gradually achieved a certain mastery over the keys and was thus able, at a time when there was neither radio nor records, to reproduce the music I loved most and thus to feel myself transported to another world in an instant. Some things I played by ear, others I first deciphered from sheets of music and then worked them out independently on the key-board as though I were composing them myself. What I played made a strange mixture. There was, for example, Offenbach (*Tales of Hoffmann*), whom I rated very highly as a composer (I still do today); then, Wagner's *Tristan,* the magnificent preludes to all three acts, the long, warning notes of Brangäne in the second act, and Isolde's death in the third; many of Schubert's songs, at least half of *Müllerlieder* and *Winterreise;* some pieces by Schumann; excerpts from Verdi's *Aida* and *La Traviata,* Bizet's *Carmen,* and some Puccini. I also composed songs of my own with lyrics written in my style of positive irony.

In contrast to Winsen, Lüneburg was an attractive old town with high walls and large wooded areas nearby. I would walk almost every afternoon to "Rote Schleuse," which was about an hour away, drink coffee there, take a ferry across the river and walk back on the other side. As I walked I would be absorbed in critical philosophy, would work out poems and scenes for dramas, and I finished a romantic story called *Traum der Treue* (The Dream of Faithful Love). At the same time I completed my essay on contract liability with no ironic overtones, either negative or positive. This paper, as mentioned before, was immediately published, but the story stayed in my drawer.

There were occasional social gatherings, games of tennis and get-togethers in the evenings. I fell in love from time to time; at that age it is possible to feel love for several women at the same time. But the strongest source of attraction still was in Lübeck.

At work I watched what others did: judges, attorneys, plaintiffs and defendants, the accused and witnesses; and I learned the art of writing case reports. Mine were considered good; difficult and involved trials were assigned to me for handling, and I thus won the friendship of judges who had at first regarded me with disapproval because of my peculiarities.

At the end of my time in Lüneburg, however, twenty-four years old, I had had enough of this prolonged education. I wanted to give up the in-service training, go to Berlin and earn money there by coaching students of law for their exams, write an "instructive commentary" on the Civil Law Code for students, and pursue my *real* inward vocation. But again my father was successful in warning me. You have held out so long, he said, carry on for the final two years as well; then, as an *Assessor* you will have many more possibilities and will thus not find yourself in the position of having done things by halves. His reasoning convinced me. So I persevered, but decided to go for the subsequent training period—to be spent in an attorney's office—to Berlin.

When I saw the tall, boring houses of the endless Berlin suburbs passing by the train windows I was overwhelmed by a feeling of aversion to the great city, or should I say a fear of it. Here there were millions of anonymous people who did not concern me. Here was the Imperial Court with its hierarchy of courtiers, its pomposity, and its arrogance. Here were the top regiments with their military splendor which meant nothing to me. Here was the top-level bureaucracy which I did not trust. And here was what at that moment repulsed me even more: the whole group of established artists and writers, clever people who knew how to operate this machine called Berlin. How could I expect to find any personal echo here, other than a smile? Ought I not to turn back?

But when I was there, when I had my own room and my piano in Marburgerstrasse 15, this aversion soon vanished. One of Berlin's most respected attorneys, Walther Lisco, cousin of Martin Richter, my brother-in-law, accepted me as a trainee. He let me sit with him in his office room in Mohrenstrasse and listen in at his conferences; I worked out individual problems for him, was occasionally to substitute for him at court sessions, and still found time for my articles in *Jherings Jahrbücher*. He was a cultured man, an expert on Goethe, and was pleasantly surprised to find similar predilections in me.

In my leisure time I did not wander around alone as I had done in Paris. At that time Gustav and Gertrud were in Berlin—she was studying music and lived wih Aunt Else Weishaupt—and so were several more distant relatives. Jürgen Fehling was preparing for a career in the theater. I looked up Alfred Kerr, who was then at the peak of his influence as a theater critic. There were numerous others we came to know, and again others who, though no personal friends of ours, were in a sense public property: actors such as Fritzi

Massary, Alexander Moissi, Joseph Giampietro, "old Pagay," Albert Bassermann, painters like Max Liebermann, Lovis Corinth, and Max Slevogt. Berlin became our spiritual home. It was an intoxicating feeling to be just "contemporaries" in this city.

We lived a Bohemian life. We went to all the exhibitions and great theater productions of the time, particularly those of Max Reinhardt, whose star was as yet in the ascendant. We read and liked Büchner, Grabbe, and Strindberg, and discussed the style in which Strindberg ought to be, but was not yet, produced. Our days usually ended in the Café des Westens on Kurfürstendamm, or the restaurant Schwarzes Ferkel, Strindberg's favorite in Dorotheen-strasse, or at Bertolini's Italian restaurant by the Potsdamer Brücke.

I still showed no interest in politics. Only once did I go to the Reichstag. The senior Hanseatic representative took me up to the box reserved for the federal states. Nothing was further from my mind than the thought that one day I myself would have business here.

When my time with Lisco was up, I stayed for the next period of my training—this time with a larger County Court—in Berlin and delighted in the first theatrical efforts of Jürgen Fehling as an actor, not yet as stage director. Then I moved to Celle, in order to finish my prescribed training at the highest Provincial Court.

Thus, after an absence of four years, I found myself once again in Celle, where I had been so happy in the period immediately before my first state examination. I lived again in a room by the Aller river—though I now had a piano, a possession I had formerly to do without—and sailed again in the same boats. I still exchanged letters with Rezia. But their tone and content began to alter. There were arguments, differences of opinion about other people, reproaches, justifications, jealousy perhaps. Since neither of us was willing to put up with less than what we had had, the letters suddenly stopped. Our feelings toward each other remained in essence unaltered, and we both knew it. But outward approaches were at an end. We exchanged only an occasional greeting.

There were brief flareups of other amours. But I never was able to transfer those deeper emotions which had belonged to Rezia for five years, to another woman. Every attempt I made, while reading Goethe or playing Schubert songs, to think of others but her was a ridiculous failure. Even Rezia, at a time when we were still on the best of terms, had had reason to be jealous of my mental image of her.

Once, during one of her short visits to Berlin, when we went to see Offenbach's *Tales of Hoffmann,* it seemed to me that the distant beloved was competing with the one sitting next to me; I found it difficult to realize that the subject of my inward longing as I listened to the music was a physical presence in my immediate vicinity.

My life so far had been an *éducation sentimentale,* an education in feeling and in art, a search for truth, and at the same time a professional education—but none at all for political activity. I had nothing to do with the German youth movement of that time, called *Wandervogel.* In order to be able to live, truly to live, I had to be alone or in the company of a few friends.

Like many before and after me I tried to unite Nazareth and Hellas; like many before and after me, I failed. Every step toward Nazareth is a step away from Hellas; every step toward Hellas is one away from Nazareth. Yet both were very strong within me.

The beauty I sought was beauty expressive of something supernatural. I looked for and found it in nature, in art, in human persons, in human interrelations. But only in tranquillity. In hallowed silence. Alone.

## 6. THE GREAT STATE EXAMINATION—DEATH OF MY FATHER—JUDGE IN LÜBECK (1910)

I WROTE my major thesis for the second ("great") state examination at home in Lübeck in the fall of 1909. My parents had traveled to Arosa in Switzerland on account of a slight relapse in the pulmonary disease which, during my childhood, had necessitated my father's going twice to Ajaccio on Corsica and Ospedaletti on the Riviera in the winter; after these visits, however, he had been declared cured.

The maid stayed behind and cared for my needs. I was joined for lunch by Georg Pfuhl, a friend of Jürgen Fehling's, who had attached himself to me, too, and accompanied me to Lübeck. He was as bizarre as a character out of Hoffmann's tales, lover of all arts, clearly unsuited to contemporary bourgeois life, yet marvellous as a companion in spinning out unusual trains of thought, and very musical. He composed beautiful songs. He also had the gift of presenting problems vividly in short plays, and eventually wrote some twenty one-act plays—among them "Hiob" and "Xanthippe"—all of which have a tone peculiar to him, but none was produced, nor even printed. We talked of everything but politics.

Two days after I had submitted my thesis my father died, at the age of sixty-eight. His heart had not been able to stand the altitude of 1,800 meters; the lung specialists had not taken this fact into consideration and, when it was discovered, it was too late to take him down to the valley. His poor condition had been concealed from me in accordance with his wishes, so that I would not be distracted from my work. We buried him in Lübeck, to the music of the funeral march in Beethoven's seventh symphony and the ringing of the bells of the old churches. Henceforth we would have to miss his clear honesty, the incorruptible objectivity of his judgment, his goodness which I had so often deceived, his profound concern for our development, the nobility of his brow and that happy ease which radiated from him on quiet evenings spent at home with wife and children. But even more painful to me was the fact that I had not been able to assuage his anxieties about my future, which had troubled him to the last. My ministerial career, which was to begin just a year later, would have put our relationship on a completely new, more mature, and for him happier, footing.

I received the news of his death late at night and, in order to be able to pull myself together, went out for a walk alone in the darkness, over the lonely walls, continuing to the Burg Gate, down by the harbor back to the Holsten Gate, past the "old station" (a new one had been built under my father's management), and past our old house in Moislinger Allee, back to the present house in Lachswehr Allee—more than two hours, walking quickly. I entered the house again long after midnight and was just going to my bedroom when there was a sudden loud continuous ringing which went on and on with no interruption. The ringing did not come from the door, nor from the telephone. It was an uncanny experience. Many years later, one evening in Cambridge, Massachusetts, when the Harvard philosophers Ernest Hocking and Ralph Barton Perry, the political scientist, Professor Arthur Holcombe, and the former Chancellor Brüning were our guests, the conversation turned to "parapsychic experiences." The two philosophers were discussing what to do with money bequeathed to the university for parapsychic research. Each of us related some experience, I that story. In reality, when it hap-

pened, I had not lost my composure but tried to trace the physical
cause of the ringing and had found it at a damaged point of the cir-
cuit, where the two wires to and from the bell crossed. But the fact
that it is possible to find a physical cause does not fully account for
the psychical experience, nor refute the possibility that God uses the
physical range in psychical happenings. When something psychical
happens to you, you must not show too much physical curiosity;
this can only cause a distraction from what is essential. We philoso-
phized about such topics. I confessed that the symbolic force of that
mysterious ringing at just that critical moment had always stayed in
my mind—like some urgent call, a wish for communication, an appeal for help or a warning signal.

On the morning of April 18, 1910—eight years to the day since
my debut at the university—I took the oral part of the examination
in the Prussian Ministry of Justice in Berlin, wearing my dress-coat,
as was the custom. Passing once again with "good," I now was seriously faced with the difficult choice of a profession. I still was ill
prepared for a decision. There seemed to me to be three separate
worlds: the worlds of thinking, acting, dreaming (poetry). All
three made claims on me. But they could not be combined. The one
impeded the other. There is a way of settling a disagreement: the
disputing persons stretch out their hands in one of three positions—
one signifying "paper" (hand flat); the second "stone" (fist
clenched); the third, "scissors" (two fingers spread). Who wins is
decided according to the formula: "Paper wraps up stone, stone
whets scissors, scissors cut paper." The relationship of dreaming,
thinking, and acting seemed to me similar. Dreaming enwraps acting, thinking cuts up dreaming, acting kills thought.

Which of the many jobs, that were open to a successful *Assessor,*
should I choose? Walther Lisco, the Berlin attorney, offered me a
vacation post in his office, but I refused despite the prospects it
opened up. For the present I took leave from Prussia and accepted
an invitation from the president of the Lübeck court system to help
out as a judge in Lübeck. Thus every week in the summer and fall
of 1910 I held my two or three sessions either as single judge in the
lower court or as a member of the three-man district court.

The burden of this work was much greater than I had expected.
It took all my energy to work through the sixty to eighty files for
the next session and to write out the opinions. My knowledge of

the law and my faculty for logical thought were sufficient, but my practical experience was small. On the whole the impression I have kept of that time is that at twenty-six one is too young to be a judge, at least the only judge at a one-man court. The practice of the Anglo-American countries, which select their judges at a later age from among tested attorneys and let their young lawyers first earn their spurs as attorneys, seems wiser to me.

High as I rated the job of a judge, I felt that I did not want to stay therein. One of Lübek's most prosperous attorneys, Emanuel Fehling, elder brother of Jürgen, offered me a partnership in his law firm. Gladly, I replied, but only half-time, for half the money. I wanted to devote the other half of my working hours to literary plans. He answered that half a Brecht is less than half, since a large part of time at work is spent in gathering information and only completeness of knowledge about people and things makes work as valuable as it can be.

Only seldom did I go to the Soederbrook's house. I had grown too old to continue the relationship as it had been. A new, younger friend had taken over the role of enthusiastic admirer. There was still a glow under the ashes. But I could no longer find a deeper meaning in my staying on in Lübeck. I longed to return to Berlin.

I wrote a letter to the state secretary of the Federal Department of Justice in Berlin, Hermann Lisco, brother of the attorney and like him a cousin of my brother-in-law. I complained to him of my indecision in choosing a profession. In the work as a judge there was something missing. "Law suits come. Judgments go." I wanted to create new law, not merely apply the old. I wanted to be able to look back on something I had created. In view of my good exam report he invited me to present myself to the Under Secretary of his department. I did this. After the latter had conversed with me politely for a time, he asked if I were prepared to enter the Department as an assistant (*Hilfsarbeiter*), in order, among other things, to undertake some of the preparatory work for the new penal code. Such a call was an affair of great distinction in imperial Germany. Delighted, I answered yes.

Lübeck obliged by releasing me from my duties. There was a farewell party at Rezia's, and suddenly, there were tears again. Then, on the 7th of December, 1910, still at the age of twenty-six, I took up my position in Berlin.

## 7. In the Federal Department of Justice (1910–1918)

The work and the surroundings in the Department of Justice were so congenial that I soon forgot my choice of a profession. This was the right place for deferring the decision. There were in the Department at that time under the direction of the Under Secretary only about eight established councillors (*Vortragende Räte*) and some six to eight aides—judges on loan from Prussia or other states or younger lawyers (*Assessoren*) like me. They were all hand-picked. The mere quality of the work made working with them a pleasure, and this was the greater because of the friendly relations between older and younger members and among the younger ones themselves. Here I began my lifelong friendship with Erich Zweigert, later State Secretary in the Republican Ministry of Interior, and with Ernst Trendelenburg, later State Secretary in the Ministry of Economics.

My work did not, however, consist of that application of creative initiative which I longed for. I first had to put together extracts of essays on penal law reform to be laid before the Commission in book form at their meeting in April, 1911. Then I became one of the three recorders of the Commission. We took turns at the three weekly sessions and spent the rest of the week working out our minutes carefully. Nevertheless, I felt the opportunity for participating at the meetings of the Commission and the friendly communication with its members and the government delegates to be an exceptional privilege. The basic questions of guilt and responsibility, nature and degree of penalties, their execution and consequences, were all not nearly thoroughly enough considered, I thought. But otherwise good work was done. Zeal was so great that once during a total eclipse of the sun, after only a brief glance at this rare marvel, work was resumed, if uneasily, with the electric lights turned on; this disrespect enraged me, but was in keeping with the Prussian sense of duty.

Other tasks occasionally fell to us assistants too: drafting minor laws and memoranda, handling complaints about lack or procrastination of justice, and the like—nothing of great importance.

Privately, I wrote my third major essay for *Jherings Jahrbücher,* "Condition and Expectation," already mentioned. The completed, handwritten manuscript suddenly disappeared without a trace. After two days of vain searching, it occurred to me that while I was working on other things at home I had put it down on a tubular wastepaper basket beside me, and had forgotten to remove it when I went out. The basket had been emptied into the garbage can and this taken away. All attempts to recover the manuscript failed. I could overcome the destructive feeling I had only by forcing myself to rewrite the entire essay—about two hundred pages—from memory and reconstruct the bibliographical references from notes. The most annoying thing was that I did not gain that inner freedom which would have enabled me to write the essay afresh, but tried continually to reconstruct the formulations I had used in the first draft. Only when the repeat performance was completed did the affair cease to haunt me. Since then I have never laid manuscripts down on wastepaper baskets.

Life at the Department was very hospitable. We assistants were in the course of every winter invited at least once by each of the older councillors, together with all the others, to a festive dinner, always in evening dress. Hermann Lisco, the head of the Department, and his friendly wife—both of them great admirers of Goethe—invited me also to their own social gatherings and asked me to help in their arrangement.

While I am writing this I can see the building in Voss Strasse 4 clearly, with the door through which we, "freely in order of seniority" (this phrase was repeated every time with a laugh), re-entered after lunch, the corridors and every room, in several of which I myself had worked for a time, and the men whose faces, figures, movements, and voices I knew so well and still do know. The building is no longer there, not even its ruins, only flat concrete, and apart from me none of the men is still alive. But in my mind they all still live, freely in order of seniority.

More important in retrospect than this sentimental memory is the fact that despite the ministerial surroundings and the nearness of Wilhelmstrasse, I still had no contact with politics.

Because of the late voting age under the monarchy (25 years) the first national elections in which I could vote were those of 1912. Although I was by then twenty-eight years old, I was completely unprepared for the election. At that time every third German voted for

Social Democrats, just as in the elections of 1898 one in four had done. But I did not think in terms of party concepts; I thought of individuals and personalities. The Social Democrat candidate for my constituency in Berlin was a far cry from Goethe, and the other candidates did not please me more. I did something stupid. I remembered that Count Bernhard Bülow had as Chancellor mustered the courage to go to the Kaiser and warn him to be cautious in his utterances. This had probably been a decisive reason for his fall from grace. I voted for Bülow. He got *one* vote. What I did was politically immature and senseless. I spoke to no one about it; the whole thing made me feel embarrassed rather than involved. I remembered it, however, when, after the discharges of Bethmann Hollweg, Michaelis, and Hertling in 1917 and 1918, each time leading members of parliament, including Stresemann and Erzberger, had their eye on Bülow for Chancellor at a time when I would no longer have considered him. They had to give up because of the insurmountable opposition of the Kaiser.

That many middle-class Germans wanted and were able to lead a non-political life was not due to their lack of political power and education alone. Intellectually eminent people, in particular the "Goethe-Germans," lived under the exalted delusion that it was not becoming for them to meddle in politics, that the entire political tumult belonged to a lower level, that it was better to be concerned with what was "essential." Even among leading government officials there were many, including Hermann Lisco, who in this manner tried with a gentle smile to rise over the harshness of political reality on the wings of Goethe.

The German intelligentsia in those years enjoyed almost all the freedom of a democratic society for their critical remarks on social and political conditions, for satirical writings and cartoons, provided the critic did not care for success in government service (as a municipal official he might pass) or for lucrative government orders in business. Only high treason and gross, crude forms of lèse-majesté, uttered aloud in public, would cause charges to be brought.

When I say that criticism in Germany was as free as in democratic countries, that is not saying enough. It was even more free, because its freedom was not checked by responsibility. Many intellectuals indulged with delight in this boundless freedom without being fully aware of how mean is freedom without responsibility, and in particular the complacent enjoyment of such freedom. For civil servants there was another excuse. To keep aloof from politics was in line with the ideal of impartiality.

Finally, there were private circumstances that kept me from paying much attention to politics. Shortly after taking up my position in Berlin I got to know my sister Gertrud's closest friend there, a slender, but well-built, sportive, yet graceful woman, seeking trust, truth, God and immortality of the soul, far from our toying with positive and negative irony, serious, lively and warm-hearted. She had brown eyes and rich brown hair which she wore in a thick, soft plait around her head. Unhappily married, having wed at the age of nineteen with no knowledge of the world, she had, before I met her, after several unsuccessful attempts to revive trust, made the grave decision to dissolve her marriage and restart her life independently. The development of our love, from its first stirrings until the end of the long period of waiting, which the formal dissolution of the first marriage and consideration for all those involved imposed upon us, is not what I have set out to describe in this book. For the first time since I had met Rezia as a twenty-year-old student seven years before, I encountered a woman who could hold her own in my mind over against Rezia's shadow.

There was a decisive turning point also in brother Gustav's life. He became engaged to a Belgian girl who was studying German and music, daughter of a deceased Belgian colonel, with some German blood from the Humboldt family in her veins. When the time for the wedding came round I took advantage of the opportunity to make a ten-day trip through Belgium with Georg Pfuhl. Then I functioned as a witness at the wedding in Brussels. When I toasted the bride at dinner in my imperfect French I tried to comfort her mother by saying that you only had to get into the right train in Berlin in the evening in order to be in Brussels the next morning, and that it would be the same the other way round, when she visited her daughter. None of us suspected what a difficult time the couple would have to live through but three years later. Norah overcame all ordeals. In the course of years she became the central figure in our family life, not only because she was Gustav's wife but because of her own charm and character.

From Lübeck I received the news that Rezia's marriage had ended in divorce. I did not learn the particular cause. I was saddened at this turn in events, which was so little in keeping with my wishes, and felt guilty. When on my next stay in Lübeck I visited her husband, he asked me before I left if I played billiards. He opened the door of his study to the neighboring room—the renaissance room with the blue walls and the heavy yellow curtains. The grand piano had disappeared. In its place in the middle of the room there stood a large, green billiard table and there were cues leaning against the wall. I held my breath. It seemed as though he were looking at me mockingly. I pressed his hand and quickly took leave, to conceal my emotion. Neither of them married again. He was killed in action at Langemarck in the first year of the war, when he was almost fifty. She, by now approaching forty, worked in German hospitals in Belgium. When I was in Brussels for a short visit in 1918 (Chapter 10), we exchanged written greetings. Then I did not hear of her for a long time.

But back to 1914. It was customary for young aides to stay at departmental headquarters for four years and then to take positions outside, so they could obtain practical experience and also in order to prevent their being promoted out of mere convenience instead of the full staff members being freely selected from the most able lawyers in the country. This was one of the many wise principles of the former German administration. Thus at the beginning of 1914, when my four years came to end, I looked round for another sphere of activity.

The old doubts and problems about a choice of profession all re-emerged. What did I really want? I travelled to Göttingen and discussed the possibility of an academic career with Professor Rabel, an authority on Roman Law. "Whose pupil are you?" he asked me. Then I was approached by the Juridical Faculty of the University of Marburg, who were looking for an assistant professor (*Privatdozent*). They offered to accept my three publications in *Jherings Jahrbücher* as an inaugural dissertation (*Habilitationsschrift*). So it only remained for me to fulfill the formality of a colloquium with the Faculty, and then to begin my lectures in the winter term. I accepted. August 4th was set as the date for my colloquium—August 4th in the year 1914. Things were to turn out differently.

# PART II
## Political Awakening

## 8. Events But Dimly Noticed

When I spoke of my continued lack of interest in politics, I did not mean that I had neglected reading the newspapers carefully. I did do that, of course, and I also exchanged comments with other people, gradually filling the gaps in my knowledge of modern history. In my own mind I built a better world. But I felt no personal responsibility for what went on around me in the political arena. What was lacking was any form of *action* on my part, whether in union with other people or in persistent personal efforts—action in support of some great cause, the cause of peace, the cause of freedom, the cause of political and social justice, or only the cause of political truth. I let it pass. I loved Germany and wished everyone well. Political events and the dates of my own life merely happened to coincide, to be contemporary.

And with how many major events had my existence already been contemporary! I shall list a few of them. Their assignment to dates of my life not only serves the understanding of one particular man; it illustrates the historical significance of a person's year of birth. The fact that the impact of major political events affects a great variety of persons at the same stages of their lives lends people of the same age group mysteriously kindred traits later on.

When I was born, William I was still German Emperor and Bismarck his Chancellor. In the year of my birth (1884) Germany acquired her first colonies, Togo and Cameroon; the dual alliance with Austria had become a triple alliance including Italy; and in Germany the Health Insurance Act, which was to become a model for the whole world, came into force. When I was three years old, Bismarck concluded the Neutrality Treaty ("Re-insurance Pact") with Russia. When I was four, the old Emperor died and, after the short episode with Kaiser Friedrich, Wilhelm II came to the throne, at the age of only 29—but all I can remember is that I got a fortress with towers and drawbridges on my fourth birthday; this is the first memory I have of anything.

When I was six, Bismarck was dismissed; the picture "The pilot leaves the ship" in *Punch,* which my father showed and explained to me, is my first *political* reminiscence. In the same year (1890) the German act outlawing Social Democrats expired without renewal and their numbers increased so quickly that, before I was fifteen, every fourth German voted for a Social Democrat in the Reichstag elections. In 1890 also the Re-insurance Pact with Russia came to an end, likewise unrenewed, so that Russia was free to come to terms with France.

The Spanish-American War (1898) passed unnoticed by me. Apart from stories about Red Indians, I knew almost nothing about America. I doubt that I could have explained the difference between Washington, Jefferson, and Chicago. Yet I well remember the day of Bismarck's death (July 30, 1898). It was during the summer holidays and I was loitering around the paddock at the Travemünde race meeting, using complimentary tickets which were given every year to my father as chairman of the railroad board. Suddenly the flags were lowered to half-mast. Bismarck was dead. The contrast between the cheerful activity on this beautiful racetrack by the Baltic under the blazing sun and the seriousness which the news of the death caused and which dominated all conversations during the following weeks, is an example of that linking of historical events with the memory of physical atmosphere which exists only in the minds of people who have experienced the events personally. Who thinks about the weather in connection with the deaths of Caesar, Alexander, or Pericles?

I saw Bismarck in the flesh only once, when I was a small child and my father received him at the station on a visit to Lübeck. He offered me his hand, but I refused, much to the horror of my mother, and crossed my hands behind my back, the way children do; it was not a *political* demonstration.

The first political shock came to me at the age of sixteen when, at the embarkation of German troops for China, the Kaiser said: "There will be no pardon. No prisoners will be taken. Just as the Huns made their name a thousand years ago under Attila, a name which in legend and tradition seems mighty even today, so let the name German become activated by you for a thousand years so that no Chinese will so much as dare to look askance at a German." After that it became clear to me that many people did not take the Kaiser seriously, at least not until after he had learned, after many setbacks, to behave with greater reserve in public. Respect for the Kaiser as a symbol of German unity was kept separate from the shoulder-shrugging, at times humorous, at times uneasy, at times bitter, criticism of the bearer of imperial dignity.

My experience as a student of tentative British moves toward an agreement on the relative size of the two navies and of Germany's rejection of these feelers was similarly passive, if I took any notice at all. Likewise, I all but ignored the subsequent approach made by England to France (1903) and the conclusion of the *entente cordiale* (1904).

German attempts to acquire a large colonial empire in Africa stand out more clearly. Southwest Africa had first to be defended against the revolts of the natives (1904–1906). When the first Moroccan crisis arose (1905) I realized what was going on. By protesting against the increase in France's African power Germany wanted to win considerable colonial compensation, but had in the end to be satisfied with minor concessions. Much to the annoyance of extreme nationalists, the Kaiser and Chancellor Bülow wanted to avoid war (Algeciras, 1906). There followed the extension of the Anglo-French Entente to include Russia (1907); the dissolution and re-election of the Reichtag with national slogans, which led to temporary losses for the Social Democrats; the dismissal of Bülow, the beginning of Bethmann Hollweg's chancellorship (1909) and the second Moroccan crisis (1911–1912). The crisis began with the dispatch of a small military vessel, the "Panther," to Agadir as evidence of the German wish for a say in the new situation created by French expeditions in Morocco. It again ended with a German failure, ill-concealed by minor concessions. The visit of the English Secretary for War, Haldane, in Berlin (the "Haldane Mission," 1912) did not end in agreement, but rather led to the exposure of irreconcilable antagonisms. Germany, as we now know, tried in vain to obtain a conclusive pledge of English neutrality in the case of attack by France or Russia on Germany; England was prepared to promise neutrality only in the case of an *unprovoked* attack. The defeat of Turkey, whose armed forces had been trained by German generals, in the Balkan War (1913) followed. Strengthening of Germany's army and the adding of two corps to her army (1912–1913) were answered by corresponding naval increases in England and the introduction of three years' military service in France.

The background to all these events was known only to few. Many details were not made public until after the war. But one thing could not remain hidden even to those with little interest in politics, namely, the groundswell in the German will to power—economic as well as political—which accompanied, and in a way surrounded, my early years. The consciousness of strength, the claim to a position in the world corresponding to this strength, and the will to secure recognition of this claim found expression in many ways, not only in the Kaiser's own defiant remarks, not only in the establishment of the Naval Union (*Flottenverein*) and the Defense Union (*Wehrverein*) and their noisy propaganda movements, but also in everyday discussions among the upper-middle classes who were liable to become intoxicated with patriotic visions of the future, although on the whole they remained as aloof from politics in general as previously. In the spirit of this atmosphere a young academic lecturer, Erich Kaufmann, afterwards a very sensible Professor of public law, wrote in his book, *The Nature of International Law* (1911), that the essential nature of the state was "the development of power" and the desire to "assert itself and succeed in history," and that the real social ideal was "victorious war." In war "the state reveals its true nature, this is its greatest performance, in which its peculiarity finds its most complete display." A "victorious war" proved to be "the final criterion which decides which of the states is right." Such views nauseated me. If a woman wearing the blue uniform of the Salvation Army came late at night into the Café des Westens or Bartolini's I would take a deep breath. Here there was a pure human being in infamous times. I would buy the Salvation Army's *War-cry* from her and not laugh (or only with positive irony) when she and her comrades sang spiritual songs to the melody of popular hits.

My suspicion that the affairs of this world were in disastrous shape was not limited to Germany. The opinions people in Germany at that time had of other countries can be easily imagined if one re-reads the following sentences from the contemporary reports of Belgian diplomats. I volunteered to put these together later (see below, Chapter 11), and I insert some of them here. If Belgians—rightly or wrongly—judged the politics of England, France, and Russia in this way, how much more so did the Germans.

Baron Greindl, the Belgian Ambassador in Berlin, wrote to his government: "The real cause of the English attitude towards the Germans is jealousy" (1905). "If England attacks Germany one day in order to get rid of a rival, then she will only be acting in accordance with her old principles" (1905). "There is no longer any doubt that it was the King of England who forced M. Delcassé into his martial policies" (1906). "This eagerness to unite forces threatened by no one (Spain, Italy) ostensibly for defence purposes can justifiably be held suspect. It is impossible in Berlin to forget the offer of 100,000 men made by the King of England to M. Delcassé" (1907). "French arrogance is becoming just as great as during the final terrible days of the Second Empire and the *entente cordiale* is to blame" (1907). "The policy pursued by King Edward VII under the pretext of protecting Europe from an imaginary German threat has only caused an all too genuine threat from France, which is of danger principally to us [Belgium]" (1908). "The customary assurances of peace have very little significance in the mouths of three powers which, as in the recent case of England and Russia, in the single endeavour to extend their power, have, without plausible excuse, waged wars of conquest in Manchuria and the Transvaal, or which, like France at the present time, set about the conquest of Morocco, ignoring solemn promises and with no other legal right than the transfer of rights from England, who never had any" (1908). "Some of my colleagues are astounded at Germany's forbearance" (1911).

Baron Greindl, to be sure, was particularly Germanophile. But similar opinions can be found in the reports of other Belgian diplomats. The Belgian Ambassador in London, Count Lalaing, wrote: "The atmosphere in England evoked by fear and jealousy . . . has not subsided in the slightest degree (1907). "A certain category of the press, known here under the name *Yellow Press,* bears a large part of the responsibility for the hostile atmosphere between the two countries [England and Germany]" (1907). "It is clear that the Government of England is pursuing a policy which is hostile to Germany and which is aiming at isolation, and that King Edward has not disdained to use his own personal influence in this matter" (1907).

Baron Guillaume, the Belgian Ambassador in Paris: "There will be much less prospect of coming to an agreement with Germany if England takes part in the discussions" (1911). "M. Poincaré is from Lorraine and lets no opportunity of remembering this pass; he was one of the collaborators and instigators of Millerand's military policies" (1913). "In the troubled times in which Europe now finds herself, there is here the danger that lies in the presence of M. Poincaré in the Elisée. Under his ministry the militaristic and chauvinistic instincts of the French people have been awakened. In this sudden development his part is clearly recognizable" (1913). "Poincaré, Delcassé, Millerand and their friends have designed militaristic and chauvinistic policies. These present a danger for Europe and for Belgium" (January 6, 1914).

Finally the Belgian Ambassador in Serbia, later Belgian Minister for Foreign Affairs, Baron Beyens: "There is no doubt that the Kaiser, the Chancellor Bethmann Hollweg and the Secretary of State for Foreign Affairs are passionate supporters of peace" (end of 1912). "In a communicative moment the French Ambassador in Berlin admitted to me how difficult it was to reckon with the highly gifted, but fickle politicians who govern the Empire [Russia] in alliance with France. . . . M. Cambon in particular complained about the continued influence of Mr. Iswolsky, who wants to have personal revenge against Austria" (1913).

This was the political world, or some aspects of it, both in and outside Germany, which I had been facing so far as a mere contemporary, a mere spectator.


## 9. POLITICAL EDUCATION THROUGH
### THE WAR'S OUTBREAK (1914)


BUT then the war came.

What was it—war? Only very old people, in the far-off days of their youth, had gone through the experience of a European war. For men and women of thirty or forty, and indeed of fifty too, the thought that there might be war, actual war, was rather unreal. Despite the grave tension preceding the war, its actual outbreak, therefore, overtook almost everyone in Germany by surprise in a great variety of private circumstances.

I had moved in July to a boarding house in a Berlin suburb, in order to escape the continual noise and the great heat in my two city rooms and to prepare myself for the Marburg colloquium. Disturbed by the news, my attitude to politics began to change. I started looking at the political events as at something I had to be concerned with, regardless of whether or not I might have any influence on it. In the first place, I felt, I had to form my own judgment.

The results of my appraisal were not particularly original in the beginning. Roughly, they were as follows. The murder of the heir of the Austrian throne was a monstrous crime committed out of political motives. Austria's insistence that the guilty persons and their supporters be punished was understandable, even necessary. The fact, however, that the formulated demands were so severe as virtually to exclude their full adoption was highly reprehensible. And when the Austrian government rejected Serbia's remarkably extensive acceptance of these demands, it was playing with fire. The fact that the German government failed to restrain Austria more firmly was a grave omission, the more so because the outbreak of the Austro-Serbian War (July 28), the result of such clumsy diplomacy, obviously brought the danger of a general European war very close. I was, however, convinced at this point that neither the Kaiser nor the Chancellor wanted war with Russia or France. The Kaiser's departure on his customary summer cruise to the north did not deceive me as to the danger, but I did not consider it to be an attempt to camouflage the real intentions of the German government.

Then came the Russian total mobilization (July 30). In the view of the German general staff, Germany was not equal to war with a fully mobilized Russia and France at the same time. Germany's only military prospect in that case was considered to lie in her making use of the long time the Russian deployment would take to strike decisive blows in the west. Would the German government really do that? Or would they continue negotiations and run the risk that in case of war Russia would be fully mobilized and ready to invade Germany? I hoped desperately that there would even now be a further attempt to avert war from Germany or at least to confine it to Russia. But any major last-minute alteration of the detailed plans made beforehand was considered impossible. So there followed the German mobilization, the declaration of war on Russia (August 1), simultaneously the ultimatum to France demanding assurance of French neutrality—with the logical, yet ignominious demand (in reality not passed on by the German Ambassador in Paris, but nevertheless picked up by French monitors) that as a guarantee of her neutrality France should allow Germany to occupy the border fortresses of Toul and Verdun—and then, after France's refusal, the declaration of war on France.

These were the impressions at that time of a German who, to be sure, was no political expert but who neither was a naïve "provin-

cial," nor a simple-minded nationalist, but a critically attuned observer; and his opinions were identical with those of the overwhelming majority of his fellow citizens in Germany, particularly
of the German working class. I have set them down here as they
were at the time. That is historically more important than noting
wisdom acquired subsequently. For this is a book of personal memories, not a piece of historical research into the causes of the war.

Today, of course, we know many facts not known to me at that
time. Above all it seems that not only did the German government
fail effectively to restrain Austria, but had actually encouraged the
Austrian statesmen to go ahead, in order to revive Austria's sinking
prestige—all along fully aware of the danger that this could lead to
war with Russia and France and consciously taking this alternative
into account.[1] All this is historically very important. But at that time
the German people knew nothing about it. They justifiably felt threatened by the Russian mobilization. Nor do the subsequent political
findings alter the fact that the Kaiser and the Chancellor had not
"intentionally brought about" the war with Russia and France (in
contrast to that with Serbia), nor had they "desired" it, but on the contrary would have been glad if things had not gone that far. Of this
I am fully convinced even today, however much I condemn German
diplomacy toward Austria at that time.

When the war thus had suddenly become reality, a tremendous inward excitement and an equally tremendous outward commotion
burst in on those many private lives which together form the life of
the nation. It was the most beautiful, hot and dry summer Germany
ever had. As usual at this time of the year, everyone who was able
to travel was on holiday, or about to set off. Overnight everyone
who was away wanted to return from the seaside and the mountains. As a result there was dreadful crowding in trains and on stations.

Nor could those who did not have to travel stand to be at home.
They streamed into the city center, women and girls in their white
summer dresses. They surged up Wilhelmstrasse and Unter den Linden in front of the palace. I can see myself standing in the summer

---

[1] Cf. Fritz Fischer, *Griff nach der Weltmacht,* Düsseldorf, 1961, pp. 63 ff. This
is, however, a disputed account. See, e.g., Gerhard Ritter, "Eine neue Kriegsschuld-
frage," *Historische Zeitschrift,* vol. 194 (1962), pp. 646–68, and Hans Herzfeld,
"Die deutsche Kriegspolitik im ersten Weltkrieg," *Vierteljahrshefte für Zeitgeschichte,* vol. 11 (1963), pp. 224–45, especially p. 228.

evening among the huge crowds in the palace square. People wanted to see the "little princes," that is, the children of the crown prince. Someone appeared and shouted down that the little princes had to go to bed. The crowd surged on.

Riding home on my suburban train, I heard a complaining voice in the overcrowded compartment, in the middle of men who would shortly have to take the field, of women who would have to take leave of their husbands and sons, the loud voice of a woman who had cut her holiday short: "Und wo bleibt meine ganze Erholung?" ("And what is going to become of all my recreation?"). I could never forget that voice and the egoism it expressed. It was a phrase I often repeated when at important moments minor, egoistic complaints are made totally out of proportion to what other people have to face.

My brother Rolf, then seventeen, was spending his first term as a law student in Lausanne. Wont to send comforting reports to calm mother's unending worries about him, he wrote on a postcard to me: "I am quite safe here." With the authority of the elder brother I replied that now he had to come back to his country. So he came, volunteered for the army, was declared too young—which happened twice more when he volunteered again—spent two further terms studying in Germany, then was accepted for service with the field artillery, trained, and sent into the field, first in the east, then in the west. He was wounded five times, each time coming home or going into the field hospital and then back into battle. But he survived and twenty years later was still strong enough to serve as a captain in the Second World War from its outbreak until a serious hip wound rendered him unfit for service and, after a long stay in hospital, he returned to his delicate wife and little son, only to have his home in Koblenz shattered by a bomb. Once again he escaped death only by a hair's breadth.

Gustav's seventeen-year-old Belgian brother-in-law, Charley, was working in Berlin. I now had to give him responsible advice as to what to do, for Gustav was not yet back home from his seashore resort. I advised Charley to return to Belgium immediately, gave him the money for the fare and took him to the station. That was on August 2. He was one of the last civilians to cross the Belgian border. I did not have the faintest idea that a German invasion of Belgium was imminent and it is on this account that I have mentioned the episode. For the fact that even a government official, who had been working in a federal department in Berlin for four years, knew nothing of the planned invasion of Belgium, serves well to illustrate the general ignorance of the German people in this respect. The result was that Charley, who, had he stayed in Berlin, would two days later have been interned as an enemy alien and would thus probably have survived the war, joined the Belgian army and was killed in his first engagement.

When Gustav and Norah arrived they approved my advice to Charley and turned to preparing their own great leave-taking; for Gustav had to report with his regiment on August 5. The day before his departure we celebrated Norah's birthday and listened to a sermon which horrified me by its warlike tone at a time when we thirsted to hear the gospel of love. Some time afterward my mother's only brother died, Colonel Ewald Weishaupt, director of the rifle factory in Spandau. The clergyman at the funeral praised the deceased for having slipped weapons into the hands of hundreds of thousands of German soldiers. My desire to hear sermons had been satisfied for a long time to come.

Meanwhile the military deployment was taking its course. What was going on about us normal mortals was equally overwhelming because of its scale, its precision, and its secret nature. When I heard the trains rolling endlessly through the night, I was overawed by the sinister magnitude of the historical process.

Then the 4th of August came, and with it Bethmann Hollweg's announcement in the Reichstag that at that moment the German army was marching through Belgium, admitting that this was a wrong, but appealing to the higher principle that necessity knows no command and promising reparation: "Thus we were forced to overlook the protests of the governments of Luxemburg and Belgium. The wrong (*das Unrecht*)—I am speaking frankly—we are thus doing, we will try to repair (*wieder gut zu machen*) as soon as we have achieved our military goal." I was standing behind the Chancellor as he spoke these words, on the government dais which, normally empty, was overcrowded. Someone beside me whispered: "That means war with England." I was too stunned to be able to understand. I thought of Charley whom I had just sent across the border and who would now fight with his brothers against German troops and they against him. The decision was obviously politically, militarily, and morally momentous. But I was not yet sure that it would cause Great Britain to enter the war, until the British decla-

ration of war was received; for I thought that the German government must have assured itself of the contrary before giving the
order for the invasion. The fact that there were no such assurances
and that vague hopes were relied upon played a considerable part in
the destruction of my political confidence.

But there was something in Bethmann Hollweg's announcement
in the Reichstag which seemed to me to be a new element in politics (and indeed it was) and which pleased me: namely that he
himself admitted that Germany was doing a wrong. He has been bitterly criticized in Germany for this admission, which was said to
have been a gross blunder; he rather ought, in the old diplomatic
fashion, to have declared that Belgium had broken her obligations
as a neutral state years beforehand. Certainly that would have been
diplomatically "clever." It would have been even more clever if Germany had never invaded Belgium at all, if Kaiser and Chancellor
had bluntly rejected the plan from the day of its conception on.
How different the world would be today! But I must admit that,
once this fateful step had been taken, the honest admission, "We are
doing a wrong," seemed to me like the dawn of a new day in politics. No one had ever spoken like this before; I can think of no historical example of a statesman admitting that his actions were unjust.

I noticed that Bethmann's frank words made a strong impression
on the Social Democrats, whose conduct was very important at this
moment. The words seemed to arouse something like confidence in
the integrity and honesty of the Chancellor. Those who condemn
his declaration as a diplomatic error should not overlook this fact. I
do not know whether this favorable personal impression played a
part in the following sanction of the war credits by the Social Democrats. Certainly two other major circumstances were decisive in this
respect: first, the conviction shared by the working class that it was
not the German declaration of war but the Russian general mobilization which had started the war; second, the spontaneous desire of
the proletariat and of the Social-Democratic members of parliament
to protect German culture and Germany's liberal and social development against the far more reactionary and brutal Tsarist regime in
Russia.

The German occupation authorities afterward found documents
in the Belgian Foreign Office which showed that Germany's opponents had long before the war made tentative approaches to Bel-

gium regarding military collaboration in case of war. These documents, from which I quoted extracts on Anglo-French policies above, made such a strong impression on me—my conscience having been greatly troubled by the invasion of Belgium—that I went to the press division of the Foreign Office and urged them to publish a short booklet putting together the most telling passages. I was asked to compile such a booklet. I did so. It consisted merely of extracts from the documents and was entitled *Thus Spoke Belgium's Diplomats.* The Foreign Office published it in Switzerland in German and French, possibly elsewhere in other languages. A few further quotations follow: In 1906 Baron Greindl, in the same letter in which he accused the King of England of having driven Delcassé into his militaristic policies, had added the words: "If there were any further doubt, this would be dispersed by the strange move of Colonel Barnadiston with General Ducarne." This referred to an attempt to reach an agreement about the transport of an English landing force in case of war. In the following year Greindl wrote again: "We ourselves must take note of the strange disclosures of Colonel Barnadiston to General Ducarne, and who knows whether there have not been other intrigues which have not come to our notice." And in 1911: "England's intentions are also made clear by the advance made to you [the Belgian Foreign Minister] by Sir A. Hardinge [the English Ambassador] in Brussels in an attempt to involve us too." In another report in the same year: "The English plan to support France by sending a landing force is not surprising. It is simply a continuation of the strange suggestions made to General Ducarne by Colonel Barnadiston some years ago." In April 1914, Baron Beyens wrote: "Do we yet have to fear that English troops will invade Belgium in order to assist us in the defense of our neutrality, thereby compromising it from the very beginning?"

The historical question as to what contact existed between the English, French, and Belgian armies and whether the Belgians remained entirely aloof I am not qualified to discuss. It is nevertheless important for other reasons to remember these things nowadays. Is it at all morally justifiable and practically possible to forbid a country which has reason to fear attack on a given flank, to discuss with other countries how such an attack might be countered, which divisions will make which moves and how their actions should be coordinated? Is not the taking of such precautionary steps, as long as they serve only defense purposes, an "inprescriptable human right" in the sense that it is a morally justifiable action, which cannot be prevented by treaties, and that treaties which make the attempt to forbid them are immoral?

On May 20, 1914 the Social Democrats had remained seated during the customary three cheers for the Kaiser with which the session was being closed. As late as July 25, less than a week before the declaration of war, the chairmen of the Social Democratic party had issued a proclamation: "Party members, we call upon you to attend mass meetings to demonstrate the unflinching desire for peace of the class-conscious proletariat. . . . Our words must echo everywhere in the ears of those in authority: 'We do not want war! Down with war! Up with the international brotherhood of the peoples!'" Refusal of war credits had been an essential part of the Social Democrat policy. The decision to vote for the parliamentary approval of war credits was, therefore, an extraordinarily significant one, both from the party's standpoint (which could, however, refer to an oft-repeated statement made by the former party chairman, August Bebel, that he himself in his old age would take up arms against Russia, the enemy and oppressor of all culture) and from the point of view of the German government, which needed the full support of the working class. After the party had decided to support the credits it was the lawyer Hugo Haase, afterward one of the revolutionary people's commissaries (*Volksbeauftragte*), who announced this decision and the reasons for it in the Reichstag, although he had been one of the few who had voted *against* it in the party caucus. For party disciplinary reasons he made an announcement which he considered wrong as though he approved it, just as German judges do, when they are outvoted in court. I came later to prefer the American practice that a judge states publicly if he has a conflicting opinion. This protects the people better from the dangers of anonymous authority and makes them clearly aware that behind decisions there are fallible human beings and not a divinely inspired oracle. In any case the ever-increasing practice in European parliaments of subordinating personal convictions to party discipline has fundamentally changed the nature and function of parliament. The theoretical arguments between supporters and opponents of this development should go to greater depth. Mere recognition of inevitability does not heal the wound.

On August 5, I accompanied my brother Gustav—who wore his first lieutenant's (*Oberleutnant*) uniform, for he had completed military service and several retraining periods—to the station. His regiment moved out immediately, and took part in the first battles on the Western Front and within the Fourth Reserve Corps approached closest to Paris. There, at the beginning of September, he was seriously wounded in the Battle of the Marne: a bullet had gone right through the abdomen, the same sort of wound our father had received in August, 1870, at Weissenburg and from which he had recovered miraculously. It was hardly to be expected that this miracle would repeat itself. In a state of fever, Gustav, with the whole hospital, was taken prisoner by the French. Five anxious weeks followed. Then came the happy news that he too had pulled through, that he was in captivity in reasonable condition at first in Brest and later on the island Belle Isle off the northwest coast, together with the famous actor Alexander Moissi and the son of the physicist Max Planck, Erwin Planck, who later became Secretary of the Chancellery under General von Schleicher, and after July 20, 1944 was executed by Hitler's hangmen as a member of the resistance movement.

Fortune had been good so far, but more than three years were to pass before the couple's reunion. In captivity Gustav passed the time by observing a strict daily routine (persuading Moissi to join in this was difficult), careful study of French, music (he played violin in chamber music recitals, clarinet in the orchestra, Erwin Planck the cello; some of the instruments were sent from Germany through the Red Cross, others were loaned to them by the mess owner, who had a business interest in music), and in solving intellectual problems; among other things he devised a formula by which it is possible to work out for any date what day of the week it was or will be.

At the end of 1917 an exchange agreement between France and Germany led to Gustav's internment in neutral Switzerland. Thus his reunion with Norah was made possible. When she crossed the Swiss border with the five-year-old Walther, the boy was strictly interrogated by the border guards. When they asked him: "Where were you born?" he answered angrily: "I wasn't born at all; the angels brought me down from heaven to mummy." The ice melted. For quite some time he called his newly found father "Uncle daddy." "Uncle daddy, can you remember when I was a little baby?"

Now back to the beginning of the war. My brother-in-law Martin Richter, who was forty-six years old and already an established staff member (titled *Geheimer Regierungsrat*) in the Prussian Ministry for Education and Culture, was reactivated as a captain in the field artillery. After a few weeks he returned with a minor wound. Of the four men in our immediate family I was the only one who had not seen military service because of a heart defect. Now I had to submit to another examination, which again ended with the decision: "permanently unfit for military service." Our mother—"old" mother as she was to us then, although only 58 years old—was living alone in Lübeck. She started work in the care of the wounded and in the Burgfeld hospitals was known as "Schwester Mutti" (Sister Mama) to many of the soldiers whom she tended with her gentle hands, practiced in the care of her children, and with a sense of duty that never faltered. Several of our cousins too were active in the war from the start. Otto Brecht, son of the mayor of Quedlinburg, a professional member of the medical corps, who had been particularly close to us Lübeck Brechts, was seriously wounded and died after great suffering. The others survived.

What happened in our family was common fate not only in Germany but likewise in France and Belgium. If there was anything special about us, then it was the fact that we played our part in the tragedy of the four great European wars (1813/1815, 1870/1871, 1914/1918 and 1939/1945) not in four or five generations, but in part in only three consecutive generations. Our grandfather, Christoph Heinrich Brecht, afterward Pastor in Ochtmersleben, had joined Blücher's army in the war of 1815 at the age of sixteen; his son, our father, had fought in 1870 (my mother's father, Theodor Weishaupt, was directing the Prussian railroads then); my two brothers and cousin Otto in 1914, and my younger brother Rolf again in 1939. It normally required more than three generations. But since there were forty-three years between the birth of my grandfather and that of my father and fifty-five between my father's and Rolf's, the four wars ran their course within a span of only three generations in our family.

Enlistment and special assignments also left great gaps in the staff of the Department of Justice. My official duties therefore changed by leaps and bounds. Naturally, I now canceled the academic colloquium which had been set for August 4 in Marburg. My first war assignment was the preparation of a decree by which courts were given the power to grant deferment to debtors. A fair copy of the text had not yet been written when the session of the Federal Council began. I rewrote the draft and rushed across with the copy to the Department of the Interior in Wilhelmstrasse, where the Federal

Council held its session. It was the first time I was present at one of its meetings.

Some thirty more decrees followed during the next few weeks. Among them was the prohibition of payment to enemy aliens, modeled on the corresponding British prohibitions, and many other measures in the spheres of law, economics, and banking. There were almost daily sessions with the representatives of the various government departments, both Federal and Prussian, of the National Bank, the non-Prussian Laender governments, and so on. This work not only strengthened my self-reliance and my knowledge of personnel; it also increased my political insight.

While my critical faculties began to stir energetically in the political sphere, I still had uncritical faith in the military conduct of the war. The succession of victories during the month of August in the west and the victory at Tannenberg in the east seemed to justify this confidence. Doubt did not come until later. Was not the East Prussian campaign, if the war is reviewed as a whole, a miscalculated action? Had not the Schlieffen plan hinged on the conception that first the enemy in the west was to be destroyed with all resources at Germany's disposal, before Germany turned to the east? That, therefore, retreats in the east had to be calmly accepted until then? The enemy in the west had been pushed far back, indeed, but was not yet destroyed. Every single division was important in the decisive battle which was now to come. Then ill tidings from the east led the German High Command to withdraw two military corps from the west, and to start their transportation to the east. Actually, they did not arrive there in time; the war in the east was fought without them. But they were missing in the west. The German advance was halted on the Marne, was reversed, and never again came as far as it had been. It later became evident that this was the turning point of the war. The war was for Germany lost at the Marne.

## 10. POLITICAL EDUCATION THROUGH THE WAR'S AIMS

SCARCELY had war broken out when discussions about the war aims began. That was not surprising; for, if there is war, then what are we fighting for? Since the great masses of the German people honestly believed that they had been attacked, their first aim was, of course, to repel the attack. But no debate stopped right at this point. The second question was sure to follow on the heels of the first: "If we win—and we shall win, for the contrary would be too dreadful —is the result that we have defended ourselves successfully to be all? Should not the guilty be punished and we rewarded? Must not Germany's power at least be so strengthened that the same thing can't happen again?" Experts and laymen took out their maps and extended Germany's frontiers. I did not take part in this game. But, after all, what did I understand of politics?

Those who thought they understood politics drew blueprints for a better Europe. The most harmless type were suggestions for establishing customs unions—pan-European, west-European, or central-European. Walther Rathenau had advocated the like before the war and did so again now in a communication to Bethmann Hollweg, the Chancellor, on August 1, 1914; similar, though differently framed, plans were pursued by Friedrich Naumann, Theodor Heuss, and Robert Bosch. Customs unions could be envisaged on the basis of voluntary agreements among the countries concerned, as they actually were to come about forty years later in the European Common Market. But most suggestions went much further. The planners wanted large areas in the east either to be annexed by Germany or to be transformed into separate states independent of Russia. They wanted to gain a large, coherent African colonial empire for Germany (now at last)—not suspecting that all colonial empires were soon to disappear. They wanted Belgium and Luxemburg either to be annexed by Germany or in some other way brought under German influence. They wanted Germany to annex the rich French mining area of Longwy-Briey in the neighborhood of Lorraine and the Saar.

Today it can be said assuredly that the outright annexation of the whole of Belgium was never an official German war aim. But an annexation of parts of Belgium was being considered by responsible government officials and by leading politicians, among them men like Matthias Erzberger and Gustav Stresemann who later won a reputation for their sincere efforts to further international amity. In a letter to the Chancellor on September 2, 1914 Erzberger declared that it was the duty of the German statesmen to take advantage of the victory in such a way that Germany's military supremacy on the Continent would be permanently guaranteed. He demanded the annexation of the whole of Belgium and of part of the French Channel coast, as far as Boulogne, of the town of Belfort, and the mining region Longwy-Briey; furthermore, the breaking down of the Russian empire into its component parts, and in addition, high war indemnities, including endowments for German generals and statesmen.[1] In October, 1914 he proclaimed similar though more generally expressed war aims in *Allgemeine Rundschau*. And Stresemann—as late as June 23, 1918, only three weeks before the breakdown of the last German offensive, three months before the final collapse—vehemently censured Foreign Secretary Kühlmann for his remark that peace for Germany could not be won by force of arms alone and that peace by agreement would have to be enough. This speech, said Stresemann, had an entirely depressing effect: "We have never had less cause to doubt that Germany will be victorious than we have now. When victory has been won, then we must make use of it to attain the necessary realistic guarantees." Not only Erzberger and Stresemann! At the end of 1915 *all* the bourgeois parties (that is, all but the socialists) in a Reichstag resolution clearly expressed their desire for an extension of German power. The resolution read: "We await in complete unanimity and with calm determination the hour that will make possible peace negotiations in which the military, financial, economic, and political interests of Germany will be permanently safeguarded, in full extent and through all measures, including territorial acquisitions, necessary to this end."

But there was from the very beginning a current that ran counter to this tendency, most widespread among members of the working class, but supported as well by many intellectuals, especially people who were religiously motivated. They saw in "peace without annexations" the only formula which could lead to a speedy settlement. This was in keeping with my own way of thinking and feeling, and it became a decisive factor in the gradual growth of my political interest and my political alignment. But within the small group of people that had any political influence, the supporters of this line of thought were obviously in the minority.

Not until the third year of the war did the conviction that it was necessary to expedite the end of the war by a show of readiness for voluntary agreement gain ground in politically influential groups.

[1] Klaus Epstein, *Matthias Erzberger and the Dilemma of German Democracy*, Princeton University Press, 1959.

This change of mind, urged on by Erzberger himself, led to the famous Reichstag resolution of July 19, 1917. Its wording I shall set down here because of its significance for subsequent events:

"What was true for the entire German nation on August 4, 1914, still is true today, on the threshold of the fourth year of the war, that is, the statement in the Speech from the Throne: 'We are not driven by an urge for conquests.' In defense of her freedom and independence, for the inviolability of her territorial status quo, Germany took up arms. The Reichstag is striving for a peace settlement by agreement (*Frieden der Verständigung*) and a lasting reconciliation of nations. Any forced (*erzwungene*) territorial acquisitions and any political, economic, and financial suppression by force (*Vergewaltigungen*) are incompatible with such a peace. The Reichstag rejects all plans that aim at economic isolation and enmity among nations after the war. The freedom of the seas must be guaranteed. Economic peace alone can prepare the way for a coexistence of nations in friendship. The Reichstag will energetically support the setting up of international legal organizations. But as long as the enemy governments do not acquiesce to (*eingehen auf*) such a peace settlement, as long as they threaten Germany and her allies with conquest and suppression (*Vergewaltigung*), the German people will stand together as one man, will persevere unflinching and will fight until Germany's right and the right of her allies to life and development are guaranteed. The German nation in its unanimity is invincible. The Reichstag is at one with the men who in heroic battle are defending their fatherland. The unending gratitude of the whole nation is theirs."

At first, in common with the general public impression, I understood this resolution to mean that Germany was giving up all claims to any annexation of Belgian territory and was willing fully to reestablish Belgium's sovereignty and integrity. That had also been Erzberger's original intention. But the right-wing members of his party (*Zentrum*) and the National Liberals had left loopholes for expansionist intentions in the words "forced territorial acquisitions" and "suppression by force." It was possible to toy with the thought that Belgium and France would *agree* to the desired revisions. The Peace Resolution, if understood this way, therefore was *not* a declaration of the unconditional decision to reestablish the sovereignty and integrity of Belgium. In spite of this the German High Command opposed the Peace Resolution vigorously, the National Liberals voted with the Conservatives against it, and even as honest an apostle of a peaceful settlement as Prince Max of Baden was against the resolution because he thought it would be interpreted abroad as an expression of weakness. Even before its adoption Chancellor Bethmann Hollweg was overthrown, partly because he had failed to oppose the Peace Resolution with sufficient zeal, partly because he had failed to support it energetically enough, partly because his share in the responsibility for the invasion of Belgium had given him a bad reputation abroad. Among those responsible for his overthrow were both Stresemann and Erzberger. But it was General Ludendorff who brought it about by presenting the Kaiser, who wanted to keep Bethmann, with the alternative: "Either Bethmann or I." Bethmann's successor, Michaelis, publicly revealed the latent ambiguity of the resolution by acknowledging it only with a qualifying, "As I understand it."

Only a few leading personalities continually and unflinchingly insisted that Germany must restore Belgium's sovereignty and integrity with no reservations. Among these were Prince Max of Baden —long before his chancellorship—and the man who later became his aide, Dr. Kurt Hahn (see below, Chapter 18), Professor Alfred Weber of Heidelberg University, and also Walter Simons of the Foreign Office, for whom this position simply followed from his sense of justice as a consequence of the German invasion of Belgium and Bethmann's declaration of August 4, 1914. Our agreement about this matter led to ever closer friendly relations. The great significance an unambiguous declaration renouncing Belgium would have for public opinion in America was pointed out by the Hamburg banker Max Warburg early in 1917. But the Kaiser and the High Command could not be persuaded to issue such an unequivocal statement, least of all during the great spring offensive of 1918 which began on March 21. Prince Max, supported by Hahn, rightly felt that the statement could have great effect abroad only if it were made during a victorious advance, not after the breakdown of an offensive. But the High Command was not yet prepared for it. Others wanted to withhold official renunciation so that it could be used for bargaining purposes in the peace negotiations. This had been, as we know now, originally the opinion also of Prince Max—in conscious opposition to Hahn—as he wrote in a letter to Conrad Haussmann on December 17, 1917.[2]

It is difficult today to realize that as late as in the summer of 1918

[2] Published in Matthias and Morsey, *Die Regierung des Prinzen Max von Baden,* Düsseldorf, 1962, p. 26.

hopes of a decisive German victory flared high again, not only in the minds of the Kaiser and the High Command, but in broad political sections as well. For the first time it was no longer a war on two fronts (Russia had in the meantime withdrawn), the offensive in the west had achieved great successes at the beginning, and submarine warfare was still well under way. In the memorable session of the Cabinet under Prince Max von Baden with Ludendorff on October 17, 1918, Vice Chancellor von Payer, a Liberal, said: "I remember the mood of the summer. No one doubted then that we would in the end be victorious." High spirits had prevailed until at least July 14, when the final large-scale offensive started—only to collapse the following day, a fact known at first to only a few people.

The first official assurance that Belgium would be reestablished did indeed not come until August, 1918 in a statement made by Colonial Secretary Solf, though the words "sovereignty" and "integrity" were avoided. Even as late as September 19, Hindenburg is said still to have expressed the hope that Germany could retain Longwy and Briey.[3]

Thus there were subdued, but smouldering internal controversies on the war aims in Germany. They brought all peace policy of any significance to a standstill.

The Germans, however, were not the only ones who openly or secretly pursued plans for annexations. The statesmen of the Entente were more than equal to them. The secret documents published by the Bolsheviks in November, 1917 brought to light that at a time when the allied governments publicly denied all egoistic war aims, they were secretly haggling with one another about their shares in the booty. Each one made the recognition of its own demands a condition for recognizing those of the others. Any new demand raised by one drove the others to increasing theirs. A German translation of the documents was promptly published by the semi-official German news agency, but what was thus obtainable was badly organized and hard to understand. I rushed to the press division of the Foreign Office and asked: "What are you doing with this magnificent evidence which has fallen into your lap?" They had no definite plans. I said what I considered to be necessary, namely: first, presentation of the documents in a reasonable order; and, secondly, a pamphlet contrasting the sanctimonious declarations of allied statesmen and the reality of their secret dealings. I was asked to

---

[3] Fischer, *op. cit.,* p. 853.

draw up both publications. In order to avoid delays I agreed. Within two days I handed over the rearranged file of documents and shortly afterward the manuscript of the booklet, to which the most important documents and several maps sketched by me were to be added. The *collection of documents* was immediately printed and distributed to members of the Foreign Office, who thus obtained their first insight into the significance of the publication, as I was told by Simons, senior adviser in the legal department. But it was several months—a matter I will come back to—before the *booklet,* entitled *"Secret Diplomacy,"* under the pseudonym Arn. Br. Hanson, appeared in Berne in German, later in French, and still later in the Netherlands in Dutch and in Copenhagen in Danish. A brief account follows.

In his speech on August 7, 1914, British Prime Minister Asquith declared that Great Britain was fighting for the principle that small nations might not be crushed by a large and tyrannical power. He said he did not believe that a nation had ever entered a war with a cleaner conscience or more firmly convinced that she was not fighting for her own selfish interests, but in the defense of those principles on the preservation of which the civilization of the world depended. Again, the note of January 12, 1917, in answer to Wilson's peace proposal, said that the allied nations were not fighting for selfish interests but to protect the independence of nations and the right of humanity, and especially "to free Italians, Slavs, Rumanians, Czechs and Slovaks from foreign rule." The reader should recall these statements—so the booklet went on—and then consider the secret agreements and negotiations of the very same statesmen at the very same time. A dramatic description followed, and from it I will relate the following.

On March 4, 1915 the government of the Tsar of Russia informed the governments of Great Britain and France of what Russia wanted. Constantinople and the entire European part of Turkey, together with several islands and a strip of land on the Asia Minor side, were to become Russian. Were the people there Russian? No. The governments of Great Britain and France will therefore protest and remind the Tsar of the great principles for which they are fighting? This does not happen. On the contrary, Britain and France more or less agree. But they lay down conditions. No doubt the condition that foreign nationalities must be respected? Not so. Great Britain demands a guarantee of British interests in Constantinople and the Straits and makes only one other condition, namely, that Russia will behave as benevolently toward Britain in other spheres of her interests.

Details soon follow. Great Britain first demands that those areas of Persia, about which she and Russia had so far come to no agreement and which are therefore called "neutral" zones (the booklet here adds in brackets that this is the British definition of neutral) should be included in the British sphere of influence; and, secondly, that British claims in the Asian part of Turkey be recognized. These claims are later specified to include Britain's receiving the major part of Mesopotamia with Baghdad and the large bay of Haifa and Akka on the Mediterranean. An additional note made clear that these were only those British wishes that referred to "the Asian part of Turkey"; other claims (e.g., regarding German colonies) fell under the clause "benevolent behavior toward Great Britain in other spheres of interest."

France also agrees to the Russian demands. She too adds the condition that her demands in Asia Minor be recognized. They include nothing less than Syria and mighty regions to the north, stretching far into the interior. France's second condition is that she must be left complete freedom in determining Germany's western borders. There is no mention of the principle of nationalities; there is not even an attempt to cloak the demands in any way, and this for good reasons, as soon becomes evident. Nor does the Tsar have any questions on this subject. He agrees to the British and French conditions obligingly and discreetly, but at the same time adds new conditions of his own: Great Britain wants the neutral zone in Persia? Then northern Afghanistan is to come under Russian jurisdiction, and the tip of Persia that separates Russia from Afghanistan, together with some towns in the neutral zone, must stay under Russian influence. England and France are interested in Asia Minor? Oh, so is Russia: just one area, several times as big as Belgium, from the Caucasus to southern Kurdistan. France wants freedom in determining her eastern boundaries? Fair enough, but likewise Russia wants complete freedom regarding her own western flank. Above all, no one is to meddle in the fate to be meted out to Poland—with pious phrases about the protection of nationalities. The government of the Tsar attached especial importance to this point. Indeed, here alone in the documents are the small nationalities mentioned. "It is absolutely necessary," so it reads, "to insist above all that the Polish question is omitted as an object of international consultation and that all efforts to place the future of Poland under the guarantee of the Great Powers must be swept aside." Great Britain and France, whose statesmen had written and said so much about noble Poland, raised no objections to this, pleased as they were to see their own conditions accepted.

Exactly what France wanted in the west can be learned from a telegram of February, 1917. Not just Alsace-Lorraine. France demanded that all areas left of the Rhine be cut off from Germany: Krefeld, Aachen, Cologne, Bonn, Koblenz, Trier, the whole wine-growing area of the Moselle and almost all that of the Rhine, Mainz, Worms, Ludwigshafen, Speyer, etc., regions which even without Alsace-Lorraine are as large as Belgium, old, established German territory. In so far as these areas were not to be incorporated into France—and this was the intention at least for an extended Alsace-Lorraine and the Prussian Saarland—they were to be transformed into an independent buffer state with no economic contact with Germany and to be occupied by the troops of the entente until further notice.

The Tsarist government acknowledged this note, repeating its own counter-conditions (freedom toward the west) and swiftly adding another: France was to agree to the annulment of the internationally imposed duty that Russia should not fortify the Aaland islands in the Baltic. Briand immediately answered that this wish would raise no difficulties. The official Russian agreement to the French demands regarding Germany's western boundaries came right after, and then in thanks France's recognition of Russia's complete freedom in determining her own western boundaries. The speed of this final exchange of diplomatic notes is remarkable: the main issue was dealt with from February 12 through 14, 1917; the last-mentioned piece followed on March 11, 1917. Four days later the Tsar was forced to resign.

Meanwhile, in May, 1915, Italy had joined the war. How the Italian government, after wavering for a long time, finally landed in the arms of the Entente, is described in a Russian memorandum. The promises made Italy by the Entente exceeded even the most daring expectations. She was not only to obtain regions with an Italian-speaking population, not only the southern tip of the Tyrol, as well as Görz, Gradiska, and Trieste. Not only Valona in Albania and the Greek-Turkish islands of the Dodecanese, but, besides all this, the whole of the Istrian peninsula and the greater part of the Austrian crown-land Dalmatia, that 240 mile-long stretch of coastal land with its rich wine and olive harvests and its highly developed fisheries. As far as the Tyrol was concerned, the claims extended right up to the Brenner, not because there were Italians living there, but on the ground that this was a "natural border"; this area embraced purely Germanic territory.

In the Allies' note on January 12, 1917 the whole series of idealistic war aims are paraded out again. At the end the note demands the dismissal of the Ottoman Empire from Europe. Why? Because Russia wants to obtain the straits? No, *because the Ottoman Empire is without doubt alien to west-European culture.* Thus the real reason was concealed and another sanctimonious one was substituted.

I have decided to present these unpleasant matters here as bluntly as I had done in that booklet because, for one thing, this is an autobiography and my suggestion to have such a pamphlet produced and my acceptance of the commission to write it myself were the beginnings of my own active participation in political events. Secondly, however, one can see here not only what effect the published documents had on me at the time; this description, I believe, has remained more or less correct. It presents a vivid counterpart to the preceding description of the debate about *German* war aims. It would be most unjust to consider one without the other, and it is important that future generations realize how imperfect, morally indefensible, and politically shortsighted the conduct of European politics was at that time on *both* sides.

Those were private activities of mine. They formed no part of my official duties as an aide in the Federal Department of Justice. This department was directly responsible for only a small section of matters relating to peace—legal matters—but it was often called in to conferences with other government departments (Foreign Office, Home Office, etc.) on politically more significant problems because of the legal questions involved.

On the other hand, almost every legal matter had its political aspect. One example: the settlement of pre-war debts. When I suggested prescribing the same rate of interest for both the German debtors of foreign creditors and the foreign debtors of German creditors, spokesmen of other departments disagreed. They wanted German debtors to have to pay less. The Ministry of War complained in an official note to the Secretary of my department about our failure to invite them to the conference. When we replied that this matter had nothing to do with the Ministry of War, they protested that they had a critical interest in the economic development of Germany after the war *because of possible subsequent wars* and therefore also in the rate of interest on pre-war debts. This was an unforgettable object-lesson to me on the tendency of the military to interfere in everything.

The treatment of enemy property was, of course, highly political. Germany had, under protest, followed the English lead in the sequestration and liquidation of enemy possessions almost step by step. These affairs were managed by the Department of the Interior, later by the newly created Department for Economic Affairs, where a very gifted aide, Dr. Vocke, was in charge. When he transferred to the board of directors of the German *Reichsbank* at the beginning of 1918 (where he stayed until he became managing director of the German Federal Bank after the Second World War; we met again in Frankfurt in 1948) his position was offered to me. I accepted and in April, 1918 took up my post in the Department for Economic Affairs.

I thus became a federal (*Reich*) official. So far I had been a Prussian official, loaned out to the federal government. I was sorry to change the title of county-court judge (*Landrichter*) for that of government councillor (*Regierungsrat*), which had in it the sound of what I did not like in the civil service.

Germany's enemies, by means of sequestration and liquidation, were able to come by much greater enemy assets in their overseas possessions and in the conquered German colonies than Germany in her retaliatory measures. The question arose as to whether or not Germany by way of retaliation should take such measures also in the areas she had conquered. At late as August, 1918 I took part in Brussels in a conference about this matter. We did not yet know that the military offensive had completely failed.

My sister-in-law, Norah, had asked me to look up the house owned by her family in Brussels, since her mother had fled to England. I found the house crowded with Belgian families. They were reluctant to talk. Here and in conversations with shopowners I encountered complete confidence that the Germans would be driven out of Belgium within a few months. They were to prove right.

## 11. POLITICAL EDUCATION THROUGH THE STRUGGLE FOR WORLD OPINION

THE more I felt drawn into the political arena, the more critical I became of official language. I deplored every statement that made agreement more difficult, as well as the failure of the German government to use facts and viewpoints favorable to Germany.

I sent suggestions for arguments that might be used to good effect in the international debate to the Chancellor or the Foreign Office. They probably never got further than into the hands of subordinate staff aides; at any rate, I never received an answer. When I attempted to talk to senior staff members of the Foreign Office personally I was referred to junior aides in the press division. It was through the press division, however, that I eventually was able to stir action on the propagandistic use of the Belgian documents regarding the origin of the war, and later of the Bolshevik publications on war aims. Even then the effect was marred by inept procedure. It was several weeks before my handwritten draft of the pamphlet on war aims (*Secret Diplomacy*) was typewritten and several months before the first printed copies in German and French appeared in Berne. Both editions were set and bound like a cheap thriller with glaring subheadings, quite unbecoming to the intended serious impression. In the meantime November, 1917 had become February or March, 1918. The Dutch and Scandinavian editions had a more dignified design, but appeared even later. When I went to Switzerland at the end of June, 1918 in order to check on sales, the booklet was not to be had in any kiosk or bookshop. The publishers believed that all copies displayed for sale had been immediately bought up by the opposing side, but they also informed me that the U.S. Embassy in Berne had purchased fifty copies and had probably sent them to Washington. I was later told in the United States that through this text President Wilson first gained precise information about the secret treaties of his European allies.

No copy was to be seen in German shops. When I complained, the press division confessed that the military authorities had forbidden distribution in Germany on the ground that the pamphlet was too "pacifistic"—and this in 1918. The reproach can only have referred to the introductory paragraphs, which ran as follows:

"The peoples' demands on their statesmen increase with the sacrifices the latters' policies require.

"In order to indicate the magnitude of the sacrifices Europe has brought during the past several years in terms of human lives, economic goods, and cultural values, it is necessary to think back to August, 1914. Everyone can remember his feelings after the first battles: now the first have been killed. Even if it was 'just one,' what sum of tragic possibilities did we envisage while we, with vivid imaginative power, put ourselves in the position of those whose fate it was to bear the loss ideally or materially to the bitter end. But the powers of imagination and sympathy are limited. In the face of a hundred cases which are never quite the same, human imagination has to be satisfied with an approximation. And soon it fails completely.

"In the meantime according to oft-recurring estimates—one hesitates to write it down—about ten million men have been killed in the war. It is about as many as the entire male population of France between eighteen and forty-five was in time of peace. In order to realize what this means, you have to think of how many men you met in Paris and in the many other larger and smaller towns, while traveling through France, and throughout the whole of the countryside too. The dead are distributed among many countries, to be sure, but their number loses nothing of its horror for this. Infinite amounts of goods, both material and cultural, have been destroyed at the same time. And ever more often the cry of serious men of all nations can be heard: the war has already lasted too long! What madness! And what for?

"*What for?*

"The people demand an answer to this question from their governments. . . ."

The deeper reason for the inefficiency of German propaganda lay in the fact that there was no clear line in official politics which might have been used to good advantage by the propaganda agencies. They were unable to encourage the desire for peace in the enemy countries by declaring that Germany would demand neither annexations nor reparations, as long as the Kaiser and the High Command were opposed to such a basis for peace and condemned its propagation as a sign of weakness.

Hence, people abroad read both militaristic and pacifistic statements side by side and inevitably obtained the impression that the pacifistic statements were mere disguise. In reality both were genuine. The nation was divided and had no political leadership.

Into this vacuum fell President Wilson's Fourteen Points. They were eagerly absorbed and discussed by the German people long before the failure of the offensive in the west in July and August, 1918 indicated the approaching military collapse and in September, when the war was lost, the German High Command declared itself ready to begin negotiations on the basis of Wilson's points.

Germany had lost the struggle for world opinion as well as the military struggle.

## 12. Constitution and Leadership

At the time of the outbreak of World War I people both at home and abroad generally believed that the constitution of Imperial Germany—the Bismarck Constitution—because of its autocratic features more fully guaranteed strong leadership in war than the democratic constitutions of the western countries. On the other hand, after the Second World War, I have heard German conservatives in the best of faith argue with the American occupation authorities that the Bismarck Constitution had been in essence democratic, because it provided for a Reichstag secretly elected on equal franchise and required its consent to all laws and to any measures of taxation; and because the basic human rights—freedom of opinion, of religion, of the press; the right to hold meetings and form associations; the inviolability of the home and independence of the courts—were guaranteed, though not by the federal Constitution itself, then at least by acts of legislation that could be changed only with the Reichstag's consent.

Both views—that Germany at that time was essentially an autocracy or that it was essentially a democracy—were equally incorrect. What made them incorrect proved decisive for success and failure. Under an absolute monarchy, whatever other faults that form of government might have, a uniform policy could have been forced upon all civil and military government authorities. The same result could have been achieved under a truly democratic constitution, whenever the government elected by the people was backed by large majorities, as Great Britain, France, and the United States have proved. Under the democratic form of government the majority of the voters not only determines the members of the legislative assembly (as they did in fact in elections to the imperial Reichstag, though not to the Prussian legislature), but also the holders of executive power, who have authority in both civil and military affairs, either by direct vote (United States) or indirectly through parliament (Great Britain and France). On this basis, unity of executive powers was effected in Great Britain under Lloyd George, in France under Clemenceau, and in the United States under Woodrow Wilson in his first presidential term. Under the Bismarck Constitution, on the other hand, there was in Germany a plurality of powers: a dualism of powers between civil and military government, because the High Command was not subordinate to the Chancellor, nor the Chancellor to the High Command; another dualism between either of these two executive branches and the representatives of the people in the Reichstag, because the appointment of the Chancellor and of generals was independent of the Reichstag's majorities; and several more dualisms between the federal government and the governments of the individual states.

Thus it was constitutionally possible in Germany for the Chancellor and the High Command to pursue different policies in major questions of war and peace (unconditional submarine warfare, war aims, internal reforms, etc.). In addition, the policies of the Chancellor or those of the High Command could be diametrically opposed to the wishes of the majority of the people, as represented in the Reichstag. Finally, the Prussian Representative Assembly could oppose the wishes—even the united wishes—of the leading federal executives and of the Reichstag majority, as it did, for example, in the case of Prussian electoral reform. Even when the Kaiser in his capacity as King of Prussia personally supported the reform of the unfair Prussian electoral system—desired by both the Chancellor and the Reichstag—the opposition of reactionary members in both Prussian Houses was sufficient to block the reform.

The worst of these dualisms was that between military and civil government. Theoretically it would have been possible to unite civil and military policy since the Kaiser had the constitutional right to appoint and dismiss both the Chancellor and the High Command of the armed forces. Had he felt within him the ability and desire for leadership, he could have used this right to create unity of policy. But in contrast to impressions prevailing abroad, the Kaiser was not nearly as Caesarean-minded as people liked to imagine him and as many of his earlier dashing utterances had indeed suggested. He was no longer the thirty-year-old young ruler; he was now almost sixty, older than Caesar or Napoleon ever grew, and he disliked making decisions against the advice of his official experts. Thus he failed to create personal harmony between civil and military leaders, accepting the advice now of the one, now of the other. Even if he had created unity between them, the dualism between the federal executive government and the people, represented in the Reichstag, and between the Reich and the individual states, would not have been eliminated. Thus the plurality of powers sanctioned by the Bismarck Constitution remained unbridged and—except by returning to absolute monarchy or Caesarism or by advancing to full democracy—unbridgeable. These facts played a decisive part in Germany's losing of the war.

The lack of political unity within the government also led to personal tragedy. Chancellor von Bethmann Hollweg was known to be an opponent of unlimited submarine warfare; he referred to it as our "Sicilian Adventure," in memory of the decision of the Athenians in the Peleponnesian War to ship great forces to Sicily, a decision which ended in the destruction of these forces, including the fleet, and finally the Athenian loss of the Peleponnesian War. The Kaiser, however, decided in favor of the opinion of the High Command, and unlimited submarine warfare began. The interesting fact is not just the constitutional point that the general staff was not subordinate to the Chancellor in such an important political matter, but also that Bethmann Hollweg, after the decision had been taken in opposition to his wishes failed to resign, as any prime minister in a democratic country would have done. He stayed in office in order to preserve the outward impression of unity, an attempt which obviously did not succeed. Had he resigned, Germany might after her collapse have had a natural leader. As it was, however, Bethmann Hollweg vanished tragically into the obscurity of second-class historical significance.

All this was for me a lesson of great and lasting importance in political thinking and especially in my attention to the significance of constitutions in the history of nations.

## 13. LIFE BEFORE DEATH GOES ON EVEN IN WAR

A MAN who dedicates himself to the struggle for a great cause does not cease on this account to have a private life. It may change decisively; it may become more shallow or more profound. But it is still there and still requires decisions to be made. It does not become less personal than it was previously; it is likely to become more personal.

Under the impact of the great events we had experienced together Clara and I decided to unite our lives. The wedding took place on Saturday, December 4, 1915 at Matthäikirche in Berlin, followed by a family dinner in a small room of the Hotel Esplanade. Over Sunday we traveled to Dresden, where it rained continually. On Monday I was at work again. For it was war.

Bride and groom normally pay more attention to other things than the words of the priest who marries them. But some of what Pastor Israel said at that time, by virtue of its simple, irrefutable seriousness, settled into my consciousness, seeped then slowly into my subconscious, and remained there until it awoke again from its slumber. He said that each should try to draw the other to heaven with him.

Fifty years have passed since that day. It is an almost metaphysical experience to recall, with all the clarity one is capable of, an event so long past, at which thoughts of the future have troubled us. Now we can do what then we tried in vain: see into the future. It lies visible before us, as it were by magic through some gift of second sight, while we are kneeling at the altar again.

Was it wise for a thirty-year-old man and a woman seven years older, however dearly they loved each other and however seriously they took their relationship, to marry? This autobiography would be worthless if I were to pretend that there had been no differences of temperament, opinion, sympathies. Nor would I want to advise others to follow our example because it turned out well for us. As a rule, it may well be best for both partners if a man marries a woman between five and fifteen years younger than himself and they have many children and later grandchildren, like my parents and my sis-

ter Editha, or the ninety-year-old Bishop Lawrence in Boston, who
received us at the door like a man of sixty—we thought it was the
butler—and proudly showed us the list of his descendants, one
hundred and fifteen names. Every third day he celebrated a birthday.

But I doubt that these rules would have suited my particular case.
I had settled on a slow-pace manner of maturing. In a world difficult to understand I wanted to find my way step by step, disinclined
to accept prearranged judgments, to feed on pre-cooked values. I
was *deliberately immature,* unable and unwilling to be a fatherly
friend and guide to an immature young woman. If I wished to
avoid short-lived relationships, then I had only the choice between
celibacy or marital partnership with a mature person I loved.

Outwardly, too, everything turned out differently from what one
could have expected. When the critical years approached, Hitler's
seizure of power drove us to America. In this huge continent, quite
unknown to us, where in an abrupt reversal of our European life
we knew no one and no one knew us, we felt happy, sheltered, and
grateful in the warmth of the twosomeness we had saved. When I
was sixty I fell seriously ill and was for several years the weaker
partner. Five years later it was my wife's turn to be stricken. A
stomach tumor had developed, making a grave operation necessary.
I could only pray that a miracle would save her. The incomprehensible miracle did happen. A few years later, both of us were almost
crushed in a railroad accident, but once again we escaped.

She is still by my side. She still has the figure, the walk, and the
movements of a young girl and more grace than most of them. She
pursued outdoor activities longer than I, playing tennis, climbing
high mountains, riding horseback, skiing, skating, and wandering
around the town or through the countryside untired. At eighty she
still drew her graceful circles and figures, forward and backward,
across the ice, and would have continued had I not had to give it up.
Though not at all insensitive to the charms of other women and
girls, I have never felt the wish to live in marital partnership with
any but her.

Consideration for her daughter Irmgard no longer stood in the
way of our union. A radiant young person, warm and earnest like
her mother, music pupil of my sister Gertrud's, Irmgard was eighteen years old and on the way to professional independence in social

work. She was on affectionate terms with both parents. Her father too remarried.

There are many decisions of secondary importance connected with every marriage, such as the choice of a home and of its furnishing. It was characteristic of my state of mind that these decisions were extraordinarily difficult for me to make, quite out of proportion to their importance. After the usual searching and sifting we were left with a choice among three dwellings that attracted us in different ways: an apartment in the so-called "old west," in the unassuming *noblesse* of old Berlin, with reminiscences of Theodor Fontane, but a little antiquated; a modern apartment in the "new west," ideal for an ambitious young government official; and, third, a small and old-fashioned, but solidly built, suburban house with ample garden, far away from fashionable quarters. We had decided to take the modern apartment in town. But on the morning of the day on which we were to sign the lease I persuaded Clara that, instead, we should move into the garden house off the beaten tracks. It was basically a choice between three different ways of life. It was the same with the selection of furnishings. You must have gained your personal bearings in great matters before you are able to decide small ones "authentically."

The spacious garden around the house gave us that daily contact with nature we both desired. After only two years, however, still well within the war, we had to move out since the owner wanted to live there himself. So we moved to Steglitz, another western suburb, into one of the attractive little houses near the city park there. The house—actually no more than the center unit of a three-home building—was small and had only a few small rooms. That did not deter us. We wanted to live on a simple scale, such as was accessible also to others, creating an environment in which the mind might have free rein. We had the two small ground-floor rooms made into one large combined dining and garden room, transformed the two bedrooms on the second floor into a small study for me and a combined music and living room for Clara (only with difficulty was it possible to get the grand piano up the narrow stairs), and we relegated our own bedroom to the garret. The garden, carefully tended by Clara, although much smaller than the previous one, left us some touch with nature. Thus we lived from the fall of 1917 until our departure from Germany in 1933.

There were holidays even during the war. In the summer of 1917 we happened to stay a few weeks in Salem, about fifteen miles from Lake Constance. Our landlord-farmer was working with Russian prisoners of war, whom he treated well. They were agitated by the March Revolution (the October Revolution was still to come) and sang melancholy songs. We liked to sit under an age-old lime tree, where the bees were buzzing, there to read and work. At that time I knew nothing of Prince Max, who lived in Salem, and with whom I was soon to come into closer contact.

In June, 1918 we enjoyed happy weeks of reunion with my brother Gustav in Switzerland. In July he, we, and Norah returned to Berlin. On July 21 all five children—three brothers and two sisters—were reunited with our mother in Lübeck. We had no inkling of the fact that in these very days the fate of Germany had been decided in France (Chapter 14).

# PART III

## Political Education through the War's End

## 14. My First Weeks in the Chancellery—Discovery of the Real Situation (October, 1918)

In October, 1918 my professional situation changed fundamentally. Chancellor Prince Max of Baden called me to the Chancellery. There, along with the normal functions of a junior staff member, I was to take over the position as secretary to the Cabinet he had formed. Walter Simons, who had become the Prince's chief adviser, asked me by telephone, without giving me the reason, to see him at the Chancellery. For the first time I entered this sacred building, inaccessible to all but a few. Although I afterward went in and out thousands of times, I have never forgotten the first impression I had when the livried doorman opened the mighty door and I beheld the empty entrance hall before me. Very lonely, I went up the stairway to the right at the rear, up to the first floor where, on stepping through a small antechamber, I was suddenly standing in the "Large Congress Hall"—so called because the "Congress of Berlin" of 1878, visited by the leading ministers of all the great European countries (among them, Disraeli), had met there under Bismarck's chairmanship, the climax of Germany's rise to the status of a great power respected in the whole world and a landmark in the peaceful settling of extremely complicated conflicts in the Balkan area. The huge hall, laid with carpets which covered the whole floor, was empty.

I had been standing there for a while when the door to the Cabinet room opposite me suddenly opened and Simons walked quickly across to me. "Herr Brecht," he said in his precise manner, "the German Reich is calling you definitively to its service." He explained my appointment and introduced me to the Chancellor, who had in the meantime also emerged from the Cabinet room, accompanied by the Secretary of the Treasury. Prince Max exchanged a few words with me and instructed me, in the form of a polite request, to take up my post the following morning. Dr. Simons arranged my release from the Department for Economic Affairs.

Thus I came to go to the Chancellery every day for three years. But what a state of affairs I found! The events of the preceding weeks were hidden from the public eye by a heavy veil, not fully removed until the official *Records of the Antecedents of the Armistice* (*Amtliche Urkunden zur Vorgeschichte des Waffenstillstands*) were published nine months later. Since it so happened that it fell upon me to put together that white book and to write the "Introductory Note"—a note of survey still pertinent today, but omitted from the second edition of 1924 (about which there will be something to be said later)—it is for both autobiographic and objective reasons appropriate that I start with it. This, then, is what I suddenly learned.

"In the middle of July, 1918," reads an entry from Foreign Secretary von Hintze, "in Avesnes I submitted to General Ludendorff the formal and precisely worded question as to whether it was certain that we would defeat the enemy definitively and completely as a result of the present offensive. General Ludendorff repeated my question and then said, 'In answer I give a firm, definite yes.' Just before the conference between the Chancellor, the Field Marshal [Hindenburg], General Ludendorff, and myself—I think it was on August 13—General Ludendorff took me on one side and informed me that he had said in July he was certain that it was possible, with the offensive then taking place, to break the fighting spirit of the enemy and force him to make peace, but that he no longer felt this confidence. To my question, what he now thought the further course of the war would be, General Ludendorff answered that we would by means of defensive strategies be able to paralyze the enemy's martial intentions and thus gradually bring him to make peace."

The changed situation was discussed in the Kaiser's Privy Council on August 14. No instructions were given then and there, however, to establish contact with the enemy immediately. On the contrary, the Kaiser decided: "We must *wait for a suitable moment* to come to terms with the enemy." Chancellor Count Hertling summed up as follows: "Contacts regarding an agreement with the enemy must be opened diplomatically *at a suitable moment;* such a moment would present itself *after the next successes in the west.*" Hindenburg—thus ran the minutes of the conference—"declares that it will be possible to hold our own on French soil and thus finally force our will upon the enemy." The first words of this entry originally read: Hindenburg *"hopes* that it will yet (*dennoch*) be possible," but this had been changed in Ludendorff's handwriting to *"declares* (*führt aus*) that it will be possible."

That was on August 14. Not until September 10 did instructions change, at least partially, when Hindenburg agreed to the mediation of a neutral power to bring about an exchange of views *"without delay."* From September 21 onward there emerges in the files the idea of appealing directly to the United States. Preparations were made. On September 29 and 30 Foreign Secretary von Hintze was again at general headquarters. His telegram to the Foreign Office in Berlin on the evening of September 29 reveals the results of the talks: "Please communicate confidentially in Vienna and Constantinople that I suggest we make an offer to President Wilson on the basis of his fourteen points and invite him to call a peace conference to Washington after request for immediate armistice. . . ."

At this time the action moved into a new phase. Whereas the High Command had originally wanted diplomatic steps towards a peace settlement postponed until the military position was consolidated, they now requested that an offer of peace should go out immediately because of acute danger in the military situation. On October 1st a series of telegrams and telephone conversations issued from general headquarters with the same content: "Troops hold the line today; what might happen tomorrow not foreseeable." The offer of peace "should be sent off at once and not wait until the formation of the new government which might be protracted." "Front line kept intact today and we are in a worthy (*würdigen*) position, but a break-through could follow at any time and then our offer would come at the most unfavorable moment." And later in the evening: "General Ludendorff told me [Baron von Lersner] that our offer must go out immediately from Berlin to Washington. The army cannot wait another 48 hours. . . . The General emphasized that the offer must be in the hands of the Entente at the latest by Wednesday evening or Thursday morning and requests your Excellency to take all possible steps." On the same afternoon Hindenburg sent word to Vice Chancellor von Payer that, if it was certain by seven or eight o'clock the same evening that Prince Max would form a government, they could wait until the following morning; if, however, the formation of the new government seemed to remain in any way doubtful, then he advised issuing the peace offer that same evening.

Prince Max of Baden objected that in this form and at the moment of a hard-pressed military position the peace move would clearly have a very unfavorable influence on the German situation in the negotiations. He reported, October 11: "On the evening of October 1 the position as Chancellor had been offered him along with the demand that he immediately requested Wilson's mediation; that he had opposed this and had wanted to wait at least one week, in order to consolidate the new government and avoid the impression that we were making our request for mediation merely because of a military collapse."

On October 2 General Ludendorff asked for a draft of the note and in the afternoon himself had a wording telephoned through, which on the whole coincided with the final text. Prince Max, however, still had misgivings. On October 3 he drew up a written list of preliminary questions, including the following: "Is the High Command aware that the commencement of peace moves while under the pressure of a military situation of no free choice (*Zwangslage*) could lead to the loss of German colonies and German territory, in particular Alsace-Lorraine and areas in the eastern provinces with chiefly Polish population?" On the same day Hindenburg, then present in Berlin, sent the Chancellor once again the written statement: "The High Command reaffirms its demand for the immediate dispatch of an offer of peace." Under this pressure the note was sent off on the night of 3rd to 4th October. In the course of the 3rd, Hindenburg and Prince Max had also discussed the dispatch of the note orally. (In the appendix to this book a letter from Prince Max to me on this conversation is published for the first time.)

Before the answer arrived the Chancellor reported to his Cabinet on October 6, as the minutes show: "I have resisted note, firstly because I considered the moment too early, secondly because I wanted to appeal to the enemy in general. Now we must consider the consequences calmly. Now . . . the situation on the front must be ascertained by experienced officers . . . the leaders of the [several] armies must be listened to." The Cabinet members expressed similar opinions. They obviously suspected that Ludendorff might have misjudged the military situation because of a nervous breakdown. Ludendorff, however, saw in consultations with other generals a sign of distrust and threatened his resignation, from which the Cabinet feared an acceleration of the collapse. A plan for a *levée en masse*, allegedly proposed by Walther Rathenau in *Vossische Zeitung*, was discussed, but dropped because military leaders, especially Ludendorff, did not expect much of it.[1]

Wilson's answer came on October 5. It demanded a more definite statement that Germany accept the President's points in the sense that on entering the discussions an agreement had to be reached only on the practical details of their application. Secondly, it demanded Germany's withdrawal from the areas occupied by her, and, thirdly, raised questions about the controlling authorities in Germany.

In a conference on October 9 Colonel Heye stated again: "It would mean playing a game of chance (*Hasardspiel*) on the part of the High Command if they failed to expedite the peace move. It may be that we could hold out until the spring, but again, a turning point may come any day. Yesterday fate hung by a thread— whether or not a break-through would succeed. Troops have no rest any more. Not possible to calculate whether they will hold or not. Every day new surprises. I do not fear a catastrophe, but would like to save the army, so that we still have it as a means of pressure during the peace negotiations."

Ludendorff chimed in, taking the point of view that Germany need not accept every demand, that in particular a possible demand for a surrender of German fortresses might be rejected. But his answers to the question as to how much longer it was possible to resist were wavering and uncertain. To the question whether the front could be held another three months, Ludendorff answered no, and to the question of Prince Max: "In case present peace moves fail and both our two remaining allies withdraw, would it be possible for us to continue the war alone?" he gave the heavily conditioned answer: "If there were a pause in the fighting in the west, yes."

The German reply to Wilson's answer was issued with the full consent of the High Command. Wilson's second note of October 15 was considerably more severe. For the first time a distinction was made between peace and armistice; the conditions for the latter

---

[1] The words *levée en masse* are in fact not used in Rathenau's article ("A Dark Day," *Vossische Zeitung,* Nr. 512, October 7, 1918). What he recommended was that, in the case of an unsatisfactory answer from Wilson, troops should be methodically regrouped, soldiers on leave or serving at home be sent to the Western Front, older volunteers should replace soldiers in physically less demanding positions, and General Ludendorff should be replaced. The article contains a remarkably accurate forecast of Wilson's reply and of the final results. Cf. Walther Rathenau, *Briefe,* vol. 2, nos. 435, 438, 450, 452, 467, 480, 518, and 580 on this article.

were to be left to the judgment and counsel of the military advisers. The note also spoke of unlawful and inhuman practices on the part of the German fighting forces and stated that the realization of peace would depend upon the definiteness and satisfactory nature of the guarantees Germany would be able to give on her internal power structure. The consternation this note caused everywhere in Germany and especially its effect upon the army were manifest. Emotional opposition was stirred, pride reared up, and the High Command wanted to back out. The grave question now arose whether it was at all possible to back out, since the disclosure of the unfavorable situation after four years of official assertions that victory was certain had in the meantime had its effect both at home and abroad.

The relative positions taken by the High Command and the civil government now changed. The High Command asked whether the German people would rally once more in a supreme effort to the last, or whether their moral power of resistance was exhausted. Foreign Secretary Solf saw in this question an attempt to shift responsibility. "Why then is there such a depressed mood? Because military power has collapsed. But now we are told: military power will collapse unless the general morale is upheld. This escape should not be permitted. . . ."

On October 17 three conferences followed. In the second the situation was discussed in all its aspects. Ludendorff expressed himself in a more optimistic manner about the possibility of holding out during the coming weeks. But his indefinite and changing statements did not arouse complete confidence in the face of the facts mentioned. While Ludendorff and Heye had only a short time previously characterized any delay in the peace moves as a game of chance, Ludendorff now said: "War is not like doing an arithmetical sum (*Rechenexempel*). There are a host of probabilities and improbabilities in war. No one knows what is going to happen in the end. When we came to East Prussia in August, 1914 and with the assistance of my colleague [General] Hoffmann the orders for the Battle of Tannenberg were issued, then we did not know how it would turn out, whether [the Russian general] Rennenkampf would march or not. The soldier's luck is a part of warfare. Perhaps Germany will have this soldier's luck once again."

To the summing-up question whether the Western Front, if strengthened by the transfer of forces from the east—a possibility which was yet doubtful—would still stand in three months' time, Ludendorff answered: "I have already told the Chancellor that I consider a break-through possible, but not probable. I feel no inward probability about the break-through. If you ask me on my conscience, I can only answer: I do not fear it." When reminded of his own earlier statements he answered: "Today too matters are such that we can be broken through and defeated any day. The day before yesterday things went well; things could also turn out badly."

The possibility of reinforcing the troops in the west by withdrawing from White Russia and the Ukraine, of getting along with the supply of equipment and produce (especially oil, of which there was sufficient supply for only a few months more) was intensely discussed. Many unfavorable factors became evident. The number of troops which could be made available by severer methods of combing out was estimated. At the end the Chancellor concluded: "So we will be able to bring together 600,000 men as replacements by next spring, and our enemies 1,000,000 new men, counting only the Americans; Italians may well have to be added to this figure. Will our position, therefore, deteriorate or improve by the spring?" General Ludendorff answered: "The numbers alone would mean no deterioration [in the relative size of troops]. But we also have to consider the impact of our withdrawal from certain areas on our economic situation; the position of our war industry will deteriorate considerably."

At the end of the session the logical thread of the Chancellor's way of thinking became clear. He pointed out that even according to Ludendorff's most far-reaching hopes—which Prince Max apparently did not share—the war could be continued for only a limited period, that in the meantime the defection of the two remaining allies must be reckoned with and that so the question arose: would matters be better or worse at the end than at present? Ludendorff held that there were no worse conditions.

LUDENDORFF: "I feel that before we accept conditions which are too hard we should say to the enemy: fight to gain them."

THE CHANCELLOR: "And when he has won the fight for them, will he not present even worse ones?"

LUDENDORFF: "There are no worse ones."

THE CHANCELLOR: "Oh yes, they may invade Germany and devastate the country."

LUDENDORFF: "Things have not yet gone that far."
The last words evaded the Chancellor's logical point. For the possibility of resistance was uncertain even in the opinion of Ludendorff, and the question was precisely what the political situation would be after further vain resistance. The Chancellor manifestly proceeded from the realistic point of view that the enemy's conditions could become even worse. True, from Wilson's last note it was to be expected that the conditions of the armistice would be severe and offensive. Even this note, however, maintained the President's points for the peace treaty. Should Germany be at all capable of continuing the war for a few more months, then after an unfortunate outcome present terms would be lost. Not only that, but death and misery would have continued to rage fearfully. Belgium and Northern France would be destroyed in battles on the retreat and then the devastation would be brought back home. France and Belgium also trembled at the thought of the destruction further advances would bring with them. Here the German government saw a strong point.

The German answer went out on October 20, this time in disagreement with the High Command, in particular in regard to the discontinuance of submarine warfare. In a conference with German representatives abroad the latter had unanimously declared themselves in favor of yielding to President Wilson's demands in the question of submarines. Hope was expressed that no American passenger ship would be torpedoed at this time. But right at this moment the news that the "Leinster" had been torpedoed was received, aggravating the hostile mood in the United States.

This, then, was the formidable reality—still completely hidden from the general public—that I was made aware of the first day when I began my service in the Chancellery. Simons handed me the minutes of the major session on October 17 and other notes. As I rode home at night with people who were reading their evening papers, in which there was nothing about the affairs I had suddenly become familiar with, a strange feeling of unreality overcame me, suddenly being in on the secret of major political events in a historic moment. In a few days I was accustomed to this duality. But my first impressions and confusions have remained all the more vividly in my memory.

At about this time Wilson's third note arrived. It ended with passages in which the President once again expressed doubts about the structure of power within Germany. As a result of this note, from the time of my entry into the Chancellery, the issue of the Kaiser's abdication moved into the center of debates.

On October 28 an amendment to the Constitution was promulgated, which had been introduced with the approval of the Kaiser and accepted by both Bundesrat and Reichstag. In only a few lines it radically altered the entire constitutional structure of Germany. The Chancellor was no longer to be selected by the Kaiser alone, but required the confidence of the Reichstag and could be overthrown by it. The same was to apply to the Prussian Minister of War, since the Reich, having no Department of War of its own, conducted its military affairs through the Prussian Minister. This amendment transformed Germany constitutionally from a semi-autocratic monarchy into a parliamentary democracy with a monarch as its nominal head. If this form of constitution had existed before the beginning of the war, then the unification of leadership in military and civil affairs in Germany would have been possible and likely, as happened in the United States, Great Britain, and France. But neither abroad nor in Germany did people recognize the almost revolutionary event of this legal textual amendment. A more visible expression of change had become necessary. Wilson had hinted at this in his last note, and in Germany demands for the abdication of the Kaiser were being widely expressed.

At that time there originated the plan that the Kaiser and the Crown Prince should abdicate voluntarily in favor of Prince Wilhelm, the twelve-year-old son of the Crown Prince, and that a Regent should head the government until the Prince came of age, that is, for six years (eighteen was the age at which a member of the royal house could take over the royal functions according to the domestic law of the Hohenzollerns). During these six years the practice of democracy could become living reality, without the necessity of giving up the form of monarchy to which people were accustomed.

This appeared to me a wise way out of a situation which had become very difficult indeed, both internally and externally. All depended on the Kaiser's being induced to abdicate *voluntarily* in time. I tried to find conclusive arguments which could be used in discussions with him. The formula which I passed on to Simons ran as follows: Abdication, seen from *at home:* today voluntary, tomorrow compulsory; seen from *abroad:* today a success for Wilson, tomorrow for Foch; seen from *Germany's future:* today merely a change of persons, tomorrow a change of institution, that is, abolition of the monarchy.

Prince Max at first kept aloof from the issue. On October 29, however, he received a letter from Prince Ernst of Hohenlohe-Langenburg, a man who was closely attached to the Kaiser, an admirer of Ludendorff and an opponent of the peace resolution. His letter eloquently presented the view that the Kaiser's abdication was a necessity. Prince Max now felt that he had at least to "inform" the Kaiser. But first he sent his adviser, Kurt Hahn, to Copenhagen to discuss the situation with two American diplomats who were staying in the north. At about five o'clock p.m., Baron von Grünau from the Foreign Office entered the Chancellor's room with the message: "His Majesty is leaving for Spa today." Prince Max asked him if he was making "a bad joke" (so he reports in his memoirs). But it was true. Prince Max sent Foreign Secretary Solf to Potsdam. When that move failed, he telephoned the Kaiser and asked to be received "on a matter of importance which cannot be discussed over the telephone." The Kaiser refused because Prince Max was ill with influenza and he, the Kaiser, must not expose himself to an infection; neither should Prince Max take chances. Then he left.

Hahn's report strengthened the Chancellor's conviction that a voluntary abdication was necessary. Without revealing his own opinion he threw the question open to discussion in the Cabinet meeting on October 31. The Liberals, von Payer and Haussmann; one of the leaders of the Zentrum, Trimborn; Prussian Minister of the Interior Dr. Drews; Foreign Secretary Dr. Solf; and, of course, Social Democrat Philip Scheidemann, all spoke in favor of abdication. Strongly opposed were: the leader of the Prussian National Liberals, Friedberg (then deputy Prussian Minister-President); War Minister Scheuch; a representative of the Zentrum's conservative wing, Gröber; Matthias Erzberger, leader of the Zentrum's left wing.

On the Chancellor's request Dr. Drews travelled to general headquarters to inform the Kaiser. Prince Friedrich Karl von Hessen, the Kaiser's brother-in-law, a man from whom greater influence was expected, was to go the following day. He had promised to do so in the morning. But when he arrived in the evening he had grown uncertain. Prince Max called Simons and told him about this change of mind. "Then Simons became angry," writes Prince Max in his memoirs. "His usual correctness and patience left him and he turned with passionate words to Prince Karl: if he was not able to step before the Kaiser like Luther before the Reichstag in Worms: 'Here I stand, I can do no other, God help me,' then he had better not undertake the trip." Prince Friedrich Karl said that he felt unable to do it. Simons went out to cancel the special train. Colleagues urged him to talk to the Prince of Hessen once more. "Then Simons struck the table with his fist: 'Leave me alone, I won't force anyone. If the advocates of the monarchic idea fail us at this moment, then we will get the republic!" However, he went back and told the Prince that he could still go. The Prince stuck to his refusal.

In the meantime threatening news arrived from Wilhelmshaven. On October 30 the sailors had refused to obey orders and had offered active resistance. The naval chiefs had intended to provoke the English fleet, despite its superiority, to a decisive battle with the German battle fleet. The sailors had got wind of this plan. They saw it as an action contrary to the efforts of the Chancellor and his cabinet to end the war immediately and, therefore, had prevented the fleet from sailing. Prince Max sent them word that their suspicions were without foundations. The most atrocious thing in this affair was the fact that he, the German Chancellor, did not know that the action had actually been intended and had been in fact under way. He had not been informed of such an important action, and learned the truth only later.

This mad, unauthorized action of the naval heads started the revolution rolling. Even the most romantic German patriot who is inclined to admire the decision of the admirals as a heroic deed should pause to think when he reads in Prince Max's memoirs that the Chancellor, had he been informed of the plan, would not have rejected it outright, but would have demanded only that the armistice conditions first be waited for. If these were to go a great deal further than Wilson's Fourteen Points, then Germany would reject them, and, after the abdication of the Kaiser and the Crown Prince and a public statement of Germany's agreement to the complete restoration of Belgium and to withdrawal from Alsace-Lorraine, would resume the military struggle in the hope that the peoples in the allied countries would then rebel against a continuance of the war. The sailing of the German fleet to a final decisive battle would then have had real meaning.

Now a further complication arose. Prince Max had not yet fully recovered from influenza. The burden of work and the importance of the decisions to be taken had completely exhausted him. He suffered a serious relapse. His doctor, wanting him to rest, prescribed a sedative which, as Prince Max writes, "had a stronger effect on me in my weakened condition than was intended and sent me into a deep sleep, from which it was impossible to awaken me for thirty-six hours." The doctor later denied that he had prescribed a particularly strong dose; he attributed the long sleep to exhaustion. That is unimportant here. The fact is that not until the afternoon of November 3 did Prince Max awaken, only to learn that Turkey and Austria had accepted the armistice terms offered by the enemy and that Minister Drews' mission to general headquarters had failed.[2] On the same day the revolution began in Kiel with the demonstration of the sailors there against the mass punishments of their fellows in Wilhelmshaven, who had prevented the fleet from sailing (see Chapter 17).

While all these events were taking place during the first two weeks of my work in the Chancellery I gradually came to see the members of the Cabinet, none of whom I had known previously, as distinct personalities. Philip Scheidemann, spokesman of the Social Democrats, was at the peak of his fame. In his popular speeches he had often given eloquent, dignified, and convincing expression to the patriotism of the working-class and to their criticism of those in charge of the country's affairs. His superior conduct at Cabinet meetings reflected his rank in the public mind. He made no wild, accusing speeches, nor any malicious remarks, but drew conclusions from events in simple words. A typical comment of his occurred in the first session at which I took minutes. Some Cabinet member had complained that Communist propaganda leaflets were being distributed among the people in large numbers; there was a strong suspicion that the Russian Ambassador received this material in big cases from the Soviet Union, but because of the extra-territoriality of the embassy the police authorities had no right to open the cases. To this Scheidemann said: "We will tell the workers who do the unloading that they should accidentally drop one of the cases through a trap-door onto the hard paving on the lower floor of the station; then we shall see what is in it." So it was done, and thou-

[2] Drew's report is rendered in the appendix of the German edition.

sands of propaganda leaflets burst out of the case. The German Foreign Office filed a complaint about the misuse of the immunity of the Ambassador, and he was recalled.

The moderation in Scheidemann's statements on the question of the Kaiser's abdication was most remarkable to me. In the session on October 31 he said:

"The situation has deteriorated considerably during the past fourteen days, in particular the morale of the army. The further away from the front, the worse. Add to this the defection of our allies. The world is seeking a scapegoat. Public opinion leans on all sorts of statements which the Kaiser made formerly and which have remained in the public memory. The repercussions of these statements are leading to ever-stronger attacks on the person of His Majesty. No defender of the Kaiser has come forward either in the bourgeoisie or among the farmers. Our workers are convinced that we shall obtain no peace which will enable our nation to continue to live as long as Kaiserism has not been ended. We have ever again tried to read into Wilson's notes that the President does not demand the Kaiser's abdication. But the Foreign Office will back me when I say that interpretations abroad are different. . . . If the [armistice and peace] conditions are so bad that we cannot accept them and must defend ourselves to the last, then we can only fight such a fight when the Kaiser has gone. It is our duty, therefore, to suggest to the Kaiser that he take this step voluntarily. I would not like to see the Kaiser brought into an undignified situation. It was not dignified that we allowed ourselves to be driven under Wilson's whip to constitutional amendments we should have made long ago of our own free will. It would also be undignified if the Kaiser were to abdicate because the people forced him to by strikes and revolts, and it will come to that. Our [Social-Democrat] press has been very restrained. . . .

"I am in complete agreement with what the Chancellor has said: that we must not put any pressure on the Kaiser, not even the Cabinet. But he must be given advice. We also must avoid the Cabinet's collapse [over this issue]. If I call it a historical necessity that the Kaiser goes, I do not mean to threaten that I shall resign from the Cabinet if it does not happen. Before I say anything of that nature, I must confer with my party colleagues, whose representative I am here.

"But there is one thing no one should deceive himself about: the demand was not first made in working-class circles, but in the bourgeoisie, particularly in Southern Germany, where the separatist movement is growing. In Bavaria they are saying now: 'Away from Prussia! Let us unite with Austria! Away from the Reich!' That would be the worst thing that could happen. The Reich must be preserved in its full greatness and weight (*Grösse und Wucht*), with one united people, who know what their fatherland is worth to them. The farmers too, especially in Southern Germany, hold that the Kaiser must abdicate; all contradictory news is false. What has surprised me most is the attitude of the Civil Service. I had never thought it possible that these people would give in so completely. Quite a number of officers also have come to see me and have expressed the same view. These were officers up to the rank of colonel. They all regretted it very much, but they said that their country is more important to them than the Kaiser's position. And that is right. If it is in the interest of the country and the people, then one has to disregard feelings—which I completely respect. It is also in the interest of the Kaiser and his name in history. He must accept the consequences of defeat and abdicate voluntarily."

On the other hand, Matthias Erzberger amazed me by the severity with which he turned *against* the abdication in the same session. He said: "Things must not be rushed; it is true that opinion for the abdication is growing, but about half the nation is of a different opinion and has so far not spoken out." He added that he himself would deeply regret an abdication. And later at the same session: "A Swiss said to me yesterday: If Germany ousts the Kaiser, people abroad will say that the Germans are brutal in victory and contemptible in defeat. And he is right here, if we make a bargain with the Kaiser. You expect to obtain better conditions as a consequence of the abdication? I believe the conditions are settled. It would be our political disadvantage if the Kaiser abdicated immediately before we received the conditions. Then it would seem as though he had fled from them and that would have a crushing effect. I know how people think of us abroad. If a German diplomat asks Cardinal Mercier whether the Kaiser should resign, then he is fit for the gallows; and if the Cardinal speaks of it of his own accord and the diplomat does not protest, then too he is fit for the gallows. If a German diplomat asks the Danish minister what he thinks about it, then I can only say how deeply I regret the fact that the minister of a foreign minor country allows himself to express opinions on a question which is a matter of life and death to the German nation. Even the English fear that the consequence of the Kaiser's abdication in Germany will be Bolshevism."

Conrad Haussmann replied that it was self-contradictory to say that only a voluntary abdication was of any value and then simply to wait until the Entente set such grave conditions that the Kaiser has to resign. Then the abdication would no longer be viewed abroad as voluntary, and the Kaiser would also lose the right to gratitude at home. At the present moment the renunciation of the throne would be a great sacrifice, made for the sake of the nation to obtain a favorable peace settlement; gratitude would outweigh the shock. Abdication because of the current conditions—i.e., on the ground that they were too severe—would create an impossible situation for the government. If the Kaiser and King considered the conditions so severe that he would rather give up the throne than accept them, ought the Government then to accept them? What would be the prospect of a final fight under such circumstances? If abdication, then it must take place before the armistice conditions were known.

In his notes to the United States, Prince Max, on the suggestion of the High Command, had pointed out that Germany accepted President Wilson's points as a basis of peace only on the understanding that Great Britain and France did the same. Lansing's note of November 5 stated that Great Britain and France had in fact taken on the same obligations, with two important exceptions: concerning war reparations and the freedom of the seas. I have always considered the fact that this documented basis for the peace negotiations was gained the greatest service rendered Germany during Prince Max's short period in the Chancellery.

On looking back to these first weeks in the Chancellery, I find that two points stand out. The first is the fact, which has remained incomprehensible to me, that Prince Max failed to go to the Kaiser personally to persuade him to abdicate in the interest of the country and the preservation of the monarchy. He sent other people. If I am right he spoke to the Kaiser only twice even on the telephone, the first time when the Kaiser suddenly left for general headquarters (see above), the other time on November 9. Such a decision should have been wrung from the Kaiser by the responsible Chancellor himself. It is true that influenza made the trip during several days impossible. But the physical possibility existed both before and after. The Chancellor's absence for one day and two nights would have been less damaging than the delay of the decision.

The other circumstance which had a strong influence on my political development was the historical fact, of which I was so close a witness, that the majority group of the Social Democrats was prepared to accept a democratic constitution with a monarch as a nominal head of state, as in England, the Scandinavian countries, and Holland, provided that a period of transition was guaranteed by the abdication of the Kaiser and the Crown Prince. When on November 9 Scheidemann closed his speech from the window of the Reichstag with the words: "Long live the Republic," this was only after the Kaiser's voluntary abdication had been delayed too long and the monarchy was in fact already lost. Even then his action was not in accordance with Ebert's wishes (Chapter 17). Prince Max's memoirs are the best testimony of the fact that the Social Democrats in the end had no alternative. Germany would have fallen into the hands of the Independents and Spartacists had the Socialist majority left it to them alone to be the spokesmen for public opinion on the question of the abdication. The patriotism of the Socialist majority shone never more brightly than during these weeks. This made an indelible impression on me. I admit that from the point of view of the Communists, what I here stress in praise of the Socialist majority must constitute ground for harsh reproaches. Here judgments of values differ. The facts are clear.

Prince Max impressed all those who got to know him as being an eminently honest and upright man, and these were my feelings as well. But for all the good will he showed, he must not be thought of as a man of democratic and republican conviction. He was at heart a supporter of monarchy. He was also an opponent of general franchise and of the outright parliamentary form of democracy. He considered a constitutional monarchy the best form of government, not only because he was "by profession," as cousin of the childless Grand Duke, the heir to the throne in the Grand Duchy of Baden; he believed in it from deep conviction on the ground that monarchy embodied what he (especially under the influence of Kurt Hahn, see Chapter 18) called the "leadership-idea," disregarding the fact that the monarch might be incapable or unsuitable. He was an honest supporter of extensive democratization in the broadest sense of the word. His ideal was not equal franchise, however, but a franchise with degrees of votes according to the maturity of the voter.[3]

The views of the High Command in September and October, 1918 seem to me now less self-contradictory than they did then. I now believe that their insistence on immediate armistice was strongly influenced by their desire to rescue the prestige of the High Command and of the army by avoiding manifest defeat on the battlefield, and that they wished to reserve the possibility of reopening the struggle, despite the threat of defeat, if the conditions proved too severe. This was no logical contradiction, but politically it was rather naïve. For the confession that Germany needed an armistice could only whet the appetite of the opponents and at the same time weaken the German defense.

## 15. Interlude: A Non-Delivered Speech

When Wilson's Fourteen Points had been accepted in the note of October 3 as a basis for peace, Prince Max decided to "interpret" them in his first speech as Chancellor two days later. He did not want to "warp" their meaning, but "to defend our rights stubbornly in every single point, as Wilson had indeed promised to honor them." For this purpose he summoned Walter Simons, the Foreign Office's chief legal expert. In his memoirs he writes: "I did not know him personally, but had heard of him years ago, of his opinions on the war, on our invasion of Belgium, on the enemy blockade, the submarine warfare, and the question of responsibility. His patriotism was such that he suffered dreadfully when he thought that his country was acting wrongly, yet at the same time he felt it to be a grave sin when Germany endured injustice and calumny without putting up any sort of struggle."

The two of them went through Wilson's points one by one. Then Prince Max asked Simons and Kurt Hahn to prepare the speech in consultation with Foreign Secretary Solf, the banker Max Warburg, the liberal Reichstag delegate Konrad Haussmann, and Colonel von

[3] See Prince Max von Baden's memoirs, pp. 122, 183, 184, 298.

Haeften, Ludendorff's representative.[1] The men began work and, under the leadership of Simons, drew up a draft. It was not finished until eleven o'clock in the evening. Prince Max added a demand for an international investigation of the responsibility for the outbreak of the war, and then had the draft read aloud to the State Secretaries waiting in the Cabinet room. They were unanimous in the opinion that he should not deliver the speech in this form; they felt that its interpretation of the Fourteen Points would endanger the entire armistice. Prince Max gave in. He writes in his memoirs: "Today I regret this decision."

The nondelivered speech was dignified in tone and, although it announced resistance to unreasonable demands, there was in every line evidence of the new spirit which now filled the leading men.[2] In later negotiations Germany did in fact raise these same objections, but then it was too late. An attempt to tune down demands before they had been formulated jointly would in my opinion have been more effective than was the subsequent attempt to rectify them.

## 16. THE LAST CABINET MEETING BEFORE THE REVOLUTION IN KIEL (NOVEMBER 2, 1918): MINUTES LOST, BUT REDISCOVERED

THE notes on the Cabinet meeting of November 2, 1918, the day before the outbreak of the revolution in Kiel, have so far been missing. This gap was due to a sudden illness of mine. I had been keeper of the minutes. During the meeting, signs of a high body temperature indicated that I had caught the influenza prevalent at the time. So I simply dictated a few notes quickly on the results of the meeting on one particular point—the armistice negotiations—and then went home exhausted to bed, where I was forced to stay for several days. Due to subsequent events the transcript remained unfinished. In preparing this book, however, I rediscovered my old shorthand notes. Despite omissions, which I can no longer reliably fill in from memory, they present such a vivid picture of the situa-

---

[1] In fact, he did not assist.
[2] The wording is given in the original German edition.

tion at the time on varied subjects (the fate of Alsace-Lorraine, the composition of the armistice commission, the fate of the troops in the East, Liebknecht's inflammatory speeches, problems regarding the Kaiser, the planned naval thrust) that I will reproduce them here. Words within square brackets have been added to make the meaning clearer.

*Text of my shorthand notes taken at the Cabinet meeting on Nov. 2, 1918*

## 1. The Fate of Alsace-Lorraine

SCHWANDER [Governor (Statthalter) for Alsace-Lorraine since October 18]: "Five weeks ago I thought it to be my duty to give Alsace-Lorraine autonomy [as one of the States within the framework of the German Reich] and [thus] to keep it for Germany. When I read the wording of the Wilson note I knew that everyone [in Alsace-Lorraine] would presume that they had already been ceded. There was not much more that could be done. The mood in Alsace-Lorraine is regrettable, but understandable. We are convinced that the Territorial Assembly [the *Landtag* in Alsace-Lorraine] is not prepared to take any steps [in matters of the future of Alsace-Lorraine]. The new [parliamentary] government will find supporters in all parties and will therefore come into existence. But what are they able still to do for German nationality? We can do nothing more for autonomy [within the framework of the Reich]. What I thought would be possible was [to stir] the population into demanding the right to self-determination. I said that I considered it undignified that [we were not active ourselves]. I wanted to win them over to cooperate in the declaration of the right to self-determination. The right to self-determination involves three questions, however [i.e., not only remaining part of Germany, or becoming part of France, but] also independence. The majority will opt for France. In Upper Alsace and in Lorraine a large majority is for France; in Lower Alsace a majority is for Germany.

"In wide intellectual quarters there are doubts about annexation to France. As a result of this, opinions in favor of independence and neutrality have increased. The idea that Germany will not tolerate Strassburg as a French town for good will have some influence. We ought not to oppose the thought of neutrality, but should give it that [gentle? The word is not easy to decipher] support which the government is capable of. I am convinced that the upper classes will be susceptible (*ausgeliefert*) to French propaganda; but I am equally convinced that the lower classes as a whole will try to maintain the connection with Germany. The old German elements could stay in the country [in case Alsace-Lorraine was granted independence]. The support [for the idea of self-determination] should not, of course, become manifest and the idea should not be launched from Germany. Occupation of Metz by French troops and of Strassburg by Americans—and then there is nothing more Germany could hope for in Strassburg. The Americans are sufficient. There will be fraternizing celebrations, entry while the populace cheers. Entente troops in Strassburg—and everything is lost for German nationality there. There are still some prospects for us if a neutral power, Switzerland for example, were to undertake the occupation. That would stimulate particularism (*Kantönligeist*)."

VON PAYER [Vice Chancellor, liberal]: "These are very unpleasant facts but we will have to take a stand on them. Whether we will have the power to avert all this no one can tell. Nor can we give the Governor any information about the armistice conditions. We shall have to wait for them. The idea of autonomy cannot be pursued any further. . . ."

ERZBERGER: "We shall have to wait until we know the conditions of the armistice. [In the meantime] complete suspension of censorship [in Alsace-Lorraine]. Withdrawal of the restrictions on the right of assembly, so that the Entente, when they move in, may have to tighten regulations. . . ."

TRIMBORN [State Secretary, member of the Zentrum party]: "Removal of protective custody?"

SCHWANDER: "I have filed applications for 400 persons in protective custody."

RÜDLIN [Secretary of the Postal Department]: "Censure of postal services will also have to be suspended; I do not know to what extent the military commanders will be in agreement with that."

SCHWANDER: "Negotiations [on this] are pending. If necessary, restrictive areas [areas in which liberties are to remain restricted] will have to be limited to the mountain region."

DREWS [Prussian Minister of the Interior]: "We proceed from the assumption that Alsace-Lorraine will obtain the right to self-determination in the peace treaty. If we grant them self-determination now, then we have already made our concessions."

VON PAYER: "That is a misunderstanding. No one wants to pass a national law. The question is only whether or not the government should oppose aspirations to neutrality."

DREWS: "The fact that the freedom [for such aspirations] is afforded suffices."

HAUSSMANN [Liberal]: "It is important for the psychological effect that we abstain from propaganda moves on our part. We are prepared to grant [Alsace-Lorraine] all the liberties as a free state."

SCHEIDEMANN: "No one will ever forget this meeting. The Governor tells us what [will happen in the case of a free plebiscite]. This represents an indictment of all previous governments, so grave that no worse one can be imagined. We have to do it [grant liberties], but there is no longer any point to it. It is too late. We must do it in Germany too, before it is too late."

SCHWANDER: " 'Too late'—dreadful words. I hope that—if we still have three or four months before it comes to occupation by the Entente—the mood might change in a certain direction, so that something can be saved for Germany."

## 2. *Armistice Negotiations*

ERZBERGER: "Armistice conditions will soon be received. We must immediately put counter-questions which cannot be answered immediately; then there remains hope for negotiations. Care must be taken that a politician is present: Foreign Secretary Solf, for example."

VON PAYER: "Herr von Hintze [former Foreign Secretary, at that time representative of the Foreign Office at General Headquarters] is there for this purpose. We will not be able to release Solf. There remains the question as to whether one of the [parliamentary] State Secretaries ought to go as well."

HAUSSMANN: "Solf must participate."

VON PAYER: "Not Solf, rather a [parliamentary] Secretary."

ERZBERGER: "Haussmann." [1]

VON PAYER: "Solf must first get in contact with the High Command."

---

[1] Actually Erzberger was selected. See German edition on the controversy as to who proposed Erzberger.

### 3. Evacuation of Troops in the East

FRIEDBERG [Deputy Minister-President of Prussia; National Liberal]: "What about our troops in the Ukraine and Rumania? Are they in danger of being cut off?"

SCHEUCH [Minister of War]: "There is some danger."

COLONEL VON HAEFTEN [Representing General Headquarters]: "I have an exact distribution of troops on the Eastern front lines, the position of the troops and their intended utilization. In Turkey 32,000 men with officers are being transported to the Ukraine. In Rumania the troops will be evacuated as soon as the transport situation in Hungary allows, or they will march back. In Hungary: 1 division and 10 disengaged battalions. In the Ukraine: [the troops] will remain for the present. In the Upper Eastern areas: the very shortest line has already been formed. In Finland: they are to stay until the Finns are able to defend themselves against Bolshevism. Then they will be withdrawn."

### 4. Liebknecht's Inflammatory Speeches

VON KRAUSE [Secretary, Department of Justice]: "On October [27th] Liebknecht made three short speeches; at three assemblies he more or less said: 'Now the moment has come to take decisive action. Decision in our hands. Call for revolution. Being prepared is everything. Action must decide. Long live the Socialist Republic. Down with the Hohenzollerns.' Although [there may have been] no direct intention to apply violence, there is nevertheless evidence of high treason (*Hoch- und Landesverrat*). One of the police officers thinks that Liebknecht only wanted to create an impression of being important. The Federal Chief Prosecutor (*Oberreichsanwalt*) [declared]: there is evidence of high treason. An indictment must be filed and a warrant for arrest must be asked for. Requests instructions. Whether military jurisdiction is involved not yet clarified. 'Adequate suspicion' suffices [for an arrest]. From the legal standpoint he is to be indicted, since he makes no denials but emphasizes. Whether the superior authorities [i.e., the Secretary of the Department of Justice and the Chancellor] are in a position to decide for political reasons that he is not to be indicted is legally doubtful. He will [probably] be pardoned [later]. In that case it would be wrong to begin proceedings. The Chancellor himself must assume responsibility."

SCHEUCH: "The question arises: what then does he have to do before he is indicted? This incidentally [since it is no business of the Minister of War]. He is liable for military service: what ought we [the Ministry of War] to do with him? I would for humane reasons like to delay the draft. [But that I cannot do.] I have given instructions today for Liebknecht to be examined and drafted in accordance with the degree of his fitness. We cannot exempt Liebknecht."

SCHEIDEMANN: Welcomes Krause's standpoint. "That police officer is right. Refusal to do military service is part of Liebknecht's program. It is true that some people have written 'he must be reinstated in his military honors.' But if you [draft him] he will become an effective subject for agitation [against the government]. Liebknecht makes no impression at all in his speeches. He can cause all sorts of nuisance, but no more than that."

SCHEUCH: "As Minister of War I *cannot* do that [i.e., except him from being drafted]. The draft is now being carried through with no regard for economic and personal conditions of extreme severity. I cannot make an exception in his case simply because his name is Liebknecht."

VON PAYER: "I am of the opinion that it is expedient not to indict him now, but otherwise one has to let the law take its course."

ERZBERGER: "Agree. Political interests are predominant."

VON KRAUSE: "I think he must be *overlooked*. That is the lesser evil."

SCHEUCH: "I am not authorized to release him. If he is fit I have no other choice than to draft him."

RÜDLIN: "Let us delay Liebknecht's recruitment for the present. Then we will be over the worst."

COUNT ROEDERN [Secretary, Treasury]: "Agree. Wait calmly another fortnight. The case of the Minister of War [military draft] and that of the Secretary of the Justice Department [indictment for high treason] are exactly parallel. In this case too we can wait a fortnight."

SCHEUCH: "If we wait it will become even more difficult. He cannot be ignored. He himself sees to it that he is not ignored."

It was agreed [among the members of the War Council] that further action should wait.

## 5. The Kaiser Question

GRÖBER [Zentrum party]: "There is need for a clarification of public opinion on the Kaiser question. The situation cannot remain like this any longer. In one way or another we will have to make clear what our attitude is. If we permit [public] discussion things will become worse. We must publish the Kaiser's proclamation [letter to the Chancellor of October 28 on the occasion of the amendment to the Constitution, see Appendix]. It must be countersigned. This second document is more important than the preceding address to the newly appointed [parliamentary] Secretaries [of October 21, see Appendix]. Publication of the proclamation [of October 28] implies a statement of the government's position, which clarifies everything."

VON PAYER: "At that time we asked Haussmann to publish the address [of October 21] in a non-official form (*feuilletonistisch*). The *Frankfurter Zeitung* rejected it."

FRIEDBERG: "I was at that time along with Delbrück [head of the Kaiser's Civil Cabinet] against publishing. His Majesty has been preoccupied with the idea for a long time and publication would be in accordance with his wishes. . . . Publication and a corroborative position taken by the government would bring about [public] reassurance and [be welcome] to the loyal press."

ERZBERGER: "The second publication must be brought out *this evening* in official form from the Chancellor's Palais. *Vossische Zeitung* and *Tageblatt* [liberal papers] are not willing to publish anything [directed against the Kaiser's abdication]. Today we must answer [the questions raised by the public]. The Liberals are also of this opinion."

HAUSSMANN: "The *Frankfurter Zeitung* [liberal] rejected it. I have it [the manuscript prepared by H.]. I could send it off any time."

VON PAYER: "We should do this. But not at once [not both at once]. First the second statement [of October 28]."

SCHEIDEMANN: "The words were well chosen; we can endorse them. But what sort of impression will it make? In the public discussion the Kaiser will fare badly. Each paper will add its own comments. Extracts from earlier speeches [will be quoted in contrast]. That will be dreadful. Revolutionary movements will not be cut off by it. "Here I stand, I can do otherwise." I warn against publication. Nothing more will be achieved by it. If it is in today's papers, you will see how people react tomorrow and the next day. We are unable to take [joint] action as the government, because our views are too divergent. Dandl [Bavarian Minister-President, who was expected for the following day] will confirm that the Bavarian Zentrum party desires [abdication]."

ERZBERGER: reads aloud the Kaiser's address delivered in Bellevue Castle on October 21 and his proclamation of October 28 [see Appendix].

VON WAHNSCHAFFE [State Secretary in the Chancellery]: "The Kaiser *demands* counter-signature."

VON PAYER: "I have proceeded from the assumption that the Kaiser was leaving the decision to us. Now the Kaiser *wants* publication. Therefore: counter-sign and publish."

GRÖBER: "The Kaiser has come around to accepting the new situation (*hat sich in die neue Zeit hineingefunden*) and has adopted a definite position. This fact must be appreciated. Bismarck said: "I too am one of those people who are learning something." Neither did we [parliamentary] State Secretaries refuse the call [to join the government], because we had [previously] wanted something else. It will make a great impression. Great effect! Discussion will be calmer after the proclamation [is published]."

BAUER [Social Democrat, State Secretary of Labor]: "If the Kaiser insists on it, we cannot well refuse it. Now that things have been taking a dangerous turn, the Kaiser begins to ask for good weather. A change in the public mind will not be brought about by this [publication]. I myself was *against* abdication. I discovered strongly radical views among the representatives of industrial enterprises. They all said: the Kaiser was the central figure (*der Träger*) of the system and, therefore, is responsible (*schuld*) for the whole affair. The most prominent representative of industry, the Association of Employers and Employees, will demand abdication. This view has support also among farmers."

ERZBERGER: "It must appear in tomorrow's papers."

SCHEIDEMANN: "The central problem is not that of the Kaiser, but: Bolshevism or not? [He recommends] an *appeal* from the new government: the new government turns to the German people; reference to the present calamity; improvement must be achieved; the new government is at work to accomplish everything [possible]; it is not possible to construct a new world in four weeks. Much has happened. Far more will happen. This and that has already been done . . . this and that will be done. Cooperation in great measure. Food supply; transport must be assured. Otherwise everything will collapse. All must cooperate. We cannot deny the Kaiser [publication of his proclamations]. But the other thing [the appeal] must come out at the same time. The *Vorwärts* [Social Democratic newspaper] will, I hope, adopt a sensible attitude. It will add no comments. But the *liberal* papers!"

Von Payer: "If the Kaiser wants it, we have no right at all to prevent it. Publish the proclamation [of October 28] today after countersignature. The address [of October 21] on Monday as an article (*feuilletonistisch*)."

Von Krause: "As the people's government (*Volksregierung*) we have no right to suppress the publication. That would be no truly democratic procedure."

Von Waldow [Secretary, Department of Food]: "Also for publication. If entrepreneurs want to remove the Kaiser, then it is disloyal and shameless. They have continually been driving the Kaiser toward a forced peace (*Gewaltfrieden*). Food supplies can be maintained only if there is *order*. The big landed estates east of the Elbe will have to deliver. Civil servants and farmers are for the monarchy. We will find passive resistance in these quarters [if the Kaiser is forced to abdicate]. Industry starving! Then no one will be able to accept responsibility. I wouldn't do it."

Von Payer: "We will immediately take care of the publication. Scheidemann must draft an appeal with the contents he has suggested."

Erzberger: "Sit down at once and complete it."

Von Payer: "Wait a little."

## 6. The Planned Naval Thrust

Ritter Von Mann [Secretary, Naval Department]: "We wanted to make a naval thrust [*Flottenvorstoss* on October 29 and 30 from Wilhelmshaven]. From two cruisers 150 men stayed behind and did not sail with us. Aboard the "Thüringen" many men refused, barricaded themselves. . . . Widely circulated in the fleet that the naval officers and the Kaiser wanted to go on fighting. 'Nothing can happen to us because there will be a general amnesty.' Yesterday and today other [alarming] conditions developed. Agitation. Uniform directives issued by the Independents [Independent Social

Democrats]: "1. Government wants peace, officers not. 2. Every naval thrust impedes peace. 3. The officers want to see the fleet destroyed or to scuttle the ships themselves." The movement has already gained much ground. Torpedoes and submarines still seem to be free. The men do not believe us. He [the speaker] is of the opinion that the government must call for order and discipline. Commander of the Fleet and Chief of Staff should be summoned. It [i.e., the call for order] must find a place in the appeal. They do not believe in the new government, which deceives them just as the old one did. Amnesty would be very difficult for me. I would not be opposed to substituting prison (*Gefängnis*) for penitentiary (*Zuchthaus*). It would be a big mistake to pardon the ringleaders."

SCHEUCH: "Those fit for military service are no longer prepared to obey draft orders. Antagonisms between government and High Command are presumed to exist. The appeal [suggested by Scheidemann] will also have a good effect in this respect."

VON PAYER: "Next session Sunday, November 3, at 6 p.m. Scheidemann's draft [of the appeal] will form the basis of the discussion. As soon as the draft is finished it will be duplicated and handed out to the individual members. On the following day [Monday, November 4] at 9:30 a.m. it must be decided upon. Into the newspapers on Tuesday morning."

### 7. Miscellaneous

VON WAHNSCHAFFE [Secretary, Chancellery]: "The doctor has once more ordered the Chancellor to stay in bed. He hopes for Monday."

# PART IV

## Political Education through Revolution

## 17. The German November Revolution

The German Revolution of November 1918 did not start in Berlin or on the Ruhr, not among industrial or rural workers, not among the leaders of the two Socialist parties, but in Wilhelmshaven and Kiel among the sailors. It began with the sailors' resistance against a revolt of the leading naval officers who were about to thwart the policy of the constitutionally legitimate, responsible government in Berlin by having the fleet put to sea secretly, in the middle of the peace negotiations, for a last great sea battle with the British fleet. The sailors' rebellion in Wilhelmshaven was suppressed. In Kiel it was victorious.

When the Kiel sailors thus suddenly held in their hands the power over the warships in the harbor and over the town, they did not know what to do next. Aimless and leaderless they walked the streets. Then, Gustav Noske, Social Democratic expert on naval affairs, whom his party sent to Kiel on November 4 at the request of the government, succeeded with great courage and skill in gaining control. The admiralty and the sailors willingly accepted him as governor of Kiel. Kiel was pacified. But the spark had in the meantime caught fire in Lübeck, Hamburg, and Bremen because groups of sailors had without difficulty won over the weak military garrisons in the Hansa cities. On November 6 all three—Lübeck, Hamburg, and Bremen—were occupied by the revolutionaries, and on the 7th Hannover as well. On the same day the revolution was victorious in Munich, independently of the sailors. Cologne, Düsseldorf, Frankfurt, Stuttgart, Leipzig, Halle, Braunschweig, and Magdeburg also fell on November 7.

The sailors had not come to Berlin. The Revolution there had rather antecedents of its own. There the masses of workers, and broad sections of the upper classes as well, waited breathlessly for the Kaiser's voluntary abdication, which Prince Max of Baden was trying day by day vainly to induce. Even as late as November 6— that is, two days after the victory of the Revolution in Kiel—General Groener, Ludendorff's successor as Chief of Staff, had found the Social Democratic leaders and the representatives of the trade unions "entirely reasonable," as he maintained in November, 1925 as a witness at the so-called stab-in-the-back trial in Munich. From no side, he said, was "a word uttered then, which might have led one to conclude that the gentlemen aspired to revolution. On the contrary, from beginning to end they spoke only of how the monarchy could be maintained." Finally Ebert, he reported, made the following proposal: "Abdication of the Kaiser was absolutely necessary, if the desertion of the masses into the revolutionists' camp and thus the Revolution itself were to be avoided. He therefore proposed that the Kaiser voluntarily announce his abdication on that very day, November 6, or at the latest on the following day, November 7, and appoint one of his sons, perhaps Prince Eitel Friedrich, Regent in the place of the Crown Prince's oldest son."

Groener added that he had at that time rejected this proposal. "And thus I plead guilty," he said, "of not having agreed to Ebert's proposal on that afternoon on November 6, and not having said: 'Herr Ebert, a man, a word. We will proceed together: I will see to it that the Kaiser abdicates and you that the Social Democrats back you and defend the monarchy.' From my knowledge of deputy Ebert I am sure he would have agreed to this. So, gentlemen, if you wish to pronounce me guilty then you are at your liberty to say: on November 6 General Groener committed the bottomless idiocy— not intentionally, of course—of not accepting this proposal made by deputy Ebert. Perhaps it would have been possible to save the monarchy, but only perhaps, for it was already rather late." [1]

At the same trial Scheidemann said: "We did not prepare a revolution, we did not want a revolution, but by simply following requests [to take over the government] and finally from our own sense of responsibility too, we were faced with the question of what we ought to do in this moment of terrible misery for our nation?"

The meeting with Groener was on November 6. It became ever more difficult to restrain the masses in Berlin, impressed as they were by the events on the coast and their spread to the south and west. On November 7, therefore, the Social Democrats sent their ultimatum to the federal government—that is, to Prince Max and his Cabinet—with the (in itself legal) announcement that they would withdraw their representatives from the Cabinet and from the government departments, if the abdication was not received by midday, November 8. The reason given: the workers would otherwise desert and go over to the Independents and Spartacists.

[1] Quoted from Carl Herz, *Geister der Vergangenheit,* Haifa, 1953, p. 190.

Scheidemann was willing to remain in the government until conclusion of the armistice, so that a government which was able to negotiate would exist. The Socialist leaders, therefore, asked the workers to be patient "for a few more hours." However, when on the evening of November 8 the Kaiser had not abdicated, the Social Democratic members withdrew from the government. On the morning of the 9th they issued the order to strike: "Out of the factories!"

Shortly before midday, November 9, Prince Max announced the abdication, on the basis of a telephone communication from Headquarters that "the decision had been made and had only to be formulated." Not until after publication did news from Headquarters arrive that the Kaiser had been willing to abdicate only as Kaiser and not as King of Prussia. Prince Max had taken action to prevent the agitated crowds from going over to the Independents and Spartacists and thus, if possible, to avoid violent revolution and the overthrow of the monarchy. On Simons' advice, in a bold but pertinent interpretation of his historical role at this hour, Prince Max now transferred the duties of Chancellor to Friedrich Ebert as the leader of the largest party in the Reichstag. "I enjoin the German Reich on you," he said. Ebert replied: "I have given two sons for this Reich." Prince Max took his leave of the officials in the Chancellery, asked them to transfer their loyal services to Ebert, and left Berlin.

The Revolution ignored this late attempt at an orderly transference of duties. At two o'clock Scheidemann, speaking from a window of the Reichstag, proclaimed the Republic to the masses waiting in Königsplatz, later Platz der Republik. "Our task now," he concluded, "is that we do not permit this complete victory for the people to be spoiled. Therefore, I ask you to see to it that our building up of the Republic will not be disturbed from any side. Long live the German Republic!"

Ebert felt annoyed about this unauthorized act, not because he preferred a monarchic to a republican constitution, but because he feared—justifiably, as it turned out—that abolition of the monarchy would drive a wedge through the German nation, so dividing it that the pro-democratic and pro-republican groups would not have a majority, whereas a German version of the English, Scandinavian, or Dutch forms of democratic monarchies would open up better prospects for democratic majorities; secondly, because according to his own line of thinking, the decision about the form of government was to be left to a constituent national assembly. Scheidemann replied that he had only sounded the usual Social Democratic call for a German Republic and that in any case it was now too late to maintain a monarchic form of government.

Be this as it may, matters could not rest with Ebert's acceptance of the Chancellor's duties from Prince Max. After the Revolution had been victorious in large areas of Germany the new government needed for its authority the sanction of the workers and soldiers. Suppression of the Revolution in Berlin by troops stationed there was no longer possible. A battalion considered to be "reliable" had been sent from Naumburg to the Alexander Kaserne in Berlin (the barracks of one of the Guards' Regiments), but on November 9 these troops took their stand unanimously on the side of the workers, and so did the men of the Alexander Regiment and of the other Guards' Regiments. At the request of the Naumburg troops, who asked for a briefing from a member of the Social Democratic majority group, Otto Wels went to the Alexander Kaserne and told the troops there that the future of the German nation depended on them; it was decisive that the military should sympathize with the Social Democrat majority and not with the Spartacus Group.

At that time the Spartacus Group was still part of the Independents, but acted separately. The leader of the Independents, Hugo Haase, was not in Berlin. He had gone to Kiel, where he could do little more than take note of Noske's measures; Noske was convinced that at this moment everything depended upon the Social Democrats and Independents working together. Deeply impressed by Noske's arguments, Haase returned to Berlin, along with a member of the Socialist majority group, Hermann Müller (the later Chancellor). On account of disconnections on many railroad lines, they did not get through and had to spend November 9 inactive in a small town in Brandenburg province.

Ebert, too, had reached the conclusion that cooperation with the Independents was necessary if a dreadful internal struggle was to be avoided and the transition to a democratic constitution was to succeed. He took the diplomatic step, on the morning of November 9, of offering the leaders of the Independents equal participation in a jointly formed cabinet, although the Independents were considerably fewer in number. He even said that he would leave the selection of persons entirely to them and, in answer to a question, added that, if they were to send Liebknecht, he would accept him too.[2]

At twelve o'clock the Social Democrat parliamentary party, following a report by Ebert, officially resolved that their leaders and those of the Independents should meet to come to terms about the composition of the government. They named Ebert, Scheidemann, and the lawyer Otto Landsberg. The Independents, after agitated discussion, delegated not Liebknecht—who did not want to have anything to do with a joint government and demanded government by Workers' and Soldiers' Councils—but their intelligent, circumspect, moderate leader, the lawyer Hugo Haase (who had still not arrived); a second moderate representative, Wilhelm Dittmann; and the left-wing Emil Barth.

All this had happened behind the scenes. The "people" had not yet spoken. They did so on the following day, November 10, at a mass meeting of workers and soldiers in the Circus Busch. How did this meeting come about, who were the "people" present, and how was it possible to outvote the radical elements? That is an interesting story from which I learned much.

On November 9, about ten in the evening, representatives of the soldiers and of the industrial workers had gathered in the Reichstag building at the invitation of the Independents. Most of them sympathized with the left wing of the Independents and with the Spartacus Group. From the Social Democrat majority only Hermann Müller had turned up by chance. They elected Emil Barth chairman and at his suggestion resolved that on the following day, November 10, a Sunday, at five in the afternoon a meeting should be held in the Circus Busch, to which every 1,000 workers from the large Berlin industrial enterprises and each battalion in the barracks were to send one representative to appoint a provisional government. Richard Müller, later nicknamed "corpse-Müller" (*Leichenmüller,* see below), spoke. Obviously, what mattered now was what delegates were sent to Circus Busch. If the radical elements were in the majority, they would not vote for Ebert and the other two Social Democrats, but for the Independents and Spartacists. Credit for the fact that this did not happen must go chiefly to one man, Otto Wels.

Ebert had asked Wels to explain the situation to the soldiers and workers in good time. Wels summoned the "men of their confi-

[2] Hermann Müller, *Die Novemberrevolution,* Berlin, 1928, p. 52.

dence" (*Vertrauensleute*), whom the Social Democrat majority group had in all major industrial enterprises, to come at two o'clock on November 10 to the house of the Social Democrat newspaper *Vorwärts*. During the same night, he wrote a pamphlet "To all military units who side with the political line of the *Vorwärts*." Forty thousand copies were printed, and helpers distributed and explained them in the barracks. The pamphlet appealed to the troops to send their representatives at two p.m. to the *Vorwärts* building. The soldiers did this, and at the appointed hour their delegates arrived, 148 men strong. The total number of soldiers' and workers' delegates was so large that the meeting had to be moved to a meeting hall in Teltower Strasse. There Wels spoke to the delegates. He warned them of surprise moves from the Spartacists or Independents at Circus Busch, explained that the decision to be made was between convening a National Assembly and a Bolshevic system, and appealed to them to stand up at the meeting for the National Assembly and, pending its convening, for a provisional government to be composed in equal parts of Social Democrats and Independents.

The delegates then marched to Circus Busch. At five o'clock there were about 3,000 workers and soldiers there. Emil Barth and Richard Müller, both of them Independents, and an Independent sympathizer, Lieutenant Walz, were elected chairmen. Then Ebert, Haase (who had returned in the meantime), and Liebknecht spoke in turn. Ebert—the only member of the Social Democrat majority group speaking—informed the crowd to thunderous applause that the two parties had come to terms about establishing a Socialist government composed of three members of either party. The prepared list of six People's Commissaries (*Volksbeauftragte*) was sanctioned at the meeting by a large majority.

Then, however, the Independents wanted an additional "Supervisory Council of Workers and Soldiers" (*Vollzugsrat der Arbeiter und Soldaten*) [3] to be elected, as a control over the People's Commissaries. They hoped in this council to obtain power. But the soldiers and workers, instructed by Wels, insisted on equal representation of both Socialist parties here also. Liebknecht and Rosa Luxemburg re-

---

[3] Literal translation of "Vollzugsrat" would be "Execution Council" or "Executive Council." However, the executive power in the usual English meaning of the term was to reside with the People's Commissaries, while the "Vollzugsrat" was meant to have supervisory functions, as the further text reveals. To avoid confusion I have, therefore, used "Supervisory Council" for "Vollzugsrat."

fused to become members of such a body. The Social Democrats and Independents each named six soldiers' and six workers' representatives—i.e., twenty-four in all—who were then elected by the meeting.

This course of events taught me what personal initiative, untiring energy, making the best of a few hours, and cautious planning can do. Wels' achievement explains the respect he held from then on in the workers movement.

When Ebert returned late that evening from Circus Busch to the Chancellery, he held a double mandate: one from the former establishment represented by the last imperial Chancellor, the other from the assembly of workers and soldiers, the representatives of revolutionary power. The one made him appear as the legitimate incumbent of governmental office in the eyes of civil servants and military officers, the other among workers and troops. The second mandate had not been given him alone; five other representatives of the two Socialist parties were to share the power with him, all of whom had equal rights, and there was also the Supervisory Council, supposed to keep a revolutionary vigilance. But the fact that Ebert alone had also been empowered by the old order assured him from the very beginning of a superior position.

During the very same night Ebert had a long telephone conversation with General Groener in Spa. This was in itself not surprising, for the armistice was due to be signed at eleven o'clock the following morning after the High Command had wired that the German negotiators ought to attempt achieving some moderation but, should they fail, ought nevertheless to sign. The armistice conditions included withdrawal of troops from Belgium, France, and Alsace-Lorraine within fourteen days and from the western bank of the Rhine within twenty-five—tremendous military tasks complicated by a threat of chaos for Germany if soldiers streamed back home irregularly.

That part of the conversation which dealt with the recall of troops resulted in a decree signed by all six People's Commissaries on November 12, stating that the prompt return of the soldiers could not be achieved unless demobilization proceeded in accordance with an "organized plan." The decree continued: "The superior position of the officers is to continue. Unconditional obedience in service is of decisive significance for the success of the return to

Germany. Military discipline and order in the army must be maintained under all circumstances."

The decree also had something to say about soldiers' councils. They were to have only "advisory" power, and even that only in matters of "provisions, leave, and disciplinary punishment." Their major duty was to work toward "prevention of disturbances and mutiny." [4]

In these respects there is no veil of secrecy over the subject matter of the conversation between Ebert and Groener. But seven years later, shortly after Ebert's death, Groener maintained as a witness at the above-mentioned Stab-in-the-Back Trial (November, 1925) that in that nightly telephone conversation several other things had been agreed upon between himself and Ebert. "On the evening of November 10," he said, "I entered into an alliance (*ein Bündnis geschlossen*) over the telephone with Commissary Ebert to combat (*bekämpfen*) the Revolution. Together—and I count this to my credit—we did combat the Revolution from the very beginning, and we did this on my initiative, in accordance with the aims I had in view, and with all the means I held appropriate to that struggle."

And again: "The purpose of our alliance which we had entered into on the evening of November 10 was the complete suppression (*restlose Bekämpfung*) of the Revolution, the reestablishment of organized government at power, the support of the latter with military power, and an early convening of a National Assembly. These were our aims."

"On the evening of the 10th we first came to an agreement for the next few days. We used to communicate by telephone between eleven and one at night, always in agreement with the Field Marshall General [Hindenburg], and we discussed matters from day to day, according to the latest developments." With ten divisions ordered by the German High Command to Berlin he, Groener, had also come to an agreement with Ebert about the military entry of these troops into Berlin: "The divisions were to be at the disposal of the government, to create order by disarming the population, purging Spartacists, etc."

This testimony caused a great sensation, especially among the working classes. Not only former Independents and Spartacists but

---

[4] Barth later maintained that he had not agreed to the decree, but that Haase and Dittman did has not been disputed.

even many supporters of the Social Democrat majority reproached Ebert bitterly for double-dealing and betrayal of the Revolution. "If Scheidemann proclaimed the Republic on November 9, Ebert finished it off on November 10," thus wrote the former Independent, Carl Herz, in his memoirs (see above). "We cannot understand the miserable course of the November Revolution unless we are continually aware of the fact that Friedrich Ebert, the leader of the movement, was secretly in the service of the counter-revolution."

Ebert could not reply to Groener's description; he was no longer among the living. As one of those who over the course of the years had come to know both of them well and who was able to observe them at close quarters in many different situations I have reached the following conclusion: The impression which a superficial reading of Groener's testimony might give is incorrect and does not stand up to closer examination. Groener never maintained that in his testimony he rendered the actual words used by himself and Ebert. What he did do was to sum up and give his, Groener's *interpretation* of the content of the conversation, namely, that they had entered into an alliance to combat the Revolution. That either of them or both had used the words "alliance to combat the revolution" was not what he said. It is highly unlikely that Ebert ever used them. Even Groener himself cannot have meant that the Kaiser was to be retained or the monarchy to be reestablished under some other prince. For at the same hearing he said that the reintroduction of the monarchy was "completely out of the question." He can only have meant, as indeed he himself said: "reestablishment of an organized government, support of this by military power, and early convening of a National Assembly."

In fact, with this type of program Ebert was on the whole in agreement according to everything he said during those months, both publicly and in private conversation. That was unquestionably his policy at the time. Abolition of the monarchy and establishment of a new type of government had been achieved by acts of revolution. The convening of a National Assembly for a completely new organization of government in Germany was to follow. Ebert did not want to combat these revolutionary measures; he rather wanted to see them carried through. What he did want to suppress he might well have termed "farther-going revolutionary plans," such as the introduction of a Bolshevik dictatorship, or "excesses" of the Revolution, but not *"the* Revolution" itself. Nor was there anything strange in the fact that Ebert telephoned Groener not only on this evening but then regularly late every night. When the people's commissaries distributed the governmental functions among themselves, Ebert had taken over military matters. So he had to be in constant contact with General Headquarters.

Groener's choice of words in his testimony was obviously influenced by the special circumstances at the time of the hearing. In the final years of his life Ebert had been compelled to defend himself against the reproach that he was a traitor, and it had been said of the Social Democrats in general that they had stabbed the victorious army in the back. Groener wanted to defend Ebert's honor as a patriot. He paid no attention to the fact that with his choice of words he was now incriminating Ebert in the eyes of his Socialist comrades and especially of the more radical workers—or at least, this did not seem to bother him.

To be sure, Ebert was no RRRevolutionary with three resounding R's. But he was no "agent of the counter-revolution" either. He was both a leader of the working classes and a patriot, a man who loved Germany and wanted to the best of his ability to protect his country from the consequences of the military collapse.

He had reached his position as leader of the workers not because of any remarkable contribution to Marxist theory, but because of his daily practical work in Bremen, where he had passionately advocated the workers' cause as a whole and the rights of individual workers, at first as a saddler and local organizer, then after 1894 as an inn keeper, and finally from 1900 onward from the party secretariate which he himself had founded in Bremen. His success was such that in 1905 he was called to the national party headquarters. He understood Marx as he was being interpreted by Socialists of the time: namely that a revolution cannot be "made" but that it comes about as a historical necessity in the course of the development of capitalism and heavy industry, and that a revolution ought never to be carried beyond that point for which the economic development is ripe; otherwise it would be choked by counter-revolution. "Do not let yourselves be provoked" was a maxim which his predecessor and teacher, August Bebel, had often impressed upon his friends. Ebert believed that Germany had at that time become ripe for the transition to democracy, to free and equal elections, free coalition of the workers (including workers in agriculture, domestic employees, and civil servants, who did not yet have this right), nationalization of coal, electricity, iron and steel, perhaps even of banks, but not yet ripe for a complete overthrow of the established economic and social order. This could be brought about, if at all, only by force through a sort of Bolshevik dictatorship with bloodshed, executions, and atrocities, and the attempt would end—if not in Russia, then certainly in Germany—either in counter-revolution or in foreign occupation.

All this was Ebert's unshakable conviction. His appearance was a suitable complement to his character—a compact figure, moderate gestures, self-control, a large head and domed brow, and above his eyes heavy arches of prominent forehead muscles, which at the time of writing reminded me of President John F. Kennedy, whom in other ways he did not resemble. A fitting accompaniment to all this was the strangely broken tone of his calm, never hurried voice in which seriousness and humor, concern for the whole and circumspection in decisions, were united with masculine warmth in intimate conversations. His voice betrayed many hours spent in smoky rooms and frequent participation in social drinking; yet he himself, with rare exceptions, drank only moderately.

The General with whom he established contact on the evening of November 10 had been his acquaintance for a long time. Groener was not a "reactionary general" in the manner of Ludendorff. He was the most democratic general, perhaps the only democratic general, of the old days I ever got to know. The form of democracy which he had in mind was one in which general franchise united workers and bourgeoisie in parliamentary procedures. But public order had to be maintained, and Germany could not afford to confront foreign countries with no defense; hence soldiers and policemen were necessary. As typical Swabian from Württemberg, Groener's appearance, manners, gestures were simple, showing none of the characteristic angular gestures of many Prussian officers. Later, when the time had come to celebrate the day of the promulgation of the Weimar Constitution, he wanted people to dance in the streets; that was more important than official celebrations, he said to me more than once. Dancing in honor of a republican constitution —this is not the language of a reactionary.

Not until November 20 did the funeral of those who had died on November 9 take place. In Berlin only fifteen had lost their lives. Seven had already been buried; the other eight coffins were carried in an endless procession to the cemetery of the "Märzgefallenen" (i.e., those killed during the revolution of March, 1848). It had been agreed that Emil Barth alone would speak at the funeral. But Luise Zietz and Karl Liebknecht, Spartacists both, spoke nonetheless. Hermann Müller writes of the funeral: "The procession [which had begun at noon] finished only toward four o'clock. It was led by sailors and cavalry. The Alexander [guards'] Regiment marched under the red flag. Over a thousand wreaths were taken along with the hearses. Red ribbons and flowers gave color and life to the gloomy picture on a dull day. The Supervisory Council and the People's Commissaries walked in the procession. Military bands played funeral music. . . . On all public buildings the red flag fluttered at half mast. The church bells rang. The personnel of the factories in Greater Berlin took part in the procession in their thousands. Since the world began, members of the proletariat have never been taken to their graves in such a fashion."

## 18. The Chancellery in the Period of Transition from Monarchy to Republic

No one is present everywhere during a major historical event. Each participant sees and hears what he sees and hears within narrow local limits. What is happening elsewhere, if only a few streets or even a few rooms away, he learns of only indirectly by word of mouth, telegrams, letters, newspapers, or much later from memoirs or historical works. During the Revolution in Kiel neither the leaders of the Social Democrat majority group—Ebert, Scheidemann and so on—nor those of the Independent Socialists—Haase, Barth, Liebknecht and comrades—were present. Even Noske arrived only on the second day. During the Berlin Revolution Noske was not in Berlin, and Haase and Hermann Müller, as we have seen, were sitting tight at a small town in Brandenburg province.

I was in my bed, in our apartment in Steglitz, still ill with influenza. My brothers, both returned to Berlin, described the scene in the town to me. Special editions of the newspapers informed me that the Kaiser had abdicated. I thought painfully: no longer voluntary, but compelled; no longer the triumph of Wilson, but of Foch. Only from the newspapers did I learn of the meeting at Circus

Busch and only later, from reports by Wels, Ebert, Hermann Müller, and from Müller's memoirs, details about its preparation.

When I was back again at the Chancellery the new state of affairs was already an established fact. Herr von Wahnschaffe, last imperial Chief of the Chancellery, had gone. His beautiful office on the ground floor facing the garden had been taken over by Kurt Baake, Social Democrat editor of the *Parliamentary Political News* (*Politisch Parlamentarische Nachrichten*), cultural expert, lover of Goethe, friend of Gerhart Hauptmann, in post-revolutionary days chairman of the People's Theater Association (*Volksbühnenverein*), a contemplative character, man of wisdom and humor, who deserves credit for the idea that Weimar should be the seat of the National Assembly. People's Commissaries also had rooms in the building. Business was divided among them. But the center of power lay soon unquestionably with Ebert, who had taken over from Prince Max the Chancellor's office room, acted as chairman at meetings, decided on the agenda, and had the advantage that the three Social Democrats always voted together, whereas the three Independents were often in disagreement among themselves.

The few old officials, with the exception of Wahnschaffe, were still there. Simons too, on loan from the Foreign Office, had remained at the wish of Prince Max and Ebert. Just as he had given his advice daily to Prince Max, he now was the principal adviser of the People's Commissaries, especially of Ebert, when matters of foreign policy, administration, or law were involved.

Simons was an unusual civil servant. His head seemed to me to be a smaller and more delicate version of Bismarck's in his fifties, a similarity which others did not notice. His manner of speaking was entirely bereft of any bureaucratic stiffness. He expressed opinions in a simple and clear manner and found excellent formulations for matters which had until then been vague and obscure. He always seemed to hit the nail on the head. His voice was authoritative merely because of its persuasive power. Like every good administrative official he had the ability to keep clear records of discussions and to draft resultant administrative orders or legislative proposals briefly and pertinently; this was an art which was, of course, very agreeable to the new rulers in the Chancellery, who had little practice in such matters, and it aided him, as it later did me, in establishing a position of trust with them.

On entering the Chancellery in October I had found one "outsider" who contrasted greatly to other members of the staff, Kurt Hahn. Only thirty-two years old (two years younger than I) he had been doing magnificent work in a joint office established by the Foreign Office and the High Command as interpreter of English public opinion, and had won the friendship of Prince Max. He had in fact been the first to recommend Prince Max in July, 1917 to several influential politicians as possible Chancellor and after two failures (the nominations of Michaelis and Count Hertling) had won through with this recommendation in October, 1918. Prince Max had taken him along to the Chancellery, at first wanting to give him some official position, perhaps as his personal secretary, but had abandoned this idea since his protégé was disliked by some of the secretaries, and had instead made him subordinate to Simons.

Since Hahn and I lived through exciting weeks together and liked each other's independent, unbureaucratic manner of thinking, we often talked to each other. It was through him that I first heard a term frequently used which was later to play a disastrous role in German history: the "Führer" (the leader), and the "Führer-principle." Hahn wanted to educate people to be leaders. Prince Max was to take over the role of a leader. Germany was to be governed in accordance with the leadership-principle. In saying this, of course, Hahn had no totalitarian hierarchy in mind, but the responsible assumption of political and spiritual leadership, based on true authority. I was naturally completely in agreement with him that a Chancellor should exercise political leadership, but I could not share Hahn's enthusiasm for planned education of young people as leaders. Since my own early days I had been filled with a deep-rooted aversion to all claims of leadership. No one ought to become a leader on the ground that he wanted to be one and because he simulated the born leader. Leadership ought to accrue as a result of achievement, perhaps quite contrary to intentions, on the only ground that a person had aroused the confidence of others in his character or ability, or both. It was, of course, possible to explain to young people how their own moral demeanour might encourage others, and to exhort them to set a good example in all situations (this was indeed Hahn's primary concern). In all fields of administration—civil life, military, industry, etc.—there had to be some form of leadership in technical administration; education in this respect was possible. But intellectual, academic, artistic, moral leadership beyond this could not be achieved by early education; it would rather be destroyed by this attempt. I often would have liked to talk about this subject to Hahn later. But fate soon separated us. He became the founder of the world-famous school in Salem, intended for the education of Prince Max's son, where boys and girls were to be educated in a new way to become independently thinking leaders. The later Prince Consort of Queen Elisabeth II of Great Britain, Prince Philip, had come to this school as a boy. So it happened that Hahn, after his emigration in 1933, was able to found a school similar to Salem in Scotland (Gordonstoun). He had a decisive part in many of Prince Max' public statements and later in the deposition of his memoirs (published 1927).

After the Revolution there were two of the former staff members still in the Chancellery, apart from Simons and myself, but they soon left us. New faces had appeared, above all Ulrich Rauscher, a former associate editor of *Frankfurter Zeitung* and adviser to the German occupation authorities in Brussels, who had taken over the role of an assistant to Scheidemann and press head of the People's Commissaries. He was an unusually capable journalist, a former member of a student's corps, who always had a ready joke, but was firm in his democratic opinions and superior to everyone else in the art of formulating appeals, government declarations, speeches, and newspaper reports during a meeting so that they needed only a signature before being given out and sometimes were published even without signature. He later became Ambassador in Warsaw, where he died still young without having lived up to the full development of his potentialities. It is said that Stresemann shortly before his death was so impressed by Rauscher at a meeting in Bühlerhöhe that he wanted to make him State Secretary in the Foreign Office.

Then there was a young Socialist revolutionary in his early twenties, who had been assigned by Ebert the task of meeting visitors at the entrance and, as far as was possible, directing them to some appropriate government agency outside the Chancellery. His name was Moser. The old chief clerk said to me, horrified: "To know where something belongs is the most difficult task in the Chancellery, and that is what he is going to do, this young man who has no idea of the organization of federal, state, or local administration?" Later Moser disappeared; I do not know where.

There was also a young Socialist journalist, Walter Oehme, who had been sent to Berlin to the Supervisory Council as the representative of the soldiers' council in Grodno. He became an assistant to

Under-Secretary Baake. In March, 1919 he left the Chancellery with his boss. After World War II he published a book in Eastern Germany *Damals in der Reichskanzlei* (In the Chancellery at That Time); it contains valuable details, but is written in the style of a penitent Communist who accuses himself for not having immediately seen through the "betrayal" of Ebert, Scheidemann, and Landsberg and who now criticizes everything these men did.

The small size of the personnel was explained by the fact that the department heads had been the Chancellor's subordinates, authorized to answer letters directed to him under the Chancellor's letterhead (*in Vertretung*) or under their departmental letterheads (*im Auftrage*), or to prepare statements for him. The most time-consuming business in the Chancellery was the forwarding of the numerous letters addressed to the Chancellor to the proper department. I employed all my diplomatic skill to avoid becoming involved in this work, which tended to consume one's time and energy.

I had less success in this respect with visitors. After the Revolution the foyer of the Chancellery no longer had its former dignified solitude. Anyone could come and ring the bell. Individual visitors and delegations did so constantly. Most of them wanted to be shown immediately to Ebert. Some could be persuaded at the door to go to a more suitable office. Those who remained obstinate were first sent to me. Often they wanted to promote the Revolution, to report observations of counter-revolutionary or Bolshevik maneuvers or to criticize and give their opinions about Socialism.

I often had long conversations of this type, to draw out information and also to satisfy the visitors that they had not hit upon a "narrow-minded," "arrogant," "reactionary" bureaucrat, but had found a sympathetic ear for their arguments, even though I might succeed in dissuading them from disturbing Ebert himself. They were often serious young people who had been active at the front or in the navy, filled with zeal to create a better Germany and a better world. One had to devote a lot of time to them to do them justice.

Barely six months away, then, from sixteen years of juridical work the question of justice continued to be my major preoccupation. It determined my interest in Social Democrat doctrines, of which I had only superficial knowledge, and in the points of conflict among the various Socialist groups. But the change from mere observation and meditation to initiative in acting now made rapid progress. I acted wherever and whenever the situation demanded. Once when it was important that a large poster be printed late at night, I did not allow myself to be put off by the fact that the men who fixed the bill posters were already in bed. I took their addresses, went from one to the other, turned them out of bed, and persuaded them to get dressed again and put up the posters all over the town. When the Chancellery was being besieged and there was no bread for the soldiers staying there for our protection, I rang up the city government and asked them to fill several fire engines with bread and send them to the Chancellery furiously ringing their fire bells. At first they objected because of doubts where the money to pay for the bread would come from. But finally two fire engines came hurtling along, were immediately allowed through by the crowd, and unloaded their bread in the garden. When after street fights "prisoners" were brought in I attended to their accommodation, and tried to prevent their being mistreated, for the excited partisans on both sides tended to this. If impromptu speeches were delivered in front of the Chancellery or were answered by one of the People's Commissaries, I took stenographic notes. I never stood by idly gaping. These were functions to which German senior officials would not normally have attended.

In foreign affairs I tried to work out plans with the press about how the newspapers could expand and intensify certain ideas so that foreign governments would be influenced. For a time I was the official spokesman of the Chancellery at the weekly press conferences, at which in those days the ministers themselves rarely made an appearance. I soon found that this was not the place to introduce an organized propaganda campaign. The great majority of the press worked for right-wing or at least anti-Socialist papers and were trying to pin down every weak point in the actions of the new government. I suppose the way I replied to such gibes was not very efficient, not only because the government's position was often difficult to defend but because I lacked experience in dealing with the press in such situations. It is with particular embarrassment that I recall the press conference after the Chancellery had been besieged by its own guards (Chapter 20). I would not wish such a situation on any of my colleagues. Only later did I learn how to speak with authority at a press conference without appearing bureaucratic. Although I had gained a number of friends among the press and a reputation for personal integrity and democratic reliability, I soon retired from this responsibility, and handed it over to a shrewd pressman, Robert Breuer, who did much better.

The dreadful consequences of the postwar blockade had to be made clear to people abroad in convincing figures, striking examples, and a form which appealed directly to their humanity. I tried to have men speaking on behalf of Germany who enjoyed a position of respect in the world, for example old Professor Wilhelm Röntgen, the discoverer of X-rays, or Adolf von Harnack, Albert Einstein, Max Planck.

My personal association with the workers' leaders also contributed to changing my way of thinking, which had so long been rooted in the abstract, theoretical, and aesthetic. I came to feel deep respect for them. Their seriousness, conviction, and character impressed me. This was above all true of the craftsman type of Social Democrat, best represented by Ebert, the former saddler; or Severing, a former metalworker; or the former printer, Otto Braun. Lawyers like Landsberg and Haase, or intellectuals like Breitscheid, were less of a new world for me than those who had sprung from the class of manual workers.

It had been a habit of mine, as is the case with many intellectuals, to pepper my conversations with ironic comments. I soon discovered that in discussion with these men this habit was disturbing and confusing. They expressed their opinions frankly and wanted to learn mine without any unclear overtones. I began to talk to them in as straightforward a manner as they did to me and was ashamed of my ironic frivolities. Only now did I become a man, it seemed.

Because of the central location of the Chancellery I witnessed many events in which I played no personal part. I also heard Karl Liebknecht. He was standing on a cart, talking to the masses which had collected in front of the Chancellery. To my surprise he did not have a harsh, rousing voice, but delivered his attacks in an unusually soft, modulated singsong tone. They always ended with the question: "Who has done that?" and the answer: "Ebert and Scheidemann," spoken like an hexameter soft and slow but with a strong rhythm and for that reason extraordinarily stirring.

The Chancellery building had its origins at the end of the eighteenth century. In the spring of 1921 when the U.S. Chief of Staff, General March, came to have tea with Chancellor Joseph Wirth, and five of us, including Walther Rathenau, were sitting round the tea table on the lawn about thirty yards away from the house, I said to General March in my hesitant English: "This house, General, is not as old as many other famous monuments, but its history makes it venerable. A youthful love-affair of William I's unfolded under these old trees, and Bismarck worked here and complained when his successor had some of the trees cut down. It was built at the time when the first Treaty of Friendship between the United States and Prussia was concluded. We hope that the time will come when there will be another Treaty of Friendship between our countries." General March looked at house and garden with interest and gave a friendly answer.


## 19. THE STRUGGLE AROUND A PROLETARIAN DICTATORSHIP


SINCE no serious attempt had been made to quell the Revolution, everyone expected that Germany would be reorganized in accordance with Socialist principles. Little versed in Socialist literature, the German bourgeoisie was ill-prepared to anticipate what forms this would take. To Socialists, however, this was the major issue of the day. Dictatorship of the proletariat on the Russian model or Democratic Socialism, based upon general franchise and a parliament with Socialist majorities, which were hopefully expected—these were the two basic alternatives. Between them there were others. The Social Democrats and the right wing of the Independent Socialists rejected the Bolshevik model of a dictatorial government by a small "vanguard" of workers. Would general elections really result in a Socialist majority? And, if not, would not a unique opportunity to introduce Socialism to Germany be irrevocably missed with a call for general elections? Indeed, even if the elections resulted in a Socialist majority, could Socialism really be carried through with parliamentary methods? Lenin said no; even today it is a moot question.[1]

One cannot, therefore, deny that the Spartacists and Independents were arguing logically when they opposed general elections for reasons of this sort. Anyone to whom the introduction of a Socialist

---

[1] See my *Political Theory,* Princeton University Press 1959 (5th printing, 1968), pp. 446 ff.

order was more important than democracy—democracy in the sense of a majority government based on free elections and individual liberty—*had to* raise warnings against free parliamentary elections. Historians and political scientists who overlook the logical necessity of this opposition and see the opponents only as rowdies and rogues are missing the point.

It was a historical circumstance of major importance that Friedrich Ebert was a Social *Democrat,* a man irrefutably convinced that Germany must as soon as possible have a government chosen in general, free, secret, direct voting, even though the Social Democrats might not obtain an absolute majority in the National Assembly. Scheidemann and Landsberg shared this opinion, but their colleagues from the Independent Socialists hesitated. Emil Barth rejected general elections outright. Haase and Dittmann wanted to postpone them so as to gain time for further revolutionary achievements. Ebert was not in a position to force his will upon the Independents. They were equal members of the Council of People's Commissaries. In the eyes of the masses of workers and soldiers this was not an Ebert government, but an Ebert-Haase government. Nor were the People's Commissaries the only holders of power. The "Supervisory Council of Workers and Soldiers," which had established its headquarters in the Prussian Chamber of Deputies, claimed the right of supervision over the People's Commissaries, and indeed, this right had been granted at the meeting in Circus Busch. Among the Independents within the Supervisory Council there were few of their right wing, to which belonged such leading Socialist thinkers as Rudolf Hiferding and Eduard Bernstein. Most were left-wingers, such as Emil Barth, Richard Müller, Ernst Däumig, Georg Ledebour.

Richard Müller—not to be confused with Hermann Müller, the later Chancellor—was a metal worker who had been a candidate for a Berlin seat in a recent by-election but had lost. He had now become Senior Chairman of the Supervisory Council. As early as November 19 he called a second meeting in Circus Busch, at which also Liebknecht, Lebedour, Haase, Ebert, and Hermann Müller spoke. It was on this occasion that Richard Müller used the famous words: "The way to a National Assembly is over my corpse," which earned him the abusive name "Leichenmüller" (Corpse-Müller), because he continued to live quite peacefully despite the National Assembly.

Däumig had been in the French Legion before the war. After his return home, he was at first a sleeping-car attendant, then editor of Social Democrat newspapers, finally with *Vorwärts*. He had believed in a German victory until 1918, but then had turned revolutionary and become a member of the *Obleute* (representatives of the Independents in the major industrial enterprises). He was party to a conspiracy of a number of Independents to begin a revolution in Berlin on November 4; they had been discovered and arrested. Now he was a leader in the struggle against a National Assembly.

Ledebour, the eldest of them, was a pugnacious character, a born revolutionary, a man who took a radical lead in public arguments, stirred up every dissatisfaction, visibly offended by the fact that the Revolution never brought him to the top, obstinate, but by no means stupid.

The representatives of the Social Democrat majority in the Supervisory Council were on the whole of minor caliber. With the exception of Hermann Müller and one or two others, they remained in obscurity.

Originally twenty-four, then twenty-eight strong, the Supervisory Council gradually reached a membership of forty-five, due to additional nominations of delegates from the War and Naval Departments, from the Eastern and Western Front and, since all of them were Social Democrats, of an equal number of Independents. Finally delegates from München and Baden also joined, since South Germany kept criticizing the fact that workers and soldiers from Berlin alone were claiming control over the government of the whole of Germany.

Day after day information arrived in the Chancellery about counter-revolutionary and Bolshevik coups which were allegedly being planned. Most of these rumors proved incorrect or exaggerated; more than once the allegedly hostile columns were in fact peaceful demonstrators with sympathetic opinions. We gradually grew indifferent to such alarms. But occasionally there was more to it. On the afternoon of December 6 there appeared at the Supervisory Council a group of soldiers, whose leader, Sergeant Fischer, maintained that he had been given an order by the People's Commissaries to arrest the Council. Only long discussion was able to persuade the soldiers to withdraw.

This event became even more mysterious because at almost the same hour armed soldiers were demonstrating in front of the Chancellery, under the leadership of the elected commander of the same regiment, Sergeant Spiro. Sailors and students were also present. Spiro delivered a speech in which he assured Ebert of the support of the troops, attacked the mismanagement in the Supervisory Council, and demanded that a National Assembly be convened. He concluded by proclaiming Ebert President of the Republic.

Ebert stepped outside, thanked them for their loyalty, and explained that he could not accept this proclamation of himself as President; such a matter would first have to be discussed by the government. That an arrest of the Supervisory Council was planned he did not yet know. In fact two sailors had come to the Chancellery that morning and had reported the rumor to young Moser and me. We had immediately sent a message to Ebert. However, since he happened to be at a cabinet meeting, he did not read it; perhaps it was left in the anteroom. We ourselves had not taken the information too seriously, but considered it necessary to inform Ebert.

There followed a joint meeting of the Supervisory Council and the People's Commissaries in the Chancellery. Ledebour said that two marines had informed Moser and me of the plan to arrest the Council. "Brecht and Moser must give an account of themselves and let us know whether they passed this information on to Ebert and Haase. If one of the People's Commissaries was informed, then this case ought to be brought before a Martial Court [he probably meant a Revolutionary Court]; if not, then it falls to the account of these two officials." He proposed that "Brecht and Moser be apprehended and brought in." Ebert opposed this mixture of political discussion and inquiry. But after long interchanges Lebedour's motion was passed by eighteen votes to thirteen.[2]

We were called and took our seats opposite Richard Müller and Ledebour. I described conditions in the Chancellery, the incessant denunciations, admitted that among them there had been one from two marines, explained why we had not taken it too seriously in accordance with our experience of such matters, but that we had nevertheless written a note and sent it up to Ebert at once.

Haase calmed the Supervisory Council ("We stand and fall with the Supervisory Council") and emphasized that none of the People's Commissaries had received any information and that news of coups was constantly coming in. Dittmann interrupted: there were five such pieces of news today. Ebert and Scheidemann finally left

[2] Hermann Müller, *Die Novemberrevolution*, p. 150.

the room in protest against personal attacks. We were taken to a neighboring room and locked in "until further notice."

Meanwhile the excited discussion continued. Another Independent member of the Supervisory Council demanded that Ebert resign from the government. "Moser and Brecht have lied to us quite shamelessly. The two marines are shocked that the two of them have told us direct lies."[3] Hermann Müller disagreed with this. Haase pointed out that the statements of the two marines and ours were quite compatible. The motion to dismiss Ebert was rejected. We were released.

We really had not been lying, but the suspicions of the Supervisory Council were understandable. That Ebert himself and the great majority of the population would have been glad to get rid of this Council, at least in its current composition, was just as obvious as the desire of the extreme Left to be rid of Ebert and Scheidemann.

Shortly before the events of December 6 the Supervisory Council and the People's Commissaries had indeed reached an arrangement that as soon as possible a nationwide "Congress of Workers' and Soldiers' Councils," to be composed of delegates from local workers' and soldiers' councils throughout Germany, should meet and should choose a new watchdog committee for the whole of Germany in place of the Berlin-born Council. They had also agreed that until then the old Council was to have control over the government, including the right to appoint or recall People's Commissaries. The latter were to wield the actual executive power. All this was being confirmed and made public on December 9.

Thus a nationwide "First Congress of Workers' and Soldiers' Councils" was elected and met in the building of the Prussian Landtag on December 16. Extremely unruly conditions dominated the scene inside and outside on the first two days. Tens of thousands had followed an appeal for mass demonstrations made by *Rote Fahne* (Red Flag), the organ of Karl Liebknecht and Rosa Luxemburg. Spokesmen pushed forward into the Congress hall, demanding the removal of the People's Commissaries and the formation of a *Rote Garde* (Red Guard).

But the members of the Congress, people with a sense of humor and steady nerves, accustomed to all sorts of tumults, managed to transact their main business without allowing themselves to be intimidated. By 400 versus 50 votes they passed a motion setting the

[3] *Ibid.*

date for the general election to a National Assembly on January 19, 1919. Much of the credit for this outcome must go to a statesman-like speech by Wilhelm Dittmann, one of the three Independent Socialists in the Council of People's Commissaries, to which I listened admiringly. Supporting the motion, he effectively rebuffed the leftist attacks upon his colleagues.

Only a few observers at the time or after were aware of the significance of this event. It was not the old regime, not the old military, not foreign governments, not domestic traitors; it was the German workers and soldiers themselves who through their own delegates with overwhelming majorities made the momentous decision that Germany should be governed not by a proletarian dictatorship but as a parliamentary democracy. Other resolutions reconfirmed that until further notice by the National Assembly the Council of People's Commissaries was to have executive power, supervised no longer by the Berlin-born Supervisory Council but thenceforth by a new "Central Council of Workers' and Soldiers' Councils," presently to be elected by the Congress. This new Central Council (*Zentralrat*) would from then on have the right to appoint and dismiss people's commissaries, who in turn were to send two deputies to each Federal Department and Prussian Ministry, one Social Democrat and one Independent.

The Independents decided not to participate in the voting for the Central Council. In vain Haase opposed this abstention. Thus the Central Council, with its twenty-seven members, consisted only of Social Democrat majority supporters under the tripartite chairmanship of Leinert (labor union leader), Hermann Müller, and Cohen-Reuss.

## 20. Lack of Power from the Top Downward

The way to general elections, to a National Assembly, and to parliamentary majority government seemed to be cleared. No further disturbances *from above* were to be expected during the short transitional period of one or two months. But it soon appeared that the transitional government lacked power to meet resistance *from below*. From this defect two serious conflicts arose.

The first was the refusal of the so-called "Marine Division"—a body of sailors who had established themselves in the Royal Palace and its adjacent stables (*Marstall*)—to obey a decision of the People's Commissaries to reduce their number. The impetus for this action had come, not from Ebert and Scheidemann, but from one of the Independents, the banker Hugo Simon, who, together with a Majority Socialist, was in charge of the Prussian Ministry of Finance, located opposite the palace and stables. In a memorandum of December 12 he had demanded the speedy withdrawal of the Marine Division from their present quarters because the sailors were plundering the works of art and other articles in the palace. He had advised unannounced and sudden action, so that stolen objects could not be removed in advance.

The People's Commissaries decided—with the assent of the Independents, at least of Haase and Dittmann—to reduce the Marine Division to six hundred. The sailors protested; they demanded to be incorporated into the Republican Soldiers' Guard (*Republikanische Soldatenwehr*) formed by City Commander Wels. They were informed, however, that from January 1, 1919, wages would be paid for only six hundred men. The government sent instructions to Wels—bearing the signature of all six People's Commissaries, including Barth's—to pay the sum of 80,000 marks to the division, but only "after withdrawal from the palace and handing over of all keys to the Commander's office." This decision was the source of operetta-like situations, which, however, soon turned deadly serious.

The leading man in the Marine Division at that time was Dorrenbach, thirty years old, originally destined for the clergy, then a worker, promoted to officer during the war, wounded several times, sentenced to two months' imprisonment and discharged for desertion. He hated Wels and therefore decided to handle the matter with a man much more sympathetic to him, Emil Barth, left-wing member of the People's Commissaries. Barth, who was in charge of social welfare, was sitting in his office in the Chancellery with the under-secretary of the Ministry of Economics, Wichard von Möllendorff. Möllendorff was trying to explain to Barth that production and consumption must be related to each other or else prices would be affected. He drew a square on a piece of paper, to represent consumption, and a second to represent production, and was showing Barth what happened when the two squares were of different sizes. A man stormed into the room exclaiming: "Comrade Barth, here are the keys." He threw them onto the table and demanded 80,000 marks. Barth telephoned Wels, who insisted that the keys be handed over to him before he could pay out the 80,000 marks. Dorrenbach grew furious, picked the keys up again, and left the room. Barth went on with his study of the squares of consumption and production with Möllendorff.

The sailors then sought out Ebert. When they did not find him, the unbelievable happened: Dorrenbach ordered the platoon of marines who, as usual, were standing on guard in front of the Chancellery, to close the gates and to occupy the telephone exchange until the demands of the Marine Division had been fulfilled. I tried to inform City Commander Wels, so that he might take the necessary steps to release the government from this situation. Since the sailors had occupied the telephone exchange, I used our direct line to the High Command and asked them to pass on the instruction to the City Commander, which they did. Wels ordered his Republican Soldiers' Guard to relieve the Chancellery. Since they hesitated, however, he asked the army Chief of Staff, General Lequis, to send the necessary troops to the Chancellery. Lequis dispatched some forty men from units stationed in the university, and ordered more from Potsdam.

In the meantime, I was witness to Ebert's confrontation with the sailors in the large entrance hall of the Chancellery. He took them to task for the fact that they, who were supposed to defend the government, were in fact besieging them here. They protested that they were completely loyal to the government; they only wanted the 80,000 marks which had been promised them. Ebert answered harshly that he could no longer use them as a guard and ordered their departure.

Dorrenbach had betaken himself to Wels and demanded from him payment of the 80,000 marks and written authorization for the Marine Division to remain in Berlin. Wels paid out the 80,000 marks but refused the document. The sailors then stormed the garrison and took Wels and his adjutant, Fischer, with them as hostages.

The Marine Guard and government troops now confronted each other in Wilhelmstrasse. Once again Ebert tried to avoid bloodshed. An agreement was reached with the Marine Division in accordance with which at ten o'clock that evening (it was December 23) the sailors and troops departed in opposite directions. But the situation remained critical because Wels, despite all our telephoned remonstrations, was still kept prisoner by the Marine Division. Finally, late at night, Ebert called Minister of War Scheuch and asked him "to take the necessary steps to free Wels." Scheuch passed the order on to General Lequis, who moved in with about 800 Berlin and Potsdam troops in the early morning on December 24 and demanded that all the sailors, who were in the palace and stables and who in fact outnumbered his troops, surrender unarmed, or else his artillery would fire on them. When the surrender failed to follow, shooting began and lasted from about 8 until 10 o'clock in the morning. The palace was taken by force; the stables were to be taken next.

In the meantime, however, the Spartacists had large masses of demonstrators advance and take up their position between the opponents. Furthermore, the so-called Security Guard (*Sicherheitswehr*), formed by Police President Eichhorn, a member of the Independents, also arrived, but took up the cause of the sailors. The troops were uncertain who was right. Then negotiators reached a compromise. Wels was to be released immediately; the sailors were to vacate the palace and to give a guarantee not to participate in further anti-government actions. On the other hand, General Lequis' division was to return to their barracks at once and the main body of the Marine Division was to become part of the Republican Soldiers' Guard.

Wels was released. He came immediately—it was the morning of Christmas Eve—into the Chancellery and told us what had happened. This vigorous and strong man was ashen. He had not only been ill-treated, but his captors had had several sailors' corpses brought into his dungeon and repeatedly informed him that his death sentence had been passed and that he was to be shot immediately. Three days later he resigned as Commander in Berlin.

The affair had not yet reached its close. On the following morning, on Christmas Day, the Spartacists and sailors occupied the *Vorwärts* press building in Lindenstrasse, because the paper had published a sharp attack on them. On its presses they printed a *Red Vorwärts*. Two days later, the *Vorwärts* was released after intervention by Däumig and Eichhorn, but only on the condition that the next edition would carry a self-accusatory statement.

The People's Commissaries and the Central Council met jointly on December 27 and 28 in the Chancellery. Haase and Dittmann agreed in principle that appropriate measures be taken against the Spartacist group and that force against the government might be resisted by force; but they demanded that in such cases only troops raised from the proletariat be used, and they criticized Ebert for having given an unlimited order to the Minister of War to use military force. They also opposed convening the National Assembly in Weimar instead of Berlin. The Central Council refused to give assurances on these matters without previous discussion with the People's Commissaries; a People's Defense Corps could not be created so quickly, they said.

Thereupon the three Independents resigned from the Council of People's Commissaries. In their place the Central Council elected Gustav Noske and Rudolf Wissell. Noske still held his office as Governor in Kiel, but at Ebert's request he had come to Berlin to discuss the situation. He planned to return on December 28, but was retained. Military and marine affairs were assigned to him, and social and economic affairs to Wissell—a completely unmilitary character, good-natured and honest, utterly devoted to his work for the improvement of living conditions among the masses. The sixth seat remained vacant, because Paul Löbe, who had been proposed for it, felt that he was not sufficiently well-acquainted with conditions in Berlin and could not easily be dispensed with in Breslau.

Thus, when the year 1918 came to its end, not only on the surveying Central Council but now also on the Council of People's Commissaries, there sat members of the Social Democrat majority group alone. At the same time the forces of opposition consolidated; on December 31, 1918 the German Communist Party was founded. Its central committee, with Liebknecht at its head, at first took the line that time had not yet come for a new revolution; the Ebert-Scheidemann government had first to be "undermined." But such "undermining" could quickly turn revolutionary, as soon became evident.

It was a deceptive peace. For now there arose from quite ridiculous grounds a second tragic conflict. After the Independents had withdrawn both from the National Government and from the Prussian ministries, the Berlin Police President Eichhorn, an Independent who had appointed himself to that post on November 9, refused to resign. He also refused to give to his superiors, the Prussian People's Commissaries, an account on various reproaches that had been raised against him, and allowed the ultimate date which had been set for a written defense, January 4, to elapse. The Prussian

Minister of the Interior, therefore, announced his dismissal on January 4. His office was to be taken over for the time being by one of the two deputies in the Ministry of the Interior, Eugen Ernst. But Eichhorn refused to hand his office over to him.

The Independent "revolutionary *Obleute*" supported Eichhorn's refusal, as did the Berlin section of the Independents and one group of the new Communist Party. For other reasons (delays in demobilization) they had already sent out a call for mass demonstrations on January 5, to take place in Siegesallee, and now were using these demonstrations chiefly to protest against Eichhorn's dismissal. One section of the crowd finally went to the press area and occupied the buildings of *Vorwärts,* of the liberal papers, and of one rightist daily, *Lokalanzeiger.*

This had not originally been planned. But now, on the evening of January 5, the representatives of the three groups decided to pursue the struggle against the government up to its overthrow. Of some seventy or eighty, only six voted against this motion, including Däumig and Richard Müller, both of whom refused to have anything further to do with this affair. A provisional revolutionary commission was then appointed, consisting of fifty-three people, headed by Ledebour, Liebknecht, and Paul Scholz.

The People's Commissaries—the official national government— still had no troops of their own. They therefore asked their supporters to gather the following day, Monday, January 6, in Wilhelmstrasse. Crowds of them came and by their physical presence protected the Chancellery from Liebknecht's groups on Monday and Tuesday. In this situation Ebert told the Central Council on January 6 in the name of the five People's Commissaries at a joint meeting that the government must create its own troops on whom they would be able to rely. When Minister of War Reinhardt suggested General Hoffmann as commander in chief, Ebert opposed. Instead Noske was called upon to take over the command. He said he was prepared to do this and then spoke the notorious words: "Someone has to become the bloodhound." This has been interpreted by left-wing Socialists as a sign that he was looking forward to playing the role of bloodhound. That is nonsense. In Kiel, Noske had kept to the basic idea that the quarrel between Social Democrats and Independents must be forgotten, that unity was the order of the day, and he had continually tried to influence both friends and opponents in Berlin to accept this line. But he foresaw that the man who would now reestablish order would be called a "bloodhound" by the extreme left wing.

At three o'clock, January 6, Noske transferred his headquarters to Dahlem, a Berlin suburb, in a boarding school for girls, the Luisenstift, which was empty at the time because of the Christmas holidays. He had a desk and telephone set up in one of the classrooms and one of the girls' narrow beds as his place for the night. From the following morning onward volunteers were accepted, weapons brought in, neighboring groups of troops assembled. Among these were sections of a Guards Cavalry Division, sent by General Hoffmann together with the staff-officer, Captain Waldemar Pabst, who later played a role in the murder of Liebknecht. General Märcker arrived with some troops, so did other small units, and they were joined by students, clerks, and workers, who enlisted. Attempts to keep troops together had originally been made to meet the threat that Communist forces from Russia would invade East Germany; they had been tolerated by the Allies, who also had an interest in checking the red flood in the east. But now these troops put themselves at Noske's disposal. Then there came a brigade, about 1,600 men, brought together by Noske himself in Kiel for the east. All companies were headed by officers; lower commanders were provided by the troops from their own ranks.

The situation in Berlin grew ever more menacing. The government was almost without protection. In the Chancellery there were a few soldiers under a non-commissioned officer by the name of Suppe. But they knew nothing about the world outside. I asked the doormen of other government buildings in the area to inform the Chancellery immediately by telephone whenever any suspicious crowds were on the move toward Wilhelmstrasse. This was a very primitive expedient.

Noske paid several short visits to the Chancellery. There he was urged to hurry. He urged patience to avoid failure. Finally he gave his troops the order to retake the *Vorwärts* building during the night of January 10–11. The move was successful. The following morning he marched at the head of 3,000 men from the suburbs to the Chancellery, then through the Brandenburger Tor back to the suburbs. On January 14 he had the northern sections of the city occupied, and other sections the following day. Peace had been reestablished. Ebert took a deep breath.

Then, however, a new complication endangered everything thus far achieved. During the night of January 15–16 Karl Liebknecht and Rosa Luxemburg were arrested by vigilants and handed over to the staff of the Cavalry Guards at the Eden Hotel. They were interrogated by Captain Pabst. He ordered them to be transferred to a prison in the northern section for further investigation. On leaving the hotel either one was struck over the head with the butt of a gun by the guard, one Runge. On the drive through the park Liebknecht was ordered to get out and march. Then he was shot in the back, allegedly because he had been trying to escape. Rosa Luxemburg was shot dead in the other car and her body submerged in the Landwehr Canal on instructions of First Lieutenant Vogel.

At the Chancellery I witnessed how completely shattered both Noske and Ebert were by this news. It was immediately clear to them that the martyr's fate their two chief opponents had met would by no means amount to a release from them, but on the contrary would endanger the prospects of establishing peace. The government ordered "strict investigation," which was unfortunately put in the hands of a martial court. Runge was sentenced to two years' imprisonment for the brutal blows with his rifle and Lieutenant Vogel to two years and four months for "illegal disposal of a corpse." But the officers who had fired the shots at Liebknecht were released because the court found the evidence insufficient that this was not a case of attempted escape. Who had shot Rosa Luxemburg was not definitely established. Vogel fled to Holland, using a forged passport.

At the time of writing, an interview with the now aged Captain Pabst appeared in the German magazine *Spiegel* (No. 16, 1962). He asserted quite cold-bloodedly that the removal of the two communist leaders was in the situation at the time a permissible and praiseworthy deed, because at that time there was no effective government in Germany. Therefore, he said, everyone had to act in accordance with his own conscience. He hinted that he himself had desired the two to be removed, but failed to give a clear answer to the question as to whether he had suggested the action himself. Nothing happened to him. He did not leave the army until the end of 1919 and was afterward promoted to the rank of major by Hindenburg.

Whoever believed that he was in this way helping Ebert and Noske was quite wrong and had in fact done their cause grave harm. It makes no difference whether the murder is regarded as a normal crime or as counter-revolutionary act or even as a patriotic deed; politically it was a stupid action and a typical example of the dangers connected with the irresponsible politics of military autocrats.

On January 19, a Sunday, the general election for the National Assembly took place all over Germany, calmly and with a very high turnout of voters. The battle for a democratic parliamentary government was won. Only those who personally experienced or carefully studied the details know how extremely difficult were the months immediately after the November Revolution, how near Germany came to a dictatorship on the Russian model, and what significance individuals and events had for the final outcome.

## 21. WHY THE OLD ARMY?
## WHY NOT A NEW PEOPLE'S GUARD?

WHY had the revolutionary government not immediately formed its own troops? There were a series of attempts to do this. But the large majority of the soldiers and workers on the side of the Social Democrat majority group were essentially averse to military service of any kind, especially against other German workers. Those who were battle-minded were almost all politically on the side of the left wing of the Independents or with the Spartacists. Had an appeal been made to them, there would have been a military workers' corps in a flash; but in this way the supporters of a Bolshevik dictatorship would have been brought to power.

Since all the regiments in the Berlin barracks had on November 9 lined up behind the People's Commissaries and now had self-elected leaders, it would have appeared natural and simple to rely on them. At first events indeed did seem to point in this direction. On the first day of the Berlin Revolution a "Soldiers' Council" was formed in the Ministry of War, consisting of soldiers who had Social Democratic or at least democratic political views; they wore black-red-gold armbands as a distinguishing mark. Ebert gave them recognition on the same day and, together with War Minister Scheuch, issued a decree that soldiers' councils were to be formed in all military units and were to take part in handling the situation. "Their

principal task is to cooperate in the establishment of order and security and to bring about closest possible understanding between
troops and their leaders." But the soldiers in the Berlin barracks
were no reliable protection for the new government: not because
they were "reactionary," but because they were always talking politics and, as soon as workers were confronting one another ready for
a fight, tended to remain neutral and to keep out of the struggle.
They now had leaders chosen by themselves, but they did not obey
them. "When they were needed, they did not come," wrote Noske,
"during one alarm there were less than one hundred armed men on
the spot."

Nor did it prove possible to permit the military units still in the
field to select their own leaders. Therefore on November 12 the People's Commissaries, including the Independents, issued the decree
already mentioned, according to which during the return of the
troops the officers were to be obeyed and military discipline to be
maintained.

There were several attempts to create reliable troops outside the
old army. On November 9, the Independent Socialist Eichhorn established himself as president of police in Berlin without meeting
any opposition from the old police force. He immediately began to
form a Security Guard (*Sicherheitswehr*) composed of Independents. The Social Democrats could not rely on this.

On November 12, the Supervisory Council (*Vollzugsrat*), at its
second meeting, passed a resolution to set up a Red Guard (*Rote
Garde*) of men with Socialist schooling and military training.
Workers ready to join were invited to have their names entered.
But this action provoked the opposition of the soldiers in the barracks. They were enraged by the implication that they were not
considered reliable. They demanded speedy convening of the National Assembly and declared themselves ready to defend the provisional government. The Supervisory Council then withdrew its resolution.

Otto Wels, who had been made City Commander of Berlin
(*Stadtkommandant*), sent an emissary to Noske in Kiel requesting
immediate transfer of 2,000 trustworthy sailors to Berlin. This was
not possible because rail traffic was blocked. But 600 sailors came
from Cuxhaven to Berlin, where they were billeted in the palace
and its stables and formed the basis of the Marine Division. We

have already seen how unreliable they were from the government point of view and how they grew more and more radical.

A few days later Wels, therefore, began forming a Republican Soldiers' Guard (*Republikanische Soldatenwehr*) to serve under chosen leaders, none of whom was to be a former officer. But since these forces were composed of both Social Democrats and Independents, they were just as unreliable as the other troops whenever violent disagreements between the various Socialist groups played a role.

On December 5, a meeting in Circus Busch of non-commissioned officers and reenlisted soldiers formed a voluntary government troop under the leadership of a sergeant, Suppe. Colonel Reinhard (not the later Minister of War) offered his services and set up two regiments in the northern barracks; they consisted in part of the men brought together by Suppe.

After the failure of all these attempts, the People's Commissaries themselves decided in December to form a People's Guard (*Volkswehr*) 11,000 men strong, from volunteers over twenty-five, who were to elect their own leaders (that had been decreed by the Congress of Workers' and Soldiers' Councils) and were to pledge their obedience to their leaders, to the German Republic, and to the government. A pertinent decree was issued. The details of this decision gave rise to grave disagreements with War Minister Scheuch and General Groener.

Groener requested that the bond between officers and men should not be broken. At the present time it was not feasible to have the military leaders elected by the troops, he said. The abolition of all badges of rank (which also had been demanded by the Congress) would let loose a storm of indignation among the officers. Then Groener continued: "If we go—for I will not allow my shoulder-pieces to be removed—then there will be a complete collapse. I am well able to understand those who formed this resolution, but its fulfillment would be catastrophic. Even Soviet Russia has introduced drill into her army and her army does not have any officers elected by the men. The way in which the German army has carried out the difficult conditions for withdrawal in the west has aroused the admiration of American officers. I am fully convinced that we must make a break with our old military system and must build up a new one. The officers especially must come from the masses. . . . I personally have very sober opinions about medals and decorations. I have never attached great significance to them. But if you forbid the wearing of medals by men who have fought at the front, then you will cause unnecessary unrest in the nation."

War Minister Scheuch had other differences with the People's Commissaries and resigned. On December 31, after the Independents had withdrawn, he was replaced by the Wurttemberg Colonel Reinhardt. Introducing Reinhardt at a joint meeting of the People's Commissaries and the Central Council, Noske declared that the formation of a People's Guard was most urgent. However, the outbreak of the fights in Berlin left no time. When the Marine Division took Wels as hostage and did not release him despite all appeals, Ebert believed that he had no other choice than to request the War Minister to take the necessary steps to release Wels with regular troops. This action ended, as we have seen, in a compromise, thanks to the intervention of the masses and the hesitation of the troops. When, on January 4, Eichhorn's challenge led to the occupation of the newspaper buildings by the radical masses, it became impossible to proceed any further by negotiation. Noske, as commander, could not create a new People's Guard within a few days; even if he had had more time to tackle the task, he would have failed again because of the old obstacle: the fact that radical workers and government sympathizers did not work together reliably in critical situations. What he did, he had to do quickly in order to be able to do it at all. Therefore he relied on the remains of military organizations and new voluntary groups, which sprang up naturally among the middle classes for their own defense.

Convinced Communists who believed the only possible deliverance for the world lay in an authoritarian Socialist system, ready to reduce the influence of the bourgeoisie by all possible means, acted only logically when they condemned and resisted the policy of Ebert, Scheidemann, and Noske. But anyone who rejects Bolshevism and approves of the transition to general elections ought not to indulge in superficial mockery of the "pitiful revolutionaries" who had not even proved able to create a revolutionary army. He ought rather to explain how that might have been done under the circumstances described. A military army of Spartacists would have inevitably led to the establishment of a Communist system in Germany; and it was this that Ebert and Scheidemann wanted to avoid. They were convinced opponents of such a system, in the interest of both the working classes and their own ideals of freedom, self-determination, justice, and culture. By far the larger section of the working classes were behind them in this and certainly have no reason to maintain that they were betrayed by them. A moderate revolution is far more difficult to carry through than one which is radical, extremist, and determined to apply any means.

I have been speaking so far only of the three months from the beginning of the German Revolution to the elections for the National Assembly. After the convening of the National Assembly, no cabinet was able to create purely Socialist troops, because the Socialists were not in the majority. The problem was then how to create a truly democratic army through cooperation between the pro-democratic bourgeois parties and the Social Democrats. Even their combined forces held a parliamentary majority for only a short time. After the elections of June, 1920 up to the end of the First Republic in 1933 there was in the German parliament neither a Socialist majority, nor even a majority of the pro-democratic parties (see Chapter 30). Is it to be expected that a nation which has no pro-democratic majority will make strenuous efforts to create a pro-democratic army or to replace anti-democratic army leaders with pro-democratic ones? Can one reproach cabinets, in which opponents of democracy hold seats or which, if composed only of democrats, have only a minority behind them, for not having taken decisive steps to democratize the army? Ought one not in this situation to direct the reproaches at those sections of the German population who cast their votes for anti-democratic parties rather than at the failure of the cabinets?

But more might have been done, and ought to have been done, in order to avert brutality in the civil war and to punish those responsible. Noske did not want brutality. But he was not farsighted enough to prevent it and after it had happened to expose and punish the guilty persons. His faults here were the reverse of his admirable courage and manly resolve. These qualities had won him the affection and loyalty of the workers and sailors in Kiel. He hoped to win over the people in Berlin in the same way. When, to his horror, many acts of violence were committed, he was victim to a temptation which many leaders have felt, from Caesar to Napoleon, to cover up for his own men in order not to lose their loyalty, or at least, not to make too careful inquiries.

The maiden-speech which Noske had delivered in the Reichstag as a young deputy twelve years previously (on April 25, 1907) was characteristic of him. "Abolition of the army," he said at that time, "has never been advocated by the Social Democrats. Rather, we Social Democrats are the ones who have mocked at and opposed bourgeois fantasies regarding disarmament, and have pointed out that the economic antagonisms that exist at present between the various nations are still so strong that no single nation can so much as think of disarming. . . . In the resolution, which was cited by the War Minister, the point is aversion to militarism. But, gentlemen, aversion to militarism is by no means the same as aversion to defense (*Wehrhaftigkeit*); militarism and resolve to defend one's country are two totally different things. What we oppose in militarism is unnecessary drill, maltreatment, the isolation of the officers as a separate caste, the army's being interpreted as a means of power to maintain superiority of the wealthier classes over the poorer ones. . . . I declare once again: our wish is that Germany be as valiant (*wehrhaft*) as possible; our wish is that the entire German nation has an interest in those military establishments which are necessary for the defense of our fatherland. But this can be achieved only when outdated establishments are no longer held fast . . ." [1]

During the critical weeks before and after the acceptance of the Treaty of Versailles, Noske might easily have become military dictator in Germany. But he was a convinced Social Democrat. He did not want to become a military dictator, although he knew that he had the capacity and that the atmosphere was favorable for him. The man had steady nerves. A mass meeting had declared that if Noske were to appear, they would make *Hackepeter* (mincemeat) out of him. Noske decided to go. I accompanied him in the car. He conversed with me quite calmly. Then, stepping before the meeting and received with a great uproar, he forced the crowd to listen to him, and by his objective, manly manner of speaking pacified the gathering.

It was not actually necessary that the connection between German democracy and remnants of the old army should lead to the collapse of democracy. If Germany had been given a peace treaty which was less challenging to all the national concepts of honor; if the honest democratic governments of Ebert, Scheidemann, Fehrenbach, Wirth, Marx, Stresemann, Hermann Müller, etc., had received

---

[1] Quoted from Carl Herz, *Geister der Vergangenheit* (see above, Chapter 17), part 1, pp. 142–43.

support comparable to that offered the Adenauer government after the Second World War—then it would by no means have been impossible to keep control over the military. That all this was to be denied the German governments, Ebert and Noske could not know during the first months after the revolution. They acted in accordance with honest democratic beliefs and the upright desire to put Germany and the German nation back on their feet after a dreadful defeat; they did this to the best of their knowledge and belief. That was my impression at the time, and it still is. Those were dreadful months.

# PART V
## Weimar

## 22. Political Education Through the Act of Voting

The elections for the National Assembly on January 19, 1919 included not only women among the voters for the first time, but also the twenty, twenty-one, twenty-two, twenty-three, and twenty-four-year-olds who had not thus far had a vote. For the first time they were held according to the system of proportional representation (P.R.). A certain number of votes cast within the whole of Germany (or in one of the large regions) for any one party, secured that party one seat each; no party therefore lost votes merely on the ground that its candidates were outvoted locally.

This time, in contrast to my views in 1912, I was in no doubt as to whom I should vote for. Owing to the conditions which I had experienced during war and revolution, I was resolved to cast my vote for the Social Democrats, officially known as the "Social Democratic Party of Germany." I did not become a party member however. According to my political views, which I still hold today, government officials, at least senior ones, ought not to take an active part in the actual business of party politics, ought not to canvass for any one party publicly, nor write or speak against other parties that stay within the basic principles of the constitution. They ought to avoid giving any impression in public of making their judgments and decisions out of party-political reasons.

This maxim, which is in accord with British and—within the civil service—also with U.S. practice, is not generally accepted in Germany. During the Weimar years, officials assumed the right to attack democracy publicly and to support other constitutional ideals, be it monarchy, an authoritarian presidency, a military dictatorship, or even some form of Fascism. After the Second World War they were not permitted this right, because support for the basic principles of liberal democracy came to be required by law of every government official—with the result that there were suddenly no longer any avowed anti-democratic officials. Otherwise, however, they were left free publicly to support one party or to oppose others. I regret this development and still adhere to the ideal of the government official's remaining aloof from party politics within the basic principles of the constitution.

This was not the only reason why I failed to enlist in the Social Democratic party. There were also differences between my opinions and official party doctrine. I was not able to agree without reservations with the official party's deep mooring in the doctrines of Marx and Engels, which was tighter than it is today. I recognized the great importance of Marx and Engels and their scientific contributions. But the assertion that it is possible to make long-term forecasts about the future and the course of history has always seemed to me to be a survival of outdated scientific thinking of the nineteenth century. Many forecasts had already proved to be false. To generalize experiences of only three economic systems (slavery, feudalism, and capitalism in its early stages) and to declare them in advance to be valid for all following systems is methodologically untenable. To disparage all value judgments except one's own, and to regard other people's values as mere ideological superstructures over their class interests, while claiming for one's own absolute truth, seemed to me to be rather naïve.[1] Nor was I able to feel or preach "class hatred." I felt contempt for class *arrogance* and would have liked to see class differences reduced, but I felt no hatred toward other classes which historically had come to exist, and I also doubted that classes could be completely avoided. The accusations later brought by Communists against new classes that kept emerging within Communist countries—especially convincingly in the book *The New Class* by the Yugoslav Communist Milovan Djilas (New York 1957)—have confirmed this doubt. Nor did I consider the policy of the Social Democrats on military affairs to be mature. Whether or not I was right in these critical points is not what matters here. I want only to give an account of my views at the time. Later, when I discussed my reservations with Hermann Müller, he answered quite rightly, apropos the "class hatred," that I had misunderstood this concept. The Social Democrats did not advocate hatred of other classes or their members, but lamented that different classes existed. I could have pursued my personal opinions on Marxist theories and military affairs within the party, he said.

What drove me as a voter to the Social Democrats despite my reservations was that old urge for justice which had guided me from childhood and now attracted me to the simple workers whose principal spokesmen seemed to me to be the Social Democrats. It was my feeling for equality, nourished by the awareness that all human

[1] See my *Political Theory*, pp. 186 ff.

beings are, despite all their differences, equal in one, the essential point: every day and every hour they can and must make the choice between good and evil. It was my contempt for class arrogance. It was a human feeling of brotherhood. It was also an acknowledgment of the growing esteem in which I had held the Social Democrats during the war, when I read essays and speeches by their leaders and murmured to myself: *"Sicut tu socialdemocratus et ego."* It was the shared experience of the months of revolution in the Chancellery. I was especially pleased by the fact that the Social Democrats were less encumbered by bourgeois prejudices and more inclined to reform than the other parties. I was thoroughly oriented toward reform. I believed in the possibility of improvements. I wanted reforms in every sphere, but realistic reforms only, the consequences of which had been carefully thought through.

In many respects I was close also to the newly formed German Democratic Party. Over the course of the years many of their leaders became my friends. But I was more attracted to the workers than to the lower middle class who were the principal supporters of the Democratic Party in Germany apart from the numerically small intellectual elite that headed the party. The lower middle class had a strongly marked class-conciousness. Why stop halfway? I also mistrusted—as in fact many members of this party did—the belief in the completely free interplay of forces in the economic sphere. I felt that a considerable degree of planning was necessary because of Germany's economic and political situation at the time. Today, in the light of the economic successes of the United States, and likewise of the Federal Republic of Germany since 1948, I am no longer so sure about this. But I still believe that only under very special circumstances is it possible for the more extreme forms of liberal economics to have a great success and that these principles are effective in the long run and are justifiable in human terms only when they go hand in hand with a high degree of solidarity and philanthropic generosity, equality in public life, and a high standard of living among the working classes. In fact in the United States the economy is subject in many ways to ever-more-expanding controls, both in times of war and peace (for example agriculture, rents, transport, and power);[2] these facts ought to be studied more carefully and

---

[2] The best treatment I have seen is Hans Staudinger, "Die neue geplante Wirtschaftspolitik der Vereinigten Staaten," *Neue Perspektiven aus Wirtschaft und Recht, Festschrift für Hans Schäffer*, ed. by C. P. Claussen, Berlin, 1966, pp. 91–114.

made known, as well as those special conditions which were of help
to the success of free enterprise in Germany (American support, the
common fight against Bolshevism) and the barriers which limit its
effectiveness in many other countries, especially in underdeveloped
ones.

What pleased me about the Zentrum, a party consisting almost
ninty percent of members of the Catholic minority, was its fusion of
all classes and its respect for transcendental values. I was politically
as close to its left wing as to the Social Democrats and the Democrats. But the predominance of the Catholic element was alien to
me, a North German Protestant and grandson of a pastor, without
my having any hostile feelings on this account.

Many of my friends voted for the German People's Party
(*Deutsche Volkspartei*), the substitute for the National Liberals of
the imperial era. Most of the senior ministerial officials voted for
this party (if not for the German Nationals, the conservative
Right). But its indecisiveness in acknowledging the democratic republic, its arrogance toward the Social Democrats, to whose resistance to Bolshevism it owed its very existence, and its only slightly
camouflaged love of power-politics and jingoistic patriotism de-
terred me. Some of their leaders, including Stresemann and von
Kardorff, with whom I later had friendly relationships, gradually
cast off this dross, but for this very reason they were faced with serious internal conflicts within their own party.

To get back to the elections of January, 1919. It appeared that the
Socialists of varying shades, even together, had no absolute majority.
Of the 421 seats the Social-Democrats gained 163, the Independents
22, totalling 185. They were thus 26 short of an absolute majority
(211). The prospect of reorganizing Germany on Socialist lines had
thus disappeared. The prospects for a *democratic* regime, however,
were good. The German Democratic Party, formed of the remains
of former Liberal groups and of new men, held 75 seats, and the
Zentrum, which was honestly prepared to work on a republican
democratic basis, 91. Together with the Social Democrats this made
a total of 329 of the 421 seats, that is, more than three quarters (78
percent). These three parties together formed the so-called Weimar
Coalition, created the so-called Weimar Constitution, and they
would, had they kept the majority—a prospect which at first all ob-
servants reckoned with—have been able not only to create a democratic constitution but also to see it carried through.

Hopes for continuous large pro-democratic majorities were the more reasonable since the election results did not differ fundamentally from those of the last national elections before the war. At that time (1912) the Social Democrats had obtained 110 of the 397 seats in the Reichstag, the Zentrum 91 (exactly the same as 1919), and the left-wing Liberals 42, a total of 243, that is almost two-thirds of the seats. Of the remainder, 28 members represented national minority groups, such as Poles, Alsatians, and Danes, who were, of course, opponents of German-Prussian conservatism. On the right wing, the 45 National Liberals were for all their Bismarck worship nevertheless sincere supporters of certain basic principles of liberalism, such as independence of judges, religious tolerance, and world trade. Further to the right, in the Reichstag of 1912, there were only 47 Conservatives, 13 Independent Conservatives, 3 anti-Semites, and 8 members of the Economic Union, a total of 71 out of the 397 members. The remaining 10 seats fell to some Guelphs (Hannoverians), and to so-called *Wilde* (freelance), who had no party membership.

To generations who did not experience that period before 1914 it is worth while pausing a moment at these figures. How was it possible for a conservative, authoritarian system to hold power in Germany, when the national elections had long shown that only a small fraction of the population had conservative views? The answer is very simple. According to the Constitution of 1871 the Kaiser was free to select the Chancellor and the department heads under him, not subject to parliamentary control. For this reason large numbers of Conservatives and many National Liberals, but very few supporters of the Zentrum, even fewer Left Liberals, and not a single Social Democrat, held office in the national administration.

The increase in Socialist votes from 1912 to 1919 was not as violent as had been hoped for or feared. Every fourth German had voted Social Democrat as far back as 1898, and every third in 1912. Now the combined Socialist votes had become considerably higher than a third, but not yet one half. Thus a coalition government between Socialist and non-Socialist parties had to be formed; no cabinet could be confirmed, no law passed, without at least one of the non-Socialist parties agreeing.

This was the situation created by the election, and the fact that it was thus ought to have been apparent to everyone on the very first day. But ways of thinking do not change so quickly. All the provisional governments after the Revolution still consisted of Socialists.

Lübeck, where the pre-war Lord Mayor, Dr. Ferdinand Fehling, Jürgen's father, the son-in-law of Emanuel Geibel, remained in office, was the only exception.

The National Assembly convened in Weimar on February 6. Eduard David, a Social Democrat, was elected its president. On February 11, on the basis of a previously accepted law on provisional powers, Friedrich Ebert was elected Reich President. The cabinet which he formed and which was approved by the Assembly consisted of Scheidemann as Minister-President (the title Chancellor was not yet used); six other Social Democrats (Noske, Landsberg, Wissell, Bauer, Robert Schmidt, David); three Democrats (Schiffer, Preuss, Gothein); and three members of the Zentrum (Bell, Giesberts, Erzberger). Foreign Affairs were transferred to a career diplomat, Count Brockdorff-Rantzau. Fehrenbach of the Zentrum took David's place as president of the Assembly. Then government and Assembly turned to their main business: creation of a democratic constitution and winding up of the war.

While matters in Weimar proceeded comparatively calmly, in other parts of Germany bitter unrest flared up. In Munich Premier Eisner, an Independent Social Democrat, was assassinated. The ensuing dictatorial regime of a council-type government reached its climax in the murder of anti-Socialist hostages (April 29), but then, after military intervention, came to a bloody end on May 2. In Berlin, Ebert was able to control the excesses of a general strike (March 3–9) by enforcing martial law with transference of executive power to Noske. Noske dissolved the remains of the Marine Division and of the Republican Soldiers' Guard, which had to some extent joined the revolt. He issued an order, which was militarily effective but highly objectionable in terms of human rights and due process of law, to the effect that anyone who was found carrying weapons and fighting against government troops was to be shot immediately. The volunteer corps, roused on account of losses in their own ranks, took advantage of this decree. There were over 1,000 dead. On March 11, for example, 31 sailors were shot without investigation. The lesson from these experiences was drawn too late— that such summary orders to shoot were not to be given.

At the end of March a revolt on the Ruhr followed. Only with great difficulty—after much shooting and ill-treatment from both sides—did Carl Severing, as appointed Reich Commissioner, succeed in suppressing it with the assistance of General Watter and his troops. Then came a general strike in Braunschweig under the leadership of Eichhorn, the former Berlin chief of police (April 19). All this showed only too clearly how important it was to pass the new national constitution as soon as possible, but also what difficult conditions were to be taken into account.

## 23. DEMOCRACY AND CONSTITUTION

WHAT is democracy? Opinions on this have changed in the course of history. That democracy has something to do with rule by the people is expressed in the term itself, but not how this rule is to be realized. The word admits of many interpretations: from the exercise of all governmental powers—legislation, administration, and justice—by the entire nation (or its adult males), united in a people's assembly, as in ancient Athens, down to the carrying out of the supposed will of the people by a dictatorial government, as in the Soviet Union. The modern concept of democracy in western countries combines three principles: the protection of human or basic rights, the independence of the courts of law, and the maxim that all *other* matters are decided or controlled by the majority on the basis of general elections, in such a way that the people, by making free use of their right to vote, can determine and change (either at any time or periodically within reasonable periods of time) both the membership of the legislative assembly and (directly or indirectly) the holders of the highest executive offices. No scientific argument can compel anyone to use the word "democracy" in just this sense. But when I go on here to speak of democracy, I mean democracy in the modern western sense that I have just outlined.

In the older western democracies the term "democracy" conjures up the image of a state in which human dignity is respected and human rights are assured—the happy image of freedom from tyrannical despotism. This is also the primary connotation of the term in Germany today, with the people looking back to the Hitler regime and sidewise to present-day Communism. But in 1919, when the Weimar Constitution was being written, things were different. Human rights had on the whole been protected in Germany before the war, not through the Constitution itself, but by virtue of national laws which, once passed, could be modified only with the Reichstag's consent (see Chapter 12). Rights could be temporarily suspended by proclaiming martial law, but until 1914 this had happened only seldom and then only in narrow geographical and time limits. When martial law became a permanent condition during the war, the Reichstag promptly issued (with the consent of the Bundesrat!) the excellent Protective Custody Act of 1916, which set down the rights of those in custody and protected them from complete arbitrariness. The really new thing in Germany at that time was not, therefore, the principle of respect for human dignity—old Kantian spiritual heritage—nor basic rights, although they were considerably extended. There had been general elections, free and secret, for over forty years, at least for the Reichstag. What was fundamentally new, because it had previously been absent, was the maxim that the people were to determine not only the legislators but also the highest executive officials, and the release of parliamentary legislation from any veto by princes, whether in a federal council, or by the monarch's right of veto.

In the Germany of 1919, therefore, the word "democracy" did not call the glory of freedom and human rights before the eye, but the far less fascinating picture of parties fighting for executive power and of frequent government crises, connected, in relation to foreign countries, not with freedom but with lack of it, to a degree which had not been known in Germany since the time of Napoleon.

Only those who were deeply filled with the *total* idea of democracy and the value of personal responsibility, and who were aware of the causal connection between the former undemocratic conditions and the outbreak of the war and its loss, were immune to the deceptive impression that the distinguished aristocratic methods of government in the imperial era had been something better than the contemporary loud and often vulgar struggle among the parties, and that the miserable situation of Germany after the war was causally connected with her new democratic form of government.

The men who formed the new national government shared the belief in the superiority of democracy. The new Minister of the Interior, Dr. Hugo Preuss, had already been appointed head of that department as early as November 15, the seventh day of the revolution, and had been instructed to prepare the draft of a democratic constitution. He was at that time one of the few, if not the only, professor of constitutional law firmly grounded in democracy and entirely familiar with its principles and history. He had for this reason never held a chair at a German university (also because he was a Jew), but taught at a business school in Berlin.

His principal task—setting down article by article the parliamentary system of democracy and the basic rights of men—seemed to him and to us at that time relatively simple. It was more difficult to reorganize the relationship between the federal government and the state governments, and to redraw Germany's political map. Preuss proposed to abolish the smaller states, with the exception of the three Hansa towns, and to combine several Prussian provinces, and also some Prussian and non-Prussian areas, within larger units. Bavaria, Wurttemberg, and Baden were scarcely to be altered, except that the Rhenish Palatinate was to be joined to the Rhineland. Berlin was, like each of the Hansa towns, to form a separate state. Since Preuss published his plan before the Treaty of Versailles, he included Austria. It was to form a single state within Germany. Vienna was to be an independent unit like Berlin.

The problem of territorial reorganization proved too difficult for the Assembly to solve in due time; it was referred to subsequent special legislation. But otherwise the Constitution was completed and passed by the end of July. Taken as a whole the Weimar Constitution, as it is generally called, was a venerable document from the democratic viewpoint, evidence of the idealistic desires which inspired its originators. But too little experience, a lack—not only in Germany, but in the whole world—of a really advanced political theory, and finally the confidence in the continuance of democratic majorities and in the democratic reliability of elected presidents, led to some fateful errors in important details. For even though the principles of modern democracy in the West (basic rights, independent courts, in other matters free decision of the majority) are the same in all western democratic states, the forms in which they are realized are different, and the fate of the individual democracies depends to a considerable degree upon this.

A few words here about the mistakes. *First:* the majority was to decide. This principle appears to be simple and unambiguous. But different methods of polling give rise to different majorities. In order to be particularly democratic, proportional representation was prescribed for all legislative bodies, and this requirement was even set down in the Constitution itself, so that it could be changed only by a two-thirds majority. For—thus it seemed at that time to many and even seems so today—what could be more just or more equitable?

Proportional representation is indeed entitled to be considered the best democratic method for the election of the constitutive assembly, since it assures all sections of the population a proportional share in the setup of the constitution. But that it be the best thing also for the recurrent parliamentary ballots is not nearly so certain. One might just as well argue that it would be most just if each governmental cabinet consisted of members proportionally selected from all parties, including the radicals on both sides. This conclusion is rarely drawn, because it is obviously incompatible with the functions of the cabinet. Proportional representation often deprives the people of that very cooperation in fundamental decisions that general elections were supposed to grant them. They are compelled to elect candidates who represent special interests or philosophies instead of persons seeking the necessary balance between different interests and philosophies. The voter cannot even decide upon the person; the party bureaucracy does that for him.[1] Thus under the system of proportional representation the independent political thinking of the individual citizen atrophies. Far from being induced to seek for union, integration, compromise, he is in fact cunningly prevented from doing so. He can at best leave such constructive decisions to his party. Proportional representation encourages the breakdown into many, or at least more than two, parties. In this way a small group, which holds the pivotal power between large parties, often influences the decisions in a degree quite out of proportion to its size, as for example the small party of the Gauche radicale did in France between 1924 and 1932, and in Germany during the Weimar Republic sometimes the Bavarian People's Party, sometimes the Economic Party, and after the Second World War, especially, the Free Democrats. This may in individual cases be good or bad, but it refutes the alleged mathematical justice of proportional representation. The worst defect: proportional representation throws the doors of parliament wide open for anti-democratic radical groups. The lowered voting age of twenty contributed to increasing the number of votes cast for radical parties.

---

[1] The party bureaucracies, for example, refused to put Max Weber and Hugo Preuss on the election tickets. The Social Democrats prevented Noske from standing again in either 1928 or 1932 (see following chapter). The people were not consulted.

In vain, Friedrich Naumann warned of the dangers of proportional representation in the constitutional committee of the National Assembly. The selfish interest of the parties and their bureaucratic machines in proportional representation is so great that after the Second World War every parliamentary country on the Continent of Europe introduced or retained proportional representation, if with some modifications, as in the Federal Republic of Germany. In 1945 I advised the U.S. occupational authorities to support P.R. in the elections for a National Assembly only on the condition that the parliamentary elections later be held according to the Anglo-American majority system. Unfortunately the official adviser of the military government at that time happened to have little knowledge of this question; he cherished the illusion that P.R. was something unequivocally good.

*Second.* In the Weimar period P.R. played an especially fateful part through the indirect influence it had upon the nomination of candidates in presidential elections. The president was to be elected not, as in France at that time, by the two legislative houses, but as in America, by general elections. This was considered the more democratic method. Even Max Weber, misunderstanding the differences, strongly advocated this procedure. In the United States, where practically the entire nation stands behind its federal constitution and where the method of legislative elections secures the two-party system, the selection of the president by national elections has worked well. However, where the constitution is attacked by strong parties on the left and on the right, as was the case in Germany, and P.R. keeps parliament split into many conflicting parties, so that no one party is in a position to carry its own candidate, then it can easily happen that in presidential elections outsiders are nominated, who enjoy great popularity but who are laymen in politics and without inner ties to parliamentary democracy. Thus popular opponents of democracy can come to power.

*Third.* Article 48 gave extended authority to the president in times of crises. It was hoped that four factors would guarantee democratic control: the power to issue emergency decrees was to reside in a president elected by the people rather than a prince; each decree required for its validity counter-signature by a constitutional chancellor or minister, who was responsible to the Reichstag and could be dismissed by it; the Reichstag was entitled by simple majority to enforce repeal of any emergency decree; finally, statutory law could regulate details such as protective custody and the length of time for which rights might be suspended.

Had these guarantees gained real significance, presidential emergency powers might indeed have been kept under democratic control. Their dictatorial abuse was made possible, however, by the broad power given the president to appoint and dismiss a chancellor. According to the wording of the Constitution he was able to dismiss the chancellor at any time, even though no motion of censure had been passed against him; and he could appoint as chancellor anyone, irrespective of his chances to receive a vote of confidence, and could then have him counter-sign a decree dissolving the Reichstag, and emergency decrees, before there was a new Reichstag to pass a vote of censure. The power to suspend basic laws could thus fall into the hands of a person not controlled by parliament. This was the more dangerous because the statutory law which might have provided some protection against abuse did not come into being; the parties had failed to reach agreement on it.

These mistakes affected only a few lines in the long text of the Weimar Constitution. The influence they had on the fate of the first German Republic, however, proved great. Had the rights of the president been more prudently defined, then in 1932 Hindenburg would neither have been able to discharge Brüning nor to appoint Papen; nor to dissolve the Reichstag with Papen's—from the democratic standpoint worthless—signature; nor to remove the Prussian ministers; nor finally, in February, 1933, entirely to suspend the constitutional protection of human rights. Had the voting system made it possible, as in England, in the United States, and at that time in France, to keep extremist candidates away from parliament by locally outvoting them, then the National Socialists and the Communists would never have had the large Reichstag representation which gave their movements such impetus. If the president had been elected by a joint session of Reichstag and Reichsrat or by other indirect methods, Hindenburg would never have become Ebert's successor in 1925 and so would not have been able to play the disastrous role he did in 1932 and 1933.

All this can be easily shown now and its significance realized, because we know now that the pro-democratic parties in Germany soon lost their majority. But when the Constitution was written there were still those overwhelming majorities in parliament for democracy, and the thought that these majorities might be lost was far from the minds of most observers. The makers of the Constitution should not be too strongly criticized for having left these loopholes, *which became dangerous only with the loss of pro-democratic majorities*. I could deny all responsibility on my own part on the ground that I took no part in the drafting. But I doubt that, had I participated, I would have recognized these errors and their full significance. Only the observation of their practical effects has made me, like many others, a "constitutional expert," and the study of other constitutions has increased my insight *ex post*. At that time I was no constitutional expert. There was no such thing in Germany as political science. Nor did foreign experts in political science draw the attention of the Germans to these errors and dangers.

Other sources of danger were much more obvious at the time. The postponement of territorial reorganization placed tremendous obstacles in the way of a healthy development of German democracy. So did the constitutional guarantee of lifelong tenure for all former officials in office. I will deal with these matters in later chapters.

In retrospect it is perhaps possible to say that due to those technical defects of the Weimar Constitution the battle for democracy, like the World War on the Marne, was half-lost for Germany as it had hardly begun. At the time this was far from certain. Democracy had strong battalions of electors behind it. As long as that was the case there was little to fear.

## 24. THE CHANCELLERY IN THE TRANSITION TO DEMOCRACY—THE STRUGGLE FOR A PLANNED ECONOMY

FOR a short time I had stayed in Berlin as liaison officer. At the end of February, however, I was being called to Weimar for a special assignment. I worked there in a rococo room of the grand-ducal palace. By the middle of March I returned to Berlin with the Cabinet. In May we all went back to Weimar. This time Clara accompanied me.

During the temporary return to Berlin, Ebert moved into the

President's palace, which had been prepared for him, and left the Chancellery building to Scheidemann. Heinrich F. Albert became chief of the Chancellery because the Cabinet wanted an experienced administrator on this post. Albert was without doubt that—and much more. Ten years older than I, he had a most unique career behind him. From a position as assistant in the Federal Department of the Interior he had accompanied Theodor Lewald, the German Commissary for the world fair, to St. Louis in 1902. His work there required political, economic, and cultural tact and resolve, and it implied far greater independence than was otherwise enjoyed by German government officials.

Later he became German commissary at the world fair in Brussels in 1910. The most unusual part of his career was to follow during the war. He and the former Colonial Secretary and banker, Bernhard Dernburg, were instructed to board a Danish ship for New York, in order to speed up the procuring of food supplies and raw materials for Germany from abroad. Dernburg was to obtain a loan of a hundred million dollars and Albert to supervise the expenditure. Purchase and transport were to be carried out privately by Hapag, the Hamburg-America shipping line. This assignment was entirely legal, since the United States until 1917 maintained a status of neutrality in the war. Equally non-objectionable from the legal point of view were Albert's various attempts, when it became evident that the Hapag was unable to carry out purchase and shipping, to use neutral middlemen. In this he had admirable initiative and ever new ideas to overcome difficulties, which consisted not in a conflict with American laws but in the fear of the American suppliers and shippers that the ships might be seized and the freight confiscated by the British. What was illegal in the German opinion was this British confiscation, since food supplies and cotton for the civilian population must not be seized according to international law. It was perfectly legal, too, for American or German firms, and even for representatives of the German government, to have American goods transported to Germany in any ships. It was also legal to try to deceive the English about the nature of the freight and its destination.

When American firms refused cooperation for fear of losing their British customers, Albert purchased the goods through middlemen, and when the normal shipping lines would no longer accept them, he founded new lines for temporary periods, or chartered individual ships, or bought them. Since the English refused insurance and the available German insurance companies set too narrow limits on their liability, he founded a pool of German insurance companies with sufficiently high limits. When Dernburg's attempt to obtain a dollar loan failed, because the large American banking houses did not want to put up German loans, in order not to lose British business, Albert attempted to bring a syndicate of smaller American firms into being. He obtained a loan of 10,000,000 dollars and succeeded in selling some 5,000,000 marks German war loans privately.

Not only did Albert try to secure transports to Germany; he strove to impede and hinder those to England. He purchased machine-tools and other materials that were in short supply through American middlemen in order to deprive British suppliers of them. Finally he helped the German embassy to have favorable reports and arguments printed in the American press, which was on the whole hostile toward Germany. He subsidized some small newspapers.

In the summer of 1915 this otherwise so wary man had the misfortune, when he had fallen asleep in the hot New York subway on his way home, to have his briefcase stolen from his lap and the contents published a few days later in the New York evening paper *World*. As far as I have been able to establish, these documents contained nothing that was in conflict with U.S. laws. But the matters there discussed had to remain secret if they were to achieve their desired effects. To be exact, there was a comparatively insignificant point in which Albert's activities contravened American regulations: in completing the shipping papers he had answered the question on the final destination of the goods (Germany) with the name of the neutral country where they were to be unloaded. The U.S. government made no complaints and Albert stayed a further eighteen months in America. But the press pursued him with attacks and suspicions. Even some twenty years later his daughter on a visit to America was asked: "Are you the daughter of briefcase Albert?" [1]

Albert's counterpart as military attaché at the German Embassy in Washington was Franz von Papen, the man who later helped Hitler into the saddle. He had on his return journey even greater ill-luck because the stubs in his checkbook, with recipients and amounts, were secretly photographed in his cabin.

[1] From Albert's *Aufzeichnungen* (Notes), which were published privately.

Not until February, 1917, shortly before the entry of the United States into the war, did Albert return to Berlin along with the German ambassador, Count Bernstorff. Here he became eventually head of the demobilization department. During an argument in the Cabinet about the best utilization of war materials he attracted the attention of Scheidemann, who then offered him the position as State Secretary in the Chancellery. After his appointment he came politely to see me. I had my doubts that it was wise to put in this position a man who was unpopular in both the United States and England. Our conversation also made it clear that he knew little about the various Socialist groups. But in fact no difficulties arose from his past activities, and the closer knowledge I had of the Socialists compensated for the gaps in his.

Of a more basic nature was the divergence of our opinions on economic matters. He was a liberal economist who wanted to see free enterprise reestablished as soon and as fully as possible, more or less along the lines this was so successfully done by Dr. Ludwig Erhard after the Second World War. I was more sympathetic to ideas of economic planning, in order to meet the particular difficulties of the German economic situation, and considered our task to lie not in simply rejecting plans of socialization but rather in modifying them in such a way that—preferably without prejudicing personal initiative—progress for the whole of the German economy would be assured. In this I was in sympathy with Wichard von Möllendorff, State Secretary in the Department of Economics. Albert once said to me: "Only children argue about principles; adults make their decisions from case to case." This sentence, tossed off casually, aroused me. Had our mistake not precisely been that we made our decisions from case to case instead of taking our bearings from principles? I left Albert in no doubt about my misgivings, a fact which he, however, magnanimous as he was, never took amiss.

Finally a Cabinet decision had to be made on Germany's economic policy. A memorandum drafted by Möllendorff and his colleagues and submitted to the Cabinet by Economics Minister Wissell recommended that economic councils were to be set up on various levels, consisting of producers, workers, and consumers; they should be authorized to fix certain rules on production and distribution. After a very lively debate these proposals were rejected. Wissell and Möllendorff resigned.

Albert asked me to draft a statement on the reasons for the government's decision. I objected that because of my sympathy with Möllendorff's plans I was not the right man for this. Albert answered that for this very reason I was particularly well-equipped, since it was an old experience that judges who had been outvoted by their colleagues wrote the best explanation for the court's decision. I stuck to my refusal. When he insisted and finally gave me a definite order to do what he had said, I answered by tendering my resignation to the Chancellor. According to regulations I had to turn it in through my superior, Secretary Albert. Albert sent for me very early the following morning and, after a few friendly words, canceled his order; I then withdrew my resignation. Thus, after preliminary mistrust and disagreements, our relationship gradually changed into one of mutual respect and finally friendship, which continued until his death in 1960.

In April, 1919 I was appointed *Geheimer Regierungsrat und Vortragender Rat* in the Chancellery, an unusually high position for an official of my age. My earlier appointments to the positions of judge in Prussia and imperial *Regierungsrat*—the latter only a year previously—had borne the pompous signature of Wilhelm II, in the first case followed simply by the letter R (Rex), and in the second by the more weighty I,R (Imperator, Rex); they were impressively set out documents, fixed with the splendid state seal. The present one was typewritten on a plain sheet of white paper and bore the simple signatures of Ebert and Scheidemann. Since there was no new seal yet, the imprint of a cheap rubber stamp served instead.

This appointment, together with that of Hans Staudinger—who later became State Secretary in the Prussian Ministry of Commerce and after the collapse of the Weimar Republic my academic colleague in New York—and that of my brother Gustav shortly afterward, were among the last instances of the title *Geheimrat* being conferred, a title which, after the Weimar Constitution went into force, was no longer given. Those who already had it, however, kept it, even along with other titles.

## 25. The Peace Treaty—Responsibility
   for the Collapse

The Allies submitted their draft for the peace treaty on May 7 in Versailles, granting but a short period (originally two weeks, then extended to three) for "written comments." The draft demanded surrender of Alsace-Lorraine, Upper Silesia, Posen, a corridor to the Baltic for Poland, and smaller territorial cessions in other areas, plus allied occupation of the Rhineland and the Saar. After the far greater territorial losses and the division of the country which Hitler's regime caused Germany, the territorial sacrifices demanded in 1919 appear comparatively small, the more so because in the subsequent negotiations Germany succeeded in winning the concession that a plebiscite was to decide on the fate of Upper Silesia, as a result of which its greater part remained German. Some moderation of provisions for the Saarland, too, was granted. But at that time the losses seemed greater than today. In accordance with Wilson's points a plebiscite had also been expected in the case of Alsace-Lorraine, or at least of Alsace, and the surrender of the Corridor was felt to be an absurd "cut into the flesh." The territorial demands were complemented by the condition of Germany's unilateral disarmament without any guarantee that the promised disarmament of the Allies would follow (and in fact this never was done); by clauses that reserved to the Allies the right to establish the amount of reparations in money and goods to be made by Germany; by the so-called "Guilt Clause," according to which Germany was to "accept the responsibility of Germany and her Allies for causing all the loss and damage to which the Allied and Associated Governments and their nationals have been subjected as a consequence of the war imposed upon them by the aggression of Germany and her Allies" (Article 231); and by the required surrender of the so-called war criminals on a list drawn up by the Allies alone.

This basic scheme of the peace conditions shocked the German people deeply and confronted the government, as we shall see, with insoluble problems. When in a speech to the National Assembly—convened on May 12 in Berlin in the hall where Fichte had delivered his speeches to the nation in Napoleonic times—Minister-President Scheidemann said that to compare the peace conditions with Wilson's points would be blasphemy, and asked "Where is the hand that will not wither (*verdorren*) when it puts these chains on itself and on us?" he was expressing the general opinion.

Indeed, how could the new democracy have been maintained in Germany had its leaders declared such conditions acceptable? The reactionary, monarchist, militarist forces in Germany were gaining strength, and so were the Communists, who shouted that Bolshevism was the only way out. Armed leagues came into being everywhere under more or less military leadership.

Feverish work was undertaken under Count Brockdorff-Rantzau, Walter Simons (as Commissioner-General), and other excellent men, among them Professor Schücking and the banker Dr. Melchior, to produce a written answer from material previously prepared by Count Bernstorff and his staff. A monumental work of tremendous industry, the German answer was submitted to the Allies on May 29.

I had no share in this work, apart from my recording functions at cabinet meetings and occasional exchanges of opinions with cabinet ministers and members of the German delegation. I was busy with the work for which I had been called to Weimar, namely, to produce an official White Book on the events preceding the German offer of peace in October, 1918. Dr. Adolf Köster, a Social Democrat journalist, had started collecting the pertinent documents, but was unable to continue, as he was to go to Schleswig-Holstein as German Plebiscite Commissioner. The White Book was to provide documentary evidence that the collapse of military hopes for a German victory had *preceded* the peace offer, and not, as was often maintained, *succeeded* it; and, secondly, that timing and character of the offer had been determined by the German High Command and not by the civilian leaders, who had considered both to be disastrous. Third, it was to testify that the German people had laid down their arms trusting in the honorable intention of the Allies to carry out Wilson's points.

I applied great care to produce a complete and well-organized collection, preceded with the prefatory note already mentioned, summarizing its contents. In it I distinguished four phases: the first from August 14 until the end of September, when the Kaiser and the High Command decided upon starting negotiations, but wanted to wait for a "suitable moment"; the second, from the end of September onward, when the German High Command was demanding that a peace offer be sent "immediately"; the third, from October 15 until the dismissal of Ludendorff (October 26), when the High Command wanted to recommence battle, but now met opposition from the Chancellor, who thought that this could only lead to worse conditions; finally, in the fourth phase, cooperation once again between the High Command and the government in concluding the armistice.

Ludendorff objected to my prefatory remarks in newspaper articles and booklets. Although his objections failed to refute any essential points, the German Cabinet decided in 1923, when right-wing parties had joined the government, to bring out a revised edition through the National Archives (*Reichsarchiv*). The revision led to no essential alterations, except that at the request of the rightist ministers the prefatory note was omitted, without either replacement or explanation, although it had proved to be quite valid; if this had not been the case it would certainly have been corrected. Even today it cannot be read without emotion. Since 1920 it has not been available in print.

The critical discussion of sources in the carefully edited collection of documents, *Die Regierung des Prinzen Max von Baden,* which appeared in 1962 (edited by Matthias and Morsey) begins: "The most important source of documents for our collection is the first edition of *Amtliche Urkunden zur Vorgeschichte des Waffenstillstandes* (Official Records of Events Preceding the Armistice) which appeared in 1919" (p. xliii). A note by the senior archivist, Veit Valentin, of September 7, 1923, says: "Objections to the first edition of the White Book were raised in particular by General Ludendorff. Careful examination of the original records and the entire documentary material has shown that the objections are not tenable. On several points [raised by L.] no documents have been found. Other points could be clarified, most of them in contradiction of Ludendorff's memories. It can be said that the collection was more comprehensive even at that early time than could have been expected" (*op. cit.,* p. li).

The meetings of the Cabinet in Weimar after the return of the peace delegation were held either in the grand-ducal palace or, if the National Assembly happened to be sitting at the same time, in the National Theater, which housed it. The door of the room where the Cabinet meetings took place was labeled: "Changing room for the ballet." No one paid attention to this grotesque inscription. Rather, the decisive meetings were marked by tragic earnestness, even despair.

Count Brockdorff-Rantzau gave a report on the humiliating circumstances under which the delegation had been forced to negotiate and on the meagre success their attempts had brought. He recommended that the peace treaty be rejected regardless of consequences. Erzberger opposed because of Germany's military impotence both at home and abroad. At the Cabinet's request Noske had asked the German High Command beforehand whether the army was capable of recommencing armed resistance. The answer was negative. "In the case of a serious attack from our enemies in the west we can hardly count on success in view of the numerical superiority of the Entente and the possibility they have to surround us on both flanks." In spite of this Hindenburg and the officers threatened to resign if the peace treaty were signed. Chaotic conditions were close when it became evident that opinions were almost equally divided in the parties between acceptance and rejection. I can still see as though it had been only yesterday, Ebert, Noske, Scheidemann, Erzberger, sitting in front of me at these nightly sessions with tired faces. This was the situation during which Noske, had he wanted, might have become dictator, not only to carry out hopeless resistance, but also in the event of the treaty's being signed, to meet the danger of chaotic disruption and to call the officers to order. Groener seriously suggested such a dictatorship. But Noske did not want to betray the democratic principles in which he believed and for which he fought.

Democratic principles? They only determined procedure; they did not tell ministers and members of parliament which decision was the best. The question to be decided could never arise in a real democracy. Full democracy means the self-determination of a nation in its own affairs. Basic affairs of the German nation, however —such as the size of its army, the treatment of criminals, the fate of parts of the country with German inhabitants—were to be determined not by the German people, but from outside. The democratic foreign governments who determined them were responsible to their own parliaments for this, to their own people, but not to the Germans. The word "democracy" had better not be used for peoples who are not free. But democratic principles of procedure can of course be followed by them within the limits in which they have still freedom. And that was what was to happen then.

At first the lead was taken by Scheidemann and Brockdorff-Rantzau, supported by the Social Democratic Minister of Justice, Landsberg. On their proposal the coalition parties were asked whether they were willing to authorize the government to request cancellation of the guilt clause and of the extradition clause, and in the case of refusal to deny signature. When the parties proved unable to reach a decision, the Scheidemann Cabinet resigned on the night of June 20. Time pressed; the deadline set by the Entente was June 23. At Ebert's request Bauer formed a new cabinet on June 21, without Scheidemann, Brockdorff-Rantzau, and Landsberg, and without the Democrats (Schiffer, Preuss, Gothein), whose party with few exceptions (these including von Payer) had opposed signing. The new Cabinet therefore consisted only of Social Democrats and members of the Zentrum. Hermann Müller became Foreign Minister, Erzberger Minister of Finance and Vice-Premier.

After it had been made clear that the government would attempt to have the two clauses dropped before signing, the National Assembly voted for the signing on June 22 with a considerable majority (237 votes to 138). But Clemenceau immediately rejected such a conditional acceptance, on behalf of the Allies, and demanded unconditional acceptance "within the remaining twenty-four hours," threatening that, if this were not done, the allied armies would march into Germany. Once again the National Assembly was consulted and, weakly and hesitantly, without a roll call, stated that the authorization given the previous day covered the present situation. The Cabinet then decided not to exempt the two clauses from the signature, but to lodge a strongly worded protest and appeal to Wilson's points.

Charged with the transmission of this momentous decision to our representative in Paris, I hurried late at night from the National Assembly to the grand-ducal palace, edited details of the text, and was present during the technical transmission to Paris. "The government of the German Republic, yielding to overwhelming power and without abandoning its view of the unheard-of injustice of the peace conditions, declares itself to be ready to accept and sign the peace conditions imposed by the Allied and Associated governments."

Hindenburg and Groener resigned. General von Seeckt, appointed in place of Groener, was made directly subordinate to Minister of Defense Noske.

Looking back on the situation at that time and wondering what ought to have been done, I am unable even now to come to a determined, logically conclusive result. Unfortunately in politics there is not always a solution. Many political problems cannot be solved. This was such a problem. The question of its solubility or insolubility had nothing to do with the form of government.

Perhaps the fear of occupation by the Allies was too great. Had they occupied the whole of Germany they would have been responsible for governing Germany and would have had to assure reasonable living conditions, just as in 1945. After great humiliation in the beginning, a quicker and more constructive cooperation between the occupation forces and the democratic parties in Germany might have evolved. Rathenau was, therefore, perhaps not entirely wrong when he recommended that the German government resign without renewing military resistance, and leaving the responsibility to the Allies. In engaging in such afterthought, however, one should not ignore the fact that the successful cooperation between the Western powers and the West German democratic leaders after 1945 was stimulated by two factors which were not at work in 1919: awareness on the side of the Western powers of the serious mistakes they had made after 1918, and the pressure exercised by the policy of the Soviet Union. Furthermore, although leaving total responsibility to the Allies might have possibly averted the need of a one-sided confession of guilt, the Allies' hold on the "war criminals" would have been probably much harsher (Chapter 29).

## 26. Erzberger in Weimar

Matthias Erzberger had led the Zentrum party from the right to the left, he had signed the armistice, and in the debates on the Treaty of Versailles he had been the leading advocate of signature. For these reasons he was the main target of attacks by the rightist parties against the government. But even among the government parties he was not particularly popular. Within the Cabinet he was a dynamic force. There were many more matters besides the peace treaty that had to be considered. When the other ministers were discussing their differences of opinion in lengthy speeches, not always to the point, Erzberger would come up with a clearly defined proposal and briefly sketch out the practical methods for carrying it out. His initiative was boundless. He had a strong influence also on the evolving new structure of German administration. It was Erzberger who persuaded the *Laender* governments to transfer the state railroads and the administration of income taxes to the federal government. He succeeded because in the non-Prussian *Laender* the railroads required large state subsidies and he made their being taken over by the federal government conditional on unification of income taxes and their administration.

It is difficult to explain why, despite his great ability and the excellence of many of his proposals, Erzberger was almost generally unsympathetic to his Cabinet colleagues and the bureaucratic staff. He knew of no humble reserve, was always "up ahead," a Jack of all trades, smilingly importunate, alternately aggressive and smooth, at times a little vulgar. But he was a passionate patriot and a man of great courage.

Once one of the most caustic and skilled public speakers in the National Assembly, the nationalist von Graefe, delivered a long, sarcastic attack on him, merciless, mocking, contemptuous, criticizing him for both political and personal reasons. While Graefe was speaking, many of the senior officials, who were standing around on the government platform, began to move away from Erzberger inconspicuously, and even his fellow ministers seemed to withdraw, so that finally he was completely isolated. Then he stood up to answer. He had a text prepared for a speech on financial and economic affairs. But he put his papers on one side and began with the surprising words: "Is that all?" and then moved at once to a counter-attack in such a skillful and destructive manner that an hour later the atmosphere in the hall had completely changed, before he turned to his prepared speech.

One evening, as we were standing in front of the palace four soldiers came riding along on horseback and shouted to the passers-by: "Where is Erzberger, the swine?" They rode into the palace courtyard and when they did not find Erzberger there, they rode out again, from hotel to hotel, looking for him. Erzberger escaped through a back door. At a Cabinet meeting he informed us pale-faced of some of the threatening letters he had received. Noske tried to reassure him goodnaturedly, telling of even more fearful letters he received regularly from Communists. That too was part of the atmosphere in Weimar. I shall return to Erzberger in Chapters 29 and 32.

## 27. LOOKING BACK AT LIFE IN WEIMAR

ON July 31 the National Assembly adopted the new Constitution by the large majority of 262 votes against only 75 (Nationalists, German People's Party, and Independent Socialists), and one abstention. On the same day the Cabinet submitted the White Paper which I had prepared on the events leading up to the armistice. These two actions set a positive and hopeful finale to the Weimar session for the friends of a democratic evolution—and they were, as figures show, at that time more than two-thirds of the members in parliament. At least they knew now according to what methods Germany was going to be governed, and they held in their hands the documentary evidence of how the collapse of the old regime had come about. Corrections of the Versailles Treaty were to be left to the future.

Before I leave my notes on Weimar, I would like to say a few words about the fascination which, despite all distress and humiliation, the place had for us. For four years we had scarcely been out of Berlin. The general misery and the frequent street fightings had made life more and more oppressive. Now we were moving around in the park and the castles of Weimar, during beautiful spring and summer days, walking between the houses of Goethe, Schiller, and Frau von Stein, and, when time allowed, through the woods and meadows, surrounded by the romantic memories of the beloved town. When I went home from work late at night I walked past fountains and we could hear the splashing of a fountain during the night.

Cooperation between officials and ministers and among the various ministries was evidently helped by the fact that only a small select group in a small area, where all distances could be easily walked, were working together on major problems, while the ministries in Berlin kept other members of their staffs ready to join the leading work-group for a longer or shorter period if called.

It was in Weimar that our friendship with Walter Gropius began, the designer of the Bauhaus, originally intended for Weimar. He was still married to Alma Mahler, widow of the great musician. To her Weimar was too provincial and Gropius, it seems, too earnest. But we shared his passion for serious enquiry and the boundlessness of the things with which he was concerned. The friendship with him and with his vivacious, intelligent, and charming second wife, Ilse, a cousin of Irmgard's on her father's side and known to Clara since childhood, continued and developed in the United States until his death in 1969.

In public affairs something seemed to be missing, something apt to fascinate, to give spiritual guidance, beyond the homely praise of democracy. I was thirsting for this "something." But in a coalition of Social Democrats, Liberals, and Catholic Zentrum the distinct ideologies of the partners made it difficult to develop creative leadership in government manifestoes beyond the repetition of general democratic ideals. Ebert was no spiritual leader, no Rathenau, no Heuss, and, of course, no Lenin. Nor did he want to be. He wanted to do good practical work, and this he did. That was good, very good in fact. But it aroused no great enthusiasm. Warm affection from the entire nation did not flare up immediately.

But then, why should all inspiring thoughts proceed from the government? Was not that an antediluvian, a pre-democratic way of thinking? *All* the minds of Germany were now free of the old bonds. Intellectual life flourished. Music and the theater, sculpture, architecture, all the arts, science, and journalism developed as never before. No one has described this better than Toni Stolper in her biography of the founder of the *Volkswirt,* Gustav Stolper.[1]

[1] Toni Stolper, *Ein Leben in Brennpunkten unserer Zeit, Wien, Berlin, New York, Gustav Stolper, 1888–1947,* Tübingen, 1960, pp. 211–13.

# PART VI
## The Loss of Pro-democratic Majorities

## 28. Vain Attempt to Escape Politics— Controversy with Ludendorff

Thus in August, 1919 we went on holiday, a peacetime holiday again at last. We hurried to Kampen on Sylt. After six years we longed to see again the beloved island which had been our summer paradise three times before. Kampen, however, was no longer as untouched as it had once been. On top of the Uwe-Dune there stood a concrete construction for a defense cannon; similar constructions along the coast continually brought the war to mind. The idyllic loneliness of the fishing village of List had been destroyed by the extension of the harbor for purposes of war.

And, then, the great world of politics caught up with us in Kampen, with the arrival of General Ludendorff's counter-declarations to the *Urkunden zur Vorgeschichte des Waffenstillstandes*. I replied in two articles, published in the *Norddeutsche Allgemeine Zeitung* (August 16 and 19, 1919). Ludendorff protested against what I had written at the end of the prefatory note on the great popularity of Woodrow Wilson in Germany at the end of the war. Ludendorff blamed the German people for admiring a foreign statesman and the government for mentioning it. But there were good reasons for this. First, it was in keeping with the truth. Second, it was to underscore the fact that the trust of the German people in Wilson's sincerity and dependability had formed the basis for the capitulation. When subsequent events showed that Wilson was not able to enforce his points, or did not want to, and that his constitutional power in the United States and his authority with the Allies were less than popular opinion in Germany had assumed, then his popularity soon vanished. It was followed by severe disenchantment, and finally by dislike that is still felt today. People tended to see a sanctimonius speech maker in Wilson, a weakling or liar. Thus they fell victim to the opposite mistake. For Wilson's honesty in the conception of his points seems to me well established; it was just his honest idealism which secured the great effect of his peace program.[1]

[1] For details see German edition.

## 29. A Winter of Unpleasantness—Kapp Putsch— Loss of the Democratic Majority (1919–1920)

THE head of government was now Gustav Bauer, no longer as Minister-President, but with the title of Chancellor. Following the almost elegant and by nature cheerful Scheidemann in office, Bauer was heavy, bull-necked, and slow. His views and decisions were reasonable. He strove hard to meet the strokes of fate and the need of constructive work confronting the government. Nonetheless his appointment revealed a notable lack in the new democracy of tested leaders of international stature.

At the end of September the National Assembly met again, no longer in Weimar but in the Reichstag building in Berlin, in order to attend to current work, until the right moment for new elections arrived. The parliamentary foundation of the government was strengthened by the return of the democrats, who had withdrawn during the Versailles negotiations.

At once the Allies began to apply the vise again. They forced withdrawal of Austria's admission to the Federal Council and assurances against any future union with Austria. They demanded immediate recall of regular troops and volunteers corps from the Baltic provinces. General Nollet moved into Berlin as chairman of the allied military commission.

The reawakening political right wing made ruthless use of the difficult situation. In addition to the main point of their attacks— the signing of the Treaty of Versailles—they based their political propaganda effectively on the accusation that the President and the National Assembly were illegally in office because the new Constitution gave the people the right to elections. Indeed, it could hardly be denied that the elections were being postponed because they would have given the opponents of democracy the opportunity to profit from the bitterness over the forced peace treaty. Time for a calming down was needed, in order to make it clear that it was not Germany's democratic reorganization but the previous lack of democracy that had led to the catastrophe; not the final discontinuance of the war but its outbreak and military loss; not omissions at the peace negotiations but the failure to begin them sooner.

A committee for investigation of the collapse had been set up by the National Assembly. Among those who during October and November appeared before this committee were the former Ambassador to the United States, Count Bernstorff; the former Chancellor, von Bethmann-Hollweg; the former Foreign Secretary, Zimmermann; the former Secretary of the Interior, Helfferich, and finally, on November 18, Hindenburg and Ludendorff. The large hall of the budget committee in the Reichstag building was packed to capacity at these hearings. Visitors were allowed to sit at the sides; behind me Karl Kautsky, the great Marxian theorist, was sitting with his wife, and we exchanged comments. Questions put to witnesses were often very cutting. The difference in type and character of the men who had once governed Germany and of the new parliamentarians was often strikingly revealed in demeanor and speech, especially when Social Democrat Dr. Sinzheimer, who conducted the hearings, put ever-more searching questions to Hindenburg and Ludendorff in his rather lisping and hissing voice. When the hearing adjourned and Hindenburg was given to understand that he need not come to the next session, he said: *"Ich werde doch meinen Kameraden nicht im Stich lassen"* (I just would not forsake my comrade). To judge from various indications, the hearings seemed to help the rightist opposition more than they did the new democracy.

The German troops in the Baltic provinces refused to comply with the order to leave. In view of the threats from the Entente to cut off all Germany's supplies of foodstuffs and raw materials, the government had to insist on withdrawal. It was finally decreed that all soldiers who had not returned by November 11 would be considered deserters. At the beginning of November new sanctions were imposed upon Germany for the scuttling of the fleet off Scapa Flow.

Several times Ebert was forced to make use of article 48 of the Constitution in order to maintain or reestablish order: for example, on January 11, 1920, during a large and hectic railroad strike in the Ruhr, and two days later in the whole of Northern Germany, because the Reichstag debates on workers' councils had occasioned serious excesses on the part of Communists and Independent Socialists demonstrating in front of the Reichstag building. When the crowds attempted to force their way into the building, the police shot.

There were some forty dead and over one hundred injured. Ebert transferred executive power in Berlin to Noske.

In January, 1920 Erzberger brought libel action against Helfferich, last Imperial Secretary of the Interior, now a German-Nationalist member of the Reichstag. Helfferich had in a series of articles in the conservative paper *Kreuzzeitung* under the heading "Erzberger Get Out"—they were also published in booklet form—directed serious personal accusations against Erzberger. They ended in the following provoking words:

"This is Herr Erzberger, who is charged on all sides with intentional deceits, not twice or three times, but ten and twenty times; who has to submit to the reproach that he dishonestly mixed political activities with personal financial interests; who does not answer all these accusations by bringing legal action, but shirks, and like a menaced cuttle-fish darkens the water, in order to escape. . . .

"This is Herr Erzberger, whose name appears rightly at the bottom of the miserable armistice agreement!

"This is Herr Erzberger, who helped the Entente during the armistice to gag us financially, who steered our merchant fleet into the harbors of the Entente!

"This is Herr Erzberger, who led us to Versailles, who made it clear to the enemy during the peace negotiations that he was prepared to sign this disgraceful, servile peace treaty (*Schand- und Knechtschaftsfrieden*) unconditionally, who, therefore, has the surrender of the Kaiser and other German men on his conscience, but who knew how to shirk signing the treaty in recognition of his work!

"This is Herr Erzberger, whose name will nevertheless always be connected irrevocably with Germany's misery and Germany's disgrace!

"This is Herr Erzberger who, if not finally stopped, will lead the German nation . . . to total destruction.

"There is, therefore, only one salvation for the German people. The country must be filled everywhere with the irresistible cry: 'Away with Erzberger!' (*Fort mit Erzberger!*)"

The criminal court in Moabit was dealing publicly with Erzberger's libel action for almost two months (January 19 until March 12). After the first week, a twenty-year-old highschool boy, a former ensign, fired two shots at Erzberger just as he was about to drive away in his car after the session. The first hit him in the shoulder; the second rebounded from his watch chain. The culprit, Oltwig von Hirschfeld, had been inspired by Helfferich's booklet to carry out his "act of riddance." Was that surprising? Was not Helfferich more responsible than Hirschfeld? The culprit was brought before a court in the middle of February and got away with eighteen months' imprisonment. Although the shot he had received in the shoulder was painful, Erzberger did not interrupt his many activities; day after day he hurried around from his Ministry to Cabinet sessions and to the court. Not until February 24, when his personal tax declaration had been stolen and published, did he take leave. Day after day the monstrous contentions in the trial brought against him, and indirectly against the government, filled the press in minute detail, including forty-two individual cases in which Erzberger was alleged to have mixed private business and politics, and numerous cases of perjury.

The verdict on March 12 imposed a fine of only three hundred marks on the accused Helfferich for libel. Unfair mixture of private business and politics was judged in 35 cases to be unproved, but proved in 7 cases, and perjury proved in 6 cases. Erzberger immediately requested legal proceedings against himself because of perjury. Investigation showed that the evidence was not sufficient to justify the commencement of a court case against him. But by then March had become June. A check of Erzberger's tax declaration showed that it had been returned in good faith. Thus, when the smoke had cleared, there remained only the political condemnation of his policy and the seven cases in which the court had seen mixing of private business and politics. Erzberger retreated and worked on his rehabilitation, based on the fact, confirmed by many persons, that he had acted quite openly with the intention of serving German interests, and never with malicious intent. But the first effect of the trial had been an immense outburst of feeling against democracy.[1]

In these same difficult months the Allies also presented their lists for extradition of "war criminals." France demanded over 300 and Great Britain 100 extraditions; Italy, Poland, and Rumania still others. The lists included the names of generals—Hindenburg, Ludendorff, and others (among them von Mackensen, von Kluck, von Falkenhayn, Hoffmann); admirals (von Tirpitz, von Scheer); Crown Prince Rupprecht of Bavaria and ex-Chancellor von Beth-

[1] For further details see Klaus Epstein, *Erzberger, op. cit.*

mann Hollweg. The chairman of the German peace commission, Baron von Lersner, who had stayed in Paris, was courageous enough to send the note back to Premier Millerand, along with the statement that it would be equivalent to aiding and abetting, if he were to accept the note and pass it on to the German government. At the same time he submitted his resignation. The French envoy then delivered the note to the German government in Berlin. The government declared that carrying out these extraditions was *impossible*. It offered to have judgment passed on alleged criminals by the German Supreme Court (*Reichsgericht*). The Allies took note of this offer and later presented a list of forty-six names of "selected war criminals," reserving to themselves the right to make further decisions according to the results.

These are but a few examples of the situation in which the democratic government found itself during that first winter after the conclusion of peace: enmity from without, enmity from within; humiliation upon humiliation; not a friend in the world offering assistance; on March 12, the catastrophic verdict in the Erzberger trial; on March 13, the explosion followed—the Kapp Putsch.

It is not correct to say, what has often been maintained and still is, that the government was completely surprised by the putsch. They knew, of course, that the nationalistic sections of the people were longing for action and that there was considerable unrest, especially among the army, which had already been reduced to 200,000 men, and was to be reduced still further, to 150,000 by October and 100,000 later. They also knew that this unrest had lately increased because of an order for the disbanding of the two marine brigades, one of which was in Döberitz close to Berlin under the command of Captain Ehrhardt. They knew that the division commander in Berlin, General von Lüttwitz, had refused to carry out this order; that he demanded removal of General Reinhardt, the army chief; and on top of that, influenced by the political opponents of the government—in particular by the former founder of the Fatherland Party, now director of an agricultural organization, Kapp—was even pressing political demands for speedy elections of a new President and of a new Reichstag. Kapp had personally submitted these demands to Ebert and Noske. But Noske believed any danger was banished for the time being. In a joint meeting with President Ebert he had rejected Lüttwitz' demands sharply and on March 11 relieved the general of his post; he had instructed the police to arrest Kapp, and also Captain Pabst, who was party to the plot. Admiral von Throta, the chief of the navy, whom he had sent to Döberitz—he had chosen this man because the disbanding of the marine brigade involved the navy—had made a reassuring report.

During the night of March 12/13 I was phoned in Steglitz at 3 a.m. from the Chancellery with the instruction that I should come to a suddenly summoned Cabinet Meeting. When I arrived, the meeting had just ended. Ebert and the ministers were coming down the stairs from the first floor. They had received news during the night that Ehrhardt's brigade was marching on Berlin. Two generals, sent by Noske to meet them, had brought back an ultimatum. When Noske asked the generals assembled around him to take military action, they had—with the single exception of General Reinhardt—advised against it, the reason being given by General von Seeckt: "The German army does not shoot at the German army" (*Reichswehr schiesst nicht auf Reichswehr*). At 7 a.m., if the ultimatum was not accepted, the rebels had said they would march in. Noske was willing to lie in waiting in the Tiergarten Park with a company and machine guns and start shooting when the rebels advanced, convinced that the whole nuisance would then be over. But the Cabinet had decided to withdraw to Dresden, so that they would not be taken prisoners and thus put out of action.

I was at first to remain behind with State Secretary Albert. Ulrich Rauscher, the government's press chief, in leaving the building with Ebert and the ministers, handed me a call for a general strike, at the bottom of which were, in his handwriting, the names of the Social Democrat members of the government, and asked me to pass it on to the press. I did so, and went to my office room.

Meantime the day began to dawn. It was a strangely ghostlike situation. I considered what I might do. I remembered how bare the first decrees of the People's Commissaries after the Revolution had looked without an authoritative official stamp. I therefore had all the metal stamps of the Chancellery brought to me and put them in my overcoat, in order to send them later to my brother Gustav's suburban apartment. At about 6:30 a.m. I phoned him. "Good morning, Gustav. I am at the Chancellery. In half an hour a putsch is going to take place. The ministers have left Berlin to organize resistance from outside. A call for a general strike has gone out. What would you do in my place during the next half hour?" He answered: "I don't know what you can do. But I do know what I'll do. I shall fill our bathtub with water." He knew from previous experience that the most unpleasant aspect of a strike was the breakdown of the water supply. In fact the filled bathtub did not help them, as the unsuspecting housemaid washed nappies in it.

Finally I went to the telephone exchange and told the girls working there to go home and not to come back until a week later. They asked if this holiday would be counted as part of their annual summer leave. "No," I said, "this is additional." When the revolt did collapse after a week and the office workers came back, they accredited supernatural powers to me for having predicted the time so exactly.

Another series of operetta-like situations followed. At seven three men entered the entrance hall. State Secretary Albert went to them. They asked him: "Are you the former State Secretary to the Chancellery?" He answered: "I am indeed the State Secretary to the Chancellery, not the former one, but the present one." He recommended that they take off their hats. One of them said apologetically they had thought this was only an anteroom. Albert still advised them to take off their hats, and they did. He recognized one of them, Herr von Falkenhausen. "We know each other," he said. There was a moment of silent consideration as to whether they ought under such circumstances to shake hands. They did not. Herr von Falkenhausen introduced the other two: Herr Kapp and Herr von Jagow, last imperial police-president of Berlin. Albert turned his back on them and went out through the garden to his residence, where we had agreed to meet later.

After a time another man with two soldiers carrying hand grenades came into my room. He asked: "Are you willing to work for the Chancellor?" I said, "I already do that." He looked at me, frowning: "I don't mean for the former Chancellor, but for Chancellor Kapp." I replied, "I know only Chancellor Bauer." He: "He has been deposed." I: "According to the Constitution he is the Chancellor. I have sworn an oath to uphold the Constitution, and I do not carry my oath in my hand as your men their hand grenades." He: "You also swore an oath to the Kaiser, yet worked for Ebert. So now you can work for us." I: "This error will be fatal for you. At that time the constitutional Chancellor, Prince Max, told us to work for Ebert just as we had worked for him. Ebert and Bauer have not asked me to work for you—quite the contrary." I put on my coat with the stamps in the pocket and left the building.

On the way to Potsdam Square I met the usual morning stream
of men and women hurrying to work, still ignorant of what had
happened. After discussing matters with Albert and other colleagues,
I went home, packed a few things in a bag, and drove to the Anhalt
station, the only one, strangely enough, which had not yet been
taken over by the rebels, and got onto a train to Dresden. There I
found Ebert, Noske, and other ministers in conference with General
Märcker, regional commander. Although Märcker was not willing
to work with Kapp, he was not prepared to back Ebert unconditionally. He offered his services to negotiate with Kapp, but Ebert
refused to give him official authority to do this.

Due to Märcker's equivocal position, the situation in Dresden did
not seem sufficiently secure. It was therefore decided to move on to
Stuttgart. We traveled by night on the scheduled train, sleeping in
our seats as best we could. Since the train went to Munich we had
to change early in the morning and wait for the train to Stuttgart.
While we were sipping coffee in the station restaurant, someone
said it would be fitting if a military unit were to receive us in Stuttgart, if possible with music. This suggestion was passed on to Stuttgart by telegram. Then someone asked: "Are we sure that the Stuttgart military units are loyal? That they won't simply take us prisoner—and on our own orders to meet us?" The telegram was canceled. We were met by the heads of the Württemberg state government without the military and music, but learned that the army in
Stuttgart had remained loyal. State and city government did everything possible to ensure a pleasant stay. Cabinet meetings were held
in the New Palace. I organized a sort of Chancellery and took part
in the meetings.

There were three main problems to be solved: first, finding out
which military units in Germany had remained loyal, which had
gone over to Kapp, and which were wavering, and how they could
be kept on our side; second, deciding whether we ought to negotiate with Kapp and whether the attempts being made in Berlin by
Minister Eugen Schiffer—a Democrat, who had stayed behind—to
persuade Kapp to step down by making certain concessions to him,
ought to be approved; and third, bringing the struggles which had
flared up, especially on the Ruhr, between Communists and the
army, to an end. All ministers agreed that there should be no negotiations with Kapp. In the Ruhr area Severing, who had been ap-

pointed Federal and Prussian State Commissioner, attempted to gain control of the situation.

Otto Meissner, who had just begun work in President Ebert's office and at first stayed behind in Berlin, joined us a few days later in Stuttgart. In order to get through with his official car, he had taken the precaution of obtaining letters of recommendation from both sides, producing either the one or the other, according to whether his car was stopped by supporters or opponents of the government. He once had the misfortune to submit his Kapp documents to the Communists. Only after long discussions did they let him go on.

After a few days Kapp had to admit defeat. The quick collapse of his putsch was due in equal measure to the shallowness of the whole venture, the resistance of the working classes, and the loyalty of most state secretaries in the federal and state ministries. These officials were not faced with the dilemma, as they were twelve years later under Papen's and Hitler's regimes, that the constitutional President himself had appointed the new Chancellor. On the contrary, the Kapp putsch was directed *against* the constitutional President. In both situations the majority of ministerial officials supported the President. In both the personal disparagement of the democratic ministers had found little response among senior officials, except in the case of Erzberger. Ebert, Noske, Otto Braun, Severing, and most of the other Federal and Prussian ministers rather enjoyed considerable personal prestige.

With the government's return to Berlin the consequences of the Kapp putsch were far from settled. The general strike had to be stopped. On March 20 representatives of the three Weimar parties came to terms with the strike leaders in Berlin, but only on condition that the Federal and the Prussian Government were to be reorganized "by arrangement with the labor unions" and that the public administration would be purged of democratically unreliable elements. Noske and the Prussian Minister of the Interior, Heine, were considered "untenable" by the labor unions, as well as by most of their party colleagues, including Scheidemann. They resigned. The unions also demanded that Schiffer be dismissed, because he had negotiated with Kapp supporters in Berlin.

Pacification on the Ruhr remained difficult. The loyal workers had risen against the commanding army officer there, General Watter. A "Red Army" had been formed, direction of which was soon taken over by Communists, and had gained control of Düsseldorf, Essen, Elberfeld, and other industry centers. Severing brought about an armistice, in accordance with which the "Red Army" was to be disarmed and disbanded, action by the regular army to be stopped, and amnesty promised. But the radicals rejected the agreement and called for continuation of the general strike. After a vain ultimatum from the government the army units attacked. A genuine civil war followed. Battles were fought; there were many dead on both sides. When the army penetrated into the 50-kilometer zone east of the Rhine, which had been forbidden in the peace treaty, French troops occupied Frankfurt and Darmstadt as a sanction, without consent of the other Allies.

On March 26 the Cabinet resigned. Bauer was replaced as Chancellor by the former Foreign Minister, Hermann Müller; Noske by Dr. Gessler, a Democrat. The new Cabinet stayed in office for barely three months. After the elections, held on June 6, 1920, it was replaced by another one without Social Democrats. In these elections the three parties of the Weimar coalition not only lost their old two-thirds majority, but even the simple majority their predecessors had had in the imperial era. Seats held by Social Democrats dropped from 163 to 113; those held by the Democrats from 75 to 45; those of the Zentrum (chiefly due to the breakaway of the Bavarian People's Party) from 91 to 69. This left these three parties a total of 227 out of 466 seats, that is, a *minority*. The Independent Socialists, on the other hand, went up from 22 to 81; the German People's Party (national-liberal) from 22 to 62; and the German Nationalists from 42 to 66. The Weimar democracy had been dealt its mortal wound, a wound which would not necessarily be fatal to absolute monarchies, to dictatorships, or aristocracies, but which affects a democracy's very core: *loss of majority* in its support.

## 30. Reflections on the Loss of a Pro-Democratic Majority Under a Democratic Constitution

I shall proceed from the banal truth with which I closed the preceding chapter—that an autocratic form of government need not be in danger solely on the ground that it is supported by only a minority of the people. This is indisputable both logically and historically. Absolute monarchies, constitutional monarchies, aristocracies, and other varieties of oligarchic forms of government have often been able to maintain themselves for a long time irrespective of the wishes of the broad masses. The world has seen not only bad autocratic rulers, but occasionally good ones, who in opposition to the momentary desires of the masses led them successfully through times of crisis. These heroic autocrats were the favorite theme of German schoolteachers and the objects of their pupil's romantic hero worship. The longing for such leaders has been rooted in the German people longer and deeper, and the risks involved less feared, than in other western nations, thanks to the successes of such bold leaders as Frederick the Great and Bismarck. It is all the more important, therefore, to be soberly aware of the fact that under a democratic constitution this longing for strong leadership, even in the absence of popular support, can be legitimately satisfied either not at all or only temporarily and tentatively—until the next popular election. A democratic government needs the support of the people both in good and bad times. It may not offend certain basic principles of its citizens, even if the majority is prepared to give their approval.

For democracy to function properly it is a necessary condition that a broad majority of the people appreciate democratic ideals and earnestly want to see democratic rules of the game obeyed, whether out of romantic enthusiasm for the will of the people, or because of a firmly held trust in the ultimate wisdom of the common man in fundamental questions of policy,[1] or simply out of fear that uncontrolled autocratic power will be misused. But democratic reality can be far from satisfying this postulate of basic popular support. Circumstances can be such that the majority of the people living under a democratic constitution would prefer an autocratic form of government, either because of a romantic desire for hero worship and for subordination to leadership, or because of the entirely unromantic, purely egoistic-realistic hope that the holders of autocratic power will do just what people want to be done in their own interest. When the *majority* of a country's population thinks like this, then that country has in fact a non-democratic majority.

One might perhaps object that logically there could not be non-

---

[1] See the fine study by Carl J. Friedrich, *The New Belief in the Common Man*, Boston, 1941.

democratic majorities, because democracy means government by the majority or in accordance with its wishes; and if the majority wants to have an autocratic regime (monarchy, dictatorship, or the like), then that type of government is democratic and so remains as long as that is what the majority wants. Seen in this light, the rule of the Roman Emperor Augustus, of the English Queen Elisabeth I, or of Prussian kings like Frederick the Great and Wilhelm I, at the peak of their success, was truly democratic, and likewise the reign of Louis XIV, Napoleon I, and even of Hitler, at the height of their popularity. Communist domination, too, whenever it is approved by the majority of the nation, would then be democratic.

As I said before (Chapter 23), there is no compelling scientific reason why the word "democracy" should not be used in this sense, except that using it thus contradicts the general usage in western countries up to the twentieth century, and that it would then not connote a distinct form of government. In this book I am using the term in its modern western sense, so as to connote a form of government in which both legislation and administration are subject to the control by the majority of the people and, in addition, certain basic rights and the independence of the courts are respected. Seen from this use of the term, a majority which opposes those three basic principles, or even only one of them, is "non-democratic" or "anti-democratic."

Non-democratic majorities may not be in a position without violence to overthrow the existing democratic constitution, because formal alterations of the constitution require larger majorities than are at their disposal, or because they are in disagreement among themselves on the alterations desired. It may then seem superficially that democracies can be maintained without majority support over long periods of time, just as autocracies. It may even happen that democratic-minded men can stay in office despite the anti-democratic majority, alone or in mixed cabinets, because the anti-democratic sections of the community cannot agree on how to fill the posts otherwise. All this was the case in Germany between 1920 and 1932. Notwithstanding these external experiences, however, the loss of pro-democratic majorities sounds the death knell of living democracy. Democracy can only have a hollow existence thereafter, because the apparently democratic cabinets cannot pursue a consistent democratic policy, either in legislation or in administration—

for example, in appointing generals and high officials. They will be overthrown when they challenge the majority.

The problematic character of a democracy in the face of anti-democratic majorities is intensified when public opinion is not only divided on the desirability of the democratic form of government but also of its republican (non-monarchic) basis.[2] For then there are four possible combinations of political ideals, all of which had considerable backing in Germany at that time. First, the combination of pro-democratic and pro-republican tendencies, characteristic of Social Democrats and Democrats, and after the revolution predominant also in the Zentrum. Second, the combination of anti-democratic and anti-republican feelings, characteristic at that time of the German Nationalists, and of most members of the German People's Party. Third, pro-democratic tendencies combined with anti-republican (monarchic) views, as in the remainder of the German People's Party and in the Bavarian People's Party; this opinion could also be found "subcutaneously" in the Zentrum. Fourth, pro-republican but anti-democratic views, the combination characteristic of both Communists and National Socialists.

The important fact here is that after 1920 there was no majority any longer in Germany for democracy, at least not for its republican type. Even so there could still be constitutional governments, of course, backed by parliamentary majorities, but none that could pursue a consistent democratic-republican policy, and no genuinely democratic style of government. This lack of a pro-democratic majority was the fatal worm, the disease that led to death. The amazing thing indeed is not that the democratic constitution in Germany collapsed thirteen years later, but that it did not do so much sooner. Until the end of the republic the three Weimar coalition parties were never able to regain their lost majority in the Reichstag. Only once did they come near it, in the elections of 1928, when they lacked only seven seats for a majority.

The main reason for democracy's survival, in form at least, was that the undemocratic majority was split into two antagonistic parts, neither of which alone had an absolute majority—the rightist parties and the Communists. The Communists always gained more seats than either the Weimar coalition or the Right needed for an

---

[2] The term "republican" is used here in its European sense of a state not headed by a hereditary monarch.

absolute majority. Coalition with the Communists was impossible not only for the Right, but also for the parties of the Weimar coalition. Even if the Social Democrats had been ready for this, as in fact some of them were, the Democrats and the Zentrum were not; and Social Democrats and Communists alone, singly or together, never had a majority in the Reichstag.

Therefore only two possibilities remained. Either a minority government could be formed, which might be overthrown at any time, or a majority government in coalition between pro-democratic and anti-democratic parties, which would suffer from internal weakness and at any rate would be unable to agree on a clearly pro-democratic policy. Both alternatives were tried in turn. During the twelve years from 1920 until 1932 there were minority cabinets for a total period of eight years, i.e., for two-thirds of the time—in fact eleven of them. Most of them included the German People's Party, which, although its leader Gustav Stresemann was coming ever closer to democracy and republicanism, was nonetheless on the whole more in sympathy with the Right. Only during one-third of the total period, for four and a half years, was the other alternative realized: the forming of a so-called "Grand Coalition," backed by a parliamentary *majority*. For this purpose either the German People's Party had to join hands in a cabinet with the Social Democrats (that is to say, the anti-democratic advocates of capitalism with the pro-democratic and anti-capitalist Socialists) or the Social Democrats remained excluded. Then the pro-democratic Catholic Zentrum had to work not only with the People's Party but also with the German Nationalists (without them there would have been no majority), who were radically monarchist and anti-democratic and, in addition, basically anti-Catholic. Both of these combinations were tried twice. Socialists and anti-Socialists were together in the Cabinets of Stresemann (August-November, 1923) and of Hermann Müller (June, 1928 until March, 1930). Democratic Catholics and anti-democratic, nationalistic Protestants were together in the Cabinets of Luther (January-December, 1925) and of Marx (January, 1927 until June, 1928). Despite their large majorities these four cabinets were intrinsically weak because of the fundamentally different opinions represented in them.

The Weimar democracy has often been criticized for the weakness of its statesmen; it has been widely scoffed at on this account. It has rarely been seen that any statesman who was willing to act in accordance with the rules of democracy was *bound* to be weak because of the missing pro-democratic majority, however great his talents for leadership might have been and however strong he might have been under other circumstances. Stresemann is a good example of this. He grew to be a strong personality, capable of leadership, as strong as any party leader can be in a democratic country. But how could he make full use of this strength, even as a member of majority cabinets, when the majorities were so precarious, so badly unified, that he literally consumed the major part of his strength in quarrels with his own party and with his coalition partners, merely to keep the majority together? If the "strong" man was not willing to break away from constitutional ties and from the democratic rules of the game, then he could not help but be politically "weak" due to the manifold divisions of the German nation at that time. No Roosevelt, either Theodore or Franklin, no Churchill, no Lloyd George, no Poincaré or Clemenceau, no Kennedy would have been able to lead such a democracy forcefully unless they overstepped the limits laid down in the constitution.

The reproach that the democratic parties failed to establish true democracy while they were in power is least justified when directed at the Social Democrats, since during the thirteen years from the spring of 1920 until the spring of 1933 they shared power in federal cabinets for only a little over three years and that in disconnected periods (May, 1921 until November, 1922; three months in 1923; and after that not again until 1928–1930), and chiefly in coalition with anti-republican parties. The rightist German People's Party, on the other hand, was represented in the federal cabinets without a break from 1922 until the end, and even the German Nationalists shared the power for three and a half years (January, 1925 until January, 1926; January, 1927 until June, 1928; and then again from May, 1932 on). As regards the preceding period from November, 1918 until the elections in June, 1920, the points that must be taken into consideration in historical judgment have been discussed at length in previous chapters.

There remain two questions. The first is: What could have been done, and who could have done it, to make a majority out of the democratic-republican minority? For the reasons here discussed it would be entirely beside the point, however, to answer this question with the usual cheap recommendation of pertinent pro-democratic measures the Cabinets should have taken, measures that would have required pro-democratic majorities backing the government to be resolved upon and carried out. Nor is it fair to reproach the pro-democratic minority—as has often been done abroad—for not being a majority without saying how it might have become one, or even to reproach the monarchists for being monarchists. There is no "guilt" attached to the fact that after a centuries-long tradition of monarchic regimes, approximately half a nation continues to harbor monarchist sentiments for a time, as the masses in England, the Netherlands, Belgium, Denmark, Sweden, and Norway do up to the present day, and as the majority of the people did even in France after the downfall of the Second Empire until 1876 or longer. A political scientist who complains that there were supporters of the monarchy after the revolution had better change his profession. Some great inspiring leader of democratic convictions could perhaps have achieved a sufficient increase in pro-democratic votes with sympathetic moral support from abroad; but split up in many groups as the German nation was, suffering from humiliations inflicted from abroad, from the terrors of inflation before 1924 and from unemployment after 1929, the task of a democratic leader wanting to strengthen pro-democracy feelings against detractors on the left and the right, without support either from the government or from abroad, was extraordinarily difficult.

The second question for political research is: What should and can a republican-democratic minority do under a democratic constitution, when it is *unable* to obtain a majority? Must it stick to the majority principle even when the majority is aggressively anti-democratic? Or ought it, since in the absence of a democratic majority no true democracy is possible, to seize the initiative in good time in order to substitute the *next-best* system of government, before its opponents have an opportunity to use their majority in a mock-democratic procedure in order to establish what is from the democratic point of view the *worst* type of government?

The classic principle that democracy is government "by the people" or at least in accordance with the wishes of "the majority of the people," was wisely modified in the Bonn constitution (*Grundgesetz*) of 1949 by articles which tend to ensure that the *parliamentary* majority will remain pro-democratic even if the majority of the *people* should once again fall for undemocratic ideas. To this end the Bonn Basic Law forbids advocating anti-democratic objectives in elections and threatens parties who infringe this rule with dissolution. Furthermore, basic rights were increased and some of them exempted from change even by alteration of the Constitution. Had these principles been in force in the Weimar period, the collapse of decent government might well have been averted. But how would it have been possible to enact these modifications at a time when even simple majorities in favor of democracy were lacking, not to speak of the two-thirds majority required for constitutional amendments?

What else could have been done? *Both German and foreign political scientists have been sadly silent on this question.* When expert advice was desperately needed, it was not offered either at home or from abroad. These problems will be discussed more concretely in Chapters 64, 73, 85, 86 and 93.

## 31. The First Cabinet Without Socialists (1920)

The defeat of the Weimar coalition in the elections of June, 1920 led to long and difficult negotiations among the political parties. Since neither the Weimar coalition partners nor the parties to their right had a majority backing them, a minority government, wholly middle-class ("bourgeois"), was finally formed, of Zentrum, Democrats, and the German People's Party, headed by Constantin Fehrenbach (Zentrum) as Chancellor. Wirth and Gessler kept the Ministries of Finance and Defense they had received after the Kapp Putsch; Dr. Simons became Foreign Minister; three members of the People's Party took over the Ministries of Justice, Economics, and the Treasury, and General Groener the Ministry of Transport.

Thus, less than a year after the birth of the Weimar Constitution, a totally changed constellation had emerged, which no one would have considered possible even a few weeks before: the Social Democrats had been excluded from the Federal Cabinet and the rightist German People's Party had taken their place. There still were two important connecting links with the Social Democrats. Ebert remained President. Although he himself pressed for the calling of presidential elections, the new Cabinet, like the preceding one, did not yet want to take this step. They had confidence in Ebert, did not consider a presidential election to be advisable before the referendum in Upper Silesia, and in any case feared only difficulties from national elections at this moment. Besides this, the Social Democrats remained in the lead on the other side of the Wilhelmstrasse, in the Prussian government. Law courts, police, schools, and municipal affairs were controlled by the individual *Laender* under the Weimar Constitution. Hence close cooperation with the Social Democrats continued to be necessary in the overall administration of Germany.

In Prussia, in contrast to the Reich, the parties of the Weimar coalition had maintained a majority in the June elections of 1920. It thus became evident that in this state, which had for so long been decried as particularly reactionary and where until 1919 under the three-class franchise the left wing had only weak representation in the chamber of deputies, the pro-democratic parties had a higher percentage of supporters than in Germany as a whole. The democratic percentage in the whole of Germany was lower because in a series of the non-Prussian *Laender* anti-democratic or anti-republican sentiments were more strongly represented than on the average in Prussia. Such was the case in the second largest land, Bavaria, because the Bavarian Catholics had remained loyal to the king and were outright anti-Social Democrat. The Bavarian members split off from the national Zentrum Party in 1920 and founded a party of their own, the Bavarian People's Party, which upheld the monarchist tradition and refused to form cabinets with the Social Democrats, at least unless right-wing parties participated. In Saxony, Thuringia, and Mecklenburg, and later (after 1930) in Braunschweig and Oldenburg, relatively more votes were cast for right-wing parties than in Prussia; other *Laender,* such as Hamburg, had a larger percentage of Communist voters, and in two (Saxony and Thuringia) both the Communists and the Right were stronger than in Prussia. Of course, the share of votes for the Right was very high in *some parts* of Prussia, too—in Pomerania, East Prussia, and Schleswig-Holstein for example—and in other areas, such as Berlin and the Ruhr, the Communist figures were very high. But Prussia, taken as a whole, had proportionally more democratic voters than Germany as a whole. Even under the terrorist pressure in the Hitler elections on March 5, 1933 the nationalistic parties (National Socialists plus German Nationalists) were not able to obtain an absolute majority in seven Prussian constituencies (Berlin, Cologne, Trier, Düsseldorf West and East, Westfalia North and South).

Thus it came about that the Weimar coalition parties kept their majority in the Prussian Landtag from 1920 until 1924 and again from 1928 until 1932. In the years between 1924 until 1928 they lacked only four seats for a majority, a deficiency which could be made up by support from smaller parties. They were therefore able in Prussia to stay in government until the end of the republic. After the Kapp Putsch (1920) Otto Braun, formerly Minister of Agriculture, had taken over the leadership of the Cabinet. He continued as Minister-President until 1933, except for a few months in the years 1921 and 1925.

But back now to the national government. In Constantin Fehrenbach, for the first time since the Revolution, a dignified elderly man —he was close to seventy—was again at the head of the government. He had been a member of the Reichstag since 1903 (when I was still a young student in Bonn), also a member of the Baden lower house, where he had moved up to the position of president; he had become chairman of the Reichstag budget committee at the end of the war, and later president of the National Assembly in Weimar. He enjoyed respect and human confidence from all sides, including his political opponents. But he did not radiate great creative energy. My friend Fehling said he looked like the "widower of Germania."

Noske's brusque departure had occasioned Gessler's selection for the post of Minister of Defense during a momentary dilemma; but now he was being firmly established there. As lord mayor of Nuremberg he had shown liberal opinions, a talent for administration, and amiable power of persuasion. It was hoped that these abilities would have a soothing effect on the internal struggles about the army. But Gessler had no gifts which impressed soldiers: neither the soldierly disposition of a Noske nor the mental superiority of the born statesman. His amiable persuasive powers were not sufficient to inspire the army with the spirit of democracy. On the contrary, his military subordinates—in particular General von Seeckt and Major von Schleicher, who was soon promoted to colonel and major general—took advantage of Gessler's good nature to have him represent the interests of the army, as they interpreted them, in the Cabinet and in the Reichstag. They needed a go-between for this, because General von Seeckt, although his conduct in Cabinet meetings was always obliging and neither arrogant nor aggressive— he sometimes showed great personal charm—quite unmistakably adhered to the old Prussian military ideals, which had developed in the officers corps from the time of Frederick-Wilhelm and his son Frederick the Great down until Moltke. No one who had ever seen this slightly built, elegant but strict officer, with his enormous monocle, stride along in front of a line of soldiers, alone, slowly, or who read his book on Moltke,[1] could be in doubt about this. They were lofty ideals, ideals of unconditional devotion to duty and ascetic self-control; I have always been far from mocking them. But they were ideals of another time, closely tied to concepts of an officers' caste that had no close contact with ordinary people beyond the barrack yard. Seeckt's manner of speaking, for all his obligingness, was militarily brief, precise, authoritative.

Gessler attempted to translate the military points of view into normal German, speaking coaxingly and sensibly. He did this, in contrast to Noske, in a completely unmilitary fashion. But he remained dependent upon the generals; as a rule he could go only so far as they would let him. The army (Reichswehr) was behind General von Seeckt and Hindenburg, not behind Gessler. It could not be otherwise, unless it was fundamentally reorganized. Gessler apparently did not seriously think of doing this, neither in matters of principles nor in the selection of personnel, with the exception of his determined dismissal of Seeckt for a special reason (Chapter 56). But even if he had wanted such reforms, how could he have carried them out with no democratic-republican majority in the nation to back him? I spoke about this at length in the preceding chapter and will not repeat myself here.

## 32. HISTORICAL TURNING POINTS—MEETINGS WITH PÖHNER, HITLER, PACELLI (1920, 1921)

A LONG series of conferences, concerned with the disarmament of Germany, which had been stipulated in the peace treaty, and the fixation of the war reparations to be paid by Germany, which had been left open in the peace treaty, began in July, 1920 in Spa. Dr. Simons, as Minister for Foreign Affairs, together with Chancellor Fehrenbach and others, now represented the Reich. Germany's re-

---

[1] *Moltke, ein Vorbild* (Moltke, a model), Berlin, 1931.

quest for permission to maintain an army of 200,000 was rejected and the deadline for the reduction to 100,000 merely deferred until January 1, 1921, on condition that the so-called *Bürgerwehren* (citizens' guards) be disbanded and the civilian population disarmed without delay. The German government accepted this condition for better or worse, supported in its decision by an ample majority of the Reichstag, and a law on the disarming of the population was passed in August.

But the decision was difficult to put into effect, especially in Bavaria. Here a former forestry ranger, Escherich, had founded an organization combined from various self-defense groups, called "Organization Escherich" (*Orgesch*). Outside Bavaria the organization was not recognized by the *Laender* governments, and in Prussia it was banned by Severing, but it flourished unhindered in Bavaria. The federal government decided not to allow this organization any special treatment in the disarmament law. At the end of the year a French note accused Germany of not having fulfilled the Spa provision on disarmament. An Allied conference in Paris at the end of January, 1921 confronted Germany with an ultimatum, according to which failure to comply by July 1 would result in the occupation of further German territory and the extension of the occupation of the Rhineland. The German government wanted to carry out the disarmament; the Bavarian government demanded its being rejected, but admitted that the decision was up to the national government.

Under these conditions Chancellor Fehrenbach sent me to Munich in February, 1921 for on-the-spot inquiries. In Munich I was advised by the excellent Prussian envoy there, Count Zech, son-in-law of Bethmann Hollweg, who introduced me to various officials. I made use of these introductions, but at the same time went my own way. I visited an old school friend from Lübeck, the sculptor Fritz Behn, a few years older than I and a well-known member of the *Ordnungsblock* (Block of Public Order) in Munich. My arguments impressed him, and he suggested putting me in contact with two people, whose names were to play an important role later: Chief of Police Ernst Pöhner and the leader of a newly formed radical group, by the name of Adolf Hitler.

We drove to the police headquarters and were immediately received by Pöhner in his office. I told him that my visit was not official, that it originated at Behn's initiative. I wanted to gain infor-

mation from people who really knew the situation in Bavaria and
to separate mere misunderstandings from real differences of views
between Berlin and Munich. He declared, somewhat hesitantly at
first, that such an attempt could only please him and that in his
opinion better information in Berlin on the atmosphere in Munich
was greatly desired. According to the notes I made immediately afterward, the conversation then went on as follows:

PÖHNER: "First of all, in Munich we have a government, and in
Berlin there is no government. That's not really a government, is
it? We would go through fire and water for Kahr; we would die
for him, all of us, to the last man. But who would die for Ebert or
for Fehrenbach or for Gessler; I don't even know the names of all
these no-bodies, I think one is called Schiffer. Gessler Minister of
Defense! *He* Minister of Defense! We can only laugh at that. I'll
tell you what people here think of him. When he was here, a captain on active service stood up and left. 'You can't sit at the same
table as Gessler,' he said to the man next to him. Gessler didn't notice that. In Berlin you are all ruled by the law of the street. There
aren't men in the government there, just cowards. You allow people
to be stirred up and thus prevent unity."

I: "You are apparently not as well informed on the situation in
Berlin as on that in Bavaria. Berlin is indeed a working-class city.
But since the split of the Independents, there has been no more terror in the streets. The present national government has no Socialists.
Foreign Minister Simons is an upright man. He opposed the signing of the Treaty of Versailles and is to throw the weight of his
good name into the scales when it becomes necessary to resist. But
the time has to be decided by the government of the Reich. In their
opinion *today* is not the right time."

PÖHNER: "Right now is the time. We submitted in Versailles and
Spa; now we cannot do that any longer. They are going to march
into the Ruhr anyway. You're saying that the working classes
would not fully cooperate in a resistance now? That is typical of
the damned double-dealing mentality of all red dogs and democrats."

I: "But that is a fact you cannot change from one day to the
next."

PÖHNER: "Of course it can be changed. Only the Berlin government is to blame. They need a few people with a determined will.
Here you can see what can be done then. Anyone who contradicts

must be shot, not the masses, but the leaders. Then the refusal comes to an end. When it comes to the point, there are not five people who—with a pistol sticking in their chests—are willing to die. When your Berlin government wants to end a big strike, what do they do? They negotiate! That's got to be changed. The leaders are to be summoned to a discussion and told that work has to start again the following morning. If the first one says no, you shoot him and ask the second one. If he says no, you shoot him too. The third then says yes. Then you have a total of two dead; with your methods of negotiation there are battles which last for weeks and thousands are dead. But you've got to shoot, not just make threats. When we stepped in to end the Communist terror here, we had these red dogs shot. Don't hesitate for long. I have taught my wife to use a gun and a pistol. When we men fail, the women have to step in. If a red dog comes, she must be able to shoot. All of us think like that. I am a simple member of the citizens' guard. In the citizens' guard a simple sergeant is my superior. I do my duty. I have five guns and a pistol at home."

I: "Hand over some guns by March 30; then we'll be quits for a few months."

PÖHNER: "Never. I put a bullet through the head of any red dog who comes to take my gun away. If you get Herr von Kahr drunk in Berlin, so that he agrees—I'm just saying that, it's impossible that he will—then men from the Chiemsee and from the Allgäu [Bavarian mountain side], etc., will march in on the same day and occupy Munich. That will happen quite automatically. Then they'll ask everyone: 'Are you for Kahr?' And anyone who doesn't say yes will be shot. We aren't particularists. The whole of Germany would think the same way, if there were a *government* in Berlin."

I: "You can't change the government in Berlin to your own measure either legally or illegally in these weeks. Stresemann and the German People's Party are behind the government. Your resistance is limited to Bavaria alone, a local, not a German movement. Go to Berlin, try and change the minds of the national government and the Reichstag; but if you don't succeed, what then?"

PÖHNER: "The Bavarian government must and will say no. You won't get any guns here. The Ruhr and Poland—all that is irrelevant. I prefer the Communists to have the guns rather than the French. Then you can get them back at the right moment; otherwise they've gone forever. When we've handed over all our weapons, then an attack will be just like taking a walk. Then they haven't got anything to be afraid of. That's what they want."

I: "Individual Bavarians could state their 'no' at meetings, but not the Bavarian government and official authorities. Otherwise they are responsible for serious consequences."

PÖHNER: "The Reich alone is responsible, if they don't go along. The legal situation is completely irrelevant, what matters is the *cause* (*die Sache*)."

I: "The Bavarian citizens' corps won't defend either the Ruhr area or Upper Silesia."

PÖHNER: "Volunteer corps will come up. In addition to that you can call up the regular army. That is a matter not for careful consideration but for impulse and passion. We have to say 'Never' at last. If the Entente attacks in the west, we shall have to invade Poland or Czechoslovakia, burn everything down, take hostages, etc. That's how it is done. It is a great mistake to think that the splitting up of the Independents makes things easier. Now the Communists have the resolute people all together. That's what is important, not the masses. The revolution has shown the value of personality once again."

So much for my notes. When Pöhner said at the beginning that everyone in Bavaria was ready to die for Kahr, but who was prepared to die for Ebert? he added: "Would you die for Ebert?" I answered: "That is the wrong question to put to a republican. A republican dies for a cause (*eine Sache*), not for a person." To which he replied: "That's just the point. You can die only for a *person.*" But two years later, after Hitler's beer-cellar putsch, Pöhner was far from ready to die for Kahr; on the contrary, he and Hitler rebelled against Kahr. In the trial that followed, he mentioned a visit from a "Berlin *Geheimrat*" who had said that he would be prepared to die for a "cause" but not for a "person," and that he had answered that one could die only for a person. He forgot that he had boasted he would die for Kahr.

This visit to Pöhner gave me more insight than all other discussions and inquiries could have. Pöhner was not just any one; he was the chief of police in Munich, the man who would have to enforce the disarmament. When we had left his office, Behn said to me: "Now you must come with me to see Hitler." I did know the name; it had been mentioned occasionally in reports on riots in Munich. But who was Hitler at that time? Less than eighteen months before he had joined, as the seventh member, the organizing body of a group he himself had thought half ludicrous, a group then called the "German Workers' Party," which aspired to a blend of Socialist and Nationalist goals and in which a locksmith (Anton Drexler), a poet and drunkard (Dietrich Eckart), a homosexual captain (Ernst Röhm), and a utopian economic theorist (Feder), played leading roles. About a year before my visit Hitler had taken over propaganda in this group, had drawn up a program of twenty-five points with Drexler and Feder, and had read it at a large meeting in the Hofbräuhaus, famous Munich beer cellar. Only a few months before my visit the party had been renamed the "National Socialist German Workers' Party," and Hitler had introduced the party badges—swastika, armband, standard. This was as far as he had gotten; he was not yet even the leader of the little group. He did not become the leader until half a year later, when he crushed the first revolt against himself by demanding "the dictatorial power of Führer" and threatening otherwise to resign. That was still part of the future; two and a half years in the future was his putsch in the Bürgerbräu cellar in November, 1923, which made him the center of world attention and resulted in his and Pöhner's arrest by Herr von Kahr. The man we visited was rather anonymous, still a little man, a rioter and mob orator, momentarily of interest to me because of my general interest in all such groups, in Munich local color, and because of the radical attitude of his men in national questions, which differed from that of other Munich circles. They condemned Bavarian particularism and called for strong German unity.

Behn took me to the Sterneckerbräu, another beer cellar, into a small, dark room at the rear, where four men were sitting around a table, putting leaflets into envelopes. One was Hitler. I spoke just as I had to Pöhner. The men raised a few of the usual objections, but not with anything like the degree of passion I had heard from Pöhner. They wore no guns, so they were possibly not quite displeased to see rival groups disarmed. My visit may have flattered them because they were not used to such attention. I cannot even remember what Hitler himself said. In any case it did not impress me. I cannot claim to have recognized his future significance.

On the same, or preceding, evening I met a man who impressed me more. Count Zech had arranged for me to visit Nuntius Eugene

Pacelli, who was later to go to Berlin and eventually to become Pope Pius XII. He received me in an ascetically bare room; the only picture in it was a simple photograph of his parents. It was nine o'clock in the evening and we spoke for an hour. I told him frankly why I had come to Munich. He asked me to understand the point of view of the Munich people, who had experienced the leftist council government and their shooting of bourgeois hostages. He took me to the window and showed me the marks of shots from that time. It was understandable, he said, that the orderly citizens of Munich did not want to hand over all their weapons, because that would leave them vulnerable to similar acts of violence; for the Communists would certainly know ways of keeping or getting weapons. He brought the conversation around to the question of reparations and strongly recommended that the government make larger payments. In the usual fashion I listed the number of things that had already been accomplished and assured him that the government intended well. He spoke with marked respect of the members of the present Cabinet.

It was not so much the content of the conversation as the personality of Pacelli that made such a lasting impression, which was intensified by later meetings in Berlin. In the summer of the same year (1921) Joseph Wirth, then Chancellor, and I as the acting chief of the Chancellery were guests of Pacelli at a small luncheon in the Hotel Kaiserhof and later were invited with a group of some twenty statesmen and church dignitaries to another Berlin hotel. The dignity and friendliness, at once ascetic and elegant, with which he received his guests and then took them with inimitable grace of bearing and gait past the band playing jazz, past the shoes, big and small, placed outside rooms in the corridors, along to his suite, took the whole company out of the all-too-human surroundings. Everywhere he went was holy. Another time I met him on the top floor of the Vox House in Potsdamer Strasse, where he, Ebert's secretary Meissner, and I had been invited to one of the first radio tryouts. I was at the time head of the division in the Ministry of the Interior which was in charge of radio affairs, and I listened, absorbed, to this new technical wonder. When we got up, Pacelli said to me quietly but urgently: "But *what* will the people be told by means of this new medium?" I have never forgotten that.

I saw him last at Ebert's funeral in February, 1925. In the black-draped room on the first floor of the President's palace he was sitting as doyen of the diplomatic corps in the first row in front of the catafalque. When the ceremony was over and everyone was going out, he stepped up in front of the coffin and opened his robe with a gesture that seemed to indicate that he was taking the son of the Church, who no longer had been a member, back into the Church in grace—it was a silent scene in the almost deserted room; then he walked out.

When Lloyd George reproached Germany at one of the international conferences for the delay in disarming Bavaria, Simons said he had heard that the oldest parliamentary government in the world, the government of a victorious country at the height of its powers, was having difficulties in carrying out its policy in one section of its territory (Ireland). He asked the Allied statesmen to have some sympathy when a young democracy in a weak, defeated country was not able to carry out its intentions in one part of the country as quickly as it wished. But the Allies remained inexorable, with no consideration for the psychological consequences of constant humiliations for the reputation of democracy in Germany.

## 33. FIGURES DIFFICULT TO UNDERSTAND

NOT only German disarmament but also the problem of reparations had reached a new phase in Spa. The German Minister of Finance, Dr. Wirth, suggested a fixed minimal sum to be paid annually for about thirty years, and in addition to this an amount according to an economic welfare index to be agreed upon, up to a maximal grand total. The matter was postponed until a later conference. The Allies agreed among themselves in Paris in January, 1921 to ask for forty-two annual payments, to amount to 2 billion marks in gold annually for the first two years, 3 billion for the next three, 4 billion for a further three years, then 5 billion for three more, and finally 6 billion for thirty-one years annually, in addition to which there was to be an export tax of 12 percent. Germany was to give her consent to this at a conference on March 1 in London.

Foreign Minister Simons rejected the Paris decisions and made counter-suggestions. He estimated the current value of the payments demanded by the Allies at 50 billion gold-marks, from which 20 billion were to be deducted for payments already made. The remaining 30 billion were to be covered by international loans on which Germany was to pay interest. In addition, Germany was willing to pay 1 billion gold-marks for five years, chiefly by payment in kind and reconstruction work in the areas which had been destroyed.

Lloyd George rejected these suggestions abruptly. Simons finally proposed a provisional arrangement, under which Germany was to pay the fixed yearly amounts asked for by the Allies for five years (2 and 3 billion per year respectively) and an equivalent for the required export charge, assuming that the imminent referendum in Upper Silesia would turn out favorably, because without the mineral resources of Upper Silesia, Germany would not be able to pay that much. Since Simons refused to accept the terms set by the Allies, Lloyd George—after vehement arguments about the sole guilt for the World War being Germany's, which Lloyd George maintained was a *cause jugée* since Germany had accepted the peace treaty—announced that the sanctions which had been decided on previously would now come into effect. On the following day (March 8) Düsseldorf, Duisburg, and Ruhrort were occupied.

Germany asked the United States for mediation and declared herself ready to accept, unconditionally and in advance, the American arbitration decision. The United States, however, rejected the role of arbitrator and asked the German government to make its own suitable suggestions; in this case the American government would consider its services.

At the end of April Dr. Simons submitted further ideas, including the payment of the Allied debts to America by Germany. But it was all in vain. The Allies countered with the London ultimatum of May 5, 1921, threatening occupation of the Ruhr area should there be a refusal. Germany was to accept within six days a reparations debt of 132 billion gold-marks. The 132 billion, which had to be deposited in promissory notes, represented the sum of the annual payments, not their current value. Actual payments were to be 2 billion gold-marks yearly in the beginning plus 25 percent of the German export value, as well as an immediate payment of 1 billion and additional extras.

The normal citizen was in no position to understand these figures, which seemed absolutely fantastic to him. Few were the experts who could claim to realize what was involved. Even Simon's suggestions for a five-year provisional arrangement were attacked after his return by the German Nationalists as far too burdensome. After the London ultimatum opposition spread to the German People's Party.

A new government was formed under Dr. Wirth. The People's Party withdrew; the Social Democrats re-entered. Simons resigned. Dr. Rosen took over the Foreign Ministry and Walther Rathenau the newly founded Ministry for Reconstruction. The new government accepted the ultimatum "in order to spare Germany from the threatened invasion and maintain peace." The period of the "fulfillment-policy" began.

During these months the referendum in Upper Silesia took place. It resulted in a majority of 60 to 40 percent in favor of Germany. The Allies decided, however, to hand over districts with Polish majorities to Poland rather than leave the entire province to Germany. Those areas which remained within Germany expressed themselves later in another referendum in favor of remaining part of Prussia rather than forming a separate land. All this was by no means accomplished with peace and quiet. There were several Polish revolts and battles of German volunteer corps, intensified on both sides by terrorist acts.

## 34. MEETING HAUPTMANN

DURING an idyllic holiday on the island of Hiddensee near Rügen in the Baltic, our friend and later brother-in-law, the violinist Ossip Schnirlin, introduced Clara and me to Gerhart Hauptmann and his wife Margarete, with whom he had formerly studied at the Berlin College of Music. The Hauptmanns lived in a castlelike house on the high dunes by the sea. We were taken to a large table with other friends, where the guests were treated to Hauptmann's favorite substance, a mixture of burgundy and champagne. I told him of the special attraction which his great novel *Emmanuel Quint* and his controversial *Jahrhundertfestspiel* (Century Celebration) had held for my friends and me, and I quoted some passages which had moved us most deeply. I then brought up the question of his attitude toward democracy. I admitted the weaknesses of the Ger-

man democracy, which with no tradition and without inspiring
leadership was fighting for its very existence. But, I continued, precisely for these reasons democracy as a form of government needed
positive and warm support from Germany's greatest men outside
the government. We argued about this for some time, in a completely friendly fashion and on a high level. Although Hauptmann
failed to take as firm a stand as I would have wished, he had apparently become rather thoughtful. His wife then played a few pieces
on the violin, which became her well. Hauptmann sat silent at a
distance. "I went out to find a kingdom, and found a violinist," I
said to him as we left. He was not offended.

I met him a few times afterward. About six months later I had
lunch with him and Walther Rathenau, in the house of Envoy Lu-
cius, quite intimately, only the four of us. On the occasion of his six-
tieth birthday (1922) I accompanied Ebert and the Minister for the
Interior, Köster, to the official celebration in Breslau. There was a
performance of Hauptmann's *Florian Geyer* with a completely
hoarse Geyer, played by Eugen Klöpfer, followed by a night with
Klöpfer, Jessner (manager of the Berlin State Theater), Köster, and
me and a never-ending string of theater anecdotes. Later I persuaded Hauptmann in the Hotel Adlon to appear as a speaker at a
memorial meeting for Walther Rathenau, together with Chancellor
Marx, Edwin Redslob, and myself, and we also met his wife and
him at the house of Rathenau's sister, Frau Edith Andreae. The last
time I saw him was on his seventieth birthday at the end of 1932
when the illegally deposed Prussian cabinet presented him their
congratulations through the Social-Democratic Minister of Culture,
Grimme, and me. He never took a clear and unambiguous stand for
democracy.

## 35. The Two Bachelors: Wirth and Rathenau

Joseph Wirth—not the older Wirth, who tried in vain to regain a
leading role in politics after the Second World War—at that time
only forty-two years old, tall and straight, was an impulsive person. Thanks to the ingenious move with which he made Walther
Rathenau, who complemented him in almost every respect, his

closest co-worker and trusted adviser, he became a historically highly influential figure as a switchman in German history. Originally a highschool teacher, who had studied mathematics and economics, he had become a member of the Baden Landtag at thirty-four, of the Reichstag at thirty-five, Baden Minister of Finance at thirty-nine, and Reich Minister of Finance at forty-one. Wirth was intellectually quite able to understand the financial, economic, and calculatory problems which he discussed with German experts and now in particular with Rathenau. He had been present at the conference in Spa and had displayed a good psychological comprehension at the international level. He was also genuinely gifted for assuming the role of a political leader. But he was basically a lone wolf and similar to his partner Rathenau in this, sharing with him also the fact that both were bachelors, which may have contributed to their mutual understanding.

Certain limits to Wirth's gift for leadership were revealed in the beginning by his failure to establish viable relations with the bureaucratic apparatus. The head of the Chancellery, Secretary Albert, found himself in the position of having to run the Chancellery and maintain contact with other ministries and the press office without really knowing what was going on. While other Chancellors had usually brought along the head of the Chancellery or his assistants to official conferences, Wirth did not. Albert therefore went up resolutely to Wirth and informed him that the machinery could not be kept running properly in this fashion. There was a sharp exchange of words. Albert declared that he could no longer run the Chancellery under such circumstances, and resigned. "This will be the source of your failure, Mr. Chancellor," he warned, not without some wounded pride, "if you want to conduct the government of such a great country privately, as it were, without the bureaucratic machinery."

During the following ten weeks when I attended to the affairs of the Chancellery as "acting head," Wirth once said to me in an apologetic manner: "You have to understand, I am simply not capable of thinking and deciding in an orderly bureaucratic fashion. When I have something to think over, I sit down on a stump or on a stone, alone, and think and brood, until I have reached some conclusion. I have to talk to people singly, not together with bureaucrats whom I don't really know and don't know what they are thinking." This was not difficult to understand and certainly not unsympathetic. From then on, however, Wirth was careful to see to it that I was either present at official discussions or was at least informed. This was perhaps easier for him in my case, since I was five years younger than he and even less bureaucratic than Albert had been.

Wirth's basic political convictions were similar to those of Erzberger during the latter period of his life, when they had been cleansed from his earlier nationalism and lust for annexation. But they were simpler, less complex in means, less meddlesome, less cunning, straightforward, from heart to heart, and not at all opportunistic. His maxim in foreign policy was an oft-repeated: "Patience, more patience, and still more patience." He believed that the main danger for Germany, in both foreign and domestic policies, threatened not from the Left, from the Communists, or even the Social Democrats, but from the Right, from nationalists, anti-Semitic rabble-rousers, militaristic leagues, which intoxicated the people with jingoistic slogans, with their vehmic courts and political murders. The existence of these movements, orders, leagues endangered not only Germany's gaining international confidence, but her inner pacification and increase in strength as well. It was natural for Wirth to form a Cabinet of the Weimar coalition. But he sought advice as little from his colleagues in the Cabinet as he did from the bureaucrats; he sought it from Walther Rathenau. As a result of this, Wirth's Foreign Minister, Rosen, played a rather meager role, until he was replaced in January, 1922 by Rathenau.

In a speech to members of the German Democratic Party in Frankfurt on October 28, 1921, Walther Rathenau said of Wirth: "I have worked with Wirth for two years and have for two years been a close friend of his. Despite this I believe, for this very reason I believe, that I can give you my opinion of this man who has been so sadly misunderstood. My opinion is—and I believe that many of you will share it, if you think about it carefully—that of the last ten Chancellors who have had the fate of the Reich in their hands, none has surpassed him in that material, that wood from which statesmen are carved. A Southern German of candid, sincere character, firm will, with a broad perspective in politics and with an indefatigable working power and great authority. That is the man; and if I emphasize the great esteem I have for his sincerity of character, it is because the stupid and frivolous saying, that politics spoils the character or even that politics requires no character, is so often be-

lieved. Quite the contrary: I have found that both in business and in
the affairs of state, in the case of equal talents only one thing is decisive—character. . . ."

Wirth's own speeches after Rathenau's murder, all of which I listened to from the government dais in the Reichstag, were so typical
that I shall quote them here: On the day of the assassination he
said: "During the bitter days when chaos passed over us, the working classes did not touch a hair of any who remained loyal to the
old regimes. I am grateful to them for that, and it will stay like this
in the future. Name a single conspicuous representative of right-
wing opinion in Germany who was harmed at all! But from the
very day when we began to serve this new form of government uprightly, a terrible poison was being fed to the people with enormous
amounts of money. Murderous agitation (*eine Mordhetze*), from
Königsberg to Constance, threatens the fatherland which we serve
with all our strength. At large meetings they scream that what we
are doing is a crime against the nation; they scream for court procedures against us, and then people wonder why blinded youths seize
weapons of murder. . . ." And on the following day he said: "If it
was possible in Germany to rely on one man, on his brilliant ideas,
and on his word, to take the initiative in the interest of our German
people, then it would have been appropriate to have Dr. Rathenau
continue his work on the crucial issue of Germany's sole guilt for
the war. Great developments have been abruptly broken off here
and the gentlemen who are responsible for this will never be able to
compensate their nation for it."

Wirth read aloud an article by the deputy Reinhold Wulle in
*Deutsches Tageblatt,* which said: "The present government is in
reality merely the employee of the Entente, paid by the German
Reich, merely fulfilling the Entente's demands and directions;
otherwise it would be put out on the street and would lose its means
of subsistence." Wirth continued: "When in the course of the year
has a word been spoken by you against the activities of those who
have really created this murderous atmosphere in Germany? . . . I
have read letters which the unfortunate Frau Erzberger received. If
you had read these letters—the lady refuses to subject them to publicity—if you knew how these letters inform her that the grave of
her husband will be despoiled merely for the sake of revenge. Are
you surprised (to the right) that letters are sent to me, under the influence of the output of your press, like the one I have in my hand

now, bearing the heading: 'On the day of the execution of Dr. Rathenau!' . . . Well, I was a witness of important discussions of our murdered friend with the most powerful of the Allied states-men in Genua. You could not have found a more eloquent advocate in small, intimate discussions—serious discussions!—in the whole of Germany than Dr. Rathenau. His manner of preparing the mood, of forming it, of bringing the treatment of problems from an atmo-sphere of passion into calmer consideration and decent thinking, no one has known how to do this as well as Dr. Rathenau. But what were his motives according to the right-wing press? Indeed, when I read in this letter that all the treaties are concluded only so that he can enrich himself and his Jewish relatives, then you will under-stand that our German fatherland is being driven irrevocably to ruin by the rabble-rousers. . . ."

This speech ended with the now famous words: "At every mo-ment democracy! But not democracy which bangs its fist on the table and says: we are in power! no, instead of that, democracy which is patiently seeking freedom in every situation! To this end every mouth must speak to do away with this atmosphere of mur-der, of quarrel, of poison! There (to the right) is the enemy who injects his poison into the wounds of the people. There is the enemy —and there is no doubt about it: *this enemy is on the right; (dieser Feind steht rechts!)*."

In describing Wirth I have unavoidably begun to describe Rath-enau. He has been analyzed so often that it might appear idle for me to give a picture of how I saw him. But the description of my own life would be incomplete without it. For not only was I acting head of the Chancellery when he became a member of the Cabinet. After his death, I also was a co-originator of the laws and decrees for the protection of the republic and a co-founder and member of the governing body of the Walther Rathenau Foundation and of the society founded in his memory. I therefore had to form an opin-ion on him and his character. In what follows I have made use of some that I wrote in earlier essays on him,[1] but now adjusted to the special context of this book.

If the usual descriptions of Rathenau were to be believed, his most outstanding characteristic was his vanity. But at the time when I got to know him—from about 1920 onward—this was not correct. During his youth he had passed through the school of vanity; that

[1] Especially "Walther Rathenau and the German People," *Journal of Politics,* 1948.

is true. This, by the way, is not necessarily a bad school, provided that one is capable of shaking off the vanity after graduation and leaving it behind, as Rathenau did. At the time when I was in contact with him he was not vain. He was living entirely for the *cause,* not for the ego. The most striking thing about him was not vanity, but his solitary life. He was relying far more on himself than most of his contemporaries. This has often been incorrectly interpreted as vanity.

In the middle of Rathenau's adult life there had been a decisive change in his way of thinking. He discovered for himself and in his own way that the soul is essentially different from the intellect. Intellect is guided by purpose and by purpose alone. It may grow, increase, and improve, but it is always controlled by purpose; and behind purpose is fear. For this reason even the greatest achievements of the intellect are bound to fail; they differ from the purpose-directed behavior of animals in quantity only, not quality. "The spirits chained to the ego are all alike, different though their faces may be," he wrote to a woman friend. There is, however, another spiritual power: the soul. It is different from the intellect; it is without desire, will, and purpose. Only by developing the soul, by abandoning one's life wholly to this compass needle, can the individual, the nations, the world, be saved.

The discovery of the soul by Rathenau—so long after Socrates and the Old and New Testaments—was in itself not new, of course. But his apostleship in the service of the kingdom of the soul is nevertheless captivating: for its non-cleric, unorthodox, entirely independent interpretation, for the radical dividing line he drew between soul and intellect, and for the many unusual images and forceful parables he used. It is also impressive that he, a German industrial leader of the twentieth century and himself an outstanding intellectual, did not shrink from confessing openly that the source of all our evils lies in disregard of the soul. His peers seemed to consider this as injuring his value as a businessman.

Rathenau's patriotism was no less fundamental than his philosophy: it emanated from his soul, not from his intellect. One can roughly say that Germans of the upper strata were either "Weimar Germans" or "Potsdam Germans" at that time. Their ideals were determined either by the cultural heritage of Goethe and Schiller, or by the military culture of the Prussian state and the example of Frederick the Great. Rathenau mirrored both Weimar-Germany and Potsdam-Germany. While deeply rooted in Weimar, he also loved—in a manner which can only be called tender—the cultural blossoms that had sprung from the hard earth of Prussia, or rather, from the sandy ground of his home, Brandenburg province. He particularly cherished the memory of Prussia as it had been during the Wars of Liberation in Napoleonic times; he acquired a country house which had belonged to Queen Luise and where she had lived then. He admired and exalted the northern type of men and women and sometimes used language which almost sounded like that employed by National Socialists later on, just as individual phrases used by Luther, Kant, or Nietzsche did.

This was, of course, particularly striking in a man of purely Jewish descent. "My people are the Germans, no others," he once wrote in answer to a letter from a friend who had referred to the Jews as "your people." He advised Jews all over the world to give up all aloofness and all characteristics which seemed strange and to adopt themselves to the culture and way of life in the nation of which they were citizens. But he refused to be baptized. That might have looked like opportunism; it would also have made it necessary for him to decide in favor of one particular Christian creed and to pledge himself to special details of dogma he did not believe in. Nor was baptism necessary for his belief in the teaching of the Sermon on the Mount. He even wanted to found a "Christian Union of Jews"; this, he said, was quite compatible with Jewry.

Rathenau's German patriotism had induced him to urge upon the Minister for War during the first days of the war the necessity of creating a systematic organization for the supply of vital raw materials, and then to take over the job himself and build up such an organization within a few weeks. He had opposed all plans for annexation and unconditional submarine warfare, but strangely enough (presumably from ignorance of international law) not the use of Belgian workers for the production of armaments. When Ludendorff appeared to lose his nerve at the end of the war, it was once again Rathenau's patriotism which had him demand that resistance be continued. When the Treaty of Versailles was presented to Germany, Rathenau advised the government not to sign, but to resign, together with the president, and to invite the Allies to move into Germany and to take over the responsibility themselves—a suggestion which was not heeded then, but which, had it been followed (as has been discussed in Chapter 25), might have produced better

results than the continual pressure of the Allies on German governments after the First World War, to judge from experiences after
the Second.

But it was not only, not even chiefly, as a politician that Wirth
sought Rathenau's advice. It was above all the expert on economics,
the bold planner. Rathenau is said to have played, for some period
of time a leading part in sixty-eight German corporations and twenty-one foreign ones, including some in Italy, France, Spain, Switzerland, Russia, and Africa. These companies produced or dealt with
electricity, metals, chemicals, railroads, telegraphs, spinning-mills,
rolling-mills, or else were banks and trust companies. He was thus
certainly in the midst of economic life—but only with one foot.
With the other he stood, or felt his way around, on utopian ground.
His books were remarkable for their (pessimistic) warnings and
their (optimistic) suggestions. More a planning engineer than an
economic theorist, Rathenau loved to express his thoughts in utopian form, in drafting plans for a new, better world, plans which
absorbed all of his realistic experience. "The utopian is indispensable
as a goal, but as a means it is to be avoided," he once wrote. A considerable number of economic-technological ideas later adopted in
Europe and America could be traced back to Rathenau.

Rathenau wanted to develop economic associations of private enterprises under democratic government control, evolving from the
existing economic setup with as little change as possible. These associations were to have a threefold purpose: first, as advisers to the
government; second, as executive organs of the government within
their respective economic fields; third, as independent administrative agencies in fields not controlled by the government. He wanted
thus, without violent changes and without sacrificing private initiative, to build up a progressive, social "common economy" (*Gemein-
wirtschaft*) from existing economic conditions. His ideas differed
from unlimited state socialism through the extensive administrative
independence of these corporations, from guild socialism through
the controlling sovereignty reserved to the government, while the
democratic form of the government not only differentiated his system from Communism, but from the Fascist corporative state as
well. Many of his ideas were in line with those of State Secretary
Möllendorff; how far they influenced one another is disputed.

If economic planning is Socialism, then Rathenau was a Socialist.
If the upholding of private initiative is Liberalism, then he was a

Liberal. In any case, his Socialism was not Marxist. It was less a scientific than an ethical sort of Socialism, in which science was to play only a supporting role and which rejected class struggles and dogmatism. Ethical considerations and his efforts to avoid any wastage of human labor made him desire also that the great inequalities of life be modified.

All this made him an extremely interesting and sympathetic adviser to Chancellor Wirth. But the reason for Wirth's needing him was not so much domestic economic planning as the international negotiations about German reparations. Rathenau, like other German experts, was of the opinion that it would prove virtually impossible to raise and transfer the total amounts the Allied had demanded. But he nevertheless advised Germany's pursuing a "fulfillment policy" honestly and in good faith and leaving alterations to the future.

In the summer of 1921 Rathenau succeeded in reaching an agreement with the French Minister for Reconstruction, Loucheur, on the help of German industry and German labor forces in the rebuilding of the destroyed areas of Northern France. He sought out Lloyd George and other British statesmen in London and impressed them with his plans for European reconstruction and general understanding, plans which included Russia. An official conference with the Allies was envisaged; it took place in January, 1922, in Cannes and led to the Conference of Genua and the Rapallo Agreement. But in the months about which I am speaking, this was still in the future (see Chapter 42).

## 36. Changes in the Chancellery and in the Cabinet

In the eight or ten weeks following Secretary Albert's resignation I took over his duties as acting head of the Chancellery. I worked at Bismarck's desk in the Secretary's room where the windows afforded a better view out onto the gardens, now filled with all the magnificence of spring. At Cabinet meetings I sat next to the Chancellor and was also present at many of his discussions with Rathenau and other ministerial colleagues.

It was probably during these weeks that we received a sharp note from England in which they demanded that the Zeppelin works on Lake Constance be closed down. The American representative invited me for lunch and gave me to understand that the United States had an interest in the development of airships for peaceful purposes and would not be shocked by German opposition to the English demand. I saw to it that the German refusal was more forceful than had been planned.

The weakening of the German currency caused me increasing concern. Up to the time of Rathenau's assassination, inflation was still kept within limits; but it was not difficult to see that it would soon run away unchecked. Together with some officials in the Ministry of Economics (in particular the later secretary in the Ministry of Finance, Hans Schäffer) I was co-originator of a plan under which the national government was to obtain a twenty-five percent share in all economic corporations and all real estate, in order to put the Reich finances on a more solid basis than the issuing of bank notes ("acquiring real value"). This government participation in ownership was to replace the corporate income tax, etc., to the same extent. We tried to work out the details. All this was quite preliminary, however, and conceived as one of several rather than as a unique remedy.

I put the proposal to Chancellor Wirth and the Cabinet. Rathenau took me aside with a gesture peculiar to him—he would lay his arm familiarly around one's shoulder and back—and walked up and down the hall with me. He asked me whether my economic plan had grown out of economic and financial considerations alone or whether it was a flareup of revolutionary fire. I said that it was the former, but that the latter would do no harm in stimulating our courage to do what was necessary. He said he did not think that it could be done like that and referred to his suggestions for a "common economy," described in the preceding chapter. I warned that the dizzy increase of inflation could not be averted in this way. I later had the sad satisfaction that, after the total collapse of German currency and the acceptance of the Dawes Plan, industrial obligations and real-estate duties on industry and agriculture at the rate of twenty-five percent of the value were imposed as a guarantee against another collapse of German currency—too late, like so many things in Germany.

In the meantime, the Zentrum party pressed for the position of Chief of the Chancellery to be filled by a party member, because it was a political, not an administrative, post, they said. I had closer connections with the Social Democrats and the Democrats than with the Zentrum. Wirth finally gave in and appointed Erzberger's former secretary, Dr. Hemmer, Chief of the Chancellery. Wirth offered me the position of State Secretary for Economic Affairs in the Foreign Office. I thanked him for his confidence, but said that, lacking experience in the foreign service, I did not feel yet ready for the task. The offer showed, however, that Wirth and Rathenau were not entirely displeased with my economic ideas and that they appreciated my initiative.

In the fall, Wirth's Cabinet collapsed, because the Council of the League of Nations had refused to leave the whole of Upper Silesia to Germany, although the majority of the population had voted in favor of remaining in Germany, but had divided it up between Germany and Poland according to local results. The Democrats withdrew from the government as a sign of protest. Nor did the People's Party want to join. There was no alternative other than to form another minority cabinet, on an even smaller basis, consisting only of Zentrum and Social Democrats. Professor Gustav Radbruch, the great jurist, took over from Eugen Schiffer the Ministry of Justice, and Adolf Köster from Koch-Weser the Ministry of the Interior, both of them Social Democrats. Rathenau had given up the post as Minister for Reconstruction because of his affiliation with the Democrats, but shortly afterward—on January 31, 1922—took over the Foreign Office, which Wirth himself had been running in the meantime.

I knew Radbruch well, as a native of Lübeck and classmate of my brother Gustav. In every class he had ranked first, Gustav always second behind him, on the ground of his intelligence and maturity but not by far equal to Radbruch's early erudition and much more intent upon life than the shyer comrade. They had both loved the same girl, Radbruch quietly waiting every day for her pleasing greeting, Gustav bolder, so that he managed to obtain a lock of hair, all or part of which he afterward swapped with Radbruch for the picture of an actress. But this happy period of youth was past. Radbruch had become a renowned teacher of jurisprudence, whose lectures, delivered without notes, formally perfect and substantially profound, drew large numbers of students in Kiel and Heidelberg. His *Introduction to the Study of Law* and his *Introduction to Legal Philosophy* had gained him widespread recognition. He had joined the Social Democratic Party as a matter of conscience. During the Kapp Putsch he had shown courage and strength of character in preventing irresponsible acts of violence. His appointment was an honor for his party. But Radbruch did not feel himself called to be a party leader. He told me he thought we intellectuals, sprung from a bourgeois background and having never lived in vital contact with the working classes nor truly identified ourselves with them, were not qualified to take over the leadership of the workers. We could only *advise,* stimulate, and warn those who were their born and chosen leaders. His arguing made a strong impression on me and influenced my own way of thinking.

Radbruch's attitude in legal matters was, of course, different. Here he was a real expert and could well claim to *lead* a staff even as excellent as that in the Ministry of Justice. He did so marvelously in the revision of the criminal law code, which had made little progress since the demise of the first Penal Code Commission, to which I had served as a secretary (Chapter 7). But even in the Ministry of Justice Radbruch was not inclined to play the lord and master. He had a justifiably very favorable opinion of his subordinates and was far too earnest a seeker after truth to cut them short when they wanted to change or modify his opinion on something. It is the job of state secretaries and staff members to present all material to a minister *before* he makes a decision, and to present their own views and recommendations clearly and boldly; but, after the decision has been reached, to carry it out loyally, even though they had previously opposed it. The senior officials in the Ministry of Justice did all this in an exemplary fashion, as did those in many other ministries.

## 37. The Anniversary of the Constitution
### (August 11, 1921)

Since German federal governments, ever after the elections of June, 1920, were dependent upon the support, or at least the tolerance, of parties of anti-democratic or anti-republican conviction, they were unable to lend democratic-republican ideals real vitality, attractive power, impressive form in public life. German democracy lacked the richness of symbols in which other democracies rejoice. The only official symbol were the black-red-gold colors. They were hectically disputed, precisely because they, and they alone, symbolized the democratic ideals. There was at that time no national anthem. There were no generally honored heroes and martyrs, unless the freedom fighters from the Wars of Liberation of 1813–1815 and the Revolution of 1848 were to be counted—but most of them were monarchists anyway. There were no days of commemoration which impressed themselves upon the national consciousness as general holidays. There was no substitute for the imperial, regal, princely deployment of splendor, of military glory, might, and discipline. German democracy had risen unadorned from the humiliation of defeat, loved by many and felt with pride to be an achievement, a precious possession gained in the midst of misfortune—by many, yes, but not by all, not even by half of the people, and yet almost by half of them, and therefore not merely an alien body in the German political community.

Even with all their inhibitions, German governments could not, however, leave the creation and use of symbols entirely to the parties and other groups which battled with one another under their separate symbols. They needed official symbols for public appearances. A starting point seemed to me to present itself in the widespread recognition of the Weimar Constitution as the actual basis for the preservation of peace and order. The charter of the Constitution was the only firm ground under the people's feet. It formed the actual basis for a community of life, fate, and work, and as such presented a broader meeting ground than the glorification of democracy and republic. Because the Constitution was the basis of lawful order, the code of the rules of the game to be heeded in the political struggle, the guarantor of peaceful settlement of domestic conflicts, the source of reassurance that one was living at least in a state of law (*Rechtsstaat*) with independent law courts, and above all the guarantor of freedom of opinion and speech, and of social benefits gained—because it was all this, the Constitution was treated with respect by many of those—especially in the German People's Party, the Bavarian People's Party, and even sections of the German Nationalists—who held monarchist opinions or for other reasons did not see final wisdom in democratic-parliamentary principles. Of course, the Constitution did prescribe the republican form of government and democratic procedures for political decisions. But it did this not in forms of ideological propaganda. It did it in a sober, matter-of-fact fashion, taking its point of departure in conditions created by historical circumstances. The Constitution allowed all Germans to have other views and to express them; even government officials could do this, as long as they fulfilled their official functions properly. In other words, the Constitution enjoyed greater respect than the form of government it laid down. Some saw in it the fulfillment of the Revolution, others the guaranty of the Revolution's end.

I therefore suggested to President Ebert and Chancellor Wirth that the day of the signing of the Constitution, August 11, be celebrated as "Constitution Day." They agreed. Who was to deliver the official address? It would have to be a person greatly respected by all, a worthy representative of Germany, not too pronounced a party man. I went first, along with the newly appointed State Secretary Hemmer, to the great liberal theologian and historian, Professor Adolf von Harnack. He fully understood our reason for not wanting to have a politician speak and for having come to him. But he was not prepared to expose himself at this celebration. He refused. Then we went to Bill Drews, Prussian Minister of the Interior under the monarchy, in the meantime president of Prussia's highest administrative court, who had made the vain attempt, on Prince Max's instructions, to persuade the Kaiser to abdicate in time and had given personal support to the new democracy. He, I thought, would understand and respect our request. But he also refused. In the end, Chancellor Wirth had to make the speech himself. German democracy was still that poor.

The scene was beautifully arranged in the great opera house built by Schinkel. The philharmonic orchestra, under a famous conductor, played at the beginning and end, sitting on stage in front of a huge heraldic eagle as a backdrop. Wirth spoke simply and straight from his heart. The celebration was a considerable *succès d'estime* (*Achtungserfolg*) for the Republic. Not only supporters of the Weimar coalition had turned up, but also the members of the rightist German People's Party and the high bureaucracy of all departments. Among the ministers, Walther Rathenau was present; it was to be the only commemoration of the Constitution in which he could participate. Ebert thanked me in a personal letter.

From the Ministry of the Interior I later organized several more of these celebrations in close collaboration with Edwin Redslob, the

federal government's art expert (see Chapter 41). The morning cer-
emonies were transferred to the Reichstag building; two huge masts
with black-red-gold flags flanked the square in front of the broad
staircase; a guard of honor stepped up. Renowned speakers came
forward readily, among them Professor Anschütz (1923) and Professor Radbruch (1928). Everywhere there were evening festival
performances in the theaters.

Although the celebrations were greeted with respect, they never
became popular holidays. That has been the fate of state celebrations in many countries, with the notable exception of France,
where the storming of the Bastille contributed a revolutionary and
exciting point of departure for really popular celebrations. That the
German federal governments did not stage anything more dramatic
was not because of our lack of imagination but, as discussed at length
in Chapter 30, because they included opponents of democratic-
republican ideals or were dependent upon their tolerance.

## 38. The Death of Erzberger

On August 26, 1921, barely two weeks after the first celebration of
Constitution Day, the retired Minister of Finance, Matthias Erzberger, was murdered. A week previously he had gone to Bad Griess-
bach with his family. While he was out on a walk with deputy
Diez, two young men had intercepted the pair and had fired shots
at close quarters at Erzberger's head and chest. Erzberger leaped
down the slope by the road, but three further shots hit him in his
lung, stomach, and leg. The murderers then ran down the slope
themselves and fired more shots at him. Diez was also hit in the
chest, but was able to return, bleeding, to the hotel and relate what
had happened.

The murderers, Heinrich Schulz and Heinrich Tillesen, escaped
to Bavaria, from whence they had been sent by the mysterious "Organization Consul," under the leadership of Lieutenant Manfred
von Killinger. The Baden public prosecutor requested the Munich
police to arrest the culprits. But Pöhner was in charge of the Munich police; instead of arresting the pair immediately, he sent them a
written invitation, thus giving them time to escape. They fled to Bu-

dapest. Hungary refused to extradite them and repeated the refusal three years later, saying that Germany had also refused to hand over the murderer of Tisza. A trial against Killinger was held in June, 1922, in which he was charged with aiding and abetting murderers; but the jury dismissed the charge for lack of evidence. Thus all three were still unpunished when the National Socialists came to power. Hitler made Killinger Premier of Saxony and later Ambassador in Rumania. When Schulz and Tillesen returned to Germany, proceedings against them were dropped on the ground of the amnesty of March, 1933. Tillesen was made a battalion leader in the Nazi Storm Troops.

Justice did not come until after the war.[1] Killinger committed suicide in Rumania in 1944, to avoid falling into Russian hands. Tillesen was sentenced to fifteen years' hard labor (*Zuchthaus*) by a court in Constance in 1947, Schulz three years later to twelve years hard labor by a court in Offenburg. Both were released on probation after several years.

Not until these postwar proceedings did it become fully clear what had really happened. The Munich "Organization Consul," to which the murderers had belonged, had as their statutory goal "opposition to everything anti-national or international, to judaism, Social Democracy and the left-wing radical parties; opposition to the anti-national Weimar constitution in word and deed." The members had to vow "to be unconditionally obedient to the leader of the organization and to my superiors and to preserve the utmost secrecy about all affairs concerning the organization." Those who betrayed this were dealt with by a secret court. Schulz and Tillesen had received the order to murder Erzberger in Killinger's office at the beginning of August, 1921. A slip of paper handed to them in an envelope said that they had been chosen by lot to remove Erzberger. "The way in which this is carried out is left to you. It is not necessary to report completion of the task." On the strength of this order they committed the murder. When they returned, Killinger obtained forged passports for them with the assistance of Pöhner. Thus they were able to escape to Budapest.

When the news of the murder was released, it was shameful to listen to reactions in bourgeois circles which, although not explicitly approving the murder, found it most important to emphasize their

---

[1] The following dates are taken from the excellent biography of Erzberger by Klaus Epstein, already mentioned.

personal disapproval of Erzberger's policies. Diez reported that as
he was hurrying from the scene of the murder back to the hotel,
bleeding himself, he met a woman who helped him but who, when
he told her what had happened, remarked drily, "What on earth
made you take a walk with Erzberger?" I experienced something
similar in June, 1934, after the murder of General von Schleicher,
when the wife of a senior government official said simply, "He
wasn't very well liked anyway." During the persecution of the Jews,
one often heard people say quite seriously, "Yes, but there really
were far too many Jewish lawyers and doctors." This inability to
distinguish between the disapproval one feels toward a person or
group of people and the unconditional demand that their basic
rights be respected was very characteristic of many people in Germany.

## 39. The End of My Three Years in the Chancellery—Taking Over the Constitution Division in the Ministry of the Interior

Shortly after Constitution Day we had gone on holiday, this time
to the Mecklenburg coast. We stayed there until the middle of September, reading, bathing, and taking in the afternoons usually the
same two-hour walk along the bay and through the woods. After
many turbulent months our life was suddenly quiet and soothing. I
often thought back to the old days before the war, to the time when
I was a sixteen- and seventeen-year-old pupil in Lübeck. All that
was so infinitely far away now. I imagined a banquet at which my
favorite student songs were sung. I longed for something innocent,
something which would bind men together, the end of all strife.

But there could be no return to romantic youth. Apprenticeship
was past. I had to take over some concrete task and personal responsibility. My work would have to be political and administrative, not
purely legal. I was well enough prepared for this.

Shortly after my return Adolf Köster became Minister of the Interior and asked me to go with him. I answered that I would like to,
although not as State Secretary, but rather as Ministerial Director

(head of a ministerial division). I did not desire to be under a young minister an even younger state secretary in a ministry whose manifold specialist tasks and whose personnel I did not know from years of personal experience. I did not want advance in a "lightning career," but time for the development of solid knowledge and ability.

President Ebert, at Köster's suggestion, promoted the head of the constitutional law (first) division to state secretary and me to head of that division, which was renamed at my request "Division for Policy and Constitution."

Initiative had been lost in the Ministry of the Interior. Creative imagination seemed to be lacking. The program I had in mind included such points as: filling the politically most important posts with adherents of democracy; political education of the German middle classes by example, writing and speeches, commemorations, symbols, and public discussions, toward a better understanding of contemporary events and active cooperation; reorganization of the interrelations between Reich and *Laender,* especially through a union of the two parallel central administrations in the Reich and in Prussia and formation of *Laender* of reasonable size; improvement of the electoral system; modernization of the antiquated inner organization of German offices, especially of their almost medieval filing system; collection of the federal laws similar to the United States Code; rewriting of the laws of associations and public meetings; and reorganization of the civil service.

With these plans, I left the Chancellery in November, 1921 after three years of service, under the seventh Chancellor I had worked for. When I left, Dr. Wirth said to me "The fact that we are putting you in this post in the Ministry of the Interior, is a program in itself."

# PART VII

Reformer in the Ministry
of the Interior
(1921-1927)

## 40. The Magic of Limited Functions

With my transfer to the new office, the rooms and gardens in the Chancellery, with which I was so familiar, ceased to be *my* rooms and gardens, to which I had had access at any time, where no one was surprised to see me enter and walk around. Nor could I any longer attend Cabinet meetings just as I wished to. When I now happened to enter the Chancellery for some official business, I stood as it were in front of my own door, whose handle I had so often pressed as master of the house or member of the family, and where I now had to knock and wait and face surprised if friendly eyes. This change in relationship to rooms that had previously been mine happened to me several times before and after—most strikingly, of course, when the National Socialists moved into the ministries—, but my awareness of it was very marked then. I am a guest on earth.

Similar experiences lay in wait for me in the substance of my work. I had been used to involving myself in almost any government business that seemed to me important: foreign and domestic, military and police, economics and labor. Now I had a field of work that was important but limited, and, however widely it might expand, it did not allow me the old freedom to interfere in other things, just as others might not interfere in my work, except where duties overlapped. In the eight federal ministries, excluding those for post, transport, and defense, there were at that time some 30 ministerial directors, supported by a total of about 400 aides, including 260 high-ranking ministerial counselors (*Ministerialräte*), grouped in some (only about 10) cases in subdivisions. The entire range of the federal administration was distributed among these ministerial directors. They all knew one another and could easily maintain contact. Each was expected to provide information at any time, at the request of his Minister or the Chancellery, on any fact, any historical or legal question within his field, either from his own knowledge or by consulting his aides. That was, and still is, the secret of good public organization. But the condition of its proper functioning is mutual respect for each other's appointed functions.

Thus *pride* in one's own field and awareness of its *limits* developed side by side.

I pursued my program (see conclusion of preceding chapter) consistently for five and a half years under eight different ministers—Social Democrats, Democrats, members of the People's Party, and German Nationalists. Although at times one or the other item had to be shelved, I was able to complete, or at least push far ahead, several of the projects. But the most important ones remained uncompleted. What blocked fuller success was, in the last analysis, always the same factor: the share anti-democratic parties had in governmental power hindered outspokenly pro-democratic political and administrative steps.

In retrospect that is clear and simple. But it was at that time still possible to hope that the next elections would change the situation, and that in the meantime education and improvements would contribute to bringing about the change.

## 41. STAFF PROBLEMS

DR. KÖSTER had brought with him, in addition to myself, the twenty-seven-year-old Dr. Hans Simons—a good choice. He later followed me to New York, and as an American citizen was to play important roles as adviser to the U.S. Military Government in Germany, as President of the New School for Social Research, and as consultant to the Ford Foundation on East-Indian and South-American cultural affairs. In the independence of his judgment and his precise diction he was very like his father, the Foreign Minister and later President of the Supreme Court (*Reichsgericht*), but he was less troubled by memories of the past in his democratic-republican way of thinking and in his dislike of nationalism, militarism, and bureaucracy. Among other qualities he had the amazing gift of committing complicated facts in every detail to memory in the shortest possible time and presenting them clearly in systematic analysis. When mixing with other people, even political opponents, he was cheerful, relaxed, of pleasant manner, and like his father never obtrusive. He listened attentively to what others had to say, without giving the impression that, while listening, he was learning from their mistakes. He had been present at the peace negotiations in Versailles, acting as secretary there. Now he was to work as Köster's personal assistant in his anteroom.

We were thus three exponents of democracy, strategically placed in the Ministry. It would be going too far to say that we were the only ones. There were a few others, above all the art expert, Dr. Edwin Redslob, who had been appointed shortly before; although his primary duties lay outside my division, thanks to his democratic-republican way of thinking, his refreshing thrusts against spiritless red tape, his excellent historical knowledge of the struggles for freedom and unity during the nineteenth century, and his ingenious, fresh, and nimble manner, he became an important aid in my own sphere of activity.

Such men were exceptions, however. Most of the officials we found in the Ministry, while highly qualified specialists, were inwardly opposed to democracy. They had been chosen for their loyalty to the old regime, were mostly conservative, accustomed to seeing Social Democracy as the national enemy and to considering democracy a necessary evil, better than Bolshevism, but not to be compared to the high goals realizable in the organized hierarchy of a monarchy. How could the spirit of public administration, and through it the spirit of the German citizenry, be reformed with such a staff?

To the average Western critic the problem was simple. One ought to have dismissed the old employees and replaced them with competent democrats. This, unfortunately, met with grave obstacles. The Weimar Constitution had guaranteed all members of the civil service protection of their "well-acquired rights." This was a most peculiar "basic right," quite extraneous to the historical and ideological context of inalienable human rights. It should never have been incorporated in the catalogue of such rights in the national Constitution. But it was there, and we were bound by it. We were only able to transfer politically unsuitable officials of high ranks to positions at least as high or higher in the government service, but not to dismiss or demote them. The rank of Ministerial Counselors (*Ministerialräte*) in the official hierarchy was so high that there were few equally high posts outside the ministries.

The most necessary change was in the post of adviser on matters of police, associations, and public meetings, which was held by a conservative staff member. We promoted him to head of the pensions' office for former members of the military. But such possibilities were rare. The Minister sent a very friendly letter to the oldest counselor, around seventy, head of a subdivision with varying duties, trying to persuade him that he might retire to make room for younger men who were more familiar with the new conditions. He was bitterly offended and refused. There was no compulsory retiring age; it took several years before one was prescribed by the legislative bodies, and for a long time there was doubt if this act was constitutional. We had, therefore, to wait for vacancies by death or apply for the creation of new posts, but the latter was almost always refused.

There was a second difficulty. The federal administration did not train its own recruits, except in the postal and the financial services. It had to turn to the *Laender* governments for properly trained personnel. The *Laender* watched jealously over their proportionate representation in the federal services. Nor did they always send their best men to the Reich, keeping these for themselves. The candidates were always well-qualified specialists, who had passed their examinations with distinction. But most of them were opponents of democracy.

## 42. THE DEATH OF RATHENAU

BECAUSE of the implications for home policies I took part in the Cabinet meetings in which Rathenau reported on his negotiations in Cannes (January, 1922) and afterward Wirth and Rathenau on the conference in Genoa and the Treaty of Rapallo (Easter, 1922). In Cannes, where Loucheur represented France, and Rathenau Germany, an agreement had almost been reached—almost, but not quite. While Rathenau was speaking to the Allied statesmen, who were listening tensely, suddenly—as he informed the Cabinet—telegrams were brought into the room and were passed around among the Allies from hand to hand. They soon became no longer neatly sealed dispatches, but loose strips of tape. Attention changed into unrest and confusion. What had happened? The telegrams informed Loucheur that the liberal French Premier, Briand, had been overthrown and the conservative Poincaré, advocate of intransigent severity toward Germany, was to be his successor. The negotiations in Cannes were broken off and a new meeting at Easter proposed.

In the week before Easter, 1922 the statesmen of Europe met in Genoa. It was the first official meeting of a pan-European character in the twentieth century. Representatives of small and great nations, victors and vanquished—all were assembled. France was no longer represented by Loucheur, but now by Barthou. The hand of the absent Poincaré, decisive in determining Barthou's attitude, lay heavy on the conference. He was said to be determined to prevent any agreement which did not separate the Rhine and the Ruhr from the rest of Germany. Officially he had insisted that Germany should not make the reparations a subject of negotiations.

Among the nations present there were the "Big Three"—at that time Great Britain, France, and Italy—others with fewer rights and again others with no rights. Long discussions at the official meetings concerned matters of procedure: whether, for example, Germany and Russia were automatically to have a place at the committees or should be invited only from time to time. Substantive issues were discussed only behind the scenes at private meetings. One main problem was whether Russia would have to pay the pre-war Tsarist debts to France and on the other hand have the right to collect reparations from Germany. Rathenau attempted to come to an unofficial agreement with the French on reparations to the West and with the Russians on a settlement in the East. When hope of a satisfactory conclusion had vanished, the Russians invited the Germans by telephone to nearby Rapallo to sign a treaty with them which had already been prepared in Berlin; both countries were to renounce all claims against each other arising from the war. After difficult deliberations during the night, first Wirth and then Rathenau decided to accept the offer. Rathenau drove to Rapallo and signed.

The Treaty of Rapallo had an explosive effect on the conference. The Germans were bombarded with reproaches. Under the leadership of Lloyd George, however, the Western powers soon reentered discussions with the German delegation and through their members, especially Rudolf Hilferding and Ago von Maltzan of the Foreign Office (afterward Ambassador to Washington), with the Russians as well. The conference came to a peaceful end, if without substantive conclusions. At the final meeting, on May 19, Rathenau de-

livered a formal address which ended with the words of Petrarch:
"I shall continue to call: Peace, peace, peace!" In honor of the host
country he quoted in Italian. The whole assembly gave him a personal ovation, in part for his gifts as a speaker, but also for the general impression all countries had that he was searching honestly and
uprightly for the way to peace in Europe, a peace which would include both East and West.

The Treaty of Rapallo led to excited arguments in Germany as
well. President Ebert was annoyed because he had not been consulted. To what extent he was opposed to the contents of the pact I
am unable to say from my own knowledge. I had the impression
that Rathenau was by no means intending to introduce a so-called
"seesaw policy" in which Germany would play the East off against
the West and vice versa just as it suited her own interest. He
wanted to compel respect for Germany, but never lost sight of his
ultimate goal: general, all-inclusive peace, which every individual
step taken by Germany had to serve.

After the first comparatively peaceful discussions in the Cabinet,
storm warnings were soon heard. Under the leadership of the
former Secretary for Home Affairs, Karl Helfferich, the German
Nationalists attacked Rathenau violently. Nationalist groups made
ever-increasing use of the theme of the "Jew Rathenau" in their agitation against democracy. We asked the Prussian police force—the
Reich government had no police force of its own, as, for example,
the United States government has at its disposal—to increase Rathenau's protection. But Rathenau refused to have a personal body-
guard. In the interest of a strong foreign policy he attempted to
come to a *modus vivendi* with his opponents in parliament. He had
a private discussion with Helfferich, but with no result. Although
Rathenau in the last speech he gave in the Reichstag, on June 23,
had strongly criticized the occupation forces, Helfferich delivered a
particularly malicious speech against him.

On the same evening Rathenau continued his efforts for understanding. The U.S. Ambassador, Alanson B. Houghton, had invited
him to dinner. From there they telephoned another of Rathenau's
opponents, the mightiest industrialist in Germany, Hugo Stinnes, to
join them. The discussion lasted to well after midnight. When on
the following morning Rathenau, later than usual, was on his way
to the Foreign Office, his car was overtaken by another; a sub-ma-
chine gun, discharged at very close range, drilled his body with nu-

merous shots, and a hand-grenade completed the work. A nurse, without knowing Rathenau, got into his car and supported him. He looked up at her but was unable to speak, since his jaw was smashed. He was taken home, where he breathed his last breath.

His murderers were immature assailants, some of them as young as sixteen, led by a former naval officer of twenty-five. All of them belonged to the Bavarian "Organization Consul," which had also been responsible for the murder of Erzberger (Chapter 38). After what they had heard and read they believed that Rathenau was a traitor and that his death was essential. Helfferich and other German Nationalists had not actually disseminated these untrue statements themselves, but they had not denied them publicly. Their own malicious attacks thus fell on ground well prepared by the poison of rumor and slander. If lies are not forcibly enough denied, they can kill. Thus Rathenau's "removal" was a classic example of that way of thinking and acting and that lack of opposition which later found general expression under the National Socialists. Erzberger had died because of it and there had been a serious attempt on Scheidemann's life. With Rathenau, however, for the first time in Germany a Jew in a prominent position had been murdered on the very ground that he was a Jew in a prominent position.

When the news reached me I could not allow myself long meditation. Pursuit of the criminals was up to the police of the individual *Laender,* in particular Prussia and Bavaria. But two other urgent tasks faced me. A fitting state funeral had to be arranged in cooperation with Redslob and the Foreign Office, and legislative measures had to be prepared to provide more effective prevention of similar crimes in the future.

I quote an entry in Count Kessler's diaries which testifies to the dignity of the funeral service held in the Reichstag building:

"The coffin stood raised in state behind the rostrum and beneath a mighty black canopy. The room was hung with black and filled with a sea of plants and flowers. . . . The galleries, and the whole room, were packed tight. No seat was empty, not even among the German Nationalists. . . .

"At twelve the Chancellor led Rathenau's old mother into the former Kaiser's box, still embellished with the W. The old lady was as pale as chalk, as if carved under her veil, but apparently completely controlled. Her face, ashen with pain, was what moved me most. She looked quite impassively at the coffin. . . . The musicians, out of sight behind the coffin in the hall, played Beethoven's Egmont overture, the stirring uprising of the people and the sweet and secret melody of love, and then Ebert spoke, stepping in front of the coffin, quietly, almost inaudible from emotion, but nobly. And after him, very clearly and movingly, Bell for the Reichstag. . . . Then the invisible instruments played the funeral march from Götterdämmerung, for the slain Siegfried, and this was the climax. . . . The effect under these circumstances was tremendous. Sobbing was heard, many around me cried, the historic tragedy in this death moved souls through music.

"Then the coffin was borne out, through the corridor onto the open staircase. Below, a company of the regular army stood, their helmets on their heads, inflexible in rank; the drums rolled; a mighty funeral march, sounding like a distant storm, swelled up; the coffin, wrapped in the national colors was put onto the hearse, which had been covered with roses. The procession slowly moved off. Despite the rain, or perhaps because of the grey veil of rain, the impression was almost greater than that in the hall. . . ." [1]

The martyr's death Rathenau had met seemed for a time to have a beneficial effect. Everyone semed to think it important to dissociate himself from the perpetrators. The German Nationalists were ashamed. Hugo Stinnes paid a visit to Rathenau's mother at her home in Viktoriastrasse, in order to express his sympathy personally. She asked him how it had been possible for him, Stinnes, to have known her son so little, to have so misunderstood and so attacked him. "Have you read his books?" she asked. Stinnes answered frankly that he had not. Frau Rathenau then brought out the six volumes of Rathenau's *Collected Works,* gave them to Stinnes, and asked him to give her his hand and promise that he would read them. What could Stinnes do? He promised. Anyone who knew him cannot imagine either that he kept his promise or that he broke it. He died shortly afterward; that may well have been the solution to this problem.

[1] Count Harry Kessler, *Tagebücher 1918–1937* (Diaries, 1918–1937) edited by Wolfgang Pfeiffer-Belli, Insel Verlag. Reprinted with the permission of the publishers.

## 43. Political Consequences of the Rathenau Murder

Two of the young men from the murderer's car took their own lives when, after a pursuit lasting several days, they were traced to the ruins of a medieval castle in Thuringia. A third, who had driven the car, was sentenced to fifteen years in prison; others were given lesser sentences. Advocates of democratic ideals, supported this time by the Communists, organized protest meetings and marches. The Right was hiding. Anyone who witnessed the demonstrations could have thought that all Germany respected and mourned Rathenau. Ten years later, when Hitler came to power, it was the Rightists who marched; the others were silent under terror. Then it seemed as if all Germans were Hitler supporters. If half of the population, or even only one third or less, become noisy and active and the others remain silent, the deceptive appearance of unanimous action is given.

Under the moral shock of the Rathenau murder we succeeded in getting an Act for the Protection of the Republic passed (July 21, 1922), even with a two thirds majority, required because some of the provisions were in formal conflict with the Constitution. The German Nationalists, the National Socialists, and the Communists opposed the law and denounced it as a monstrous repressive measure. But its major purpose was to close intolerable gaps in existing legislation. Persons who participated in an association whose purpose was to kill someone—as, for example, in the "Organization Consul"—were not punishable, unless it could be proved that concrete steps had already been taken for the plan to be carried out. Coarse abuses of the colors and insignia of the Weimar Republic were not punishable. Anyone could approve and glorify acts of violence or treason against the republican form of government without risking penalty. The new act made such deeds punishable and increased the penalties for other acts already punishable under existing law—for example, acts of violence, if directed against members of the government, and provocations to acts of violence, if directed against persons because of their political activities. Secondly, the new law empowered the police to take prompter action against unconstitutional meetings and publications. They had been forced to stand by inactive when meetings for illegal purposes were called until the illegal deeds had actually been committed and tolerated by the leaders of the meeting. The new act authorized the police to forbid a public meeting, if "definite facts justify the fear" that illegal acts will take place. Newspapers through which treason or deeds contrary to the new law had been committed could be confiscated and forbidden to appear for up to four weeks (in the case of weeklies up to six months).

The federal government was empowered to forbid members of families who had been formerly sovereign to stay in Germany, in order to prevent their becoming a center of counter-republican movements. A special "Court for the Protection of the Republic" was formed at the Supreme Court (*Reichsgericht*), before which the most important infringements of the act could be brought. There was ground for doubts if the ordinary courts, whose composition could not be changed, would enforce the act as energetically against the extreme Right as against the Communists. The composition of the new court was perfectly fair. The chairman was a senate president of the Reichsgericht, Dr. Hagens; members were two other justices of the Reichsgericht and six persons named by the Reich President, including a law professor of the People's Party and the former Chancellor Fehrenbach. With these two the judges from the Reichsgericht had a majority. The Democratic and Social Democrat members, too, were sensible men, not fanatics.

The preparation of the act lay with me, in cooperation with Erich Zweigert of the Ministry of Justice, who later became Secretary of the Ministry of the Interior. I was chairman of the pertinent Reichsrat committees and had to represent the federal government at the meetings of the Reichstag committee.

The act was limited to a period of five years. When this time ran out in 1927 a two-thirds majority for its prolongation could be obtained only for two more years and only after canceling the special Court for the Protection of the Republic. The extension act was signed by Hindenburg. In 1929 no qualified majority for further extension was available; only a weakened version could be passed by simple majority, which gave back the broad freedoms of the Weimar Constitution to the opponents of the republic. The police were no longer empowered to take preventive measures against public meetings of the Nazis. The special provision against the members of formerly sovereign families was abolished. Again two years later it became evident that this liberality was untenable. Chancellor Brüning reintroduced several preventive measures and added new ones but, since there was no two-thirds majority available, he was able to do this only by resorting to the emergency powers of the President under article 48 of the Constitution.

The lack of a two-thirds majority was, however, only a lesser evil compared to the fact that even simple majorities in favor of the democratic republic were not available either in the Reichstag or among the people at large. This lack, along with the political composition of the civil service and the courts, was a serious obstacle to energetic action by the police and the law courts against the extreme Right. Even the federal Ministry of the Interior, which was responsible for enforcing the act, passed into the hands of German Nationalist ministers three times (Schiele, 1925; von Keudell, 1927; Baron von Gayl, 1932); two of them turned the pertinent division, which had been in my hands until 1927, over to German Nationalists (Chapter 57).

In addition to the act for the Protection of the Republic we also succeeded in having an act passed on the duties of government officials to protect the republic. Every government official had to "abstain from anything that is not compatible with his position as a government official of the republic." In particular he was forbidden "to promote maliciously (*gehässig*) or provocatively public aspirations which were directed toward a restoration of the monarchy or against the continued existence (*Bestand*) of the republic, or to support such aspirations by slander, abuse, or scorn (*Verächtlichmachung*) of the republic or of members of the government. . . ." On a superficial reading this sounds as though officials were forbidden to oppose democracy in public or private life. But there was no two-thirds majority available for such prohibition. Officials were not forbidden to support the monarchy or produce propaganda for anti-democratic measures either in private or publicly; they were only forbidden to do this "maliciously" or "provocatively" or by telling conscious lies, by slander, abuse or scorn. They were free to belong to anti-republican associations, unless in an individual case that did conflict with official duties entrusted to them.

The celebration of Constitution Day after the Rathenau murder (August 11, 1922) still profited from the widespread feeling of shame and serious desire for unity against sham patriotism and lawless terror. Germany yet had no national anthem. At my suggestion President Ebert on this day proclaimed the third stanza of the popular *Deutschlandlied* with its praise of Unity, Justice, Liberty (*Einigkeit und Recht und Freiheit*) henceforth to be Germany's national anthem. The proclamation stated that the poet (Hoffmann von Fallersleben, 1798–1874) had been a fighting liberal all his life and had sung his hymn against all oppressors of freedom and justice. We ought not to allow his song to become the battlesong of those against whom it had been directed. "Just as once the poet, so we today love Germany above all else." At the end of the morning celebration the stanza was sung with visible emotion by all those present. The words *"Einigkeit und Recht und Freiheit"* shone from the wall behind the government dais and appeared for the first time on the once-most-popular coin, the *Taler* (three marks).

## 44. EDGING TO THE RIGHT—BLACK-RED-GOLD— STRESEMANN'S FLAG-DAMASCUS

IF the reactions to the Rathenau murder had some favorable consequences in home policy, its impact on foreign relations was catastrophic. The exchange rate for German currency was falling ever more rapidly. The foreign powers doubted that the promises of the Wirth government were truly representative of Germany. Discussions therefore began on replacing it with a "great coalition" including the rightist German People's Party. But the latter had misgivings about Wirth, because he had spoken so bitterly against the Right, and the Social Democrats refused to cooperate with the People's Party. Leading businessmen spoke of the need for a Chancellor whose signature would be considered "discountable" on the international market. It was being suggested to Ebert that the director general of the Hamburg-America line, former senior staff member (*Geheimrat*) in the treasury, Dr. Cuno, be appointed Chancellor. Wirth resigned. At the end of November Dr. Cuno formed a cabinet without Social Democrats. It consisted of members of the People's Party, the Zentrum and the Democrats, joined by a member of the Bavarian People's Party, by three ministers who belonged to no

party, and a few days afterwards by the former Lord Mayor of
Essen, Dr. Luther, as Minister of Food. Stresemann, the leader of
the German People's Party, was not yet a member of this Cabinet.

Ebert guaranteed a certain degree of continuity of policy and at
the same time a moderating influence on the Social Democrat opposition. He had still not been elected by the people. But the previous
opposition to him had given way to a widely held respect. It was in
fact neither he nor the Social Democrats who wanted to see the
election postponed; that was the wish of the parties in the middle
and at the moderate Right. Ebert, on the contrary, pressed for immediate election, and the old Cabinet under Wirth had proposed to
the Reichstag (October 5, 1922) to hold it on December 3. The Social Democrats were in favor of this. But the parties in the middle,
including the People's Party under Stresemann's leadership, were
opposed. Stresemann had good reason to worry that elections held
in this year, after the Rathenau murder and Ebert's decision to
make the *Deutschlandlied* the national anthem, would give Ebert
seven further years as President, especially since the Right was not
able to agree on a suitable opposing candidate (he himself thought
of Hindenburg or Bülow). Finally, all the parties except the German Nationals, the National Socialists, and the Communists agreed
to extend Ebert's term by constitutional amendment without popular election until June 25, 1925—a day he would never see. The
amendment was accepted by 316 to 64 votes. There is no better testimony to the widespread respect Ebert enjoyed.

The alterations in the Cabinet's composition affected the freedom
of action of the Ministry of the Interior. We could do nothing that
would offend the feelings of the new Chancellor or of the German
People's Party now represented in the Cabinet. Then we hit on a
constructive idea. The German revolution of 1848 and the first all-
German National Assembly that convened in St. Paul's Church in
Frankfurt the same year would reach their seventy-fifth anniversary
in 1923. Although it is not the custom to make much out of seventy-fifth anniversaries, we wanted to do so in this case; it gave us an
unusual opportunity to combine historical instruction with a glorification of the black-red-gold flag. In order to blunt party opposition,
Redslob and I flanked Stresemann in the Reichstag restaurant early
in January and tried to win him over to our plan. When he hesitated, because he perceived that such a celebration would revolve
around the black-red-gold flag, we reminded him that he himself as

a student had once carried that flag at an anniversary for the *Märzgefallenen* (those who died in the 1848 March revolution). We showed him a newspaper cutting about it. He then agreed, laughing and willing, apparently convinced by the plan and by the historical support he expected from the celebration for his own policy of active cooperation with the Weimar majority parties.

Stresemann was won over to the Weimar Republic there and then. The preceding two years, with their check on Social Democrat ascendancy on the one hand and growing rightist extremism on the other, had made a "rational republican" (*Vernunftrepublikaner*) out of him. But now he became inwardly engaged. Now there was involved more than mere opportunism, mere rationalism. While we were talking to him about St. Paul's, he suddenly looked like the former idealistic student again, who had carried the black-red-gold flag in honor of the *Märzgefallenen*. His hidden inclination toward the democratic republic was clear in his shining eyes. The Stresemann of Wilhelminian expansionist policies—Stresemann the First, if you like—who had supported the Kapp Putsch, was dying. Stresemann the Second was born, not a mere "rational republican," but—even though he might not say so openly to his party colleagues—seriously involved. Externally his attitude remained ambivalent; it had to, because his party stuck firmly to their monarchic ideal. At any rate he made sure that the Cabinet members from his party did not oppose our plan. He could easily reassure them by pointing to the fact that most of the deputies in St. Paul's had been supporters of a parliamentary monarchy.

So we went about our work. The celebration was being prepared for in a number of booklets and essays. On the anniversary of the opening of the Frankfurt National Assembly (May 18) President Ebert and the heads of governments of the Reich and the *Laender* assembled in the Frankfurt town hall opposite St. Paul's in the old Emperor's Hall, at that time still undamaged. Hindemith and his quartet played the work by Haydn from which the melody of the *Deutschlandlied* is taken. At the same hour as seventy-five years before, the guests formed a procession which marched, accompanied by the ringing of bells and led by the old black-red-gold flag which had been preserved, across to St. Paul's Church. There was organ music, Bach at the beginning, Beethoven at the end. President Ebert spoke, followed by a member of the German People's Party, Dr. Riesser (himself the nephew of a member of the National Assembly

of 1848; he described the influence of the St. Paul's assembly on subsequent history), by the Vice President of the Austrian National
Council, Dr. Dinglhofer. Professor Alfred Weber concluded. He
warned that what had been an established fact to the men of St.
Paul's—the spiritual basis of Europe—had become problematic in
Europe, more so than in America. After the service there was a popular celebration on the Römerberg. President of the Reichstag Paul
Löbe spoke from the balcony of the Emperor's Hall, Ebert standing
on his side. Great exultation followed. The *Deutschlandlied* swelled
up. In the evening there was a torchlight procession. From the balcony of the opera house Ebert spoke once more. We had succeeded
in making the German people more aware than they had been of
the liberal tradition in their own history.

## 45. OCCUPATION OF THE RUHR—REVOLT IN BAVARIA—

### HITLER PUTSCH—

### THE HUNDRED DAYS OF CHANCELLOR STRESEMANN

EVERY hope, however, for a recovery was crushed by other events in
the course of the year 1923. On January 11, France had sent a control commission of engineers, accompanied by French troops, to the
Ruhr, in order to check on deliveries of coal, with which Germany
was slightly behind. These arrears, along with others in the delivery
of telegraph poles, served as a pretext for Poincaré's action. Germany should never have offered him this excuse. Belgium participated in the French measures. England showed her disapproval, but
took no decisive action against them. The Cuno government announced a policy of "passive resistance." Entrepreneurs and workers
refused to work for France under French command. The French
then cut off all deliveries of coal to Germany from the Ruhr. The
federal government paid the idle workers and compensated the entrepreneurs. Inflation soared. Active resistance, which flared up in
several places, was put down by the French with cruel reprisals.
The Cuno Cabinet was not equal to the situation. Inflation reached
such proportions that for this reason alone the moral condition of
the Germans came near to madness. The dollar, once worth 4.20

marks, quoted at about 400 marks at the time of the Rathenau murder, was equal to 4,000 marks five months later (November, 1922); 4 million in August, 1923; 4 billion in October, 1923, and in November even 4 trillion (thousand billion) marks. Dr. Alvin Johnson, then editor of the *Encyclopedia of the Social Sciences* and first president of the New School for Social Research in New York, who landed in Bremen at about this time in order to look for contributors among German scholars, liked to tell how he gave a newspaper boy an American ten-cent piece for a paper and received several million marks change. How could anyone convince a nation of the value of democracy in such a state of hell?

When Constitution Day came around for the fourth time on August 11, 1923, the failure of the policy of passive resistance in the Ruhr was obvious. On the eve the Social Democrats had withdrawn their confidence from Cuno. The morning celebrations in the Reichstag building, at which Professor Anschütz, Germany's foremost constitution expert, delivered the speech, therefore passed in exceptionally serious fashion, but still as a public demonstration of goodwill and need of concentration.

Cuno resigned the following day. Stresemann became his successor for the short period of about one hundred days, decisive for Germany's recovery. In the face of violent opposition not only from the German Nationalists, but also from a large section of his own party, Stresemann had the courage to form a "great coalition," which included the Social Democrats, in order to obtain a broad enough basis for his Cabinet to end the adventure in the Ruhr and to stabilize the currency. He himself took over the Foreign Ministry. Wilhelm Sollmann, Social Democrat, became Minister of the Interior; Rudolf Hilferding, a former Independent, but on the basis of his book *Das Kapital* generally recognized as an expert on financial matters, Minister of Finance; Radbruch, Minister of Justice again; another Social Democrat, Minister of Reconstruction. To the horror of the German Nationalists and the right wing of the People's Party, this was a total of four Social Democrats. The Zentrum took over three ministries, the People's Party that of Economics, and Dr. Luther—classed as without party, but close to the People's Party— Food. Dr. Gessler stayed as Minister of Defense.

On September 26, President Ebert and the Stresemann Cabinet announced the end of passive resistance on the Ruhr. On the same day the Bavarian government invested dictatorial power in Gustav von Kahr. This action was based on Article 48 of the Federal Constitution which empowered the *Laender* governments to take emergency measures in a case so urgent that intervention from the federal President could not be waited for. President Ebert answered, on the suggestion of the federal Cabinet, by conferring dictatorial authority over the whole Reich upon Defense Minister Gessler, who appointed the regional commander of the federal forces in Bavaria, General von Lossow, to take the necessary steps in Bavaria. On October 19, Gessler forbade further publication of the National Socialist paper, *Völkischer Beobachter,* which appeared in Munich, but met with refusal by General von Lossow on the ground that the Bavarian government did not approve of the prohibition. When Gessler, who showed himself to be a true defender of the federal Constitution throughout this story, dismissed the General and appointed another in his place, the Bavarian government, under its temporary head, Commissioner von Kahr, went so far as to reappoint Lossow. General von Seeckt, chief of the military command in the federal Defense Ministry, sent a proclamation to the Bavarian troops, exhorting them to be loyal to the oath they had sworn to the Reich and to the national Constitution. The Bavarian government had the troops swear an oath of loyalty to the government of Bavaria, saying they were acting "as trustees for the German people" until an agreement with the federal government was reached.

These events formed the background for the Hitler putsch on November 8, 1923. It was precisely the time when the exchange rate of the dollar had reached about 4 trillion (4,000,000,000,000) marks. Hitler used the universal despair and indignation and the precarious situation in which Kahr and Lossow found themselves to his own advantage. He forced his way into the Bürgerbräu beer cellar while Kahr was speaking there, fired off a shot into the ceiling, and by his terroristic manner made Kahr and Lossow recognize a national dictatorship under himself and Ludendorff. As soon as they were free again, however, Kahr and Lossow broke with Hitler. They ordered the National Socialist Party in Bavaria disbanded and mobilized the police against Hitler, Ludendorff, and their supporters, who were marching to the Feldherrnhalle the following morning. There were a number of deaths. Hitler and Ludendorff were arrested.

Since the situation within the army had become so critical, President Ebert transferred executive authority, on Gessler's recommendation, to General von Seeckt, who promptly dissolved the National Socialist Party on November 23 within the whole of Germany. The Prussian Cabinet had already done this within Prussia a year before, on the basis of the Act for the Protection of the Republic. After long negotiations Kahr and Lossow resigned, but not until February 18, 1924. The federal government once again made concessions. They promised to consult the Bavarian government in the future before military commanders in Bavaria were dismissed (consultation in the case of *appointment* had been the rule before), and also when Bavarian troops were to be put into action outside Bavaria. The oath to be sworn by the Bavarian troops was modified. The new wording was as follows: "I swear loyalty to the Constitutions of the German Reich and of my home state, and as a brave soldier I promise solemnly to protect my *Vaterland* and its legitimate institutions at all times and to be obedient to the Reich President and to my superiors." The duty of obedience to the Constitution as the highest law was thus not changed.

But now back to November, 1923. A few days after the failure of the Hitler putsch, stabilization of the German currency was achieved. On November 15, a new currency called *Rentenmark* began to be circulated; one *Rentenmark* was to be equal to 1 trillion (1,000,000,000,000) marks, guaranteed by first-rank mortgages on all German real estate and on gold-bonds to be issued by industry, trade, and banks. The *Reichsmark* soon took the place of the *Rentenmark*.

I am one of the few members of the older generation who claims no credit for the currency stabilization. The Ministry of the Interior had nothing to do with it. I noted with satisfaction, however, that the plan was similar to the basic idea I had supported so actively in the last year of my work in the Chancellery, because it provided for the support of German government credit by mortgaging the "real values" in agriculture and industry (Chapter 36).

A few days before the Hitler putsch, the Social Democrats had announced their withdrawal from the federal Cabinet because of the "weak attitude" the government took toward the Bavarian government. They pointed out that Stresemann had shown greater energy in calling the Socialist governments in Saxony and Thuringia to order, when Communists had entered the cabinets. In these cases the federal government had sent a commissioner, Dr. Heinze, to the spot, who had deposed the *Laender* governments with the help of the armed forces. This undesirable difference in treatment only emphasized the fact that the danger of Bavaria's seceding from Germany was more serious than that of Saxony's or Thuringia's and, secondly, that a section of the regular army was involved in the Bavarian rebellion, so that the army would have had to shoot at members of its own body.

Along with Ebert I considered the decision of the Social Democrat Party to withdraw its members a serious mistake. Presumably they would not have done it a few days later, after the Hitler putsch and the currency stabilization. That they did it at all was due to the pressure from the former Independents, with whom they had just been reunited.[1]

Stresemann's rump cabinet stayed in office only a few more weeks. On November 23 it toppled. The leader of the United Social Democrat Party, Otto Wels, asked the Reichstag for a vote of censure against the government because of the two-sided policy against Bavaria, Saxony, and Thuringia and for the appointment of a member of the People's Party, Dr. Jarres, as Minister of the Interior, in the place of the Social Democrat Sollmann. Stresemann, not satisfied with the likely rejection of the motion for censure, demanded a positive declaration of confidence. This was refused by 230 against 115 votes. Stresemann resigned.

Within the hundred days of his chancellorship Stresemann had become a superior statesman, recognized as such at home and abroad. He remained Foreign Minister in all subsequent cabinets until his death in 1929, but he never again became Chancellor.

## 46. Changes in the Ministry of the Interior

WILHELM SOLLMAN, one of the most admirable characters I have come to know—manly, courageous, straightforward—unfortunately remained Minister of the Interior for only three months. In or out of office he felt himself fortunate to live in a Germany striving for renewal, to be the contemporary of many important men and women, including those of other parties and classes. But he died as an American citizen. At the beginning of the Hitler regime gangs

[1] See German ed., vol. i, p. 328.

of National Socialists took him to the Cologne Braunes Haus (Nazi headquarters), interrogated and tormented him, driving him up and down a staircase past a huge open window, in the expectation, no doubt, that he would leap through it—which he did not do. When he lay stretched out on the floor, one assailant sank a long knife slowly into his body and then drew it out again. Sollmann assumed that he would die in pain. He was rescued by the regular police, which still existed at that time, and taken to the hospital, where the doctor told him that the stabbing must have been done by a skilled surgeon, for he had stuck the knife in at just that one point where it was not dangerous. Sollmann had to flee Germany, and he found refuge in the United States. The Quakers took an interest in him and got him a post as a teacher at their institutes and as a speaker at a hundred places all over the United States. He also took part in training American soldiers going to Europe. After the war he remained a United States citizen, but went to Germany every year, calling for the establishment of free associations for the protection of civil rights. When he died, his last care—which I shared with him and which he urged on our mutual friend, the historian Felix Hirsch, on his deathbed—was that Germany must not fail to engage in practical negotiations in good time with its Soviet opponents on the reunification of Germany. "Negotiate! Negotiate!" was the last advice of a dying patriot of two countries. But that was thirty years later.

Sollmann was a Social Democrat. Jarres, who followed him into office in November, 1923 for a year and two months, was a member of the People's Party, a supporter of monarchistic ideals, nationalistic traditions, military concepts of honor, politically the opponent of Social Democracy. As a manly and candid person he was not unlike his predecessor; like him he respected the honest political convictions of others. Since we spoke to each other frankly our official cooperation was most pleasant on the personal level and often beneficial objectively; Jarres frequently accepted my arguments and made himself their advocate. He made several changes in the Ministry's organization and personnel that were obviously aimed at the pro-democratic trend to which his party was opposed. This was made easy for him because an "economy act" passed by the Reichstag authorized the federal government to transfer officials to lower posts, where they kept their former titles and salaries. He removed the outspokenly pro-democratic director of the Civil Service Division, appointed by Köster and particularly unpopular among older officials. Jarres transferred civil service affairs to my constitutional division, split off from my division a "political office" for purely political affairs, and transferred this section to Hermann Kuenzer, who had been "Commissioner for Public Order" under the Interior Ministry since 1920. My division was renamed "Division I, for Constitution, Administration and Civil Service."

Kuenzer, twelve years older than I, had been colonel and commander of the police forces in Baden and chief of a regiment during the war. He was politically a member of the Democratic Party, not the People's Party, to which Jarres belonged; both had formerly been National Liberals. In personal manner and ways of working he was a typical representative of the moderate Southern German Democrats. Attacks on the Constitution, including German Nationalist and National Socialist thrusts against it, were just as energetically repulsed by Kuenzer as by me. As a native of Baden he also was a born friend of the black-red-gold colors. But he showed less initiative and tended not to keep too close a watch on the military.

My "Division I" in its new form gave me such a large and politically important field that there was nothing for me personally to complain of in the reorganization. My influence in the federal administration increased.

My tasks included: interpretation and application of the Constitution, national elections, national symbols, Reichstag, Reichsrat, federal reorganization, relation between Reich and *Laender,* public administration and its reform, administrative law, civil service. New drafts for federal acts on associations, public meetings, and the press were to be worked out in my division, not in the political office. There was enough, then, to satisfy the greatest zeal for work. I rushed into most of these problems at once, carefully planning the various stages of work so as not to lose control. I will discuss only two of these here—Germany's reorganization and the reform of election methods.[1]

[1] Others are dealt with in the original German edition.

## 47. GERMANY'S REORGANIZATION (REICHSREFORM)

UNDER the Bismarck Constitution there had been a threefold personal union of offices between the federal and the Prussian government. The Kaiser was also King of Prussia; the Chancellor (with three brief exceptions) also Prussian Minister-President and Prussian Foreign Minister as well. These three bridges no longer existed in the Weimar Republic. According to the Constitution of 1919, the Prussian government was independent of the Reich government. There were no structural connections between the two, no bridge from one side of the Wilhelmstrasse to the other. As long as both governments were composed of members of the same parties, the party organizations could work toward coordination of federal and Prussian politics. But when the Social Democrats left the Reich government while continuing to be predominant in Prussia, and when other parties, such as the German People's Party, and several times the German Nationalists and the Bavarian People's Party, had a share in the Reich government but not in the Prussian, then the party link also disappeared. The party organizations tended to become sources of discord rather than conciliation between the cabinets. Coordination depended after that on good will alone. That it was achieved to a considerable degree was to be credited above all to the statesmanship of the Prussian Minister-President Otto Braun, who practiced great reserve in opposition to the Reich government, in order to avoid Germany's political collapse. As long as Ebert lived, he too exercised a moderating and conciliatory influence.

A second basic difference in Germany's constitutional structure before and after the war lay in the fact that during the imperial era the federal government had essentially claimed only legislative functions and not administrative ones, leaving the latter, with the exception of the navy and the postal service (in Bavaria and Württemberg the postal service too) completely to the *Laender* governments. Even the collection of custom duties—an important source of federal income—and the military administration was left to the *Laender,* if under federal regulations. Only in a war did the *Laender* armies pass under the Kaiser's command and executive power. After the war all this had changed. The Reich had taken over the administration of the army, of railroads, canals, customs, major taxes (especially the income tax), and social security administration. Consequently, while there had formerly been no federal office buildings in the *Laender,* except for the usually ugly post offices (and in Bavaria and Württemberg not even these), now the Reich eagle shone out everywhere on barracks, railroad coaches, railroad stations, national finance buildings, national labor exchanges.

The power of the *Laender* could no longer be compared with that of the Reich. "Prussia is really only a huge village now," State Secretary Albert once said to me in the Chancellery. That was, to be sure, a great exaggeration, for the *Laender* continued to be responsible for the administration of justice, of the police force, of education, and the control of local government. But this division of power between Reich and *Laender* in important branches of administration led to friction that had not been disturbing internal relations formerly.

In addition, the senseless differences in the size of the *Laender* blocked the path to rational reorganization. Prussia embraced about three-fifths of the total population of Germany, Bavaria and Saxony together a further fifth, and all other fourteen *Laender* the final fifth. The four smallest *Laender* (Lippe, Lübeck, Mecklenburg-Strelitz, Schaumburg-Lippe) together had less than half a million inhabitants, about as much as an average-sized city. More than half the *Laender,* in fact nine, had a total of less than three million inhabitants, less than *one* Prussian government district, that of Düsseldorf, or the city of Berlin.

The need for reorganization was emphasized in various parliamentary resolutions and in writings by leading men. Now it was being brought up officially in a memorandum handed in by the Bavarian government on January 5, 1924—right in the middle of the conflict between the federal and the Bavarian government. This paper did not express any separatist tendencies. Indeed, it recognized that whatever "the Reich needs for its existence externally and its effective operation inwardly, it must keep" including any functions "in the exercise of which unified regulations would improve and strengthen the situation of the citizens."

The basic thesis of the memorandum was the following: The Bismarck Constitution had been ideal for Germany and had brought Germany to her peak. "It was a federal type of government in the full sense of the term." "Defeat and revolution were independent of the Bismarck Constitution." The opposite was true, so the argument went on, of the Weimar Constitution. In the preamble great goals were declared. "But what had come about is the opposite . . . never has the Reich been further from internal and external peace than it now is; there is nothing to be seen of social progress." Increasing unitarism actually endangered German unity, the more so because of the change in the form of government. "There the strong cement of the monarchy, here the weak binding powers of the republic." "What was intended to be a clamp to hold the new Reich together [increased unitarism] has proved to be dynamite."

The historical comparison elaborated in the Bavarian memorandum suffered from one intrinsic contradiction. It extolled the Bismarck Constitution as the guarantee of ultimate wisdom for Germany. It asked for a return to its tested principles. But the actual proposals were in complete contradiction of the Bismarck Constitution, precisely at its central point. For Bismarck's Constitution proceeded from the greatness and supremacy of Prussia, on which the internal power of the Reich was to be based. Prussian supremacy was guaranteed by the three personal combinations of federal and Prussian offices already mentioned, and by Prussia's undivided votes in the Bundesrat, not yet split between state government and provinces. In addition, Prussia had an unconditional right of veto in military matters, in customs, and in questions of indirect taxes. It is scarcely comprehensible how the Bavarian memorandum could present the Bismarck Constitution as an ideal compared to the Weimar Constitution, without mentioning those points. What the memorandum suggested was quite different from a return to the Bismarck Constitution. The Reichsrat was to recover the greater powers of the old Bundesrat, but Prussia was not to regain the position it had held there. The assertion that the Bismarck Constitution had nothing to do with the German defeat was highly contestable (see Chapter 12).

The task of drafting an answer to the Bavarian memorandum fell to me. I replied to its general argument in the manner just outlined and asked the individual federal Ministries to deal with the suggestions of the Bavarian government within their respective fields according to a unified scheme, so that first the situation under the Bismarck Constitution, then the changes under the Weimar Constitution, then any apparent defects, and finally the Bavarian suggestions were to be discussed. In this way we obtained a carefully grounded answer within a very short time. Together with the Bavarian memorandum, our answer was to play a considerable role in the further work on reform in the Reich.

I did not advocate reintroduction of Prussian supremacy, of course. I rather emphasized that the duplication of Germany's central administration by federal and Prussian Ministries and the absurd differences in size of the *Laender* must be abolished. The Prussian central administration was in part to be transferred to regional units and in part to be combined with that of the Reich. In other words, the Prussian central administration was to disappear. Prussia was to be divided territorially into medium-sized *Laender,* and the smallest *Laender* were to be joined with neighboring *Laender* or provinces.

Work on the reply to the Bavarian memorandum made me familiar with every detail of the constitutional problems involved. Thus I eventually became what I had previously not been, one of the best-informed experts in the field, and I was being consulted more and more on these matters. There was from the start one difference in my approach. I tried to find solutions which had *a prospect of being accepted* in Reichsrat and Reichstag with the majorities necessary for constitutional changes. It was comparatively easy to think up ideal solutions one way or the other. But solutions that could be realized constitutionally without force were not so easy. I shall return to this point later.

## 48. ELECTORAL REFORM

LET us assume that in the United States, Great Britain, France, and Germany there was, in each of them, one constituency in which 100,000 of the voters had cast their vote for a Conservative candidate, 90,000 for a Liberal, 80,000 a Social Democrat, and 70,000 a Communist. Then this constituency would in the United States and Great Britain be represented by the Conservative. In imperial Germany there would have been a second ballot between the two top candidates, which would have probably ended in favor of the Liberal. In the France of the Third Republic (until the Second World

War), where second ballots were not restricted to the two leading candidates, either the Liberal or the Social Democrat would have made the running; the result would be largely the same today in the Fifth Republic. In the Weimar Republic, however, all four would have gained a seat, since each of them had more than the quota necessary at that time for a seat (60,000 votes).[1] Hence, despite exactly equal division of views in the electorate, a Conservative would be elected in one country, a Liberal in another, a Social Democrat in a third, and in a fourth all three and a Communist as well.

The defects of proportional representation have been discussed in Chapter 23. Its splitting effect was particularly disastrous in a country with political opinions so diversified as in Germany at that time, where people were not even agreed on the constitutional foundations. Rather, ideals of authoritarian monarchism, democratic republicanism, National Socialism, and Communism were combatting one another. The Anglo-American rule that the relative plurality decides who is elected would have forced the German voter to cast his vote, unless he wanted to waste it, for a candidate who had a chance of obtaining a relative plurality and thus to join forces with other people with whom he agreed on essential points. Under a system of proportional representation, carried through mathematically, and especially under its Weimar version, this was quite different. The voter could cast his vote for a program which corresponded to his particular interests and be sure it would not be wasted, provided that his interest group received at least 60,000 votes. The voter was not, therefore, brought up to a citizen's duty to join with others peacefully. He could leave that—even *had* to leave that—*to the members elected*. They in turn felt themselves representatives of a closed group with specific interests or ideologies and were afraid that they would forfeit their chances of reelection if they failed to support these special interests or ideologies firmly.

The many historical factors that had shaped the composition of the German people were reflected in as many different parties. There was a special party for every attitude to life. This was paradise for statisticians, hell for statesmen. Nor could, under proportional representation, right and left-wing extremists be kept out of parliament by being outvoted locally. In France's Third Republic this was possible, and also happened as a rule. This fact alone ex-

---

[1] So it would still be today in the Federal Republic (except for the outlawing of the Communists) and in almost all democracies on the Continent of Europe.

plains why there were only a dozen Communists and a handful declared monarchists in the French Assembly, when a system of proportional representation would have supplied sixty or more Communists and numerous monarchists.

Great Britain had large government majorities in the House of
Commons for more than twenty-two of the twenty-five years between 1918 and 1943. Under methods of proportional representation
there would hardly ever have been firm majorities in that period;
rather, constant three-cornered struggles would have removed all
possibility of a strong leadership. The large parliamentary majorities made it possible for the British parliamentary system to meet
grave crises, as in the general strike of 1926, the transition from free
trade to protective tariffs in 1932, and the abdication of Edward
VIII in 1936, not to mention Chamberlain's Munich policy in 1938.
Had Great Britain lived under a system of proportional representation, the course of her history—and of world history—would have
been different.

In the United States, too, the plurality system has kept Communists, special ethnic parties, nationalistic groups, and other fanatic
minorities (Townsend, Father Coughlin) as such out of Congress.

Along with our official expert for electoral affairs, Dr. Kaisen-
berg, I sought a way out. Abolition of proportional representation
was not feasible, since it was prescribed by the Constitution. We
suggested increasing the number of constituencies to almost five
times the original number, from 35 to 156, in order to replace the
enormously large constituencies with their long lists of candidates
for each party by considerably smaller ones. In these the number of
candidates any party could nominate was to be limited to two. In
this way we hoped to influence the selection of candidates—more
personalities, fewer party secretaries, and more youthful candidates.
The proportional character of the electoral system was maintained
by a clause saying that any excess number of votes received by a
party in one constituency could be credited to a member of the
same party in a neighboring constituency.

The Cabinet and the Reichsrat accepted our draft (1924). In the
Reichstag, however, while the party leaders, who had nothing to
fear for themselves, were prepared to accept it, the bulk of the
anonymous members was not. No argument could convince them.
For to the question: "Why should the law be altered?" the real answer was: "Because you are not good enough; because we want bet-

ter representatives." No deputy is prepared to vote for a law, the purpose of which is that he shall not be elected again. A leading article which I published on September 19, 1924 in the Social Democrat paper *Vorwärts,* supporting our proposal, had no success. The law was not passed. A second thrust, undertaken in 1930, after I had left the Ministry of the Interior, also failed. The system of proportional representation stayed.

## 49. Easing of International and Economic Tensions—The Dawes Plan— Further Jolt to the Right

The year 1924 brought decisive political changes in Great Britain, France, Russia, and Germany, although in different directions. In January Lenin died—an event to which little attention was paid in Germany. Stalin took his place. Three days after Lenin's death Great Britain got her first Labour Cabinet, under Ramsey MacDonald. Later in the same year, after a large swing to the left in the elections, Poincaré resigned as Premier of France. The victorious Left, led by Herriot, attacked President Millerand for his support of Poincaré and forced him to resign. Doumergue—for the first time a Protestant—was elected President. Herriot became Premier.

In Germany the trend led in the opposite direction. The election on May 4, 1924 inflicted an even more depreessing defeat upon the democratic-republican parties than they had suffered in 1920. Social Democrats, Democrats, and Zentrum received a total of only 193 from 472 seats, far from a majority (237). The parties to their right had 217 seats, the Communists 62. The German Nationalists, with 106 seats, were stronger than the Social Democrats, who had been reduced to 100. They demanded a place in the government and the exit of Stresemann, whom they hated for his republican collaboration. But Chancellor Marx refused to give up Stresemann and continued to govern with largely the old Cabinet.

On the question of reparations a decisive step was taken. A conference in London in August led to the acceptance of a reparations plan worked out by and named after the former director of the

United States Budget Bureau, Dawes. Further developments in Germany cannot be understood without some knowledge of the Dawes Plan, scarcely familiar today even to the older generation and completely alien to the younger. I will describe it here as simply as possible. The reparation payments were to consist of three main items: payments from a bonded debt imposed on German railroads, from another bonded debt placed on the German industry, and payments from the federal budget. For this purpose the railroads were to be turned into an independent corporation, on the supervisory council of which the creditor states were to have half the seats and which was to be debited with a bonded debt of 11 billion gold-marks for the benefit of the creditors. This debt was to have an interest rate of five percent—although only from the third year onward, in order to give a brief pause of recovery—and to be paid off at the rate of one percent from the fourth year on. The new railroad corporation therefore had to pay 660 billion gold-marks annually to the reparation creditors from the fourth year on. A five percent industrial debt was to be redeemed at a rate of one percent from the third year on. Payments from the federal budget were to begin in the third year only and, gradually increasing, were to amount to 1¼ billion gold-marks in the fifth year and thereafter. On top of this a traffic tax was to be levied in favor of the reparation creditors. Total payments according to the Dawes Plan would amount to 1 billion gold-marks (800 million of which was to be advanced as a reparation loan by the creditors) in the first year and then increase gradually, until in the fifth year they would be 2½ billion gold-marks annually. From the sixth year on, with increasing prosperity, there was to be added a sum to be determined according to a prosperity index. All amounts were to be paid in Germany currency and were to be transferred, "as far as possible," to the foreign countries in foreign currency by a transfer committee under the chairmanship of a reparations agent, the young and gifted American, Parker Gilbert. There were to be foreign commissioners for the note-issuing bank, for the railroads, for certain budget revenues that were to be pledged as pawns (custom duties, taxes on beer, tobacco, sugar, and brandy), and trustees for the railroads and industry bonds.

The Dawes Plan left Germany with alarming prospects for later years. But for the moment a pause for recuperation was guaranteed, and one could hope, if necessary, for new negotiations in the future. The Reichstag accepted the Dawes Plan at the end of August, 1924.

The German Nationalists opposed it passionately, Helfferich condemning it as a "second Versailles" (a few days before his death in a railroad accident). But their approval was not necessary for reaching simple majorities, and the two-thirds majority necessary for one of the laws (the railroads act) was obtained when almost half the German Nationalists, in order to avoid a collapse, from which they themselves could find no way out, voted in favor—the beginning of the later split in the party.

The government announced in an official statement that the assertion in the Treaty of Versailles that Germany alone was responsible for the First World War was a contradiction to the historical facts and that they did not acknowledge it.

Home politics also grew calmer. In February, Commissioner von Kahr and General von Lossow in Bavaria had finally resigned. From February until April, Hitler and his accomplices were tried in the people's court in Munich. Hitler and Pöhner were sentenced to five years' confinement in a fortress for high treason, Röhm and Frick to one year and three months for aiding and abetting. Röhm and Frick were granted probation. Ludendorff was discharged. Hitler and Pöhner were pardoned soon after (December, 1924), but for the moment they were imprisoned. Legal proceedings were also begun against members of "Organization Consul," these cases being heard before the special court created by the Act for the Protection of the Republic. Several of the accused were sentenced to various penalties on charges of being members of a secret illegal society.

In this year Constitution Day was celebrated with particular verve. At the morning ceremony in the Reichstag, the last at which Ebert was present, he was joined in his box by Otto Braun, Hugo Preuss, and Vice President Riesser (People's Party). Hamburg's Lord Mayor, Carl Petersen, delivered the official address. "Anyone who abuses the black-red-gold flag," he said, "is abusing the ideas of national unity." Vice Chancellor Jarres (People's Party), representing Chancellor Marx, who was away in London, stated in the name of the government, "that we, as is our duty, are resolved and able to defend the Constitution with all means and with no reservations against any attempt at illegal or violent change, from whatever side such an attempt might come." After the ceremony Ebert walked down the broad front staircase. The military band played the "Deutschlandlied." The march past of the guard of honor followed.

In Weimar, Preuss, Fehrenbach, and Heuss spoke; in Stralsund, Thomas Mann.

Thus the horizon seemed to clear on all sides. But the German People's Party demanded extension of the Cabinet to include the German Nationalists. Stresemann himself supported this demand. Marx would yield only if the Social Democrats were drawn into the Cabinet; they for their part were demanding previous recognition of the republican constitution by the German Nationalists. Negotiations broke down. The Reichstag was dissolved.

After the new elections in December, 1924 the Social Democrats returned stronger by a third (131 as against 100 seats), the Communists weaker by more than a fourth (45 against 62). The "Racists" (substitute for the banned National Socialists) had less than half their former strength (14 against 32). The German Nationalists kept about the same number of seats they had obtained in May. On the whole the election marked distinct advance on the way to recovery. Stresemann's party showed a slight increase, from 44 to 51; the Democrats from 28 to 32; the Zentrum from 65 to 69. Löbe became Reichstag President again, having had to relinquish the post to a German Nationalist in May.

However, the three democratic-republican parties were still short of a majority. Marx was unable to win sufficient support for either a minority cabinet of Zentrum and Democrats, or a great coalition including both Social Democrats and German Nationalists. On Stresemann's recommendation Ebert thereupon asked Hans Luther, formerly Lord Mayor of Essen and Federal Minister of Food and Finance to form a new government. For the first time after the Revolution the German Nationalists entered the Cabinet, even four of them. Martin Schiele became Minister of the Interior in place of Jarres; other German Nationalists occupied the Ministries of Economics, Finance, and Food. Stresemann remained Foreign Minister; Gessler, Minister of Defense. The Cabinet, including the German Nationalists, declared that the legal basis of its work was the republican Constitution, and that it would oppose vigorously and prosecute as high treason any attempt at change by *illegal* means.

In the Ministry of the Interior the slip to the Right was especially notable. Only a year previously had a member of the People's Party replaced a Social Democrat minister, and now a German Nationalist had become his successor. We awaited him with a sort of amused tension, for it was indeed strange that the Ministry of the

Interior under the Weimar Constitution was to be headed by a representative of its enemies. On the other hand, since he had sworn an oath to the Constitution and had approved the government declaration, a step toward consolidation could be seen in his appointment. Was not Ebert still Reich President so that a link from the Social Democrats to the German Nationalists had now been established, quite apart from the continued rule of the Weimar coalition parties in Prussia?

## 50. EBERT'S DEATH

THEN Ebert died (February 28, 1925), barely fifty-four years old. The medical cause was peritonitis following appendicitis. But I think his closest friends were right when they said that his death had to be traced back to two other links in the chain of cause and effect. One was the fact that against the urgent advice of his doctors he had put off the operation too long, because he was involved in a legal dispute, after a radical nationalist in Munich had shouted the accusation at him in the street that he had been "a traitor to his country" (*Landesverräter*). The second was Ebert's bitter grief about the spread of such slander (in 1924 alone he brought more than one hundred suits for slander) and its lenient treatment in the German courts, and more generally the hostile attitude of broad sections of the German middle classes. Even many workers had shown hostility, though for different reasons; they accused him not of high treason, but of betraying the working classes. His former great physical power of resistance had been broken.

After the Munich incident Ebert brought suit against the offender, but refused to go on the witness stand himself on his role in the munitions workers' strike of 1918, which constituted the basis for the slanderous reproaches. It was well known in all politically interested circles, he said, that he had condemned this strike vigorously and had finally joined the leaders of the strike only in order to bring it to an end as quickly as possible. He considered it below the dignity of the President to justify himself personally on this to any person who came along. The only alternative in German law to appearing as a witness was to withdraw the suit for slander. This he

did. But now the real trouble began. The offender declared in an
open letter that Ebert had admitted his guilt by withdrawing the
suit, and a Magdeburg newspaper published the letter with words
of editorial agreement. Ebert then brought suit against the editor.
Proceedings in the Magdeburg district court lasted two weeks,
ending the day before Christmas Eve, 1924. The court sentenced the
editor to two months' imprisonment for slander, without summon-
ing Ebert as witness. But in its opinion it also stated that Ebert, by
joining the strike leadership, had actually committed treason in the
sense of the penal code, although politically, morally, and historically it might be possible to judge his action differently. Ebert immediately appealed, but the appeal was never heard because of his
death.

He was in my opinion more than necessarily disturbed by the
Magdeburg verdict. The testimony to his patriotism, which after
the Magdeburg case and then again after his death came from all
sides, was overwhelming. Chancellor Luther and the Cabinet delivered memorial addresses and articles in his honor, no less strong
than those from his own party. I was personally much affected by
his death. What had drawn me to him—from external characteristics to the unerring firmness of his policy and to his natural dignity,
which kept him from any affected, artificial, or theatrical gestures—I
have spoken of before. I was proud to have his confidence. In difficult questions I liked to turn to him. In his political insight he was
far superior to most of his friends and opponents, and in particular
to average middle class Germans who were so proud of their better
school education.

It was my task after Ebert's death to organize a dignified funeral
in cooperation with the President's office and Edwin Redslob. The
ceremony took place in the black-hung hall of the President's palace
in the Wilhelmstrasse. Chancellor Luther spoke with vigor and
emotion. Nuntius Pacelli, the doyen of the diplomatic corps, later
Pius XII, sat in the first row in front of me. I have already described how, after the ceremony, he stepped up in front of the coffin, spread out his robe, and seemed to be receiving the dead President back into the Church in mercy. Then the long procession
moved through the Brandenburg Gate to the Reichstag, where
Reichstag President Löbe spoke, and on along the street which afterward became Friedrich Ebert Strasse, to the Potsdam Station. It
was a grievous leavetaking, and the German people, at least the

great majority of them, obviously shared the emotion. On the following day Ebert was buried in the beautiful hillside cemetery of his home town Heidelberg.


## 51. HINDENBURG's ELECTION: THE APPARENT AND THE REAL SURPRISE

Now, at last, the first national election of a Reich President, which had been put off for so long, was to be held. National elections were under the care of my division. We issued the necessary instructions. In the intervening period the President of the Federal Supreme Court, Dr. Simons, was Acting Reich President. I therefore went to him, as I would have gone to Ebert, when the head of the police division in the Prussian Ministry of the Interior asked me whether I would accept an appointment as chief of police in Berlin. I owed this question, which took me by surprise, to the reputation I had acquired as an expert on the Constitution and the laws on associations, public meetings, the protection of the republic, and emergency decrees. Simons thought my work in the federal Ministry of the Interior to be more important, as in fact I did myself. Ought I to make things so easy for the new Minister to appoint a German Nationalist replacement for me? I asked not to be put on the list of persons available for the police post.

When the Constitution came into being I had, like so many others, accepted the American principle of popular presidential elections as a further prop for true democracy. But the question had not been thought through carefully enough. In the United States, where the entire nation, almost without exception, approves the republican-democratic constitution, no party can dare to nominate a candidate about whose loyalty to the basic principles of the constitution there is any possible doubt: such a candidate would have no chance. But in Germany three, later four, constitutional concepts were competing for the favor of the people: democratic-republic, monarchy, Communism, National Socialism. None of them was backed by a majority. Furthermore, in Germany proportional representation provided for some twenty parties in parliamentary elections. Parties do not like to unite under the leader of another party.

Wherever there are many parties there is an inherent danger that in presidential elections political outsiders, who enjoy popularity as generals, heroes, artists, inventors, etc., are nominated as vote catchers and elected.

That none of the party candidates proposed for the first ballot would be anywhere near the necessary majority was obvious from the outset. The votes were 7.8 million for the Social Democrat Otto Braun; 4 million for the Zentrum candidate, Wilhelm Marx; 1.6 million for the Democrat, Hellpach. This made a total of 13.4 million for candidates of the old Weimar coalition parties, less than half. The joint candidate of the People's Party and the German Nationalists, Dr. Jarres, collected 10.8 million; the representative of the Bavarian People's Party 1 million; General Ludendorff, candidate of the National Socialists and other anti-semitic groups, only 0.2 million; Communist Thälmann, 1.9 million.

It is worth noting that the referendum indicated no *fascist* preferences in the German nation at that time; Ludendorff's failure was outright ridiculous. The pro-democratic parties' most dangerous rival was not a fascist, but Dr. Jarres, moderately right of center, known to be an unconditional supporter of government based on law and independent law courts (*Rechtsstaat*).

A second ballot had to follow, in which a relative majority was enough. The Weimar parties agreed on the Zentrum leader, Dr. Marx, since it was certain that all Social Democrats would vote for him against the Right, but not that the supporters of the Zentrum would all vote for a Social Democrat, had he been selected as joint candidate. The right-wing parties, doubting that any party man would be able to attract sufficient votes from other parties, now put up a popular outsider: Field Marshall Hindenburg. He obtained 14.7 million votes; Marx, 13.8; the Communist Thälmann, 1.9. Hindenburg was thus elected.

Four circumstances helped him: first, his great popularity; second, the fact already mentioned that many voters preferred to vote for a non-party candidate than for the leader of another party; third, the hesitation many Protestants felt to vote for a Catholic, which along with the hero cult caused many Protestants, women especially, to vote for Hindenburg; fourth, the stubbornness of the Communists, instructed by Moscow, in presenting their own candidate for the second ballot instead of casting their decisive votes for Marx against Hindenburg.

The real surprise was not Hindenburg's victory, which in view of the lack of pro-democratic majorities was quite logical, in case the Communists abstained. The real surprise came later. It was the unexpected fact that Hindenburg subjected himself quite loyally to the Weimar Constitution and maintained this attitude unhesitantly during his first term in office. Both sides had expected his support for right-wing attempts to restore the monarchy, to abolish the colors of the democratic republic in favor of the former black-white-red, to reduce the rights of the working classes, to reintroduce more patriarchal conditions. The great surprise—disappointment on the one side, relief on the other—was that he did *not* do any of this. During the election campaign he said that now he had read the Constitution for the first time and had found it quite good. "If duty requires that I act as President on the basis of the Constitution, without regard to party, person, or origin, I shall not fail." Campaign promises are often mere sedatives; no one trusts them. But the Field Marshall kept his for seven years. He swore an oath to the Constitution before the Reichstag. He had the black-red-gold standard fly above his palace and on his car and made no attempt to show the black-white-red colors instead. He made no step toward a monarchistic restoration. He performed his presidential functions conscientiously in the manner prescribed by the Constitution. During the first five years, he did not even once make use of the President's emergency power under article 48, as Ebert, much to Hindenburg's annoyance, had done repeatedly, and then did so only at Chancellor Brüning's request. For seven years he dismissed and appointed chancellors in strict accordance with the Constitution without regard to his personal preferences; the Social Democrat Hermann Müller was chancellor under him for two years (1928–1930). He signed all acts passed by the Reichstag, whether or not he liked them, even the first extension of the Act for the Protection of the Republic in 1927, though with a little grumble about the paragraph on the further exile of former royal families, the "Kaiser-Paragraph."

Only once did Hindenburg refuse his signature. That was when a law passed by the Reichstag subjected duels on matters of honor in the military to disciplinary punishment. Had the Reichstag insisted, Hindenburg would either have had to sign, or to put the law to a referendum, or to resign. The majority parties, however, wisely avoided a presidential crisis on this relatively trivial matter. They did not insist. Hence there was no infringement of the Constitution.

Hindenburg's election thus gave the German democracy a new lease on life, just at the moment when its demise had been expected. *That* was the real surprise, not the fact that the general had been elected. In France, too, in 1876 a popular general had been elected president, Mac Mahon. Unlike Hindenburg, Mac Mahon at once actively supported the opposition to democratic institutions. He tried to force his personal followers on parliament as premiers, pressure which Hindenburg—during his first term—did not apply. After many humiliations Mac Mahon finally resigned when he was asked to put his signature to the replacement of all anti-democratic generals by pro-democratic ones. That was actually never asked of Hindenburg; if it had been, he would probably have reacted as did Mac Mahon.

For once, then, the Weimar Republic had good luck. Hindenburg's election led to the disillusion of his monarchistic-nationalistic electors, not to the abolition of the republic. His great popularity and his military appearance satisfied a widely felt desire to see a person of splendor and glory at the head of the Reich. The memory of a thousand victories, and strangely enough not that of defeat, was associated with Hindenburg. The desire to see the Kaiser return gradually grew weaker. Hindenburg was more popular.

One of the drawbacks that have been associated with the election of popular generals to civil posts has been their lack of knowledge of personnel suitable for civilian functions. Correct assessment of political and administrative qualities is possible only on the basis of knowledge of strong and weak points in practical work, and this knowledge is acquired only by long observation and cooperation. A general has knowledge of military personnel, but not of civilian. There he depends on advisers and wire-pullers. This defect has been clearly seen in all generals. It was especially evident in Hindenburg during the Weimar Republic. At one of the first evening receptions he gave as President, he stood upright at the entrance and received each of his many guests—members of parliament, journalists, senior officials—who were introduced to him, with a gracious handshake. Then he strode through the crowd of guests in the manner of a great landowner, addressing friendly words to some. What could he say? I overheard his remarks when he said to the best-known journalist in Berlin, Georg Bernhard, editor of *Vossische Zeitung* and chairman of the weekly press conference, "Well, do you also live in Berlin?"

## 52. Continuing Work Under Anti- and Pro-Democratic Ministers—Luther's Defeat on the Flag Issue

I HAD no personal difficulty in my work under the new German-Nationalist Minister of the Interior, Herr Schiele. Frankness, a sense of humor, and mutual tact helped us to get along well. My current work on reconstruction of the Reich, administrative reform, reform of the civil service acts, the law on associations and meetings, codification of the federal statutes, went on undisturbed. Nor did Schiele or Hindenburg object to the celebration of Constitution Day. They took part, although other members of the German Nationalist party stayed away. Professor Hermann Platz (Bonn) delivered the official speech along the lines of "on the one hand, on the other hand," devoid of any spark.

Of course, militant plans for the protection of democratic-republican ideals could not be carried on in my official work. In view of the frequent change of ministers, that was not very important. In any case, as long as I was there, I could prevent my division being used *against* the democratic republic.

Stresemann's diaries have revealed that Schiele made an attempt to have the Foreign Office send me as ambassador to Vienna. He wanted in this case to give my division in the Ministry of the Interior to a member of the Zentrum (to give it to a German Nationalist did not seem to him quite proper), and to have in turn installed a German Nationalist as Ministerial Director in the Foreign Office. Stresemann called this "unscrupulous" (*ein skrupelloses Personalgeschäft*) and refused to have anything to do with it.[1]

Indeed, Schiele's rule did not last long. At the end of October the German Nationalists withdrew from the government as a protest against the Locarno Pact which reconfirmed the cession of Alsace-Lorraine to France by *voluntary* agreement in return for rather vague promises of a speedier end of the Rhineland occupation. Min-

---

[1] Stresemann, *Vermächtnis,* ed. by Henry Bernhard, Bern, 1932, vol. 2, p. 309, entry of August 5, 1925; quoted in the German ed. of these memoirs, vol. 1, p. 515.

ister of Defense Gessler took over the Ministry of the Interior, the sixth minister under whom I worked there within four years. But that, too, was only a short interlude. On January 19, 1926 Luther's second cabinet was formed, a minority cabinet of the middle parties, without either German Nationalists or Social Democrats. The Lord Mayor of Dresden, Dr. Külz, Democrat, became Minister of the Interior, my seventh.

Less than four months later Luther was forced to resign on an issue that was under my division's particular care: the flag. President Hindenburg, on Luther's suggestion, had issued a decree on May 5 to the effect that all German missions overseas, and also those residing in European harbors, were to fly the black-red-gold national flag along with the trading flag, which had retained the old black-white-red colors of the imperial era, if with a black-red-gold jack in the top inside corner. In a letter, presumably asked for by Luther, the President expressed the hope that a reconciliation on the flag issue would soon be reached. The decree was attacked by the Social Democrats on principle, and the attempt to involve the President was strongly criticized by the Democrats. When Luther, who tried to defend the decree in the Reichstag, abruptly rejected any delay, the Social Democrats asked for a vote of no confidence, which was passed. Luther's decree was a comparatively modest attempt at a compromise. But it could not be imposed by surprise action from above. Only a much more circumspect procedure might have achieved internal appeasement here, if that was at all possible.

Hindenburg now asked Gessler to form a cabinet. Gessler turned to Konrad Adenauer. The great man of the future could thus have become Chancellor then. But he did not want to form a coalition without the Social Democrats, a type of move he was later particularly fond of. He declined the appointment. Thus Wilhelm Marx became Chancellor for the third time. The middle parties stayed in power, without Social Democrats and without German Nationalists. Külz remained Minister of the Interior.

With Marx as Chancellor, Külz as Minister of the Interior, Zweigert as State Secretary, Kuenzer, Schulz, and myself as division heads in political and cultural affairs, Redslob as adviser, Germany's inner affairs were in 1926 once again in democratic hands. But our official initiative and language continued to be limited out of consideration for the minority basis of the Cabinet. Although we could rely upon Stresemann's personal sympathies, which were now more or less on the side of democracy, we could not expose him to blows from his own party, the majority of which still supported anti-democratic ideals.

In our efforts to uphold constitutional order we were not alone. Police duties were well attended to in Prussia with Severing as Minister of the Interior. The Prussian Ministry of Culture and Education was headed by an intellectually prominent supporter of democracy, Professor Carl H. Becker. These and other Prussian ministers under the leadership of Minister-President Otto Braun were on the alert. In May, 1926 Severing's police discovered that certain groups were toying with the idea of bringing about a reactionary change in regime with the help of article 48 of the Weimar Constitution. They were waiting for a left-wing putsch which, if it did not come about of its own accord, would be induced by provocation. Then the President was to establish a military dictatorship by using emergency powers under suspension of the constitutional guarantees of basic rights. Braun revealed these discoveries, with evidence, in the Prussian Landtag, adding that Hindenburg had told him that he, of course, had nothing to do with them.

In July there was a national party rally of the new party founded by Hitler, the National Socialist Worker's Party; but the number of members was so small and remained small for some time that the event attracted little attention.

In heavy industry, too, support was forthcoming for the constitutional order. At a conference of the National Association of German Industry, Dr. Silverberg, my brother Gustav's predecessor as managing director of Rheinische Braunkohlen AG (Rhenish Brown Coals Ltd.) and then chairman of the supervisory board, gave a speech in which he said that German business rejected all extremist tendencies from the Left *and the Right*. German government could no longer rule *against* the Social Democrats, and no longer *without* them, he said. Other industrial leaders dissociated themselves from this speech, especially Fritz Thyssen. I had a long private conversation with Silverberg, in which I advised him not to retract or modify a single word of his speech, for he would otherwise fall between two stools. Our conversation, which covered the entire situation, obviously impressed him; but he would probably not have retracted anything anyway.

Germany's influence abroad improved. On September 10, Germany joined the League of Nations and obtained a permanent seat on the council. Stresemann and Briand delivered conciliatory speeches in the grand manner and some time later held discussions together privately, from which new hopes of international appeasement rose (Thoiry).

Minister of Defense Gessler showed that he was not prepared to tolerate everything the officers did. The eldest son of the Crown Prince had been given an assignment as ordnance officer in one regiment without Gessler's having been informed, let alone his consent having been obtained. Gessler ordered an investigation. It turned out that General von Seeckt himself had arranged the matter "in the interest of tradition." Whether or not it was considered suitable for the grandson of the Kaiser to be put in the ranks of the republican army, the minister responsible for the army ought to have been informed beforehand. Gessler refused to act the puppet. He asked General von Seeckt to tender his resignation. Seeckt did so. President von Hindenburg signed the dismissal. General Heye was Seeckt's successor.

## 53. Dismissal by My Eighth Minister—
### Appointment in Prussia

After all this, one could have cherished the illusion that the constitutional order in the Reich developed satisfactorily. But it failed to do so. The Cabinet represented only a minority and was exposed to political winds blowing from opposite directions. In December, 1926, therefore, Marx began negotiations with the Social Democrats about their joining. The surprising result was the entry not of the Social Democrats, but of the German Nationalists. Scheidemann had accused the army of accepting payment from Russia and of thwarting Stresemann's foreign policy with such machinations, also of accepting money from industrialists for the training of extra-budgetary troops, and maintaining relations with organizations hostile to the Constitution. With these disclosures, preceded by others in the Prussian Landtag, mutual accusations of treason grew ever stronger on both sides. Right-wing groups declared that anyone who made public secret military attempts at strengthening the German army was a traitor; the Left found high treason in the thwarting of official foreign policy, which was aimed at establishing international trust.

In answer to Scheidemann's disclosures, Marx said that the relevant events had happened long ago and did not give an accurate picture of present conditions. The Social Democrats, genuinely convinced that the extra-legal practices of the army might lead to a catastrophe, now made the mistake of not stopping at criticism, but of moving a vote of no confidence. This motion, to everyone's surprise, was carried by a large majority, because the German Nationalists, although substantially backing the Ministry of Defense, voted against the government, in order to take advantage of its overthrow to get back into government themselves. Thus the great weakness of the Weimar Constitution became evident: parties of diametrically opposing views could overthrow a government without being able to establish a new one.

Six weeks passed before a new government was finally formed in the last days of January, 1927. The German Nationalists reentered the Cabinet while the Social Democrats were excluded, as were this time the Democrats as well, with the exception of Gessler, who withdrew from the Democratic party in order to stay as Minister of Defense.

This was the fourth cabinet with Marx as Chancellor. It included two further members of the Zentrum; in addition to Stressemann as Foreign Minister one further member of the People's Party (Curtius, economics); a member of the Bavarian People's Party; and no less than four German Nationalists. Thus the result of the foolish Social Democrat vote of no confidence was that the Ministry of the Interior, responsible for the Constitution, lost its Democrat minister, Külz, and once again obtained a German Nationalist head, Herr von Keudell. He belonged to the moderate wing of his not yet divided party, but had, as a Prussian official, put himself at Kapp's disposal during the Kapp Putsch.

After Herr von Keudell had left me undisturbed in my work for about ten weeks, he summoned me shortly before Easter, 1927, and informed me that he had asked President Hindenburg to appoint a member of the highest administrative court in Prussia, von Kameke, a political and personal friend of his, as head of "Division I" in my stead. He complimented me on my work and answered my question whether he had found fault with it in any respect in the negative, saying that the political situation made the change necessary.

Keudell's move was constitutionally not objectionable. State secretaries and ministerial directors—in contrast to ministerial counselors and officials of lower rank—could be retired at any time by the Reich President on the suggestion of their minister and with the agreement of the Cabinet. So far, however, no minister had taken advantage of this provision in the case of a ministerial director. My dismissal therefore attracted a great deal of attention, the more so as it obviously only served the purpose of removing an official of democratic and republican leaning from the control of the constitutional division. A political storm broke. The newspapers reported the news beneath large headlines and added extensive comment.

It turned out that I enjoyed on all sides, even the Right, a reputation for being an objective worker with sound knowledge in many fields. From colleagues in other ministries I received letters of regret and sympathy, often interspersed with misgivings as to the consequences this move might have. The officials and employees in my own division gave me ovations far exceeding the normal.

I turned over my division and my large corner room on the second floor of the Ministry—the room which had once been Ludendorff's and Groener's, for the building had formerly housed the General Staff—to my successor, informed him of current work, handed him a well-organized pile of draft laws and memoranda, and transferred the winding up of my own affairs to another room.

During Easter week I received a series of widely varying offers. The federal Cabinet wanted to clear itself of the charge that "one of the best officials," as the press put it, was left unemployed at age forty-three. Economy Commissioner Dr. Saemisch, with whom I had often worked on the best of terms, proposed to me that I undertake the investigation of several federal departments with the aim of possible economizing. The head of the mighty association of government officials sought to win me as head of its legal department. The wife and heiress of the founder and editor of the weekly *Weltbühne*, Siegfried Jacobsohn, wanted me to become the paper's chief editor.

At the end of the week the Prussian Minister-President, Otto Braun, asked me on behalf of his Cabinet, to enter the Prussian State Ministry as one of Prussia's three chief delegates to the federal

Reichsrat, in particular to assume the duties of the Reichsrat's "rapporteur general" for the federal budget. This position offered me an opportunity as a critic of the national budget to continue my work in federal affairs, in all branches, not only in home policies. I accepted, but asked for four months' leave before commencing my new tour of duties, to allow me to study French and British administrative practices. Meantime the excitement about my appointment would die down, so that I could begin my work in a neutral atmosphere.

With the appointment as delegate to the Reichsrat I also obtained the privilege of traveling free on all German railroads. I, therefore, had personally no reasons for complaint. When my friend Zweigert expressed his anger at my dismissal, I pointed to the Tiergarten Park brilliant in its spring green. When did an official of our age ever have the opportunity for long travels abroad? But it was no spring day in the calendar of democracy. It was rather a widely visible symptom of the deadly disease spreading in German democracy —that lack of democratic majorities which had already led to the election of a non-democratic President and twice to the appointment of German Nationalist Ministers of the Interior, and which was now having its effect on the control over the constitutional division.

When I went home on the evening of my dismissal, unable to reach Clara, who was visiting friends in Hannover, I stopped at the house where my seventy-year-old mother lived. I lay down on the old, long sofa and put my head in her lap, as I had often done on the same sofa as a child. Clara said that my mother told her afterward I had tears in my eyes. That may be, but not for myself.

When Clara arrived in Cologne, she had not yet heard of the dismissal. "Haven't you read the newspapers?" asked my sister-in-law when she met her at the station. No, said Clara, she had been reading Eckermann's conversations with Goethe in the train. My sister Gertrud and her husband, Ossip Schnirlin, also spent Easter with us in Cologne. She felt everything that affected me very deeply, just as she had as a child. When we were listening to Bach's St. Matthew Passion with Hermann Abendroth conducting, she said to me tenderly, she had thought of me at the words, *"Er hat uns allen wohlgetan."* To accept such a comparison for a person like me, a bundle of imperfections, would be blasphemy. But on Gertrud's lips this expression of feeling touched me.

During my study trips to France and England the passive renown

and active sympathy roused by my dismissal proved useful. In Paris
the German embassy did all they could to help me. This time we
lived in the Hotel Quai Voltaire, opposite the Louvre. I spoke to
deputies and senators, enjoyed the hospitality of several of them,
was present at parliamentary sessions under the animated chairmanship of Herriot, made the acquaintance of André Siegfried, among
others, and obtained a good picture of details in French parliamentary and administrative methods, especially of the relationship between government and bureaucracy.

Things were similar in London. Nothing has ever made the difference between England and France so clear to me as the seven-
hour train journey (including the Channel crossing) from Paris to
London; the difference is more striking this way than when one
travels separately to the two countries. In London, too, the German
embassy was helpful, especially by contacts they opened for me with
officials in the Treasury and the Home Office. Personal recommendations brought us to the poetess Edith Sitwell—on one occasion in
her simple home—also to Professor Herman Finer, who had visited
me in Germany and later moved to the United States; and Harold
Laski, who was at that time the leading spirit in political science. I
was not content with studying government practice in general, but
delved into the relationship between government and bureaucracy
and into administrative practices down to filing methods, for critical comparison of administrative structures and processes. And, as
in France, I studied the influence which even small differences of
constitutions can have on the history of nations.

From London we traveled back to France on the "Majestic,"
which had once been the German ship "Vaterland," across the
Channel to spend August in the delightful seaside resort Port Ma-
nech in Britanny. Here I arranged the material I had collected and
wrote the new edition of my commentary on the Law of Associations and Public Meetings. We became friendly with a lobster fisher-
man who had called his boat "Berceau de l'Exploité" (cradle of the
exploited) as a protest against the small amount he received for
catching lobster in comparison with what the Paris restaurant
owner demanded of his guests. "Are you a Communist?" we asked.
"Even a militant one," he replied.

Then I returned, still forty-three years old, strengthened mentally and physically, from the private into the public sphere of life.

# PART VIII

## Across the Wilhelmstrasse—
## Working for Germany
## from Prussia[1]

---

[1] The Reich Chancellery, Reich Presidency, Foreign Office, formerly also the Home Office, and other federal office buildings were located on the western side of Wilhelmstrasse. The Prussian State Ministry, the Prussian Ministry of Justice, and the Prussian Ministry of Culture were across the street on its eastern side.

## 54. Prussia in the Twenties

So now I was no longer an official of the Reich, but of Prussia. At first I could not get used to it. For a long time I found the change degrading. It was like a stab in my heart when the press began to refer to me as "the Prussian Ministerial Director Brecht." My inward home was Lübeck or Berlin or Germany—above all Germany —and not Prussia. I felt like being a "must-Prussian," as people from Frankfurt, Hannover, Hesse, and even the Rhineland liked to call themselves because they had become Prussians through Prussia's annexation of their home countries. The reason for my aloofness was not alone an inner coolness toward Prussian history and glory which came from my having grown up in a Hansa city and from my basic political beliefs (Chapter 4). Nor was it the result of my general dislike for all militarism, "hurrah politics" and subordination ideals—this dislike would no longer have been justified in republican Prussia, and also the shadows of the past were lightened by the brighter sides of Prussian history. The ultimate reason was rather my awareness of the declining political importance of Prussia and my realization that in the new republican Germany there was no longer any real ground for maintaining Prussia as a separate entity.

Every day my personal experiences confronted me with the difference between the political importance of Prussia and the Reich. All those factors that had constituted Prussia's glamor—such as the royal court, Prussian military splendor, Prussian power in foreign policy, economic, social and financial policies, even the splendid Prussian railroads—no longer existed. They had either disappeared or been transferred to the national government. Federal legislation limited the power of the Prussian police, established the rules governing the civil service, and levied the income taxes. Consequently Prussia had become politically a feeble shadow of what it once had been. This impressed me the more because many of my Prussian colleagues still harbored remarkable illusions. They tended to overlook the limitation of their political role and bolstered their pride with emphasis on their administrative powers and on the remnants of political power in certain areas like culture.

This Prussian pride was effectively supported by the fact that Prussia, owing to its centralized administration, assured administrative unity between east and west. For Prussia was the only German state which stretched from the farthest west to the farthest east of the Reich territory. Much has been said at home and abroad about the antagonisms between north and south, but those between east and west were stronger and deeper. They were less conspicuous when viewed from outside because they were at work within one state only, but within the Prussian central administration one of the most important tasks had always been to decide questions having to do with these contrasts. In the time of the monarchy decisions were more apt to favor the east; in the republican period, the west. But they always constituted an important part of the art of governing Prussia. After the Revolution they became even more significant on the ground that the western provinces usually had pro-democratic majorities (at least until 1930); the eastern—except Upper Silesia —anti-democratic ones. If each province had been able to form its own government according to parliamentary principles the administration of the east would have been reactionary and of the west democratic, and this difference would have shown most distinctively in their respective administration of police and schools, and the control of local government. Only because of the centralized administration of Prussia was it possible to carry modern democratic trends to the east. This gave additional nourishment to the self-respect of the Prussian administration.

Last but not least, the stability of the Prussian Cabinet under the almost continuous chairmanship of Otto Braun—often called, whether appreciatively or ironically, the "uncrowned king of Prussia"—did a great deal to cover up the fact that Prussia had become politically second-class. According to the Prussian Constitution the Minister-President, once elected by the Landtag, was free to name the other ministers as he pleased and to dismiss them; he was limited only by the risk of his overthrow by a vote of lack of confidence in the Landtag. He was also free, within the frame of the law, to appoint civil servants, to advance them, and to dismiss them. Braun made unabashed use of these powers whenever it seemed to him to the point and useful for the state. This gave him great authority over the members of the Cabinet, the bureaucracy, and even the Landtag. The autocratic character of his governing was reflected in his outward appearance—the tall, slightly stooped figure; the strongly chiseled, beak-like nose; the dark, heavy eyebrows; and his resolute, sometimes grim but at the same time humorous way of speaking, and the firmness with which he stated and defended his opinions. From a worker's family, he had become a printer in East Prussia, where, before the November Revolution of 1918, the farm workers were not allowed to organize politically and where, as he recalled, it was then the custom for wives of the farm workers to kiss the hand of the lord of the manor. He agitated among the peasants for political reforms, learned to make friends with dogs so that they would not chase him away, and eventually became the editor of a Social Democratic newspaper. He developed a clear, simple style of writing and was soon thrown into the political life of Berlin. He often told about how he first came to Berlin, poor as a churchmouse, and smelled such enchanting aromas floating out from the Hotel Kaiserhof that his mouth watered and he rushed to the next baker's shop to buy a few rolls which he gobbled up in the street. In the Revolution the Social Democrats delegated him to the Supervisory Council, but he left the next day to take over the Ministry of Agriculture in Prussia. From there he advanced to the position of Prussia's Minister-President in 1920 and remained in it, with two short intermissions in 1921 and 1925, until the end of the Republic.

Braun's position toward the Reich was basically determined by his loyalty to it. Only in exceptional cases and then for important reasons did he enter into active opposition to the federal government in questions pertaining to the Reich. But as a born East Prussian he was proud to be a Prussian. His memoirs, published during his exile in Switzerland in 1938, closed with the words: "What the National Socialists are doing now has as little in common with the real Prussia and the real Germany as has the Nazi philosopher Rosenberg with Kant and the Nazi poet Johst with Goethe. Even though the beauties of nature in my exile [Ascona in Switzerland] have helped me to overcome bitterness, I still long for my harsh Prussian homeland. I am proud to be a Prussian and a German and I long for the day when those who today rule Germany so that she has become a menace to Europe will disappear from the political scene. That day will come."

Braun's loyalty to the Reich was rooted not alone in his patriotism but above all in his conviction that Germany must become a unitary state (*Einheitsstaat,* see Chapter 58) and that the leadership of the Reich should be impeded as little as possible by Prussia because otherwise it could not be successfully governed. This statesmanlike discernment gave his presidency its particular character.

Braun's Cabinet contained other remarkable men with whom very few of the federal ministers could be compared. Chief among these was Carl Severing, Prussian Minister of the Interior until 1926 and again from 1930 to 1933. His manly head was one of the most expressive I have seen. My relation to him, first in the Prussian Cabinet, where I sat next to him, then through our work at the reform of the Reich's structure, finally during the common fight against the National Socialists, became ever closer and the feeling I had for him developed into what can only be called love.

Another impressive character was Finance Minister Hermann Hoepker Aschoff. Formerly a judge at a Prussian court of appeal, he had been elected to the Prussian Landtag and from there called to the position of Finance Minister. At the time I entered the Prussian service he fully mastered the problems confronting his ministry. He impressed me by his deep love of Germany and his affirmation of democratic ideals.

No less important was the Minister of Culture, Carl H. Becker. In his ministry, where he had originally been in charge of university professorial appointments, he had continuously held a leading position from the year 1919, first as State Secretary, then in 1921 temporarily as Minister, then again as State Secretary under a parliamentary Minister, and from 1925 once more as Minister. His particular academic field of research had been the world of Islam, but his spiritual horizon was much wider. It embraced the simultaneous and successive existence of divergent world cultures, the special worth of each, their varied assimilation of classical elements, and their testimony for universal human values. He wanted to see the human personality developed in its entirety. Nonrational sources and tendencies—especially those of religion, art, and humanity—should be cultivated along with rational and scientific ones. He emphasized the significance of the concrete personality and the subjective and artistic factors in man and in his achievement, even in scientific work, and along with that the artistocratic aspects of every culture. After his death in February, 1933, the psychologist and democratic politician Willy Hellpach said rightly that even if everything

Becker did had been wrong (as some of his opponents claimed), still Prussia had not had a better Minister of Culture for over a century.

The political influence of the Prussian government centered in the *Reichsrat* (The Federal Council). In addition to the leading Prussian delegate—the first in line to cast a vote for the Prussian government, at that time State Secretary Weismann—there were three standing delegates who attended all the Prussian Cabinet meetings so that they were thoroughly oriented. In view of my length of service in the Reich, I was their senior; next was Hermann Badt, a Social Democrat; third, a member of the Zentrum Party. Actually the three of us, as well as Dr. Weismann, were only *deputy* representatives. The real representatives were the eight Prussian Ministers, but on the basis of a practice going back to imperial days they did not perform this function personally. Each one of us three standing delegates was at the same time assigned to one of the ministries closely involved with the Reichsrat, I to the Ministry of Finance. My work was soon concentrated on participation in the meetings of the Prussian Cabinet and of the Reichsrat, and in the committee meetings and plenary sessions of the Reichstag. Gradually I was drawn into other major tasks, such as representing Prussia in the Commission on "Reichsreform" (Chapter 58) and before the Constitutional Court (*Staatsgerichtshof,* Chapter 76 ff.). I was deputy chairman of the Commission on the Federal Debt, member of the Trustees (*Verwaltungsrat*) of the Postal Service, later member of the Board of the Society for Public Works, and several others. Hence, personally I had no grounds for complaint about the minor importance of my field of activity.

## 55. THE REICHSRAT (FEDERAL COUNCIL)

THE Reichsrat of the Weimar Republic was historically a descendant, as it were a grandchild, of the Frankfurt Bundestag of 1815, in whose plenary sessions the original 39 member states (1817) had 69 votes: the six kingdoms (at that time Austria, Prussia, Bavaria, Saxony, Wurttemberg, Hannover), 4 each; Baden, Kurhesse, the duchy of Hesse, Holstein, and Luxemburg, 3 each; Brunswick,

Mecklenburg-Schwerin, and Nassau, 2 each; and all of the rest, 1 vote each. After several of the original units had lost independence and Austria, Lichtenstein, Luxemburg, and Limburg separated from the German Bund (1866), 25 states remained. Their voting strength in the Federal Council (Bundesrat) of the Reich after 1871 remained generally the same as it had been in the plenum of the Frankfurt Bundestag, with the important exception, though, that Prussia had its votes increased to 17 over its former 4 by adding those of the incorporated states of Hannover (4), Kurhesse (3), Holstein (3), Nassau (2), and Frankfurt (1). Saxony and Wurtemberg retained 4 votes each, just as in the Frankfurt Bundestag, Baden and Hesse 3 each, Mecklenburg and Braunschweig 2 each, and all of the other states 1 vote each. This gave the totality of members of the German Bundesrat of 1871 fifty-eight votes.

Under the Weimar Constitution (1919) the number of votes was no longer determined by historical happenstance but by population. Each *Land* (as the former states were henceforth called) got one vote for every 700,000 citizens, but at least 1 vote even when, like Schaumburg-Lippe it had only 50,000 inhabitants. In order to limit the overwhelming influence of Prussia the Constitution decreed that no *Land* could have more than two-fifths of all votes and that furthermore half of the Prussian votes were to be distributed among the Prussian provinces. Toward the end of the democratic period the votes were distributed as follows:

> 13 votes: Prussian state government (without the provinces)
> 11 votes: Bavaria
> 7 votes: Saxony
> 4 votes: Wurttemberg
> 3 votes: Baden
> 2 votes each: Thuringia, Hesse and Hamburg
> 1 vote each: the other 9 *Laender* and the 13 Prussian provinces including Berlin
> Total: 66 votes

In spite of the rational distribution of votes according to population, the relative strength of the *Laender* in the Reichsrat remained similar to that in the old Bundesrat except for the transference of half of the Prussian votes to the provinces. The representatives of the provinces were named by provincial committees, but in their voting were independent of the regional government, whereas the *Laender* representatives had to vote according to the instructions of their governments. This division of the Prussian votes between the state government and the provinces occasionally had a decisive influence on the decisions of the Reichsrat, especially when the conservative representatives from the eastern provinces joined with the Bavarian government to vote against the democratic Prussian state government. Altogether the influence of Prussia remained dominant and overshadowed that of every other state and even groups of states. Bavaria's strength in the Reichsrat, too, was essentially the same as in the old Bundesrat; it was actually improved, especially owing to the division of the Prussian votes (see Chapter 47).

The most important change from imperial times was not the redistribution of votes but the reduction of the Reichsrat's powers. In contrast to former rules, the Reichsrat's consent to legislation could be replaced by that of a two-thirds majority of the Reichstag. Furthermore the Reichsrat had no way of opposing legislation by presidential emergency decrees under Article 48 of the Constitution, whereas the Reichstag could demand recall of any such decree by a simple majority. One should not overestimate the powers of the imperial Federal Council, for, while it had to give its consent to every new law to make it effective, it could not without the consent of the Reichstag recall or change any laws already enacted. To that extent even the old Federal Council had been powerless against a simple majority of the Reichstag. Legally established human rights, for example, could not be set aside or limited by the old Bundesrat alone.

At any rate, the powers and rights of the Reichsrat, and of Prussia as its leading member, were by no means negligible during the Weimar period. The fundamental tendency of the Prussian Minister-President, Otto Braun, to avoid causing difficulties for the Reich (above, Chapter 54) was noticeably helpful.

Although the delegates of the *Laender* were subject to instruction by their governments, in practical application it often happened that the delegates instructed themselves or proposed to their governments in writing or by telephone just how they wanted to be instructed. Hence the votes frequently reflected the political views of the delegates rather than those of their governments. My colleague Badt conceived of the idea, before important decisions, of writing letters to sympathetic members of the governments of other *Laender* asking them to instruct their delegates to vote with Prussia. In several cases this worked.

Personal relations among the delegates were in general very friendly. They invited one another to social affairs, usually together with federal and *Laender* Ministers and high government officials. Aware of each other's diplomatic difficulties, knowing well that colleagues had to represent the opinions of their governments and not their own, they avoided treading on political toes but felt free to trade harmless jokes and in private conversations to talk about personal views.

## 56. Rapporteur for the Federal Budget— International Comparison of Public Expenditures

The Reichsrat's most important business every year was its discussion of the federal budget, the governmental draft of which it received usually in the fall for the coming fiscal year. A "General Rapporteur" (*Generalberichterstatter*), traditionally supplied by Prussia, introduced the debate, sounded the keynotes for critical analysis, coordinated the work of the committees, and later delivered the integrating report in the plenary session. In addition, there were special reporters for the budgets of the individual federal departments.

The role of General Rapporteur fell to me from September, 1927 until January, 1933 for five budgets. In the beginning I almost felt like a swindler, because I had never before dealt with the totality of governmental financial problems. I was familiar with single positions, and I had acquired a solid overall knowledge of the federal administration. That was all. Now I was to be the first to analyze and criticize the entire federal budget in public. How could I possibly perform this function adequately, especially in the first year? "Work will help me," I said to myself, as I often did in similar situations. Boldly I decided to change—within the two weeks available between my receiving the budget and the first Reichsrat meeting—

from an ignoramus into an expert by working from early morning into late night.

Instead of following the lists of items before me, I formulated my own questions, a method that has often helped me in life. I started out not from the single positions, but from total expenditures. I deducted from them expenditures for the liquidation of the war (reparations, cost of occupation, veterans' pensions, etc.) and the cost of tax collection, debt service, etc. The remainder was to serve federal and *Laender* purposes. How much of it was to go to the *Laender* as their appointed part of income and sales taxes (raised by federal tax agencies) or as federal contributions to police and welfare expenditures? Only after deducting these items, too, was one left with the amounts available to the federal government for its own services: armed forces, foreign affairs, social security, agriculture, economic, and cultural purposes. A small remainder was left for "everything else."

This a priori scheme I completed by going over the budget item by item. I added comparative figures for former years, including the last prewar year. My penciled notes went to the federal printing office to be set up in print. A summary table, a small piece of hardly half a page, preceded the detailed columns for a quick survey. The entire work, neatly printed, was distributed before the beginning of the committee meetings and formed the basis of my critical introductory speech. My listings made evident that out of a total budget of roughly three and a quarter billion dollars (RM 11 billion), no more than half a billion (RM 2 billion) remained available to the federal government for its own services, including defense (at that time between RM 700 and 800 million, equal to less than $200 million, for army and navy together; today annually more than RM 18 or $4.5 billion!), foreign affairs, economics, all federal ministries, Reichstag, etc. It pleased me to do a service to Germany by pointing out this austerity. It became evident as well that a number of non-recurrent income items were to be used for recurrent expenses so that a considerable deficit for the next fiscal year was to be expected. Unfortunately this prediction proved correct.

The separation between recurrent, non-recurrent, and "extraordinary" expenses (the latter to be financed by loans) was the more misleading as the classification was frequently changed. Thus, in 1926 shipbuilding and most of the reparations were listed under extraordinary expenditures (loan-budget), but in later years under ordinary expenses. Likewise, canal building was listed in 1931 in the extraordinary budget, in 1932 in the ordinary.

My report was well received both in the Reichsrat and by the domestic and foreign press. The international Commission on Reparations under the leadership of Parker Gilbert acknowledged its value and awaited the forthcoming annual reports with interest. My greatest satisfaction, however, was the decision of the federal Minister of Finance to add my report and my tables to the material submitted to the Reichstag. This had never been done before and was the more gratifying because it was done by the same federal government that had dismissed me only a few months before and had censured my call to Prussia as an unwelcome act.

In subsequent reports I detailed and extended my analysis. The last one, in 1932, had tables of expenditure and income, both federal and Prussian, for several comparative years and, in addition, a list of all public expenditures (federal, *Laender,* and local governments) for the different purposes. It also listed public expenditures *per capita* of population and discussed the reasons for the frequently striking difference from land to land and community to community. This led me to formulate the "law of progressive parallelism between density of population and public expenditures," proving that with greater density of population public expenditures per capita rise. For instance, in 1927, public expenditures were in Reichsmark pro capita in Saxony 142, Bavaria 131, Oldenburg 83, Schaumburg-Lippe only 77, decreasing with decreasing density of population. Within Prussia (1929) they were in Berlin 260, in other cities of more than 100,000 inhabitants 200, in towns with 20,000–50,000 inhabitants 164, and so on down to towns of below 2,000, where they were only 24 per capita.[1]

These studies formed the basis for my comparison of public expenditures in various countries.[2] Apart from the differences that were to be expected on the ground of the differences in density of population, it appeared that the public expenditures of U.S., Great Britain, France, and Germany diverged dramatically in four areas: (1) army and navy; (2) internal debt service; (3) reparations; and (4) social emergencies. Items 1 and 2 were far higher in the U.S.,

---

[1] I drew up similar tables for the US later on. See "Three Topics in Comparative Administration," *Public Policy,* vol. 2 (1941), pp. 289, 304 ff.

[2] See my *Internationaler Vergleich der öffentlichen Ausgaben,* Teubner, Berlin, 1932.

Great Britain, and France than in Germany, whereas in Germany items 3 and 4 ranked highest. I discussed the reciprocal influence of public expenditures in these four areas.

In particular, these comparisons brought out very impressively the double-edged impact of Germany's almost complete annulment of her domestic debts. Those of the old federal and states securities issued in mark still in the hands of their original buyers (*Altbesitz*) had been converted into new Reichsmark securities at the rate of 12½% of their original amount; but no more than 26 billions of the 90 billions mark securities participated in this relatively high revaluation. The remaining 64 billions were no longer in the hands of the original buyers. About one third got a nominal revaluation of 2½%; the remaining two thirds had in the meantime been paid back or repurchased in valueless paper money. As a result, by the end of the twenties, Germany's domestic debt service amounted to no more than about $125 million (RM 500 million) annually. Great Britain's was 12 times as much, and even France's 6 times.

These $125 million included Germany's total annual debt service for prewar, war, and postwar loans, and also most of the *Laender* debts, which had been taken over by the Reich. Prussia paid only about $17.5 million annually for domestic debts. Germany had freed herself of her enormous domestic war debts by the bottomless inflationary process (see Chapter 45). But the effect was the same as if Germany had taxed her domestic creditors to the full amount of the securities they held. After this huge bleeding to which the large reparations were added, Germany stood financially exhausted. The result was great scarcity of private capital.

From this analysis I drew the conclusion that a considerable increase in domestic debts for public purposes was justifiable. I suggested raising the domestic debt by "even a billion or more" to be used for fighting unemployment by huge public work programs.[3] I shall return to this in Chapter 69.[4]

---

[3] *Op. cit.,* pp. 16, 17.

[4] My budget analyses were published annually as brochures by Carl Heyman, Berlin. Even four months after Hitler came to power, the *Vossische Zeitung* published two full-page articles on the German financial situation under my name (June 13 and 14, 1933). The last democratic federal Finance Minister, Hermann Dietrich, asked me at that time to write an anonymous pamphlet *Die Sanierung des Reichshaushalts im Kabinett Brüning-Dietrich,* which was widely distributed as a private printing.

## 57. THE MYTH OF THE POCKET BATTLESHIP

CRITICAL examination of the federal budget for 1928 required, in the first place, discovery of possible savings. The only major item that could possibly be omitted was RM 9.3 ($2.3) million, a first installment for building a new type of battleship, temporarily named "Panzerschiff A." The treaty of Versailles had permitted Germany to keep six of her old battleships and to replace them gradually by new ones, each of them limited to 10,000 tons water displacement (the displacement of a medium freighter). Neither German nor allied military experts expected in the beginning a battleship of such limited size to have any fighting value. But the German admiralty soon found out that even so small a battleship might become a dangerous adversary if it was quicker to move than big battleships and equipped with better guns and armor than the average cruiser. Such a ship would be able to keep her distance beyond the guns of enemy battleships while attacking cruisers effectively. Therefore the federal Defense Ministry had requested an installment for the first of these "pocket battleships," as foreign countries termed them. In the following years further installments were to follow for this first and at least three more ships of the new type.

Reporting on the new federal budget in the Prussian Cabinet, prior to the first Reichsrat meeting, I suggested that the Prussian government authorize its delegates to propose the elimination of this item. This would prove to the Allies Germany's utmost austerity and, at the same time, her peaceful intentions. The political effect of such a double gesture seemed to me much more important than the relatively small military value of the ship. It would strengthen Germany's position not only in financial affairs but in her claims for reciprocity in disarmament as well.

Minister-President Braun immediately backed my suggestion. So did all the other Prussian ministers, not only the Social Democrats and Democrats but those of the Zentrum as well. They authorized me to move for elimination.

At that time the federal government of Marx-Hergt-Keudell-Stresemann-Gessler was still in office (Chapter 53). Defense Minister

Gessler, of course, opposed the elimination. With the sympathy of the other *Laender* delegates evidently on his side he felt confident of getting a majority. My colleague Badt, however, wrote letters to Social Democrats and Democrats in various *Laender* governments in good time to instruct their Reichsrat delegates in favor of the Prussian move. The effect was a 36 to 32 vote for elimination of the position from the federal budget.

Leaving the meeting, Defense Minister Gessler said to me: "Today I've learned something from you." At first I thought he meant to express his anger about Prussia's influencing the other *Laender*. There would have been little cause for moral indignation on this account, because attempts of *Laender* governments to influence each other's votes were entirely legitimate. The Defense Ministry had often resorted to less legitimate devices in handling its own affairs. Minister Gessler may indeed have intended honestly to acknowledge my firmness in opposing a military request even against the pressure of nationalist propaganda, since he found himself constantly in similar situations. At that very moment it had become public knowledge that the Defense Ministry had occasionally given incorrect budget figures to Reichsrat and Reichstag in order to squeeze out some additional millions for covert expenditures they considered desirable in the national interest. They had been getting into an untenable position by the speculations of one Captain Lohman, who had used funds of the Defense Ministry for buying shares of a movie concern in the interest of the Ministry. Gessler was disinclined to defend his Ministry in that case as he had done in others before; he resigned. This happened before the battleship item reached the Reichstag.

Gessler's successor was General Groener. In his *History of the Weimar Republic* (vol. 2, p. 194) Eric Eyck writes correctly, "Groener had learned from Gessler's bitter experience that all the veiled and opaque methods of budgeting had to be stopped." Groener ordered that no one in the department would henceforth be permitted to spend money for secret purposes without the Minister's knowledge; he was going to report any such proposal to the Cabinet for taking the responsibility. Yet he adhered to the first installment for the new battleship.

The Reichstag then approved the building of the ship against the votes of the Social Democrats, Democrats, and of course the Communists. The Zentrum decided the matter by voting with the Right.

Now the question was up to the Reichsrat again, which had the constitutional right of vetoing a decision taken by the Reichstag. But the veto could be directed only at the budget as a whole, not at any single position. To delay the entire budget was highly undesirable. Therefore I helped formulate a resolution which enjoined the federal government not to start with the building before September of the year, to permit the newly elected Reichstag and the new Cabinet to take a stand in the matter. This resolution was accepted, after Groener had concurred on behalf of the federal government.

The new elections brought a great success for the Social Democrats, who in their campaign had stressed their opposition to the new battleship. They received 153 instead of their former 131 seats. The new Cabinet, which was formed under Hermann Müller, chairman of the Social-Democratic parliamentary party and included three more Social Democrats, now had to take a stand on the issue of the ship. It was clear that despite the increased strength of the Left the majority of the new Reichstag, including the Zentrum, would again vote for its being built and that the new Cabinet would collapse if it withdrew from that position, since Groener and the Volkspartei would not accept such a reversal. Therefore, Hermann Müller and the majority of his Socialist Cabinet colleagues decided to leave the question alone: i.e. not to interfere with the beginning of the work.

This should have been the end of the matter, but it was not. The issue, reasonably debatable from the two opposed viewpoints, had become a matter of principle, stirring up passions to their depths. Opposition to the navy program was decried as lack of national dignity and patriotism, or even as treason, its support as militarism, anti-republicanism, and revanchism. The Social Democrat party officials publicly disapproved of their colleagues' yielding in the Cabinet. The Communists moved for a plebiscite. The Social Democrats disassociated themselves from this action so that the Communists gained merely a fraction of the votes that were necessary to get the plebiscite under way, indeed only one third of the votes they had received in the elections a short time before. But in order to retain the respect of the masses the Social Democrats moved in November, 1928 at the first meeting of the new Reichstag that the building of the warship be stopped. Their party caucus even went so far as to subject all party members, including the Cabinet members, to this decision. Hermann Müller thus found himself in the embarrassing situation of having to vote on the floor against the policy he had condoned as Chancellor. But this could not change the outcome since the Reichstag majority was sure to vote for the building of the ship. And so it happened. The motion of the Social Democrats was rejected with 257 against 202 votes.

Had the Social Democrats wished to break up the Great Coalition, their action would have made sense. This, however, was not their intention. They wanted the Cabinet to stay in office with their leader Hermann Müller as Chancellor and Stresemann as Foreign Minister. Under these conditions it was a capital blunder to press the matter to the utmost in view of inevitable defeat. The action dealt a heavy blow to the Chancellor's authority in the very beginning of his term. He could have strengthened his personal prestige by either resigning as Chancellor or leaving the party. Either action, however, would have meant the end of the Great Coalition on which so much depended at that time. Therefore he voted with his party against his own Cabinet—without success.

In view of these developments I came near regretting having ever made my proposal to eliminate the new warship in the 1928 budget. But the usual assertion that the attempt to renounce building the ship had damaged democracy, adding votes to the Right, is a myth. As mentioned, the Social Democrats increased their mandates from 131 to 153. The German Nationals, on the other hand, who had passionately fought for the navy program, reduced their mandates from 103 to 73 or, according to different manners of counting, from 109 to 78. Only twelve National-Socialists were elected.

Nor should it be overlooked that the Prussian proposal and its acceptance by the Reichsrat proved to the world that Prussia, still considered the center of militarism abroad, was in reality a bastion of pacifist intentions in its democratically elected government.

# PART IX

## The Struggle for Germany's Reorganization (Reichsreform)

## 58. Fitting Prussia and Bavaria into Germany's Reorganization

From the beginning of my work in Prussia I considered it my natural task to promote Germany's reorganization, to which I had given so much thought during my federal service (Chapter 47), now from the Prussian side. It was evident to me that Prussia held the keys if the reform was to be carried through with constitutional means. Of course, Bavaria and other southern *Laender* should not be driven to secession; however, the Constitution did not require their affirmative vote for every detail of constitutional reform. Even Bavaria could be outvoted. It would not secede from the Reich on that ground unless its life center was affected. But no constitutional reform at all was possible against Prussia's objection. The Prussian vote in the Reichsrat, amounting to more than one third, could block any change in the Constitution. Prussia's opposition would also prevent two-thirds majorities in the Reichstag from gathering. Nor could a popular referendum be hoped for as a remedy against a Prussian veto. For a referendum to be carried would need approval by the majority not only of all those voting but of all those *entitled* to vote. This made it necessary to look for a solution that had a chance of getting Prussia's agreement in the Reichsrat without driving Bavaria into secession.

Shortly before my entering the Prussian administration Minister-President Otto Braun had talked to the students in Berlin about federal reform on February 24, 1927 (published under the title *Deutscher Einheitsstaat oder Föderativsystem?*). He wanted Germany to be transformed into a unitary state (*Einheitsstaat*), although with strong decentralization and broad self-government of its component parts. For the realization of this plan he insisted that Prussia must remain unified. Prussia could be given up only within the framework of a total solution which would for the other *Laender,* too, mean their disappearance within a unitary state of Germany.

It was clear to me that one could not force Bavaria and the other southern *Laender* into such a unitary state of Germany, even if that was considered the ideal solution. On the other hand, one could not postpone the reform indefinitely. I therefore risked stepping into the limelight by talking on October 27 at a Stettin meeting of public administrators on the subject: "Reich and *Laender*—Facts and Next Steps." I described the disadvantages resulting from the twofold central governments of Germany and Prussia in Berlin, from the inadequate size of many *Laender,* and finally from overlapping administrative responsibilities—three defects which together had the effect of making the total German administration a dark continent. I pointed out that Germany's conversion into a unitary state could not be achieved with constitutional means, because the *Laender* would dissent. I suggested that the solution would not necessarily have to be the same for all parts of Germany. A big step in the right direction would be the voluntary combination of Prussia's central government, and that of all those *Laender* prepared to go along, with the federal administration, retaining broad self-government for the Prussian provinces and cooperating *Laender.* The southern *Laender* might remain in their present statelike position. "This would be tolerable. The river Main is no longer a dividing line in Germany. For Germany is at any rate unified north and south of the Main River insofar as its foreign affairs, its army, its railroads, its postal service, custom duties and income taxes, its law-court system and judicial proceedings are concerned. We would just have two types of *Laender* then, for the time being." But this reform, too, would require a long time. In the meantime it would not do for us to stand still. I recommended a "personal union" between Reich and Prussia. By identical decisions of President, Reichstag, and Prussian Landtag the functions of Reich Chancellor and Prussian Minister-President could be entrusted to the same person. Several federal and Prussian ministries, too, could be combined under the same minister. We could even declare all federal ministers at the same time Prussian ministers (without portfolio if necessary) and vice versa all Prussian ministers federal ministers. This would result in having about 19 national ministers as compared with the 21 members of the British Cabinet. If this arrangement was maintained by party discipline for just one year, public opinion would insist on its ratification by constitutional amendment, the preparation of which had to be the main task of the combined Cabinet from the beginning.

In January, 1928 a joint conference held at the suggestion of the Prussian Minister-President and Hamburg's Lord Mayor (Carl Petersen, a Liberal) between the federal Cabinet and all the presiding *Laender* ministers discussed the question of Germany's reorganization and agreed on its urgency. It decided to install a constitutional committee of ten experts to be appointed from the Reich and ten from the *Laender,* one each from the ten who were members of the Reichsrat's constitutional committee.

While the other nine *Laender* appointed their respective presiding ministers, the Prussian government appointed me. The reason for this was not—although people used to misinterpret it this way —any desire on the side of the Prussian government to hinder the committee's success. Rather the opposite. Minister-President Braun expected no progress from endless repetitions in political arguments over the merits and demerits of a unitary and a federal organization between himself and the Bavarian Minister-President. Nor did the members of the Prussian Cabinet see eye to eye in this question, the Zentrum members being more inclined toward a federal setup and the Democratic members toward compromise. Therefore the Prussian Cabinet preferred waiting for concrete proposals from the work of experts in the constitutional committee. By appointing me as a member, the Prussian government unmistakably revealed its positive position toward federal reform, since I was known as an enthusiastic advocate of reform and enjoyed at the same time the reputation of a constitutional expert.

The ten members appointed by the Reich included four federal ministers of different parties, two well-known professors of public law—Professors Triepel of the University of Berlin and Anschuetz of Heidelberg—and Dr. Heinrich Brüning, at that time not yet Chancellor. In its first meeting (May 4, 1928) the committee decided at Professor Anschuetz' suggestion to ask for material on the *gravamina* (points of complaint). Immersing myself at once in this preparatory work I came up with two memoranda in May and June, the one on "The Shortcomings and Their Implications" and the other one on "Procedural Proposals and Substantive Recommendations." The first distinguished four groups of shortcomings: (1) number, size, and borderlines of the *Laender;* (2) overlapping responsibilities; (3) duplication of central governments in Berlin; (4) financial questions. Systematic discussion under these four headings resulted in an impressive picture of the calamity within six mere folio pages.

In the second memo I combined procedural proposals with practical recommendations. First I pointed out "possible yet insufficient" steps, such as the elimination of enclaves, the merging of smaller northern *Laender* with Prussia, the sharper separation of responsibilities between Reich and *Laender* under the present constitution. Then I turned to those steps which were "sufficient yet politically not possible," at least not at the present time, namely the two extreme proposals of return to a setup with no regional and local agencies of federal administration, similar to the setup in Bismarck's time, or transformation of the Reich into a unitary state. Then followed the main section on "possible steps capable of overcoming the shortcomings." We would get no common basis for discussion in the committee, I wrote, unless we agreed that no *Land* should be forced to change its relations to the Reich against its own wishes. This might lead to two types of *Laender* or even more. I warned against the inclination to equalize everything everywhere. Prussia was not likely to permit its provinces getting the status of *Laender* with the same degree of independence the southern *Laender* enjoyed, because this would lead to perilous differences between east and west. I recommended the summary transfer of all those administrative functions that were performed by Prussia's central government from Prussia to the Reich, and the gradual devolution of these functions as far as appropriate to the former Prussian provinces. To this end the Prussian and the Reich government should be combined.

Both my memoranda showed my endeavor to find solutions that had a chance of being accepted by Reichsrat and Reichstag, and that meant a chance, especially, of being accepted by the Prussian government.

## 59. DEATH OF MY MOTHER

OUR mother, who had been suffering from pernicious anemia, passed away in her seventy-second year during these eventful first months in 1928. Since she could eat less and less, her strength gradually left her. There were no vitamin B-12 injections at that time, which now keep anemic patients alive for indefinite years, as we learned later in Clara's case. Despite her weakness she kept sharing her children's and grandchildren's daily joys and sorrows. The attacks in the budget committee on my dismissal from the federal Ministry of the Interior, and the praise given me in the discussion, did her well. Even during the budgetary debates on the pocket battleship she sided with me, although formerly she had been inclined to yield to nationalist emotions. "What good would it do against France, anyway," she whispered. Finally she could not speak any more, just caress us.

The end came on March 8, while I kept her hand in mine. We brought her to Lübeck, where we laid her to rest next to our father at the Burgfriedhof. When at the Berlin railroad station the coffin had been placed into an empty freight car to wait for hours at a siding I shuddered at the loneliness that ends a human life.

Yet I did not interrupt my work. The day before she passed away I delivered my lecture on the structure of Germany at the Hochschule für Politik. When I tried to say "fatherland" the word became "fatherland, motherland, children's land" as in a poem by Dehmel. My voice broke at "motherland"; but no one seemed to notice. On the day of her passing I had to give a talk in the budget committee of the Reichstag.

## 60. Declining Appointment to Chief of the Chancellery

The elections on May 20, 1928 had resulted in an overwhelming victory of the Social Democrats and the defeat of the German Nationalists (Chapter 57). The Marx Cabinet with its sprinkling of German Nationalists resigned. Hermann Müller, leader of the Social Democratic Reichstag party formed a Grand Coalition Cabinet of Social Democrats, Democrats, Zentrum, German People's Party, and Bavarian People's Party. During his negotiations Müller called me into his office to offer me the position of State Secretary in the Chancellery. "You have not only," he said, "my full confidence but that of my party in both its wings as well, and also that of the Democratic party and of the moderates in both Zentrum and People's Party." This was one of the decisive moments in my life. Had I accepted, my life would have developed differently, without doubt. Half a year before, I would have accepted. But now I refused. It was not that I disapproved of the broad basis of the new government or of its Social Democrat leadership, both of which I had wished for. However, I did not want to give up my recently accepted responsibility as Prussian representative on the constitutional committee of the conference on Germany's reorganization. I had just presented my proposals as a member of this committee (Chapter 58). I believed in my mission and was full of hope to obtain majority support for a constitutional federal reform without the use of force. My advice to Müller was to continue with his predecessor's chief of the Chancellery, Hermann Pünder, since this would help him in his relations with the Zentrum. He followed my suggestion.

Was this the right decision? Müller stayed in office much longer than expected, fully two years. During these years my work in the constitutional committee enjoyed considerable success (see the following chapter), but got stuck afterwards. In the meantime Müller's Cabinet solved many important tasks in foreign affairs; Pünder played his part as mediator with the Zentrum well and served Müller faithfully. I could hardly have done better; only in the final phase I might have been able to do more to prevent the Cabinet's breakdown (see Chapter 66). Bigger problems would have faced me in the Chancellery under Brüning. But the Zentrum certainly would have insisted that one of its own members be chief of the Chancellery then.

Two other positions were being offered me at that time. The Democratic Party's leader Koch-Weser asked me to accompany him to the federal Ministry of Justice as his State Secretary. Severing, who followed Keudell as Minister of the Interior, asked me to resume my former position as head of the constitutional division; this was not meant to exclude my rising to the position of State Secretary later, he added. I declined both offers in favor of my position in Prussia and in the Reichsrat.

## 61. The Triumph of Cooperation

The Prussian opposition to the "breakup of Prussia" (*Zerschlagung Preussens*) into mutually independent units is likely to sound strange, narrow-minded, and old-fashioned today, because after World War II there has come to pass exactly what the republican

Prussian government had wanted to avoid: that part of Prussia which is located in the Federal Republic has been divided up into several *Laender,* each with the same rights as Bavaria, and things seem to be working out just as well. Prussia as an autonomous state has disappeared and is almost forgotten. Paul Löbe, formerly President of the Reichstag, told me of his introducing Otto Braun, who had come from his exile in Switzerland for a visit to Bonn, to Bundestag President Köhler. "This is Minister-President Braun," Löbe said. Köhler looked embarrassed. "From which of the *Laender?*" he asked.

It is difficult to recall a time in which not only Prussian conservatives but democratic political leaders as well opposed the breakup of Prussia. They saw great advantages for the development of a good and economically sound administration and the growing up of civil servants with a wide horizon in the traditional Prussian setup. Above all, however, they feared on good grounds that the Prussian provinces north and east of the Elbe, except Silesia, might end up with reactionary governments once they lost central leadership. This problem does not exist for the Federal Republic of today, bereaved of Prussia's eastern provinces, and probably would not exist in the future even in the event of reunification.

At that time, however, the Prussian ministers were not prepared to grant the provinces full autonomy in matters of the judiciary, the police, the schools, and the control of local government. Not only Minister-President Braun and his Social Democrat and Democratic colleagues shared this view; the Zentrum too felt this way. Although this party's attitude was principally favorable to federalism, they understood very well that their own influence in the Protestant north and east depended on their great influence in the Prussian central government and the Reich government and that it would be lost if the provinces obtained full autonomy.

When the constitutional committee met for the second time, October 22, 1928, with Chancellor Hermann Müller presiding, the *Bund zur Erneuerung des Reiches* (League for Germany's Renovation) organized by Dr. Hans Luther, former Chancellor, had just published its first major volume (October 7). This work helped interest wider strata of the public in the need for reform. Yet its recommendations failed to show understanding of the necessity of gaining a two-thirds majority in Reichsrat and Reichstag; it rather endangered the reform by its basic political naïveté. The league proposed to make Prussia a "Reichsland" (Reich territory)—reviving the highly embarrassing memory of "Reichsland Alsace-Lorraine" —to be governed by the Reich. My own memoranda of May and June, too, had proposed eliminating Prussia as a centralized state and combining its government with that of the Reich. But I had taken great care to make this solution acceptable to Prussia by simultaneously determining the Reich's relations to the other *Laender* in a way Prussia could accept. This care the Renovation League had failed to take. Its slogan "Reichsland Preussen" appealed, intentionally or subconsciously, to anti-democratic prejudices against the continued rule of the Weimar coalition in Prussia. It was clear (and should have been from the beginning to the Renovation League) that Prussia would refuse a solution transforming it into a sort of Alsace-Lorraine. And without Prussia's votes it was impossible to obtain a constitutional majority in the Reichsrat. Nothing but romanticism and a lack of realism could hope that a two-thirds majority in the Reichstag might declare Prussia a Reichsland over the Reichsrat's veto, or that a referendum might do so.

These reasons compelled me to oppose the formula of the Luther League in the constitutional committee's second meeting. "That's not the way to proceed." I succeeded in getting unanimous acceptance of a resolution saying that the dualism between the Reich and Prussia had to be dealt with "within an over-all solution (*Gesamteösung*), not isolated."

Two subcommittees were set up, one to deal with territorial changes, the other with the responsibilities (*Zuständigkeiten*) of Reich and *Laender*. These subcommittees appointed two sets of reporting members, one for organization, the other for responsibilities. I was the only member appointed for both sets. This gave me a key position, which enabled me to push the deliberations ahead and to influence their trend. The other reporting members in the subcommittee on organization were the representatives of Saxony, Wurttemberg, and Hamburg; in the subcommittee on responsibilities, those of Bavaria and Baden and Minister Koch-Weser, one of the ten members appointed by the Reich. In addition to these we coopted the head of the Rhine Province (*Landeshauptmann*), Dr. Horion, as an expert on provincial home rule.

We succeeded in producing "joint reports" (*Gemeinschaftsreferate*) in both sections. That is to say, we did not produce four or five individual memoranda but agreed on joint proposals, each signed by four of us, with the exception of the Bavarian Minister-President Dr. Held, who submitted a separate report on responsibilities. The fact that the representatives of Saxony, Wurttemberg, and Baden, as well as Dr. Horion of the Rhine Province, did not vote for the Bavarian report, but agreed with me on common proposals, was the decisive constructive step likely to lift the federal reform program from its nebulous wishful phase into the realm of reality.

There appeared little ground for apprehension that acceptance of our "joint report" would drive Bavaria to secession, because her position, just as those of Saxony, Wurttemberg, and Baden, was to remain essentially unchanged under our joint recommendations. But there was another difficulty arising from the understandable desire of the medium- and small-size *Laender* for constitutional guarantees similar to those to be given the big southern *Laender* and Saxony. We had to ask for their confidence that the federal government and the Reichstag would delegate enough authorities to them just as Prussia had to trust that the federal government and the Reichstag would withhold autonomous authorities from its former provinces that might hinder the development of a democratic Germany.

The third and last plenary session of the constitutional committee took place on June 21, 1930 in the congressional hall of the Chancellery with Dr. Brüning, the new Chancellor, acting as chairman. Authorized by both subcommittees, I presented the summarizing report. I said:

"The majority proposals of the subcommittees amount to the complete elimination of the dualism between Reich and Prussia at both upper and medium levels, where the responsibilities of Reich and Prussia will be combined. There will be only *one* central government and the duties of today's Reich and Prussian state authorities will belong uniformly to Reich authorities, as far as they are not left to the provinces and local government.

"Secondly, these proposals also present an overall solution (*Gesamtlösung*). For not only the Reich's relations to Prussia are detailed here, but also those to the other *Laender,* especially to the other four major ones: Bavaria, Saxony, Wurttemberg, Baden. Their status is to be constitutionally determined. In the following points the federal power toward them is going to be increased: all law courts to become federal courts (*Verreichlichung der Justiz*) [1]; federal legislative powers to be extended to matters of administrative judicature, to the principles of administrative structure and administrative law, to the structure of local government, and to matters of examinations and recognition of examinations.

"Whether the recommended inclusion of the southern *Laender* into the total solution is adequate has remained controversial in the subcommittees and will certainly be the subject of new debates and motions today.

"As regards the other twelve *Laender* of medium and small size, their territorial reorganization is being suggested. The larger ones among them, and possibly the Hansa cities, may be granted appropriate peculiarities as to their responsibilities and organization. Their special status, however, is not—according to our proposals—to be fixed in the Constitution but to be determined by simple acts of federal legislation, just as the degree of delegation of power in Prussia will be left to simple acts of federal legislation. The majority of the subcommittees believe it impossible to bring into being a uniform medium type, since in the north the situation from west to east is so different from that in the south, requiring tighter co-ordination. . . .

"If compared to the situation of today, our proposals will, in the majority's opinion, lead to great simplification in public administration, especially by combining federal and Prussian authorities, and beyond Prussia by combining in the north the central authorities controlling police, municipal government, education, and commercial activities. . . .

"The subcommittee rejected with 8 to 3 votes the Bavarian Minister-President Dr. Held's motion to adopt a basic resolution opposing the differentiating over-all solution. . . ."

Once again the battle around the medium-sized *Laender* was flaring up. The old motions demanding constitutional guarantee for their status were brought in again. I had to apply heavy artillery to save the deliberations from breaking down. I said:

"We now have reached a decisive point. . . . Our deliberations so far have tended in the direction of granting four major *Laender* the

---

[1] This recommendation was rejected in the subsequent deliberations of the full committee with respect to the four major *Laender* in order to meet their wishes, although the majority favored the recommendation.

constitutional guarantee of their rights, giving Prussia and the other twelve *Laender* in the north no constitutional guarantees regarding future acts of federal legislation. Prussia is to leave to federal legislation the degree of delegation of power [to regional or local government]. . . . You, gentlemen, who represent the medium and small *Laender,* do not want to risk this leap into the future, trusting federal legislation. If you do not have this confidence and insist on constitutional guarantees, then I feel compelled to move, and I do so move, in case your proposal was accepted, that the following clause, too, be inserted into our decisions: 'In the present Prussian territory no power shall be delegated to the new *Laender* except as provided for in these decisions.' If you should vote for your proposal while defeating mine, I would be unable to vote for the totality of our recommendations. On the other hand, if you vote for both your and my proposals, all our deliberations would have been in vain, since the outcome then would be: for the four southern *Laender* everything will be constitutionally guaranteed, for the smaller *Laender,* too, as far as they feel capable of existence, and for Prussia that it remains as it is. Our recommendations will be ridiculous. That is the situation. . . ."

Here former State Secretary Dr. Busch, one of the committee members appointed by the Reich government, interrupted me, "I want to say just one thing: I agree in every word with Dr. Brecht."

After this, constitutional guarantees for medium-sized *Laender* were rejected again so as to leave the degree of decentralization to simple federal legislation exactly as in the Prussian territories. In the final count, the total recommendations were accepted by the great majority of 15 against 3 votes and 2 abstentions. Nine of the ten members selected by the federal government voted yes; so did, on the side of the *Laender,* in addition to myself, the representatives of Saxony, Wurttemberg, and Baden, i.e. all the major *Laender* except Bavaria, and in addition the representatives of Hamburg and Anhalt. Against the proposals voted, on the side of the *Laender,* only Minister-President Dr. Held of Bavaria and the recently appointed Minister-President of Mecklenburg-Schwerin, a German Nationalist, whose predecessor had voted with the majority. Thuringia and Hesse abstained. The only member selected by the federal government voting no was Dr. Schätzel, like Dr. Held a member of the Bavarian People's Party.

The overwhelming majority of the affirmative votes made a deep

impression on all those present. To me it meant the successful conclusion of three years' work toward a solution that had a good
chance of being accepted in a strictly constitutional procedure,
avoiding dictatorial force. The six *Laender* whose representatives
had voted yes in the committee (Prussia, Saxony, Wurttemberg,
Baden, Hamburg, Anhalt) could count on two thirds of the votes in
the Reichsrat as well. They needed only one additional vote from
one of the smallest *Laender* to have a two-thirds majority, provided
all Prussian provinces agreed. In case some eastern provinces should
object, other *Laender* would be sure to come to the rescue with
their votes. The great majority of Prussia's provinces favored the
plan. Besides, there were other combinations possible that commanded a two-thirds majority; for instance, if Thuringia and Hesse
voted yes, no additional votes of smaller or smallest *Laender* would
be needed.

In order to get the legislative procedure started, our recommendations first had to be couched in legislative language. This was done
by me and my Saxon colleague Poetzsch-Heffter in two drafts published in the journal *Reich und Laender,* summer, 1930 (vol. 4).
They differed merely in a few details which would have arisen in
the Reichsrat deliberations. Rather late, the federal Ministry of the
Interior went to work on producing an official draft. It contained
three or four clauses or omissions that were sure to lead to counter-
proposals from Prussia in the Reichsrat. But all this was relatively
unimportant. The main thing now was the speedy introduction of
an official draft in the Reichsrat by the Reich Cabinet. Chancellor
Brüning had attended all sessions of the committees and had always
voted for the recommendations along with me. He had chaired the
final session, helping energetically in bringing it to a favorable end.
There was good reason then to be optimistic.

## 62. BAVARIA'S DISSENT

ALTHOUGH Bavaria's Minister-President voted against the totality of
the recommendations in the final session of the committee, he had
agreed to many details before. No doubt, Bavaria would also keep
up its opposition in the forthcoming official deliberations of the

Reichsrat. But quite as surely it would not consider legislative acceptance of the recommendations a cause for secession, especially since the "differentiation" guaranteed Bavaria its accustomed status in the Reich. Bavaria's moderation was clearly demonstrated in Dr. Held's memorandum: [1]

"Just as the political union of the various German tribes was once the ardent desire of all Germans, so we are all at one now in the desire to preserve a powerful Reich. The delegates of all the *Laender* have confessed to this need for strong federal power. Strong federal power is inconceivable without some sacrifices of sovereignty on the side of the individual *Laender;* the power of the central government in a federal state exists at the cost of the member states united in the federal country. Division of governmental powers, however, between the central government and the authority of the *Land* government, and the concurrent existence of the two powers, do not signify any deficiency in a country's structure. The federal form of government is different from, but not inferior to, the unitary form. Proof of this can be seen in the prosperity of the political and national life in those commonwealths, both large and small, that live under a federal constitution. . . .

"It can be stated as a guiding principle, in line with the Bavarian Memorandum of 1924, that federal power should include whatever is necessary for the preservation of the entire nation and for its efficiency abroad, and for all those matters that need uniform order and administration at home, but that the individual states are entitled to everything that does not require such uniformity. . . ."

The main difference between Bavaria and the majority concerned not the old but the new *Laender*. The Bavarian delegate saw no reason for dismembering Prussia. Since this must sound strange to anyone who is aware of the typical antipathy felt by Bavarians against Prussia I shall render hereafter some passages from a draft resolution submitted by the Bavarian representative:

"The so-called dualism between Prussia and the Reich is being exaggerated as to causes and effect. The difficulties and shortcomings are not so deep-seated as to necessitate a fundamental change of the Constitution. They can be taken care of by such changes in the Constitution as Bavaria has proposed for creating clear legal conditions, permanently guaranteed by the Constitution. The so-called differentiating overall solution is dangerous politically because it would

[1] *Materialien des Verfassungsausschusses*, p. 432.

split, legally and politically, the Reich into two uneven parts, abandoning the federal principle of the legal equality of all constituent parts. This would not eliminate dualism but only shift it. A new dualism would be created between the north and the south, with much greater difficulties and dangers than the old one."

There was danger, so the proposed resolution went on to say, that in the long run all *Laender* would be adapted to the type now proposed for the Prussian provinces. Therefore the dismemberment of Prussia was not advisable. Should this course be taken in spite of Bavaria's warnings, then the new *Laender* must obtain the same rights the old ones held under the Weimar Constitution. Dr. Held agreed, however, to grant the Reichstag the right to "withhold or take back" the rights of the new *Laender* "according to national necessities (*Staatsnotwendigkeiten*)." Hence he agreed that the rights of the new *Laender* should not be guaranteed in the Constitution, as the rights of the old ones were.

This resolution was skillfully worded. It tried to profit from the considerable resentment felt in Prussia against Prussia's dismemberment; at the same time it satisfied public opinion which obviously preferred a uniform type of *Laender*. In general, though, the idea that Bavaria of all the *Laender* should be the one to protect Prussia from division was considered absurd. Public opinion in the north wished to see fewer rights granted the new *Laender* than the Bavarian delegate wanted them to have. It was precisely these local differences of opinion which had caused the other reports to propose a "differentiating" solution.

The subcommittee rejected the Bavarian resolution by 8 against 3 votes. Only the two members of the Bavarian Volkspartei—Dr. Held representing Bavaria and Dr. Schätzel, appointed by the federal government—and a German Nationalist—the Minister-President of Mecklenburg-Schwerin—voted for it. They were the same three committee members who voted against the majority in the final vote on the totality of the recommendations.

## 63. Backstage in Prussia—My Relations to Minister-President Braun

None of the Prussian Cabinet members criticized my way of conducting the deliberations. Minister-President Braun in particular gave me his full confidence. I did not, however, rely on this personal confidence alone. I tried to meet any unfriendly reactions backstage by confidential reports, not published. Here is an excerpt from one of them:

"Confidentially I may add to my report on the factual course of events the following. . . .

"Being the only Prussian to nine representatives of other *Laender* I had from the beginning reached the conclusion that it would be hopeless for me to fight against all the other major *Laender* with any chance of success. I would only have forced all of them, major and small ones, into a common front with more extreme views supporting each other and would have had completely isolated myself. Therefore, I have seen my attainable goal in a different direction, namely (1) to isolate not the Prussian but the Bavarian representative, i.e., to have the other southern *Laender* for the first time clearly dissociate themselves from the Bavarian ideology; (2) to separate the medium-sized and small *Laender* from the major ones to the extent that they could not expect support for their special constitutional wishes from the major *Laender;* (3) to prove the undesirability of completely eliminating central legislation and administration for the Prussian provinces in the process of melting Prussia into the Reich.

"All this has been achieved. I pursued these three aims with all available means and greatest obstinacy. . . .

"Of special importance was the fact that I was able to win the third point—maintenance of central legislative and administrative authority—purely through the convincing force of my reasoning, although all the other delegates originally held other opinions. . . .

"Of particular significance, furthermore, was the acceptance of the total recommendations in the final vote by the minister-presidents of Saxony, Wurttemberg, and Baden, although any *super*constitutional guarantee of their rights had been rejected. . . . There will be no right of *veto* for the southern *Laender,* neither singly nor jointly. There will be no "reserved rights" (*Reservatrechte*) in the former sense. . . .

"I suggest that the Prussian government (1) desist from official response to the decision of the constitutional committee; (2) that it rather wait for what proposals the federal government may make, whose obvious task it is now to take the initiative; (3) that it refrain from summarily rejecting any proposals the federal government may submit if they are based on the recommendations of the constitutional committee with regard to northern Germany."

There is neither logical nor psychological justification for the widespread belief that Minister-President Braun would have rejected a federal reform based on the constitutional committee's recommendations. Never did he say either officially or privately that he would reject the reform if he could not obtain anything better. He had decided to accept, as the following chapter will show.

## 64. THE FAILURE OF THE FEDERAL REFORM

THE official draft of the federal Ministry of the Interior was being submitted to the Cabinet in Summer, 1931—a full year after the final session of the committee had passed. In personal talks I tried to urge Chancellor Brüning to have the Cabinet pass on the draft and then introduce it in the Reichsrat. He basically backed the reform. In the subcommittee he had voted with me for the recommendations. Yet he was too deeply involved in foreign and economic affairs (Chapter 67 ff.) to tackle the federal reform as well, he said. I replied, the more great problems he attacked, the stronger his backing in the German nation was going to be, and the better his chances of solving some of them. I feared there was not much time left, I added. Yet he postponed action. He meant to proceed as soon as the reparations had been dealt with. But by that time he was no longer in office.

Together with Poetzsch-Heffter, my Saxon colleague, I went to Dr. Wirth, then Minister of the Interior, whom I knew well from his term as Chancellor. "Dr. Wirth," I said, "you know as I do how short a time a Federal Minister is in office as a rule—often no more than three months. When it is over, he meditates on what he could have done but failed to do. In your case that which you someday would regret may well be having failed to introduce the Reform Bill. If you do it now, the merit will always be yours; if you do not, you may always regret it." Yet the only thing he did was make a speech.

In a similar way I tried to urge Minister Groener, when he took charge of the Ministry of the Interior (Chapter 52). It was all in vain. During the tumultuous events of those days, Germany's reorganization was considered of secondary importance. I thought differently; but no one could predict what the future had in store for us.

Then, on July 20, 1932, there came the senseless coup of Chancellor von Papen, ruining all preparations for non-violent federal reform, when he made elderly President Hindenburg order the combination of the Prussian with the Reich government by emergency decree on the basis of Article 48 of the Weimar Constitution, dismissing all Prussian ministers and replacing them by federal commissars (Chapter 76). This move looked simple from the outside, but it was an unconstitutional act, morally contemptible and politically naïve. Prussia could accept it the less since Papen tried to justify his action by the false assertion that Prussia had neglected fulfilling its duties toward the Reich, whereas his real aim was the fight against democracy, against the Weimar coalition, and especially against the Social-Democratic Party.

Papen's coup did considerable damage. Nevertheless, when the Supreme Constitutional Court (*Staatsgerichtshof*) unambiguously stated that there had been no neglect of duties toward the Reich on the part of Prussia, that the Prussian Minister's dismissal had been unconstitutional, and that their right and duty to represent Prussia in the Reichsrat could not be canceled by emergency decree (Chapter 81), and when thereafter Papen was dismissed and Schleicher appointed Chancellor, I made a last attempt to bring about a constitutional federal reform peacefully. I suggested to Braun and his Prussian Cabinet that they now take the initiative by submitting a suitable draft bill to Chancellor Schleicher. Realizing that all three of the prepared drafts were too long and too complicated for political action at this critical moment, I wrote a short draft strictly in line with the recommendations of the constitutional committee.[1] It was accepted by Braun as well as by the Prussian Cabinet in a special session. Braun submitted the draft to Schleicher around December 20, 1932, and a slightly amended text early in January urging him to present it to the Reichsrat and Reichstag.

Chancellor von Schleicher recognized this draft as a possible solution. He meant to talk about all details with me at a confidential meeting, for which he set aside several hours on January 26 in his rooms in the Ministry of War, to avoid premature publicity by a meeting in the Chancellery. The date then was postponed to January 28. But this very day decided Schleicher's fate. He had to resign (Chapter 84). Two days later, Hitler became his successor. He replaced democratic reform by brutal totalitarian force.

When Hitler deprived the Prussian government, on February 6, 1933, of its remaining rights by another constitutionally untenable emergency decree, we presented to the Supreme Constitutional Court the legislative draft we had submitted to Schleicher as the clearest proof of our sincere attempt to achieve a legitimate solution of the Prussian problem (Chapter 89).

The postponement of constitutional action on Germany's reorganization was not only the most tragic event in my professional life— that is unimportant historically—it proved to be the fatal disaster for Germany, for it was the unsolved dualism between the Reich and Prussia over which the Weimar Republic broke down. Papen's coup led to the dissolution of constitutional order in Germany, to the incurable break with the embittered Social Democrats, and to Hitler's ascendancy to power.

---

[1] The German text of this draft is rendered in the original German ed., pp. 95 ff., and an English translation in my book *Federalism and Regionalism in Germany—The Division of Prussia,* New York, 1945, appendix H, pp. 182 ff.

# PART X

## From Young Plan to Brüning's Dismissal

## 65. The Young Plan and Dr. Schacht's Leaving the Democratic Band Wagon

GERMAN reparation payments, gradually rising under the Dawes Plan, had reached the annual amount of 2½ billion gold-marks in 1928. They were to continue at this rate for an indefinite period of time, subject to increases in line with a "prosperity index" (Chapter 49). In view of the growing difficulties in Germany, the countries concerned agreed in the Council of the League of Nations, chiefly at the instigation of Parker Gilbert, Reparations Agent, to ask a board of experts to prepare a final solution of the reparations problem.

The experts, selected by the respective governments, among them Dr. Schacht, President of the Reichsbank, as one of the Germans, met in Paris in February, 1929. Under the chairmanship of Owen Young of the U.S. Federal Reserve Board, they kept deliberating for four months and, after weathering several crises, finally (June, 1929) settled for a compromise proposed by Young, which reduced the annual payments by an average of 500 million marks and limited them to a total period of fifty-nine years.

The thorniest problem was the transfer in foreign currency. This transaction had been carried through successfully so far, but only on the ground that billions of foreign currency had flowed into Germany as loans for private projects or to local governments for community purposes, among them planetaria and other luxuries. These sources of foreign money would not continue to flow forever; rather, the obligation to pay interest in foreign currency and eventually to repay the loans was sure to lead to stiffer competition in demand for foreign currency in the future. Responsible for the handling of the transfer had been the Reparations Commission. The New Plan was to change this. The first 660 million marks annually were to be paid unconditionally in foreign currency. As to the remaining sum of about 1,300 million, provision was made that the transfer could be withheld in cases of emergency (see below).

Although the German experts considered the total payments still unbearably high and the missing transfer protection for 660 million a constant peril for the German currency, they—including Dr.

Schacht—had agreed for several reasons. In the first place, rejection would leave the far higher annual obligations under the Dawes Plan in force. Secondly, the Young Plan abolished the special bondage of German industry and of certain categories of internal revenues, as well as the placement of foreign personnel in the directory of the German railroads, etc. (Chapter 49). Thirdly, early evacuation of the Rheinland from foreign occupation was hoped for as a political concession. Breaking up the negotiations now with the hope of gaining better conditions later would expose the German economy and the value of the German currency to immediate catastrophe. Even Dr. Schacht was not prepared to accept these consequences, so he reluctantly agreed.

In order to put the recommendations of the experts into effect, however, the governments had to adopt them. This involved new bargaining on two conferences in The Hague, held in August, 1929 and January, 1930. The first ended with further concessions by Germany, especially her agreement that the unprotected amount be raised from 660 to about 700 million. On the other hand, the allied governments promised to evacuate the Rheinland not later than July 30, 1930, that is, five years earlier than agreed in the Versailles Treaty. The second Hague conference regulated details.

In the meantime, violent opposition to the Young Plan had been building up in Germany. Hugenberg, leader of the German Nationalist Party, aligned himself in September, 1929 not only with the mighty organization of the Steel Helmet (*Stahlhelm*), but in addition with Adolf Hitler, who had not yet been considered worthy of partnership by responsible statesmen (*bündnisfähig*), and whose public image received a considerable uplifting from the association with those conservative gentlemen. They joined forces in a *Volksbegehren* (demand for a referendum) against Germany's "enslavement" by the Young Plan. The bill to be submitted to the referendum, called *Freiheitsgesetz* (Freedom Act), went so far as to request in its Article 4 that any Chancellor or Minister signing such a treaty was to be declared guilty of high treason.

If the demand for a referendum was supported by ten percent of all those entitled to a vote—and it just received this amount of support—the Reichstag had to vote on the requested bill, which, if it failed to gain parliamentary adoption, was to be submitted to the popular referendum. On November 30 the Reichstag rejected the bill by a majority of five-sixths (323 against 82). In the subsequent referendum it suffered an even greater defeat, since merely 13.8 percent of the people entitled to vote supported it, whereas acceptance required affirmative votes by the majority. A side effect of this whole affair was that the moderate wing of the German Nationalist Party revolted against the party leader Hugenberg. They formed a working group (*Arbeitsgemeinschaft*) within their party. Shortly afterward one of the most respected party members, Graf Westarp, resigned as chairman of the parliamentary group in protest against the party leader. The party was split.

After successful conclusion of the Hague conferences in January, 1930 the German government submitted the results for ratification, first to the Reichsrat. As its rapporteur I had a mere twenty-four hours to prepare the first public statement of the legislative bodies. The huge material included beside the chief document—"Act on the Hagues Conferences of 1929/1930," filling 343 printed pages—a separate agreement with the United States, nine agreements with several countries on the end of liquidations, and two laws amending the German Railroads and Bank Acts. Since the acceptance of the Young Plan was to become an important factor in the subsequent historical development, several paragraphs of my report in the Reichstag are inserted here.

"Germany's total reparations debt under the New Plan will be equal to a debt of about 34 billion reichs-marks (8.5 billion dollars), on which $5\frac{1}{2}$ percent interest is to be paid. It is incorrect, simply adding up the annuities, to say that Germany's debt will amount to over 100 billion. Foreign Minister Dr. Curtius was perfectly right when he referred to the analogous case of a mortage of 34,000 marks, on which 2,000 marks are to be paid annually as interest and amortization. In that case no one would speak of a total debt of more than 100,000, simply because addition of the annuities would amount to such a figure.

"The proposed reduction of the debt to payments whose present value would be about 34 billion recalls the offer made by the German government Fehrenbach-Simons in March and April, 1921 in London of 50 billion gold-marks to be reduced by the value of previous German deliveries and performances; their value was to be estimated by international experts. This would, according to the German estimate, have left a debt of about 30 billion present value. The allied creditors rejected that offer almost scornfully, demanding instead a total of 132 billion gold-marks, to be paid in annuities of 5 billion from 1929 and 6 billion from 1932. The German refusal at that time was answered by the occupation of additional German cities. Only the practical attempt to satisfy the claims of the Allies (*Erfüllungspolitik*), as announced by the government of Wirth and Rathenau, and continued by their successors, was capable of gradually making the world better aware of the limited possibilities. Lining the dreadful detour road of these nine years are the graves of Erzberger, Rathenau, Ebert, and Stresemann. . . . The German bonds of 132 billion gold-marks are still in the hands of the creditor nations. According to Appendix II of the new agreement they are to be definitely withdrawn and destroyed.

"No word is needed to explain that the Reichsrat's committees were unanimous in their regret that it has not been possible to achieve a further reduction.

"But it is not only the absolute amount of the annuities that counts for our decision. High as they are, they are much lower than those imposed in the London agreement of 1924. Were we to refuse the new treaty the old one would remain valid for an indefinite period. This is the core of the matter that cannot be ignored.

"The committees have satisfied themselves that according to the New Plan it will depend solely on our own judgment whether or not to make use of the transfer protection clause for the chief part (about two thirds) of the total annuity. . . . In such a case we will gain by our own decision two or three years' time for recovery of our currency and for new negotiations, which will be set in motion automatically by our decision to postpone transfer. The Special Advisory Committee will then meet immediately to examine and to report on the situation 'under every point of view.' . . . Even without announcing transfer postponement we are entitled to have the Special Advisory Committee called, whenever we consider our currency in peril.

"Finally, the New Plan will terminate the undignified control of Germany by foreigners. Even before Easter the Reparations Commission will be dissolved and the following agencies will depart, along with their large administrative staffs, namely, the Agent General for Reparations Payments, the Transfer Committee, the Commissioner for the pawned international revenues, the Railroads Commission, the Commissioner for the Reichsbank and Controller of Banknotes, the Trustees for Industrial and Railroads Obligations, and the foreign members of the administrative councils of the Railroads, of the Reichsbank, and of the Bank for Industrial Obligations.

"These four reasons have caused the committees to recommend acceptance of the agreements. . . . To be added to the financial reasons is the evacuation of Rheinland by the occupying forces prior to June 30, 1930. . . .

"No one has shown us how we can reach these aims by any other method."

The plenary meeting of the Reichsrat thereupon accepted the Young Plan with large majorities. Only Thuringia, where Dr. Frick, a National Socialist, had just taken over the Ministry of the Interior, and four of Prussia's provinces voted against it. Bavaria abstained.

Stormy debates arose in the Reichstag. It was one of the few occasions when I made use of my right as a delegate to the Reichsrat to speak in a plenary meeting of the Reichstag. I did so to answer Dr. Frick's attacks, pointing out that he had been the only one of the *Laender* delegates to cast his vote against the government bill in the Reichsrat. On March 13, 1930, the tenth anniversary of the Kapp Putsch, the Reichstag accepted the new plan by 270 against 90 votes. It was a major victory for the government.

Yet there had been a fatal desertion from the government supporters. Immediately before the final vote in the Reichstag, Dr. Hjalmar Schacht resigned his position as President of the Reichsbank and joined the opposition, although he had agreed to the experts' memorandum. To lose this man, who had been admired everywhere for his intelligence and independence, was a heavy blow for German democracy and an invaluable support for Hugenberg and Hitler. He gave as his reason that he was unable to accept the changes made at the Hague conferences, especially the rise from 660 to 700 million of the payments not protected against untimely transfer. Yet these changes were relatively unimportant if seen in the perspective of the total problem. The impression prevailed that his real reason was an opportunistic attempt to join the growing rightist forces. His public image had always been that of a man not only very intelligent but also extremely ambitious and conceited. These are not unusual qualities, of course, nor is a politician necessarily to be blamed when he quits a group that is fighting for a cause he considers lost. Since there was no pro-democratic or pro-re-publican majority in the Reichstag, permitting a really democratic policy (Chapter 30), one could call it a move of intelligent anticipation that Schacht changed sides after reaching an earlier and deeper evaluation of the situation than did his former democratic friends. But there was no intelligent anticipation, nor any reasonable attempt on his side to introduce the "next-best form of government" when he henceforth lent his weighty support to the National Socialists, until they actually reached governmental power. I have no right to doubt his good intentions. But his famed intelligence failed him here. His high self-evaluation, personal ambition, and independence, paired with limited political talents, became attributes dangerous for Germany.

## 66. STRESEMANN'S DEATH AND THE END OF THE GREAT COALITION

DEATH, the great reaper, sometimes seems to forget his harvest; then suddenly he collects it in bushels. Gustav Stresemann died in Berlin on October 3, 1929; in the same month, Prince Bülow died in Rome; in the following month, Prince Max of Baden in Constance and Clemenceau in Paris. Among them, Stresemann alone had still been active in politics. Germany lost in him a first-rate leader, who might have succeeded in solving problems that could not be solved without him. In August he had brought the negotiations at the Hague to a successful end, accomplishing his main purpose: evacuation of the Rheinland.

He had spent his last strength in an effort to preserve the government majority in the Reichstag, especially to keep his own party from defecting to the Right. The very last day before his death, he had been busy persuading his party not to vote against the increase of contributions to unemployment insurance from 3 to $3\frac{1}{2}$ percent (see below). In the night he suffered two strokes and succumbed, only fifty-one years old.

Yet he had lived to see and enjoy the hour of his greatest triumph when Aristide Briand, on Stresemann's balcony in his hotel in the Hague, overlooking the Northern Sea, gave him at long last the promise that on June 30 the last occupation troops would leave the Rheinland. Paul Schmidt, who attended the conference as interpreter, reported on this momentous dialogue years later with lyrical enthusiasm: "The sun suddenly was brighter, the sea more radiant, the light reflected on the faces of the two statesmen who had struggled so hard with each other and their nations for a solution. They both hoped in this hour that a new time was at hand for France and Germany to become really good neighbors." [1]

At the time of Stresemann's death, growing unemployment began to pose a major problem for the German government. The number of unemployed soared from 1½ million in December, 1929 to 2½ million in January, 1930. The semi-independent federal agency "for employment and for unemployment insurance" faced large deficits, which the federal government had no choice but to pay from general resources or governmental loans. The Reichstag had just granted, after difficult negotiations, an increase in contributions from employers and employes from 3 to 3½ percent, which by February proved insufficient. Therefore Finance Minister Moldenhauer proposed to raise the contributions to 4 percent. All other government parties agreed; only the German People's Party objected. A compromise proposed by Dr. Brüning and Oscar Meyer, a democrat, to raise the contribution merely to 3¾ percent was accepted by the other parties, except the Social Democrats. This fight for one quarter percent broke up the coalition. Neither the People's Party nor the Social Democrats were willing to yield further.

It has become traditional within the German bourgeoisie to blame the Social Democrats for their obstinacy. One can just as well blame the People's Party for theirs, the more so since four months later Brüning as Chancellor requested a further increase of the contributions to 4¼ percent, imposing it by emergency decree, and even to 6½ percent in October.

A year later, a similar situation brought about the fall of the British Labour government. There, too, the Labour members in the Commons refused to accept reductions of payments to the unemployed, which Prime Minister Ramsay MacDonald had asked for. MacDonald reacted by quitting the Labour Party and staying in the government in order to save the currency, voting with the Conservatives against Labour. Hermann Müller, the German Chancellor,

[1] Quoted from Erich Eyck's excellent history of the Weimar Republic.

however, while likewise objecting to his party's position, resigned from his government position, remaining in the party. Müller's submission to party discipline did not even permit an open fight in the parliament.

Too much party discipline may destroy parliamentarism. Yet it must be admitted that an open parliamentary fight with Müller losing (as MacDonald lost) would not have been able to save a truly parliamentary regime in Weimar-Germany, because there was no loyal conservative opposition, as Great Britain had, ready to assume governmental power either alone or together with the defecting Labour ministers. There was only one way out in Germany: that of forming a minority government.

## 67. Brüning

Since this book is meant to present memories rather than the results of scientific research I am not going to analyze Brüning's personality here on the basis of all the materials now available to historians. I shall simply relate how he appeared to me at the time.

When I was working at the Chancellery after the war, Brüning held a minor position in the Prussian Ministry of Welfare. As a volunteer, and later an officer, at the front he had won the reputation of a man with a strict sense of duty. In the service of the Christian labor unions he had acquired a deep understanding of the working class. Elected to the Reichstag in 1924 he still remained little known outside the house and the unions, or at least little talked about. We hardly got acquainted before I entered the Reichsrat in 1927. From then on, however, we often met because of his quickly rising importance as budgetary expert in the Zentrum Party and also because he was a member of the Committee on Constitutional Reform (*Verfassungsausschuss der Laenderkonferenz*), whose sessions he attended regularly (Chapter 58 ff.).

What kept Brüning so long out of the public eye was precisely his very virtues—modesty, avoidance of any appearance of pushing, objectivity, lack of gesturing bravado, quiet sense of duty. As a type— if one can speak at all of type here—he was the extreme opposite of Matthias Erzberger. Like Rathenau and Wirth, he was and remained a bachelor. His personality had my greatest respect, a respect which grew with the years.

Still unknown in wider circles, Brüning was elected leader of the parliamentary group of the Zentrum in the Reichstag in 1929. It was from this position and because of his knowledge of financial problems that President Hindenburg summoned him after Müller's resignation in 1930, and—attracted also by Brüning's soldierly qualities—asked him to form a new cabinet as removed from party influences as possible.

This at once placed him in the limelight of history. Only forty-four years old he gave the impression of being older. I, too, had been looking up to him as to a man older than I, although he was actually one and a half years younger. He was the first Chancellor after the war who had seen front service as a soldier.

When talking with him I had noticed, from the beginning, a peculiarity which later became more pronounced. Not only did he always speak in a low voice; he kept looking around cautiously like one who is afraid of being overheard. I do not know the origin of this habit. A similar tendency is sometimes found among persons who are members of a minority group, such as Catholics in Protestant surroundings or Protestants in Catholic; they feel suspected and watched, consciously or unconsciously. This attitude may have played a part in Brüning's development. During the war, his duty as an officer—to be wary of listeners and traitors in all military and political conversations—may have added to his caution. Finally, embarrassing experiences at the end of his chancellorship, which seemed to torment him in his waking and sleeping hours, contributed to his diffidence. At any rate, as a political leader he never radiated that serene and winsome charisma and personal warmth which contributes so much to popularity.

The more admirable are the great qualities of leadership he displayed during his two years as Chancellor, starting as he did from almost anonymous beginnings. Three days after Müller's resignation he had formed a cabinet. It consisted mostly of the same ministers as the last one, minus the Social Democrats, who did not join. Although the new group of the *Volkskonservative* and the Economic Party were added, the cabinet lacked a parliamentary majority. In vote after vote it had to rely on support by the Social Democrats or by the Right and could be overthrown any day by a vote of "no confidence" supported by both. He knew this well, as did every member of the parliament. This was his source of weakness as well as strength, because awareness of the potential consequences of a cabinet crisis made the Social Democrats hesitate to vote against the Chancellor, and because everyone knew that the President was resolved to grant Brüning the use of his emergency powers, dissolution of the Reichstag, and new elections.

Notwithstanding its weak basis, the new government started energetically on its program of austerity and taxation. When his major financial bill failed to get a majority, Brüning resorted to the presidential power to issue emergency decrees, which Hindenburg had never made use of before (article 48 of the Constitution). Such a decree had to be repealed whenever a simple majority in the Reichstag demanded it. In the present case the combined opposition of Right and Left did request repeal. Hindenburg and Brüning obeyed. They recalled the emergency decree, but at the same time they dissolved the Reichstag. In the subsequent parliamentary vacuum the President, at Brüning's request, put into force the measures the Reichstag had just rejected, by new emergency decrees with minor modifications. With the Reichstag dissolved there was no parliament to request repeal. The date for new elections was set as late as the Constitution permitted, on September 14.

This course of Brüning's policy aroused painful apprehensions in me, as it did in others. Difficult as it was to obtain a parliamentary majority for an adequate financial program, a compromise seemed to me preferable to the prospect now confronting us. Dissolution of the Reichstag and resort to emergency decrees for the realization of projects just rejected by the Reichstag evidently offered tempting arguments to all enemies of parliamentary democracy. They could point to the fact that it had proved impossible to put measures considered absolutely necessary by the government into effect with parliamentarian methods. They could easily blame the foreign policy of the democratic governments for the economic crisis that had not yet been recognized as worldwide. And they could use Brüning's practice as a model for themselves.

When Cicero at the height of his consular power in 63 B.C. used legally objectionable devices against five of Catiline's followers, one of the senators rose to say: "All dangerous cases of precedence have originated in good causes. However, when a less intelligent or less honest man [than Cicero—Brüning] gains power, then the new procedure will pass from just causes to causes where it is not justified. Not that I fear that from Marcus Tullius [Cicero] or in our time. But in a great commonwealth there are many and different minds. It may well happen that in another time, under some other consul, who also may have an army at his disposal, something wrong will be deemed right. If that consul then uses today's precedence to draw his sword, who will stop him, who will stay his arm?" [1]

That speaker's name was Julius Caesar, still young and not yet famous at the time. He later used this precedence himself and created new ones.

But is a statesman required to refrain from helpful measures in a critical situation in his country just because he may be setting a precedent for a potentially evil successor? This question cannot be answered in absolute categories.

Measured in figures, the new elections proved a great failure for democracy, greater even than feared. On the Left, as expected, the Communist mandates jumped from 54 to 77. On the Right, however, it was not the German Nationalist Party which gained; on the contrary, their seats were reduced from 73 to 41 and those of the German People's Party from 45 to 30. It was the National Socialists who won 107 instead of their former 12 seats; this meant a nine-times' growth and a tremendous gain in prestige.

This success of the National Socialists came as one of the greatest surprises in the history of the Weimar Republic. They themselves had counted on only 40 to 50 seats. I used to believe that Brüning, had he foreseen this tremendous growth, would not have dissolved the Reichstag. The old Reichstag, elected in 1928, could have gone on working for two more years with its twelve National Socialists, before the Constitution required new elections. But Brüning wrote me on August 6, 1944, after my *Prelude to Silence* had appeared, that he had indeed anticipated such a growth, even counting on a possible growth up to 140 seats, and had acted nevertheless the way he did in the conviction that they would grow even far more if no one else provided strong leadership (see appendix to Chapters 14 ff.).

Remarkable as their growth was, the National Socialists were still backed by merely a fraction of the population. In none of Germany's 35 large election districts did they get even 30 percent of the

---

[1] Sallust, *The War With Catiline*. Loeb Classical Library, pp. 95, 97. H. J. Haskell, *This Was Cicero*, New York, 1942, p. 192. I pointed out this parallel in my *Prelude to Silence*, p. 28, but without the modifications added in the text here.

votes, and only in one—Schleswig-Holstein—more than 25 percent. Professor F. A. Hermens has proved [2] that they would have had no majority even in any of the about 400 smaller election districts, into which Germany would have been divided, if there had been a majority-election system—one representative for each district—as it exists in the United States and in Great Britain. In the overwhelming majority of these smaller districts they would have had far below 20 percent. Only in 23 would they have had more than 30 percent, in none more than 40. Had the mandates gone to the candidates with the relatively highest votes, the National Socialists would probably have won only about 20 seats, since in all other districts other parties or groups of parties would have had the relative majority. Such would also have been the result under the old French election system and that used in the German Empire with their run-off elections, both of which enabled the moderate parties to exclude extremists by local alliances (see Chapter 48).

Be that as it may, by their numerical success the National Socialists had suddenly become an important *parliamentary* group, which they had not been with their twelve seats before. Whatever crisis had existed in the German parliamentary system before 1930 had resulted not from the presence of that handful of National Socialists in the Reichstag but from the lack of a working majority either on the pro-democratic or on the anti-democratic side (Chapter 30). The parliamentary struggle had centered around "republic or monarchy," not "democracy or fascism." Only after the election of September, 1930 can we speak of a political struggle against fascism in the Reichstag and in German governmental politics.

This new orientation involved major tactical changes. When the new Reichstag convened Prussian Minister-President Otto Braun, statesmanlike, wrote in *Vorwärts* that the Social Democrats were now facing the historic task of keeping the German Republic from sliding into the abyss of a fascist dictatorship; they would have to act with responsibility, unafraid of being unpopular. Under the leadership of Dr. Breitscheid, a former Independent (*Unabhängiger*), the Social Democrat Reichstag Party did indeed engage in a moderate political course. Consequently the Right suffered defeat after defeat. In vain the National Socialists tried to oust Social Democrat Paul Löbe from his position as President of the Reichstag. In

[2] *Democracy or Anarchy?* With an introduction by C. J. Friedrich. Notre Dame, 1941.

vain they proposed votes of "no confidence," which failed because they were not supported by the Social Democrats. In vain did they introduce a motion that the Reichstag should declare its confidence in Brüning's Cabinet, hoping that a majority would reject it; it was not even admitted, evidently judged as not meant in earnest. In vain they requested repeal of emergency decrees; the Social Democrats did not support their motions but either abstained or voted for the decrees. Enraged, the National Socialists finally left the parliamentary hall, followed by the German Nationalists, and did not return until the Reichstag adjourned, leaving the other parties among themselves.

As a result, Brüning had gained the position of a strong leader within a short time, and he used his power vigorously. His prestige was quickly rising at home and abroad.

Had then dissolution of the Reichstag and legislation by decrees been the right step after all, justified by success? Elsewhere (Chapter 30) I raised the question as to what the friends of a democratic form of government should do if their country, although blessed with a democratic constitution, harbored anti-democratic majorities electing anti-democratic representatives. I answered that the friends of democracy should not wait for their adversaries to gain the power to destroy democracy; that they should rather introduce the "next-best" form of government before others could replace it by the worst. Germany seemed to be in this situation at the time of Brüning's Government. Anti-democratic or anti-republican majorities had been elected. Could it be that Brüning's form of government was that "next-best" one, prudently to be established before the worst was to happen?

For one year and a half it looked indeed as if this ruling by presidential decree under parliamentary control was the "next-best" form of government for Germany. But this was to forget that its stability depended not on Brüning, nor on the Reichstag, but on the changing views and moods of an elderly general, whose term as Reich President was nearing its end. Before pursuing this line of thought, however, I shall first turn to Brüning's actual work.

## 68. Brüning's Fight Against Reparations and Germany's Unilateral Disarmament

Shortly before Brüning became Chancellor, the Reichstag had rati-fied the Young Plan providing for the payment of about 2 billion gold-marks annually for fifty-nine years (Chapter 65). Two years later, on July 1, 1932, all reparation payments came to an end. None had even been made in the preceding year. How had this unex-pected change come about that soon?

Four factors led up to it: Germany's impending economic col-lapse; her heroic attempt to save herself by her own effort under the whip of Brüning's austerity measures and emergency decrees (see the next chapter); the extraordinarily favorable impression of Brüning's personality abroad, especially in Great Britain and America; and President Hoover's generous offer of a one-year mora-torium for all international reparations, as announced on June 20, 1931. There was a fifth factor, of which it is hard to say whether it operated for or against an international agreement: the fear of irra-tional forces in Germany, the fear of what Pierre Viénot in a widely read book called *incertitudes allemandes.*

The imaginative but failing attempt made in March, 1931 by Brüning and his Foreign Minister Dr. Curtius, Stresemann's succes-sor, to create a customs union between Germany and Austria met with energetic protests by France, whose government interpreted it as a step toward *Anschluss,* forbidden by the peace treaties. The project, dubbed by State Secretary Albert a "Maria Stuart—beauti-ful but unhappy," had to be dropped. There followed a withdrawal of large amounts of foreign money from both Austria and Germany on grounds difficult to determine whether they were economic or political. This withdrawal led to the first debacle of private financial corporations, that of Oesterreichische Kreditanstalt, the leading Vienna bank (March 12, 1931), which had to be helped by the Austrian government at the rate of 100 million shillings. In Germany, Brüning put in force radical economy measures (decree of June 5, 1931), at the same time publicly requesting alleviation of the "unbearable" reparation debts. Impressed by his personality, the

British government invited him to London, to lend him moral support. Together with Dr. Curtius he deepened this favorable impression at informal talks in Chequers, although he frankly warned his hosts that in November at the latest Germany would have to initiate negotiations for a reduction in reparations.

Hoover's moratorium offer (June 20, 1931) followed like a ray of sunshine from a cloudy sky. It could not prevent, however, three days later, the beginning of a series of economic breakdowns in Germany. One of her biggest textile enterprises, the Norddeutsche Wollkämmerei (*Nordwolle*) in Bremen, discontinued its payments. This entailed the threatening bankruptcy of one of Germany's biggest banks, the Darmstaedter and National Bank (*Danat Bank*), which had been widely engaged in Nordwolle and was now hard-pressed by its creditors. The German government guaranteed all deposits at this bank, but the storm threatened other banks. Hence the government decreed several bank holidays to stop the withdrawal of deposits. The stock exchange closed down for some time to prevent a bottomless decline of stocks. Free trade in foreign currency was replaced by official distribution of foreign exchange. An exodus of capital to foreign countries was subjected to a tax of 25 percent.

International negotiations were resumed, first in discussions among Brüning, Curtius, and Laval, held in Paris to forestall French irritation, and then continued in London at the London Conference (July 20-23, 1931) under the chairmanship of Ramsay MacDonald. The British and French governments agreed to keep foreign creditors from withdrawing their funds from Germany at the present time ("standstill agreement"). Friendly feelings were underlined by visits of the British, and later the French, Ministers to Berlin.

On November 20, 1931, the time had come for Brüning to submit an official request for convening the "Special Advisory Committee," provided for in the Young Plan (Chapter 65), in order to have the problems discussed in their entirety. The recommendations of this committee, presented by Christmas, were favorable to continued cessation of reparation payments. There remained, however, an open question as to whether Germany was to resume payments after the present crisis had been overcome and, if so, to what extent. This point of uncertainty delayed the beginning of the final conference in Lausanne until June, 1932, with Papen instead of Brüning representing Germany. An agreement was reached that Germany was still to pay a total of three billion marks, that is, only about one and a half the annuities to be paid under the Young Plan for fifty-nine years. These three billion were quietly forgotten in the course of time. So the books of reparations were actually closed by July 1, 1932.[1]

This reversal in the international attitude had chiefly been brought about by the impression of objectivity, reliability, intelligence, and energy which Brüning's personality had made on the foreign statesmen. Sir Horace Rumbold, the British Ambassador, Frederic Sacket, U.S. Ambassador in Berlin, Montagu Norman, governor of the Bank of England, Prime Minister MacDonald had become his friends and admirers. Without Sackett's reports the Hoover moratorium would hardly have been possible. The high esteem in which Brüning was held abroad was the more remarkable as he challenged it repeatedly, for example in the question of the pocket battleships. He had put into the federal budget of 1931 the first installment for the second warship of this type, as requested by the Ministry of Defense. When Sackett suggested eliminating this item in the current period of austerity, Brüning refused because it would cause Hindenburg to resign. He likewise reacted negatively when he was asked to give assurances regarding Germany's resignation in questions concerning the eastern boundaries, especially the Polish Corridor.

France's fears concerning future German governments unfortunately have been justified by historical developments. At that time it was the Harzburg meeting of the German Nationalists, the Steel Helmet organization, and the National Socialists (October 11, 1931), which troubled the French. At this occasion Hjalmar Schacht, now "without a party," made a speech against the prevailing system of government. At the end of November, the so-called "Boxheim documents" were discovered, guidelines for the leaders of the National Socialists of Hesse, as agreed upon on their meeting at the Boxheimer Hof near Worms. They stated that after gaining power any resistance would be punishable by death, and that no food was to be supplied to Jews.

---

[1] As regards the additional three billion, the parties had reached an agreement—prepared by Brüning—that the German promissory notes were not to be sold below 90 percent of the par value. If they could not be sold at that minimum price for fifteen years—as they actually were not—they were to be destroyed. The fifteen years were up in 1947. See G. R. Treviranus, *Das Ende von Weimar-Heinrich Brüning und seine Zeit,* Düsseldorf, 1968, with rich material on the negotiations.

Although French apprehensions did not thwart the end of the reparations they still blocked agreement in the thorny issue of armaments. Brüning had won the British and the American support for plans of modifying the existing situation, either by international disarmament or by doubling the armed force permitted to Germany. His argument that only by reaching sensible progress in this question could he hope to get control over the nationalist movement in Germany convinced the British and Americans. In France, however, fear prevailed, possibly nourished by the war industry. Had Brüning's dismissal (Chapter 74) not interrupted these discussions, providing at the same time new reasons for the French apprehensions, he might well have succeeded in this matter too.[2]

## 69. Brüning's Fight Against Unemployment— His Policy of Deflation

FOLLOWING the stock market crash in the United States (October 29, 1929), many countries—including the United States—experienced heavy unemployment. But in Germany unemployment grew worse than anywhere else. Only one out of ten labor union members had been unemployed in 1928. In 1930 more than two were, in 1931 more than three, and in 1932 more than four. These figures do not include those only partly employed. When four out of ten were fully unemployed, there were two or three more who had only part-time jobs and only three were fully employed.

Brüning, by emergency decrees, reduced welfare payments and introduced the examination of personal need after six weeks of unemployment compensation. Nevertheless, public expenditures for care of the unemployed rose from 1.2 billion reichs-marks in 1928 to 3 billion in 1932, not including expenditures for public works. There was no value produced by these 3 billions, no road or canal built, nor even a park kept orderly. At the same time, federal revenues dropped from 9.3 billion in 1928 to 6.6 billion in 1932 in spite of ten additional taxes which Brüning introduced, among them an in-

---

[2] See Herbert Hoover (then U.S. President) and Hugh Gibson (chief U.S. delegate to the Disarmament Conference of 1932), *Problems of Lasting Peace,* Gordon City, 1942, pp. 167–68, reprinted in my *Prelude to Silence,* pp. 37–38.

crease in the sales tax from 0.80 to 2 percent; abolition of the refund of income taxes raised at the source in case the final return did not justify the deduction; an additional per capita tax (*Bürgersteuer*), and several other additions to the income taxes; a new salt tax; doubling of the sugar tax; a tax on capital flight. Despite all these additions the tax revenues fell by about one third.

Rising expenditures with diminishing revenues threatened the federal budget with a deficit of 4 billion reichs-marks. To prevent this, Brüning and Hermann Dietrich, his Minister of Finance, cut federal expenditures by about one third of the 12 billion spent in 1928. Half of these savings were made possible by the end of reparations. The other half resulted from the reduction of salaries and pensions; they were cut in three stages by 19 to 23 percent. To soften the impact of these measures the government, again by emergency decrees, reduced prices by about 20 percent. Dr. Goerdeler was appointed "Price Commissioner."

Fully thirty-eight out of a total of fifty emergency decrees issued during Brüning's chancellorship dealt with economic and financial questions. Each decree was duly presented to the Reichstag, with Brüning ready to repeal it in case the Reichstag requested, or to resign. But none of the frequent motions for repeal brought in by the opposition received a majority. The Social Democrats, although often disinclined to approve decrees explicitly, always refrained from voting against them, since this would have produced a political crisis. They just abstained; positive support was not necessary under the Constitution.

It has become a highly controversial question whether Brüning's policy of deflation was the right one. Lowering the cost of production by 20 percent was apt to improve Germany's competitive position on the world market, provided other countries did not meet this challenge by appropriate counter-moves. Great Britain indeed answered by three measures of her own. She devalued the pound by more than 20 percent in September, 1931; she reduced the salaries of civil servants and public employees by 10 to 15 percent in the same month; and she introduced protective tariffs in 1932. These measures more than met the German challenge on the foreign market.

The United States had already increased protective duties in 1930. Therefore Germany did not gain much on the world market. Inside Germany, on the other hand, the reduction of wages, salaries, pensions, and unemployment payments irritated and antagonized the great mass of the German people who depended on these payments for their meager livelihood, and made them an easy prey for anti-democratic propaganda from the Right and the Left, especially since the whole system was built on mere emergency decrees.

Even the soundest economic measure may be unreasonable if it overturns the political equilibrium to such an extent that the country is thrown into the confusion of revolt and revolution. Could a different economic policy have produced better results? In this auto-biography I can merely relate that I watched the rigorous consist-ency with which the plan of simultaneously lowering wages and prices was being carried through, with considerable amazement, even admiration, but with growing concern about political conse-quences. I thought it urgently necessary at almost any cost to re-move the unemployed from the streets to places of employment be-fore they were all turned into political radicals. To say this sounds rather trivial today, and it was no less trivial at that time. For the real problem was how it could be done.

I saw two possibilities, as mentioned before. One was stretching the available work by radically shortening the work hours. The other was making jobs available on a grand scale by organizing public works to be financed by those billions of marks that would be saved in unemployment compensation by spreading available jobs among more workers, and by loans, if necessary compulsory loans. My comparative research on public expenditures in the main countries had convinced me that Germany in consequence of her an-nulment of interior war debts had unjustifiably low domestic debts. No political or economic objections could be justly raised if these domestic debts were increased by billions of marks for the purpose of giving jobs to unemployed workers (see Chapter 56).

Prussian Minister-President Braun sent a letter to this effect to Chancellor Brüning in April, 1932. I had drafted it together with State Secretary Hans Staudinger (Prussian Ministry of Commerce) and Ministerial Director v. Leyden, expert for communal affairs in the Prussian Ministry of Interior.[1]

Mastering the situation was by no means simple. Although it is widely recognized today that in order to create jobs for unemployed workers a country's government, as practiced for instance under Franklin D. Roosevelt in the New Deal, can finance public works

[1] The text of this letter is rendered in the appendix of the German ed., vol. ii, pp. 421 f.

by loans without thereby starting an inflationary process (Keynes), there did not yet exist any scientifically grounded theory of this type in 1930. It was, rather, generally believed that every spending of public money for production of a non-self-liquidating character would lead to inflation. And the fear of inflation was overwhelming in Germany, with the memory of the unlimited inflation of 1920–1924 still vividly alive. Nor was the floating of long-term loans in Germany as easy as it was in the United States. Even borrowing small amounts for undisputed projects frequently proved impossible. To provide billions of reichs-marks for unprofitable projects would have required additional printing of paper money or financial methods yet untried.

Brüning wrote me in his letter of August 6, 1944 (Chapter 67) that the Allies had forced him to engage on a course of deflationary policy. Only a few days before Great Britain abandoned the gold standard, the British Ambassador had submitted a note to him demanding a further decrease of wages and salaries. Circulation of federal bank notes had been narrowly limited by the creditor nations strictly depending on the amount of gold reserves. At all conferences they had insisted that Germany had to prove first that even her greatest efforts were insufficient for making the transfer of reparations possible, before reductions of the reparation debts could be considered. This imposition of a deflationary policy on Germany had indirectly forced all other countries into a deflationary policy. Had Germany begun to spend large additional sums for non-self-supporting public works, the creditor nations, who always insisted on reduction of expenditure and a balanced budget, would have violently objected, Brüning wrote.

These are strong arguments. Yet the political dangers of Germany's huge unemployment figures had become so evident even for the creditor nations that insistence on the need of additional public works could hardly have failed to impress the foreign statesmen.

In defense of his policy Brüning, of course, can point to the fact that he was not permitted to complete his program but was maneuvered out of his position "a hundred yards before the goal." After reaching his primary aim of having reparation payments abolished at the June conference he could and would have used bold new methods for a drastic reduction of unemployment. In his letter he referred to the "Accept and Guarantee Bank" his government established in 1931, which had been able to make available credits of 2.5

billion reichs-marks without widening the circulation of banknotes.

In conclusion I want to add, autobiographically, that I recommended absorption of unemployed workers by shortening of working hours and additional public works as early as October 26, 1930, in a long lead article in *Berliner Tageblatt* with detailed calculations, and that I repeated these arguments as late as January 10, 1933, immediately before Hitler became Chancellor, in my last speech before the budgetary commission of the Reichstag.[2]

## 70. Brüning's Frontal Attack on National Socialism

Effective foreign, economic, and financial policy appeared more important to Brüning in the fight against National Socialists than legal or police measures. In this basic conception he was certainly correct.

But the ever-growing threat of violence and terror forced Brüning, from the spring of 1931 onward, also to resort to measures of frontal attack against the extremists. A series of emergency decrees, issued from March, 1931 to April, 1932, served this end. They ordered all public meetings held outdoors and all parades to be announced to the police forty-eight hours in advance, and permitted their prohibition if facts substantiated the fear that public peace and safety would be endangered. They ordered all posters, tracts, and leaflets to be submitted to the police first, who could forbid their dissemination for the same reason. They banned the use of trucks in political parades since trucks had often been used as armored cars. They authorized the police to prohibit private uniforms and badges of political organizations, since the Reichsgericht had questioned the legality of a Prussian ordinance issued without federal authorization. Later (in November, 1931), a federal decree imposed such a ban directly for the whole of Germany, therewith making the wearing of the National Socialist brown shirts in public illegal everywhere. The police were entitled also to close down any gathering place from which violent actions had started.

[2] Both, the article and the talk, are rendered in the appendix of the German ed., vol. ii, pp. 418, 423.

Penalties for high treason against the Republic were increased, as well as those for withholding the names of editors or printers of publications endangering peace and safety. The wearing of arms at places where that was forbidden, especially at public meetings or parades, could lead to arrest. The arrested person was entitled to ask for a trial only on the question of whether he had violated this prohibition; if he had done so he could not dispute his detention up to three months.

Hindenburg signed all these emergency decrees as submitted to him by the Brüning Cabinet. The ever-growing number of violent acts became threatening indeed. Most of them occurred in fights between National Socialists and Communists, yet clashes with the defenders of the Weimar Constitution, too, caused shedding of blood. Every month a growing number of persons were killed in such clashes or secretly slain (Chapter 77).

## 71. The Prussian Government's Fight Against National Socialism

The Weimar Constitution gave the federal government no police power unless the president by emergency decree under article 48 placed branches of the state police under his authority. In most of the *Laender* the police proceeded against violations of the law by Communists fairly regularly, but not against violations by Rightists. Prussia was leading in dealing equally with violence from either side, yet could do so only to the extent permitted by federal laws protecting freedom of opinion, freedom of the press, freedom of assembly and organization. Other limits resulted from the fact that reactionary members of the law courts frequently favored Rightists.

The National Socialist Party had been dissolved by the Prussian government in November, 1922. This had been done not on the basis of general police authority to dissolve organizations which pursued "illegal purposes," but on special authority given the police by the Act for the Protection of the Republic of July, 1922 (Chapter 43). After Hitler had been imprisoned in 1924, Prussia had permitted the police order to lapse, but had repeated the ban against the Berlin branch of the party in May, 1927, this time because of its "illegal purposes." This prohibition remained in force until March, 1929, but because of the insignificant success of the National Socialists in the elections of 1928 was not renewed.

When the struggle with fascism grew serious in 1930, the special powers given the police in the original Act for the Protection of the Republic had become invalid. Prussia could dissolve the party and its storm troopers thereafter only on the ground of "illegal purposes." But the Prussian government, afraid of the position the highest court might take toward a general dissolution order, preferred waiting for a ban of the National Socialist Party and its Storm Troops by an emergency decree of Hindenburg-Brüning based on article 48 of the Constitution, a ban which would also have the advantage of being valid for the whole country, not for Prussia alone.

I urged no further delay in dissolving the Storm Troops on the ground of their "illegal purposes," for I felt fairly certain that the numerous murders committed by the Storm Troops would cause the Reichsgericht to confirm the dissolution. Minister Severing, however, was afraid that a triumphant revival of the Storm Troops, in case the Reichsgericht declared the dissolution illegal, would make matters worse. When Hindenburg finally dissolved the Storm Troops in April, 1932 by emergency decree (Chapter 73), but repealed his own decree in June, the Storm Troops indeed experienced a "triumphant revival." A dissolution based on general law and supported by the Reichsgericht would have been less exposed to arbitrary presidential actions.

Lacking more radical powers, the Prussian police concentrated on preventing acts of violence and prosecuting violations of the law, case by case. Beyond this, the Prussian government took three steps in 1930. It decided that the Prussian state authorities would deny confirmation for any National Socialist or Communist elected mayor of a Prussian town; it forbade any Prussian civil servant to be a member of either of the two parties (a constitutionally debatable measure as long as these parties were not legally prohibited); and it prohibited the wearing of uniforms by the National Socialists and its branches.

However, Prussia was unable to prevent Thuringia and Brunswick from accepting National Socialists as members of their governments (February and September, 1930, respectively), nor to prevent Brunswick from appointing Hitler a state official (*Regierungsrat*) in February, 1932 in order to make him a citizen. This gave Hitler the right to become a candidate for the presidency. The Weimar Constitution, while adopting the American principle of general elections, had failed to insert the rule that only a person born as a citizen could become president. Ironically this condition had been omitted in order to make it possible for an Austrian to become president.

## 72. Personal Commitment—Deutschlandbund

Although action by the police was necessary, it was not enough. The police could not be present everywhere. Their measures were unable to cope with systematic irritation and inflammation. They could hit symptoms only, not cure the malaise.

One of the most efficient methods used systematically by the National Socialists was their constant circulation of lies, which it often was difficult to correct on the spot because of complicated details. It also was difficult to reach people beyond the readers of pro-democratic newspapers.

Up to 1929 or 1930 I had underrated the danger which was spreading from the National Socialist movement in view of their poor results in the Reichstag elections of 1924 and 1928 and of Ludendorff's miserable failure as a candidate for the presidency in 1925. I believed the German people in its majority was not so stupid as to fall for National Socialist doctrines and propaganda even though Bavarians of the beer-cellar variety had done so. I awoke from my illusions after Hugenberg's fraternal kiss had received Hitler in good society in their joint fight against the Young Plan (Chapter 65), and after their votes had jumped in the election of September, 1930. Professor Hermann Heller, then a young political scientist from Frankfurt, who had just returned from a research trip to Italy, communicated to me his alarming impression of successful terrorist methods. We exchanged our anxieties and ideas with people of the same convictions (among them Grimme, Prussian Minister of Culture), at regular meetings in the House of the Press in Berlin. There was no lack of awareness any longer, nor of ideas. What was lacking was a central organization, and money.

Considerable private funds were not available before the spring of

1932 when Dr. Hermann Dietrich, federal Minister of Finance, succeeded in collecting several million reichs-marks—I believe four—from private sources, especially from the large banks, for the campaign in favor of Hindenburg's reelection. He passed on about half of this money to the Prussian ministers for the same purpose.

On April 6, 1932, the Prussian government, at Severing's suggestion, decided to put an amount up to 2 million reichs-marks at the disposal of the Prussian Ministries of Interior and Finance for use in the struggle against the vitriolic propaganda spread by the National Socialists. Any use of these means for party purposes was explicitly barred. The funds were to be budgeted, for orderly control, under the existing budget title for "fight against crime." The chairman of the budget committee in the Prussian diet was being informed. Whether these funds were identical with Dietrich's private funds or to be supplied out of the Prussian budget was not entirely clear. I did not attend that meeting.

But these various funds were not available until the spring of 1932. Only a relatively small amount of 200,000 reichs-marks, released at the end of 1930 by the Prussian Minister of Finance for propaganda purposes after an urgent letter by Severing, was at our disposal prior to 1932. The Finance Minister asked me to control the use of this fund. Means from it were transferred to a private account opened under my name at the Prussian state bank (*Seehandlung*). Thus we obtained an opportunity to spend modest sums in the fight. Leaving other activities to my colleagues in the Ministry of the Interior, I concentrated on the project of establishing a center from which truth could be spread against the growing flood of lies, and decency in public affairs supported against shamelessness.

This led to the organization of the "Deutschlandbund" (literally "Germany League," in the sense of "Friends of Germany"), a loose association with no "members," to which anyone belonged as long as he himself identified with it. It had a working center called "Bureau Deutschlandbund" in Berlin, Linkstrasse.

To serve as its manager I found a man of sterling character, prepared to descend into the gutter (*Drecklinie,* as he called it), Dr. Foehr, formerly on the staff of the renowned *Koelnische Zeitung* (national-liberal). He was the very incarnation of the idea of the Deutschlandbund by inclination, experience, and decision. He conducted its individual activities with energy and circumspection, presiding over the public meetings, editing the *Blaetter des Deutsch-*

*landbundes* (see below), sending them out from his office to a large and well-selected number of people, and assuming financial responsibility under the control of an auditor of my choosing. From our funds I gave him modest amounts of about 10,000 reichs-marks each time, at irregular intervals, from person to person without any official documentation, just against his receipt. There were no fees for members, but voluntary contributions arrived all the time. He also elicited funds from the federal government, derived from Dr. Dietrich's private funds, as I learned later.

We contacted Helmut von Mücke, former lieutenant-commander (*Kapitänleutnant*) in the German navy, who had become world-famous by his adventurous voyages with the cruiser "Emden" and the captured British Schooner "Ayesha" in the war. For a while he had joined the National Socialist Party because the pretended combination of national and socialist aims appealed to him. There he had become familiar with Hitler and his intimates, but had left the party when he experienced the lies and other evil practices of the party leaders, especially of Hitler himself. He was not only willing but eager to speak about these experiences from a worthy platform. He did not know fear.

After these preparations, the Deutschlandbund presented itself to the public on December 18, 1930, at a mass meeting in the Sport Palace in Berlin, where the National Socialists used to hold their mass meetings. Commander von Mücke's passionate speech aroused a strong response from the audience as a truthful report and a patriotic expression of honest convictions. He spoke for the Deutschlandbund with similar success during the following two months at Hannover, Hamburg, Kiel, Flensburg, Rostock, Stettin, Breslau, Dresden, Leipzig, and other cities. His popularity was too great to permit any disturbances. Later the sponsorship of the Deutschlandbund was replaced by that of the democratic organization Reichsbanner Schwarz-Rot-Gold. His meetings were always announced by huge bill board posters with his name as the speaker and a list of his gravest accusations against Hitler.

At a second mass meeting of the Deutschlandbund in the Sport Palace on February 6, 1931, the speakers included Hermann Dietrich (Democrat), Wilhelm Sollmann (Social Democrat), and Joos (Zentrum Party). On that occasion the first issue of *Blaetter des Deutschlandbundes* was distributed. It listed purpose and aims as follows:

"The Deutschlandbund is not a party; it is a community of people with similar moral convictions (*Gesinnungsgemeinschaft*). It is based on the fact that there are common principles and aims within and outside the political parties for which no party can claim a monopoly and which for this very reason needs a center to prevent them from trivial neglect or debasement in the daily political struggle. The Deutschlandbund wants to be this center. . . . Its aims are: decent political mores; a strong, just, clean state; a Germany, free, confident, and of high culture.

"The Deutschlandbund has no policy of its own, but wants to help create the moral conditions for good German policy. To this end it will combat

1. lies and calumnies, selfishness, and corruption in public life;
2. violence and terror in political strife;
3. conducting political debates by mere slogans;
4. political apathy and discouragement, yet also political self-inflation and economic dilettantism;
5. any attempts at exploiting economic and personal calamities for political adventurers.

"The basis of the Deutschlandbund in this combat is love of Germany, respect for the Constitution, and faith in our nation and its future. . . ."

The *Blaetter,* published twice a month, were sent by thousands to carefully selected addresses—students, teachers, physicians, housewives, and anyone who cared to get them. They contained corrections of lies, information on problematic issues, excerpts from the most repulsive pages in Hitler's *Mein Kampf* ("My struggle"), significant addresses and articles, such as a radio speech by Hugo Eckener, an essay by Theodor Heuss on the presidency, and the like. Issue after issue, they are documents Germany need not be ashamed of.

The activities of the Deutschlandbund lasted from December, 1930 until August, 1932. They then were drastically stopped short by the unconstitutional Papen coup against Prussia, after which the funds at the state bank were no longer at my disposal. The last inspiring issue of the *Blaetter* appeared on August 11 (Constitution Day) of 1932. Words cannot express what a folly it was to suppress these attempts at saving decency in German political strife.

After the National Socialists had come to power, half a year later, Dr. Foehr took his own life on Starnberg lake near München, on which he had rowed out far from the shore. His last act was throwing into the water all the files of the Deutschlandbund except the monthly statements by the auditor. He was one of the best Germans I have ever met. The final fate of Commander Mücke has not become known to me.

Apart from my current official functions and our propaganda activities against National Socialism, I delivered many speeches all over Germany on federal reform and on the financial situation; I published the essay, already mentioned, on international comparison of public expenditures, and completed the third edition of my commentary on associations, public meetings, and article 48 of the Constitution. I used every opportunity to urge the federal government to go ahead with federal reform and alleviation of unemployment, warning time and again against the tragedy of "too little and too late" which had so frequently decided the fate of Germany.

These activities often took me on the same day into the Prussian Cabinet, the Prussian Diet, the Reichsrat, and to committee meetings of the Reichstag. At each of my appearances, however short, I attempted to contribute something worthwhile, if possible.

## 73. PRESIDENTIAL ELECTION, 1932—HINDENBURG'S RE-ELECTION—DISSOLUTION OF HITLER'S STORM TROOPS—BRÜNING'S TRIUMPH THWARTED— THE TRAGEDY OF A RULE TOO WEAKLY GROUNDED

HINDENBURG'S seven years in office ended in April, 1932. Since he was in his eighty-fifth year of life, it seemed a matter of course that he should be replaced by a younger man. He himself wanted rest. There had already been symptoms of beginning senility. Brüning told me later—and published it as well—that Hindenburg several times failed to recognize him. Although Hindenburg's State Secretary Meissner has disputed the truth of this assertion in his own memoirs, Brüning ought to know better. Anyway, the old field marshal frequently came up with confused ideas, which Brüning had to straighten out. Even the best Hindenburg owned, his character, began to disintegrate under the influence of old age. Fated as he was like all of us at the end of a long life to become a mere ruin of himself, was it not a grave wrong committed against him and against the German people to make him a candidate once more for this office whose decisive significance had just been so clearly revealed?

Unfortunately, the fear that any other candidate could be defeated by Hitler persuaded the political leaders of the middle, moderate left, and moderate right parties that it would be best to extend Hindenburg's time in office either by a constitutional amendment or by reelecting him in regular presidential elections.

From the outset I was strongly opposed to this psychosis of fear. It was indeed improbable that an outspoken adherent of the former Weimar coalition would receive an absolute majority in presidential elections. But neither would Hitler. In the run-off election no absolute majority was needed; relative plurality sufficed. A candidate of great human stature and nationwide popularity, politically known to be a little to the right of Weimar but hostile to fascism, had a good chance of defeating Hitler, provided he could count on the votes not only of the middle parties but also of the Social Democrats.

Such a man I saw in Dr. Hugo Eckener. He was sixty-three years old, director of the Zeppelin works in Friedrichshafen since 1924, commander of the first Zeppelin flight to America in the same year —three years before Lindbergh's first crossing of the Atlantic—and of the first passenger flight to America in 1928, even of a flight around the world in 1929. All this had made him very popular. He was greeted with enthusiasm wherever he went. My Prussian colleague in the Reichsrat, Ministerial Director Hermann Badt, had joined him on his trip to America in 1928 and had become an admirer of his human qualities, intelligence, and balanced judgment. I met him first in Badt's home. There, and later as our guest in Steglitz, I too was very favorably impressed by his personality and political views. We informed Severing and arranged a meeting in Kroll's restaurant between the two men. Severing shared our favorable impression and election prognosis. He had no doubt that in the run-off elections all Social Democrat votes would go to Eckener, as well as those of millions of people from the moderate right who were unwilling to vote for Hitler.

Unfortunately fear prevailed. At first Brüning tried to pass a constitutional amendment to prolong Hindenburg's time in office.

When the German Nationalist Party denied their cooperation, the leaders of the other major parties from the Social Democrats to the German People's Party decided to back Hindenburg as their common candidate in a regular election. Time was running out; there was nothing else possible.

Considering Hindenburg's record in his first term of office, the decision to reelect him was—apart from the age factor—by no means unreasonable. The general confidence in him was reflected in the proclamation of Prussia's Minister-President, Otto Braun, published in *Vorwärts* on March 10, 1932, three days before the election:

"Hindenburg or Hitler? Between these two the voters have to choose. Can that choice be difficult? Look at them! Hitler, this prototype of political adventurer, whose demagogic agitation, fed from dark financial sources, has gathered around him all despairing, hopeless people, as well as those who out of capitalistic lust for profits, reactionary habits of thinking, or political stupidity are deadly hostile to our present popular form of government, and who has won their support for his nebulous Third Reich, which promises to everyone everything he wants, to each at the cost of the others.

"Facing him, Hindenburg: embodiment of calm firmness, manly loyalty and devotion to the fulfillment of his duties toward the entire nation; whose life lies clear before everyone's eyes; who has shown, and by no means least so during his seven years as President, that all those can rely on him who want to deliver Germany from chaotic conditions and to lead us upward out of our economic misery, in peaceful cooperation of all classes bound together in a common fate . . .

"Although my world view and my political standpoint separate me from Hindenburg by a deep chasm, human values, all too often neglected in political life, have built a bridge across it uniting us in the desire, each according to his conviction, to promote the welfare of the people. I have come to know the President as a man on whose word one can rely, a man of pure intentions and mature (*abgeklärtem*) judgment, filled with a Kantian sense of duty, which has caused him once more to place himself at the German people's disposal and to assume the heavy responsibilities of his office in spite of his age and his comprehensible yearning for rest.

"Just because, true to his oath, he has stood by the people as defender of the Constitution they [the National Socialists] now pursue him with their venomous hatred, showering him with abuse and calumnies. That is why I stay by him. I vote for Hindenburg and I call on the millions who voted for me seven years ago, and beyond them on all those who have confidence in me and my policy: Do the same, defeat Hitler, elect Hindenburg."

With this proclamation he threw the 7 to 8 million Social-Democratic votes into the scale for Hindenburg. Consequently, even in the first round, Hindenburg lacked only a few votes to absolute majority. In the run-off election, on April 10, 1932, he received 19.4 million votes against 13.4 millions cast for Hitler and 3.7 for Thaelmann, the Communist candidate.

The picture Braun had drawn of Hindenburg was accepted as correct by everyone. Friedrich Stampfer, then editor-in-chief of the *Vorwärts,* wrote later in his book *The Fourteen Years of the First German Republic:* "Otto Braun met with no contradiction when he wrote in the *Vorwärts,* 'I have come to know the President as a man on whose word one can rely.' Everyone saw him this way."

Hindenburg himself had said in his campaign speech that he accepted the candidacy to prevent Hitler's election, whom he characterized as a man "of extreme and one-sided views." "He, Hindenburg, would rather be misjudged and personally attacked than see our people, who suffered so much in the last decade and a half, run into new civil war."

And, indeed, three days after the election, Hindenburg resumed his frontal attack against fascism. At the recommendation of General Groener, Defense Minister and Minister of the Interior, he signed a decree dissolving the National Socialist Storm Troops (SA) and Elite Troops (SS) on April 13, 1932.

Brüning's triumph seemed assured. In his own words, he found himself "just one hundred meters from the goal." Suddenly Hindenburg changed his mind, and Brüning's rule came to an end. It would be a false metaphor to speak of a house of cards toppling at a gust of wind. Brüning's house was massive and artfully built. Yet it had been built on thin ice and was swallowed by the floods when the ice broke. That which had appeared to many observers at home and abroad as perhaps the best possible form of government for Germany—next best to a truly democratic government supported by pro-democratic majorities, non-existent in Germany at the time— namely, rule by presidential emergency decrees under parliamentary control, had suddenly been revealed as a deceptive illusion, because its functioning depended on the moods of an old and senile man.

Much had been accomplished, though. Subsequent events should not be permitted to obscure this fact. The Allied troops had withdrawn from the Rheinland five years ahead of the original plan. The agent general for reparations and other control authorities had left Germany. The reparations were about to be voided so that they did not need to be included in the budget for 1932–1933. The disarmament conference had not yet achieved a final success but there was a strong trend toward a decision in Germany's favor. The foreign governments felt friendlier toward Germany than at any time since the war. At home the monthly nightmare of the Finance Ministry—no funds for current obligations—had disappeared. The public debt was extremely low, and the deficit from all former years was lower than 2 billion reichs-marks.

These and other achievements would have become of prime importance in the fight against fascism, had there been more time. Unemployment, it is true, was still on the increase; but the government would now have made it its foremost concern, and could have done so on a large scale since the financial situation had so much improved. The Reich Reform Bill was before the Cabinet and Brüning was ready to expedite its introduction in Reichsrat and Reichstag (Chapter 64). Braun had offered him his position as Prussian Prime Minister (Chapter 81, and Braun's memoirs, p. 355), in order to bring about a personal union.

In concluding this chapter I will note that I kept up contact with Eckener. New presidential elections were likely to be held in the near future in the event of Hindenburg's death or retirement. He had explicitly reserved his right of early retirement. We had to be prepared.

It certainly was sensible to think through, in detail, all possibilities in good time. But since history moved in another direction, it is not worthwhile to report here what we discussed in December, 1932 with many "ifs" and "buts." Eckener or another Reichspresident of his caliber would not have dismissed Groener or Brüning in May/June, 1932; would not have made Papen Chancellor; nor would he have readmitted the dissolved Storm Troops; nor chased from office the Prussian ministers in violation of the Constitution and under personal assaults. Brüning could have fulfilled his mission.

This is no mere speculation, but a well-grounded statement of political science.

# PART XI

## Why into the Abyss?

### (1932-1933)

## 74. Hindenburg's Ominous About-Turn

But why *did* Hindenburg suddenly perform that tragic about-turn in April and May, 1932? Why did he do things then which he had been expected to do after his first election seven years previously, but which—great surprise (Chapter 55)—he did not do either at that time or later during his first term in office? The man who had been reelected President with the help of Brüning's devoted exertions and of Braun's public testimony to his reliability, the man who in October had entrusted the Ministry of the Interior to his old comrade in arms, Minister of Defense General Groener, and in April at the latter's request had disbanded the Storm Troops of the National Socialists, now dismissed first Groener and then Brüning and entrusted the post of Chancellor to an elegant outsider presuming to seigneurial privileges, Franz von Papen, who, although he was a nominal member of the Prussian Zentrum Party, had no real parliamentary support nor the prospect of gaining any, not even that of his own party. With this gentlemanly amateur's counter-signature, worthless from a democratic point of view, Hindenburg dissolved the Reichstag, only to gain an even worse one in the elections on July 31; allowed, on June 14, the Storm Troopers of the National Socialists to reband, only to be thanked with a series of terrible acts of violence; drove, on July 20, the Prussian Minister-President Braun in disgrace from the office he had held for more than twelve years—thus setting the snowball rolling which was to bury decency in Germany for the next twelve years.

The causes of this change, apparent to close observers in broad outline at once and since well documented for historians, have already been described in my *Prelude to Silence* of 1944. A major role was played by differences of opinion on the granting of assistance, provided for by legislative action, to the great landowners in the east (*Osthilfe*) to avoid their financial breakdown. In agreement with the Prussian government Brüning wanted to limit assistance to property where a sound financial reconstruction was at all *possible* and to combine it with the cession of parts of the soil for the settlement of small farmers. The aristocratic land proprietors called this "agrarian Bolshevism." (After World War II, they were to learn the hard way what Bolshevism really means for landed proprietors.) A valuable gift recently made by them together with major industrialists to President Hindenburg of the estate Neudeck in East Prussia, which had formerly been owned by his forebears, subjected him, as grateful recipient and close neighbor, more than ever to the influence of the landowners. Some of them said later that, although Hindenburg was staying at Neudeck at the time, they had no political discussions with him or did not even speak to him at all during the critical days in May. But precisely such a social boycott may have had a deep effect.

As a matter of fact, however, one of East Prussia's most distinguished representatives, Freiherr von Gayl, did write Hindenburg a warning letter in those critical days, on May 24, which must have had a strong effect. There Hindenburg read passages like these: "The whittling down of morale (*Zermürbung der Seelen*) makes dreadful progress in the east. It more and more affects the power of resistance in those groups that up to now have been the pillars of the national will of defense against Poland."[1]

Even more important, perhaps, than these attacks on Brüning's agrarian policy were the accusations from the Right, which Hindenburg heard daily, that he had disbanded the Storm and Elite Troops of the National Socialists (SA and SS, trained with a view to overthrowing the Constitution), but not the republican organization of the Reichsbanner Schwarz-Rot-Gold (founded for the defense of the Constitution). Groener had said that there was no constitutional justification for doing the latter, and he stuck to his opinion.

Another fateful factor was the influence of General von Schleicher, who was close to Hindenburg's son Oskar. Schleicher, too, had performed an about-turn from his former position. He attacked his old and previously abundantly praised friend and superior Groener from behind, demanding that he resign the "politically irreconcilable" dual position as Minister of Defense and Minister of the Interior. Groener took his leave, not, however, as Minister of the Interior, but as Minister of Defense. Hindenburg wanted to appoint Schleicher Defense Minister, but the latter declined to enter Brüning's Cabinet. He left no doubt that he no longer felt Brüning to be the right man to lead the government.

[1] Published in *Vierteljahreshefte für Zeitgeschichte,* 1953, p. 276.

In other words, wire-pullers had got hold of Hindenburg. Signs of increasing senility suggest that he was no longer entirely clear about what was going on around him. In his memoirs the Prussian Premier Otto Braun describes the impression he had on his last visit with Hindenburg in October of the same year: "I had not seen the President for a long time. At this discussion, the last I had with him, Hindenburg made a shatteringly senile impression, so that my indignation at his decree of July 20 [removal from office of the Prussian Cabinet, see Chapters 75 and 77] was replaced by compassion for this old man, whose sense of duty had led him to assume once again the burden of the presidency and who was now being taken advantage of in this infamous way by unscrupulous people."

The personal reasons for Hindenburg's sudden change of direction are in retrospect not the most important thing. There will always be human weakness, whether it results from old age, vanity, mental disturbances, or corruption. There will always be intriguers and wire-pullers in the environment of men in power. Political desires and opinions will always clash with opposing desires and opinions. However unique each individual embodiment of these factors may appear to those involved and to historians, they are the ordinary elements in the history of governments. They are what led to the drawing up of *constitutions,* in order to check abuse of power. What matters now in retrospect is, therefore, whether the German Constitution made sufficient provision for such controls and how they were used.

According to democratic and parliamentary concepts Brüning's dismissal was not justified. He had suffered no defeat in the Reichstag. Quite the contrary, in the middle of May a vote of no confidence against him had been rejected by 287 votes to 257 (National Socialists, German Nationalists, Communists). Papen was not the recognized leader of the opposition, but an outsider, who obviously had only a few votes at his disposal in the Reichstag. Hence Hindenburg's change of chancellor was a flagrant violation of parliamentary principles.

It was not, however, an equally flagrant violation of the wording of the Weimar Constitution, which formulated the right of the President to appoint and dismiss the Chancellor very broadly. The only limitation lay in the clause that the Chancellor must have the confidence of the Reichstag. But the Constitution did not say that this confidence must have been expressed *before* the appointment. It did not even stipulate that the Chancellor could not be dismissed as long as he enjoyed this confidence. It was, moreover, questionable whether Brüning did in fact have it. Although the majority were not prepared to express their lack of it, neither had they given affirmative expression. Had Hindenburg replaced him by a man for whom the majority expressed confidence in a formal vote, no objection could be raised. In fact, however, there was no sign that such a vote of confidence in Papen would be forthcoming. Yet here again it could be argued that the President had the right to find out whether or not a new chancellor would obtain a majority, and that he could even cause new elections to be held for this purpose. The wording of the Constitution made such an interpretation possible. Furthermore, Brüning was not formally dismissed until he had requested release from his office. He did that when the President told him that he, Hindenburg, was no longer prepared to sign the emergency decrees Brüning submitted to him. The Chancellor would have to work through normal legislative channels, he said. Since Brüning had neither a majority in the Reichstag ready to pass the laws he considered necessary, nor an assurance from the President, he tendered his resignation. This was on May 30, and the dismissal was signed on June 1.

The letter of the Constitution was, therefore, not violated. As to its spirit, there was in the history of the young republic no precedent applicable to this situation. It was the first time that a president made use of his authority in this way. It was, therefore, the first opportunity for the Reichstag—or rather for the people, since the Reichstag was being dissolved under Papen's counter-signature and new elections were set—to create a precedent *against* Hindenburg's interpretation. Such a historic answer the French nation had given fifty-five years before in a famous election, when, also in the month of May another popular general had made use of a comparable ambiguity in the French organizational laws. He was President Mac-Mahon, who in 1877 dismissed a premier who had the support of the majority, the republican Jules Simon, and appointed in his place a monarchist, the Duke of Broglie, whom he authorized to dissolve the house. The nation's answer under Gambetta's inspiring leadership was reelection of a house with a two-thirds republican majority. MacMahon had no choice except to submit to the decisions of this majority or to resign. He subjected himself to the will of the majority for two years and then resigned when he was asked to dismiss the monarchist generals.

Although the majority of the German people clearly rejected Papen in the parliamentary election of July, 1932, there was not as positive an expression of support for parliamentary democracy as there had been in France in 1877. On the contrary, the election only brought to light that in Germany political ideas went into four different directions—toward Communism, Democracy, authoritarian Monarchy, or Fascism. None of the groups obtained a majority in July, 1932, not even the Democrats and Monarchists together, as had been the case in previous elections. But more of this later.

## 75. DILETTANTE METHODS

WHEN Hindenburg appointed Papen, neither of them intended to submit to totalitarian theories and to allow the National Socialists to establish a one-party state. Rather, both of them wanted to check National Socialism. They thought they would be able to overcome it if they steered a more conservative course than had previously been pursued. They were ready to recognize the strength of the Hitler party by offering them seats in a coalition cabinet and thus to transfer to them a share of power and responsibility, but only on condition that the party drop its absolute and totalitarian demands.

How strong Hindenburg's opposition to these demands was is shown by two communications from the President's office on August 13 and November 24 on negotiations between Hindenburg and Hitler. On August 13, an official communication stated that in a discussion on the entry of his party into the Cabinet, Hitler had demanded that Hindenburg "transfer to him the leadership of the government and the whole power in the state (*die gesamte Staatsgewalt*)." The communication continued: "President Hindenburg rejected this demand very forcefully, declaring that he could not bear the responsibility before his conscience and his duties toward the fatherland if he conferred all governmental power exclusively on the National Socialists, who intended to use this power one-sidedly."

Hitler disputed that he had demanded not only the chancellor-

ship but full power in the state. That this, however, was his ultimate goal, has been shown clearly enough by subsequent events. At
any rate, the official announcement shows that Hindenburg and
Papen did not at that time intend to pass total power into Hitler's
hands.

After the November election the President again discussed the
formation of a cabinet with Hitler and again rejected the latter's
proposals (November 24). The official communication gave the reasons as follows: "The President rejected these proposals, because he
believes he cannot resume responsibility before the German nation
for granting his presidential full powers to the leader of a party
which has continually emphasized its exclusiveness, and the President, therefore, fears that a cabinet leaning on presidential powers,
led by Hitler, would automatically lead to a party dictatorship with
all its consequences for an extraordinary intensification of the antagonisms among the German people. The President felt he could not
bear the responsibility under his oath and before his conscience for
bringing about such aggravation."

The oath to which the President referred was his oath of loyalty
to the Weimar Constitution.

Criticism of Hindenburg, Papen, and Schleicher cannot, therefore, be justly based on the accusation that they intentionally
brought Hitler to total power, but it must be limited to the charge
that their dilettante methods resulted in bringing about precisely
what they had wanted to avoid. It is not evil intent but political
folly that they may be reproached for—the imprudence of political
dilettantes let loose on Germany at Germany's expense, combined
with breach of the Constitution, with weakness of character in critical situations, and with a more than average self-confidence, in Papen's case based on a strange mixture of piety and personal vanity.

The idea of taking the wind out of the National Socialist sails by
a swing to the Right was in itself neither stupid nor rash. That was
what to some extent Brüning, too, had wanted. But Papen and
Schleicher thought—in a manner common enough among military
politicians (Papen was still the elegant cavalry officer of whom
Briand is said to have remarked that the longer he looked at him
the more he admired his horse)—that the right thing to do was to
attack the whole problem with a strategically simple plan. That, of
course, pleased the old general. Toleration of the National Socialists
up to a conceded agreement with them on their reciprocal tolera-

tion of Papen's Cabinet (Chapter 77); suspension of frontal attacks on them—instead, directing frontal attacks against the Left alone, and there not only against the Communists but against the Social Democrats as well; bold neglect of constitutional misgivings, whenever they stood in the way of these plans—Papen and Schleicher thought these the best methods of overcoming Hitler.

Many a German reader may ask himself even today: why not? These seemed to be good plans in the opinions of many millions of Germans. From the democratic point of view they were of course bad, but from the point of view of an opponent of democratic "equalization ideas" they were good. Whether good or bad—this cannot be decided by the writer. And as far as the Constitution is concerned, you yourself, Arnold Brecht, have said that friends of democracy must, when the majority proves to be anti-democratic, try to change the democratic form of government into the next best thing in good time, as long as they are in a position to do so (Chapter 30). Why, then, shouldn't opponents of democracy be permitted to do likewise?

My answer is that, even if Papen's and Schleicher's policy in the spring and summer of 1932 is not rejected on principal grounds from the very beginning, the possibility for a beneficent judgment dwindles when one turns to the actual performance and notices that it brought about precisely what it wanted to avoid: total power of the National Socialists.

Since Papen obviously had no majority in the Reichstag, Hindenburg dissolved the Reichstag with Papen's—I repeat, democratically worthless—counter-signature. Over the same signature he repealed on June 14 the decree forbidding the wearing of private uniforms and the disbanding of the National Socialist Storm Troops (SA) issued by himself only two months before. The SA took up their deployment and activities. The Prussian police, which had been striving for two months to keep them off the streets, now had to march at their side in order to protect them in their regained rights from attacks by embittered Communists, whose Red Front Organization was still forbidden. On the same day Hindenburg-Papen repealed most of the other decrees passed in the Brüning period against the National Socialists for the preservation of public order. Another decree, of June 28, forbade the governments of the *Laender* to pass such measures themselves. At a conference of all the *Laender* called by the Federal Minister of the Interior at Prussia's request all of them protested—with the exception of one of the smallest, if I remember rightly—against the new measures.

The indirect effect was a multiplication of bloody street fighting and other overt or secret acts of violence in the entire country (Chapter 77). After a few weeks Papen felt impelled to reintroduce several of the repealed decrees and on August 9 even to threaten the death penalty for participation in political encounters at which people were killed. Although he did not disband the SA again, he forbade public parades and meetings in the open air, including those of the brown shirts. But that was only after the blow against Prussia.

The ineptness of the first part of Papen's policy cannot be illustrated more clearly. It was not different in the case of the second part: the frontal attack on Social Democracy (see next chapter).

On June 24, 1932, the anniversary of Rathenau's assassination came round for the tenth time. I did not consider it right that the anniversary be passed over in a cowardly fashion. As chairman of the Rathenau Foundation and the Rathenau Society I saw to it that the murdered man was honorably remembered. Laying a wreath at the spot where the murder had taken place, I summed up Rathenau's life as follows: *"Leben ist Sichhingeben. Sichhingeben ist willig sterben"* (Life is surrender. To surrender oneself is to be ready to die). A platoon of the pro-democratic Reichsbanner marched past with Ebert's son Fritz at its head (today the Lord Mayor of Berlin-East). At the foundation celebration in the afternoon in the Rathenau House in Königsallee Koch-Weser, Severing, Redslob, and Count Kessler were among those present. I said that Rathenau had loved Germany, as one only could love with closed lips, not with a mouth wide-open. I spoke again at a large general celebration in the Reichstag building at night. I mentioned the deeply rooted aversion to Jewish names. Recently leafing through an alphabetic list of all the men with Jewish names who had been killed in the war, I saw to my shame that the name Cohn filled dozens of pages.

Also in the course of June, 1932 I delivered for the last time my general report on the budget in the Reichsrat.

## 76. Germany's Reorganization by Force

The Prussian Landtag, elected in 1928, had not been dissolved in the middle of its normal legislative period, as was the Reichstag by Brüning in 1930. It continued to function until the normal end of its term in April, 1932. The Weimar coalition parties there had a majority, unlike the Reichstag, where they were seven seats short of it (see Chapter 31 on the reason for this difference). The National Socialists had only nine seats.

It was clear beforehand, though, that the Weimar coalition would lose its majority in the new election arranged for April 24, 1932. The first function of the Landtag would be to select a new minister-president. According to standing orders the successful candidate needed only a so-called "relative plurality"; that is to say, he had to get more votes than any of the other candidates, not the absolute majority. This ruling could have made it possible for the right wing to have a National Socialist elected premier with a mere minority, and for this man then to appoint another National Socialist Minister of the Interior and thus to put the Prussian police in Hitler's power. In order to prevent this, the old Landtag changed the standing orders at the eleventh hour to the effect that an absolute majority was required for the election of a minister-president. This question had not been settled in the Prussian Constitution, but had been left open for standing orders.

In the election, on April 24, the National Socialists obtained 162 seats in place of their former nine, so that, as was the custom, the post of Landtag President fell to them, now the largest party. The three Weimar coalition parties suffered great losses, especially the Democrats (now State Party), who obtained only two seats, and the Social Democrats, who went from 137 down to 94, losing almost a third. The Zentrum Party lost four of its 71 seats. Despite these losses, with 163 seats the three parties together still had one more than the National Socialists.

The German Nationalists went down from 71 to 31, that is, to less than half—in percentage a loss greater than that of the Social Democrats—the People's Party to 7, while the Communists increased from 48 to 57. Neither the Weimar coalition nor the parties to their right had an absolute majority. That majority could be attained by the Weimar parties only with the support of the Communists and by the right-wing parties only through a coalition with the Zentrum. Both possibilities were discussed behind the wings, but in general in the negative sense.

According to the Prussian Constitution the old Cabinet had the right and the duty to conduct business until a new minister-president was elected. Until then there would exist in Prussia merely an "acting government" (*geschäftsführende Regierung*), as was at that time also the case in Bavaria, Wurtemberg, and Baden. The Prussian ministers were not pleased with the task that had fallen to them in this way, least of all Minister-President Braun, who withdrew to his house in Zehlendorf, leaving the chair to his deputy, Minister of Welfare Hitsiefer of the Zentrum Party.

In this situation Chancellor von Papen saw a unique opportunity to strike the blow against the Social Democrats which he and General von Schleicher had planned as a major part of their program and had probably even promised the National Socialists as a consideration for their being tolerated by the latter. Papen later maintained that he had only struck against the Prussian government in order to gain control of the Prussian police before the National Socialists. Had this really been his only motive it would have been enough for him to put the Prussian police under the control of a national commissioner. But that was not enough for Papen; he wanted the whole governmental power in Prussia.

On July 20, 1932, three days after the bloody Sunday in Altona, on which the National Socialists had provoked an out-and-out fight by demonstrating in Communist sections of the town (see next chapter), Papen announced his appointment as Reich Commissioner in Prussia by decree of the Reich President with considerably greater powers than merely police authority. He had obtained Hindenburg's signature during a visit to Neudeck, accompanied only by General von Schleicher and the German Nationalist Minister of the Interior, Baron von Gayl, who had joined him in assuring the President that the decree was fully compatible with the Constitution. The decree empowered the Chancellor, in his capacity as Reich Commissioner for Prussia, to "remove the Prussian Ministers from their offices," to take over the functions of the Minister-President himself, and to entrust other national commissioners with the conduct of the other Prussian ministries.

On the morning of July 20, Papen informed three Prussian ministers, who had under some pretext been invited to the Chancellery (Hirtsiefer, Severing, Klepper) of Hindenburg's decree, adding that for the moment he had confined himself to dismissing Braun and Severing. A few hours later he published a second decree, proclaiming a state of emergency in Berlin, which he had brought with him from Neudeck to meet all contingencies. Executive powers were given to General von Rundstedt.

The government based the decrees, as the published text made clear later the same day, not only on the second section of article 48 of the Constitution, which provided for special measures to be taken in the case of a serious disturbance of public safety and order, but explicitly also on the first section, which allowed executive steps to be taken against a *Land* that had failed to perform its duties under the national constitution or national statutes.

As for the reasons, the Reich government gradually referred to more and more, among them: the changing of the Landtag's standing orders immediately before new elections; the inability of Prussia to elect a new minister-president; the "key position" the Communist party held in the lower house; the bloody disturbances all over the country ("civil war conditions"); the allegedly insufficient measures taken against the Communists; the equality of treatment the Prussian government applied to infringements of the law by National Socialists and Communists; alleged negotiations by Prussian officials with the Communists to secure their support for the Weimar coalition parties; improper attacks which Prussian officeholders were said to have directed against the Reich government during the election campaign.

The Prussian ministers learned most of these reasons from the evening papers and from a radio speech Papen delivered at seven p.m. It had not been considered necessary to discuss any of these complaints with them beforehand, to demand corrective measures, or to threaten the appointment of a national commissioner in advance. The dismissal of state ministers went far beyond what the second section of article 48 allowed; as far as the first section was concerned, no act had so much as been asserted which represented a violation of duties by the *Land* Prussia toward the Reich.

At the time in question, on the morning of July 20, a Wednesday,

I was busy opposite the Chancellery building in the State Ministry, where we were as usual discussing the agenda of the next Reichsrat meeting with the provincial delegates, in order to achieve as unified a delivery of the Prussian votes as possible. Here we received the news. "Violation of the Constitution!" I said. "Why?" my colleague Nobis intervened, "if Hindenburg decrees it?" "Because he does not have the right to make such a decree."

After some delay due to our meeting I went across to the Ministry of the Interior in Unter den Linden, where I found the three ministers in conference with their colleagues. They had agreed to appeal to the Staatsgerichtshof (Supreme Constitutional Court) and asked me what in my opinion would probably be the court's decision. I answered that it would likely declare the putting of the Prussian police under a national commissioner valid, but the dismissal of ministers and voiding of their right to represent Prussia in the Reichsrat unconstitutional. I considered it a matter of course that we should appeal to the Constitutional Court, since the Constitution had provided for this judicial decision in controversies like the present one.

Whether active resistance should be resorted to was not discussed after I came. It had been shortly debated, I was told, but all the ministers had rejected this idea, perhaps with the exception of Finance Minister Klepper, as he himself later maintained, but Severing disputed. I shall return to this issue later (Chapter 79).

The ministers asked me to draft a letter of protest to the Chancellor and to inform him of the appeal to the Supreme Constitutional Court. Unable to find a quiet place to do this on the spot, I went across to the Ministry of Finance, drafted the letter in my office, and then took it to the ministers, who were waiting impatiently. It read as follows:

"The Prussian government is firmly convinced that the measures of the Reich government announced in the Chancellery today, July 20, to Ministers Hirtsiefer, Severing, and Klepper, constitute an infringement of the Constitutions both of the Reich and of Prussia. The Prussian government has therefore appealed to the Staatsgerichtshof for a decision and at the same time asked the tribunal for an interim order, whereby the measures in question be provisionally put out of force.

"In so far as the measures taken by the Reich Commissioner on the basis of Article 48 of the Reich Constitution interfere, whether directly or indirectly, with Article 17 of the Constitution—for example in dismissing ministers or in appointing new ministers—or with article 63, according to which the Laender are represented in the Reichsrat by members of their own governments, the Prussian government will regard such measures as invalid and nonexistent; for it is generally recognized in judicial decisions and legal theory that the Reich President may not interfere with these articles on the basis of article 48, but on the contrary, is bound by them."

In the two paragraphs I had distinguished between measures regarding which we would wait for a decision from the tribunal—as, for example, the legal validity of the President's decree as a whole and of putting the Prussian police under a Reich commissioner—and those we considered null and void immediately—such as the dismissal of ministers and the usurping of their rights in the Reichsrat.

During my absence a letter under the heading "The Prussian Minister-President" and signed "von Papen" had arrived asking the ministers to attend a "session of the state government" on the "internal situation." The use of the title "Prussian Minister-President" and the description of the intended session as one of the Prussian government aroused the particular indignation of the ministers. At their request I added a third paragraph to my draft, rejecting the invitation. It read:

"The Prussian government is, therefore, not in the position to comply with the invitation received to a 'session of the state government' under the chairmanship of the Reich Chancellor or Reich Commissioner; for a session of the Prussian government can only be held under the chairmanship of a Prussian Minister."

The words "session of the state government" were not at first within quotation marks; I added them by hand at the wish of the ministers, in order to make it clear that they did not reject negotiations with the Reich government altogether but only the presumption that it was a case of a session of the Prussian government.

Papen, however, made use of this rejection of his invitation as a pretext for dismissal of the six ministers who had so far not been removed from office.

On the same day the Prussian government asked me to represent them before the Supreme Constitutional Court, together with my colleague Badt from the Ministry of the Interior and professors of public law. Although it was clear to me that my answer would affect the whole course of my life, I said yes without hesitation. I felt it to be my manifest duty—as a human being, as a German, and as a government official—to defend the Prussian ministers who had been unjustly accused. Many of my acquaintances resented my decision. My sister Gertrud was deeply moved; she saw an *imitatio Christi* in it. But I was not motivated—not consciously in any case —by religious impulse, but simply by my desire for justice and truth.

As soon as July 23 the hearing on the proposed interim order took place in Leipzig. It was the first time I pleaded a case before the Supreme Court. We lost. The tribunal declared, referring to precedents, that in an interim order it could not take the part of one of the parties, but must wait for the fully prepared hearing of the case. It also considered it not appropriate to divide the public power in a state by interim order.

One of the Reich Commissioner's first actions was to have several of the democratically minded senior officials provisionally retired; these included several state secretaries, ministerial directors, chiefs of police, presidents of regional and district governments—a number which grew daily. Other officials were promoted or newly appointed, and indeed, not only provisionally but permanently.

At first I was not one of the officials affected. But when I had taken over the case for Prussia, Papen sent me, on July 25, the day of the tribunal's decision on the interim order, a letter informing me that the "State Ministry" had decided to "give me temporary leave." Two days later came a telegram and a letter, saying that the State Ministry had decided to put me into temporary retirement, with the added note, "Your further employment is left to the future" (*bleibt vorbehalten*). At the same time Papen published a statement in the press to the effect that my entering the legal conflict for the opposing party would bring me into conflict with official duties and, therefore, forced him to take this step. Just as after my dismissal five years previously by Herr von Keudell (Chapter 53) not only the democratic press, but also a section of the right-wing press, regretted my removal from office and expressed the wish that it would only be temporary.

I answered (July 28):

"I have handed over my secondary functions in the Prussian Ministry of Finance to my deputy this morning.

"As regards my primary functions as an authorized delegate to the Reichsrat I have, after thorough and conscientious examination, reached the conclusion that the Chancellor has not the power, either as such or as Commissioner, appointed on the authority of article 48 of the Constitution, to withdraw them from me. While it is not in general proper for officials to contradict the orders of a superior, it is in this particular case the official's duty to examine whether the person who gives him the order *is* his superior or otherwise legitimized to give him orders. This duty to examine applies in the case of emergency decrees under article 48 very rarely, but it does apply precisely with regard to the Reichsrat. To my great regret I am, therefore, placed in a position most embarrassing for an official of having to decide to the best of my knowledge whether your instruction or that of the state ministers is binding for me. This is a duty which I have sworn to fulfill when I took my constitutional oath.

"I have for years advocated a personal union in leading offices and other devices of closer contact between the Reich and Prussia. Now as then I consider this to be a healthy goal worth striving for. I trust, however, I am at one with the President and with you, the Chancellor, in saying that this goal may not be pursued through infringements of the Constitution. In any case, political desires do not alter my constitutional duties.

"I am, furthermore, a member and deputy chairman of the Reich Debts Commission, acting for President Saemisch, who is ill. I cannot hand over these duties either, since I was made a member of the Commission by the Reichsrat."

I sent a copy of this letter to President Hindenburg. We now began feverish work on drafting the suit. We had lost our office rooms and, therefore, had to work in very noisy surroundings in the Landtag building, with excited visitors continually coming to us with questions and suggestions. I often fled into the empty plenary room, in order to be able to work there undisturbed.

The Social Democrat party group in the Landtag joined the suit as an independent appellant, appointing Professor Hermann Heller to represent it, as did the Zentrum party, which named Professor Hans Peters. The Bavarian and Baden governments brought independent suits with the aim of having the violation of the Constitution through Papen's measures juridically determined.

Before I pass on to the further course of events, I will give extracts in the next chapter from the narrative I delivered at the first session of the Staatsgerichtshof on October 10, 1932. This is not only a memorable autobiographical item; it will also help to preserve the public memory of these events which grew so fateful in German history.

## 77. The 20th of July, 1932—My Speech at the Supreme Constitutional Court

"In order to give a clear picture of the events on July 20, I must first say a few words on the crisis in parliamentary life in the course of which they took place.

"Ever since the September elections in 1930 we have found ourselves in a unique crisis of parliamentary life, not only in Prussia, but also in the Reich, and in the majority of the other German *Laender*. Not every crisis in parliamentary life is at the same time a crisis in parliamentarism, just as every crisis in economic life during the past hundred years was not at the same time a crisis of capitalism. That there has been a crisis in parliamentary life, however, cannot be disputed.

"What is the peculiar nature of this crisis? It resulted from the fact that the 'National Socialist German Workers Party' showed increasing election success, to such an extent that after the elections in September, 1930 it might have seemed appropriate and desirable in accordance with parliamentary principles to give those who had gained such a victory a share in the government; not only on grounds of chivalry, but because precisely this is the deeper meaning of the parliamentary system, namely, that the movement which is victorious should also take over the government, should bear responsibility, and that in this way its ideologies be subjected to the correcting influence of practice.

"But two circumstances prevented this. There were serious doubts about the legal exercise of the governmental power by the NSDAP.[1] Moreover, the party itself raised demands in line with the maxim: 'All or nothing,' stating that, if it were to be given governmental power, then this must be done in such a way that there would be practically no countervailing power.

[1] NSDAP stands for the National Socialist Party (National-Sozialistische Deutsche Arbeiter-Partei).

"The problem as to whether it is proper under these circumstances to hand over governmental power to the NSDAP has been for two years, and still is today, the great problem in internal politics. The NSDAP holds *no majority,* either in the Landtag or in the Reichstag. In the Landtag it has 162 of 423 seats, the Weimar Parties (Zentrum, Social Democrats, and State Party) have 163, the Communists 57, the German Nationalists 31, other smaller groups 10. In July it obtained in the Reichstag 230 of 608 seats, the Weimar Parties a total of 212, with the Bavarian People's Party 234. The NSDAP thus does not have a majority; in both parliaments it is in the *minority.*

"So far all the responsible authorities—this is of particular relevance in our context—have *refused* to give the decisive power to the NSDAP *while it is still a minority.* This was refused by the Reich President and by Chancellor Brüning from September, 1930 until May, 1932; it was likewise refused by the Prussian Landtag before and after the new elections, from spring 1932 until today; it was again refused by the Reich President and by Chancellor von Papen in the middle of August, 1932, and once again by Chancellor von Papen at the end of August during the negotiations on a coalition government composed of the NSDAP and other parties. The official communication on August 13, 1932, contains the following sentences on this point [already quoted in Chapter 75, ending with the words that the President 'could not bear the responsibility before his conscience and his duties toward the fatherland if he conferred all governmental power exclusively on the National Socialists, who intended to use this power one-sidedly']. And Chancellor von Papen said on August 28, 1932 in his speech in Münster, which was broadcast: 'The lack of any restraint (*Zügellosigkeit*) disclosed in the appeal of the leader of the National Socialist movement suits ill the claims to leadership in the state. I do not concede him the right to regard that minority in Germany which follows his flag alone to be the German nation and to treat all others as fair game.' Von Papen went so far as to thwart through his political counteractions serious attempts of the NSDAP and the Zentrum to reach some parliamentary government basis at the end of August.

"There was a certain uniformity of attitude in this course of things. All former governments of the Reich had applied the parliamentary principles of 'equal opportunity' which I cannot describe better than in the following words from the latest book by Professor Carl Schmitt [sitting opposite me during the proceedings] *Legality and Legitimacy* (p. 37): 'The principle of equal opportunity (*der gleichen Chance*) is of such a sensitivity that even a serious doubt about the full loyalty of thinking of all participants makes its application impossible. One can, of course, keep open equal opportunity only to those of whom one is certain that they would keep it open to himself. Any other handling of such a principle would not only mean, practically, suicide, but would violate the principle itself.'

"This quite steady course of events has been interrupted by an episode, *the episode of agreement between Chancellor von Papen and Herr Hitler* or, more precisely, between the President, the Chancellor, and Minister von Schleicher on the one hand, and Herr Hitler and his party colleagues on the other. This episode lasted from the beginning of June until August 13, 1932. It began with a sort of contract. The National Socialists promised to support Chancellor von Papen and his government as a presidential Cabinet, without participating in it and for the duration of the rule of this Cabinet. This fact was originally disputed, but is now no longer controversial between the parties; for in the above-mentioned official government communication of August 13, 1932 it is said: 'He—that is, the President—regretted that Hitler did not feel himself to be able, *in accordance with his statements made prior to the elections,* to support a national-minded government called into office with the confidence of the President.' And in the later official communication on August 15, this was specified as follows: 'The undertaking to support a presidential cabinet of the Reich President has been given not only by Hitler, but by other controlling leaders of the NSDAP as well. The form in which this happened left no doubt that this promise of toleration was not limited to a definite period, but was to be valid for the entire duration of the rule of the Cabinet which the President had appointed as the government that had his confidence. This promise of the National Socialist leaders was afterward repeated to Chancellor von Papen, and this not privately, but in the presence of irreproachable witnesses.' The National Socialist leaders did not, of course, give their promise of support, if I may put it like this, out of pure affection for the government (*um der blauen Augen der Reichsregierung willen*), but, self-evidently, only on the basis of certain assurances. These assurances provided for: (1) the repeal of the ban on the wearing of uniforms, (2) readmission of the banned

Storm Troops, (3) a change in the Prussian government, in particular in the control of the police.

"This agreement, too, is no longer disputed, we believe. Should it be disputed, we must name the gentlemen concerned as witnesses.

"In pursuance of these agreements, the repeal of the ban on uniforms and the readmission of the storm troops came on June 14, and on June 28, the decree forbidding the *Laender* to issue similar bans. In Prussia, first the Chancellor got in touch with the National Socialist Landtag President, Kerrl, to bring about a right-wing government in Prussia, and finally, when this attempt failed, there followed the appointment of a Reich Commissioner for Prussia.

"I am now turning to the *significance of this episode from the point of view of the police* and in the wider sense from that of the *Laender* altogether. Here it is necessary to remember that legally the Reich confronts the *Laender* as one and the same (*eine Einheit*), irrespective of form and time. Whether the question is about an action by the President or by the Chancellor, by the Brüning government or the Papen government—as far as the *Laender* are concerned, every action on the part of the responsible organs of the Reich government is an act of the same Reich.

"In March, in July, in August, and in October, 1931 the Reich government issued severe decrees for the reestablishment of peace and order. In these decrees a series of measures were provided for, in order to stop the dreadful terrorist activities and disorders. They included the following:

the duty to give previous notice of all public political meetings, allowance for preventive prohibitions of such meetings, prohibition of political demonstrations on trucks,
permission to ban the wearing of uniform dress and badges,
the duty to submit all posters and leaflets beforehand,
prohibition of the distribution of demoralizing pamphlets (*Zersetzungsschriften*) of unknown origin,
permission to shut down centers of activities hostile to the state.

"This was followed by a general ban on the wearing of uniforms —not passed by the Prussian government, but by the Reich government, namely, the Reich President, on December 8, 1931—and on April 13, 1932, the disbanding of the Storm Troops of the NSDAP, again not through the Prussian government, but by the Reich President.

"The reasons for the decree of April 13 were published officially, and there it was said that 'such a militarily organized force leads logically to clashes and finally to conditions similar *to those of a civil war (bürgerkriegsähnlichen Zuständen)*.' Here for the first time the words 'civil-war-like conditions' were used, when the President disbanded the Storm Troops of the NSDAP.

"In addition to the above-mentioned decrees of the Reich since October, 1931 there has been a general prohibition of political meetings and parades out of doors in Prussia.

"This was the legal basis for attempts to suppress disturbances of public order. On this basis the police went into action, on this basis they did their difficult work both day and night. The battle was in full swing. We know that this battle cost a regrettable number of deaths month by month. Eight were slain in February, 3 National Socialists and 5 others, 3 of them Communists, in April six, in May seven, three until the middle of June. . . . Such was the situation, when on June 14, in the middle of this battle, the Reich President repealed, at the request of the [Papen] government, all the measures taken which I have just enumerated. Repealed were: the duty to give advance notice of public political meetings; the permission of preventive injunctions against such meetings; the prohibition of the use of trucks for political demonstrations, the ban on wearing uniform dress and badges, the obligation to submit political posters and leaflets; the prohibition of disseminating demoralizing writings of unknown origin, and the permission to shut down centers of activities hostile to the state. At the same time, on June 14, the general ban of uniforms and the disbanding of the Storm Troops were repealed; uniformed Storm Troops were readmitted. Indeed, even more: on June 28 the *Laender* were forbidden to pass such measures as the ban on public meetings and on the wearing of uniforms. All this in the middle of a civil-war-like situation.

"What did this mean for the *Laender* and for the police? In the middle of this battle the police suddenly had to turn about. I do not want to speak of the centers of activities hostile to the government, which had been closed on the instructions of the President and now had to be reopened by the same police force and could once more resume their activities, but only of the following. Until that day, June 14, it had been the duty of the police to prevent parades in the streets, to keep the Storm Troopers of the NSDAP from appearing on the streets in uniform. And then, quite suddenly, from one day to the next, they had to allow these parades and NSDAP uniforms, not only allow them, but to walk alongside, to protect them from attacks that sprang from the sudden wave of hostile feeling which had thus been aroused.

"A uniform protest from the large *Laender* and most of the small ones followed. There was a meeting in Berlin, at which the *Laender* protested vigorously. They said: at this moment there is no real danger of a sudden flaring up of the Communist movement, but if you do this, then there will of course be such a danger. The *Laender* protested most strongly on the ground that they themselves were forbidden, in fulfilling their police duties, should it become necessary, to pass decrees prohibiting public political meetings and the wearing of uniforms. On this point there was only one opinion among the *Laender*. All *Laender* ministers declared that it was not possible for them in this way to perform their police duties, to maintain order and safety.

"And what happened? What had to happen, did happen: the clashes increased. I have already listed the sad number of deaths in previous months. These figures were taken from the statistics the Reich Commissioner himself has just published. According to them there had been on average 6, 7, or 8 deaths per month in the preceding months. In the first half of June, that is, before the decree on June 14, there had been 3. But in the second half, that is, after the repeal of the ban on uniforms and after the readmission of the Storm Troops, there were 17 deaths as a result of disturbances, 12 on the National Socialist side and 5 among the Communists. In July the number increased to 86, among them 38 National Socialists and 43 others, including 30 Communists, two thirds of these before July 20, and one third after.

"The clashes in Altona on July 17 were especially characteristic. In Altona the National Socialists wanted to have a parade and, despite the mood of excitement prevailing at the time, to march through the narrow streets of precisely that section of the town inhabited by the embittered Communists. On the ground that the new regulations did not permit them to forbid this parade, the police let it take its course. They protected it with all their forces. Official reports, printed in the briefs of the Reich government, describe how exemplary the police behaved in their protection of the National Socialists during the parade. Even the right-wing press recognized this fact. But there occurred heavy shooting from the windows and there were a large number of regrettable deaths. The

only fault was that the parade was allowed to take place at all despite the hectic excitement. This, however, was done to meet the
new policy of the Reich government.

"Very soon the Reich government had to withdraw from its new
decrees. As early as June 28, it was compelled to reintroduce the obligation to give advance notice of public political meetings, and on
July 18, on the day after Altona, unfortunately too late, to reiterate
the general ban on meetings and parades out of doors. From July 31
until August 31 any public political meetings were prohibited. Finally, on August 9, special courts had to be established, and the
death penalty was pronounced for clashes that resulted in slaying.
Due to the preceding decrees, public appearances of the Storm
Troops had already been suppressed since all public meetings out of
doors were forbidden. But only the threat of the death penalty and
the establishment of special courts sent the curve of disturbances of
the peace down again. Before that, the bloody clashes continued
during the end of July with 23 deaths, including 6 National Socialists
and 17 others. Every day lists of regrettable victims were published.
Thus it continued also from August 1 to 10. [There followed a description of the worst acts of violence in this period.]

"The causal nexus between these events is manifest for anyone
who is willing to see. The causal nexus between the repeal of the
ban on uniforms and the readmission of the Storm Troops on one
side and the subsequent increase in disturbances of the peace on the
other is quite obvious, and equally obvious is the causal nexus between what happened on the occasion of the formation of the government von Papen and its support by the National Socialists, on
one side, and the measures directed against the Prussian government on the other. . . .

"Now, how did what happened on July 20 look from the *standpoint of the Prussian ministers* in particular? For weeks open and
concealed demands had kept appearing in the right-wing press for
the Reich government to appoint a Reich commissioner for Prussia.
These suggestions were justified in different ways, but the relevant
point was always that the ministers in Prussia were to be removed
and that their place was to be taken by the Reich Commissioner.
Any intention to do this was most strongly denied by the Reich
government, even on the day immediately before the deed. The
Reich government failed to direct any demands to the Prussian government, and to warn them that nonconformance would lead to se-

questration through a Reich commissioner; quite the contrary, right until the end they denied having any such intention. By means of a casual office invitation, giving as subject to the one minister 'finances and agriculture' and to another 'internal politics and finances,' the Ministers Hirtsiefer, Severing, and Klepper were asked to come to a meeting in the Chancellery on July 20. The gentlemen came at ten o'clock in the morning. They were merely informed by the Chancellor that he had just dismissed Minister-President Braun and Minister Severing. To their astonished question why, they were simply told that things in Prussia were not as the Reich government wished, that there was nothing to be done now, that he himself was very sorry, but that they had to go. When they objected that it was necessary to explain why the discharges were being made and that those affected must at least be heard, the answer was a mere shrug of the shoulders, and the ministers were sent home.

"They did not learn the reasons for the dismissal until the Chancellor's radio broadcast that afternoon. . . . The broadcast reproached the Prussian government on the ground that in the Landtag 47 percent of the deputies were members of the NSDAP and of the German Nationalist Party, 37 percent members of all other parties, except the Communists, and 16 percent of the Communist Party, and that, therefore, there was no majority for the government, unless the Communists were to join the 37 percent of the other parties. Hence the Communists held the key position. But in reality every large party in the Landtag has a key position. How can one say that such a distribution of seats constitutes a violation of duty on Prussia's part? And how can just the Reich government use this argument?

"When we are criticized on the ground that the Prussian government is supported by no more than 37 percent of the Landtag members, you cannot be surprised, gentlemen, that we answer by stating that the parliamentary basis which the Chancellor had in the Reichstag elected on July 31 and now dissolved, was considerably smaller. The call for a vote [on September 12, see Chapter 80] may have not been in order, but the vote was taken, and the result was that out of 559 votes cast the Chancellor had 510 [more exactly, 512] against him and no more than 42 for him, with 5 abstentions. What, under these circumstances, does the reproach mean that the parliamentary basis of the Prussian government depends on the tacti-

cal moves of the Communist party and this is said to constitute a violation on the side of Prussia of its duties, and indeed of its duties
toward the Reich, toward the Reich Constitution and the Reich
law! . . ."[2]


## 78. EQUAL TREATMENT OF NATIONAL SOCIALISTS AND COMMUNISTS?


IN his answer on behalf of the Papen government Herr Gottheiner,
Ministerial Director in the federal Ministry of the Interior, said that
the bloody events could be traced back to a considerable degree "to
the entirely one-sided treatment which had been bestowed upon the
National Socialist movement." He said that Papen's measures "were
intended to serve the purpose, and have served the purpose, of opening a valve for the excitement that had been dammed up in the National Socialist movement as a result of this one-sided treatment.
That was the purpose: to prevent a sudden outburst of this excitement and thereby the outbreak of civil war." The policy of the
Prussian government had given the impression that "they were willing to combat the Communist danger, as decisively as the situation
demanded, only on condition that National Socialists and Communists were treated equally. The Reich government, however, is unable to see any justification for this equalization."

Professor Carl Schmitt stated: "I do not consider it correct, or at
least not exhaustive, when Ministerial Director Brecht says: 'Where
acts of violence occur, we intervene; there are neither Christian-
German acts of violence nor Communist acts of violence; there are
just punishable acts, and there are individuals who commit them.' "
The relevant question was rather, he said, whether a party was legal
or illegal. "The decision whether a party is legal or illegal can be
made only by an independent government, since the very source of
all our trouble is that the one party declares the other to be illegal.
. . . The Reich government's motive was not to howl along with
the wolves or to take the wind out of anyone's sails, or the like, but
principally to do something much more simple and obvious, to be

---

[2] My introductory speech before the tribunal, which discussed many other relevant points, is more extensively rendered in the German ed.

*just and objective,* and to invalidate the insulting equalization with the Communist party on behalf of a party with which not only millions of Germans sympathize, but for which they have cast their votes." He then raised the question: "How far does this right of a land go to pursue a policy deviating from the policy of the Reich?"

I answered:

"We will be all at one in our resentment that it is extraordinarily difficult to govern in Germany, with seventeen *Laender,* all of which under the Reich Constitution have the right within the framework of their functions—and these include the police—to pursue differing opinions in matters left to their judgment by the law. And we also will all agree that these conditions must be changed through appropriate political means, be it by a change in the Constitution, be it by mutual agreement or the like. But we are concerned here with the question as to who has violated a legal obligation under present legal conditions, and this is quite a different question. The bloody events in June and July—so the representative of the Reich government has said—were caused by the one-sided treatment of the National Socialists in Prussia. There could be no doubt, he added, that the Communists are a party whose goals are antagonistic to the state, a party hostile to the state, in contrast to the National Socialists. The fact that the Communists are enemies of the state, he said, has been confirmed in numerous decisions handed down by the Supreme Court (*Reichsgericht*). No doubt that is so. But where did the evidence for these judicial decisions come from? The Prussian Minister of the Interior, Severing, and his predecessor in office, Grzesinski, have passed the evidence for the treasonal and illegal activities within the Communist party to the courts. . . .

"Professor Schmitt says that only the proper government authority can judge whether a party is legal or illegal, and that not just anyone can have a say in this matter: that is, for example, not the Prussian government—he can only have meant it this way—but solely the Reich government. That is not correct. The *courts* have the final decision on this. How opinions have changed within the Reich government in the past three months I have described this morning! The decree on the prohibition of the Storm Troops was passed by the Reich President on the ground that this organization must lead to civil-war conditions. In other words, the one-sided decree against the Storm Troops of the National Socialists was passed because the President was of the opinion that the available evidence made a special move against them necessary. . . .

"The Prussian state ministers are by no means of the opinion that the Communist and National Socialist movements are of equal character. No one knows as well as they that there are great differences between them and what they are. But why one ought to differentiate between the acts of violence that occur, acts, I hope, not approved of by the leaders, why acts of brutal ferocity committed by the National Socialists ought to be dealt with somehow more mildly, why one should turn a blind eye to them from the point of view of Christian culture—this is a mystery to us.

"Among the accusations against Minister Severing a new one has emerged. . . . Some weeks before the appointment of the Reich Commissioner he is supposed to have said that the appointment of a commissioner was unavoidable. He is supposed to have said—the Prussian Minister of the Interior to the Reich Minister!—"Do appoint a Reich commissioner in Prussia as soon as possible, otherwise it will be too late!' Has the factual part of our argument really been lowered onto a level where such assertions can be made? . . . A Reich commissioner who was to dismiss the eight Prussian ministers in the way it has happened, such a man is supposed to have been asked for by Minister Severing? This is expected to be believed? But I state that this assertion has been made.

"And this new assertion is joined by another one, in regard to Minister-President Braun: 'What great wrong has been done him?' you suggest. 'His salary was paid to him in full; he enquired about this, and then he was content.' I will make no answer to this.

"But I have here a letter written to me on August 29 by Minister-President Braun in Bad Gastein. Braun lost his only son in the war; his wife is severely crippled. He wrote from Gastein:

" 'Here I am only slowly getting over the bitterness which fills me because of the method of my removal from office and the reasons given. For more than ten years I have supported the Reich policies without regard to the composition of the various Reich governments, precisely in order to lessen injury to the Reich from the Reich-Prussia dualism. I have often done so at the expense of my own party's public image (*Werbekraft*), when they in the Reichstag were violently opposing measures of the Reich which I supported in the Reichsrat in the interest of harmonious cooperation between the Reich and Prussia. We have often lent support to the

Reich government, at its request, against Bavaria and other *Laender,* when it would have been in the better interest of Prussia to have joined the other *Laender* in an oppositional front. We have done so in the higher interest of Germany. And now, because of failing to fulfill obligations toward the Reich, to be driven out of office like a servant who has stolen and may no longer enter the house, this is amply bitter. And the more so since it happens at the order of a man [Hindenburg] on behalf of whose uprightness (*Lauterkeit*) and loyalty to the Constitution I have intervened publicly with all my strength and who owes not the least part of his reelection as President to this. From more than forty years activity in politics I know that in politics there is no gratitude. But a certain measure of respect is nevertheless a prerequisite for political cooperation. . . .'

"One of the gentlemen from the side of the Reich government has said that *Prussia's fronde in the Reichsrat* was intolerable in the long run, that it led to intolerable conditions. Is this meant to assert another infringement of its obligations by Prussia? Is it meant to maintain that Prussia has formed a sort of fronde in the Reichsrat and therewith failed to fulfill its obligations so that according to article 48, paragraph 1, executive steps can be taken against it? . . . In reality things are very different: Prussia has over the course of the past ten years supported the Reich government and joined forces with it in the Reichsrat, neglecting political antagonisms to such an extent that I count it a great honor to be able to bear witness here to the wise moderation the Prussian government has shown under the leadership of Minister-President Braun.

"What were the most recent events in the Reichsrat under the present Reich government prior to July 20? Not a single conflict had occurred, not even during the debates on the Reich budget in June, 1932, where Prussia had charge of the general report. The deliberations not only proceeded without any disharmony, but in the final plenary session, in which only Prussia spoke, Baron von Gayl, the Reich Minister of the Interior, expressed the thanks of the Reich government and of the Reichsrat to Prussia and the Prussian representative! And yet, precisely during the budget debates would there have been an opportunity to assert opposition. In only two questions did differences of opinion gain any significance: Prussia wanted 20 million more spent for the settlement of small farmers and unemployed in East Prussia; the Reich government had deleted this sum in the estimate, but afterward complied with our suggestion by granting the means as a loan. And the second point: Prussia was of the opinion that available jobs should be spread among more workers by shortening the working hours in order to lower expenditures for unemployed workers and to set large sums free for public works. The *Laender* will back me if I say that we had very impressive committee meetings on this matter, with the result that the representatives of the Reich said: we must do something about this. . . . This is the sort of objective cooperation which we have cultivated continually in the Reichsrat."

## 79. Active or Passive Resistance?

At their first discussion of the issue the Prussian Ministers had rejected the idea of resistance through violent actions. Was that decision politically wise? Should they not have called up the police and the population in general to resist, and proclaimed a general strike? Should they not at least have resisted in person, instead of allowing their offices and files to be taken over by Papen and his deputies without any struggle?

In fact Minister Severing, in reply to Papen's question whether he would vacate his post voluntarily and hand it over to Commissioner Bracht, had replied that he would yield only to force. But when Papen proclaimed martial law in Berlin and Bracht appeared in Severing's office with a new chief of police just appointed and two police officers, Severing considered this to be sufficient evidence of the use of force and left the building. A heroic scene, a physical struggle, ending in ill treatment, wounding, or killing, would have been easy enough to stage at this point. Anyone who knows Severing will realize that it was not lack of personal courage which restrained him. What did restrain him was the responsible consideration of a former union leader that such a gesture would have become the signal for an uprising of the Social Democratic workers, which would have been met with military force, and that on the following day a military dictatorship—Hindenburg-Schleicher-Rundstedt—would have been established.

For the same reason I kept Minister-President Braun from a personal fight into which he was about to rush when, coming with me from Unter den Linden, we were passing his office. Rage seized hold of him; he wanted to go in and make his way to his room on the second floor by force. "I want to see who will dare to stand in my way." I advised against this for the same reasons for which Severing had foregone a heroic martyr's scene.

A flag is easily attached to a pole, but not so easily hauled down honorably. If the way of active resistance was to be taken—resistance not only against the Chancellor, mind you, but against the President—then it had to be taken after careful consideration of the consequences and not to be drifted into at the expense of others. To allow oneself to be thrown out violently, to be led away or struck down, was to incur a humiliation which a responsible workers' leader could undertake only when he intended thereby to give the signal for a general revolt and to set off the resulting street fights between well-armed military units and unarmed workers. Braun did not want this any more than did Severing, and if they had wanted it, then the members of the Zentrum party in the Prussian government would not have followed suit.

Most critics are at one in condemning the abstention from violent resistance as politically wrong and woefully inadequate. To quote only two of the most distinguished books on the Weimar Republic, the one says: "Whatever good reasons can be brought for that passivity . . . it remains unpleasant nevertheless. Whoever subjects himself without fighting is judged wrong in public opinion. . . . Whether the republic's downfall could yet have been halted in any way it is impossible to say. But the fact that no hand was raised to ward off this downfall makes it not only tragic but also deeply depressing" (Eyck, vol. 2, p. 611). In the other book, the author sums up by saying that Braun and Severing "did not react by giving concrete evidence of that political responsibility which was theirs according to their democratically based positions" (Bracher, p. 595). True, only a few pages later he does write (p. 599) that it would be difficult to deny "their motives and thoughts human respect," but then again he continues that "they nonetheless failed to act according to political necessities. There remained the possibility of a sustained demonstration, evidence of the unbroken desire for self-assertion of democracy even in the face of temporarily prevailing acts of violence." Indeed, comparing July 20, 1932, with July 20, 1944, the date of the revolt against Hitler, he goes so far as to speak of twelve

years of destruction, a destruction "for which both sides bear responsibility—the one for its scruples and passivity, the other for its
delusion of power and authoritarian experiments," thus equating
the responsibility for the lack of a revolt in July, 1932 with the responsibility of Papen and Hitler (final note to Chapter VIII).

The most striking point in these critical verdicts for me is that
they refer to the lack of revolt, not when Hitler seized power in
January, 1933, but in July, 1932, when Hindenburg, Papen, and
Schleicher still wanted to avert Hitler's access to power; and, sec-
ondly, that they usually speak only of the passivity of the Social
Democrats, and not of the middle and upper classes as well. Are
the workers always the only ones who have to do the dirty work?
Twelve years later, on July 20, 1944, one did not think that way.
Why so in reflections on July 20, 1932?

But my main objection aims at something else. It is a basic requirement of historical and political science that in allotting guilt
the critic must proceed from the situation as it appeared at the time
of the action, and not from one that developed afterward but could
not be foreseen.

Considered as of today, with all our knowledge of what happened later, it is entirely plausible to say that an uprising of German workers on July 20, 1932, would have been better for Germany's future than a mere appeal to the Supreme Constitutional
Court. Not only would a heroic struggle for freedom, even bloodily
suppressed, have been a source of self-respect for the working classes
and all friends of democracy in Germany later on, and also a source
of strong and lasting sympathy abroad, but, furthermore, the dictatorship that then would have come about as early as July, 1932
would not have been Hitler's, but Schleicher's. This would have
been less ominous.

But it is unjustified to accuse the Prussian ministers on this
ground. For in the summer and fall of 1932 Hindenburg, Papen,
and Schleicher were seriously combatting National Socialist supremacy. At that time it was highly unlikely that the President would
entrust Hitler with the Chancellor's office (see the official announcement of August 13, Chapter 75) and just as unlikely that Hitler
could gain governmental power against Hindenburg's will. Bracher
himself has said explicitly that it was not only subjectively quite ex-
cusable for the Prussian ministers to believe that Hitler could be
kept from power, but that such a belief was objectively justified, as

the considerable drop in National Socialist votes in the November elections showed. *Speaking objectively,* Bracher said, *Hitler's access to power was unlikely, and remained unlikely, until the beginning of 1933.* But if this was so, why should the Prussian ministers have provoked a blood-bath for the workers and the setting up of a military dictatorship by engaging in violent resistance? They could not yet know that in January, 1933 Papen would attack Schleicher from behind in the latter's fight against Hitler (Chapter 84). On the other hand, they were reasonably certain that violent resistance would end with defeat; indeed, they had good reason to fear that this struggle would lead to the Storm Troops' joining the regular army, and subsequently to the participation of the National Socialists in the dictatorship. Active resistance would therefore have brought about precisely what they wanted to avoid. They still remembered Bebel's firm warning: "Do not be provoked!"

Elsewhere in his book Bracher blames the Social Democrats on the ground that they did not in good time try to come to terms with Schleicher on establishing a viable form of government of a less strictly parliamentarian type, especially in December, 1932, when Schleicher wanted to bring together the military, the labor unions, and the moderate wing of the National Socialists (Chapter 84). Eyck also launches this reproach. "They seem not yet to have understood that Hitler was *ante portas* and that in comparison with him even a conservative general, though suspect as an intriguer, was a comfort" (p. 564). Seen from this standpoint, which is in line with my ideas on a "second-best" form of government (Chapters 30, 85, 86), it is contradictory to scold the Social Democrats for not having started a hopeless civil war in July, 1932.

The assertion, formerly often heard, that Hindenburg and Papen would have yielded to any manly resistance on the part of Braun and Severing is now, rightly enough, repeated only rarely. Bracher too thinks it is false. He admits that the active resistance which he recommended would in all probability have been suppressed (pp. 596 f.), because Hindenburg, Papen, and Schleicher had expected it and made preparations, and were even surprised that none came. The Prussian police, although to a large extent loyal to Severing, knew that the President had the right (often made use of by Ebert) to put them by emergency decree under the command of a commissioner or a military general. It is therefore unrealistic to believe that they would have fought against Hindenburg.

And the general strike? With more than half the workers out of work or on part time, including millions of young people who had been waiting in vain for years for their first jobs and many of whom had gone over to the National Socialists and Communists, who promised them work, a general strike, not like the one after the Kapp Putsch called by the President himself, but *against* the President, not like the former one supported by most of the state secretaries and the majority of government officials—what would its prospects have been? The prospects were that it would have collapsed miserably.

I trust that, in due course of time, historiography will correct the condemnation—psychologically understandable, but objectively unjustified—of the Prussian ministers for their passive resistance on July 20, 1932. I have blamed the Social Democrats and other parties for their policy in many other situations, but in this matter I must defend them. On the question whether they could have and should have looked for a workable alternative to parliamentary democracy, see below, Chapters 85 and 86.

## 80. Intermezzo—Papen Caught in His Own Snares

The Reich government, of course, tried as well as possible to justify its assertion that it had upheld the Constitution. Since we watched their further moves closely and, whenever they gave reason, denounced them as evidence of the unconstitutional aims of their decrees, the President and the Reich government tried hard to avoid anything that might sustain our accusations or might otherwise have an unfavorable influence upon the decisions of the Constitutional Court. These indirect consequences of our appeal to the Court—to me one of the chief reasons for conducting the trial at all —have so far not been sufficiently appraised.

Papen drifted from one difficulty to another. The Reichstag elections on July 31 (Chapter 77) had the catastrophic result that without National Socialists or Communists, who together were in the majority, no majority government could be formed. Of 608 seats the

National Socialists obtained 230 (instead of previously 107), the Communists 89 (instead of 77), the Social Democrats 133 (10 less than before), the Zentrum 75 (6 more), the Bavarian People's Party 20 (1 more), the Democrats (State Party, 4 instead of 14), the German People's Party 7 (30 before), the Economics Party 2 (11 before), and the German Nationalists 37 (41 before).

The two Socialist parties had stood the test well if their seats were counted *together;* they now had 222 seats as against 220 in 1930 and 207 in 1928. Since the National Socialists had no majority, either alone or together with the German Nationalists, or even with the inclusion of the People's Party, and since all the bourgeois parties taken together, from the Democrats to the German Nationalists, even together with the Social Democrats, did not have a majority, there was under the parliamentary rules of the game no other solution than that Zentrum and National Socialists formed a coalition government, with or without the inclusion of the German Nationalists. The two parties did indeed begin negotiations. This put Papen in a dilemma. Ought he to promote such a coalition, which would have thrown him from the saddle, since neither the Zentrum nor the National Socialists wanted to have anything to do with him? In a passionate article he turned against such a coalition as insincere.[1] He insisted instead on the continuation of "presidial governments," based on the President's confidence and power.

When the new Reichstag assembled on August 30, Papen and the National Socialists were therefore in a state of war with each other. Göring, elected Reichstag President as the representative of the strongest party, spoke in his first address as the defender of the Constitution and of parliamentary rights in contrast to Papen's presidential authority. The House adjourned until September 12. When it reconvened, there came the tragic-comic scene in which Papen tried in vain to announce the dissolution of the Reichstag, before Göring had put a Communist proposal to a vote, which demanded repeal of a presidential decree passed on September 4 on economic needs, and at the same time expressed the Reichstag's lack of confidence in Papen. Since no opposition was raised from any party, Göring set the roll call going, rejecting Papen's request to speak with the remark that they were in the middle of voting, and bestowing com-

---

[1] *Deutsche Allgemeine Zeitung,* September 1, 1932. See German ed. for the text, vol. II, p. 219.

plete inattention on the presidential dissolution order, which first Papen himself and then his state secretary Planck held out in front of him. Göring read it out only after the completion of the vote.

The vote was 512 for the expression of no confidence and only 42 against, with 5 abstentions. Papen had therefore obtained only 42 of the Reichstag's 608 votes. But with the Reichstag dissolved he continued to govern through presidential emergency powers.

Under these conditions the proceedings began before the Supreme Constitutional Court on October 10, 1932.

## 81. Proceedings Before the Supreme Constitutional Court—Its Decision (October 10–25, 1932)

At the end of August the former Prussian Finance Minister Höpker-Aschoff handed me a suggestion for a settlement out of court. The Reich government was to withdraw its dismissal of the Prussian ministers, but the Prussian ministers were to give up their government jobs voluntarily and with the Landtag's approval to recommend to President Hindenburg the transfer of the functions of the Prussian state government to the Reich government by emergency decree.

This was well intended. But it required of the Prussian ministers that they gave to the Papen-Schleicher government, which had so severely insulted them and accused them of failing to fulfill their duties toward the Reich, voluntarily what the two men had tried to take by violating the Constitution.

Minister-President Braun, whom I informed by letter to the alpine resort Bad Gastein, where he was taking a cure, answered on August 29, 1932. The aim which Höpker-Aschoff had in mind, he wrote, had been his own aim for many years. He had told Brüning at the beginning of 1932 that he, Braun, would for health and other reasons under no circumstances remain in office after the imminent Landtag elections. "For this reason I would rather resign now and suggest to the Landtag that they elect him, Brüning, Prussian Minister-President." This would strengthen Brüning's position. "Above all this action would most strongly further realization of the idea, which was uppermost in my mind, of the union Prussia-Reich." Brüning, however, after careful deliberation had informed him that he would have to decline Braun's suggestion out of regard for President Hindenburg, who could hardly be expected to approve it.

Braun's letter then continued as follows: "You may see from the above, which I am writing down here for the first time, what I think of uniting Reich and Prussia under common leadership; this will also explain to you why I am not committing myself in the legal struggle with the Reich with so much verve as may appear desirable to you and Badt, who are defending our rights in a manner deserving much gratitude and requiring great sacrifice. I have inner inhibitions, resulting fom the fact that the state of affairs which has now been established is in accordance with my basic idea, although, true enough, I do not approve of the way it has come about and even less of the caricature (*Zerrbild*) it is. I would therefore not be opposed to negotiations with the goal of a sensible combination of governmental powers in the Reich and Prussia, the less so because the outcome of the legal conflict will be only slightly satisfactory anyway. It is true that the pre-condition of a settlement, which would arrange for uniting the governmental powers in Prussia and in the Reich in some reasonable form, would be that the odium would be removed from Prussia that it had not fulfilled its duties toward the Reich and not secured peace and order in Prussia. That historical action must not remain encumbered with this argument, which is not true to the facts and a grave insult to me, my colleagues, and our loyal fellow-workers. I cannot go into the details of a possible settlement here; I would be very pleased if you could come here so that we could discuss this more fully."

More eloquent evidence of Braun's basic agreement with a union of Prussia and Reich and of his generous way of thinking and love for Germany can scarcely be imagined. I went to Gastein immediately. After thorough discussion of all aspects of the matter we reached the conclusion that we could not make a pact with Papen in the way suggested by Höpker-Aschoff, although perhaps with his successor, and that the Landtag, too, would not give approval to that deal with him. The court proceedings had first to be gone through.

In Leipzig my attention was so much taken up by the study of the comprehensive material for the hearings that I forget which hotel we were staying in, which street we were in, and which way we walked several times each day the quarter of an hour's distance to the Reichsgericht building.

On the first day of the proceedings we went early to the large court hall. I decided singlehanded to sit with my Prussian colleagues in the box intended for the accused, suggesting to the Bavarian and Baden representatives who were accompanying us that they take their places apart from us in the middle between the disputing parties at a sort of table for witnesses and experts, which gave them the outward dignity of impartial advisers. Afterward I wondered why I did not wait to see which seating arrangements Reichsgericht President Bumke, the chairman of the tribunal, had worked out. But no one questioned my arrangement, and the Bavarians declared it to be "statesmanlike."

After the chairman's introductory words and an excellent report by one of the justices on the briefs I said:

"I would like to ask permission, before we enter the agenda, to say a few words about the meaning of the Prussian suit.

"What does Prussia want with its suit? Prussia does not wish to direct any attack on the person of the Reich President. The Prussian state ministers entertain no doubts about the basic desire of the President to uphold (*zu wahren*) the Constitution. They all voted for the President, and they have done everything they could to secure his election. They continue to hold him in that respect which he as the German head of state has deserved in a special degree. But they do most decisively question the correctness of the information given the President and of the interpretation of the Constitution presented to him.

"The subject of our suit is not—as the chairman of the tribunal has already said—the *political expediency* of the Reich government's action, not even its good intentions, but only the *legal permissibility* of its action.

"The subject of the dispute is, above all, clearing Prussia and its ministers of the accusation, which deeply offends the honor of the *Land* and of its representatives, that Prussia has failed to fulfill the duties which fell to it in accordance with the Reich Constitution and the Reich laws and on this ground could be and had to be sequestered (*sequestriert*). Prussia and the Prussian ministers are not surpassed in loyalty to the Reich by anyone, whoever he may be.

"The Minister-President and the State Ministers are awaiting with confidence a decision from the Tribunal in accordance with which the decree, in the form in which it has been issued, must be withdrawn. Then it will be a matter of political skill to find another solution until the Landtag nominates a new government, and especially, if possible, to continue the union of Prussia and Reich in another better form, and to give it constitutional expression. The Ministers are pursuing no personal interest in this matter. Its peaceful settlement will not fail because of quarrels about personalities.

"Marshalling those political problems is not, however, the business of these proceedings, whose only concern must be—and in this we are entirely in agreement with the chairman of the court—to say what is the law (*Recht zu sprechen*)."

I considered it advisable to make this statement in advance for several reasons. First, dragging the person of the Reich President into the legal argument would have considerably lessened our chances of winning. Furthermore, I expected the statement to keep him aware, and strengthen his understanding of the necessity for strictly fulfilling his constitutional duties. Lack of time had prevented me from submitting the statement to the Prussian ministers beforehand; I was acting in accordance with my conscience as their appointed representative.

I will not give an account here of the further proceedings, interesting though they were. They lasted for six days, from Monday the 10th, until Monday the 17th of October, with sessions both in the mornings and afternoons; Saturday and Sunday remained free. I shall select only two points.

The Reich government had disputed the truth of our assertion that Papen and Schleicher had aroused expectations on the part of the National Socialists of moves against the Prussian government as an acknowledgment for the toleration of the Papen government. We asked that witnesses be heard. The tribunal's chairman, Dr. Bumke, referred to the official communiqué of August 13, which included the following sentence that seemed to him "particularly relevant": "He (the Reich President) regretted that Herr Hitler did not feel himself to be able, in accordance with the statements he made prior to the Reichstag elections, to support a national-minded government called into office with the confidence of the President" (see Chapter 77). Then the chairman continued:

"I think that my memory is not deceiving me when I say that shortly before July 20 a letter from the Prussian Landtag President,

National Socialist Kerrl, to the Chancellor expressed the urgent desire of the National Socialists that the present Prussian government be removed. It is a fairly voluminous letter written in a fairly firm tone, if I am not mistaken. . . . It therefore seems to be hardly disputable that there were threads of contact between the NSDAP and the Chancellor, and that within the NSDAP one of the most essential desires was to bring the former government in Prussia to an end. Now I do not know whether it is usual to carry on political negotiations in such a way that mutual concessions are taken down paragraph by paragraph, or whether they are not carried on rather so that certain possibilities are discussed by both sides, certain expectations expressed, certain possibilities suggested by the other side, and when I keep all this in mind, then I doubt whether witnesses will help us essentially in this point. . . ."

One of the accusations made by the Reich government was that the Prussian goverment had spent large sums of money (two million reichs-marks) from public funds for party purposes. The Prussian ministers informed me that the money had come from private sources, collected by Reich Minister of Finance Dietrich for Hindenburg's election, and that its use for party purposes had been explicitly excluded (Chapter 72). Out of consideration for the Reich President and the confidential nature of the matter I did not use this information at a public session, but during a private discussion with Herr Gottheiner in the presence of the chairman of the court. Thereupon the Reich government dropped the charge.

On October 25, 1932 President Bumke, at a formal session of the Supreme Constitutional Court delivered the court's decision which had been awaited with great excitement. It read as follows:

"The Decree for the Restoration of Peace and Order within Prussia, issued by the Reich President on July 20, 1932, is compatible with the Reich Constitution, in so far as it appoints the Reich Chancellor Reich Commissioner for Prussia and authorizes him temporarily to take away official functions from Prussian ministers and either to assume these functions himself or to transfer them to other persons as Reich commissioners. This authorization, however, could not be extended (*durfte sich nicht darauf erstrecken*) to taking away from the Prussian State Cabinet and its members the power to represent Prussia in the Reichstag, in the Reichsrat, or otherwise over against the Reich, or over against the Prussian Landtag, the Prussian Staatsrat, or the other *Laender*.

"In so far as petitions are not herewith granted they are rejected."

Many had traveled to Leipzig in order to be present, among them Höpker-Aschoff and Radbruch. When I heard the decision a pleasant thrill ran through me. I had achieved everything I had expected, for I had not expected more than this. Papen writes in his memoirs, which bear the title *Der Wahrheit eine Gasse* (A Path for the Truth), only two sentences about the court proceedings: "My decree," he writes, "was neither a coup d'etat nor an act of violence. On 25.10.1932 the Staatsgerichtshof, in answer to a suit brought by Prussia, decided the constitutional validity of the decree of the President and of his Chancellor" (p. 210). This is a rather narrow path for the truth. For in the court's decision there follows after the words "is compatible with the Reich Constitution" not a period, but a comma, and then the words *"in so far as* it appoints the Reich Chancellor Reich Commissioner for Prussia and authorizes him *temporarily* to take away official functions from Prussian ministers," etc. In the following sentence the Court states explicitly to what the Commissioner's authority could *not* be extended.

The most important point for us was that the court, in the reasons given for its decision, stated in great detail that the *first* section of article 48 was inapplicable, because there had been no case in which Prussia had failed to fulfill its duties toward the Reich.[1]

The press had given ample space to the six-day verbal proceedings, most dailies on their first pages, and they also printed the decision and the reasons for it in full. Since the proceedings took place shortly before the elections on November 6, the facts we had brought to light and our arguments exerted considerable influence, which turned chiefly against the National Socialists and Papen.

There was no official court report. Yet a private stenographer sent by the labor unions, Hans Pregel, had taken down the whole proceedings in full. The unions' publishing house (Dietz, Berlin) published this report, at the end of the year, with an introduction written by me at its request, under the title *Preussen contra Reich* (Prussia versus Reich). My offer to the Reich Ministry of the Interior to edit the report jointly and publish it with a jointly written introduction was, strangely enough, declined.

[1] Reprinted (*italics*) *extenso* in German ed., pp. 230 ff.

## 82. The Myth of the Court's Failure

WHEN I returned to Berlin on October 25, 1932, I was quietly wrapped up in myself, filled by the awareness that I had been present at one of the greatest constitutional trials in history and had won a victory for truth, justice, and freedom, my old ideals in life. Now, much would depend on the elections of November 6. I hoped that we had contributed to a better result there too.

On the next morning my negotiations on the consequences of the court's decision began with Dr. Bracht, Papen's deputy commissioner. They developed in a most unsatisfactory fashion. Unavoidable as they were, they appeared to me of only secondary importance. For the Prussian government, robbed of its administrative functions, could not expect to take any part in the solution of the great political problems faced by Germany. Only the fact that Papen and Bracht continued to snub them kept the Prussian ministers in the limelight.

"Macht bricht Recht" (power breaks right) says an old German proverb. "Bracht bricht Brecht" (Bracht breaks Brecht) was a witty variation of this, coined by a journalist in those weeks. I have always believed the opposite: in the long run, if only in the distant future, justice will break power. Where is it now, the power of Papen and Bracht, of Hitler, Goebbels, Göring, and Himmler?

It has become common to say that the division of power between the National Commissioner and the old Prussian government, as laid down by the Supreme Constitutional Court, was absurd; that it was practically impossible to govern with such a division of powers. The court, it is said, ought to have declared the appointment of the Commissioner either fully constitutional or fully unconstitutional.

Yet either of these extreme decisions would have been incompatible with the Constitution. Perhaps the court could have stated that the decree, in the form in which it stood, was as a whole unconstitutional because it went too far. But then the President would have been able to issue another decree immediately, which took away only those powers he was allowed to; that would have included the Prussian police and even all executive powers (or almost all). Hindenburg would have done this, of course. The result would have been the same division of powers.

Is it justified to level the reproach at the Constitution? Would it have been better if the Constitution had given the Reich President the right to dismiss ministers in the *Laender* and to have their right in the Reichsrat exercised by national commissioners? Then the Reich government would have been able, with the help of the President, to make the Reichsrat its puppet by appointing national commissioners in the *Laender,* as was actually done by Hitler afterward (Chapter 92), thus securing the affirmative vote of Prussia and Bavaria, etc., to any change in the structure of Germany the Reich government wanted to have. As long as Germany desired to be a federal country, the Constitution could not establish such an arrangement of powers.

Be that as it may, I consider the principal objection that the division of powers was *practically unworkable* to be *wrong*. With a bid of good will all legitimate purposes of the Reich government could have been reached with the ample powers left the commissioner under the court's ruling. Instead of carrying through the court's decision honestly, however, Papen and Bracht used every imaginable trick to carry through their own illegal political purposes.

A loyal execution of the court's decision would have led the President to issuing a new version of the decree, omitting the reference to section 1 of article 48 (violation of duties by the *Land* Prussia) and the authorization of the National Commissioner to dismiss Prussian ministers, both of which had been declared incompatible with the Constitution by the court, and including in the wording the other limits enumerated by the court. This, however, did not happen. The President left the text as it was.

It would also have been fitting, after the court had annulled the dismissal of ministers as unconstitutional, for the National Commissioner to put their office rooms at their disposal again. Some of the ministers were indeed allowed to return to their offices, but the two Social Democrats Braun and Severing had theirs withheld and were instead shown to rooms in the old senate house in Leipziger Strasse 3. It was the same with Finance Minister Klepper. Braun sent word to Papen that he would be satisfied with using his ministerial residence (Wilhelmstrasse 64) which was next to the Minister-President's offices (Wilhelmstrasse 63). But Papen and Bracht rejected this too, allegedly because it would lead to street demonstrations in

Braun's favor. They stuck to this, although Braun assured them that he would move into his rooms without attracting any publicity and pointed out that the Wilhelmstrasse was part of the precinct in which demonstrations were not allowed.

After the unsatisfactory discussions between Bracht and me on the first two days, Braun went the following day, October 28, to Hindenburg, who received him in Papen's presence. This was Braun's last meeting with Hindenburg, the one at which he had the shattering impression of the latter's senility which he later described in his memoirs (Chapter 74). Braun told Hindenburg that, although he would have wished the court's decision to be different, he accepted it loyally and intended to carry it out fully on the Prussian side. Hindenburg asked both parties for loyal execution. He did not, however, go into details, leaving them to further discussion between the parties, which were not successful. Papen still expressed himself negatively to all complaints in a letter to Braun on November 30. But then his chancellorship came to an end, and General von Schleicher became his successor (see following chapter).

Early in December Braun suggested personal discussions to Schleicher, and these took place at once. It was agreed to wait first and see if the imminent session of the Landtag would lead to the election of a new premier; if it did not, personal discussions were to be continued.

When the Landtag again failed, Braun submitted to Schleicher on December 20 a list of ten points of complaint, asking him to take a stand on them, so that the Prussian ministers could decide whether it was necessary to appeal once more to the court. I will shortly enumerate these ten points here in order to show that—with the exception, perhaps, of the last one—they were of no considerable importance, but mostly formal and could easily have been cleared. They were: (1) alteration of the text of the President's decree, making it agree with the court's decision (see above); (2) permitting all ministers the use of their personal office rooms (see above) and (3) of the official gazettes for publications within their remaining functions; (4) independent disposal of the necessary means, both personal and financial; (5) correct signing of official letters by the commissioners, who continued to sign as Prussian ministers instead as agents of the Reich government; (6) no opening by the commissioners of letters addressed to Prussian ministers; the ministers would agree, however, to having letters opened by joint clerical offices which would sift them according to functions, subject to later correction; (7) current information; (8) recognition of the right of the ministers to cooperate with the Landtag in establishing Prussia's annual state budget, without detriment to the right of the commissioners to deviate from it; (9) no use of the official Prussian seals, especially of the Great State Seal, by the commissioners; they should use Reich seals; (10) recognition that the right of pardon still fell to the Prussian State Ministry, or joint petition for a decision by the Supreme Constitutional Court on this point.

Who had the right of pardon (point 10) depended on whether or not according to the Reich Constitution this right could be transferred to a national commissioner. We suggested that the Reich President explicitly exempt the right of pardon from those transferred to the commissioners; then the legal situation would have been clarified. Otherwise it could be clarified only by a special decision of the court.

On December 23 Schleicher proposed new personal discussions early in the new year. They took place on January 6, 1933. Schleicher and Braun decided to attempt in all seriousness to come to an agreement on the complaints and if necessary to submit the question of pardon to the Supreme Constitutional Court.

On January 23, Schleicher's State Secretary Planck informed me that the Chancellor wanted to discuss the details with me personally, including our suggestion to legalize the union Reich-Prussia by submitting our short draft of a Reich Reform Bill (Chapter 64) to the legislative bodies. Schleicher then invited me to his office rooms in the Ministry of Defense for the afternoon of January 26, adding that he had made sure he would be "free for several hours." At the last minute, however, the appointment was postponed because of the beginning chancellor crisis, first until January 28, and then until January 30. On this day Schleicher resigned and Hitler took his place.

A peaceful settlement had been well under way. On January 31, I called on the new State Secretary in the Chancellery, Dr. Lammers, a former subordinate of mine in the Ministry of the Interior, to inform him of the state of negotiations. But the affair then took a new, violent turn (Chapter 89).

## 83. Back in the Reichsrat—Refusal of Promotion to State Secretary

After Papen's coup on July 20 the Reich government had tried in vain to hold sessions of the Reichsrat with Papen's representatives in Prussia's seat. At the first committee meeting, July 27, Bavaria and other *Laender* had immediately protested. At the subsequent plenary session—on August 2—the seat of the Prussian government remained unoccupied. Bavaria's representative stated: "Bavaria is of the opinion that the present composition of the Reichsrat is not in accordance with the Reich Constitution and that the Reichsrat in its present form is not in a position to exercise the rights it has according to the Constitution." The majority of the other *Laender* and of the Prussian provinces made similar statements. The extended agenda, which included no controversial points, was then dealt with, but decisions were made with "reservations."

After this defeat the Reich government had not dared to summon another session. The next did not take place until November 10, after the decision by the Supreme Constitutional Court. The former spokesman for Prussia, State Secretary Weismann, had voluntarily resigned from his position in the Prussian State Ministry in order to avoid being dismissed by the Commissioner. The spokesmanship now fell to me. Thus, on November 10, I sat uncontested on the Prussian seat next to the chairman, Reich Minister of the Interior Baron von Gayl. Before entering into the business of the day I reported on the essential points of the court's decision and protested against the disregard of the decision in various of the commissioners' actions. There followed statements by the other *Laender,* pleading for loyal execution of the court's decision and reserving further comment. Otherwise the session passed without dissonance.

As a legitimate Prussian delegate to the Reichsrat I also took part again in the sessions of the Reichstag and its committees, especially the budget committee, in which I still spoke occasionally, for the last time on January 10, 1933, on the problem of unemployment.[1]

When Dr. Bracht, Papen's Deputy Commissioner in Prussia, was

[1] Reprinted in the German ed., vol. II, p. 423.

being elevated to the position of Reich Minister of the Interior in mid-December, it fell upon me to welcome him as the chairman in the next Reichsrat meeting. This I did, to general amusement, by saying that we liked to see him here as the legitimate occupier of the seat with the highest back in the room rather than in the more modest Prussian seat.

At one of the first Cabinet meetings after the court's decision Minister-President Braun suggested my promotion to State Secretary, since the position as first adviser of the State Ministry and leading spokesman of Prussia in the Reichsrat had always been filled by a state secretary. I asked that this step not be taken, because I did not want to give the impression that I tried to draw personal profit from the sad situation. At first Braun objected to my viewpoint, but then gave in. It is to this event that I owe my promotion to "retired state secretary" more than twenty years afterward, dated back to April 1, 1933, by the Adenauer government in 1953.

But these things had nothing to do with the great political issues of the time. It all was—excepting the work of the Reichsrat—merely an unpleasant fulfillment of duties which had to be attended to until politics had found a way out. I will now return to the major problems.


## 84. Hope and Lull—Stab in the Back— Papen's Triumph, and Hitler's

The Reichstag elections on November 6, 1932, twelve days after the decision of the Supreme Constitutional Court, let in a ray of hope. The votes cast for the National Socialists went down by 2 million and their seats by 34, from the 230, which they had won in July, to 196. On the other hand, the seats of the Communists increased from 89 to 100, so that the two totalitarian parties, on the left and the right, together still had the majority in the house (with its total number of seats decreased from 607 to 583), and the other parties were still unable to form a majority government, even if they had all united. The Social Democrats lost about as many seats as the Communists gained. They obtained 121 (instead of 133) seats. The Zentrum lost 6 (now 70) and the Democrats (State Party) 2 of their 4. The three "Weimar" parties together kept a total of only 193, that is, three less than the National Socialists had even in their shrunken state. The German Nationalists showed an increase, from 37 to 51, and the German People's Party from 7 to 11, evidence of the fact that some of the National Socialist voters had returned to the more moderate right-wing parties.

The decrease in National Socialist votes was a serious blow to Hitler's hopes. On election day Goebbels made the following note in his diary: "Every message brings a new defeat." On the following day: "A great deal of despair prevails among the electorate." On November 11: "I have received a report on the state of funds of the Berlin organization. It is quite desperate. Only ebb, debts, and commitments, at the same time the complete impossibility after this defeat of obtaining adequate amounts of money anywhere." On December 6: "The situation is catastrophic. In Thuringia we have suffered almost 40 percent losses since July 31." On December 8: "Great depression prevails in the organization. Money problems make constructive work impossible. We are all deeply depressed, above all because there is now the danger that the entire party will disintegrate and all our work will have been in vain." On December 15: "It is high time that we come to power. At the present, however, not the slightest prospect is evident."

Had, then, the Prussian Social Democrats really been so wrong when they appealed to the Supreme Court rather than to the naked fists of the workers? Papen's prestige, too, had fallen so low as a result of his moral defeat in the Prussian law suit that the President soon had to drop him. He did not, however, do that immediately. He first clung to Papen, who fooled himself and Hindenburg into believing that the decrease in the National Socialist votes was to his, Papen's, credit, whereas it actually was a result of the barbaric crimes which had been widely publicized by the court proceedings. Papen's only contribution had lain in his return, since the beginning of August, to the policy of Brüning and Groener in combatting the crimes of the National Socialists rather than minimizing them. On the whole, the elections were from his point of view anything but a success, since the two Socialist parties, against which he had principally directed his energy, had together just as many seats as beforehand, despite decreased total voting figures, and the Communists had even won votes, so that together with the National Socialists they could still hold up any Reichstag resolution—always able to tip the scales.

In spite of all this, Hindenburg authorized Papen to negotiate with the parties. Yet Papen was snubbed on all sides. The leaders of the Zentrum were particularly outspoken in making it clear that they were not prepared to work with him. The Social Democrats went so far as to decline discussion. After Papen's behavior toward them and toward the Social-Democrat members of the Prussian government, this was humanly understandable, but politically and tactically unwise because the legitimate Reich President had authorized Papen to negotiate with the parties and a refusal to talk to him was an offence not only to Papen but also to Hindenburg, whose dislike of the Social Democrats would thus be nourished.

When Papen was thus thwarted the cabinet decided, at Schleischer's suggestion and very much against Papen's wish, to resign (November 17). Renewed negotiations between Hindenburg and Hitler failed (see the official report, Chapter 75). When Hindenburg—now proceeding quite logically—asked the Zentrum's leader, Dr. Kaas, to find out whether it was possible to form a parliamentary majority cabinet, which could have been done only by including the National Socialists, Hitler and even Hugenberg declined to speak with Kaas, just as impolitely as the Social Democrats had with Papen.

Papen then suggested to Hindenburg (December 1) that he let him continue as Chancellor with presidential emergency powers. He would, he said, negotiate with the Laender (i.e. in Prussia with himself, and not with the Prussian ministers) on Reich reform. But how could the vote of no confidence, which had to be expected from the newly elected Reichstag, be met? Hindenburg asked. Papen recommended dissolving the Reichstag the third time and governing without it for an unlimited period. That was an outright breach of the Constitution. He would also disband the National Socialist and Communist parties, perhaps even all the parties; the latter move, at least, would also involve a breach of the Constitution.

I do not want here to denounce planned breaches of constitution without suggesting alternatives (see the following chapter on this question). I only want to relate why Hindenburg refused to reappoint Papen. Schleicher countered Papen's plan with the suggestion that a new government be based on the army, the labor unions, and the moderate wing of the National Socialists (they, he told Hindenburg, under Gregor Strasser, were amenable to these plans). The Reichstag would likely tolerate such a government, he said, since the parties themselves could not think of any better way out. Thus breach of constitution would be avoided. Papen maintained that Hindenburg nevertheless asked him to go forward on the basis of his own ideas. But Schleicher still had a trump up his sleeve, and he now played it. He stated at a Cabinet meeting the following day— and had this confirmed by another competent officer—that the army was not in a position to maintain order in a civil war against National Socialists and Communists at the same time, especially if Poland were to make use of the situation to attack in the east. Upon this Hindenburg regretfully dropped Papen ("I had a comrade," he wrote on the picture he gave him) and appointed Schleicher as Chancellor.

Schleicher found a supporter of his plan in Leipart, the leader of the Social Democrat labor unions. He also had the satisfaction that the Reichstag meetings from December 6 to 9 passed calmly without a vote of no confidence and ended with a voluntary adjournment for an indefinite period, in order to give the new Chancellor time. Indeed, the whole of the month of December remained peaceful. Schleicher's negotiations on a cabinet formed of labor unions, army, and National Socialists, however, soon ran into difficulties. At the request of the Social Democrat party Leipart withdrew, as did Gregor Strasser, when he met violent opposition in his party from Hitler and Goebbels. Strasser resigned his important position as the party's organization leader, thereby losing most of his power.

Schleicher did not give up. He attempted to gain confidence by constructive work. The first refusals did not have to be final. Since no one—apart from the totalitarian parties—had a recipe for a solution of the crisis, it was not unreasonable to hope that with more time for careful preparation a climate more favorable either for negotiations or for dictatorial decisions would evolve.

While I had not been personally acquainted with Papen at the time of his appointment in June, I had a fairly accurate idea of Schleicher's gifts, character, strength, and weakness. I had known him personally ever since he had drafted the first troops for the People's Commissaries under Ebert in 1919, then as a major working with Noske (Chapter 16). I had indeed fought many a fight with him, from my positions in the Chancellery, in the Ministry of the

Interior, and in the Reichsrat, and we also had exchanged many a jest. Throughout these years he had studied the game of parliamentary government carefully and often taken a hand in it in his own way. "In his own way" had always meant to him: without any inner commitment toward democracy and its ideals, both of which he simply did not take seriously. Constitution, parliament, parties, cabinets—all were to him mere obstacles or diversions that had to be overcome. His was the military way of thinking. Whenever one had chosen a goal—a patriotic goal, of course—then the task was quite simply to reach it in the quickest and most direct way; if that path was blocked, then to overcome one's opponents with a strategic outflanking maneuver or to subdue them by force. In legal or moral questions for him the end—if the end was patriotic, or a strengthening of the army—justified the means. What was patriotically good or bad he himself decided, or "the Army."

His intrigues against leading men whom he formally had patronized, such as Groener and Brüning, and against the Braun-Severing government in Prussia, his using government officials as spies on their superiors, and the like, were to his way of thinking entirely permissible, even meritorious, since they served what he considered to be patriotic purposes.

He also entered the Chancellery in the sincere belief that he was doing something useful for Germany. His political prospects were better than Papen's. He had, except for the high rank the army held in his thinking, fewer prejudices than the latter, was definitely less set in his political likes and dislikes, and was, when his attention was drawn to wrong calculations in good time, more pliable.

In agreement with Braun I saw to it that tensions with the Commissioner's offices were not aggravated at the moment. I drew up the brief text of a Reich Reform Bill already referred to (Chapter 64), intended to bring about the union of Prussia with the Reich in a legitimate manner. Braun passed it on to Schleicher with the suggestion that it be submitted to the Reichsrat as quickly as possible.

Day-to-day operations often assumed the character of a musical comedy, for example when we reproached the Post Ministry for the post offices' handing out letters addressed to the ministers to persons to whom they were not addressed. Gerhard Hauptmann's seventieth birthday (November 15) was celebrated a few days before Papen's resignation. Papen and Bracht had been so tactless as to invite him, without previous consultation with the Prussian ministers, to a state ceremony at which Deputy Commissioner Bracht was to present him with the Prussian Golden State Medal. The Prussian Minister of Culture, Grimme, and I called on Hauptmann in the morning in his hotel and handed him, in the presence of his wife, Margarethe, a congratulatory message from the legitimate Prussian government. We were sure, we told him, that the spirit of this homage to his poetic work for freedom and justice would be more important to him than the Great Seal of State, which the Commissioner was illegally keeping from us. We asked him to accept the Golden State Medal in the evening as though it were coming from us. As we were departing, he took me at one side, pointed upward, and said in his characteristic, cryptic manner of uttering incomplete sentences, only the words "Higher up." If one remained aloof from politics, it was easy to climb higher up. But was it right in times like these, as I had done in my youth, to leave the political arena to others and to flee from it oneself? He had no answer, and we did not expect one from him.

All this was incidental. The main political problem was in the hands of Hindenburg, Schleicher, and the party leaders. I saw no possibility at present of fruitful activity for me. On the contrary, I felt I had to dispel the error that I, crowned with the laurels of the trial, was now in a position to solve the crisis of the Reich government. When I showed up at meetings, I was given ovations before I uttered a word. In order to escape from such misunderstandings about my personal importance, I left Berlin for a short trip to Switzerland with Clara over Christmas, where we spent about ten days in a small guest house above St. Maurice, skiing and visiting Herman Heller in nearby Celerina. Then we returned to Berlin.

On January 4 the political situation worsened because of an unexpected conciliatory meeting between Papen and Hitler at the home of the banker Curt von Schröder in Cologne. Unable to get over his political defeat Papen had made an about-turn in his policy by taking up contacts, behind Schleicher's back, with Hitler, whom he had rebuffed in August and November. He afterward maintained that he had only wanted to persuade Hitler to cooperate with Schleicher and had not been thinking of himself. However that may be, at any rate Papen became active from then on in striving to appease Hindenburg's aversion to Hitler, minimizing the dangers that threatened from him.

We did not learn of Papen's unexpected move until later. Nor was Schleicher's position immediately shattered by it. Rather, almost the whole of the month of January passed before Hindenburg yielded to Papen's new suggestions. Papen told Hitler as late as January 18 that it was beyond his, Papen's, power to persuade Hindenburg to appoint Hitler as Chancellor. Papen has even maintained that he suggested to Hindenburg as late as January 23 the inclusion of Hitler in a cabinet under Schleicher, not under himself. Until January 22 even Hindenburg's son, Oskar, and State Secretary Meissner were opposed to Hitler's chancellorship. Only on this date did Hitler succeed in winning over Oskar during a long private discussion at Ribbentrop's.

On January 23 Hindenburg senior was still opposed, although he allowed tentative contacts to be made behind Schleicher's back with the Nazi sympathizer General Blomberg as successor to Schleicher in the Ministry of Defense. Not until the 25th did Oskar report that Hitler's candidature was not "without prospect." On the 26th Hindenburg still failed to agree. Indeed, even on the 27th he said to Generals Hammerstein and Bussche: "You surely do not think that I shall appoint this Austrian first-class private Chancellor." On the same day Hitler declined meeting Hindenburg, because he feared the President would give him a brush-off damaging to his reputation, as he had done in August and November.

Current political business in Berlin thus went on into the last days of January as though Schleicher would continue as Chancellor. The Reichstag committee negotiated on the budget. On January 10 I delivered there the speech already mentioned, on the overcoming of unemployment by public works and shortening of working hours. The discussions between Braun and Schleicher and between the latter and myself also continued (Chapters 64, 84).

Not until the 28th of January—two days before Hitler's actual appointment—did Hindenburg change his mind after, as Bracher puts it, "long and respectable resistance." Not only we, but even Schleicher, who was normally well informed, had not expected this, and we did not learn of it immediately. Schleicher, when his plan to associate with Strasser and Leipart in a cabinet had failed, was prepared to declare a "national emergency" (*Staatsnotstand*) and to govern an indefinite period without Reichstag, if Hindenburg gave him the necessary backing; this was similar to the suggestion made by Papen at the beginning of December. He now dropped his scruples that the army was not equal to such a situation, provided that he remained Chancellor and was supported by Hindenburg. Some people maintain that he toyed with the thought of acting over Hindenburg's head; others (Papen), that General von Hammerstein, the army's chief in command, urged him on to such an action, but that Schleicher had not been able to make up his mind. In any case, Schleicher, right up to the last moment—until his successor Blomberg, appointed by Hindenburg without Schleicher's signature, was standing at the door—believed that he would at least remain Minister for Defense and would therefore control the army as a powerful check on Hitler.

In explaining Hindenburg's ultimate capitulation, Bracher says (p. 718): "Papen's intervention on Hitler's behalf and the change of mind of Meissner and Oskar von Hindenburg certainly played an important part. Similarly, the NSDAP threats [i.e., they would bring a case against Hindenburg, for breach of constitution, to the Supreme Constitutional Court] seemed to have had some effect. But also the growing number of acts in which friends like Oldenburg-Januschau, and finally the *Reichslandbund* [a league of landowners] intervened with Hindenburg in favor of a Hitler cabinet, cannot have been without influence. In addition there was the fact that only Schleicher presented an alternative solution [see above and Chapter 85] which, however, meant the breach of constitution so feared by Hindenburg, and that the party leaders, who were now also consulted by Hindenburg [that is, the leaders of the right-wing parties and the Zentrum, not the Social Democrats] expressed themselves to be as much against Schleicher's proposal as against a new Papen experiment and stated more or less explicitly that Hitler would have to be given responsibility with all possible precautions and so the NSDAP be led *ad absurdum*."

Since no one suggested a way out which Hindenburg was prepared to accept, he appointed Hitler German Reich Chancellor on January 30, 1933. Only two National Socialists were appointed with him: Dr. Frick as Minister of the Interior and Hermann Göring as Reich Commissioner for Air Traffic and at the same time Deputy Commissioner for the Prussian Ministry of the Interior, where the Prussian police was at his disposal. Goebbels was not yet a member of the Cabinet; he made his propaganda still as head of the party propaganda machine.

Papen became Vice Chancellor and also Reich Commissioner for Prussia again (though only until April 7, when Göring became

Prussian Minister-President); Hugenberg, Minister of Economics, Food and Agriculture (until his resignation on June 27); von Blomberg, Minister of Defense; the leader of the Steel Helmet organization, Franz Seldte, Minister of Labor; Baron von Neurath, Foreign Minister (as under Papen and Schleicher); Count Schwerin von Krosigk, Minister of Finance (as under Papen and Schleicher); Baron Eltz von Rübenach, Minister of Post and Transport (likewise); Franz Gürtner, Minister of Justice; as Bavarian minister of justice he had arranged the early pardon of Hitler. None of these eight was a National Socialist.

## 85. What Were the Alternatives?

Before turning to questions of guilt, it is advisable to compare and contrast the alternatives among which the leading men had to choose in January, 1933. As we have seen, with the Reichstag as it was, it was impossible to establish and maintain a government constitutionally, unless one of the two totalitarian parties was either included or willing to support it. Had the Reichstag been dissolved, the prospect of obtaining a better one was, after the increase in Hitler's stature, thanks to Papen's policies since January 4, 1933, meager, unless the two totalitarian parties were banned on the grounds of their illegal purposes. Whether this could have been done without civil war, and whether the government would have kept the upper hand in this case, was controversial.

If all theoretically imaginable courses of policy are counted, constitutional or not, then a solution to the crisis could be sought in one of the following six alternatives of action:

1. Splitting the National Socialists and forming a government which included the moderate wing of the National Socialists and was supported or at least tolerated by a Reichstag majority.

2. Forming a majority government by coalition of Zentrum and National Socialists either with or without the inclusion of other parties.

3. Forming a government supported or tolerated by a Reichstag *minority* only, composed of National Socialists, German Nationalists, and non-party experts, combined with a dissolution of the

Reichstag, either in the hope of a majority for the government being won in new elections, or (violating the Constitution) under postponement of new elections.

4. Forming a government *without* National Socialists and, therefore, supported or tolerated by a Reichstag *minority* only, combined with a dissolution of the Reichstag, either in the hope of winning a majority for the government in new elections—a chance possibly to be promoted by banning totalitarian parties on the grounds of their unlawful aims—or (unconstitutional) under postponement of new elections.

5. Establishing a *military dictatorship,* combined with a dissolution of the totalitarian parties, either by the President or (unconstitutional) over his head.

6. Reestablishment of a *monarchy,* either under maintenance of a democratic form of government, as in Great Britain, the Scandinavian countries, the Netherlands, etc., or in more authoritarian forms.

From these six possibilities, all of which were discussed at the time, and from their sub-alternatives, those involved had to choose.

Schleicher had first striven for solution number 1 (splitting off the moderate wing of the National Socialists) and, after failing with this, had finally suggested number 4 (new elections under dissolution of the totalitarian parties). He had also considered numbers 2 and 3 (coalition with the National Socialists) if he kept the Ministry of Defense, and perhaps had also toyed with number 5 (military dictatorship).

Papen, at the time of his departure from office, had considered number 4 the best solution, but later, after his meeting with Hitler on January 4, had concentrated on number 3 (minority coalition of the Right, including the National Socialists) and had violently opposed all other solutions, especially number 2 (majority coalition of Zentrum and National Socialists).

Solution number 6 (reestablishment of a monarchy), which Brüning had considered a possible ultimate solution and which Hindenburg, of course, would have welcomed, could obviously not be brought about from one day to the next. Hence there was, after the failure of solution number 1, practically only a choice between numbers 2 to 5, when Hindenburg finally decided for number 3 under Papen's influence (minority cabinet of National Socialists, German Nationalists, and non-party experts, and new elections).

From the standpoint of democratically minded republicans each of the six alternative expedients was undesirable. But they were undesirable in different degrees. Number 3 was the worst. Which, then, was to be supported?

I considered (and still do so today) "second best" to genuine democracy, which had become impossible (or not yet possible) in Germany, a sort of "oligarchic democracy," in which governing power is reserved constitutionally to adherents of the democratic constitution as against totalitarian opponents: for example, as it was later done in the Bonn Basic Law, by outlawing parties and candidates that advocated totalitarian aims or means, so that pro-constitutional majorities in *parliament* are guaranteed even when they do no longer constitute the majority within the *population*.

But with the situation as it was in January, 1933, especially with Hindenburg in the key position of Reich President, this solution could not be realized right away. It could at most be "steered toward." Under these circumstances I saw the best temporary solution in a continued presidential government with Schleicher as Chancellor, if neecssary under dissolution of the Reichstag and a ban on totalitarian parties—that is, solution number 4. I believed, and still believe today, that this temporary solution, after the setback the National Socialists had suffered in the November elections, had a fair chance of success. But this chance had, of course, been considerably affected after Papen had increased Hitler's prestige, recommending him to Hindenburg.

Before selection of alternative number 4, an attempt could have been made with number 2 (majority government Zentrum-National Socialists). But that would in all probability soon have led to a repetition of the crisis.

I did not consider the matter only theoretically. As related in the preceding chapter, I worked for a sort of pragmatic understanding with Schleicher, and in December had another discussion with Hugo Eckener (see end of Chapter 73) on the succession to Hindenburg in the case of his decease or resignation. All this formed part of a preparation for a "second best" solution.

But I was no party chief. The Weimar parties, above all the Social Democrats, have been accused of a "senseless clinging to the legality principle." This reproach is justified in so far as since July, 1932 there was no strictly constitutional solution at hand, a fact that had caused the opponents of democracy to act earlier than its supporters. Despite their justified annoyance, the Social Democrats ought not to have declined negotiations with Papen and Schleicher or forbidden the labor unions such negotiations (see the preceding chapter). Rather, they should have participated more actively in the search for a viable "second best" form of government, painful though it might have been. But I can find no indication that this would have led to tangible results. Their holding back may deserve blame, but it has had no part in the negative result. The Social Democrats, after all, did tolerate and support Schleicher in December and January by refraining from a vote of no confidence and by agreeing to the Reichstag's long adjournment, just as the Prussian government did by refraining from bringing a second law suit in the Supreme Constitutional Court and offering assistance for a legitimate union of Reich-Prussia. Even with the positive support of the Social Democrats, Schleicher would have had no majority against the totalitarian parties. Had he decided to dissolve the National Socialist party (alternatives 4 and 5), the Social Democrats would certainly not have hindered him. Therefore, if the accusation of passivity is meant to imply that otherwise a better way out would have been possible, then this assertion lacks evidence.

## 86. REFLECTIONS ON THE RESPONSIBILITIES FOR HITLER'S APPOINTMENT

WHO was to blame for the fact that on January 30, 1933, Hitler was appointed German Chancellor?

For an objective discussion of this question to be possible, one must first realize that the allotment of "guilt" implies three assertions. The first is that the appointment was at that time reprehensible. No one asks who was "guilty" in the appointment of Theodor Heuss as President. If Hitler had shown true statesmanship after his appointment and had benefitted Germany and the world, or had been prevented from doing evil by Hindenburg, the army, and the non-Nazi members of the Cabinet, then no one would be interested in who was to blame for his appointment.

The second assertion implicit in the allotment of guilt is that the person accused of guilt did see, or could see and ought to have seen, the evil consequences in advance—if not necessarily *all* the evil consequences, then at least enough to find him "guilty."

The allotment of guilt, thirdly, implies the assertion that another behavior, which would have had less evil consequences, was possible and that the accused person ought to have been aware of this.

The question as to who was to blame for Hitler's appointment must finally not be confused with another question: namely, who after his appointment was to blame for not having prevented him from doing evil things and for his final assumption of total power.

If this analysis of the question of guilt is accepted as valid, the attempt to answer it runs into a series of difficulties. All the men at the top who were closely involved—that is, principally Hindenburg himself, secondly Papen, thirdly Hugenberg, Oskar von Hindenburg, Meissner, and General von Blomberg (the only one of the generals who said to Hindenburg that "a national concentration under Hitler was the best solution and would be welcomed by the regular army" and who denounced Schleicher's plans for a frontal attack on the National Socialists as "hopeless and, above all, an unendurable demand, especially to the young officers"; Bracher, p. 714)—would deny that the various assertions implicit in the allotment of guilt applied in their case. They had expected that Hitler would develop true statesmanship or would be checked. "We'll enframe him" (*Wir rahmen ihn ein*), said Hugenberg, "We engage his services for us" (*Wir engagieren ihn uns*), said Papen. They had neither desired nor foreseen the evil consequences, and knew no better alternative. I do not feel entitled to question their good faith.

The only accusation which then remains to be discussed is that the persons named above, or some of them, acted with extraordinary negligence, with irresponsible thoughtlessness, when they exposed the well-being of Germany, of their fellow men, of themselves too, to the grave *risk* which was involved in Hitler's being appointed Chancellor. This charge applies especially to Papen. But it is logically conditioned by the assumption that there could have been better ways out of the crisis and that Papen was, or should have been, aware of it.

If we turn from the search for "guilt" to that for "responsibility," then we cannot but reach the conclusion that the *constitutional* responsibility was Hindenburg's alone. The other players in the game were only advisers without constitutional responsibility. They can be considered responsible only in a moral sense, or with reference to vague duties implied in citizenship. It is perhaps possible to speak of an intensified moral responsibility in the case of Papen, because he was the special confidant of Hindenburg, and in the case of Hugenberg, because he was a party chief, and in the case of Blomberg, because he was responsible for behaving as a loyal soldier, of Meissner, as a loyal official.

They were all, as we have seen, faced with the fact that both elections in the year 1932 had resulted in a situation from which there was no constitutional way out without the cooperation or at least toleration on the side of one of the two totalitarian parties, since these parties had together an absolute majority in the Reichstag. The only alternative to this association which had a chance of being accepted as constitutional by the German courts was a ban on both the totalitarian parties on the grounds of their unlawful purposes. Taking this path, however, threatened a civil war, especially after Papen had brought Hitler back into the foreground, thereby intensifying the expectations of his supporters to the highest possible degree.

This constitutional calamity had not existed before July, 1932. It is true that since 1920 the Reichstag had not had a pro-democratic/pro-republican majority (Chapter 30). But up to 1932 there had always been a majority in favor of a *constitutional* form of government based on respect for human dignity and human rights, the rule of law, and the independence of the courts. Only after July, 1932 were there no longer majorities that agreed on these basic principles —only majorities of anti-constitutional, totalitarian mixture.

The direct cause of this calamity had been Hindenburg's dismissal of Groener and Brüning and his appointment of Papen in the spring of 1932 and the subsequent dissolution of the Reichstag two years before the end of the regular legislative period. That dissolution had resulted in the former 107 National Socialists becoming 230 in July, and still 196 in November. Without it the Reichstag would not have had the totalitarian, anti-constitutional majority in 1933.

In other words, Papen himself bore the constitutional responsibility for the fact that in his own personal opinion and finally also in that of Hindenburg, Hitler's appointment as Chancellor became necessary in January, 1933. For this reason—more than for his attitude in January, 1933—not only a moral but also a constitutional responsibility for Hitler's appointment falls to Papen to a considerable extent.

So much for the responsibility of the men at the top. Hindenburg's own constitutional responsibility for the situation that forced him to appoint Hitler was shared not only by Papen but also by the *electors* who cast their votes in July and November, 1933 for the totalitarian parties. I will go more deeply into their responsibility here for reasons that will become clear in the course of the discussion.

The basic principle of democracy is that the people choose their own government. The ultimate constitutional responsibility for the majorities that exist in parliament falls to the electors. Strangely enough, most people forget—especially in the oral tradition of the Weimar story—to point out the voters' responsibility for the debacle. They speak with contempt of the Weimar Republic, of its incompetent foreign and home policies. They criticize individual politicians and parties, especially the "Social Democrats"—because they were too radical, or because they were not radical enough; this always finds a willing echo in the middle and upper classes. But the electors are forgotten.

This is less surprising when one remembers that to consider the voters would mean that the critics would point responsibility at their own homes. Almost every large family unit in Germany—all uncles, aunts, nephews, nieces, cousins included—had some National Socialist voters even before 1933. It is only human to spread the cloak of silence over this embarrassing fact. I have no quarrel with that and sometimes conform myself. I am here objecting only to the practice of leaving the primary responsibility of the voters *unmentioned even in debates on the question of guilt*. Their responsibility for Hitler's appointment is in one sense more fundamental even than that of Hindenburg, Papen, and their colleagues, who in January, 1933 were faced with that gruesome fact that no coalition in the Reichstag could have a majority without National Socialists (or Communists). The final responsibility is to be borne by those who voted for totalitarian parties; Hindenburg, Papen, and Hugenberg had not.

I do not doubt that many sincerely believed that casting their vote for the Hitler party was the best thing, or relatively the best thing, they could do for their country. Their good faith, though, can at best have an effect on the measure of their moral "guilt," not on their constitutional responsibility.

Even regarding their moral guilt, things look worse for the voter in January, 1933 than for Hindenburg (if we leave aside for the mo-

ment Hindenburg's later failure of keeping Hitler under control,
see Chapter 93). If anyone cast his vote for the party after the publication of Hitler's *Mein Kampf;* after speeches by Goebbels,
Streicher, Kube, etc. and by Hitler himself; after the dreadful
threats against certain sections of people, then this is evidence of his
own partial dolus or at least irresponsible thoughtlessness, rather
than of his good intentions. Such a voter did not have Hindenburg's
excuses—Hindenburg believed when he finally appointed Hitler
that he was *not able* to act otherwise (the voters could have voted
otherwise) and he hoped to keep Hitler under his control—anyone
who *voted* for Hitler voted for a man who *did not want* to be controlled, and those who voted for him knew this. The fact that the
voter disliked Stresemann or Brüning or the Social Democrats, and
made them responsible for the political situation, is no excuse for
the fact that he voted for Hitler, Goebbels, Frick, Streicher, Himmler, Heidrich, and Heines. Neither is he excused by the fact that
he wanted a renewal of Germany "from the bottom up." Renewal
by whom?

It is a mistake to suppose that the major part of the 14 million
National Socialist voters in July, 1932 came from the 6 million unemployed. Most unemployed workers stuck to their traditional parties, and the rebels among the Social Democrats went mostly over
to the Communists, rarely to the National Socialists. This is shown
by the fact that the total of Social Democrat and Communist voters
did not decrease (Chapter 80) and that the National Socialists had
comparatively little success in constituencies with large amounts of
heavy industry, as in the Ruhr areas, in Berlin, and in Hamburg;
they obtained less than 30 percent there in November, 1932, and in
Berlin, North and South Westphalia even less than 25 percent. On
the other hand, the phenomenal setback of the German Nationalists, from 103 seats in the Reichstag in 1924 to 37 in July, 1932, and
the even greater drop of the People's Party from 51 to 7, shows that
to a considerable extent the gains of the National Socialists came
from middle-class and agricultural voters.

This is also shown through the regional distribution of the votes.
The highest percentage of National Socialist votes (40 percent or
more) was in November, 1932 in the two vertical (north-south) agricultural stripes which stretched from Schleswig-Holstein via Hano-
ver and Hessen to the Palatinate and from Pomerania via East
Brandenburg to Lower Silesia.

Almost all those who thronged to the National Socialists from the middle and upper classes, whether for idealistic or egoistic reasons, had in common one flaw—or, if you like, one excuse—without which the course of events would be inexplicable: the political immaturity, ignorance, shortsightedness of the average German citizen, not least the women, regarding the special risk of uncontrolled authoritarian government. Spared in the past those upsetting experiences with dictatorial governments the English had in the 17th century and the French in the 17th, 18th, and to some extent still in the 19th, most German middle-class voters, especially Protestants (Catholics and Social Democrats were more weary), were entirely blind to the dangers threatening their nation and themselves if they were to transfer unlimited power to one man or group. The German kings in the time of absolutism and enlightenment had been either humanly too good, or politically too successful, or too insignificant, to serve as warning. The many foolish Germans, who kept saying since 1930 "Just let them try" had not yet learned to see that the major question is how *to get rid of* those to whom one has given absolute power—army, police, bureaucracy, legislation, press, broadcasting, etc.—if they misuse their power.

Two reconciling points remain. All indications suggest that, after the experiences in the Hitler period, which were much more terrible than the historical sufferings of the English and French under their own dictatorial regimes, German voters will not cast their votes in the forseeable future voluntarily in considerable numbers in favor of granting all power to a single man or group without effective control, as a third of the voters did in 1932, with no guarantee, with no desire for control.

Secondly, it would be unfair not to mention the fact that there was only *one* constituency in Germany where the National Socialists *alone* had a majority before 1933—Schleswig-Holstein in July, 1932 (in November they dropped there too to less than a majority) —and that there were large areas of Germany where the National Socialists did not even gain a fifth of the votes before 1933 (Cologne-Aachen and Lower Bavaria) or a fourth (Berlin, Westphalia North and South). In the constituencies Cologne-Aachen and Koblenz-Trier the three parties of the Weimar coalition still obtained an absolute majority together in all free elections, including those of July and November, 1932, and in many other constituencies these parties in 1928 still had at least an absolute majority (so in Berlin and Hamburg) together with other parties as against the National Socialists until the end of 1932.

In general it is possible to say that the whole of southern Germany, and western Germany at least west of the Ems river, and also Upper Silesia, Berlin, Hamburg, and Leipzig still had anti-National Socialist and anti-German Nationalist majorities up to the elections of 1932 and to a large extent (see above) even longer.

Even taken *together,* the two nationalist parties (National Socialists and German Nationalists) obtained a majority in only one of the 35 German constituencies before 1932, namely in Pomerania since 1924. Even with the pressure they used in the elections on March 5, 1933, they still did not achieve a majority together in 12 of the 35, including Berlin, Hamburg, Leipzig, Rhineland, Palatinate, Upper and Lower Bavaria (see Chapter 91).[1]

But these comforting considerations do not help us past the fact that in the last free elections—November, 1932—a third of all Germans voted for the National Socialists and a sixth for the Communists and thereby made government with constitutional majorities impossible. Anyone who voted National Socialist cannot complain, cannot accuse others, because he got a National Socialist government; this was his own doing. In view of the consequences he can of course say, "I hadn't intended this." But this does not relieve him of his share of responsibility for Hitler's appointment and for the risk this involved. The present chapter has been concerned only with this particular responsibility. In this respect the National Socialist voters do not have merely to *share* the blame; but their responsibility was, under a democratic constitution, of a *primary* nature.

Who was responsible for the fact that Hitler after his appointment as Chancellor was able to assume total power and to use it as he did, without anyone preventing him, is a different question, to which I shall return later (Chapter 93).

[1] See my *Federalism and Regionalism in Germany,* Oxford University Press, New York, 1945, pp. 31 ff., for maps and details on these figures.

# PART XII

## From Hitler's Appointment to His Obtaining Total Power

## 87. How Far Will Hitler Go?

WITH the sudden appointment of Hitler as Chancellor, an appointment which a few weeks, even a few days, before had seemed to be most unlikely, even entirely out of the question, the total political picture changed by leaps and bounds—not only in Germany, but in the whole world.

At first, at least, the majority of the German people remained opposed to National Socialism. But the *conditions* in the fight against Hitler and against his political views were suddenly completely reversed, to a degree whch is difficult to describe and make comprehensible. The uninhibited agitator, anti-Semite, protector of political murderers, originator of the Bürgerbräu Putsch of 1923, prisoner of Landsberg, author of *Mein Kampf* with its grotesque exaltation of political deceit and of violence—he was now the legitimate German Chancellor.

The endless torchlight parade of the SA and the Steel Helmet organizations, which marched past him and Hindenburg on the night of January 30, was the prelude to an ecstasy of raptures not among his followers alone, but among all nationalistic or militaristic-minded Germans. Hindenburg was overwhelmed. There it was again: the nationalistic jubilation of the crowd, their enthusiasm which he had been accustomed to from wartime and had had to do without for so long. When a third or more of the people demonstrate in the streets and the others remain silent, as had happened on the Left after the Rathenau murder and was happening now on the Right, the impression is given that the entire nation backs the activists. The impression had been false on June 24, 1922; it was false on January 30, 1933. But it had its effect both at home and abroad.

It was not, however, this nationalistic inebriation alone that was decisive for the absence of any resistance. Dreadful paralysis was caused by the fact that Hitler had come to power, not by usurping it against the will of the President as Kapp had done in 1920, but as the legally appointed Chancellor, appointed by the President, who had himself been legitimately elected by the people and had the constitutional right to appoint anyone chancellor if he was convinced that his candidate could win the majority in the Reichstag, either the existing one or one to be elected. *This* was what crippled any stir of resistance, the more so because Hitler had sworn the oath laid down in the Constitution immediately after he had been appointed. He had sworn: "I will work with all my strength for the benefit of the German People. I shall abide by (*wahren*) the Constitution and the laws of the German nation, fulfill the duties that fall to me conscientiously, and conduct my office impartially and with justice toward everyone."

In order to establish whether or not the nation was behind the appointment, the President dissolved the Reichstag, as he had done previously in similar circumstances. The earliest possible date, March 5, was set for the new elections.

No one really believed that Hitler would *actually* uphold the Weimar Constitution, to which he had sworn his oath. Neither his supporters nor his opponents believed that. But if his opponents had now answered his appointment with active, violent resistance or a general strike, then that would have made *them* the "flagrant violaters of the Constitution." The regular army, the Steel Helmet organization, the SA, the police, and the bodies of officials, always inclined to submit to formal legality, would have opposed them and have branded them as traitors to their own Constitution, would have mowed them down or locked them up.

Looking back with the knowledge we have today of subsequent events, we might like to believe that there could have been no serious doubt about the deception that was being displayed. Vague fears, indeed, persisted in about half the population. But there is a great difference between mere apprehensions and established facts. Apprehensions may prove wrong.

Many circumstances could be cited to show that those dark presentiments were unnecessarily pessimistic. First, Hitler had not obtained complete or absolute power with his appointment. The power given him was only that of the Chancellor under the Weimar Constitution. Second, the great majority in his Cabinet did not consist of National Socialists, but of Conservatives—conservative Catholics like Papen, conservative Protestants like Hugenberg and Seldte, conservative government officials like Count Schwerin von Krosigk in the Ministry of Finance or von Neurath in the Foreign Office. These men, one could argue, would do their best to prevent terroristic methods and arbitrary despotism. Third, there was still Hindenburg, whose constitutional power had proved, during the course of the preceding two years, to be superior to that of the Chancellor. Fourth, there were still independent courts, the body of government officials, and the army. It is true that the army was on the whole nationalistic and militaristic in outlook, but it was filled with traditional concepts fundamentally different from those of the National Socialists, and violently opposed to giving the Storm Troops greater authority than the army. Fifth, the foreign countries would in their own interest see to it that no despotic and militaristic regime took the place of constitutional government in Germany. Opponents of National Socialists had, therefore, some reasons left for hope that the worst would be averted.

The new Cabinet's first proclamation, issued on February 1, seemed to justify a more optimistic outlook. It did set the destruction of Communism in Germany very clearly as its goal, and did not lack threats to the Social Democrats if they supported Communism, but otherwise it contained no threats of any kind. The Jews, against whom it had been feared there would be brutal acts of violence—even wholesale butchery within the first night—were not even mentioned. As to the Cabinet's constructive plans, the proclamation stated that the government would overcome the economic crisis through two major four-year plans, one of which was to save German farmers, the other to bring unemployment to an end. Within four years both goals would be reached. "So, German people, do give us four years' time and then judge and pass sentence on us!" Reference was again made to legality. "Loyal to our oath," declared Hitler and his Cabinet, they turned to the German People for election, thus indicating that they did not seek extra-constitutional powers. The proclamation appealed for "reconciliation." Only the Communists were to be excluded from it. The rearmament problem was mentioned only negatively. "Great as our affection for our army is, we would be happy if the world by limiting their own armaments were to make an increase of our own weapons forever unnecessary." The value of tradition was praised and the religious basis of the government's moral standards emphasized. "May Almighty God," thus the proclamation was closed, "grant His mercy to our work, shape our will the right way, bless our insight and grant us the confidence of our nation." No democratic government proclamation had ever used such pious language. The signatures brought the fact to mind that only three of the Cabinet members were National Socialists and eight were not.

Nor was it quite certain whether Hitler would pursue the path of Fascism to the very end and even surpass his Italian model. He had sworn several times to keep within the limits of the law. His type of personality was completely unfamiliar, not to foreigners only but to Germans as well. In his very outward appearance and bearing there were strange contrasts. He seemed in turns to be frank and sly, soldier and mystic, intelligent and mad, well-disciplined and hysterical. When he was addressing a large audience, his voice was harsh and his threats sounded barbaric. In smaller, private circles, however, his voice could be soft and pleasant and his eyes could have a friendly and candid look. Anyone who believed he could judge people from their faces was presented with a puzzle. Hitler's face seemed to be completely blank—"the blank face of a waiter," Ernst Trendelenburg said to me. Perhaps Hitler cherished the ambition, now he had come to power, to go down in history as a great and constructive statesman, open to reasonable advice.

His party was not of one mould. Two or more distinct groups could be discerned. There were the extreme rowdies, who were after adventure, revenge, brutality; but there were others who, although intent on realizing certain basic principles, were in other respects open to advice and serious in their arguments. Much would depend upon whether Hitler would act under pressure from the extremists or use the great official power he now had to render them harmless. Everyone would wish him success if he were to try that.

In discussions with Cabinet members, ministerial officials, or industrial leaders Hitler made use of an extremely clever formula to mark his position. He was quite willing, he said, to govern legally. But there was a national revolution under way; this movement was a fact with which he had to reckon. Even he was not in a position simply to call off the national revolution. Rather, he would have to proceed with utmost caution in order to avoid the worst. It was not advisable to meet every infringement of the law by his party followers with the usual means of punishment. This simply would not work. Every attempt of this nature would merely lead to dreadful excesses. Rather, he would have to show by action that a new method of government had really begun. After that he might hope to direct the uncontrolled forces of the national uprising into the channels of the new order.

One of the main reasons, he would continue, for the uprising of his party comrades was the mildness that had been shown toward the Communists. The nation as a whole wanted to be rid of Communism. This was absolutely necessary for the reestablishment of peace and order, he insisted.

The proclamation of the Cabinet had followed much the same line. There it read: "If Germany is to experience this political and economic revival and fulfill her duties toward other nations conscientiously, one decisive act is necessary: to overcome Germany's disintegration by Communism." Strong as these threats to Communism were, they were still compatible with Constitution and law. The Supreme Court had often stated that the Communist Party was pursuing illegal goals and that its plans were sufficiently substantiated to justify its dissolution, as soon as this was desired by the government. The police ministers in many of the *Laender,* especially Carl Severing, had often emphasized the illegality of the methods used by the Communists and had provided the court with evidence. To be sure, Severing and the Supreme Court had come to the same conclusion in regard to the National Socialists. But the Court had left the question open as to whether Hitler himself approved the illegal methods of his party, since in September, 1930 in a case brought against three army officers, he had stated while under oath that he pursued his aims only in a strictly legal manner.

Hitler seemed to take his course in keeping with the Court decisions. He could have disbanded the Communist organization right away, but he did not go that far. The Communists were allowed to put up their candidates for the election on March 5. Their party and their candidates obtained their places on the government-printed ballots, as provided for by the election law for lawful parties. Only in the final weeks of the campaign, especially after the Reichstag fire (Chapter 90 below), were Communist meetings banned and the Communist candidates imprisoned. Even then the candidatures were not quashed and a vote for Communists not forbidden. Acts of violence against Communists that occurred were classed among those revolutionary acts from below which one had to handle carefully in order not to stir up something worse.

A few personal impressions from these first days have stayed in my mind. When I was visiting the newly appointed State Secretary in the Chancellery, Lammers, in order to inform him of the state of the negotiations in the Prussian question (Chapter 82), the Chancellery already presented an exterior appearance determined by SA uniforms and "Heil Hitler" greetings with extended arms.

On the same day, January 31, there was a meeting of the Reichsrat which had been called before Hitler's appointment, and at which Dr. Frick, the newly appointed Minister of the Interior, an old National Socialist, took the chair for the first time. In his opening address he emphasized his Bavarian origins and his understanding of federal traditions. I answered on behalf of the Reichsrat coolly and formally, expressing the hope that he would succeed in solving the present constitutional conflict within the framework of the Constitution and in gaining the confidence of the Reichsrat.

When I met Siegfried von Kardorff, a vice-president of the Reichstag, in Unter den Linden, he said, "This will all end with a tremendous international humiliation for Germany." A few steps further, I met the former Minister of Justice, Eugen Schiffer, who seized my hand, saying: "It feels good to shake hands now with an honest person." I assured him of the same. Other acquaintances I met suddenly had urgent business to attend to in directions other than the one in which I was going.

The imperial black-white-red and the National Socialist swastika flags were appearing everywhere in the western suburbs. The republican black-red-gold disappeared. I met SA troops who had taken away black-red-gold flags and were carrying them along triumphantly. There were stories of people being taken off to some cellar and thrashed. They had been forced to say "Heil Hitler" or to sing National Socialist songs. Sometimes the regular police still intervened. My friend Ernst von Harnack, although in danger himself as a Social Democrat, was especially courageous in intervening with irregular crowds, pursuing them when they led someone away, and demanding his release. He was to die by Hitler's hangmen in the last weeks of the regime, twelve years later.

Göring had been appointed National Commissioner for the Prussian Ministry of the Interior, the police ministry. On the way to a luncheon at the Hamburg legation in the Platz der Republik I met a platoon of uniformed policemen marching through the Brandenburg Gate behind a swastika flag—Severing's police, now Göring's police. They did not look happy. I shuddered.

At a social gathering in the house of the Bremen Reichsrat delegate I was sitting at table with Frau von Oheimb-Kardorff and a few other guests, when Hjalmar Schacht came up. Frau von Kardorff greeted him in her usual direct manner with the words, "Herr Schacht, you were a Democrat once, weren't you?" "I still am," he answered and turned his back on her (see Chapter 23 on the use of the word "democracy").

How far would Hitler go? How far would his Cabinet colleagues and Hindenburg follow him? This was the main question during those first days.

## 88. HITLER IN THE REICHSRAT (FEBRUARY 2, 1933)

As early as February 2—the third day after his appointment, the first after the publication of the government proclamation—Hitler presented himself to the Reichsrat, as though he wanted to emphasize the observance of old tradition. It was his first official public appearance in his capacity as German Chancellor.

The Reichsrat did not allow itself to be diverted from its normal business manners. Before the opening of the meeting the delegates stood around in casual groups or sat in their seats. But many spectators had appeared, and for lack of space they had to stand along the walls or in the middle section of the horseshoe-shaped table. Among them was Count Helmut von Moltke, later executed as a resistance fighter, and his wife.

When Hitler entered there was no special stir. The Braunschweig delegate, Herr Boden, senior member in the Reichsrat, introduced to him individual delegates they passed together. When they reached the Chancellor's seat, he also introduced me, since my place was next to him. Hitler held my hand firmly for a considerable time and looked at me fixedly without saying a word. This gesture lasted for so long that it attracted general attention and gradually became embarrassing. His glance seemed to pose a question, "Can't something be done with you?" Did he remember my visit to the Sterneckerbräu in Munich in 1920 (Chapter 32)? Did he want to let his magnetism work? I felt none. I finally withdrew my hand slowly, we sat down, and the meeting began.

His address to the Reichsrat was sober and differed little from other speeches which had been delivered from the same seat on similar occasions. Being the delegate from the largest *Land,* Prussia, I had to answer for the Reichsrat. Proceeding from Hitler's references to tradition and legality, I said:

"Mr. Chancellor! In keeping with old custom it devolves upon me to reply to your address in the name of the Reichsrat. The room in which we now find ourselves is the unaltered room of the Old [imperial] German Bundesrat, which the Bundesrat used more and more frequently since the inauguration of the Reichstag building in 1896, instead of the old meeting place in the Ministry of the Interior. Today, as at the time of Bismarck, the *Laender* are seated in much the same order in the Reichsrat, Prussia on the Chancellor's right, Bavaria on his left, followed by the other *Laender,* their number recently enriched by the representatives sent by the Prussian provinces, sitting on the other side of the table. Not only the arrangement of the meeting, but also the procedure in plenary and committee meetings has remained the same. Even today there are persons among us who sat here before the war. Their ranks have been thinned slowly, not all at once after the war.

"Tradition, then, and a specially German tradition, is at home in this room. This applies also to the spirit of the deliberations and the personal relationship among the members of the Reichsrat and between them and the Reich government. Objectivity, temperate argument in controversies, the cultivation of good personal relations—these have been the custom, and we are not aware of any violation of it.

"This atmosphere, which only seldom bursts into thunderstorms, is imperative because of the Reichsrat's organic function which—if not in a strictly legal sense, yet in actual fact—is that of a first, or should I say more modestly, of a second chamber. The Reichsrat is meant to be the balance in the German clockwork, not its motor or spring. It is meant to be a refuge of strict objectivity, the government's conscience in disturbed and excited times. Not a block to progress, but a block to outbursts of passion and overheated struggle. A support for all objective work, above all a support for the Reich government in such work.

"The experience and opinions of all the German *Laender* and regions are gathered here. We are asking you, Mr. Chancellor, to be aware of this institution's high value and to use it, as befits the Reichsrat in accordance with the constitution and with its functions.

According to the Constitution the Reichsrat is called upon to cooperate not only in the Reich's legislation, but also in its administration: it is to be kept informed by the Reich ministries on the conduct of Reich business, and its committees are to be consulted on all important matters."

Turning to Hitler, who was sitting next to me, I continued: "You, Mr. Chancellor, have taken the grave step from your position as the leader of a movement grown in rigid opposition, to that of the responsible chief of the German Reich policy. We all feel that this has been an extremely serious decision for you personally as well. For it means that you have taken over the grave duty and confirmed it by a solemn oath, to use your strength for the benefit of the *entire* people, to uphold the *Constitution* and the laws of the Reich, to fulfill your duties conscientiously, and to conduct your office *'impartially and with justice toward everyone.' The entire Reichsrat will support you in the fulfillment of these duties, firmly and with understanding.*

"The Reich government faces difficult problems, especially overcoming unemployment, which is prevalent not only in Germany but, for example, also in the United States and England, countries of a completely different political situation. At the present moment we do not want to examine why measures taken during the past five years have met with no success. Agreeing with the Reich government on the priority of this question, the Reichsrat considers constructive cooperation here especially important.

"In the name of the Reichsrat I ask you, Mr. Chancellor, to cooperate closely with the *Laender* in the Reichsrat. At the same time I wish to express, at the request of the Reichsrat, our appreciation that you have taken this early opportunity to present yourself to the Reichsrat."

During a discussion with the representatives of the other *Laender* beforehand, replying to their question as to what I was going to say, I had briefly sketched out the content of this speech. I had said nothing about the reference to Hitler's oath and the promise of the Reichsrat to support him in the fulfillment of the duties assumed therewith. But no one objected to these words.

That was the last free speech in the Reichsrat. Hitler did not answer. It was probably the only time that he failed to give an answer. He stood up hesitantly, made a slight, rather stiff bow to the Reichsrat, offered me his hand briefly, without looking at me—very much in contrast to his greeting before the meeting—and left the room with the four or five party members who had accompanied him.

On the same evening State Secretary Lammers rang me up from the Chancellery to tell me that the Führer was very indignant about my speech and the men who had accompanied him were furious. I asked why. I had only assured him of the support of the Reichsrat in the fulfillment of his duties. Lammers uttered a grumbling "Well, hum," and was silent. On the following morning the liberal and socialist press printed my speech with headlines expressing respect or praise. The National Socialist papers, on the other hand, spoke of a scandalous challenge with headlines such as "Brecht gives Hitler advice" or "Impudence of Ministerial Director Brecht."

## 89. RENEWED DISMISSAL OF THE PRUSSIAN CABINET— UNCONSTITUTIONAL DISSOLUTION OF THE LANDTAG (FEBRUARY 6, 1933)

THE Prussian question now came back into the foreground. It was the cause of Hitler's first, for the moment single, formal breach of constitution. Instead of hindering him in this, Papen and Hugenberg were the driving forces. Papen had not yet recovered from the wound which the Supreme Constitutional Court had inflicted on him. He was passionately desirous of obtaining those rights of the Prussian ministers that had remained theirs after the tribunal's decision. Taking them away was not only a matter of satisfying a personal resentment; it was also desirable for two very realistic political reasons. For in contrast to the generally held opinion that the Prussian ministers had no longer any power, they, and they alone, had at their disposal the thirteen votes of the Prussian government in the Reichsrat, which would soon enough be all important for passing an Enabling Act, and the Minister-President had one of the three votes in the *Dreimänner-Kollegium* (three-man board), which could pronounce or decline the dissolution of the Landtag. Of the other two members the one, Landtag President Kerrl, National Socialist, was in favor of the dissolution; the other, Konrad Adenauer, President of the Prussian State Council, opposed it. As the third member, therefore (or as the first), Minister-President Braun had the decisive vote, and he was opposed to the dissolution because, like Adenauer, he had no confidence that elections at this moment would be really free. Hence the dissolution, desired by the rightist parties, was rejected by two votes against one.

On February 6, therefore, urged on by Papen and Hugenberg, and with the consent of the whole Cabinet, Hindenburg issued a new emergency decree against the Prussian government, once again based not only on the second paragraph of article 48 (danger for public safety and order), but also on the first (violation of duties), relieving the Prussian ministers of all rights they had retained, and explicitly transferring the vote of the Minister-President in the three-man board to Papen as the newly appointed Reich Commissioner for Prussia, and nominating Papen also Prussian representative in the Reichsrat. Significantly, it was Papen, not Hitler, who countersigned this decree.

Since the Supreme Constitutional Court had established in October that Prussia had not violated its duties toward the Reich (Chapter 81), the Reich government now boldly stated that the Prussian ministers had done this *since* by their attitude regarding the Court's decision and by their refusal to dissolve the Prussian Landtag, although new elections were necessary on the ground that the Landtag had proved unable to form a new government for almost a year.

We had got wind of the new decree beforehand. I had, therefore, gone to State Secretary Meissner to warn of such a step and to advise Hindenburg to hear Braun first. Braun had also requested Hindenburg for this by letter. Hindenburg declined brusquely, along with promulgation of his decree, on account of urgency. Papen and Kerrl, now ignoring Adenauer's and Braun's protests, thereupon dissolved the Landtag on February 6. New elections were set for the same date as the Reichstag elections, March 5.

Although the breach of constitution was in this case even more notorious than on July 20, no one as far as I know has ever accused the Weimar parties and the labor unions for not having put up active resistance or declared a general strike at this moment. Not only was actual power so overwhelmingly in the hands of those who had broken the Constitution; there were also certain points which were difficult for the man in the street to understand, even more difficult than the year before: a struggle against general elections, in order to keep alive a government which had run aground; a struggle for

Prussia's rights, no longer including control of the police which admittedly could be transferred to a Reich commissioner by emergency decree of the President; a struggle for Prussia's political independence from the Reich, a struggle in which the Democrats, by tradition supporters of national against particularistic ideals, were fighting for Prussia and the Conservatives and National Socialists for the Reich. These were prospects which could not inspire democratically minded sections of the population in a struggle for life or death, or rather in a one-sided struggle to the death.

With my colleagues I immediately drew up a new law suit, which we sent to the Supreme Constitutional Court on the same or the following day. I quote from it:

"The assertion, made in the text of the decree, that 'confusion in public affairs (*im Staatsleben*) which endangers their conduct has come about *because of the attitude of the Land Prussia* toward the decision of the Staatsgerichtshof of October 25, 1932' is not true. The truth is, rather, that after the Court's decision Prussia placed herself firmly on the basis of the decision and strove to achieve a peaceful settlement of differences of opinion. In the interest of such a settlement the State Ministry has maintained extreme patience and reserve even in the face of obvious violations of its rights and of insulting forms of treatment not common in the relations between governments. Evidence of this is given in the exchange of letters [a copy of which was enclosed] and in the fact that until today the Prussian government has not approached the Supreme Constitutional Court again.

"Plans for a permanent change in the relations between Reich and *Laender* must be pursued by submitting a bill for amending the Constitution to the legislative bodies or by a plebiscite. Six months have passed since July 20, 1932, without any attempt at this having been made by the Reich government. In December and January Premier Braun submitted to Chancellor von Schleicher drafts based on the recommendations of the Constitutional Committee of the Conference of the *Laender,* which could have served as a basis for discussion in the Reichsrat."

A few days later we added the text of the January draft to a second brief.

It was not difficult to draw up a legally convincing law suit. But legal victories were not enough. And not even the legal procedure could be carried through. We urgently petitioned the President of

the Supreme Court to have a decision made at least on the legality
of the dissolution of the Landtag before the date set for new elections. After oral discussion lasting several hours Dr. Bumke declared it impossible to pass judgment before March 5. When I objected that after the election it would be too late (*fait accompli*)
and that under these circumstances it was the duty of the tribunal
to make at least a preliminary decision, President Bumke shrugged
his shoulders regretfully. They were judges, he said, who had to
concern themselves with the past in a trial conducted in an orderly
fashion. He could not be persuaded to change his mind on this
point.

After the elections it was indeed too late (Chapter 91).

## 90. My Dismissal Repeated—The Reichsrat Disemboweled—Braun and Severing Charged with Fraud—The Reichstag Arson (February 27)

A few days after the Prussian ministers had been divested by presidential emergency decree of their remaining rights I received two
letters from Papen. In the first, of February 10, I was requested "to
refrain from attending to any official functions"; the second, on the
following day, informed me that I was being temporarily retired
(*einstweiliger Ruhestand*).

Both these actions were, in so far as they were meant to apply to
my functions as an aide to the Prussian ministers and as their delegate to the Reichsrat—and I performed no other functions—unconstitutional and legally invalid. Papen had no say in these matters.
The suit brought by the Prussian ministers was also directed against
these measures. They were being partially limited by a directive issued by the Commissioner himself, which put me at the disposal of
the Prussian ministers in their legal proceedings.

At the following meeting of the Reichsrat, on February 16, my
colleague, Ministerial Director Nobis, and other officials who were
prepared to cooperate with the Nazis, appeared. The session began

with vigorous protests from Bavaria and Baden and other *Laender* against this participation of the Commissioner's representatives in Reichsrat negotiations. Similarly, Dr. Hamacher protested on behalf of the Rhine province and six other Prussian provinces. To the surprise of the presiding Reich Minister Dr. Frick and the *Laender* delegates, he announced that he was making his statement also on behalf of the Prussian state government. We had given him documentary authority to represent the state ministers because, had any of us put in an appearance, the chairman would not have given him the floor.

Despite these vigorous protests the meeting came to a feeble end. The five largest *Laender* after Prussia and the three Hansa towns moved adoption of the following resolution:

"The Reichsrat takes note of the appointment of representatives for Prussia by the Reich Commissioner, without expressing an opinion on the legal basis for these appointments.

"Since the validity of the appointment is dependent on the decision of the Staatsgerichtshof in the legal proceedings between the Reich and Prussia, we request that the deliberations and resolutions of the Reichsrat be limited to matters of extreme urgency until the decision be made and, in so far as the Reichsrat resolutions are not unanimous, that the number of votes cast for and against be listed in the minutes."

According to the minutes this resolution was adopted by 39 votes to 26, with one abstention, counting for the Prussian government the votes cast by the Commissioner's delegate, not those cast by Dr. Hamacher. Otherwise the resolution would have been rejected 39 to 26. This was the lame end of all protests in the Reichsrat. With all the *Laender* governments soon brought under the control of National Socialists, protests stopped (Chapter 93). There were still eight meetings in 1933. Then, with its own agreement, the Reichsrat was abolished (Law of January 30, 1933).

After Hitler's appointment as German Chancellor there appeared on the Berlin advertising pillars enormous white posters about four to five feet high, bearing at first in large print only the words "Two million stolen," but then, a day or two later, in equally large print the addition "by Braun and Severing." Underneath this was printed a statement signed by Ministerial Director Nobis, averring that the

Prussian state ministers had resolved at a secret meeting in April, 1932 to spend two million reichs-marks of state funds allegedly for combatting crime, but in reality for the election campaign.

I immediately went to Papen and requested that in his capacity as Reich Commissioner for Prussia he intervene against these posters, since on the basis of the statement I had given to his representative in the presence of the President of the Supreme Court (Chapter 81), he knew that the assertions made on the posters were incorrect. But Papen already did not have the actual power to stop such actions by the National Socialist propaganda machine. He gave me a statement, however, signed by him, that no accusations could be made in this matter against the personal honesty of Braun and Severing. I handed it on to the press. He furthermore agreed to pass my request on to Hitler, but this, of course, meant nothing.

At the last meeting of the old Landtag on February 4, 1933, the National Socialists, in a state of megalomaniac ecstasy since Hitler's appointment and behaving like drunkards, took advantage of the misleading disclosures by Nobis. No one who did not witness their Landtag leader's Kube speech and the reaction of his party comrades on the spot can imagine the brutality of the scene. Kube screamed sentences like the following at Severing: "You had the effrontery to call us criminals." "You do not constitute a political case for us; you constitute for us a criminal case." Severing rose from his deputy's seat to the howling of his opponents and walked, small and slender in stature, with his usual quiet but firm bearing, very much alone, up to the platform to answer, but was continually shouted down. The meeting had to be interrupted.

Having watched the scene from the government bench, I spoke to the acting vice-president and some of the more sensible National Socialists, saying they ought to be decent enough to let Severing reply. But when the meeting was reopened the perpetual screaming continued. Severing was unable to make himself heard. I feared the worst for him as soon as he was to leave the building. But he kept his self-control, although he did grow pale. Actually he impressed his opponents even at this moment, and no one used physical violence against him then or later.

At one of my discussions with Deputy Commissioner Dr. Bracht in the Minister-President's office, Ministerial Director Nobis was present. I asked him why he had not voiced his objections at the ministers' meeting in April, 1932, where he was present, or at least expressed them to his superior, Braun, immediately after it. Would he also under the present regime keep to himself his objections to what he watched, in order to accuse his present superiors to their successors? His face turned red. I was very sorry to have to say such hard words to my old colleague who was obviously confused by the events, but his denunciation had caused such trouble that I felt I could not act otherwise.

Papen's statement, for which the Prussian ministers were very grateful to me, was printed readily by most of the newspapers, but it failed to halt the mischief caused by the posters. Braun and Severing had no choice but to appeal for court injunctions against the posters in each single case at the local courts. This was the more cumbersome since the posters had been distributed not only within the jurisdictional areas of several Berlin courts but also at many other places throughout the country. The ministers had to pay the fees, etc., themselves, except where their party took this over. The various court hearings were attended to in Berlin by the lawyer of the Social Democrat Party, Dr. Franz Neumann, afterward Professor of Political Science at Columbia University, a highly unpleasant function in view of the National Socialist threats, but one which he discharged bravely and with dignity.

On February 27, there was one of a number of monthly discussions on the political situation in the Hotel Kaiserhof under the joint chairmanship of Seeckt, Simons, and Solf (former Colonial Secretary and Ambassador), a so-called Se-Si-So-meeting. It was well attended. I was sitting next to Professor Emil Lederer, whom I did not yet know personally, but with whom I was to be closely connected in the New School for Social Research half a year later up until his death. When we left between ten and eleven o'clock at night the Wilhelmstrasse was blocked. We were told that the Reichstag was on fire. We were able to penetrate to Ebertstrasse, but there too found the street to the Reichstag blocked. It proved impossible to learn any details. On the next morning the newspapers reported that the Reichstag had been set on fire at the instigation and with the assistance of the Communists.

In the whole history of mankind I know of no comparable coincidence of a political situation charged with extreme tensions and a mysterious crime which took place right at the center of these tensions. Even today, as I am writing this—February 27, 1965, the 32nd anniversary of the fire—the facts have not been completely disclosed. Two myths are opposed to each other and to truth. Which are the myths; which is the truth? Either the half-mad Dutchman, Marinus van der Lubbe, caught in the act, who confessed, was convicted and executed, committed the crime on his own, or not on his own, and in the latter case his accomplices were either the Communists or the National Socialists. Supposing that the fire was laid by Lubbe alone—and most recent research seems to incline to this opinion, especially Hans Mommsen's critical essay in *Vierteljahrshefte für Zeitgeschichte* in 1964 (No. 4)—then it was nonetheless unavoidable that at the time few would believe that. In this respect the murder of President John F. Kennedy in November, 1963 forms a striking parallel; yet this crime did not occur at a moment equally charged with tension and the U.S. government itself soon took the view that Oswald had no accomplices. If members of the German government or their parties really had no part in the Reichstag fire, then it was understandable that they assumed their radical political opponents, the Communists, to be the originators and accomplices. It was just as understandable that opponents of the National Socialists suspected them to have arranged the fire themselves in order to obtain a plausible reason for severe action. The large majority of Germans among the middle and upper classes believed that the Communists were behind it. To the average respectable citizen it was incredible that members of the government, who had recently called for God's blessing in their solemn cabinet proclamation, could be so base as to have the Reichstag set on fire by their own supporters, in order to be able to blame the Communists for it, and afterward to have the audacity to bring the case to the court and to pillory the infamy of those who were spreading rumors against the National Socialists. The first words with which Göring opened the newly elected Reichstag in the Kroll Theater opposite the Reichstag building, were: "Due to a dreadful crime we have been forced to move from the building once built 'For the German People.' The meeting hall has been destroyed by a criminal act. You all know that this criminal act was only a consequence of that agitation against Reich, people, and the state which has been going on for decades. This act was to be the sign for producing chaos and anarchy in Germany at a moment when the onset of a new order and reconstruction of the Reich was becoming evident." He thanked the Chancellor for the reestablishment of the basic principles of "honor and cleanliness." Two days later Hitler himself said: "The fire in the Reichstag building, unsuccessful attempt at a large-scale action, is only a token of what Europe would have to expect from a victory of this devilish [Communist] doctrine. If some branch of the press —today in particular outside Germany—is attempting, in keeping with the political untruth which has been made a principle by Communism, to identify the national uprising in Germany with the crime, then this can only strengthen me in my resolve to leave no stone unturned to atone for this crime as soon as possible with the public execution of the guilty incendiary and his accomplices. Neither the German nation nor the rest of the world is sufficiently aware of the whole extent of the actions intended by this organization. Only by lightning action has the government been able to prevent a development which in the case of a catastrophic outcome would have shattered the whole of Europe." In the same speech he spoke once again of the fact that the government "considers Christianity the immovable foundation of the ethical and moral life of our nation."

If the eternal principles of Christianity had really been recognized in National Socialist ways of thinking and acting, then there would never have been any suspicion. But the predominant doctrine of the party was, "What is useful for the German nation is right." With this principle, if it was not limited by general ethical standards, all sorts of devilish methods, including the hypocritical disavowal of their use, could appear right, as soon as the men in power considered them useful for Germany. In accordance with this principle the National Socialists *could* have arranged the fire, they *could* also have denied it afterward in the way that happened, if they had considered this to be useful for the nation, or for their own party, whose victory was a priori considered of advantage to the whole nation. What is relevant here, then, is not the acts of individual criminals but a deeply immoral political doctrine.

As regards the Communists, the facts were cleared up relatively soon. The Supreme Court discharged the Communists who had been accused, in December, 1933. A former National Liberal, ex-Premier of Saxony, Dr. Buenger, served as chairman. The justices apparently did not take the rumors that the National Socialists themselves had arranged the fire seriously. They considered it beneath the dignity of the court to pursue such a suspicion against a German government thoroughly. But they had the courage—and cour-

age was necessary—despite the propaganda and the terroristic demands of the men in power, to discharge the accused Communists.
The acquittal, however, announced in December, came far too late
to affect the increase in power which the National Socialists had obtained as a result of the fire. I will now turn to this increase in
power.

On the very day after the fire Hitler, Frick, Göring, and Goebbels
extracted Hindenburg's signature for the so-called "Reichstag Fire
Emergency Decree," which had been prepared by Frick. Based on
article 48 of the Constitution it suspended the guarantees of personal freedom in Germany. This meant that the police were able to
arrest people, to keep them under arrest for as long as they liked, to
search and confiscate private property, to suppress or censor newspapers, to disband associations and forbid public meetings, without requiring special authority in individual cases, and without any court
supervision. Article 117 of the Constitution, which guaranteed the
inviolability of person, was among the articles that could be, and
were, suspended.

Ebert, too, had made use of this authority at critical moments
during the first troublesome years after the war, but always for only
a short period and under the constant control of a Reichstag which
had not been dissolved, and his decrees were counter-signed by
chancellors who were supported or at least tolerated by majorities.
Moreover, Ebert's decrees, several of which I had drafted myself,
when valid for more than a few days, always contained a clause
which stated that the old Protective Custody Act, which had been
passed by the Reichstag during the war in 1916, was applicable.[1]
This meant that any person taken into protective custody must be
heard by a regular court within 24 hours after the arrest; that the
person arrested had a right to have legal counsel and that the latter
might inspect all documents; that complaints might be submitted to
a special tribunal, which had the right to release the person arrested
at any time and without the consent of which the person might not
be kept in custody for more than three months. This tribunal could
also award damages from state funds and was under obligation to
do this if the arrest had not been in its opinion necessary for the security of the state. The old Protective Custody Act had appointed
the highest military court, composed of judges and officers, to be

[1] In Ebert's decree of September 26, 1923 this clause was missing, but was added
later by decree of December 23, 1923.

that special tribunal. Ebert replaced the military court by a board composed of civilians.

The decree of February 28, 1933, however, failed to declare the Protective Custody Act applicable. This omission implied dreadful consequences. It meant that there was no longer any limit to measures the National Socialist Party could take against their foes. The police might arrest them and extend the period of their custody without limit. They could leave the relatives uninformed about the reasons and the subsequent fate of the person. They could prevent a lawyer or other persons from visiting him and from inspecting the documents. They could exhaust him with work, provide him with insufficient food and poor accommodation, force him to use the Hitler salute or sing Nazi songs, torture him in order to obtain confessions or denunciations, and finally in the case of a refusal to obey or of a nervous breakdown, they could beat or shoot him. In order to "reestablish order" in the concentration camp they could even punish him for deeds which not he but his fellow-prisoners had committed. They could do all this under the one condition that their superiors backed them, and their ultimate superiors were Göring and later Himmler. In addition they could prevent the prisoner from making any contacts with any court or other agency and the world outside from hearing anything at all about what happened to him. No law court would find the case in its dockets. Once the basic rights had been suspended there was no writ of habeas corpus. This suspension of basic rights freed the police not only from the limits laid down in the Constitution itself, but also from those fixed in other laws as, for example, the Code on Criminal Procedure and the Press Law. All the commentators on the Constitution were at one on this.

When he signed the decree Hindenburg was obviously not clear about this gap and certainly not about its legal significance. It would have been the duty of his non-National Socialist advisers, especially Papen, Hugenberg, Gürtner (the Minister of Justice) and Meissner, to point this out to him. They failed to do that, or at least did not insist on it.

There was yet another essential difference. Former emergency decrees of this sort presupposed that the police, freed from control by the courts, would proceed impartially against *every* breach of the peace, regardless from which side it came. This principle, always difficult to enforce, was now given up as a matter of course. Göring, in charge of the Prussian police, issued instructions in which he warned the police that the government measures were meant to suppress the Communists, not the National Socialists, "as a defense against Communist conspiracies and for the complete extermination of this source of danger." A few side remarks indicated that those who "cooperated" with the Communists were also included. The police were directed not to apply the decree against members of right-wing organizations. "To avoid blunders I wish to point out that measures which are necessary against members or institutions of parties and organizations *other than* Communists, Anarchists, and Social Democrats, are to be based on the decree of February 28, 1933, only when they serve to prevent Communist aspirations in the broadest sense. In other cases, procedure is to be ruled by the decree of February 4, 1933." The previous decree of February 4 had left basic rights and legal guarantees in force on the whole. But as soon as February 10 an edict of Göring's had included the following passage: "The decree (of February 4) has not been issued to hinder those groups which, backing the government of the National Uprising, offer their welcome and necessary cooperation in the furthering of the government's lofty aims."

On February 28, President Hindenburg issued a second emergency decree "against treason to the German nation and traitorous conspiracies," which threatened imprisonment and under certain circumstances the death penalty for acts described in an extremely vague manner, such as "the dissemination of rumors and untrue information" and "informing foreign governments," which might well affect any publication, and "treasonable conspiracies," including incitement to strikes in essential industries or to general strikes and treasonable conspiracies committed "in some other manner."

On the basis of the two decrees of February 28 thousands of Communists were arrested, including all the Reichstag candidates, in so far as this had not already been done. Since the Weimar Constitution did not forbid the arrest of former members of parliament between dissolution and a new election its letter was not violated. Votes could be cast for the arrested candidates on March 5, and indeed about three quarters as many votes did go to Communists as in the November elections (see the following chapter). But the newly elected members could not appear when the house convened. The Reichstag had the constitutional right to demand their release, but this right was not exercised.

The Reichstag fire thus played a decisive role in the increase of National Socialist power. The two presidential decrees of February 28 provided the National Socialist police ministers with the almost unlimited authority I have described, and they did so for the whole period of the regime, for they were never repealed. Moreover, the fire caused many citizens to cast their votes for the National Socialists, who had promised to protect them from the Communists.

## 91. BRAUN CROSSES LAKE CONSTANCE TOO SOON— THE ELECTIONS (MARCH 5, 1933)—EVICTION FROM OUR QUARTERS—RESIGNATION OF THE PRUSSIAN MINISTERS—THE END OF PRUSSIA

BETWEEN the Reichstag fire (Monday) and election Sunday there remained only five days; between the issue of the emergency decrees (Tuesday) and election Sunday, only four. A wave of arrests which grew daily swept the country.

On Tuesday or Wednesday Braun came to see me in our exile-offices in Leipzigerstrasse 3, which he had visited only rarely, and informed me that he had decided to drive to Switzerland; his crippled wife would travel by rail there to join him after she had cast her vote. He assumed that he would be one of the next to be imprisoned or done away with if he stayed. He was unable to engage in politically significant actions in Germany in view of the constant threats from the SA, he said. Hindenburg had warned him that he could not guarantee his safety. He would postpone further decisions for a few weeks. In order to avoid premature publicity and to have his car at his disposal for his wife in Switzerland, he intended to make the trip by car, which my colleague Hermann Badt had agreed to drive.

Braun left Berlin on Friday. He and Badt had secured voting slips authorizing them to cast their votes outside Berlin. Arriving in Friedrichshafen on Lake Constance at midday on Saturday they committed the serious political blunder of crossing the lake at once on the regular ferry to Romannshorn. It was 3.45 p.m. Braun obviously acted in line with the old rule that whatever occurs after the

evening papers on the last day before an election are out has no influence on the results. This had been true before the time of radio,
but it was false now with the radio under National Socialist control.
Goebbels personally announced on the radio that Braun had fled to
Switzerland, adding that the workers could now see what pitiful
leaders they had, who left at the moment of danger. The news was
repeated several times during the night and in the morning.

After the first announcement I received telephone inquiries from
the major liberal and Social Democrat papers. Concealing my own
embarrassment I answered that Braun had taken his car to Switzerland for his sick wife, but would be back on the German side of the
Swiss border on Sunday to cast his vote, and in Berlin at the coming session of the newly elected Reichstag.

Badt actually did travel to Constance on Sunday and cast his vote.
Braun, however, after Goebbels' radio announcement, decided not
to expose himself to the danger of an arrest by the SA. The election
results could no longer be influenced by his going or not going to
Constance. I do not believe, incidentally, that any Social Democrat
deprived the party of his vote because Comrade Braun, whose dangerous position all were aware of, had left for Switzerland. The voting figures (see below) give no evidence of this. Many Communist
and Social Democrat leaders, and also non-Socialist politicians,
crossed the border during these days.

Further developments during the following days soon drew attention away from him. A few days later I received a package from
Switzerland with a laurel twig. Sender: Otto Braun.

Despite deceit and terror the election on March 5 failed to result
in a general German plebescite in favor of National Socialism. Of
647 seats the National Socialists obtained 288 (in July it had been
230 out of 607), considerably less than half. The German Nationalists received 52, about half as many as at the time of their zenith, in
1924. Only jointly did these two parties have more than half (340
out of 647); even together they were far from the two-thirds majority. The Zentrum obtained 74 seats, four more than in November,
1932, more than it had ever had before 1932, and only two less than
the maximum of 76 they had in July 1932. With 120 the Social
Democrats stayed by only one seat below what they had in November, 1932 and still had four-fifths of the maximum strength they
had obtained in 1928 (153). Despite all the measures taken against

them, the Communists could still claim 81 seats, more than they had ever had before 1932, and four-fifths of their maximum in November 1932 (100). The People's Party had melted to only two. The State (formerly Democratic) Party had pulled up from their two seats in November, 1932 to five.

In other words: while it is true that more than a third of the German people did cast their votes for the National Socialists, it also is true that, despite lies, violence, and terror, considerably more than half did not. When we blame the former we must not neglect to praise the latter and to record their existence in world memory.

In 12 of the 35 German constituencies the National Socialists and the German Nationalists did not obtain a majority even together. These 12 were Cologne-Aachen, Coblenz-Trier, Düsseldorf West and East, North and South Westphalia, Upper and Lower Bavaria, the Palatinate, Berlin, Hamburg and Leipzig. This list of honor ought not to be forgotten either. The Federal Republic of today consists to a very large extent of territory in which even in the March elections of 1933 the majority stood firm against terror. This historical fact is evidence that the present-day pro-democratic policy of Bonn is no mere opportunism, but can claim respect for its genuine nature.

However, insolence conquered statistics. The National Socialists behaved as though the entire German nation had decided by huge majorities in their favor, for their aims, their methods, and their leaders. Under the stream of propaganda which reached every house by radio—the same radio on which people had previously been accustomed to hear relatively objective news—the population was so stupefied and confused that the National Socialist victory was believed to be true and people reacted with a feeling of impotence and resignation.

Misinterpretation of the election results was most effectively supported by the second breach of the Constitution (the decree against the Prussian government had been the first, see Chapter 89): changing the national flag. Two days after the election, the Cabinet decided that the black-white-red flag was to be hoisted on government buildings along with the constitutional black-red-gold one. This was a comparatively tame measure; it adopted at home the arrangement introduced for German missions overseas by Chancellor Luther (Chapter 52). But it did not stop at that. On March 12, precisely a week after the elections, a decree of Hindenburg's stated that, until there was a final decision on the Reich colors, the black-white-red flag and the *swastika* banner were to be hoisted together. With this the constitutional black-red-gold flag was practically abolished as the national flag. This was a breach of constitution since the president could not change the national colors even on the basis of article 48.

The practical significance of this decree was extraordinary. Wherever the black-red-gold flag appeared, it had been torn down even before this new decree. But Hindenburg's equating of the swastika banner with the imperial black-white-red flag went much further. It raised the wanton feelings of superiority on the part of the National Socialists to new heights. Now anyone who flew solely the black-white-red flag, without hoisting the swastika flag alongside, was suspected as an enemy of the new state, an opponent of Hitler *and of Hindenburg*.

A few days later the Landtag President Kerrl, a National Socialist, let me know that the SA was highly indignant about our still occupying office rooms in the building; they had threatened to evict us by force, he said. I called Papen in his capacity as National Commissioner for Prussia and asked for his protection. He answered that he was not in a position to prevent such actions, but he offered us adequate rooms on the ground floor of the State Ministry (Wilhelmstrasse 63), where we would no doubt be safe against terrorist measures. I had our papers, after eliminating basketfuls of them, taken across to the familiar building of the State Ministry and took possession of the rooms allocated to us.

The Prussian ministers awaited the first meeting of the new Landtag before further decisions. In the meantime they met no longer in the Landtag building, but in restaurants. These were ghostly meetings. No one knew whether the others were still at liberty, nor whether the SA would not throw us out. But somehow we had to maintain contact until the situation was clarified.

At its first session on March 22, which I attended in the gallery, the newly elected Landtag decided by majority vote, *with the consent of the Zentrum Party:* "The Landtag, while reserving its right to elect a Minister-President, declares its approval of the arrangement that the affairs of the government are temporarily attended to by the national commissioners appointed by the Reich President." In view of this decision the old ministers, meeting on the following day for the last time in a hotel near Friedrichstrasse station, decided to lay down their function as Acting State Ministry. I phoned Braun in his Swiss hotel, in order to inform him and to ask for his consent. He agreed. I then advised the president of the Staatsgerichtshof in Leipzig, Dr. Bumke, by telephone of the Prussian ministers' resignation. Although this act did not preclude continuation of the proceedings now pending before the Staatsgerichtshof, no further steps were intended from our side at the moment, I told him. Relieved, he took note of this.

On the following day Severing was arrested, but soon released tentatively under an injunction to keep himself at the disposal of the new authorities for further hearings.

I remained a few more days in the rooms of the State Ministry to wind up our affairs. On March 31st I left, literally the last government official of the democratic republic. I had handed over official deeds and private files to the chief clerk, asking him that the latter be kept as my private property, because I thought they would be safer there than in my home. I do not know what has become of them. As I closed the door behind me, the history of the independent state of Prussia had ended.

Papen continued as National Commissioner for Prussia for only a few days. On April 7, he was replaced by Göring, newly elected Prussian Minister-President, nominal premier of a *Land* which, while still called Prussia, no longer had any independence, not even an independent vote in the Reichsrat such as I had cast for Prussia until February 2, 1933.

## 92. FROM THE ENABLING ACT TO ONE-PARTY RULE

ON the first Sunday after the election Hindenburg had signed not only the flag decree, but also made the propaganda boss of the National Socialist Party, *Gauleiter* of Berlin, Josef Goebbels a member of the Reich government by appointing him Reich Minister for Enlightenment and Propaganda. A mere nine days afterward, on March 21, anniversary of the opening of the Bismarck Reichstag in 1871, Goebbels produced his masterpiece in the arrangement of the great day in Potsdam, the day of the "National Uprising." The myths of the dead Frederick the Great and the living Hindenburg were ingeniously harnessed together to enhance Hitler's prestige in a deceptive maneuver, designed to distract attention from the total seizure of power by the National Socialists which was taking shape behind these sentimental scenes.

Potsdam and Sanssouci! Every adult German was, in some corner of his heart, at least in his childhood memories, an admirer of Frederick the Great. Adding to the glory of the past was the pleasant location of the place chosen. Only those who lived in Berlin before Germany was divided can understand the affection Berliners had—especially West Berliners, for North and East Berlin were closer to other excursion spots—for the place and the scenery in Potsdam, most popular goal for day trips, now inaccessible for West Berliners.

Bells ringing throughout the whole of Germany on the morning of March 21, services in all churches, Hindenburg and (separately) Hitler and the members of the Cabinet driving round in Potsdam, military parades—everything a nationalistic heart could desire. Then the great moment in Garnison Church: Hindenburg in the seat of honor, flanked by Hitler in tails and Göring in uniform, the Crown Prince couple, even a chair symbolically left vacant for the Kaiser, and around them the deputies of all parties except those "without a fatherland," the Social Democrats and the Communists. Solemn proclamations by the Field Marshal, a speech by Hitler honoring him, descent of Hindenburg to Ferderick's tomb. . . . It was not possible to titillate nationalistic feelings more effectively, and to screen the truth that power was no longer in the hands of the senile Hindenburg and the German Nationalist members of the Cabinet. Potsdam-Germans, Luther-Germans, Kant-Germans, even Weimar-Germans—not all of them, but many—embraced one another and were deeply moved, looking into one another's moist eyes. Seldom has there been a bigger catch.

Thus prepared as best as possible, the Reichstag passed an Enabling Act with a two-thirds majority, giving the Hitler government the power to pass laws of any sort by mere decree, even if they diverged from the Weimar Constitution. No clause in defense of human rights limited this authority. According to all commentaries any act, however much in conflict with the Constitution, was legally valid if passed by a two-thirds majority in the Reichstag and Reichsrat. Rejection by the Reichsrat could be overcome through repeated resolution by a two-thirds majority in the Reichstag.

A two-thirds majority in the Reichstag, however, could be obtained only if the Zentrum Party voted for the act. This the Zentrum did do, with the Bavarian People's Party and the few remaining members from other bourgeois parties following suit, bringing the total of yes-votes to 444, against only 94 no-votes from the Social Democrats. True, 81 Communists and 26 Social Democrats had been prevented from attending by arrest, flight abroad, or, in a few cases, illness. Even if these 107 votes were added to the no's—there would then have been a total of 201 no-votes—the yes-votes would still have been considerably above the two-thirds majority.

A decisive factor for the yes-voters was no doubt the fear of what would happen if the Enabling Act failed to pass. They were convinced, and had good reason for this opinion, that the National Socialists would then proceed along *illegal* paths and would, in an orgy of horror and bloodshed, create a position of power for Hitler which no longer knew any limits. The Enabling Act, on the other hand, did provide for at least a few limits to Hitler's power. It did so by five limitations which it was hoped would prevent too great abuse. The first was that the Act did give power not to Hitler personally but to his existing cabinet. It was automatically to go out of force "when the present Reich government will be replaced by another." This, so members of the Zentrum hoped, would leave vital decisions in the hands of non-National Socialists, who held two-thirds of the Cabinet positions and could by their resignation bring "the Reich government" to an end and thereby the validity of the Enabling Act. Second, the Enabling Act was restricted to four years. Third, fourth, and fifth, the Enabling Act declared all deviations from the Weimar Constitution invalid "in so far as they have as their subject the institutions of the Reichstag or of the Reichsrat as such" or in so far as they encroach upon "the rights of the Reich President." The presidial rights included the right to dismiss the Chancellor at any time, and the President's supreme command of the army.

Hitler had allowed these five limitations. Explicit clauses for safeguarding human rights he had, however, stubbornly rejected. Prelate Kaas, as spokesman for the Zentrum party, found reason for hope in the references to Christian principles and in other conciliatory passages Hitler had interwoven in his own remarks during the course of the debate. The Zentrum's left wing, too, which had under Brüning's leadership up to the end refused its consent in the party caucus (including Wirth, Joos, Bolz, Dessauer), did finally cast yes-votes in the plenary session, in order to maintain the unity of their party.

Only the members of the Social Democrat Party voted against the Enabling Act. All 94 present did so. This required great personal courage. It required even greater courage to mount the rostrum after Hitler's speech and say what the leader of the Social Democrat Party, Otto Wels, then said:

"One can take our freedom and our lives, but not our honor. After the persecution that has been the lot of the Social Democrat Party recently, no one can fairly demand or expect of it that it will vote for the Enabling Act as here introduced. . . .

"Our achievements in the reconstruction of the country and its economy and the liberating of the occupied areas will stand the judgment of history. We have established equal rights for all and a social labor law. We have helped to create a Germany in which not only princes and barons, but also members of the working classes, could come to state leadership. . . .

"The attempt to turn back the wheel of history will fail. We Social Democrats know that it is not possible to do away with the facts of power politics by mere protests. We do see that in terms of power your rule is an actual fact at present. *But the people's sense of justice (Rechtsbewusstsein) is a political power, too.*

"The Weimar Constitution is no socialist constitution. *But we hold fast to the basic principles of a government based on law (Rechtsstaat)*, of equality of rights, and of social law, as therein established. At this historical hour we German Social Democrats confess solemnly our adherence to the principles of humanity and justice, of liberty and Socialism. *No Enabling Act gives you the power to destroy ideas which are eternal and indestructible.* . . .

"We salute those who are persecuted and afflicted. We salute our friends in the country. Their steadfastness and loyalty deserve admiration. Their courage of confession, their unbroken faith, vouch for a brighter future."

The limitations which the Enabling Act had put on the government's power were carefully observed in the first two months. They did not prevent the Cabinet from abolishing the permanent tenure of civil servants or the independence of judges, from disbanding the labor unions, from forbidding journeys abroad without special permit, nor from passing brutal laws against the Jews. The flag decree, which gave the swastika banner equal rank with the black-white-red flag (see the preceding chapter), could have been passed under the Enabling Act without exceeding the government's authority. Only on July 7, 1933, when all Social Democrats and members of the State (formerly Democratic) Party were deprived of their seats in the Reichstag, and more definitely a week later, when on July 14, 1933 all political parties with the exception of the National Socialist Party were disbanded by decree-law, did the Hitler government overstep the limits drawn by the Enabling Act. In Germany, so the decree-law of July 14 declared grandiosely, "the only political party is the National Socialist German Workers' Party," continuing, "Whoever attempts to maintain the organization of any other political party, or to form a new political party, will be punished with hard labor (*Zuchthaus*) for a period of up to three years, or with imprisonment (*Gefängnis*) of not less than six months and not more than three years." This did not exclude a person's being transferred to a concentration camp after he had served his sentence.

Prohibition of all parties except the one which was under Hitler's command violated the clause in the Enabling Act according to which deviations from the Weimar Constitution were not permissible if they affected "the institution of the Reichstag as such." A parliament which consisted of only one party—with members nominated by the party itself to the exclusion of any selection from other quarters, while at the same time other parties were outlawed and anyone who attempted to found another party was threatened with penal servitude and concentration camp—such a parliament was no longer the "Reichstag" in the sense of the Enabling Act even though the name was ascribed to it. When the Enabling Act prescribed that "the institution of the Reichstag as such" could *not* be made the subject of a decree, it was referring to a body in which the various political opinions of the German nation were represented by members who were freely elected by the people, and in which free exchange of opinions was possible. A decree which limited the representation of the nation to one party, and to the very party which the Reichstag was meant to control, however slightly, such a decree had the institution of the Reichstag as its subject and was, therefore, according to the Enabling Act invalid.

With this one decree all five of the safeguard clauses of the Enabling Act collapsed. For from now on a newly elected "Reichstag" —the one-party Reichstag—could always provide the two-thirds majorities necessary for any further changes of the Constitution and for further Enabling Acts. And so it was. At the first opportunity, on January 30, 1934, the newly elected Reichstag unanimously adopted a law abolishing all sovereign rights of the *Laender* and empowering the Reich Cabinet to pass new constitutional laws *without any limitation*. This act was duly submitted also to the Reichsrat, which, of course, being newly constituted, voted for it unanimously, thereby digging its own grave. Relying on this new source of legislative power, the Reich Cabinet passed a decree two weeks later abolishing the Reichsrat—almost exactly a year after I had taken part in its meetings the last time (Chapter 88)—thus removing the second barrier set up by the Enabling Act.

When the four years to which the Enabling Act had limited its own force were about over in 1937, pedantic attention was paid to having the "Reichstag" adopt a new law with two-thirds majority (or, rather, unanimously), extending the validity of the first Enabling Act. This game was repeated in 1939. Later on Hitler decreed the extension singlehanded.

A different course was adopted for curtailing the powers of the president. One prerogative after another was taken from Hindenburg, as in the second Reichstag Fire Decree the right to appoint national commissioners (see the following chapter), and in the Enabling Act the right to issue decree laws. As for the balance, Hindenburg's death was awaited. When he did die in August 1934, Hitler could have had himself or some puppet elected president. But he preferred combining the two offices of president and chancellor by decree, subsequently sanctioned by plebiscite.

Thus after July 14, 1933 all organized opposition was not only suppressed *in practice*, it was henceforth *forbidden by law*. No objections which presented opposition against the supremacy of the National Socialists were tolerated. Only *friends* of the regime, or people who were able to act the role of friend or of unpolitical adviser convincingly, were still able occasionally to express carefully chosen words of criticism in public. *Opponents* were no longer able to speak the truth within Germany—except very softly in private, and then with an anxious glance over the shoulder—without exposing themselves to martyrdom. Even private comments could lead to severe punishment whenever the discussion partner passed on what had been said to others, mentioning names or revealing them under torture.

All open resistance against National Socialism and the Hitler regime had thus come to an end. I cannot describe the significance of the decree-law of July 14, 1933 more pertinently today than I did in 1944 in *Prelude to Silence:* "The curtain had fallen—the Great Silence had begun."


## 93. REFLECTIONS ON THE RESPONSIBILITY FOR HITLER'S OBTAINING TOTAL POWER

IN the first place it was, of course, the National Socialists themselves who were responsible for Hitler's gaining total power. Many of them deeply regretted later that all controls, even internally within the party, had been eliminated. I am not going to say more about their share here. Second, all those responsible for Hitler's being appointed Chancellor were therewith also responsible for the opportunity he obtained to misuse and to extend his powers as Chancellor.

These men, beginning with Hindenburg right down to Meissner and including above all Papen and Hugenberg, had justified the appointment, both before their own conscience and to others, with the assurance that gross misuse of power and its extension to total dimensions could, and would, be prevented by Hitler's colleagues in the Cabinet or by Hindenburg as President. Therewith they assumed a particular responsibility to the German nation, to God and to man, that they would actually do everything possible to prevent the misuse and the extension of Hitler's powers. Did they fully live up to this particular responsibility? When in the following I am speaking of "failure," I refer to actions or omissions which were at odds with that responsibility.

The first, and perhaps the most serious, failure was handing the army, the Prussian police, and the radio service over to men subservient to Hitler (Blomberg, Göring, Frick, Goebbels), thus giving the National Socialists complete control of the means of power.

The second failure was Papen's and Hugenberg's action in not only permitting, but personally instigating, the first great breach of constitution after Hitler's appointment—robbing the Prussian ministers of the rights which the Staatsgerichtshof had declared to be inviolable. Thereby within the very first week they destroyed legality and constitutionality as criteria of permissible use of power.

The third failure was that Papen, Hugenberg, Gürtner, the other Cabinet members, and the cooperating government officials failed to advise Hindenburg against signing the Reichstag Fire Decree unless it contained the usual guarantees for the preservation of minimal standards of human rights, such as formulated in the Protective Custody Act of 1916 (Chapter 90).

It was, fourth, a failure of those who bore particular responsibility in allowing the Flag Decree to be issued on March 12, which ordered hoisting of the swastika banner alongside the black-white-red colors (Chapter 91); fifth, that they did not insist upon clauses for the preservation of human rights being included in the Enabling Act (Chapter 92); sixth, that they allowed discriminating decrees to be issued against Jewish and "nationally unreliable" officials.

Seventh, it was a great failure to accept the fact that at Cabinet meetings no votes were taken, but decisions were left to Hitler. In later years there were no Cabinet meetings at all.

Eighth, they did not do everything, they did not stake their professional and private lives on preventing the dissolution of all parties except the National Socialist and the prohibition on the forming of new parties in the decree-law of July 14, 1933. Hugenberg alone took his leave under protest beforehand. Thereafter Hitler had practically gained total power.

I would like to add a few comments on the responsibility of judges and administrative officials. After Hitler's constitutional appointment as Chancellor by the legitimate Reich President and after the acceptance of the Enabling Act by the majority required to make it valid under the Weimar Constitution, there seemed to be no other choice for officials and judges than either to obey or to resign. Their very *professional duty* seemed to demand of them that, if they remained in office, they should apply all decrees issued under the Enabling Act with no regard of their own approval or disapproval.

Professor Hans Schneider has disputed the legality of the Enabling Act on the grounds that the Reichsrat, when it decided not to object to the Enabling Act, had been artificially filled with supporters of the new regime by a series of unconstitutional transactions. This is correct; and no one could be more convinced of the vulnerability of that no-objection resolution of the Reichsrat than I, who fought to the last against the doctrine that Prussia's votes in the Reichsrat could be cast by national commissioners. This procedure had not stopped at Prussia. Reich Minister of the Interior Dr. Frick took advantage of the authority given him by the second Reichstag Fire Decree of February 28—the power, namely, "to take over the functions of the supreme *Land* authorities temporarily" whenever a *Land* had failed to take "the necessary measures for reestablishing security and order"—to bring the governments of Bavaria, Wurttemberg, Saxony, Hessen and the three Hansa towns, which were still resisting the new course, into line. For this purpose he usually appointed national commissioners, as for example, in Saxony the Erzberger murderer von Killinger (see Chapter 38, and further details in the essays by Bracher and Schulz). All this was done in violation of the Constitution, which did not permit interference with the representation of a *Land* in the Reichsrat. But immediately before the passing of the Enabling Act the new Landtag in Prussia had approved the transference of government functions to the national commissioners with a large majority which included the Zentrum party, and the old Prussian government had laid down its functions (preceding chapter). In Bavaria and in the other raped *Laender* the existing governments had resigned in the face of the appointment of national commissioners. There was therefore no other Reichsrat than the one which actually worked and gave its consent to the Enabling Act. Moreover, under the Weimar Constitution a two-thirds majority of the Reischstag could overrule objections raised by the Reichsrat, even in the case of laws changing the Constitution, and the two-thirds majority was notoriously present for the Enabling Act. Under these circumstances it seems to me asking too much of judges and administrative officials that they should have declared all decrees passed under the Enabling Act invalid because of the questionable legitimacy of the Reichsrat.

The story of the Hitler regime has led to grave objections against the whole positivistic doctrine according to which a judge is bound to apply any law the passing of which had been formally correct, irrespective of moral considerations. I, too, have combatted this doctrine, particularly so in my essays on legal philosophy and in my book *Prelude to Silence* (1944). I consider it erroneous, however, to base objections against legal positivism on attempts to derive "scientific" proof for the validity of moral principles from "nature." This could be done successfully, without going in vicious circles, only when the divine origin of nature could be proved scientifically. I hold that it is quite unnecessary to claim *scientific validity* for the thesis that certain moral maxims are absolutely valid, in order to deny *legal validity* to atrocious government decrees. Which governments are considered legitimate, and which of their orders *legally* valid, legally binding, and which not, is in ultimate analysis a decision of human volition.[1] Nations are able to deny legal validity to certain types of government orders simply because they do not recognize the right of any government to give such orders. From this basis German judges and administrative officials might have refused recognition of flagrantly immoral decrees as legally binding. But at that time the prevailing legal opinion did not permit criticism by judges of laws the passing of which had been formally correct.

Moreover, the functions of government officials rarely included the execution of morally detestable directives. Terroristic methods, forced training in obedience in concentration camps, extermination of Jews and the like were not entrusted to men who were professionally in government service, but to the party organizations. Democratically minded officials who had held key positions or handled matters of personnel had been replaced by National Socialist supporters. The great majority of officials were pleased that they held morally neutral positions, such as the handling of economic matters, taxes, social insurance, statistics, post or railroads—in short official business which in general included nothing the officials considered immoral. If such matters turned up occasionally, decent officials would attempt to treat the victims as best they could. The fact that they were still able to perform such services was a moral comfort and excuse to them for staying in government service.

Of course, government officials or judges could have tendered their resignations. Had all officials done so at the same time, the re-

---

[1] For details see my *Political Theory,* pp. 191 ff., 431 f. and my articles *"Die Tröstungen der strengen Wissenschaft"* (The Consolations of Scientific Method) in *Festschrift für Eric Vogelin,* Munich, 1962, pp. 49 ff. and "The Ultimate Standard of Justice" in the volume "Justice" of the annual *NOMOS,* ed. by Friedrich and Chapman, New York, 1963, pp. 62 ff.

gime would have collapsed. Before the Enabling Act, however, no government decree had been so flagrantly unethical that a general strike on the part of the officials could have been provoked. Whoever resigned of his own free will lost his right to a pension. For a man who had no other income, especially for an older man with wife and children, the decision to resign, therefore, was a difficult one. The bondage of German officials to their pensions has always seemed to me a special evil; I have fought for a better system, which would assure officials of a proportionally adjusted pension in cases of voluntary retirement.[2] But there was no such law then; there still is not one in Germany today. Bondage to pension was clearly what kept government officials, even those in opposition, in their jobs if the National Socialists did not eject them. There were only relatively few, *really voluntary,* exceptions.

The legal situation did not change basically until the decree on the prohibition of all non-Nazi parties on July 14, 1933. At the time little heed was paid to the legal significance of this decree, since terror had driven most of the parties to disband even before the decree was issued. But the German judges at least must have recognized that the decree violated the Enabling Act. They should then—from the purely legal point of view—have declared any law passed by the one-party Reichstag and any additional authority it granted to be legally invalid.

In fact, though, the question of the legal validity of the decree of July 14 came before the courts only rarely during the first few years. The principal method of suppressing political groups was the concentration camp. Similarly, laws passed by the illegitimate one-party Reichstag—there were only seven such laws altogether, four of them before 1937—also came seldom before the courts. Only when the authority of the original Enabling Act was extended by the one-party Reichstag in 1937 were the courts more frequently confronted with the question of the legal validity of further government decrees. From then on every new government decree could be contested for the reason that the extension of the Enabling Act by a one-party Reichstag was invalid. But it was far too late then to cast legal doubt on Hitler's authority for constitutional reasons. For by

[2] See my report on the Weinheim Conference on Reorganization of the Civil Service of December, 1950, reprinted in *Neues Beamtentum,* Frankfurt, 1951, especially pp. 15 ff.; and "Personnel Management" in *Governing Postwar Germany,* ed. by E. H. Litchfield, Cornell Univ. Press, 1951, especially pp. 285 ff.

1937—if not by July, 1933—it could be argued that a new form of government had established itself which could no longer be contested on the basis of the Weimar Constitution.

When blaming German officials and courts, one ought not to forget that they were not the only ones who were deceived or hindered in acting by the formally legal camouflage of the Hitler regime. Foreign countries and their ambassadors paid respect to the new regime, although they were not threatened with concentration camp and death had they refused recognition. If Wilhelm II had returned to Germany to ascend the throne again, the Allies would certainly have intervened. But when Hitler's party seized power with their far more extremist principles, the Allies remained calm. Their calmness in turn influenced the German officials and judges. For it seemed to signify that in the meantime a new form of government had come into being, a government no longer based on the Weimar Constitution, but on the facts of revolution, its legitimacy supported by a factor regarded in legal and political theory everywhere as being of prime importance, namely, recognition abroad.

## 94. PERSONAL FATE AMIDST IMPERSONAL DISASTER— ARREST—DEPARTURE FROM GERMANY (NOVEMBER 9, 1933)

THE following record of my personal fate cannot lay claim to historical importance. It is of purely biographical nature and has beyond that merely illustrative value.

Living in Germany and in Berlin during the first months of the Hitler regime was for someone who was in no way attracted by the "new spirit," but who saw lack of spirit, deceit, brutality, and barbarism bursting over Germany, was, of course, an experience entirely different from that of people who imagined the opposite. For them it was—fantastic illusion—a time of awakening, of regeneration through and through. Did they not see the barbarism all around them? "Yes, but that can't be helped: when a plane is being used, shavings are bound to fly." The shavings, that was the others, thank God, one was not included among them, thank God. But what if you will be among the shavings tomorrow or the day after? "But we haven't done anything wrong!"

For us, the others, it was a bad nightmare from which one tried to awaken. Was it really true? Was this Germany? If one forgot the tragedy for a moment, the whole thing appeared incredibly ridiculous. "Heil Hitler," Germans were suddenly saying to one another, people who had so far been quite reasonable. *"Der Führer,"* they said, with accents of awe and power worship, gratitude in their voices that everything was now all right, now that there was a "Führer." Hadn't they felt it for a long time, deep down below, that this was what was lacking, a "Führer!" But how do you get rid of a Führer, when he misuses his power and leads us to misery? "Oh, keep quiet, you man of little faith, he won't misuse it." He is already misusing it. "Ah well, when a plane is being used, shavings are bound to fly."

At the same time normal life around us, unchanged. That was almost the strangest thing about it. You lived in the same house, with the same trees, the same neighbors, the same shops, the same owners, the same employees. The same tramways with the same numbers, traveling along the same tracks. The same newspapers delivered in the mornings, the same theaters playing the same plays at night. Our small car—I had obtained my driving license in 1931, Clara even before me—continued for some weeks to bring me by the same route to the same building. I went through the same gate, past the same doorman, and had lunch in the same club.

One day a friend from childhood days in Lübeck, Consul Hans Kroeger, managing director of the Possehl Works, called me up. He had come to Berlin to learn from me what was happening and what it was all supposed to mean. We had lunch in a restaurant. Due to a serious attack of laryngitis I was only able to speak in a whisper. We sat there for an hour and I whispered. Other guests looked worriedly across to our table. Anyone who whispered was a griper, a traitor, with one foot in prison and the other in a concentration camp.

Little had yet happened in Berlin to the Jews. Communists, Social Democrats, militant politicians from the liberal parties and even from the Zentrum were worse off than Jews at that time in Berlin. Whenever I felt I was in danger I went to my sister Gertrud and her Jewish-born husband Ossip Schnirlin near Potsdam Bridge in the center of the city. A favorite sport of irregular groups of National Socialists was searching apartments for papers and books with suspicious contents. Houses from whose chimneys rose a sudden short burst of smoke aroused suspicion that papers were being burned there. People therefore avoided burning papers and instead took the trouble to tear them into thousands of little pieces and flush them down the toilet, thereby arousing the suspicion of neighbors. I tore up a letter which Severing had written to Höpker-Aschoff, the Finance Minister, asking for funds in the fight against the National Socialists, into little pieces and flushed it down the toilet at the Schnirlins'.

Not until April 1st, the day after my final departure from office, did the scene change for the Jews in Berlin. The National Socialist Party had announced for this day a one-day boycott of all Jewish shops. There was hope that the government had permitted this merely as a valve for bottled-up anti-Semitic feelings, in order to avoid worse acts of violence. A young colleague of mine, Ministerial Counselor Dr. Wüllenweber from the Prussian Ministry of Finance, went ostentatiously into a number of Jewish shops on the day of the boycott, doing his shopping there. He was given temporary leave from his post by the Minister of Finance on account of this "unseemly behavior" and soon dismissed. He then lived a poor emigrant's life in Switzerland.

On one of the following days, Goebbels, in his daily slander campaign, said something about me on the radio. He spoke of me as the government official who was allegedly irreproachable, whose uprightness and honesty the Weimar Democrats had boasted of. It had now turned out, he said, that I had embezzled a sum of some four thousand marks of state funds and used them for my own purposes. At first I attached no significance to the matter, for I was sure that no one who knew me would believe a word of it. The money in question was presumably the balance of the fund for propaganda against National Socialism, which had been paid into my account at the Prussian State Bank. The account had so far not been closed, since we did not recognize the discharge of the Prussian ministers. To avoid complications I sent a report on the fund and its use to the president of the audit-office, Dr. Sämisch. Dr. Sämisch thanked me for the information.

At this time—formally dressed in dark jacket and bowler—I took my leave of my colleagues in the Reichsrat and some others, including Count Schwerin von Krosigk, now Minister of Finance. He asked me about my plans. I answered that it seemed to me best for either side that I did not seek public service. When I visited his Prussian colleague, Minister Popitz, he said to me that one ought not to be too disturbed by the current irregularities: "in the long run reason will always rule." I expressed my apprehension whether there would not be more destroyed before the return to reason than could ever be made good again. Popitz was fated to die by Hitler's hangmen twelve years later, before reason returned.

On April 6, when I was with State Secretary Schleusener in the Prussian Ministry of Finance, two police came into the room, showed their cards, and explained that they had an order to arrest me and bring me to police headquarters. I was driven there and brought before the temporary head of the secret police, a government official by the name of Diels, whom I had severely attacked in the Papen trial as an informer against his own superiors. With some embarrassment he told me that my arrest had not been his idea, and in answer to my questions informed me that three accusations had been made against me: first, that I had been guilty in the Reichsrat of "encouraging Jewish immigration from the East," second, that, when I was still in the Reich Ministry of the Interior (that is six years before), I had used my influence to the effect that a pardoned Jewish prisoner of Polish descent should not be expelled from Germany after his release; and third, that I had cooperated in the illegal paying out of state monies for the suppression of National Socialism. I explained the facts in all three cases. In the Reichsrat it had been up to the *Laender* governments to decide whether German nationality could be granted to immigrants from the East after twenty-five or only after thirty years of residence in Germany; in Prussia's name I had voted for twenty-five years, as had several of the other *Laender*. The desire to avoid the expulsion of the pardoned prisoner had been broached to me in a favorable testimony from the prison rabbi; I had passed the suggestion on to the proper official in the Prussian Ministry of the Interior and, when he told me a few weeks later that the man had been punished for several cases of burglary, had answered that they should reach their decision in accordance with the facts and that I did not want to interfere. I also informed Diels about the sources of monies spent in defense against National Socialism (Chapter 72).

Diels wanted to keep me in a "room" (cell) until further arrangements were made in my case. But when he was told that all rooms were "occupied," he permitted me to stay in his office, where I was for an hour able to observe his work. Then I was driven by the same two policemen who had brought me to police headquarters to the Ministry of the Interior, where I was taken to a young official, called Volk, by profession a public prosecutor. I asked him whether this was to be a police inquiry, or a judicial preliminary investigation, or a revolutionary procedure. I would arrange my own behavior in accordance. When he avoided giving a clear answer and only said that he had to wait for some person by the name of Hall, presumably a member of the Party, I explained that I wanted to phone Reich Commissioner von Papen, a thing he did not dare to prevent me from doing. However, since it was by now half past one, I was told by the State Ministry that Papen had just gone out for lunch, they did not know where. The same thing happened when I called State Secretary Lammers in the Chancellery.

After we had waited for about an hour, Herr Hall turned up. The two policemen, who had watched me attentively the whole time, were dismissed. When they had got as far as the door, one of them came back to me and said: "Sir, I just want to tell you how sorry I am that we had to bring you here." Some good spirit prompted me to answer him with a handshake, "Thank you very much for your correct and tactful behavior." Then the other came and said that he, too, would like to tell me that he was sorry. I had the pleasant feeling that there were still angels around. Hall and Volk said nothing. Then I was taken into a small adjoining room to be questioned; one wall was covered with a swastika banner.

The examination, conducted by Volk, lasted for several hours. It centered upon the spending of state monies in the fight against National Socialism. I was to tell where the money had come from, when I had first been occupied with this, and similar things. My answer was truthful: that I had not learned anything of the sources until the accusation was made at the Papen trial before the Supreme Constitutional Court by the Reich government that the Prussian government had spent state monies for party purposes. I had thereupon inquired about the sources and had been told that the money in question came from a fund collected by Reich Finance Minister Dietrich from private contributors for the election of Hindenburg. I had passed on this information in Leipzig to Ministerial Director Gottheiner, counsel for the Reich government, in the presence of the president of the tribunal in camera, and thereafter the accusation had not been pursued further. Prosecutor Volk had me relate the story several times, with many interruptions and questions, in order to catch me out in some contradiction. But he did not succeed. After a few further details I was supposed to sign a summary which he had drawn up. I demanded that a series of alterations be made. When I had signed, he turned to the wall and said: "You may go home."

I walked from the examination room and out of the building as slowly as my patience would allow me, and telephoned Clara from nearby to tell her I was free and intended only to collect our car which had been left at the Ministry of Finance. She begged me to leave the car alone, but I walked along Unter den Linden to the Ministry of Finance, found the car, and was just going to get into it, when two SA men rushed toward me, shouted "Stop," and asked me whether I was Herr Brecht, the Ministerial Director. Ah, I thought, if only I had taken Clara's advice; now I am going to be arrested again. At their request I produced my driver's license. Good, they said, and stepped back. Why did you do this? I asked. They explained that State Secretary Schleusener had instructed them to keep an eye on my car, to avoid its being stolen.

During the next ten weeks we found a heavenly refuge which we seldom left in the spacious official residence of my brother Gustav in Lindenallee, Cologne, with its large garden, swimming pool, and tennis court. I am unable to describe adequately how hospitably he and Norah harbored us for this long period, although it complicated Gustav's own situation to give me shelter. Their eldest son, Walther, who was studying elsewhere, visited us occasionally. The two younger ones, Wolfgang and Christoph, were a constant source of youthful regeneration for all of us.

I wrote two essays on Germany's financial situation, which appeared full-page in two consecutive numbers of *Vossische Zeitung*, on June 13 and 14. This was my last publication in a German paper until the end of the Second World War. At the request of Brüning's Finance Minister, Dr. Dietrich, I also composed the anonymous booklet on the financial policy of the Brüning-Dietrich cabinet, already mentioned in Chapter 56 (end). An essay on Reich reform, sent to the periodical *Reich und Länder,* of which I was co-editor and in which many of my articles had appeared, was returned—the first time I had a manuscript returned. The periodical had been brought "into line."

In the middle of June, I received in Cologne a telegram from the Prussian Finance Ministry with instructions to return to Berlin immediately for the investigation on expenditures for the suppression of National Socialism. The concentration camp was coming near. I obeyed.

The hearing was conducted by a judge in the building of the Finance Ministry. My evidence of the use I had made of the monies drawn consisted mainly of receipts signed by Dr. Foehr. My most vulnerable point was a small item of about 400 reichs-marks, which I had at the request of State Secretary Weismann spent on obtaining and disseminating a letter in which captain Röhm, chief of the Storm Troops, had expressed his homosexual delight in the strapping youths of the Storm Troops. The receipt had been made out by a former National Socialist, who had defected. Röhm was the most powerful man in the party, second only to Hitler, and a disclosure would have exposed me to the revenge of the SA. I was saved by first giving exhaustive verbal informations on each expense in order of magnitude. Only toward the end, when the judge was duly tired, was it the turn of that small item; I referred to it casually, saying that I had a receipt but had promised not to show it to anyone. I was prepared to submit it, if necessary, to the president of the federal audit-office or the Minister of Finance, or to repay the item personally. This statement was recorded, but the matter was never again referred to afterward.

In July we went to the island Wangeroog on the North Sea. After mysterious telegrams, Hans Speier, an academic of about twenty-eight years, came by air from Berlin to visit us. He passed on an invitation extended to me from Dr. Alvin Johnson to join a newly established graduate faculty at the New School for Social Research in New York. I had until then not thought of emigrating, knew little of America, and nothing about the New School for Social Research. After long discussions I delayed answering, but returned to Berlin, where Speier introduced me in the Café Josty at Potsdam Square to Karl Brandt, to whom he had given a similar invitation. I went to the American Ambassador, the historian William Dodd, and inquired about the New School. He received me as though I were still an important person, doubtful as to whether he should recommend that I go to New York. Strangely enough, one of his comments was that it was not possible to say whether there would not be an explosion in America someday, too, and that then it might be even worse than in Germany. This was obviously an over-pessimistic reaction to the great depression. Anyhow, I could not yet make up my mind to leave Germany. I wanted first to finish the struggle for my insulted honor and for the Prussian ministers, in particular Severing, who was in manifest danger.

At the end of July I received a letter from Minister-President Göring, informing me that he intended to dismiss me definitively under curtailment of my pension by one-fourth, as being *national unzuverlässig* (nationally unreliable) in accord with section 4 of the recently issued "Law for the Re-establishment of Professional Government Service." I did not simply accept this action, but protested in a long letter. It seemed the proper thing to me to put down on paper for anyone who read it, why the accusation that my national loyalty was faulty was in blatant contradiction to the clear facts, as I understood national loyalty. I obtained testimonial references from the former president of the Supreme Court, Dr. Walter Simons, from the senior member of the Reichsrat, Herr Boden, Dr. Jarres (rightist candidate for the presidency in 1925), and others, but was dismissed nevertheless as unreliable on August 30.

It became more and more clear that I would be able to live in Germany only in a state of bondage, watched in every move, unable to pursue any profession, to speak frankly, to publish books or articles, or even to meet friends without endangering them, liable any day to be taken off to a concentration camp. I submitted our passports to obtain permission to make a trip to the North Italian lakes. I was ordered to appear at the headquarters of the Gestapo (Secret State Police) in Albrechtstrasse and examined about my travel plans. A few days later we were informed that permission to leave could not be granted. Our passports were withheld.

The loss of our passports began increasingly to annoy us, especially Clara. We were no longer able to leave Germany. I recalled Alvin Johnson's invitation to New York. I sent him a cable, veiled as family news to "Uncle Alvin," saying that I would like to visit him if he still wanted me. He cabled back on October 4, "Come immediately, Uncle Alvin."

But the invitation was not all that was needed. I had to try, with the assistance of my friends in the Foreign Office, to recover our passports and permit to leave. After careful deliberations I wrote to Dr. Johnson that circumstances made it necessary for me to obtain three statements from him before I could leave: namely, that the work involved was not political but purely scientific; that the faculty was not a "university in exile," because I had not been exiled;

and that I would be able to return to Germany at any time after I had fulfilled my academic duties. Johnson understood immediately and sent a cable back on October 26, saying that the work was purely academic, that the term "university in exile" was not an official name, but a description thought up by the press, and that every member was at all times free to go wherever he wanted. On the basis of this letter, the Foreign Office succeeded in obtaining our passports from Göring with a permit to leave, signed not by Göring himself but by his state secretary, Körner.

Ambassador Dodd gave us a visitor's visa. In order to avoid arousing suspicion, we left furniture and everything else that was not necessary for a comparatively short visit behind at home and kept our small apartment in Steglitz.

Immediately before our departure I received a letter from the Gestapo informing me politely that the Secret Police was unable to recommend giving me permission to leave. I answered in an equally polite letter that Minister-President Göring had already given permission for my departure; but I posted the letter so that it would not arrive until the day after we had left. On November 9 we went aboard the Hapag liner "Deutschland" in Cuxhaven. Before stepping onto the gangplank we had to file past two SS men who had every passenger produce his papers and then checked in a thick book to see if the name was on their party's detention list. We were allowed to pass.

Thus, on November 9, 1933, in my fiftieth year, we left Germany on a boat called "Germany." We scattered flowers on the North Sea, a symbol that we would return.

"How long is it going to last in Germany?" the president of Columbia University in New York, Nicholas Murray Butler, asked me when I visited him with a letter of recommendation.

"According to the historical magnitude of things, I am afraid some fifteen years," I answered. "Without war. With war, possibly less."

"Strange," said Butler. "A Chinese philosopher was just sitting in the chair you are sitting in now. I asked him the same question for China. How long will it last? He said that in China something like this usually lasts about two hundred and fifty years."

In Germany it lasted twelve. With war.

# PART XIII

## In the United States
## (Since 1933)

## 95. Role Change in Mid-Life

WHAT I have related so far is the story of the first fifty years of a life which by now has passed eighty. A man's life seldom ends, like that of a hero in classical plays, at the moment of a dramatic climax or nadir, of fulfillment of all plans and hopes or their collapse, or even in a state of lyrical ecstasy. If life lasts long enough, it outgrows lyrics and drama and turns *epos*. The life's Iliad is followed by its Odyssey.

After my departure from Germany I played no active political role, either in the United States or in Germany, apart from occasional political advice offered orally or in writing. Nor have I aspired to such a role, not because there was no opportunity—it would hardly have been difficult for me to return to politics in Germany after the fall of the Hitler regime, and I could possibly have assumed some political function also in America as we shall see presently. But I had committed myself, body and soul, to science, and the proper discharge of this commitment commanded the undivided man. This was incompatible with an active political role. An active politician may have lightning-like scientific insights but cannot elaborate them in a scientifically binding way. Aphorisms are not science. Be that as it may, my abstention from active politics was not, as it had been in my youth, the result of thoughts far removed from politics (see Part I). Rather it was the consequence of my resolution to make the most essential contribution to political thought of which I was capable.

Only once was I seriously tempted to resume an active political role. During tea at the home of Ernst and Marie Luise Spiegelberg, a mutual friend proposed that I should establish a German government-in-exile together with Heinrich Brüning and Max Brauer in order to intensify the resistance against the Hitler regime within Germany and to direct it from afar: Brüning as former Reich Chancellor and representative of the Zentrum, Brauer as representative of the Social Democrats, and I as representative of the German government officials and the Protestant democratic citizenry.

I was startled. While the speaker had no mandate he was a man of some prominence, who had thought through his proposal carefully. I could have answered that I did not feel equal to the task, but I did not want to be guilty of evading responsibility. Hence I gave much thought to the plan, irrespective of personal questions. Yet I decided against it. I was afraid that, even with the list of members changed or supplemented, the formation of a German exile government, rather than uniting all opponents of Hitler, would have split them into friends and foes of the exile government. I also was deeply averse to demanding, from a safe American haven, heroic deeds of martyrdom from those who were exposed to the dreadful reality of brutal terror, and to subject my family to the vengeance that Himmler wreaked on the relatives of anti-Nazis, or to force them to deny me under public protestations of their loyalty to Hitler.

Later I had doubts about the wisdom of my refusal. A German government-in-exile could have become a center for negotiations with the Allied governments during the war and could have tried to persuade them to promise the German people more favorable peace terms in the event of an inner revolt. But originally that had not been the intent of this proposal. Such thoughts cropped up only after Roosevelt's proclamation of the demand for "unconditional surrender" in Casablanca. Many of us, individually, tried thereafter to influence Washington in the aforementioned sense, but to no avail. Perhaps a government-in-exile would have been more successful. But there ought to be no illusions about this matter. Roosevelt's demand for unconditional surrender had a very realistic ground, namely, the fear that with any attempt of the Allies to agree on their peace conditions before final victory, the alliance, especially that with the Soviet government, would fall apart and the victory itself be put in jeopardy (Chapter 98).

The political proposals which I made in memoranda and articles dealt especially with the following questions: world organization and regional organizations; establishment of a European federation; limited-purpose federations; international agreements on minimal protection of persons taken into protective custody or interned in concentration camps; Germany's reunification; establishment of a "security belt" in Europe reaching from Scandinavia through Germany to Turkey; limits of neutrality; the composition of the Security Council in the United Nations, especially the transformation of the permanent Chinese seat into a rotating seat for an East-Asian group, to which India and others should belong; defense of the United States in Europe. In addition there were a great number of papers on the reform of public administration and civil service in the United States and Germany.[1]

Preparation for a European federation brought me together with Count Coudenhove-Kalergi in the United States. We differed on two grounds: first, he envisioned a strictly Continental federation, whereas I deemed it politically wrong and ethically unfair to exclude Great Britain; second, in his enthusiasm, he immediately demanded a tight union, fashioned after the model of Switzerland, whereas I considered this demand utopian and proposed to begin with establishing federal institutions for special functions (which I called "special-purpose federations"), to be supplemented by overall economic agreements and the joint guarantee of basic human rights, only gradually to be developed to a full-type federal government, less close than Switzerland. Such has, in fact, been the trend until today.

My paper on "European Federation" in *Harvard Law Review,* 1942, was to my knowledge the first to mention Strasbourg as center of a European federation.


## 96. Risky Visits to Germany Before the War

Before turning to my experiences in America I shall continue to spin the thread of my German yarn, which never broke.

When I boarded the "Deutschland" on November 9, 1933 in Cuxhaven, I did not mean to stay in America for good. I intended returning to Germany as soon as the situation warranted it.

Even before the war we spent year after year, with only one exception in 1938 (Clara went even then), several weeks or months in Germany during the summer. How was this possible? Was I not *persona non grata* with the Nazis, because I had been co-author of the hated law for the Protection of the Republic, had spent public funds to fight them, had pilloried Nazi atrocities in the Papen trial, had publicly presumed to teach the Führer his duties, and finally

[1] See the listing of papers in the appendix.

had brought charges against him in the Staatsgerichtshof? Under these circumstances our journeys were indeed undertaken at great risk. But my longing to see life behind the curtain with my own eyes and to evaluate the chances of an upheaval from what transpired on the spot was stronger than fear. As a contribution to contemporary history I shall describe how we did it. At the time I could speak about it with no one, for any rash word would have jeopardized our lives and those of others.

We had kept our small house in Berlin-Steglitz with all furniture and had sublet it to a Baltic emigrant lady—secretary of my friend Trendelenburg—on the condition that we could live there during our sojourns in Berlin. In this way we had retained a legal residence in Germany. Regular returns were in accordance with my declaration at the time of my departure that my trips to America were taken only in my capacity as a scholar. I carried with me friendly letters written by the German consul general in New York, Dr. Borchers, and Ambassadors Dr. Luther and later Dieckhoff—all three at the time secretly opposed the Hitler regime, or at least its atrocities. These letters attested the purely scientific character of my own activities and those of our Graduate Faculty and declared that I had stood up against "lies being spread about Germany." This was a highly ambiguous praise, because the principal lies about Germany which I attacked emanated from the Nazis themselves, such as those claiming unanimous support of the German people, those concerning the Jews, and those on German history—loss of the war, revolution and Weimar Republic—a tissue of crude untruths which I constantly fought in my lectures on German history, democracy, and dictatorship.

But I never had to show these documents. Far more important for the success of our trips was the fact that I decided not to timidly evade contact with the German authorities, which only would have led to summons and hearings, but to grab the bull by the horns, or better said, to accustom the authorities to my presence.

When we came back the first time—it was the end of June, 1934—Papen had just delivered his courageous Marburg speech protesting the excesses of the regime. I immediately walked to the Foreign Office, the Ministry of Culture, and several high-ranking personalities as, for example, Hjalmar Schacht, and reported *truthfully* on the general mood in America and—only thinly disguised—on the New School for Social Research. In the Foreign Ministry there were still many officials, especially in the cultural section, who at bottom were as opposed to the totalitarian regime as I was, and who welcomed material from abroad which could serve them to counsel reason and moderation.

During my visit to the Ministry of Culture great commotion indicated that something unusual had happened. Hitler had clamped down on the leaders of his Storm Troops (SA) in Bavaria. Several of the leaders, among them Röhm, chief of staff, had been executed on the spot. When I left the Ministry and got into our small car, which we had taken out of winter storage, I found many streets closed off. I stood sandwiched between hundreds of cars for an hour until I reached Steglitz by many detours. We then drove on the Potsdam road, several times overtaken by SA cars whose occupants scrutinized us, to join Ferdinand Friedensburg and his wife, the Redslobs, and the young Simons in the suburb of Nikolassee. We discussed the news, rumors, and possible consequences. Was this the beginning of a split of the Nazi party? Was it a determined step by Hitler to free himself from the pressure of radical and immoral followers? It was only weeks later that we learned from the Sunday edition of the *New York Times,* which was sent to us regularly, the whole extent of the June 30 murders, and that they had included General von Schleicher and his wife, and an aide of Papen.

Nothing happened to us. Apparently my case was considered closed by the hearings before my departure (Chapter 94) and the granting of a departure visa through Göring's deputy. There were more important things for the Nazis to do than to bother with a liberal official of yesterday, a traveling professor. Ignorance about America prevailed, apart from the Foreign Office, but there also may have been a certain hesitancy to lower the prestige of the Hitler regime in America even farther by taking action against me.

Thus I was able to move freely in Berlin. I talked at length with many opponents of the Nazis, for example, the former president of the Reichstag, Paul Löbe, the former ministers Höpker-Aschoff, Albert, Wissell, Walter Schreiber, Severing, Grimme, the former chairman of the Reichstag's budget committee, Hugo Heimann, the former state secretaries Zweigert and Trendelenburg (who still occupied his official post with the League of Nations), my former colleague in the Reich Chancellery, Wever, now director in the Finance Ministry, and Olscher, chairman of the budget division of the Finance Ministry, Ernst von Harnack and his sister Agnes von

Zahn, also Finance Minister Schwerin von Krosigk and the former President of the Reichsgericht, Walter Simons.

The former State Secretary of Chancellor Schleicher, Erwin Planck, visited us in Steglitz. He declared with sober solemnity that he regretted having supported Papen's and Schleicher's policy against the Prussian government in 1932. He had now realized that human rights can be preserved only by strict and impartial observance of the Constitution. Ten years later he was hanged as a member of the resistance against Hitler, after courageously enduring tortures without betraying his collaborators.

There was no lack of tragicomic situations. I once boldly entered the building of the Prussian State Ministry to deliver a letter in which I requested a retrial. The doorman, still the old one, rushed from his basement door and asked surprised: "How is old Braun?" At this moment Göring and his entourage were coming down the staircase without recognizing me. When I got into my car, which I had parked in front of the Foreign Office, an SA man dashed toward the car and tore the door open. But all he said was, "Please, give me your BZ (the Berlin midday paper), comrade; I can't leave my post." I gave it to him.

We soon left Berlin in our inconspicuous car, which brought us across Germany toward the south, to Mittelberg, a tiny Austrian enclave in the region of Allgaeu. There we learned about the resignation of Papen from the Hitler Cabinet, the assassination of Dollfuss in Vienna, and the death of Hindenburg, and later, in Walchensee in Bavaria, the results of the plebiscite on the combination of the offices of President and Chancellor. There we met General Groener with his young second wife and the young son of this marriage of which Hindenburg had disapproved. At the Starnberg Lake we visited Mr. and Mrs. Andreae, Rathenau's sister, and Germany's last democratic ambassador to Washington, von Prittwitz. In Heidelberg we were guests of Professor Gustav Radbruch, who had already been dismissed from his university chair, and of Gerhard Anschütz, leading commentator of the Weimar Constitution—evenings of penetrating analyses.

Although we had not been allowed to take German money with us to the United States (except ten reichs-marks), we could use it for crossing on German ships and for expenses during our stay in Germany.

Every time we got back to the United States safely. But on

the pier we had to pass the two SS men each time—always a tension-ridden moment.

## 97. The Death of Gertrud and Ossip (July, 1939)

In July, 1936 we were present at the wedding of my younger brother Rolf with Vera Donner in the home of the bride's parents in Frankfurt. Brothers and sisters from both sides were present, including Gertrud and Ossip. On the wedding eve there were the traditional performances and I sang a couplet which I had written and put to music. It contained a stanza which was clearly directed against Goebbels. "Arnold," Ossip said in a low voice but so that everyone could hear it, "think of the presence of the waiters!" Up to then the conditions of Jews who had enough money to live had remained relatively tolerable in Berlin. But during our joint trip back —this time by train—from Frankfurt to Berlin I not only noticed Ossip's nervous restlessness, which Gertrud tried to calm down, but also that our fellow-travelers recognized the artist as being Jewish and took notice of it without, however, any apparent animosity. Jewish passengers had become a rarity. Ossip, who had been accustomed to be welcomed and loved everywhere, who made friends at first glance with the young and the old, nature's true child, an artist in his every nerve, flooded with music, communicating with people and things either intimately or not at all, was helpless in this change of atmosphere that surrounded him.

It was not until the fall of 1938, though, the only year before the war I did not go to Germany, that the situation for the Jews in Berlin deteriorated to the point of becoming unbearable. Large numbers of Jews were sent to concentration camps in reprisal for the assassination of a German Foreign Service official by a young Jew in Paris. Decrees imposed humiliating, even outright sadistic, measures upon Jews: they had to add "Israel" or "Sarah" to their first names, to wear a star of David visible to all, and they were not allowed to sit on public benches in the parks, only on benches specially designated for Jews. One could only shudder over such an excess of human meanness. Most of my Jewish aquaintances had left Germany before or were doing so now, often sacrificing large amounts

.

of money in order to buy their travel permit. The fate of Gertrud and Ossip also was becoming more desperate. Because of his advanced age, and because of the general esteem and affection he had enjoyed as artist and human being, because of his German wife, who cared for him tenderly, and Gustav's protection and support, they had not yet given serious thought to emigration. They sought and found refuge in the realms of music and poetry, which was their real home, in their close contact with relatives and friends, and in nature. But even this had lost its blessing for them. "Nature doesn't speak to me anymore," said Ossip.

They sat for hours in front of their radio, using ear phones to avoid the attention of their neighbors, anxiously waiting for news about further measures against the Jews. They panicked every time the door bell rang. Was it the SA? Had they come for Ossip?

Before we had realized the full dimension of this new situation, we left at the beginning of February, 1939 for our long planned tour through the United States (Chapter 100). In June, after that trip's completion, we intended to go to Germany and make plans with Gertrud and Ossip. In my mind's eye I saw her seated at the grand piano, playing my favorite Chopin polonaise, when I would clandestinely enter behind her and stroke her full blond hair. During our short stay in New York I obtained from a distant relative of Ossip's the promise of an affidavit for him and Gertrud. Because the immigration quota was filled, this could only lead to permission to immigrate after four years, but in the meantime it could serve as a basis for interim immigration to Denmark or for a preliminary visitor's permit to America. When our boat approached Le Havre I was about to mail a letter to Gertrud and Ossip starting with the words "We have the affidavit!" But I took the letter back and replaced it with some furtive greetings because I was aware of their fear the German censor would use any allusion to their emigration for measures against them. Therefore I wanted to bring them the good news personally.

This postponement had tragic consequences. In Cologne, where, as usual, we first spent one or two days with Gustav and Norah (during which we listened to Radio London and Moscow, forbidden under highest penalty) a phone call from our sister Edith in Berlin informed us that Gertrud and Ossip had gone to a hotel near the Anhalt Station the preceding night under assumed names and had tried to commit suicide by taking an overdose of sleeping pills.

Our nephew Max-Walther Richter had brought them to a hospital in the north of Berlin, in a state of unconsciousness.

When we arrived by night train, Ossip was dead. Gertrud lived for three more days. Although she never regained consciousness I was convinced that she experienced, as in a dream, what was going on around her, and understood what was spoken, but was not able actively to give a sign or form words. (In New York the victim of an accident who was restored to life after a similar coma had impressed me with that story unforgettably.) So I talked to her words of love, of repentance, of comfort, of tenderness. She gave signs of being startled a few hours before her death when dishes fell on a neighboring balcony and shattered noisily. We reassured her. Then her face was suffused with complete calm and looked like that of a Gothic saint.

From her letters of farewell, written in the hotel room when Ossip was asleep—one for each of us—we gathered that his nerves had not been able to withstand the constant humiliations and anxieties and that therefore he had ever more urgently wanted to do away with life. She was resolved to die with him in order to make it easier for him. On his desk he had left a book of memoirs on Tolstoy, opened to the page where it was described how Tolstoy made a day-long trip on foot in foul weather in order to take back an article he had sent to a newspaper with passionate condemnation of an anti-Semite, because he realized that the man had not acted out of meanness but out of stupidity and ignorance.

This was the deepest personal grief of my life, which has never left me.

Because of the danger of war we left for New York earlier than planned, on August 8, 1939 on board the "Bremen," one of the two big 50,000-ton liners of the North German Lloyd, the penultimate passenger trip of the boat. On its next trip, war broke out while she was in New York and she had to make an adventurous journey by way of the Polar Circle to Norway in order to escape being captured.

## 98. The United States and Germany:
## During the War and Shortly After

The war interrupted our visits to Germany for nine years. I kept my German citizenship, hoping for a *coup d'etat* planned by the military of which I had heard in Germany. But when the coup failed to materialize and when Hitler in 1940 subjugated almost the whole western part of the continent without yet having repeated the decisive Napoleonic blunder of attacking Russia (June 22, 1941), we asked for our first papers in the beginning of 1941. When the United States entered the war, we kept our case pending because our hopes for the collapse of the totalitarian regime in Germany began to rise again, nor did I want to appear to change citizenship out of sheer opportunism during the war.

Half-German, half-American—but in truth not two half persons but a complete man, who inseparably belonged to both worlds—I had a natural function now, which required strict self-discipline. I had to help, despite all excitements, to find the truth, to spread it, to adhere to it. What was the truth about the Germans? The fallacy soon spread that the courage and unity of the German people in the war was a sign of their universal support of the Nazi regime. Time and again I had to point out that the Germans were in a position almost without a way out, between the devil and the deep blue sea. Defeat meant mutilation, if not the end of Germany. Victory meant consolidation of the Nazi regime. Trying to overthrow the government from within during the war meant bloody civil strife and loss of the war with all its consequences. Therefore one could not deduce from their unity in fighting the war that all Germans supported the regime.

Every month a famous psychologist in Boston, in the interest of authorities in Washington, tried to measure the internal resistance of the Germans against the Hitler regime by sending to all real or alleged experts on Germany a drawing of a thermometer scale with 100 degrees. They were asked to mark the height of the mercury which indicated to what degree the German people supported the

Nazi regime. I protested against questionnaires of this type and suggested that *two* thermometer scales should be used rather than one. One scale would serve to mark the degree of the people's determination not to lose the war, the other their degree of support for the National Socialist regime (Hitler, Goebbels, totalitarianism, etc.). The answers, then, would have indicated an ever-lower mercury level in the second, but a very high level, dropping only slowly, in the first.

The logical consequence would have been to offer more favorable peace terms to the Germans in the event of an overthrow of the totalitarian regime from within. Unfortunately, three circumstances stood in the way of this strategic move: first, the failure to distinguish between the determination to ward off defeat and internal support of the regime; second, that an overthrow of the regime was conceivable only under the guidance of the German military, and the United States was as little disposed to tolerate German militarism as totalitarianism; and, third, the formula "unconditional surrender" had, as mentioned before, the advantage of sparing the Allies disputes over war aims in the middle of the war, which could easily have led to a falling out between the Allies, especially between the West and Russia, and Russia's support was needed for a victory over Germany.

My book *Prelude to Silence,* published in March, 1944 (Oxford University Press, New York) [1] tried to correct errors about the history of the Weimar Republic and the rise of the National Socialists. The book received very favorable reviews in all academic journals, in the *New York Times* (Dr. George Shuster), and in the *London Times.* A part of the daily press, on the other hand, and also some officials in Washington criticized it as too favorable to Germany. It was only two or three years after the end of the war that its presentation found general recognition in Washington and the U.S. military government in Germany.

Five of my articles on legal philosophy (*Relative and Absolute Justice, The Rise of Relativism, The Search for Absolutes, The Myth of Is and Ought* and *The Impossible in Political and Legal Philosophy*) appeared between 1939 and 1941, the first three in *Social Research* and the last two in the *Harvard Law Review* and the *California Law Review.* Along with another article, "The Latent Place of God in 20th Century Political Theory," they were

[1] Reprint edition, 1968, Fertig, New York.

later published in book form on the initiative of my students under the title *The Political Philosophy of Arnold Brecht.*[2] The key emphasis of these essays was the importance of truth as an absolute, basic element of justice. See also my "Political Theory," part IV, and, below, Chapter 101.

Other articles, written at that time, warned against the tendency of seeing all salvation in democracy. Democracy was bound to fail if the majority of the population was anti-democratic in its orientation (Chapter 30). Again, others tried to formulate international minimum guarantees of respect for human dignity as protection from brutal state violence in future.

Another book, *Federalism and Regionalism in Germany—The Division of Prussia,* which appeared the day of the German surrender in 1945 (Oxford University Press, New York), described, in a current comparison with the United States, the struggle between centralizing and decentralizing ideas in Germany in the twentieth century. It recommended that the victors supplant dangerous plans for dividing Germany by more rational plans for dividing Prussia.

In addition, I had a varied lecture program outside my faculty. I gave instruction courses on Germany to soldiers and later also to officers, organized by the United States government at Harvard, Yale, City College in New York, and other colleges. This activity compelled me to spend five hours traveling by train to Harvard weekly, and two hours to Yale. Since I also had to give my regular lectures, it was not unusual for me to speak for six hours on any given day, always on different matters. I was also involved in the reform of public administration in the United States, especially at departmental headquarters (Chapter 100), and in research at the Institute for World Affairs, associated with the New School and headed by my colleagues Staudinger and Lowe.

The upshot was a breakdown through overwork. A puncture of the spine showed a slight admixture of blood in the liquid of the vertebra, a serious medical indication. I was brought to Mount Sinai Hospital, where the distinguished brain specialist, Dr. Joseph Globus, diagnosed it as "subarrachnoyic bleeding," a kind of meningitis. I spent four weeks in the hospital, following which I was ordered to stay absolutely quiet for six months. For a long time it was doubtful whether I would survive and, in any event, it appeared improbable that I would be able to take on a big work load

[2] Ed. by Morris Forkosch, New York, 1954.

again. Nevertheless in the fall I was able to resume lecturing in my faculty, and I gradually regained much of my strength.

In 1942 the press announced the destruction of Lübeck by English bombers in the first terror attack not directed against military targets. Almost all the old churches had been destroyed. Brüning, who in the meantime had moved from London to Harvard, sent me a large aerial photo of Lübeck from an English newspaper, which had been taken after the destruction. I sat for hours bent over the picture with a magnifying glass and tried to make out what was still there, but I was unable to read the vertical picture. Thenceforth I was haunted by dreams in which I found myself somewhere in Lübeck, when suddenly it occurred to me that now I could go out to see the extent of the destruction. I would look and see the town in distorted form, with completely alien elements, and I would wake up in sweat. This dream often recurred with slight variations.

On July 20, 1944, exactly twelve years to the day after Papen's coup d'état against Prussia (and not unrelated to it causally), we got the news of the uprising against Hitler and its failure—one of the greatest tragedies in history. We took part in it as if we had been on the spot, full of admiration and thankfulness for the heroic courage of the participants, deeply shaken by their failure and personal fate, which involved many of our personal friends and acquaintances.

After Germany's surrender it took a long time before we received news from our relatives. The first came in August, 1945 from daughter Irmgard. We had not learned anything yet about brother Gustav. Only after a personal letter to General Patton, in which I requested an investigation as to whether my brother had perhaps fled to Bad Wiessee in Bavaria, where he owned a summer house, did we get a positive answer signed personally by the general. As regards Rolf we learned that he was critically wounded and that his house in Koblenz had been destroyed.

In 1946 we went through the final steps of acquiring United States citizenship. My illness had weakened me to such a degree that the doctors declared I was not in a condition to settle in Germany and to be reintegrated there. Berlin, my old field of activity, was divided. My work in America and the friends we had made there, especially in the Graduate Faculty, had bound us closely to the United States. I felt more at home in New York than in any German city outside Berlin.

I sorrowfully realized the backwardness of earthly conditions which do not take into consideration the creative reality that one can be at home in two nations, and which allot him to only one. But I decided not to let the burden of decision break me down.

My call to Germany as adviser to the Occupation authorities—at the request of General Clay—was still hindered by my weakened health. The U.S. Military Government did, however, arrange for a German edition of my *Prelude to Silence*. At the same time the British Military Government bought the translation rights to my *Federalism and Regionalism in Germany—The Division of Prussia.*

After two more years, to the surprise of the doctors, I gained my strength almost in full—under strict abstinence from alcohol and tobacco. The desire to see Germany again grew. In 1947 it seemed near fulfillment when the Senate of the City of Hamburg, at the suggestion of its mayor, Max Brauer, appointed me by formal decision "on condition of my acceptance" as Hamburg's representative to the bizonal government in Frankfurt. They generously stuck to this decision even when I pointed out that I was an American citizen. The State Department, however, advised me not to accept because it feared conflicts would arise from the work of an American as German representative.

## 99. Postwar Problems—Germany's Reunification

So it was that I did not go back to Germany until spring 1948. At that time I was nominated "Expert to the Secretary of the Army" in Washington and American member of an international group of five scholars who were to study the federal reorganization of Germany and to discuss it with appropriate Germans in the U.S. Occupation Zone. The other four in the group were the French Professor Lazare Kopelmanas of the *Centre national de la recherche scientifique* in Paris; the Australian Professor Zellman Cowen, who lectured at the time at Oxford University in England; Professor H. L. Beales, Economist at London University; and Donald Grant of the University of Edinburgh.

Deeply moved, I set foot on European soil for the first time again in Cherbourg, and drove through destroyed Normandy to Paris and from there to Frankfurt. In the Frankfurt headquarters of the United States Military Government the staff of the "Governmental Structures Branch," headed by Hans Simons, had ably prepared the grounds for the talks. Day after day we met the most varied German spokesmen, among them members of the *Laender* governments and diets in Hessen (Wiebaden), Wurttemberg (Stuttgart) and Bavaria (Munich), representatives of the universities of Frankfurt (where Professor Hallstein was the Rector at that time) and Heidelberg (Radbruch, Walter Jellinek, Alexander Rüstow, Alfred Weber, and others). We also met with the trade unions and naturally with the leading officials of the bizonal government, especially Hermann Pünder and Ludwig Erhard.

In Stuttgart I saw Hermann Dietrich, Brüning's Finance Minister, again, and also Theodor Heuss, who had turned very thin. At an official luncheon, offered by the U.S. Commissioner, I singled out Heuss to give us the benefit of his views on the federal issue, therewith renewing our old-time friendship. We also met with the minister-presidents of the *Laender* in the British zone. Then I took part in the international summer university in Munich and was present when the Parliamentary Council opened in Bonn. Here I saw Konrad Adenauer, Hermann Höpker-Aschoff, Paul Löbe, and many others again.

During the negotiations on the German federal structure, I made use of my familiarity with pre-Hitler work for Reich reform. In my recommendations I was not hindered, as formerly, by the consideration that constitutional reform of the Reich was possible only with the consent of Prussia. For Prussia no longer existed. Instead I had to take into account that the new structure had to have the consent of the Allies, who were pressing for a federal structure and would not tolerate such a strong centralization of powers as the Reform Committee had recommended in 1930 (Chapter 61). It was too late for this now. The United States government had not given me any instructions. Indeed, I worked in complete freedom from official agencies. But I knew what the bells had tolled and tried to save what there was to save.

My French colleague, the bright Professor Kopelmanas (we called him "Kopel" because "two syllables are enough," said our Australian friend) tried to persuade the Germans to break Germany up into autonomous states. This, of course, brought him into conflict not only with me but naturally also with our German partners in the discussion. "If it is so wonderful for a nation to be broken up into autonomous states," said Alfred Weber, "why do you not give us an example in France?" Compassionately, I referred my colleague to later discussions in Bavaria, where at that time there existed a strong tendency toward state independence to be gained by transforming Germany from a federal state into a federation of states. However, separatist recommendations were rejected, with no less firmness than in Heidelberg and Stuttgart, also in Munich at a big evening session with members of the Bavarian parliament. Professor Kopelmanas realized the hopelessness of his efforts. He had no doubt kept his government constantly informed so that this experiment in futility was of indirect value. No one on the western side ever again brought up division of Germany into autonomous states.

Our common report pointed basically toward a federal Germany. I was able to keep the door open for sufficient federal power in police and financial matters. I gave a detailed special report[1] and, in addition, prepared a compilation of the most important reform proposals made by Germans, which was distributed at the opening session of the Parliamentary Council.

The next year (1949) we were not able to travel because Clara had to undergo a grave stomach operation. Miraculously, she was spared from relapses, and also recovered from the serious consequences of a train accident on Thanksgiving Day in November, 1951. Apart from these two years we have been in Germany every year since 1948.

In 1950 I visited Lübeck. I finally saw the picture of the destruction which had so often appeared in my confused dreams, in its full reality. Many buildings were still undestroyed. My glance gratefully went over each stone which was still standing. The house of my childhood, Moislinger Allee 22, also was still intact with its quadrangle tower. The same iron garden gate led over worn tiles to the entrance door, the lock of which I could open now, as formerly, with a simple nail. Inside I found all the well-known corners and niches, bubble-creating faucets, banisters on which one could glide down, brass handles at the balcony door in which one could see his nose reflected as in a distorting mirror, and in the garden the same

[1] Rendered in full in the German ed., vol. II, pp. 464 ff.

wooden fence. The old linden tree had been cut; it served as fire-wood. The present owner, a doctor, did not know that a family named Brecht had ever lived in the house.

On Easter Sunday, in a side chapel of the gravely destroyed St. Mary's Church, we participated with great emotion in the communion service. I had received communion for the first time in this church in 1899. In the old city hall the new mayor, unknown to me, recognized me from my speech on Constitution Day, 1928 and gave us official souvenirs of the old patrician city.

We also saw Berlin again that year. We found our house in Steglitz undestroyed, occupied by responsible refugees. The fine pastel painting by Rathenau, which his sister had given to me, had disappeared from the dining room and no one confessed knowledge of how and when it disappeared (all other paintings were still there). The Russians had taken my camera and probably also my clarinet; my old suits had served as camouflage for youngsters from the SA. Otherwise, everything was still there, while the apartments of my brothers and sisters who had remained in Germany had been destroyed by bombs. Mayor Reuter and Friedensburg, at that time his deputy, invited me for lunch with the Senate.

Stationed in Frankfurt, I worked that year on the reform of the German Civil Service as adviser to the U.S. Office of Military Government. At a December conference in near-by Weinheim I gave two reports, one on the U.S. Civil Service, the other on the future German Civil Service Law.

In Bonn I had a discussion with Chancellor Adenauer on the question of a coalition between his party of Christian Democrats and the Social Democrats, if not in the federal government, at least in the largest *Land,* North Rhine Westphalia, where at that time a new government was to be formed. He flatly rejected such a coalition as being alien to the spirit of parliamentarism, which required a separation of government and opposition, he said. The second topic of our conversation was my proposal of a mutual withdrawal of foreign troops, kilometer by kilometer, from the center of Germany, without an obligation to neutrality imposed on Germany herself (see below). This idea, too, he rejected decidedly, because the Soviet Union could not be trusted. But he had no plausible alternative to offer.

Every year I also visited the first postwar leader of the Social Democrats, Kurt Schumacher, whom I had known as a young member in the old Reichstag. I admired his exemplary conquest of physical handicaps—he had lost a leg and an arm—by the power of the spirit, and the consistent way he had led his party so that Communism did not take the workers away from it although he liberated the party of out-dated Marxist maxims. In the new Germany he missed what he called "Geist." The "Geist" is missing, he said, stressing the slowly spoken word "Geist." [2]

A few weeks before his death I had a last two-hour conversation with him in his garden on the Venusberg in Bonn. He was brought on a stretcher to our garden table. While he sipped one cup of black coffee after the other, we talked about all major political problems. I said that from New York one could admire Adenauer and him— the two great antagonists—at the same time. I have indeed always regretted that Adenauer never found a human path to this man who suffered so much physically. The essential part of our talk revolved not around politics, however, but around death, science, and faith. He did not fear death, he said; rather, he feared what would come before. I told him that it had been important to me to realize that, although science could make no statement on whether or not there was a God, it could say one thing quite definitely: the anxiety, so fashionable in our day, that after death one stands before nothingness is unfounded. We shall either stand before God or we shall not stand at all; we shall not stand before nothing. Upon taking leave from each other, he said to me in a heart-warming way that our talk had done him much good. He died a month later, peacefully and without agony.

Every year we were guests of President Heuss in Bonn. Once he also visited us in Heidelberg. On that occasion I asked him whether he was satisfied with the regulation of the office of president in the Basic Law or whether, after his experiences, he would prefer a different delineation of presidential rights. He answered that he would wish the president granted somewhat greater rights; in relation to the Cabinet, for example, that important sessions could be held under the chairmanship of the president. I warned him that under a parliamentary system of government, as soon as the President had any kind of substantive rights, a tug of war unavoidably resulted over limiting or extending the exercise of these rights. Only when he had no powers could he dedicate himself wholly to the task of being purely and spiritually a leader and representative of the Ger-

[2] The German word *Geist* denotes mind, spirit, *esprit*, idea, all in one.

man people, as indeed Heuss had so exemplarily become. I also urged him not to seek or allow an anti-constitutional extension of his period of office. We exchanged letters regularly on our birthdays.

In 1950 I delivered three lectures in the old *aula* of Heidelberg University on "Misunderstandings of the German Constitution in America and of the United States Constitution in Germany." From 1952 to 1957, I was a guest professor in Heidelberg at every summer semester, with lectures and seminars on comparative constitutional history and political theory. I was successful in persuading the university to establish a chair for political science and later cooperated in arranging for Professor Carl J. Friedrich of Harvard to occupy this chair for one semester each year.

Our summers in Heidelberg were marked by a lively exchange of thoughts with Alexander Rüstow, Alfred Weber, and many others, greatly enriching our lives. In the summer of 1957, at the invitation of the juridical faculty, I gave three lectures on "reunification" published by Nymphenburger Verlag in München (see below).

The highlight of our European trip year after year was a stay of one week or more with Gustav and Norah at their house in Bad Wiessee near München, until Gustav, eighty-five years old, youthful to the last, passed away unexpectedly after a brief illness in October, 1965. We had seen each other last at a performance of Wagner's "Tristan" in München in July, sixty-two years after our first joint attendance at a performance of the same opera in Berlin.

In 1953, the Adenauer Cabinet promoted me *ex post* to the position of a retired state secretary because, but for the illegal interference of the Nazi regime, I would have reached that position in 1933 (Chapter 83). In 1959, at the age of seventy-five, President Heuss presented me, along with my colleagues Staudinger and Simons, with the Great Cross of Merit. In 1964, at eighty, the New School for Social Research conferred the honorary degree of Doctor of Letters on me. President Lübke, Chancellor Erhard, ex-Chancellor Adenauer, and Foreign Minister Schroeder honored me with congratulatory cables. Heuss had died a few weeks before. President Heinemann added the Star to the Cross of Merit in 1970.

On Germany's reunification I have consistently pursued an entirely unorthodox basic idea, which has found little grace either in Bonn or in Washington. If I mention it here I do so not as a politician who wants to put across his political will, but in order to include a relevant item in my autobiography.

From the beginning of the occupation of Germany by the four powers—and also in 1948 when I saw Germany again for the first time—I asked Germans and Americans: "What would you think if after the restoration of order in Germany the major powers agreed that foreign troops (especially those of the Western allies and the Soviets) on both sides were to be withdrawn step by step the same number of kilometers, with the understanding that if one of the parties again moved forward, the other could do likewise, even if the party that moved forward first should assert that it had been invited by the German government?" To this very day I believe that this would have been the best pre-condition for a reunification, and that it still is. Although this was, as I have just said, an entirely unorthodox political line, no one prevented me from pursuing it and justifying it scientifically as an alternative, as I did in the little book *Wiedervereinigung* in 1957, to which I must refer here for details, especially the important question of neutrality.

This solution presupposes, though, that a sufficiently strong defense line is to remain west of the Rhine with American help, in order effectively to meet through counter-attacks any forward push of the Soviet Union or her allies into the security belt cleared of foreign troops. If France rejected such an organization, the plan would collapse unless the Western powers declared beforehand that they would answer any serious attack on the belt immediately with the use of atomic weapons or, in the course of time, a relationship of mutual trust could be successfully established with the Soviets in this respect. This was to be the ultimate aim. Be that as it may, negotiations between West and East over the withdrawal or thinning-down of foreign troops remain meaningful so long as they are conducted with the immediate aim that no side is to gain military advantages.

Negotiations—and that means negotiations on *acceptable* proposals—are the only way to make progress in the German question. The widespread fear of negotiations rests, I believe, on an inferiority complex, culminating in the secret fear that we (the West, especially Germany) will be tricked during negotiations. This unworthy anxiety overlooks the strong arguments available to us, which the enemy has every reason to fear—the rejection of a form of government in which there is no guarantee against cruel misuse of power. Our superiority is the greater because we are not bound by a fallacious doctrine such as the so-called scientific Marxism in the Bolshevik interpretation, and can offer nations the great blessing of freedom.

The readiness for talks should not limit itself to Moscow, but extend to Pankow. It should be based on a proclamation, formulated with extreme precision, of about the following substance:

(1) At the time being in those parts of Germany whose occupation the Allies reserved to the Soviet Union, the Communist group existing there actually exercises governmental power—directly or through the SED (Socialist Unity Party).

(2) According to our information this Communist group represents only a tiny minority of the population. Its rule also is approved only by a tiny minority. Therefore, according to our concepts of the nature of democracy, its rule is not legitimate.

(3) We are prepared to establish contacts with the actually ruling group in the interest of the whole population in any appropriate manner either on individual issues or through permanent representatives without, however, thereby in the least recognizing the legitimacy of this group. Rather, we demand the establishment of a legitimate regime through free elections.

I know well that such thoughts are viewed as either heretical or naïve. But I have neither heard nor found any better ones. They are based upon the awareness that in all probability the Soviet Union will not voluntarily give up the Soviet Zone in Germany and that an overthrow of Communism in favor of free enterprise and civil rights in either the Soviet Union or in the Soviet Zone in Germany is not to be expected. But we can expect practical modifications. Whoever bases his country's policy in a vital question on the expectation of an event not wholly impossible but extremely improbable —such as the overthrow of Communism in the Soviet Union or the voluntary abandonment of the zone by the Soviet Union—acts like a gambler who stakes his whole fortune on the expectation that when the dice are cast the two sixes will be up. This is not impossible, but very improbable. Ulbricht may be removed, as Stalin and Khrushchev have been removed, but his successor will again be a Communist, as the successors of Stalin and Khrushchev have been, and at best a Gomulka or Tito.

Nor should it be considered taboo that permanent representatives —for example, state secretaries—would be exchanged between Bonn and Pankow. Other countries could be left free—through an appropriate modification of the Hallstein Doctrine—to exchange envoys on condition that they refuse to recognize the *legitimacy* of the Pankow government.

If we want to be free of barbed wire, mines, walls, and guard towers between East and West Germany, we must clearly realize that a Communist regime *cannot* allow full freedom of opinion and emigration, without digging its own grave or calling into question its own successful development. Therefore we must learn to think with awareness of Communist headaches and come up with practical proposals that open a way for a Communist-ruled country to give up or modify the brutal measures against border crossing—measures which in fact are highly embarrassing for the Communist regimes themselves—without endangering them. Probably the answer is that the more living conditions improve economically and ideally, the more will the inhabitants of Communist-ruled countries be willing to remain there voluntarily, and the sooner travel prohibitions will be relaxed.

Other subject matters for negotiations are: formation of mixed commissions of Germans from both parts for clarification of common problems; formation of a mixed parliament with functions that will be small at first, but constantly extended; establishment of joint courts for the protection of minimal standards of human rights and human dignity (see my proposals in the aforementioned book *Wiedervereinigung*).

All this is based on the presupposition that we shall continue to contest, in the most vigorous manner, the *legitimacy* of the zonal government as the proper representative of the population ruled by it; that we shall continue to pillory this shortcoming and demand its removal by the introduction of free elections; and that we shall insist on reunification, whereby we can offer concessions for the protection of the socialist measures carried out and enter into other commitments.

I have, in the matter of reunification, nothing better to offer than these thoughts.

## 100. Personal Experiences in the United States

Since that first arrival in November, 1933, we have now been living in the United States for thirty-six years, half as long again as previously in Berlin and, indeed, eight years longer than the total time I had spent in government service in Germany, from the beginning of my in-service training (1905) up until my dismissal under Hitler. These thirty-six years represent about one-fifth of the history of the United States since its founding. Crossing the Atlantic has become a routine experience for us. We have done it almost fifty times, always by sea, since I am under medical instructions not to fly.

In November, 1933, however, we were traveling to America *for the first time,* and this is something very different from repeated visits. Anyone coming for the first time is his own Columbus; he discovers America.

During the passage I had little time to concern myself with America, however. From early morning until late at night (including the twenty-fifth hour one gains every day on the west-bound voyage) I was busy preparing lectures in English on public finance, public administration, comparative constitutions, history of political institutions, and jurisprudence.

But with my inner eye I saw America. At first the whole of the two continents. The nearer we came, the narrower became the goal. Soon it was only North America, then just the United States, the east coast, New York, and, finally a certain pier on the west side of Manhattan in the Hudson.

Walther Becker, the oldest son of the former Prussian Minister of Education, who had died in February, was traveling on the same boat to New York, in order to collect his bride, daughter of the New York manager of the North German Lloyd, Hans Schroeder (see below).

After many days of flat horizon, there finally emerged the vertical towers on the southern point of Manhattan, like a giant's toy castle —a miracle of magnificent beauty, especially on a November evening like ours, when the golden lights from a thousand windows gleam clear and clean, and the early dusk still allows a glimpse of the whole.

The Statue of Liberty welcomed us with the joyful gesture of her torch, a moving greeting for anyone who is fleeing from dictatorship to America. His eyes grow moist. Whatever else may lie in wait for us, there will at least be freedom. Germany, I thought, when will a statue of liberty greet foreigners and returning Germans coming to you? When, oh when?

At that moment the Captain called from the bridge: "Hold tight!" The "Deutschland" sailed right into a freighter crossing the harbor at right angles to her own course and tore a big hole in its side. It first listed and then slowly sank. The bow of the "Deutschland" was bent. The other boat refused assistance and succeeded in reaching the shore under its own power. Since we had an American pilot on board, there arose no question of the captain's being to blame.

We sailed up the Hudson River and docked at a pier on the west side of Manhattan, surrounded by journalists, as were the prominent passengers of every major liner arriving at that time, when there was no other way of coming than by boat. Karl Brandt of the faculty awaited us. He had our entire baggage, including two heavy crates of books, stowed into a single taxi, which took us in ten minutes from our pier across Manhattan, across Fifth Avenue, Madison, and Park Avenues to our hotel on Lexington Avenue, the Shelton Hotel, where Clara refused to move into the sixth floor and demanded instead the thirty-second. There we spent our first night, looking at the tops of other skyscrapers, like peaks in the high mountains. The Empire State Building rose in front of us like the Matterhorn seen from the Breithorn. Our own tower seemed to sway, probably a projection of the heavy swaying motion of the ship.

It was cold and bare in New York. In the preceding nights storms had torn the last leaves from the trees. But our German friends enthused about the wonderful Indian summer of the previous weeks.

Three days after, on November 22, I participated for the first time at a meeting of the Graduate Faculty in the building of the New School for Social Research, 66 West Twelfth Street. Max Ascoli was also present for the first time. We were the tenth and eleventh members. The others were Emil Lederer of the University of Berlin, formerly Heidelberg, our first dean; Arthur Feiler of the University of Königsberg, formerly business editor of the *Frankfurter Zeitung;* Gerhard Colm of the Institute of Economics in the University of Kiel; Max Wertheimer, the creator of *Gestalt*-Psychology, of the University of Frankfurt; Eduard Heimann, economist and sociologist from the University of Hamburg; Frieda Wunderlich, sociologist, former member of the Prussian parliament; Karl Brandt and Hans Speier, already mentioned. Professor von Hornbostel, sociologist of music, was hospitalized and died before taking up his new functions.

Lederer, Feiler, Wertheimer, Wunderlich, Heimann, and Colm have also passed away since. Brandt, Speier, Ascoli found other spheres of important activity in the United States. Of the crop of 1933, I am now the only living emeritus member.

But many others have joined us in the meantime, among them my old Berlin comrades Hans Staudinger and Hans Simons (who was later to become president of the New School for ten years); the sociologists Albert Salomon (d.), Carl Mayer, and Julie Meyer; the economists Alfred Kahler, Adolf Lowe, Hans Neisser, Jakob Marschak (temporarily); the philosophers Kurt Riezler (d.), Leo Strauss (temporarily), Alfred Schütz (d.), Hans Jonas, Aron Gurwitsch, Werner Marx (now in Freiburg), Hannah Arendt; and for a short time also the lawyer Rudolf Littauer. In 1938 several Austrians joined us, the philosopher and logician Felix Kaufmann; Dr. Schüller, specialist on international trade treaties; and Erich Hula, professor of public and international law, soon a particularly close friend. From Italy, as well as Ascoli, came the historian Salvemini (temporarily); the sociologist Nino Levi, who was killed when thrown by his horse onto hard concrete; and Alexander Pekelis, political scientist and lawyer. Pekelis was the one among us who had "fled most": in 1919 he fled from Bolshevist Russia to Berlin, in 1933 from National Socialism on to Vienna, then to Italy (where he married a beautiful and intelligent Italian girl), then with his Russian mother and Italian mother-in-law (who were able to communicate with each other only in French) to Paris, then to England, and finally to New York, where he studied American law at Columbia University for two years, became the editor of its *Law Review,* and then—still young—was killed in airplane accident in Shannon (Ireland).

There were also two Spaniards, the profound humanist, Fernando de los Rios, formerly Spanish Minister of Education and Republican Ambassador in Washington, and Luis Recasens-Siches, sociologist, now in Mexico. American-born scholars soon began to enter the faculty, beginning with Horace Kallen, the philosopher. Today they far exceed in number the immigrants in a faculty that has grown to more than forty active members. But the tradition has been maintained. A *Volkswagen* Foundation endowment for a Theodor Heuss chair, made in 1964, ensures that each year a German guest professor joins the faculty.

When we ten or eleven began to work in the fall of 1933 we had, apart from the lecture rooms and one general office, no rooms at our disposal. The cloakroom served as a meeting ground among the professors and between them and their students. It was adventurous and wonderful, for what mattered was spirit only and not comfort. Only after World War II did Hans Simons as president succeed in adding two new buildings, which gave us more rooms, and not until 1969 did the Graduate Faculty move into its present separate quarters on Fifth Avenue at 13th Street.

Every Wednesday evening we held a "general seminar," at which all members were to be present. Many guests from other universities used to listen, among them frequently Paul Tillich (d. 1965), the philosopher of religion, and Kurt von Fritz, classical scholar and all-round academic of highest standing, now in Munich. In the general seminar we got to know one another better, and learned much from one another.[1]

In March, 1934 the first number of our quarterly *Social Research* appeared. There are now thirty-five volumes.

Alvin Johnson, director of the New School and founder of the Graduate Faculty, welcomed us. He was then fifty-eight years old; in December, 1969 we celebrated his ninety-fifth birthday. Only in the course of time did a genuine friendship develop from mutual respect between us, but then and ever after it was the more deeply rooted. Through him I first learned to understand differences in background and manner between great men in America and Europe. Normal career paths are rarer in the United States. Johnson was born in the wild and lonely area of Nebraska, had been reared on ground made cultivable by his father, a Danish emigrant, had

---

[1] The general seminar functioned in this manner for about twenty years, was then reduced to one term only, and later replaced by a gathering held once a month in the early afternoon.

taught himself—with the encouragement of an uncle—Latin and Greek from books, had become a young university instructor, obtained his doctor's diploma at Columbia University, taught at universities in Nebraska, Texas, California, and in the East. He had become an editor of *The New Republic* along with Walter Lippmann, founded the New School for Social Research after the First World War with Charles Beard and others, for the preservation of academic freedom, and was executive director of the Encyclopedia of the Social Sciences. At the time of our arrival he published a semi-autobiographical novel, *Spring Storm,* a description of his youth, later an autobiography of his adult years, and two volumes of informative, beautifully written stories of the Middle West. His wife, who herself had graduated from college, was the only teacher for all seven children in every subject until they went to college.

Johnson's procedure in establishing the Graduate Faculty illustrates other differences between America and Europe. He had no means, either public or private, at his disposal when he invited the first ten members. He trusted the worthiness of the action and at the same time began to collect the 200,000 dollars which were necessary for the first two years. He obtained them principally on the basis of a cable from a major oil industrialist, Hiram Halle, who was so enthusiastic and generous as to send him not only a considerable sum, but to guarantee the rest.

In Johnson's behavior there was nothing that expressed his importance. He was simple in manner and without any presumptions, always active, never resting on his laurels. In the United States what one has done in the past is less important than in Europe; more important is what one is doing now or intends to do. That with the founding of the Graduate Faculty, Johnson also had acted as a true friend of Germany, has long since been officially recognized. On his eightieth birthday he was awarded an honorary doctorate by Heidelberg University, and on his ninetieth by the Free University of Berlin. He also received the Great Cross of Merit of the Federal Republic.

We had to start our new life in a city, country, continent, where we knew no one, and no one knew us. Even among the members of my Faculty there were no old acquaintances. A German friend, Julie Braun-Vogelstein, at that time on a visit to her brother, Ludwig Vogelstein, president of the American Metal Company, introduced us to him. On January 26, 1934 we celebrated my fiftieth birthday there together with hers, which fell on the same day. She helped us find two furnished rooms in the Peter Stuyvesant Hotel with a view over Central Park and took us to the Cloisters Museum high above the Hudson. Later she too emigrated to the United States, and we have been living there in close friendship.

In the very first week we were present at the wedding of Walther Becker in the Schroeder house in Montclair, N.J., and at the subsequent dinner aboard the Lloyd liner "Europa," at which we also saw the former Reich Chancellor and President of the Reichsbank, Hans Luther, then Ambassador in Washington, again for the first time. We became close friends of Hans Schroeder and his English-born wife, Jessie, often celebrating Christmas Eve with them in Montclair and, after her death, with him alone at our apartment, until he too died in 1966.

Luther invited us to a dinner he was giving in Washington in honor of Chief Justice Hughes. We met there, among others, Senator Wagner and Franklin D. Roosevelt's closest advisers, Harold Ickes and Harry Hopkins, also the second son of the former German Crown Prince, Prince Louis Ferdinand.

The American sponsors of the New School did all they could to help us feel at home. In spring and fall they invited us to their country homes. There was an amazing chain reaction. Each host introduced us to another: Ludwig Vogelstein to William Shepard, professor of cultural history at Columbia; President Butler to Lindsay Rogers, Arthur Macmahon, and Maude Huttman (modern German history, Barnard); Miss Hutman to Charles Beard and James Shottwell; Shottwell to Robert MacIver. John Foster Dulles received us on a letter of introduction from Heinrich Albert. And so it went. The circle of acquaintances grew rapidly.

And yet the great new world remained rather strange to us for a long time. What were the people one encountered on the street thinking about; what tunes were they humming to themselves? Instead of Weimar-Germans, Potsdam-Germans, Kant-Germans, Mozart-, Bach-, or Wagner-Germans, we learned to distinguish Anglo-Americans, German-Americans, Italian-Americans, Irish-Americans, Scandinavian-Americans, Negro-Americans, etc.; first-, second-, third-generation Americans; true-bred Americans, Bostonians, Southerners, Middle Westerners, Republicans, Democrats. . . .

But that was not enough. It said nothing about what united them all—love of freedom, and love of country. And it said nothing about the cross-fertilization among them, nor about the differences within the individual categories.

"It will take ten years before you can give America of your best," said Alvin Johnson. This seemed to me too long; I thought I could do it more quickly. But it was too short. Today what Charles Beard once said makes good sense to me: that in order to understand America completely one had to have lived there for three hundred years. But after thirty-five years I have come nearer to understanding; I also know roughly what the people I meet are thinking about.

With growing understanding, my admiration for the tremendous internal and outward achievements of the United States in times of peace and war also grew, along with my affection for its history, with which I now familiarized myself, and above all for its constitutional history. I came to understand the United States system of government as a fourfold separation of powers, a separation in four dimensions, of which the familiar separation of executive, legislative, and judicial powers was only one, and not even the most important one. This quasi-horizontal division, if ever so imperfectly realized in practice, is surely a characteristic feature of United States government, but it is supplemented by three others. There is, of course, secondly the quasi-vertical separation of powers between federal, state, and local government. A third, and well the most significant separation of powers, is that between proper spheres of government activities and spheres inaccessible to public government—the private sphere of opinion, religion, art, science (especially what is protected in the first, fifth and fourteenth amendments to the U.S. Constitution). This, too, constitutes a separation of powers, although it is rarely spoken of in this way, a separation as it were in the dimension of depth. And then there is the most basic of all democratic separations of powers, the separation in time, in the fourth dimension, between the government of today and that of tomorrow, from election to election, from vote to vote. Separation of powers in the first two dimensions did not exist in every democracy, for example hardly at all in Great Britain and France. But the third and the fourth are of the essence of democracy. I have bestowed many comments on each of these four dimensions in my lectures and have found this a very fertile frame of reference.

"How can any cultured man like living in America," an old colleague from the German Foreign Office said to me, "in that materi-

alistic world." This catch phrase is only superficially true; in essence
it is misleading. Nowhere does one find more idealism—both ideological and active—than in the United States, idealism such as expressed in the Hoover supplies to Belgium in the First World War,
in the Marshall Plan in 1949, in the establishment and the activities
of many great foundations—to name but a few. In the cultural
sphere, too, Europeans can only marvel, if they care to look more
closely, at the development of an independent, characteristically
American culture in a country inhabited by people of so many
races. To be sure, there are few geographically circumscribed cultural centers such as delight us in Europe. But there is a community
of adepts, greatly receptive, and of major achievements, within
every cultural sphere. This community has to be sought out, but if
sought for seriously will be found.

Soon mutual sympathies in the pursuit of human, cultural, or political values and in academic tendencies evolved, sympathies that
associated me not with *all* Americans, but with enough to remove
my feeling of strangeness.

What repels many Europeans—the chequered mixture of the population living on the whole peacefully together in mutual respect for
democratic principles—particularly pleased me as a constant re-
minder of the existence of other traditions and standards, keeping
me from complacent provincialism.

Slowly, but constantly, we increased our geographical knowledge
of the country. We began with a Christmas trip to Virginia and
Tennessee, with spring trips to the Great Lakes and to Niagara Falls,
with trips to Boston and Massachusetts, to the resorts on Long Island, Cape Cod, Martha's Vineyard, Nantucket, and Desert Island, to
the White Mountains, and Lake Champlain, to the sites of aristocratic culture in the southern states, such as Charleston and Savan-
nah. We took part in the Republican convention in Cleveland in
1936 and, of course, were frequently in Washington.

Finally, when I had my first sabbatical leave in 1939, we undertook the crossing of the continent in our car, from February until
June. This took us in February and March into the early spring
along the coast to Florida, which we crossed from Jacksonville to
Tampa, then along the Caribbean coast to New Orleans, through
the enormous spaces of Texas (the first road sign read: "Beaumont 8
miles, El Paso 850 miles"), through New Mexico and Arizona,

through the blossoming desert (for most of the desert there is not sand desert, but a cactus desert, and the cacti blossom in pastel shades with the most delicate flowers in the most unlikely places) to San Diego on the Pacific, and then northward via Los Angeles to Carmel. There we spent four weeks in almost daily company with Julie Braun-Vogelstein, who had moved to the West Coast for several years and who had us as her guests almost every afternoon and evening in her delightful house up the hills. Then via San Francisco, Yosemite Park, through the forests of giant trees, across the Sierra Nevada to Death Valley and, after crossing this, to Nevada (Las Vegas), the Grand Canyon of the Colorado River, the Petrified Forest, Santa Fe, the upper reaches of the Rio Grande (here a tire burst on the most lonely stretch of the most dreadful road) to the Indian reservation of Taos, then through thunderstorms and cloudbursts over to the east slope of the Rockies and, northward along them, to Colorado and Denver. You think you are already in the plain, but you are still 6,000 feet high. Almost unnoticeably the plain drops down to the Mississippi.

In St. Louis I fulfilled a childhood dream: to stand at the confluence of the Missouri and the Mississippi rivers, a few miles north of the city. The countryside was not unlike that of eastern Holstein near my native town of Lübeck: fields, meadows, and hills. No one had thought of establishing an "American Corner" here, with restaurants, like the "German Corner" in Coblenz at the confluence of the Moselle and the Rhine. In June we returned to New York. We had driven more than 11,000 miles, more than a third of the circumference of the earth, but never very much on one day. Every two hours we took turns at the wheel.

This year 1939 was the climax of our travel, because after the double crossing of the American continent we spent six weeks traveling around Germany (Chapter 97). In mid-August, after our return, we were for two days guests of the widow of Professor Kuno Franke, of Harvard, in Gilbertsville, N.Y., which had been founded by her grandfather, a mill owner. I realized that many towns in America, even in the East, have existed only for three generations, so that family history runs parallel to place history, in contrast to Europe, where the history of almost every town by far outdates human memory. Then we spent three weeks in Gay's Head on Martha's Vineyard at the house of a negress who sang Brahms and Schubert in German, and another four weeks at a farmer's home on the mainland in Vermont, before we returned to New York at the beginning of the fall term.

Two years later (1941) we drove once more to the Rocky Mountains, to spend six weeks in Estes Park, a wonderful nature reserve at about 9,000 feet, but still within the most abundant flora of huge firs and fresh flowers, with numerous mountain streams, elk and beavers. From here we could drive comfortably over the 12,000-foot pass—the Continental Divide—and then down into the valley of a small, pleasant brook which was in fact the upper course of the mighty Colorado River.

These trips, including smaller ones in the following summers, which we spent in the Catskill mountains because of the limited gasoline allowances during the war, made us well aware of the greatness and many-sidedness of the United States and the tremendous achievement of its cultivation.

In Pasadena, near Los Angeles, a mutual friend had invited us to lunch with the great astronomer Hubble, discoverer of the phenomenon known as the expanding universe. We watched the polishing of the large lens for the Palomar Observatory. I asked him: "How do you know that the most remote galaxies you see are not our own Milky Way seen once around the curved universe?" I was so excited by this idea that I forgot or was unable to understand what he answered.

Thus increasingly converted from the indifference of ignorance to love of the *gestalt* and history of the United States we gradually sank our roots into the new soil, helped particularly by my growing contact with American university life and by personal friendships. Both had their natural center in our faculty. The core of our social life was formed from its members, exalted by a community of fate and by shared, constructive work, made ever anew refreshing, enjoyable, and lofty thanks to the high standards of our conversations.

From there our contacts extended to other universities. Professor Carl J. Friedrich of Harvard, fifteen years my junior in age, but ten years my senior in American experience since he had gone to Harvard as a student, and his charming and intelligent American-born wife, were among the first links in a long chain of outside university friends. He invited me to individual guest lectures. On the basis of articles I had published in *Social Research* on "Constitutions and Leadership," "Government in Economics," and "Civil Service" I received invitations to guest professorships for the spring term of 1937 in the University of Chicago by Professor Charles Merriam, and in Harvard. I accepted the invitation from Harvard, to lecture there on European constitutional history and to conduct a seminar on American "Government and Economics," a subject with which I had been much engrossed in the meantime and which later was also the subject of one of my major lectures in our own faculty, together with those on comparative government, institutional history, administration, and political theory.

In order to be able to give my lectures in Harvard and at the same time fulfill my duties in New York I went every week to Cambridge for three days. During a further term as guest professor in Harvard in the spring of 1940 I did the opposite: we lived in Cambridge, I rode every Thursday morning to New York, where I held two two-hour lectures from six until ten at night, and then returned to Boston by sleeping car, to give lectures in Harvard at nine and eleven on Friday morning and other lectures on Mondays and Wednesdays. Such shuttle service is not tiring for a week or two, but becomes increasingly so when repeated for fifteen weeks. I also gave single guest lectures frequently at other colleges, especially in Columbia and Barnard and also in Wells, Bard, Haverford, and Williams colleges, etc. This activity increased during the war, when I regularly gave lectures on Germany to American soldiers in City College and to American officers in Harvard and Yale. In addition I worked on research projects in our Institute for World Affairs at the New School and on the publication of my book *Prelude to Silence*—altogether a great strain which led to my breakdown in the spring of 1944, mentioned in Chapter 98.

An invitation by Mrs. Kuno Franke in Cambridge led to the beginnings of our friendship with the philosopher W. Ernest Hocking. We often also met his colleague Ralph Barton Perry. At the invitation of another friend of ours, Mrs. Reed, we visited her father, the ninety-year-old Bishop Lawrence in Boston. We lived in close contact, in addition to Professor Friedrich and his wife, especially with the architect Walter Gropius and his wife, Ilse, a cousin of Clara's daughter; with the classical philologist, Werner Jaeger, who had just published his *Paideia;* with the pedagogic philosopher, Robert Ulich, and his first wife, the unforgettably radiant Elsa Brandström (called "the Angel of Siberia" because of her devoted work for prisoners of war in Russia); with ex-Chancellor Brüning, who had just moved from England to America; the physicist, Otto Oldenberg, and his wife; and with my American colleagues in the field of political science, in particular Arthur Holcombe and William Elliot. The great lawyers Roscoe Pound and Felix Frankfurter also invited us.

I joined the American Political Science Association. At the first annual meeting in 1934 in Washington, I still wandered around a mere stranger, but then from year to year I gained friends by active cooperation. I was often a member, and five or more times chairman, of sessions or round-tables, and in 1946 I was elected a vice-president. Later my active participation receded, because the APSA moved its annual meetings from the end of December to the beginning of September, a time when I was usually not yet back from Europe.

Other contacts arose from my interest in public administration and civil service. I was a founding member of the American Society for Public Administration in 1940 and became chairman of a special committee for comparative administration set up under the Social Science Research Council by William Anderson, in cooperation with Fritz Morstein-Marx, Hermann Finer (at that time London), Arthur Macmahon (specialist for the United States), Walther Sharp (for France), John Hazard (for the Soviet Union), and Donald Stone, then in the Bureau of the Budget. At several conferences in Washington we discussed the administrative structure of departmental headquarters and overall coordination with heads and leading officials of federal departments—among them Secretary of War Patterson, Secretary of the Navy Forrestal, Price Commissioner Leon Henderson, and the director of the Budget Bureau—and made suggestions for reform. The meetings, which I had the honor of chairing, were usually preceded by a dinner at one of the Washington clubs. I also presided over a round-table of the American Political Science Association on the theme of "Streamlining Departmental Headquarters."[2]

Friendly relations also arose outside academic and administrative spheres, of course. I will mention only three of these because of their contributions to our American education. An import trader of German descent with wide cultural and political interests, Louis Marburg, and his American-born wife, Gertrude, whom we had

[2] My suggestions in the field of public administration are available in my articles, as cited in the appendix.

met at Maude Huttman's, became precious friends of ours and often invited us to their Montclair house. They acquired an old empty farmhouse about sixty miles south in the mountainous part of New Jersey near a small village called Hamburg. They leased the farm-land to a neighboring farmer, but kept the old house and spent a large part of the summer there with those of their five children who were available. By an old unused quarry, in which an attractive, deep lake of the purest water had formed, they had a bungalow built, and on the top of a hill their children built another with their own hands. For many years we were their guests there for several weeks. At first we were embarrassed and at a loss as to what to say about the acquisition of this rickety old house. Gradually we learned to live in its rather empty rooms, which were filled with furniture only slowly, and to do everything ourselves. We breakfasted magnificently under an old maple tree, swam in the lake, wandered through fields and meadows, read and worked. Often we were alone during the week, for the Marburgs came out at the weekend. Once a week I drove to New York for lectures at the summer school, two hours by car, and back at night—the lectures ended at ten o'clock—to sink at midnight, awaited by Clara, exhausted into bed. The friendship with the Marburgs extended to their children, whose experiences and problems we shared. They called us "Arnold" and "Clara" and not Uncle and Auntie Brecht, as would have been the case in Germany. Their father had sent them all to Germany for a few years, to the Odenwald School, and one daughter has done the same later with her children. The youngest Marburg son in particular, whom his father had called Rolland out of admiration for the French writer, Romain Rolland, held our love. He made long trips to South America or to the northwest without any money, earning his keep by doing casual work. He died when on a wild stream in Connecticut he turned to shoot the rapids. His boat capsized and he was drowned.

A friend of Dr. Johnson's, Dr. John Martin, former co-founder of the Fabian Society in London, invited us, together with his wealthy wife, in July to his summer house in the White Mountains in the north. He had become a hater of all things German, without distinguishing Nazis and non-Nazis. For hours we argued about the reasons for Hitler's rise to power and the character of the German people. In winter the couple lived in Winterpark in Florida, where we visited them on our cross-country trip. Instead of the grapefruit, which grew to enormous size in his garden, he gave us prunes for breakfast, because he considered them to be better-tasting and healthier, and he was perhaps not entirely wrong in this; if prunes cost a dollar each, all rich people would have them for breakfast.

To the north of New York, in Connecticut, other friends of ours —Albert Roothbert, art collector and humanitarian of great qualities, and his wife, formerly Toni von Horn, a well-known photographer—owned a beautiful country place, Topstone Farm. After my grave illness in 1944 they invited us there to convalesce. We stayed about five weeks. There were no servants. Despite their resources the wife did all the housework and cooking herself.

Since we had left our furniture in Germany, we did not set up— unlike almost all our colleagues—an apartment of our own in New York, but lived in two medium-sized, furnished hotel rooms, the first ten years at the park corner of West 86th Street in the Hotel Peter Stuyvesant, thereafter for twenty-five years a few blocks farther south, at 81st Street in the Hotel Standish Hall, later called the Hotel Excelsior, also close to Central Park, where we would take about an hour's walk every day before lunch. We used both rooms as living rooms, each with a couch to be made up as bed for the night. We arranged the furniture so that the rooms had personal character, hung our own engravings and prints, including watercolors by Clara, on the walls, and accustomed ourselves so well to this way of living that we kept it even after the war, because we had learned to value being able to move around easily. "I am a guest on earth." In February, 1968 we moved to Hotel Alden, 225 Central Park West, where we permitted ourselves a third room.

Until well into the Second World War our life in New York was even more mobile, since every year in April we put the larger part of our possessions into the hotel cellar, gave up the city apartment, and moved to the Edgehill Inn with its large garden, delightfully situated on the highest point of a hilly quarter in the north of the town, called "Spuyten Duyvil" by the Dutch. From there I drove to my New School work along the Henry Hudson highway—at that time newly opened—past the George Washington Bridge, the sailing ship harbor, and under the bows of the ocean giants lying by the piers—the "Queen Mary," "United States," "Bremen," "Liberté," etc.—a marvellous drive, the beauty and grandeur of which always made our hearts swell with joy. In the fall, after returning from our trips to Europe, we would live again in Edgehill Inn and move back to our "city apartment" only with the beginning of the cold season at the end of November. We later had to abandon this custom, since Edgehill Inn was closed and the town hotels demanded payment during our absence.

These descriptions of our way of life may leave a rather restless impression. This would be correct were it not for the fact that my life kept inner coherence through our community within the Graduate Faculty and my passionate devotion to the scientific work I had set myself to do (see the following chapter).

Within the framework of this book it is not possible for me to relate in detail how present-day America gradually revealed itself to me with its social, economic, cultural, and political conditions and problems. This cannot be done, if one really knows America, with trivial generalities or witty aphorisms. It would require another voluminous book, which in tone and content would have little in common with this autobiography.

I would like to say only one thing more in this context. Germany ought not to let herself be dazzled by the exemplary understanding that prevails between her own and American statesmen into forgetting that the United States is not a country ruled dictatorially by a president and his cabinet, but a democracy in which political decisions—at least in so far as they are not limited by formal treaties—are ultimately dependent on the voice of the people. The United States president certainly has a lot to say. He can do a great deal to influence public opinion, guide it and restrain it in its outbursts. But in the final resort it is nevertheless public opinion which determines the further course of American politics. Foreign statesmen who know what "Washington thinks" do not automatically know what undercurrents of opinion there are among the American people in the various regions of the country, currents which can sooner or later lead to changes in the political course.

## 101. Science, Practice, and Faith

More than everything else it was my association with the Graduate Faculty of Political and Social Science at the New School for Social Research—this was its official name—which made the United

States my new home and New York my third home town, after Lübeck and Berlin. To sing the praises of this faculty, to tell anecdotes of our groping around in a world new to us, of stammering in a language as yet insufficiently mastered, of our first misunderstandings of America, and gradually overcoming these handicaps; to discuss the merits and failings of our activities and rules would be most tempting, but it would shift the focus of this chapter. My feelings of respect for all members of the faculty and of a community of fate shared with them in a great adventure of the spirit grew over the course of the years to all-embracing love.

At the beginning it often happened during our discussions in the general seminar that we exchanged meaningful glances when we heard the sirens of the ocean giants docking or departing on the Hudson, reminding us of where we were—in the United States, in New York, in the great world of the West.

Americans are often more tactful than their visitors. When at some social gathering our students in an improvised sketch made our general seminar the target of their jokes they satired the differences in our opinions and methods, but none of them mimicked the failures in our speech, as German students would certainly have done in a similar case. When I expressed my surprise at this, Dr. Johnson said only: "Why should they do that? They admire your struggle with language difficulties. They don't see anything funny in it."

It was my great personal fortune in the midst of misfortune that my appointment gave me the opportunity to devote myself to science. This meant first of all that I tried to gain a better knowledge of the history of political institutions in many countries. My experiences at close quarters with German history under three fundamentally different constitutions in the twentieth century had sharpened my understanding. I focused attention on the influence constitutions had on history. After ten years my material was so abundant that I dared to give a course of lectures on "The World's Constitutional History," which I improved and extended from year to year.

Not only the history of political *institutions* had to be mastered. The history of political *ideas* was just as important, and even more attractive. Socrates, Plato, Aristotle, Polybius and Cicero, Augustine and Thomas Aquinas, Hobbes, Locke, Rousseau, Montesquieu, Hegel, Marx, etc., were all studied zealously, as were the Federalist papers, and contemporary works on constitutional monarchy, democracy, communism, and fascism in all its forms. Once again an unending subject for study, inexhaustible source of reflection. Pleasures of scholarship!

If a young student is able to acquire the professional knowledge of these subjects within three years, how much more an adult man who begins his work with a great deal of practical experience and continues this study over thirty years!

But all this was only basic preparation. What I was really after was the great thing of science itself. I wanted to find out what assistance science could render practice. Many of my academic colleagues were more or less frustrated practicians. They longed for practice; I, the practician, longed for theory.

When we were preparing our first book together, the two members who had been entrusted with its editing wrote in the introduction, "We all believe in democracy and in science." I objected. The word "belief," I argued, in the sense of believing *in* something, was not proper here. The sentence "I believe in God" was a statement made on a personal creed, not a scientific contribution. Even as a personal creed, it was not true of myself that I "believed" in democracy and science. I loved both. But I believed in their ability to solve political problems only to a limited extent.

Yes, I *loved* democracy, because it gave free rein to my own ideals of freedom, truth, and justice; I loved it as the opposite of forms of government which subjected me to authoritarian powers which I could not respect. But I did not "believe" in democracy as a cure for all political ills, for I knew only too well that it had failed in so many cases; indeed it must fail, for example, when the majority prefers other forms of government (Chapter 30). It could lead to satisfactory results only when a whole series of historical and moral conditions were given (see *Political Theory,* Chapter xiii). There were problems which even then it could not solve.

I *loved* science. Science was, so to speak, my hobby. I also believed that it could make many important contributions to politics. That was why I engaged so eagerly in its pursuit. But I was far from believing that all problems of politics and community life (not to speak of private life) could be solved by science. On the contrary, I knew only too well that precisely the most important questions could not be answered by it, not only whether there is a God, and what sort of God, but also what our aims should be.

My objections were ignored. The sentence I had protested against remained unchanged in the introduction.

What is science?

I am unable to convince any scholar, by purely scientific means, on how to use the word science. If he calls everything the truth of which he is convinced of "knowledge," I cannot force him to alter his usage. But I can make him and his readers or listeners aware of the fact that not all real or supposed knowledge can be transferred to others as "knowledge." This led me to the distinction between *scientia transmissibilis* and *scientia non transmissibilis*. Even transmissible knowledge is transmissible as knowledge only under certain assumptions (I call them "methodologically immanent assumptions"), for example, that our senses give us similar impressions and that we have a certain minimum of freedom to be able to choose between true and false. These assumptions can be clearly expressed and are generally comprehensible.

The systematic pursuit of these questions through a period of more than thirty years made me well acquainted with the history of the philosophy of knowledge, from the pre-Socratic philosophers, the Sophists, Socrates, Plato and Aristotle, down to the pragmatists, the relativists (Max Weber, Radbruch, Kelsen, Lasswell, etc.), the neo-positivists, linguists, sociologists of knowledge, existentialists, and their opponents. I also studied the theory of causality in all its branches and tried to rid it of the confusion which had arisen under the influence of quantum mechanics and of the linguistic mannerisms of the neo-positivists.

I gave particular attention to the phase of scientific work which has been most neglected, the phase of *acceptance* (or *non-acceptance*) of observations and descriptions as "executed accurately," and of what has been observed and described as "real" ("actual").

I was surprised to discover that the early history and gradual development of "scientific value relativism," both before and after the famous essay by Max Weber in 1904, had been investigated so little and that the distinction between it and other forms of relativism (skepticism, agnosticism, positivism, neo-positivism, historicism, pragmatism, physical, philosophical, and legal relativism) was still ill-defined. There was no coherent presentation of these fundamental problems. I therefore decided to write one myself. I did this first

in several essays on relativism (Chapter 98) and afterwards in my
*Political Theory,* the subtitle of which is "The Foundations of
Twentieth-Century Political Thought."

At the same time I tried to cast more light on so-called "higher
law" and "natural law." Anyone who believes in God is logically
bound to accept as "possibly true" the traditional doctrine that there
is a divine law and that this perhaps is expressed somehow in nature, which has been created by God. Since, however, the existence
of God cannot be proved in a strictly scientific manner, neither can
the existence of a "higher law" or "natural law" created by God
(and not by man) be so proved. No morally binding order can proceed from an uncreated, inanimate nature.

What limits scientific work does not, however, bind either philosophical speculation or religious belief. To assume the contrary
would be an inadmissible confusion.

Nor does the fact that science cannot establish the truth of absolute value judgments compel us to accept—for example, as judges,
lawyers, government officials—any orders given by the government
in power in due procedural forms as *legally valid* regardless of their
contents. This is not a *scientific* decision, although it has often incorrectly been considered such. It is basically nothing more than a
decision of the *will* of people as to what authority they wish to
grant or deny their governments—deny, whether it be for religious
reasons, or for pseudo-scientific reasons, or simply for fear that the
powers be misused, or for the realization of an order of human
things they aspire to. But here I am repeating myself (Chapter
93).

It is also possible to investigate scientifically (anthropologically,
phenomenologically, sociologically, etc.) whether any "universal"
(generally human) and "invariant" postulates can be observed in
the field of morals and justice and what they are—and this I now
did. I concentrated on the postulates of the sense of justice (or of
the "feeling for justice") and arrived at the conclusion that, according to the large amount of evidence available—which, of course,
had to be checked by further observations—the desire for justice is a
human category of universal character and that the invariant elements of this desire include the requisite of *truth*—objective justice,
objective truth; subjective justice, subjective truth (veracity). Other
universal invariant elements of the sense of justice demand like
treatment of like cases and respect for the limits of possibility—it is

not just to accuse someone of not having done something that was impossible for him to do.

"But, Professor, politics is a matter of refined intuition (*Fingerspitzen*), and not of science," a Heidelberg student said to me in the first session of my seminar on political science. "Just think of Bismarck and Metternich," he added. To be sure, much of good politics is art, skill, and not science. But a good statesman does have to *know* something, in fact a good deal, in order to be able to produce good politics. He must know the experiences of the past, the facts of the present, of human nature, etc., and must not fail to see relevant consequences. Bismarck knew a great deal and foresaw a great deal, but not enough, nor did Metternich.

Scientific work can above all help to ascertain the *facts* of present conditions in the world—whether by means of statistics, questioning, sociological investigation, or by any other means—and the facts and trends which tend to influence the future, and also help awareness of those special risks which are involved in certain institutions or decisions. Scientific work can investigate alternatives of action in good time and indicate and analyze *neglected alternatives*.

Science can clarify in advance that it is not possible to carry out certain radical changes in the economic structure of a large country, such as the industrialization of an agricultural nation, with purely democratic means within a short time, and that it can be done much more quickly with dictatorial means. But science is unable to decide whether the disadvantages of a dictatorial administration weigh heavier in the scales of value than the advantages of quicker industrialization. It can, however, point out the disadvantages, and especially the risks involved, and give warning of them.

This is one of its most important tasks. For the disadvantages of a dictatorship include the fact that, once complete power is in the hands of one man or of a small group, there is no guarantee against an objectively unreasonable or a morally crude use of power. There is no guarantee that the man who emerges as the victor from the struggle for dictatorial power is morally good and intellectually wise, and that, if he be so today (a thing which is rare, but not impossible), he will still be so tomorrow (corruption, senility, mental illness), and even less, that his successor will have these rare qualities. This is a strictly scientific argument against dictatorship, and it is the strongest and most effective of all arguments, because it cannot be refuted and does not depend upon personal value judgments, as do most other arguments. We could extend it by the further argument, scientifically equally faultless, that the dictator of a large country needs hundreds of thousands of subordinates, whose encroachments, because of the limited human span of control, he is unable either to prevent or remedy; in numerous cases he will learn nothing of them, as long as there are no freedom of speech, no freedom of the press, and no independent judges.

I will not pursue these thoughts, which I have discussed more fully in the book mentioned and elsewhere, any further here, but let it suffice to report, autobiographically, that I have pursued them as consistently as I could.

Political *practice* can greatly profit from political science. But practice is always bound to be more than just applied science. The practical politician pursues *goals*. The choice of goals is not the proper business of science. Science can examine—as Max Weber already made quite clear—what consequences the pursuit of any particular goal will or may have, which other goals will be precluded from realization or affected by this one, what means are suitable or unsuitable to achieving the goal, whether it can be achieved at all, and (a thing I have put in the foreground) which special risks are involved in the setting of this particular goal or in the choice of these particular means (such as dictatorship). But all the information and analyses science can offer—considerable as they are—will rarely if ever limit the choice of goals to only one, nor the choice of means to only one.

What guides the practician in his choice of goals may be personal preference, fondness for innovation, desire for fame, pseudo-scientific conviction, ideology, religious belief, creative urge, the genuine desire to build a better world—it is never science alone.

The fact that science alone cannot determine what are the proper goals of policy, unless we define what we mean by "proper," does not imply that reason has no function in setting goals. Nothing could be farther off the mark than this foolish doctrine, an entirely unwarranted inference. On the contrary, the first conclusion to be drawn from the impotence of science alone to determine the proper goals is the inference that we have the choice between either leaving the determination of goals to chance, to human instincts, to individual resolutions of men in power, and the like, or realizing that we have the *possibility* and the *responsibility*—at least the *causal* responsibility if we do not care to recognize a *moral* one—of shaping and propagating goals, be it singlehanded or be it through reasonable cooperation with others. We can sit down together and examine what sort of possible development of man and the world would please us most, and in so doing decide what we mean by "please"— not our own selfish pleasure but something concerning the development of man and mankind in general, or of our nation, or whatever else we consider most important. In other words, we can try to help *create a world that we would consider worth living in.*[1]

Even in this stage there is plenty of opportunity to apply scientific methods in order to take stock of the conditions of men as they actually are and to investigate the possibilities or impossibilities of change in the desired direction. Once we have decided on our goals and directions within the range of possibilities, we can reason in a fully scientific manner on the means suitable to achieving these goals and pursuing these directions. In all this, however, it is never science alone, but science plus responsible volition which sets the proper goals and determines the proper means.

My emphasis on the limits of science went against the trend of the time, particularly in Germany, where a sweeping change in approach had evolved as a result of the Hitler regime. While at the turn of the century the sociological situation in Germany had made the critical treatment of traditional, conservative value judgments by the advocates of scientific value relativism appear as an act of liberation, the sociological situation after the Hitler period was exactly the opposite. Everything seemed to demand of science that it oppose absolute moral principles to the amorality of the Hitler theories. Social scientists were expected to proclaim absolute moral values *qua* science. And they succumbed—from the most honorable motives, I must add immediately—almost man for man to the undertow of this new sociological situation, to some extent even their illustrious leader, Gustav Radbruch.[2] With few if any exceptions they turned

---

[1] Much on this is in my *Political Theory*, e.g. pp. 20, 274, 287 ff., 331 ff., 449 ff., 487, 490–92. More in "Die Tröstungen der strengen Wissenschaft," *Politische Ordnung und menschliche Existenz* (Festgabe für Eric Vogelin, München, 1962) pp. 49 ff., especially p. 58. For closely kindred thoughts for economists, see Adolph Lowe, *On Economic Knowledge: Toward a Science of Political Economics*, New York, 1965.

[2] On the four phases of his way of thinking, see *Political Theory*, pp. 357 ff.

from being political scientists to becoming ethical philosophers or
theologians (if not simply bad logicians) and *they called this science,* although at that particular moment the strictly scientific criticism of totalitarian theories would have been so important and
promised so many gains—and was fortunately pursued by a few on
the side.

"What!" exclaimed Alfred Weber (four years younger than his
brother Max, but his survivor by thirty years at that time) on my
visit to Heidelberg in 1950 indignantly, pounding the desk with his
fist, when I answered his question as to what I presented as political
science to Americans by politely mentioning his brother's methodol-
ogy, which in 1933 had been scarcely known in America. "What!
You are telling the Americans this old nonsense. Relativity of values? The first thing I tell my students is what the highest values
are"—namely spiritual values. I answered that his brother's metho-
dology allowed him to tell his students what values he put at the
top, if he added why and how and investigated the origins, consequences, and risks of various estimates of value—for example, the
consequences of disregard of spiritual values. I did not teach, I continued, and according to my interpretation neither had Max Weber,
that all values *are* relative—no one who believed in God or in the
possibility of there being a God, could do that—but only that the
contributions of science in this point, in contrast to the contributions of belief and philosophical speculations, could be only of a relative character.[3]

I sometimes came across an objection which seemed to me very
primitive, namely, that a theory which was already fifty years old
could no longer be correct. Indeed, it had not been *completely* correct, and in my own and other works it has been given a series of
corrections. But the objection that a theory is too old to be correct
cannot be taken seriously, not in respect to Socrates, Plato, or Aristotle, nor to Max Weber. Most old theories have been surpassed to
some extent, but not all old theories entirely.

My approach to *faith* and religion (Chapter 4) has basically remained the same. Aware as I am of the lack of scientific evidence
for the existence of a God who makes demands on me and watches
me, nevertheless the belief in such a condition of life has remained

---

[3] I have analyzed the different approaches of the two brothers more closely in
*Political Theory,* pp. 272 f., 350 ff.

constant with me in my vegetative, if I may call it such (plant-like, unreflecting), life. I have not struggled against it or tried to suppress it, after I had become convinced that the non-existence of such a God was just as impossible of scientific proof as his existence, in fact even more impossible, since one day God's existence may become manifest, but never his non-existence. "Probability" and "improbability" are categories of thought that cannot be applied here in a strictly scientific sense, where only transmissible forms of evidence are valid. These lines of thought have been pursued in my *Political Theory* (Chapter xiii) with the detail they deserve.

But the intensity of my belief in God has been subject to variations. After the brutality of the Hitler regime, after the death of my sister Gertrud (Chapter 97), my own serious illness which brought me so close to death (Chapter 98), in the following period of recovery, then again after Clara's operation and her miraculous recovery, and after our railroad accident, when a block of concrete threatened to crush us to death (1951)—under the impression of these experiences my religious life intensified between my fiftieth and seventieth years, my faith grew stronger and ever more independent of intellectual doubts. This was the result of daily thoughts of life and death, the daily confrontation with the metaphysical world, the awareness of the closely limited time granted us for good deeds and use of the talents allotted to us, a new wonder at the grace of life—the first branch of lilac in the spring of 1944, when I feared it would be the last; the first bars of good music I heard again; the comfort of biblical language; the inner truth of the most beautiful sacred songs.

My closeness to God at that time is shown in a series of poetic notations. I gave expression to my feelings in this way, in order to fix the experience for myself, so that I would be able to bring it to mind again later. They were "reference verses" (*Merkverse*), as I called them.

Thus it was then. My belief has remained, but it has—I must report this here just as honestly—not remained as strong as it was in those years. Perhaps the strictly scientific work of my major publication has played a part in this recession of metaphysical closeness, although in that book did I describe not only the great *potentialities* of science but also its *limitations,* vindicating religious faith against all pseudo-scientific arguments and revealing the frequent coexistence of belief and doubt at various levels of human consciousness.

Expressed in religious terms, I am no longer as much "in grace" as I was then. Or I am "in grace" in a less vital manner. Or is this true grace? Who can say?

My now deceased friend, Professor Alexander Rüstow, in a note in his major work *Ortsbestimmung der Gegenwart* (Orientation of the Present Time) blamed St. Theresa for having stuck firm to her belief after she no longer really had it. He said this was an insincerity, an untruth. I realize that from the standpoint of someone striving for truth it is possible to reach this opinion. But I do not share it. I feel that I do not have the right to ignore a great experience of faith in the past because I am unable to repeat it in the present, unless I have evidence that it was an error. But there is no such evidence.

Thus I serve the unknown God in my own way—very incompetently, very defectively. But I do serve him, patiently waiting for his grace.

Whenever and wherever God is being spoken about, this concerns me most deeply. I do not let any superficial or mocking remark pass, and likewise no empty preaching. The subject is too serious for either.

As long as I try to bear *what* is good in mind and strive to realize it, I feel I cannot go completely wrong, even if he *who* is good seems to withhold his grace.

The Christian doctrine of the Trinity holds no trouble for me, though for reasons that would hardly find approval among either theologians or philosophers. Whenever my concept of God (God the Father) is threatening to fade into contradictions and anthropomorphisms, I switch to the Holy Ghost, flee to him and feel safe. When he seems to escape me in obscurity and distance or seems to lead me astray as a mere abstraction, then I turn to Jesus, who is real and concrete before my eyes, exemplifying true goodness through his life. The doctrine of the Trinity encourages me to this changing, authorizes me to it, gives it deeper meaning.

Brought up in a Lutheran family in a Lutheran town, baptized and confirmed in the Lutheran Church, I found myself in related circumstances in the United States in so far as the great majority of North Americans are Protestants. But only a small fragment is Lutheran. The great majority belong to other Protestant communities, which were strange to me and remained so. The Lutheran Church also gained a new image for me. It no longer was *the* Protestant Church, but attained the characteristics of a provincial German-Scandinavian sect among other Protestant sects, historically significant but without general validity.

I was unable to make up my mind to enter one definite Protestant Church in the United States, because I could not and did not want to decide among them. I desired a union of all Protestant, of all Christian Churches. Was I to wait for this? I deeply regretted the splitting up of Christianity at the time of the Reformation; yet at the same time I was on Luther's side here, at least under the circumstances that then existed. Would he have done it again today, now that the Catholic Church has purged itself of the forms of corruption then prevalent? But after the split existed, how could it be removed? I knew that the reunion, if it ever took place, would not occur until five hundred years after my death at the earliest. Individual conversion to Catholicism could not solve the problem since it, too, such as it was, was not all-embracing. I did not feel equal to the change of convictions, or should I say of non-convictions, that conversion would involve, much as the rich community life of the Catholic Church attracted me. If the Churches were to grant all Christians the possibility of belonging to the Catholic and one or several Protestant Churches at the same time—and to a Jewish Synagogue, too—it would make me feel happy. Could not this idea at least be realized sooner than in five hundred years, perhaps even in our century? It would be a big step toward reunification of Christianity.

Our private religious life is very simple. Every night we say the Lord's Prayer together and each adds a silent prayer. Every Sunday morning we read the Bible together; for many years we have done so regularly, later less regularly, usually the texts read on that day in the Protestant Churches, sometimes using several lists at once. Following this we would read one or two hymns, slowly and with devotion—not sing, but read aloud, not discussing what we read, but letting it affect us, just as it was.

I report these things autobiographically, without claiming that we did well. On the contrary, I have always felt that this was not enough, that true religious service requires joining a large community. I waited for the renewal of religious community life and saw to it that nothing in my life's work stood in its way. Whenever the door for God's entry into community life or into private life threatened to close I have put my foot on the threshold and have reminded scholars who undertook such attempts in the name of science, of the *limits* of science.

# EPILOGUE

TODAY it has become fashionable to inquire into one's own identity. The answer to the friendly question, "Who are you?" is not rarely, "I don't know who I am."

Sometimes a deep break has destroyed old identity. "This is no longer I," says a woman in a play by Barlach, as she meets the boy friend of her youth.

Sometimes it is the opposite way. We feel that we have not yet achieved our real I. "I am not yet I," we could then say, playing on a favorite theme of the philosopher, Ernst Bloch, that man is not yet what he could be according to his potential. ("S is not yet P," the subject is not yet the predicate; this is how he expresses it.)

"I don't know who I am," "I am no longer I," "I am not yet I"— these are conflicting ideas which accompany every true autobiographer in his work, indeed, which alone can press the pen into his hand legitimately. I cannot pursue them here for all people, or for modern man in general; I can do so only for myself.

At my age I feel I no longer have the right to say, "I am *not yet* I," great and demanding as this challenge to completion sounds. What I once was, but no longer am; what formerly I was not, but now am; and what I always have been and still am—this is all I have to show. I can hardly change it noticeably any more. My personal alphabet stands written down in longhand by myself from A to Z or, at least, from A to Y. I ruefully confess that I have failed fully to develop the human potentialities whose germ I felt in me.

"I am no longer I," I could well say of myself in many respects, fortunately so with regard to some of my former traits, unfortunately as regards others. Much as I have changed, though, and much as have changed the things around me, I have maintained an unerring feeling of identity. *"Und keine Zeit und keine Macht zerstückelt/Geprägte Form, die lebend sich entwickelt"* (Goethe, *Urworte*).[1]

*Gestalt* and speech, the struggle for truth, justice, freedom, the

[1] And neither Time nor brutal Force destroys/The form, once coined, developing in life.

love of music and poetry, are still there. So is that questioning after the consequences and risks of doing or not doing something, with an ever greater emphasis on the consequences for others. In my leisure time, there is still something of the tendency to playfulness which marked my early years.

Among things no longer with us, there is an object without which I was previously unimaginable: the grand piano. Once a daily, hourly refuge from the writing desk, it has disappeared since our move to the United States. Thrown into a world entirely new to me, I had to make use of every hour in finding my way around. There was no time left for dreaming at the piano. Nor was there space for a grand in our two rooms, not even for an upright piano of regular size. Not until thirty years later did we acquire a small instrument again, one on which the highest and lowest keys were missing, and for which, thus shortened, there was just enough space left.

But along with it came tragedy. I was no longer I. My fingers had forgotten their lessons. I was able only to play a few pieces—Schubert and Schumann lieder, Offenbach, own compositions—otherwise I had to put melody and harmony together laboriously (even of my own compositions) with many mistakes, more torment than pleasure. The little finger of the left hand, accustomed to strike mighty octaves, knocked the wooden edge of the shortened keyboard or grasped thin air. I soon gave up. The piano stands there almost unused; only occasionally do I try a new melodic line, a new composition of my own.

A second sacrifice was legitimate theater. We lacked time and energy to become as deeply absorbed in theater as we had been in our younger days, and the plays were rarely of such high standards that seeing them stood comparison with the great events in the Berlin theater of our youth. Now as formerly, however, I read everything about the theater I get hold of. Only to the opera did we go regularly, in recent years increasingly often, both in the old and the new Metropolitan Opera in New York and during visits to Germany.

What has affected my ego more deeply than these changes in old habits—and there have, of course, been many more—has been the loss of human contacts. Of loved companions who are no longer there, some lost their young lives far back in the First World War. After that, the leaves fell more slowly. I have no grounds, as do many less fortunate people, for complaining that my family were torn from me unusually early. When my father died I was twenty-five years old, certainly not particularly young, at the death of my mother forty-four, at that of Gertrud fifty-five, of Edith seventy-three, of my brother Gustav even eighty-one. My younger brother, Rolf, and Vera are still with us. (Norah died in November, 1969.) We four friends from the Göttingen and early Berlin period—Jürgen Fehling, Georg Pfuhl, Julius Flechtheim, and myself—were all four still alive when the German edition of these memoirs appeared in 1967. (Fehling and Pfuhl have since passed away.) Above all, I have Clara living with me still, slender like a girl, graceful and easy in her motions as ever, if from time to time somewhat confused now in her mind about present-day affairs.

Many of the younger generation preceded us, though, including two of Gustav's three sons in World War II. All four of Edith's daughters have long since lost their husbands, and, more recently, daughter Irmgard hers too. My colleagues in the German Department of Justice, the Chancellery, and almost all those from the Weimar period, passed away, as indeed it had to be expected since I had been among the youngest at every stage.

All these facts, so important to me, are mere curiosities for others, with no significance for them except perhaps as comparison. Far from destroying my consciousness of identity, they have, on the contrary, tended to strengthen it. They have made me more my real self, this particular self, inexchangeable.

Old as some of us have grown, none of us who saw the year 1900 will see the year 2000. In this we are all alike, and we know it. In this we are characteristically different from all of you, younger friends, who have the right (as John and Robert Kennedy also had) to reckon with the year 2000 as a plausible date within your life span. Babies in their mother's arms or in their carriages with whom I like to exchange tender smiles may even see the year 2040 or 2050, years we do not even think of, sealed as we are in the present. For, as I now well know, living to be eighty is not unusual. Do live to be eighty! Do carry my salute to 2000 and 2050!

Those future years, too, so unattainable for me, will someday be part of the past. For time does not stop. I know full well, though, that what is done or omitted now will have a causal effect in the future, both the good and the bad. From this the only conclusion I can draw for myself is that the short span of time granted us on earth is in no sense of property "our" time. It is the time granted us, which can be better or worse because of us.

The scale of time used by octogenarians is a large one. Galileo, who was born in the same year as Shakespeare, in 1564, is separated from me by only three other octogenarians. When he died (1642), Newton was born (1643). When he died (1727), Kant had already been born (1724), and when he died many were already alive who were still so when I was born in 1884, such as Moltke (1800–1891) or Cardinal Newman (1801–1890). Surely, then, beneath the smile exchanged between octogenarians and babies world history melts considerably—from the Reformation up to the present day to only six generations, since Charlemagne to fifteen, since the birth of Christ to twenty-five.

Younger people use shorter scales when they measure history. Whatever individuals have achieved, as "generations" they failed. For the world is still in a bad state. You, you youngest generations, have not yet failed. This is the most important difference between you and us.

# APPENDIX

To CHAPTER 14

*Letter from Prince Max of Baden on the influence of the German High Command on the peace offer*

Salem, October 7, 1919

Dear Herr Geheimrat,

Thank you very much for your letter of September 26. . . . At the meeting on October 3 [1918], the Field Marshal [Hindenburg] did indeed use several phrases that did not seem to be completely in accordance with the catastrophic mood from which the demand for an armistice had resulted. But every time I wanted to draw practical consequences from one or the other of his more optimistic expressions: [such as] I want to pursue home policies first, to draw up a detailed program of war aims without turning directly to the enemy, etc., the Field Marshal insisted on the demand for an offer of armistice. I assume that the answers mentioned by General Ludendorff were intended as a basis for the meeting on October 3. He [Hindenburg] did not pass them on to me, though, nor, as I distinctly remember, did he read them out. I may add that the decisive impressions of the opinion the High Command had on the military situation were submitted to me not by way of written answers, but orally by what the Field Marshal said to me, either in the presence of others or when we were alone. I would also suggest that Colonel von Haeften be consulted on Hindenburg's alleged answers.

With best regards, I remain
Yours most sincerely,
Prince Max von Baden

To CHAPTER 16

*Speech of Kaiser Wilhelm II to the Parliamentary State Secretaries in Bellevue Palace (October 21, 1918) shortly after, for the first time in the history of the Empire, he had appointed leaders of the Reichstag majority to these positions*

Gentlemen! I am welcoming you to your new posts, to which you have been called as the men who have the confidence of the people (*Vertrauensmänner des Volkes*). With my decree of September 30, on the basis of which you have been given your appointments, I took the de-

cisive step in leading the German people to new constitutional forms
(*neue Verfassungszustände*). In the dreadful storms of the world war
the task has developed upon us of securing the structure of the Reich by
new and broader foundations. The impacts of the war have made us realize where the supports of the house which shelters us all are weak and
obsolete, where they are in need of renovations. But they have also revealed to us the fresh, surging founts that in our nation strain toward
the light. The impressions I obtained during the first days of the war
have remained unquenchable in my memory, and only more deeply have
they imprinted themselves during these years of struggle in which our
nation has shown a truly sublime greatness in the defense against an
ever more pressing superiority of forces working under increasingly
difficult conditions, suffering from ever more severe need. A people
which has fought so heroically, has performed such superhuman feats,
will always have honor. All this is written deep in my heart, and today
I bear witness to it again.

In a series of proclamations I have corroborated my resolve that there
shall be a new order in keeping with the new time. The German people
shall, in comprehensive manner, be assigned their part in the forming of
their destiny, inferior to no other people on earth in political freedom,
fearing no comparison as to their inner morale (*Tüchtigkeit*) and solid
patriotism (*fester Staatsgesinnung,* sense of duty toward the state).

You, gentlemen, have the task of cooperating in leading Germany
into the new conditions. I know that there is none among you who is
not aware of the greatness of this task and his tremendous responsibility.
But I desire from my heart to tell you at this moment that it is my firm
resolve for my part to do everything to achieve, with you and the people's
representative assembly, the goals set down in the decree of September
30. With you, gentlemen, to whom as my fellow-workers I address my
greetings for the first time today, I know myself to be at one in the holy
resolve to lead the German Reich from the distress of this time back to a
calm and peaceful development. I hope that, joined in warm love of
our fatherland and the feeling of heavy responsibility, we will succeed
in paving the new Germany a way to a bright and happy future. This
we will strive for with our whole strength, ready to take the path of
peace, but ready also to fight to the last breath, to the very last blow,
should our enemies not desire otherwise.

*Decree of the Kaiser to the Chancellor of October 28, 1918, after the
Amendment to the Constitution had been passed by the Reichstag*

. . . At the moment of this step which is so significant for the further
history of the German nation I desire to express what I feel. Prepared by
a series of government acts, a new order is now coming into force which
transfers basic rights from the person of the Kaiser to the people. There-

with a period will be closed which will continue to stand in honor in the eyes of future generations. Despite the struggles between traditional powers and new forces aspiring for their share, it has made possible for our nation that grandiose development which has been imperishably revealed in the achievements of this war. But in the dreadful storms of the four years of war old forms have been destroyed, not to yield to ruins, but to make way for new styles of life. After the achievements of this period the German people can claim that no right be withheld from them apt to guarantee a free and happy future. The bills [for the amendment of the Constitution] submitted by the federated governments [of the German states], and accepted and extended by the Reichstag, owe their origin to this conviction. I myself accede to these decisions of the people's representation along with my high [federated] allies, firmly resolved to cooperate toward their full realization in what I have to do, certain that I am thereby serving the welfare of the German people. The function of the Kaiser (*das Kaiseramt*) is service to the people. May the new order set free all the good forces our people need in order to pass the grave tests which have been imposed on the German Reich, and to gain, firmly stepping forward from the darkness of the present, a brighter future.

Berlin, October 28, 1918
(signed) Wilhelm I. R.

(countersigned)
Max Prince von Baden

To Chapters 58 ff.

*Federalism as a defense against totalitarianism*

After the war the opinion that countries with a centralized structure were more likely than federal countries to fall victim to totalitarian dictatorship was widespread. This thesis is of dubious validity, however. The very weakness of the central power in a federal country and the splintering of power between federal and state governments may lead in times of emergency to the call for a dictator. As a defense against the assumption of total power by a dictator other elements of the constitutional structure are more important than federalism, such as provisions against the intrusion of anti-democratic majorities into democratic parliaments, the guarantee of minimum standards of basic rights even in the face of emergency measures, and guarantees against the overthrow of a parliamentary government by a majority unable to establish an alternative government—problems which on the whole have been well solved in the Basic Law of the Federal Republic of Germany in 1949. See my essay "The New German Constitution," *Social Research,* vol. 16 (1949), pp. 425–473.

To Chapters 67 ff.

*Text of the letter, frequently mentioned in these chapters, written by ex-Chancellor Dr. Brüning on August 6, 1944, after publication of my book "Prelude to Silence."* [1]

> Lowell House E-11
> Harvard University
> Cambridge, Massachusetts
> August 6, 1944

Dear Dr. Brecht,

I apologize for not thanking you earlier for your book. . . .

I naturally read your book with very great interest, and fully recognize and appreciate its tenor. It is very difficult at the present moment to create a better understanding of events in Germany after the last war [1914–1918]. . . . Any attempt to explain the situation will provoke violent reactions at the present moment, but that may change after the [present] war is over, even though not immediately. The change may be too late to affect the fate of Germany.

I am always amazed that writers ignore the fact that the greater part of Germany's economic and financial and also international policy was dictated by the terms of the peace treaties. No one realizes that currency questions were under the legal sovereignty of the reparations creditors. While I was in office this sovereignty was exercised not only on general lines, but also in the details of the budgetary and monetary policy of the Reich. I would wish, if you will allow me to say so, that as the financial expert of the Prussian government you could have said something further about this. Perhaps in a second edition you could include, for example, the fact that even a few days before Britain left the gold standard the British Ambassador brought me a note peremptorily demanding the further reduction of wages and salaries in Germany. It would also be important to mention, possibly in connection with your position in the Reichsrat, the law limiting the circulation of Reichsbank notes to a very low relation to the gold and foreign exchange reserve, of which you are aware. This might make people understand that the so-called deflationary policy was imposed on Germany. At all conferences it was made clear that the revision or cancellation of reparations would not be open to discussions unless the German government demonstrated that the greatest efforts within the frame of international conditions laid down in the Young Plan did not permit the transfer of reparations. I am always surprised that the German economists who are now in exile,

---

[1] Published with Dr. Brüning's consent. He had dictated the letter to his American secretary in English; hence this is not a translation but the original wording.

especially, seem to have forgotten these facts entirely. Apparently they have never read the classic article by Sir Henry Strakosch about the enforcement of a deflationary policy on all the countries of the world through its initial enforcement on Germany.

What strikes me even more in this connection is the fact that no German emigrant seems willing to study the consequences of our setting up a new Reichsbank—the Akzept- und Garantie Bank—which permitted us to make one of the largest credit expansions known, without which we would not have been able to survive the crisis of 1931. The technique we evolved was the model of every subsequent credit expansion. I obtained the consent of the Bank of England, and after three weeks negotiation I was able through Wallenberg to induce the French government to ignore though not to approve the establishment and policy of the institution. The credits extended by the Akzept- und Garantie Bank, together with the grant of Russian export credits, created within five months a total credit expansion of 2,500 million marks, without increasing the circulation of bank notes. We were the first to make a large-scale credit expansion, but in this way nevertheless remained within the legal restrictions of the Young Plan.

I will not bother you with the aims of the Fourth Major Decree. I will only mention that it was not so much a further step in a deflationary policy as a necessary operation to make good for the mistakes made in the preceding periods, first of monetary inflation and then of credit inflation based on short-term foreign loans. It was a redistribution of national income to make survival for everyone possible, and to prevent a breakdown of the mortgage banks.

There is another point about which it would perhaps create a wrong impression for me to remain silent. I am interested in the statement only because you make it, as I am utterly indifferent to the mass of emigrant books and the others based on them. You seem to think that the use of Article 48 together with the dissolution of the Reichstag was a new interpretation of the Constitution and was responsible for the large increase in the Nazi vote. Any further postponement of the Reichstag dissolution would have increased the Nazi vote even farther. It would have been much better for the Prussian authorities to have accepted my advice to dissolve the Prussian Diet at the same time. The elections in Thuringia and other states and communities before I came into office showed an enormous rise in the number of Nazi votes. All our information from the country at large and my own impression since the summer of 1929 convinced the government unanimously that the postponement of the election would lead to disaster. We were not surprised by the results, as I had calculated a possible 140 seats for the Nazis in the Reichstag.

Hermann Müller had promised Hindenburg to use Article 48 to carry through the financial reforms entailed by the Young Plan on the responsibility of the government. It was only after a year of struggle for any budget at all that President Hindenburg became aware of the dangers of the financial evolution and refused to sign the Young Plan unless the budget was balanced at once. In this situation Hermann Müller pledged Hindenburg his word that he would introduce the necessary measures by Article 48, even against the opposition of his own party, and risk elections. Discussions about the constitutional aspect of the action, based on discussions in the fall of 1923 and certain measures taken after the second Reichstag dissolution in 1924, were carried on by the Hermann Müller Cabinet, including Zweigert and Joel [State Secretaries in the Reich Ministries of the Interior and Justice]. They agreed unanimously that this measure was in complete conformity with the Constitution. I had some doubts about its practicability, and therefore advised Hermann Müller and the Cabinet to accept the compromise I worked out with Oscar Meyer [a democrat deputy], which would not really balance the budget, but which I persuaded Hindenburg to accept for the time being. When the SPD voted against the SPD ministers, with the exception of Wissel, and refused to accept the compromise, Hermann Müller called the Cabinet together and proposed to use Article 48 and to dissolve the Reichstag if any difficulty occurred. Then Meissner inquired of the President and reported that he would no longer give Hermann Müller power to use Article 48 and dissolve the Reichstag after his own party had voted against him.

I cannot state all the reasons why I did not use Article 48, but tried to carry through an improvement of the budget by way of a junctim, which succeeded the first time. I would have used it a second time if the SPD leaders had not promised us that they would pass the financial laws of June and July 1930. As the result of intrigue . . . while I was sitting with the President over the crisis resulting from the ban on the Stahlhelm in the Rhineland, the SPD members suddenly changed their minds and voted against the financial laws, Hilferding and Hermann Müller being absent. If we were to avoid a discussion of sanctions against Germany, always possible under the Young Plan agreement, I had to use Article 48, as we could not otherwise have continued to pay salaries and unemployment benefits. When it became doubtful whether there was a majority in favor of the decree, I advised the SPD to ask first for a vote of censure against my Cabinet, so that all the strictest traditions of a parliamentary regime would be brought into effect, and conflict with the President would be avoided. This the SPD refused to do, saying that they had no interest in playing into the hands of the Right. It is not necessary for me to comment on this policy, but such facts must be considered in the writing of an objective history.

Without wanting to pester you any more, I will add only one remark. The Center Party has never been a Roman Catholic or clerical party. It has always tried to hold Protestant members, and in western and southern Germany it had from 7 percent to 10 percent Protestant voters. The term "Roman Catholic" is very likely to be used further in abuse of me, and I am sorry that you did not realize that our policy was entirely independent of any influence by the German episcopate or the Vatican, and that sharp clashes, such as that over the Concordat, frequently arose between the Vatican and the bishops on the one side and the Center Party on the other. To mention this is only my duty to people who have stood in the fight against every form of totalitarian government, and who have suffered more than others, not only physically, but also from slander.

Please forgive me for these remarks. My only aim, as I have said, is to present my point of view, as I feel it necessary to do in the face of a publication of a person of your position and qualifications, which I have always highly respected. Please give my kindest regards to Mrs. Brecht.

With all best wishes for a fully successful convalescence,

Very cordially yours,
(signed) H. Brüning

To Chapter 91

*Letter from Prussia's former Deputy Minister-President, Dr. Hirtsiefer, after the resignation of the old Prussian Cabinet*

Berlin, April 18, 1933
Prinz-Albrecht-Str. 5

Dear Dr. Brecht,

After I expressed the thanks, both of myself and on behalf of the other state ministers, to you and the other government officials and employees at the ministers' conference on March 22, 1933 [when the old Cabinet decided to resign], for your work during the last difficult months, I feel urged, dear Dr. Brecht, to offer thanks to you especially. For thanks are due to you above all. After the events of July 20, 1932 you immediately spoke up for the Prussian government selflessly and without consideration for your own person, in defense of the rights constitutionally granted them. If we succeeded in gaining recognition for the principles of legality before the Supreme Constitutional Court and achieving all that could possibly be achieved under the prevailing circumstances, then this is primarily due to your excellent knowledge of constitutional law, to your painstaking and conscientious preparation of the case, and your firm yet tactful demeanour before the tribunal. During the subsequent difficult period of juxtaposition between the Prussian government and the national commissioners for Prussia, too, you rendered the Prussian government and thereby the state of Prussia most excellent service in your work as intermediary and with your wise advice. The Prussian government has therefore with confidence entrusted you again with representing them in the legal dispute arising from the decree of the Reich President of February 6, 1933. Even if this legal dispute should never be settled, this will not lessen our thanks to you for your faithful readiness to stand up once again for the preservation of justice.

On behalf also of the other state ministers I should like to close with the sincere wish that your exceptionally valuable gifts be made use of again in the near future for the benefit of our German people and our German fatherland we all love so dearly.

In deep regard and with the assurance of exceptional esteem, I remain

Yours very sincerely

Dr. Hirtsiefer

To Chapter 93

*Papen's self-criticism. Extracts from his memoirs, "Der Wahrheit eine Gasse" (A Path for Truth)*

What was demanded above all [in the German General Staff, where Papen had served several years] was independent judgment and the taking over of complete responsibility for the resolve reached. I have often been criticized in later years and in performing my functions as a statesman for the suddenness of my decisions and the directness of my actions. It may be that they are less proper for a politician—but I am unable for a moment to deny that origin of my education (p. 35).

When we formed the Hitler government it was clear that . . . it would not be easy to put Hitler and his party on the road of statesman-like responsibility. But we hoped that the influence of Christian principles would prevent a development toward radicalism. When I spoke to Hindenburg about these worries on January 29, he had tried to calm me: "I really do not know what could yet happen. You are Vice-Chancellor and at the same time Prussian Minister-President. With the exception of two ministerial posts all government departments are directed by our people. On top of this you will be present at every one of Hitler's reports to me" (p. 289).

Amorality, unscrupulousness, and the negation of all traditional concepts . . . were considered by us transitory revolutionary phenomena. We believed in the necessity, and in that Hitler, too, would recognize it, that he, having attained power and responsibility, would do everything to direct the revolutionary passion of his movement slowly into organized channels. The actual expressions of goaded mass instincts made it clear that this would not happen from one day to the next. It would not be possible to avoid excesses. Nevertheless, we believed—foolishly, perhaps—that a development toward statesmanlike responsibility would take place with Hitler and the party. . . . (pp. 290 f.).

We further overlooked the fact that Hitler aspired to unlimited power. . . . (p. 291).

Looking back it is clear to me that in many cases I should have appealed to the authority of the Reich President in the very early stages of certain developments. I did not do so because I myself and my colleagues in the Cabinet were of the opinion that the development would be from radical to moderate and not vice versa (p. 292).

A man of such great gifts and such exceptional strength of will [as Hitler] would, I hoped, grow out of the shoes of the party leader into those of the statesman. I recognized too late the lack of the character traits necessary for this. The complete unprincipledness of his ethics in comparison to Christian ethics made him believe that the deception and lies he considered practicable in domestic party disputes were also permissible in the constitutional life of nations (p. 294).

I have striven from the very beginning to establish a relationship of personal confidence [with Hitler] and to rid him of the feeling that he was confronted with an enemy. . . . In these discussions he had often delivered long monologues, but was open to every counter-argument and was never offended when I interrupted him. Though I often did not have the impression that I had convinced him, he nevertheless seemed to me to be susceptible to influence. Therein lay my hopes.

How strong his influence on other people was became clear also in the case of the Reich President. The latter's originally deep mistrust quickly gave way to a sort of confidence (*einem gewissen Vertrauen*), so that as soon as April Hindenburg asked me to give up the joint reports of Hitler and myself which had been agreed upon on January 30. He said that Hitler felt this to indicate mistrust of himself and that he did not want to offend him (p. 295).

What point [the development] finally reached is clear if one considers that from 1937 no Cabinet meetings took place any longer and that afterward extremely important decisions, such as on war and peace, were made without the knowledge of most of the ministers (p. 295).

The election result [March 5, 1933] was in any case the signal for the beginning of a revolutionary development, which rose from below, and although dampened externally by the National Socialist leaders, was internally welcomed and supported by them (p. 305).

Only in 1945 in Nuremberg did I learn of the horrors of the concentration camps (p. 331).

There is in history no "might have been" (*"hätte"*). Therefore I, too, have to bear the responsibility. For seventeen months [i.e. from January, 1933 to June, 1934] I had maintained the belief that I could put Hitler on the right path. This was an error, and one may accuse me of lack of political instinct. Yet one cannot accuse me, as in Nuremberg, of intending to deliver my country and my people into a despotism (*Gewaltherrschaft*) which later threw Germany into chaos (p. 366).

*Letters from Otto Braun, former Prussian Minister-President (Excerpts)*

Locarno, February 5, 1953

Dear Herr Brecht,

There is a great deal to be said about world political events, but the Russian problem cannot be solved so easily. . . . Whereas under democracy the struggle for political power is played out on the public stage, under a dictatorship it takes place in the small circles of those in power, withdrawn from the public eye; and here mostly with greater unscrupulousness and brutality to the point of physical extermination.

The ruling power is thus able for some time to appear to the public in more secure fashion, but in the long run this system leads to internal attrition and weakening. But one may not, nevertheless, reckon with an early collapse of this Russian-Asiatic dictatorship, for the Russian time measure varies greatly from that in western Europe.

I am therefore not expecting much of negotiations with the Russians, since "serious acceptable offers from the Americans" [which I had recommended] would become an issue of the clique struggle in the Kremlin and be rejected. Nor do I expect any clarification [from such offers], for Russian propaganda, which works excellently, would make sure that the guilt for the failure fell to the Western powers, whom they have been denouncing as warmongers for years. How the Russians think of such negotiations was made clear by their suggestion for the agenda of the four-power conference, on which the first point was the peace treaty with Germany. If that had been accepted, the Russians would have come to the conference with a draft for a peace treaty which included extensive concessions to Germany, but which [for other reasons] would naturally at the conference have met with the resistance of the Western powers; this would have led to a failure of the conference but would have given Russian propaganda an excellent grade for peace.

The Russians are masters at negotiations; they negotiate on everything and as long as possible to gain time, if their negotiation partners master sufficient patience. But they do not allow any result to be reached, as the negotiations on the Austrian state treaty show,[1] for they have time. Their western allies in the Second World War, with incredible short-

---

[1] Actually, the negotiations on Austria did finally lead to a treaty with the Soviets. A.B.

sightedness and complete misunderstanding of their [the Soviets'] far-sighted aims, granted them so many extensive concessions and positions of power, where they are now sitting tight and which they cannot be negotiated out of. Since they are self-sufficient in their enormous empire and their satellites have to be at their disposal economically, they yield only to force and no one is prepared to take on the odium of having used this, not even the Russians. For, although the idea of the Communist world revolution has not yet been entirely abandoned in the Kremlin, they yet shun warlike aggression, which would cost them much in goods and blood and with which they would risk their dictatorial system of power (*Gewaltsystem*), since they could not rely on their own people, languishing under brutal police pressure, even less on their satellites.

The "cold war," that is, the propagandistic disintegration of the non-Communist world through their jackals (*Handlanger*), who are supported by millions [of money], costs them little and they risk nothing; they have time enough. They therefore hold a constant cloud of the threat of war over the non-Communist world, thus forcing the latter to tremendous armament projects, which eat at the prosperity of the people and thus fertilize the ground for the lies of Soviet propaganda. This propaganda, which swaggers even on the rostrum of the United Nations with audacious lies and insolence and is mostly answered only with diplomatic politeness, ought to be met with much more massive language. For the Russians understand nothing else, and it has gradually been having the desired effect on other nations, too. . . .

I am in tolerable health. . . . Against growing old, and what is connected with it physically, I have no defense, and my doctor knows no remedy either. . . .

Yours,
Otto Braun

Locarno, November 2, 1953
Via Teatro

Dear Herr Brecht,
Korea, Indo-China, North Africa, Trieste, and Adenauer-Germany are particular problems difficult enough, but they are merely parts of the total problem, the struggle between the Communist and the capitalist world, in which the rulers in the Kremlin, who are in a strong position, attempt to ignite little fires everywhere in the world and to keep them smouldering. Therefore, they negotiate on everything, but never allow a concluding satisfactory result to be reached. Your opinion expressed in your letter, that they might grow weary, I am unable to share. I know the Russians better than that; with negotiations they are in their element.

Grotewohl [Social Democrat in Germany's Soviet zone] and consorts are mere marionettes hanging on Moscow's strings. Thus further notes are exchanged; there are even negotiations on place, time, and participants of conferences. Meanwhile the world bleeds itself, in the armament race, to the point where people begin to feel: rather an end with horror than horror without end. Both sides fear the "end with horror," for it means death for both victor and vanquished. . . .

I do hope, of course, that the synthesis will be found to make peaceful coexistence between the two opposing poles, East and West, possible. I shall probably not live to see it because, since I have passed my eightieth year, I feel my life energies are rapidly shrinking and I entertain fearful doubts whether I shall live to see my eighty-first birthday in January. . . .

I am pleased to hear that you still take long walks, swim, and even skate. I wish that it will continue to be so for a long time and, aware of our old ties, I send my very cordial regards to you both.

Yours,
Braun

Locarno, February 16, 1955

Dear Herr Brecht,

I was very pleased to receive your letter of 24th. I thank you and your wife for your good wishes on my—unfortunately—eighty-third birthday. . . .

My main trouble is my age and that unfortunately cannot be helped. Thus I sit here condemned to passivity, disputing with fate, that so many younger friends have already passed on, while I still have to lumber around here. More than a year and a half ago I had to cut short my annual visit to Germany in the Black Forest and at the urgent advice of the doctors return to Locarno, whence I have not escaped since. At that time I had intended to visit Frau Ebert, but unfortunately could not. Now death has seized her, too; only I stay behind, as always, though no one would weep for me. My wife and children are dead and I no longer have any brothers or sisters either. My housekeeper attends to my physical wants very well. . . .

Sitting here in peaceful Switzerland I come more and more to the impression that the policies of America and the western world are predominantly influenced by the threatening Russian cloud. According to the old principle "If you want peace, arm for war," with which every military proposal was justified during Wilhelmian times, but which did not save us from two world wars, countries are arming again and boasting of the greater number of destructive atomic and hydrogen bombs. I rather feel that the people in the Kremlin are not of a mind to take the risk which is connected with military aggression to spread Communism.

Nor do they need to, for, thanks to Roosevelt's aloofness from Europe and the shortsightedness of the so-called Big Three, which is valid only for the two anti-Communists, they have acquired so much since the end of the Second World War that they have not yet been able to digest it. . . .

As long as many people on earth are still starving and are forced to live under conditions unworthy of human beings, Communism will find fertile ground even without hydrogen bombs. Half of the billions spent today on military arming, if used on raising the social situation of those millions living in need, would be more effective in the struggle against Communism than the piling up of military instruments of destruction.

Enough about this, I have to be brief, and cannot change it either. I would love to speak to you about all these things, but this wish, it seems, will not be fulfilled. I shall not be able to travel to Germany any more. . . .

Yours,
Otto Braun

PUBLICATIONS WITH POLITICAL IMPLICATIONS
AFTER 1933

BY ARNOLD BRECHT[1]

I. On World Organization and Regional Organization

"Sovereignty," in the collective book of the Graduate Faculty, New School for Social Research, *War in Our Time,* ed. by H. Speier and A. Kähler (New York, 1939), pp. 58–77. Outlines history and present meaning of sovereignty, with emphasis on national boundaries. Calls for gradual softening of the significance of boundaries by steps toward supernational institutions for the protection of minimum standards of human rights.

"Limited-Purpose Federations," *Social Research,* vol. 10 (May, 1943), pp. 135–51. Recommends functional special-purpose federations on a regional basis within world organization, especially for humanitarian, economic, and security purposes.

"Distribution of Powers Between an International Government and the Governments of National States," *American Political Science Review,* vol. 37 (October, 1943), pp. 862–72. Contribution to a symposium with Count Sforza, Edvard Hambro, and others. Warns that the U.S. will not surrender its own decision on war and peace to a supra-national body.

"Regionalism within World Organization," *Regionalism and World Organization,* American Council on Public Affairs (Washington, D.C., 1944), pp. 11–26.

"Fairness in Foreign Policy: The Chinese Issue," *Social Research,* vol. 28 (1961), pp. 95–104. Recommends transformation of the Chinese permanent seat in the Security Council of the United Nations into a rotating seat for an East-Asian group, to which India and others should belong.

II. Establishment of a European Federation

"European Federation—The Democratic Alternative," *Harvard Law Review,* vol. 55 (February, 1942), pp. 561–94. Recommends a "functional" approach through the establishment of supra-national boards, etc., for specific functions, and an overall parliament with gradually widening functions. Proposes Strasbourg for capital.

"Limited-purpose Federations," see above at I.

III. Reorganization of Germany

*Prelude to Silence—The End of the German Republic,* Oxford University Press (New York, 1944, reprint ed. with additions, 1968 by Howard Fertig, Inc., New York). Analyzes the causes of the collapse and the weakness of

---

[1] For publications prior to 1933, see the listing in *The Political Philosophy of Arnold Brecht,* as cited under IX, below, pp. 161 ff.

democracy in the absence of pro-democratic majorities. Also in German, Vienna, 1948.

*Federalism and Regionalism in Germany—The Division of Prussia.* Monograph Series of the Institute of World Affairs, New School. With a preface by Adolf Lowe. Oxford University Press (New York, 1945). Historical analysis, including reform efforts, especially for 1900–1945. Recommendations for postwar Germany. Maps on the strength of pro- and anti-democratic parties and votes 1919–1933 in the various parts of Germany.

"On Germany's Postwar Structure," *Social Research,* vol. 11 (1944), pp. 28–44.

"The Future of Germany," *Bulletin of the National Peace Conference,* vol. 9 (October, 1949), p. 5.

"Reestablishing German Government," *Annals of the American Academy of Political and Social Science,* vol. 267 (January, 1950), pp. 28–42.

"The New German Constitution," *Social Research,* vol. 16 (1949), pp. 425–73; also separately published as Occasional Paper of the Institute of World Affairs, New School, 1949. Discusses all aspects of the Basic Law.

"The German Army in Retrospect," *Social Research,* vol. 20 (1953), pp. 358–65.

IV. On the Soviet Union and Our Relations to Her

"The New Russian Constitution," *Social Research,* vol. 4 (May, 1937), pp. 157–90. Analyzes the USSR Constitution of 1936, with particular attention to the economic system and human rights.

"The Idea of a 'Safety Belt,'" *American Political Science Review,* vol. 41 (October, 1949), pp. 1001–09. Suggests a pact with the Soviet Union on the mutual withdrawal of foreign troops from a "safety belt," and abstention from unilateral entrance into that zone, in Germany or, preferably, all through Europe, from Scandinavia to Turkey. Counsels against imposing neutrality on the respective zonal states themselves, in particular in case other states should become attacked.

"Letter to the Editor," *The New York Times,* April 13, 1949. Same theme.

"United States Defense in Europe," *Social Research,* vol. 19 (March, 1952), pp. 1–22. Political implications of the decision to defend the U.S. in Europe, especially the pros and cons regarding Germany's remilitarization, and alternatives of action. Suggests the use of a more "strategic" diplomacy through proposals that are not on their face unacceptable to the Kremlin. Discusses details of the proposal of mutual withdrawal of foreign troops from a European security zone.

V. The Division of Germany

Proposal to divide, not Germany, but Prussia, see III.

Proposal of mutual withdrawal of foreign troops, see IV.

"Gangbare und ungangbare Wege," *Aussenpolitik,* vol. 6 (November, 1955), pp. 685–94.

"Alternativen der Wiedervereinigung," *Die Gegenwart,* vol. 10 (1955), pp. 554–56.

*Wiedervereinigung,* three lectures given at the University of Heidelberg at the invitation of the Juridical Faculty in July, 1957, published by Nymphenburger Verlagsbuchhandlung, München, 1957.

See also this book, Chapter 99, at the end.

## VI. Concentration Camps, Protection of Minimum Standards

"The Concentration Camp," *Columbia Law Review,* vol. 50 (June, 1950), pp. 761–82. Discusses the use made of "preventive detention" and camps in U.S., Great Britain, France, Germany, and USSR, and criticizes the lack of provisions to limit or control such practices in international covenants on human rights. Submits concrete proposals.

See also the papers cited under I and II, and "The New German Constitution," cited under III.

"Democracy, Challenge to Theory," *Social Research,* vol. 13 (June, 1946), pp. 195–224. Recommends the establishment of "amendment proof minimum standards" in national constitutions (last section).

## VII. Public Administration

"Democracy and Administration" in a cooperative book of the Graduate Faculty, New School, *Political and Economic Democracy,* ed. by M. Ascoli and F. Lehman (New York, 1937), pp. 217–28. Discusses particular problems of administration that arise under the democratic form of government, especially the conciliation between people, bureaucracy, and defense forces.

*The Art and Technique of Administration in German Ministries,* with Comstock Glaser (Harvard University Press, 1940). Discusses the differences of administrative procedures in Germany and U.S. and presents a translation of the German "Code of Administrative Procedure in the Federal Ministries."

"Three Topics in Comparative Administration—Organization of Government Departments, Government Corporations, Expenditures in Relation to Populations," *Public Policy,* Harvard Graduate School for Public Administration, vol. 2 (1941), pp. 289–318. Discusses the differences between the European practice of separating departmental headquarters as "ministries" from the bulk of departmental activities and the U.S. opposite tradition, the different construction of government corporations, and the parallelism between growing population density and growing public expenditures per capita.

"Smaller Departments," *Public Administration Review,* vol. 1 (Summer, 1941), pp. 363–73. Recommends a better organization of departmental headquarters, as above, with expert aides for advice, liaison downward and sideward, and as departmental memory.

"Organization for Overhead Management," correspondence with Paul Appleby, then Under Secretary in the Department of Agriculture, concerning above proposals, *Public Administration Review,* vol. 2 (Winter, 1942), pp. 61–66.

"Comparative Overall Administration," mimeographed report on conferences held in Washington, D.C., on May 1 and 2, 1942, by the Special Committee on Comparative Administration (chairman A.B.) of the Social Science Research Council with a group of top-level administrators, including

Harold Smith, Robert P. Patterson, Leon Henderson, Arthur Altmeyer, Arthur Fleming, Pendleton Herring, Donald Stone.

"Regional Coordination," memorandum by the same Special Committee, drafted by A.B., March, 1943, 46 pp.

"The Streamlining of Departmental Headquarters," report on another conference of the same committee, held May 29, 1945.

"Government Departments," *Encyclopaedia Britannica,* 1951.

VIII. GOVERNMENTAL PERSONNEL

"Civil Service," *Social Research,* vol. 3 (May, 1936), pp. 202–21. Discusses examination, promotions, patronage, and training in various countries comparatively, calls for an "examination of examinations" on an international basis, and submits reform proposals, especially on in-service training in a variety of operational services.

"Bureaucratic Sabotage," *Annals of the American Academy of Political and Social Science,* vol. 189 (January, 1937), pp. 48–57. Discusses various types of unwitting or purposive sabotage on a comparative basis.

"The Relevance of Foreign Experience," in *Public Management in the New Democracy,* ed. by F. Morstein-Marx (New York, 1940). Compares U.S., British, French, and German personnel management and makes recommendations for the U.S.

"Memorandum on Civil Service Reform in Germany," August, 1946. Mimeographed.

"Civil Service Reform in Germany, Problems and Suggestions," *Personnel Administration,* vol. 9 (January, 1947), pp. 1–11. Critique of denazification laws and proposals for civil service reform.

*Probleme des öffentlichen Dienstes in England, Frankreich und den Vereinigten Staaten,* Deutsche Gesellschaft für Personalwesen, Frankfurt, 1941, pp. 32–38, 44–50.

*Neues Beamtentum.* Report on Weinheim Conference, Deutsches Institut zur Förderung Öffentlicher Angelegenheiten (Frankfurt, 1951). Speeches by A.B., pp. 5–25 and 69 ff.

*German Civil Service Today,* report and recommendations. High Commissioner's Office (Frankfurt, 1950). Mimeographed 52 pp.

"What Is Becoming of the German Civil Service?" *Public Personnel Review,* Chicago, vol. 12 (April, 1951), pp. 83–91.

"Personnel Management," in *Governing Postwar Germany,* ed. by E. H. Litchfield (Cornell University Press, 1953), pp. 263–93. Systematic description and critique of basic differences in the civil service of the U.S. and that of the West-European countries. Discusses nine unique features of the German civil service in great detail, otherwise not available in print, and the attempts at reform after the war.

"How Bureaucracies Develop and Function," *Annals of the American Academy of Political and Social Science* (February, 1954). Types of bureaucratic power, historical examples of strong and weak bureaucracies, peculiarities of U.S. bureaucracies. Critique. Remedies.

"Bürokratie," article in *Staatslexicon* (6th ed. Freiburg, Germany, 1960).

Concept of bureaucracy, historical types, phenomenology of bureaucracy, particularities in various countries, bureaucracy in business, parties and labor unions. Remedies. Healthy functions of bureaucracy in a democracy.

IX. POLITICAL THEORY AND ITS RECENT HISTORY

"Constitutions and Leadership," *Social Research,* vol. 1 (August, 1934), pp. 265–86. Compares U.S., British, French, and German constitutions regarding the combination of democracy and leadership. Points out fatal defects of the Weimar Constitution.

"Federalism and Business Regulation," *Social Research,* vol. 2 (August, 1935), pp. 337–52. Describes the trend toward a "New Federalism" and its rationale.

"Relative and Absolute Justice," *Social Research,* vol. 6 (1939), pp. 58–87.

"The Rise of Relativism in Political and Legal Philosophy," *Social Research,* vol. 2 (1939), pp. 392–414.

"The Search for Absolutes in Political and Legal Philosophy," *Social Research,* vol. 7 (1940), pp. 201–28; *erratum,* p. 385.

"The Myth of Is and Ought," *Harvard Law Review,* vol. 54 (1941), pp. 811–31.

"The Impossible in Political and Legal Philosophy," *California Law Review,* vol. 29 (1941), pp. 321–31.

*The Political Philosophy of Arnold Brecht,* ed. by Morris Forkosch (New York, 1954). Includes reprints of the five aforementioned articles and of "The Latent Place of God in 20th Century Political Theory," a paper read at the general seminar of the Graduate Faculty, New School, in 1950, and at the American Political Science Association, in 1953.

"Democracy, Challenge to Theory" (1946), as cited under VI, above. Calls attention again to the problem of "non-democratic majorities."

"Beyond Relativism in Political Theory," *American Political Science Review,* vol. 41 (1947), pp. 470–88. Report on a panel discussion at the December, 1946 meeting of the American Political Science Association.

"A New Science of Politics," *Social Research,* vol. 20 (Summer, 1953), pp. 230–35. Discusses theoretical problems raised in Eric Voegelin's book *The New Science of Politics,* Chicago, 1952.

*Political Theory—The Foundations of Twentieth-Century Political Thought,* Princeton University Press (Princeton 1959, fifth printing, also as a paperback, 1968; also German, Spanish, and Portuguese editions). Attempts a full treatment of pertinent problems in four parts: systematic, genetic, polemic, at the borderline of metaphysics. Offers a theory of scientific method, of scientific value relativism, and of justice. Discerns precursors and cousins of scientific value relativism, such as skepticism, positivism, neo-positivism, historicism, pragmatism, Marxism. Introduces the concepts of *scientia transmissibilis, scientia non transmissibilis, scientia mere speculativa.* Analyzes the revolt against relativism and recent attempts to identify highest values. Seeks reconciliation of schools. Probes into factual, not logical, links between Is and Ought, and into universal, invariant, inescapable reactions of human feelings. Dialogue on "impossibility" between Communism and democracy. Simultaneous feelings of belief and doubt.

"Liberty and Truth," *Nomos,* vol. 5 on Liberty (1961), pp. 243–61. Critique of Mill.

"Die Tröstungen der strengen Wissenschaft," in *Politische Ordnung und menschliche Existenz, Festgabe für Eric Voegelin* (München, 1962), pp. 49–56. Scientific method claims no limitation of religious, philosophical, or legal thought. The role of human *responsibility* where science leaves off.

"The Ultimate Standard of Justice," *Nomos,* vol. 6 on Equality (1963), pp. 62 ff. Pursues these ideas further.

"Political Theory," article in *International Encyclopedia of the Social Sciences* (New York, 1968). Sub-topics: 1. What is "theory"? 2. What is "scientific theory"? 3. Transmissibility of knowledge. 4. Distinction of theory from practice, description, hypothesis, law, philosophy, reason, models. 5. History of political theory. 6. Scientific relativity of political values. 7. Scientific and legal validity distinguished. 8. Meeting grounds of natural law and scientific political theory. 9. Political goals. 10. Basic units of political theory. 11. Changes in theoretical topics, sovereignty. 12. Scientific theory of democracy.

SYNOPSIS OF CHAPTER NUMBERS
IN THE GERMAN AND AMERICAN EDITIONS
OF THESE MEMOIRS

Note: The two volumes of the German edition (*Aus nächster Nähe,* 1966, and *Mit der Kraft des Geistes,* 1967) are cited as vols. I and II, respectively.

| American Edition | German Edition | American Edition | German Edition |
|---|---|---|---|
| Chaps. 1–42 | same numbers | Chaps. 72 | II 21 |
| 43 | I 43, 44 | 73 | II 22 |
| 44 | I 45 | 74 | II 23 |
| 45 | I 46 | 75 | II 24 |
| 46 | I 47 | 76 | II 25 |
| 47 | I 48 | 77 | II 26 |
| 48 | I 49 | 78 | II 27 |
| 49 | I 53 | 79 | II 28 |
| 50 | I 54 | 80 | II 29 |
| 51 | I 55 | 81 | II 30 |
| 52 | I 56 | 82 | II 31 |
| 53 | I 57 and | 83 | II 32 |
|  | *Nachwort* | 84 | II 33 |
| 54 | II 1 | 85 | II 34 |
| 55 | II 3 | 86 | II 35 |
| 56 | II 4 | 87 | II 36 |
| 57 | II 5 | 88 | II 37 |
| 58 | II 6 | 89 | II 38 |
| 59 | II 7 | 90 | II 39 |
| 60 | II 8 | 91 | II 40 |
| 61 | II 9 | 92 | II 41 |
| 62 | II 10 | 93 | II 42 |
| 63 | II 11 | 94 | II 43 |
| 64 | II 12 | 95 | II 44 |
| 65 | II 13 | 96 | II 45 |
| 66 | II 14 | 97 | II 46 |
| 67 | II 16 | 98 | II 47 |
| 68 | II 17 | 99 | II 48 |
| 69 | II 18 | 100 | II 49 |
| 70 | II 19 | 101 | II 50 |
| 71 | II 20 | Epilogue | II *Nachwort* |
|  |  | Appendix | I and II *Anhang* |

The following chapters of the German edition are omitted in the American:

I 50 (Freedom of Association and Assembly),

I 51 (Administrative Reforms),

I 52 (Reform of Civil Service, Codification of Federal Legislation, Establishment of a Supreme Administrative Court, Unified Stenography, Particular Measures for the Protection of the Republic),

II  2 (The Tight Centralization of the Prussian Administration), and

II 15 (Democracy and Personal Individuality, Bargaining about Cabinet Seats, etc.).

Also omitted are most sections of the two appendices of I and II. Other chapters have been amply rewritten, with omissions and additions as required.

* Since the purely autobiographical data are scattered throughout the entire book, separated by stretches of historical narrative and political contemplation, they are listed under the entry "Brecht" on chronological order.